SOLIDARITY AND DIFFERENCE

For Caroline, Emily and Catharine

Solidarity and Difference

A Contemporary Reading of Paul's Ethics

David G. Horrell

T & T CLARK INTERNATIONAL
A Continuum imprint
LONDON • NEW YORK

BS
2655
.E8
H67
2005

Published by T&T Clark International
A Continuum imprint

The Tower Building
11 York Road
London, SE1 7NX

15 East 26th Street
Suite 1703
New York, NY 10010

www.tandtclark.com

British Library Cataloguing-in-Publication Data
A catalogue record for this book is available from the British Library.

ISBN 0-5670-8334-9 (hardback)
     0-5670-4322-3 (paperback)

Library of Congress Cataloging-in-Publication Data
Horrell, David G.
    Solidarity and difference : a contemporary reading of Paul's ethics / David G. Horrell.
        p. cm.
    Includes bibliographical references and indexes.
    ISBN 0-567-08334-9 (hardcover) – ISBN 0-567-04322-3 (pbk)
        1. Paul, the Apostle, Saint–Ethics. 2. Bible. N.T. Epistles of Paul–Theology. 3. Ethics in the Bible. I. Title.

    BS2655.E8H67 2005
    241′.0412′092–dc22   2004066068

Typeset by Tradespools, Frome, Somerset
Printed on acid-free paper in Great Britain by Cromwell Press, Wiltshire

CONTENTS

PREFACE

This book is an attempt to engage in some detail with Paul's ethics, not only in a way which is exegetically serious and historically informed, but also in a way shaped by debates in the contemporary field of ethics, specifically the debate between liberals and communitarians. Underlying the study is the conviction that biblical texts are worth taking seriously in contemporary ethics generally, and not only in Christian ethics. They are, after all, 'classic' texts that have been – and continue to be – profoundly influential in Western culture and its traditions of ethics. And Paul, I want to maintain, for all his faults and foibles, is worth wrestling with as a practical moral philosopher.

The perspective developed in this book has been quite a long time in gestation, and some studies of particular related topics have appeared in a number of essays that have been produced along the way. Some of these previous publications are incorporated in part in what follows, though revised for inclusion here; none of them, however, is wholly reproduced below, nor does any one of them constitute a chapter as such (see below for a list). I am nonetheless grateful to the various publishers and editors who have given permission for material to be reused. I have also on occasion made further reference to these (and other) earlier essays, where they provide fuller discussion of a point covered more briefly here, or further references. Bibliographical references are given using the Harvard system, which helps to keep the text and footnotes more concise than might otherwise be the case. All items mentioned can be found in the bibliography, except for those listed under "Abbreviations" below.

Douglas Harink's book, *Paul among the Postliberals* (Harink 2003), came to my attention only as this project was nearing completion. Consequently there is only minimal interaction with it in what follows, despite some points of similarity in the tasks we attempt (see further my review: Horrell 2004). Harink also seeks to open up a conversation between Paul and contemporary thought (in Harink's case, contemporary postliberal theology) and – as in what follows below – Stanley Hauerwas is a key figure in this conversation. However, the conversation Harink develops is restricted to bringing Paul alongside the postliberals and thoroughly affirming this theological movement as representing the most faithful appropriation of Pauline theology in our time, the means by which Paul's gospel to the nations is now being heard (cf. Harink 2003: 18–20). Comparisons with other approaches in theology and ethics are not attempted, and any supposed parallels between Paul and liberalism – such as are explored here – are swiftly dismissed (p. 84 n. 29; cf. p. 92). I hope to show in what follows the fruitfulness of engaging Paul's thought with various traditions in contemporary ethics, in a way that indicates how the Apostle's theology is rather more multi-faceted, complex, and indeed problematic, than Harink's marriage of Paul and postliberal theology allows.

Still less have I been able to engage with Jeffrey Stout's highly important work of public philosophy, *Democracy and Tradition* (Stout 2004). Focused on the subject of democracy in the USA, Stout is concerned to articulate a way 'beyond secular liberalism and theological traditionalism' (p. 294), 'an acceptable path between the liberalism of Rawls and Rorty, on the one hand, and the traditionalism of MacIntyre and Hauerwas, on the other' (p. 296). For Stout, '[d]emocracy is a culture, a tradition in its own right', the programme of which 'is to involve strangers and enemies, as well as fellow citizens, in the verbal process of holding one another responsible' (p. 13). He offers, *inter alia*, a brilliant and penetrating, though not altogether unsympathetic, critique of Hauerwas (esp. in ch. 6, pp. 140–61), highlighting the problems with Hauerwas's diatribal anti-liberal rhetoric and 'uncharitable attitude toward the world, especially in its democratic forms' (p. 156). Hauerwas, Stout claims, 'seems no longer to be moving in the direction of a world-engaging conversation about the biblical injunction to build communities – ecclesial, familial, and national – in which justice and peace visibly embrace' (p. 154). So much more of Stout's critique bears repetition that I must simply encourage readers to read it for themselves. If – by showing the various ways in which Paul's ethics resonates with, but also differs from, both liberal and communitarian forms of ethics, leaving a complex and diverse legacy that does not, *pace* Harink, simply affirm a Hauerwasian anti-liberalism – this study can add a supporting footnote to the project Stout so ably articulates, I will be pleased enough.

In producing this book I have incurred many debts. I am grateful to all those, too many to mention, who have discussed its ideas with me, either privately or on the occasions when I gave a paper related to the topic. There are, however, some individuals and institutions whom I should like specifically to thank. I would like to express my general appreciation to all of my colleagues in the Department of Theology at the University of Exeter, for the friendly and stimulating environment they and our students together provide. I am grateful to John Rogerson, without whom I probably would never have started to think about Habermas's discourse ethics, to Martin de Boer, Richard Fermer, Mike Higton, Bill

Jordan, Alistair May, Stephen Plant, Annette Weissenrieder and Mark Wynn, all of whom offered valuable comments on earlier versions of lectures, papers, and sections of the book, and to Richard Burridge, for enjoyable and stimulating conversations as he worked on his own (much broader) New Testament ethics project. I am especially grateful to the friends and colleagues who have commented on ch. 2, where their expertise greatly exceeds mine: Graeme Gilloch, Stephen Plant, Nigel Pleasants, Geoff Thompson and Mark Wynn. I am conscious of the extent to which a number of their questions remain inadequately addressed, and can only hope that this book at least contributes to the kinds of ongoing conversations I have enjoyed with these friends, in which those with different areas of academic expertise dare to tread into one another's territory in the hope of making connections and enabling fresh insights.

In terms of opportunities to present my ideas, while I cannot mention every relevant occasion, I would like to express my thanks for the invitations to give a course of lectures at the Vacation Term for Biblical Studies in Oxford, 1998, the Boundy Memorial Lectures at the University of Exeter, 2000, and main papers at the British New Testament Conference, 2002, and the Society for the Study of Theology, 2004. I am also grateful to the Bethune-Baker Fund (of the University of Cambridge) for a small grant to enable a short research visit to Heidelberg in 2000, and to Fernando Enns and all at the Oekumenisches Wohnheim for their hospitality on that occasion.

My greatest academic debts, however, are to the people and institutions who made possible my year of study leave in Heidelberg, from February 2003 to January 2004, as a Research Fellow of the Alexander von Humboldt Foundation. I am grateful to the Research Committee of the University of Exeter and the Study Leave Scheme of the Arts and Humanities Research Board for allowing and enabling me to spend a year away from Exeter. I am grateful to the Alexander von Humboldt Foundation for the award of a research fellowship, and for all the care and friendly support which the Foundation provides. I am grateful to the University of Heidelberg, particularly the Wissenschaftlich-Theologisches Seminar and the various *Neutestamentler* there, for welcoming me as a *Gastwissenschaftler* and making their research resources available to me, and to the staff of the University Gästehaus for their friendly assistance throughout. Most of all, in this regard, I would like to express my heartfelt thanks to Gerd Theissen, for his willingness to act as my *Gastgeber*, for his friendly hospitality – here my thanks to Christa Theissen too! – and for stimulating and enabling my work in many ways. I am especially grateful for the opportunity to co-teach a course of seminars on *Ethik des Paulus* where my ideas about Paul's ethics in relation to liberalism and communitarianism were discussed alongside Theissen's (different but comparable) ideas about Paul's ethics as a synthesis of biblical *Gebotsethik* and Greek *Einsichtsethik*.

My last and most profound words of thanks are reserved for Caroline, Emily and Catharine (our Heidelberg baby!) not only (though fundamentally) for so greatly enriching my life, but also for agreeing (at least in Caroline's case) to share the adventure, and accept the demands, of a year in Heidelberg. As a small token of appreciation, this book is dedicated to them.

July 2004

Parts of the following publications are included, in revised form, below. I am grateful for permission to reproduce them.

'Paul's Collection: Resources for a Materialist Theology', *EpRev* 22.2 (1995): 74–83.

'"The Lord Commanded ... But I Have Not Used ..."' Exegetical and Hermeneutical Reflections on 1 Cor 9.14-15', *NTS* 43 (1997): 587–603.

'Theological Principle or Christological Praxis? Pauline Ethics in 1 Cor 8.1–11.1', *JSNT* 67 (1997): 83–114.

'Solidarity and Difference: Pauline Morality in Romans 14–15', *SCE* 15.2 (2002): 60–78.

'The Peaceable, Tolerant Community and the Legitimate Role of the State: Ethics and Ethical Dilemmas in Romans 12.1–15.13', *RevExp* 100.1 (2003): 81–99.

'Idol-Food, Idolatry and Ethics in Paul', in S.C. Barton (ed.), *Idolatry in the Bible, Early Judaism and Christianity*, London: T.&T. Clark International, forthcoming.

ABBREVIATIONS

1. *Biblical and Other Ancient Texts*

Abbreviations for biblical and other ancient texts, and for modern biblical translations, utilize standard or easily comprehensible forms, generally following the conventions given in *JBL* 116 (1998): 555–79.

2. *Additional Abbreviations Used in Footnotes*

The following additional abbreviations are used in the footnotes:

ABD	*The Anchor Bible Dictionary*, 6 vols, D.N. Freedman, ed., New York: Doubleday, 1992
BDAG	W. Bauer/F.W. Danker et al., *A Greek-English Lexicon of the New Testament and Other Early Christian Literature*, 3rd edn, Chicago and London: University of Chicago Press, 2000
LSJ	H.G. Liddell, R. Scott and H.S. Jones, *A Greek-English Lexicon*, 9th edn, Oxford: Clarendon, 1940
NA^{27}	E. and E. Nestle, K. and B. Aland et al., eds, *Novum Testamentum Graece*, 27th edn, Stuttgart: Deutsche Bibelgesellschaft, 1993
NW 2.1	*Neuer Wettstein. Texte zum Neuen Testament aus Griechentum und Hellenismus, Band II, Texte zur Briefliteratur und zur Johannesapokalypse, Teilband 1*, G. Strecker, U. Schnelle and G. Seelig, eds, Berlin, New York: De Gruyter, 1996
OED	*The New Shorter Oxford English Dictionary*, L. Brown, ed., 2 vols, Oxford: Clarendon, 1993
Str-B	H.L. Strack and P. Billerbeck, *Kommentar zum Neuen Testament aus Talmud und Midrasch*, 3 vols, München: C.H. Beck, 1926
TDNT	*Theological Dictionary of the New Testament*, 10 vols, G. Kittel and G. Friedrich, eds; ET G.W. Bromiley, Grand Rapids, MI: Eerdmans, 1964–1976

TDOT	*Theological Dictionary of the Old Testament*, 12 vols, G.J. Botterweck, H. Ringgren and H.-J. Fabry, eds, Grand Rapids, MI: Eerdmans, 1974–2003
TWNT	*Theologisches Wörterbuch zum Neuen Testament*, 10 vols, G. Kittel and G. Friedrich, eds, Stuttgart: Kohlhammer, 1933–1978

3. *Bibliographical Abbreviations*

Abbreviations used in the bibliography are as follows:

AB	Anchor Bible
AGAJU	Arbeiten zur Geschichte des antiken Judentums und des Urchristentums
ANRW	*Aufstieg und Niedergang der römischen Welt*, H. Temporini and W. Haase, eds, Berlin and New York: De Gruyter
BBR	*Bulletin for Biblical Research*
BETL	Bibliotheca ephemeridum theologicarum lovaniensium
Bib	*Biblica*
BibInt	*Biblical Interpretation: A Journal of Contemporary Approaches*
BJRL	*Bulletin of the John Rylands University Library of Manchester*
BNTC	Black's New Testament Commentaries
BTB	*Biblical Theology Bulletin*
BZ	*Biblische Zeitschrift*
BZNW	Beihefte zur *Zeitschrift für die neutestamentliche Wissenschaft*
CBQ	*Catholic Biblical Quarterly*
CR	*Critical Review of Books in Religion*
DPL	*Dictionary of Paul and His Letters*, G.F. Hawthorne, R.P. Martin and D.G. Reid, eds, Downers Grove, IL/Leicester: IVP, 1993
EKKNT	Evangelisch-Katholischer Kommentar zum Neuen Testament
EpRev	*Epworth Review*
ETL	*Ephemerides theologicae lovanienses*
ExpTim	*Expository Times*
FRLANT	Forschungen zur Religion und Literatur des Alten und Neuen Testaments
GNS	Good News Studies
HDR	Harvard Dissertations in Religion
HNT	Handbuch zum Neuen Testament
HTKNT	Herders theologischer Kommentar zum Neuen Testament
HTR	*Harvard Theological Review*

HUT	Hermeneutische Untersuchungen zur Theologie
ICC	International Critical Commentary
Int	*Interpretation*
JAAR	*Journal of the American Academy of Religion*
JBL	*Journal of Biblical Literature*
JR	*Journal of Religion*
JRE	*Journal of Religious Ethics*
JSNT	*Journal for the Study of the New Testament*
JSNTSup	*Journal for the Study of the New Testament*, Supplement Series
JTS	*Journal of Theological Studies*
KEK	Kritisch-exegetischer Kommentar über das Neue Testament
NEchtB	Neue Echter Bibel
NICNT	New International Commentary on the New Testament
NIGTC	New International Greek Testament Commentary
NovT	*Novum Testamentum*
NovTSup	*Novum Testamentum*, Supplement Series
NTAbh	Neutestamentliche Abhandlungen
NTOA	Novum Testamentum et orbis antiquus
NTS	*New Testament Studies*
OBO	Orbis biblicus et orientalis
RAC	*Reallexikon für Antike und Christentum*
RB	*Revue biblique*
RBL	*Review of Biblical Literature*
RevExp	*Review and Expositor*
RGG^4	*Religion in Geschichte und Gegenwart*, 4th edn, H.D. Betz, D.S. Browning, B. Janowski and E. Jüngel, eds, Tübingen: Mohr
RRT	*Reviews in Religion and Theology*
SBLDS	Society of Biblical Literature Dissertation Series
SBLSP	Society of Biblical Literature Seminar Papers
SBS	Stuttgarter Bibelstudien
SCE	*Studies in Christian Ethics*
SCJ	Studies in Christianity and Judaism
SEÅ	*Svensk exegetisk årsbok*
SJT	*Scottish Journal of Theology*
SNTSMS	Society for New Testament Studies Monograph Series
SNTW	Studies of the New Testament and Its World
SR	*Studies in Religion/Sciences religieuses*
SUNT	Studien zur Umwelt des Neuen Testaments
THKNT	Theologischer Handkommentar zum Neuen Testament
TToday	*Theology Today*
TU	Texte und Untersuchungen
TynBul	*Tyndale Bulletin*

VT	*Vetus Testamentum*
WBC	Word Biblical Commentary
WUNT	Wissenschaftliche Untersuchungen zum Neuen Testament
ZNW	*Zeitschrift für die neutestamentliche Wissenschaft*
ZTK	*Zeitschrift für Theologie und Kirche*

INTRODUCTION

Despite the wealth of publications dealing with Paul's letters, and many studies of specific aspects of Paul's ethics, there have been surprisingly few book-length attempts to deal with his ethics as a whole. Victor Paul Furnish's *Theology and Ethics in Paul*, published in 1968, remains a significant landmark in this respect. Also somewhat lacking, as occasionally noted by those seeking to remedy the lack, are studies which seek to bridge the gap between biblical studies and contemporary Christian ethics. More lacking still are studies which attempt to bring the study of Pauline ethics into conversation with contemporary approaches in ethics and ethical theory, beyond the realm of specifically Christian discourse. In this latter regard, Daniel Boyarin's book, *A Radical Jew: Paul and the Politics of Identity* (1994), is a striking exception. Although Boyarin's book is not primarily or explicitly a study in 'ethics', its central concerns raise fundamental issues for a reading of Paul's ethics in the context of contemporary political debate.[1]

These introductory observations begin to indicate already the basic agenda for this study. My aims are to provide a reading of Paul's ethics that is exegetically serious and detailed – this remains the primary focus; to undertake this reading in the light of issues and questions raised by contemporary debate in ethical theory, specifically the debate between so-called liberals and communitarians; and thus to consider how Paul's approach to ethics might help us think about the strengths and weaknesses of these contrasting approaches and to outline some possibilities for the ways in which Paul's ethics might shape our ways of doing ethics today.

Outlining these aims is important to clarify what this book is and is not. Because of the particular contemporary debates from which the chosen questions and issues arise, the exegetical studies are orientated fundamen-

---

1. For detailed documentation and justification of the points in this paragraph, see ch. 1 below. I intend no distinction between 'Pauline ethics' and 'Paul's ethics' but vary the expressions simply for stylistic reasons. The former term could of course be taken to refer to the longer-term development of Paul's ethics in the deutero-Pauline and Pastoral letters, but the focus throughout this work is on the undisputed letters: Romans, 1–2 Corinthians, Galatians, Philippians, 1 Thessalonians and Philemon.

tally to essentially socio-political questions about the moral values and character of Pauline ethics. It is thus a study of Paul's ethics as social or political ethics, by which I mean ethics concerned with the formation and maintenance of human community, and with reflection on the ways in which this human sociality should rightly be sustained.[2] Indeed, the engagement with contemporary ethical debate is intended to enable us to consider how Pauline ethics might contribute to our thinking about issues of community and ethics in our diverse, plural, modern societies.[3] The inquiry is concerned to discern the key moral values of Pauline ethics, and to explore whether, and how, Paul's discourse constructs forms of human solidarity, sustains difference within the community, fosters a sense of group identity, and deals with boundaries and interaction in relation to 'outsiders'. Unsurprisingly, 1 Corinthians provides much material for such a study, though all of the undisputed Pauline letters are considered (see n. 1 above). This particular focus, and the concern to bring Pauline ethics into conversation with contemporary approaches, beyond the realms of specifically Christian discourse, means that I have cast the discussion in more widely meaningful terms rather than specifically Christian ones, talking, for example, in terms of corporate solidarity, other-regard, and so on. This also means that this book does not give much explicit attention to outlining the theological framework per se, within which Paul does his ethics, except insofar as this is relevant to considering his approach to community-formation and moral argument (cf. also §9.1.6 below). The reader will not find sections devoted to eschatology, the Spirit, and so on –

2. For this understanding of 'political' as concerned with the formation of community, cf. Hauerwas 1981: 224, for whom Christian beliefs are political in the sense that they form a particular kind of community. On Hauerwas's description of the Church as an 'alternative politics', see §2.3 below.

3. It is worth noting here, despite contrasting approaches and occasionally conflicting arguments, the extent to which this concern with the arena of *public* discourse is shared with Markus Bockmuehl (2000). Bockmuehl's focus is historical, on the ways in which by drawing on Jewish ethical traditions, specifically the traditions relating to ethical obligations incumbent on Gentiles, the early Christians formulated not only their own ethics but also a 'public moral discourse' (p. xiii): '[t]he cumulative result of the studies in this book, then', Bockmuehl writes, 'seems to be the remarkable extent to which early Christianity adopted the Jewish tradition of a "public" or "international" morality, which alone renders ethical dialogue possible' (p. xiv). My own approach looks more to contemporary debate as the context in which to read Paul, in order to reflect on his possible contribution to our thinking about contemporary public ethics; and I remain unconvinced by Bockmuehl's depiction of a Torah-loyal Paul whose rule is for Jews (including Jewish Christians) to keep the whole Torah and for Gentiles (specifically Gentile Christians) to keep what pertains to them (p. 171; cf. §1.2 below). But we share, it seems to me, the conviction that reflecting on Paul's texts (*inter alia*) is important in relation to the possibilities for public moral discourse now.

these are already rather well-worn topics in the study of Pauline ethics[4] – but will find an approach which seeks to do justice to the extent to which Paul's ethics are thoroughly rooted in the theology which constitutes the community-forming myth on which Paul draws (see §3.1).

The particular agenda which guides the exegetical study also means that Paul's ethics are not studied here with a view to setting out his convictions concerning what are sometimes referred to as his 'concrete ethics': marriage and divorce, homosexuality, slavery, sexual equality, and so on (cf. e.g. Schrage 1988: 217–39). Attempts to do this, at least when the underlying goal is to commend the same convictions today, often represent a naïve and anachronistic approach (cf. Meeks 1993: ix; §9.3.1 with n. 9 below). Insofar as these issues arise here, they are dealt with in terms of the wider subject of community-formation. Thus, like the two modern authors who form the main foci in my discussion of the liberal-communitarian debate, Jürgen Habermas and Stanley Hauerwas, my treatment of Paul's ethics eschews the all-too-popular focus on what Hauerwas calls 'moral quandaries' (1983: 4) and focuses instead on what I take to be prior and more fundamental questions about the formation of human communities, within which ethical dilemmas may be debated and resolved, or left unresolved and treated as matters of tolerable diversity. In fact, I think that Paul has less to offer us in terms of resolving these specific quandaries than is sometimes supposed, and rather more to offer in terms of our efforts to think about the kinds of values a community needs, in order to maintain both solidarity and difference.

To acknowledge explicitly that the questions guiding the exegesis arise from certain contemporary debates may invite the charge that the texts are read in an anachronistic or 'modernizing' manner. This potential criticism has little force, however, not least because all exegesis – whether the fact is acknowledged or not – is guided by the questions, methods, and presuppositions which form the contemporary context of the researcher.[5] Furthermore, in reading Paul in the context of the liberal-communitarian debate, I do not pretend that Paul is a modern ethical theorist, but aim to consider both how Paul's patterns of moral argument compare with the emphases found in certain liberal and communitarian approaches to ethics and also how Paul might stimulate our thinking about ways of doing ethics. I do not of course intend to imply that appealing to the ways in which Paul does ethics could resolve contemporary debates in ethical

---

4. Cf. their treatment in, e.g., Schrage 1988: 167–86; Sampley 1991: 7–24; Hays 1997a: 16–36.

5. Well known on this point is the classic essay of Rudolf Bultmann, 'Is Exegesis without Presuppositions Possible?' (see Bultmann 1985: 145–53). For a powerful demonstration of the shaping of historical exegesis by contemporary concerns and anxieties, in depictions of Judaism and Hellenism, see Martin 2001b.

theory. Only a naïvely biblicistic view would pretend that this could be so. Rather, I hope that a study of Paul's ethics can generate some pertinent reflections when set in the context of contemporary debate. This is, to use the overworn metaphors of Hans-Georg Gadamer, to foster some kind of conversation between (if not fusion of) the horizon of the reader and the horizon of the text. The conversation is, then, two-way: on the one hand, the contemporary debate shapes the kinds of questions with which the exegesis is concerned; on the other hand, the engagement with Paul's thought is intended to generate critical and constructive reflection on the issues raised in this debate. The hermeneutical stance that is thereby presupposed requires, I think, no more long and sophisticated justification than the pithy and felicitous description given by Francis Watson: 'in the last resort, to interpret is *to use the texts to think with*' (Watson 2000a: viii). The function of the canon, Watson insists, is not to restrict or foreclose thought, but to generate it. This 'thinking with' Paul – which certainly does not imply always agreeing with him, and may include some thinking against him – is no more anachronistic than, say, a reading of Aristotle, which seeks to develop and learn from his thought, without slavishly following it. Indeed, what I attempt to do with Paul is broadly comparable, methodologically and hermeneutically, with what Alasdair MacIntyre aims to do with Aristotle, and with Aquinas: to engage with a tradition which may be developed in response to contemporary dilemmas and discussion (cf. Porter 1993: 525).[6] Furthermore, part of the value of reading the past, even when it is the past of our own tradition(s), consists in the fact that it represents, as William Countryman notes, a strange world which can valuably 'relativize the present', can destablize our taken-for-granted world and render *it* strange (Countryman 1988: 238).[7]

The first chapter below offers a survey of various approaches to the study of Paul's ethics. As such, it indicates where this study fits within the

---

6.   MacIntyre comments, concerning a tradition of thought: 'the past is never something merely to be discarded, but rather … the present is intelligible only as a commentary upon and response to the past in which the past, if necessary and if possible, is corrected and transcended, yet corrected and transcended in a way that leaves the present open to being in turn corrected and transcended by some yet more adequate future point of view' (MacIntyre 1985: 146). To this I would add that reading the past is one way to engage critically with the present in the interests of further development and 'correction'.

7.   I am also reminded here of Theodor Adorno's remarkable statement about the task of philosophy, which, according to Adorno, should represent an attempt 'alle Dinge so zu betrachten, wie sie vom Standpunkt der Erlösung aus sich darstellten'. This means developing perspectives 'in denen die Welt ähnlich sich versetzt, verfremdet, ihre Risse und Schründe offenbart, wie sie einmal als bedürftig und entstellt im Messianischen Lichte daliegen wird' (Adorno 1980: 281 §153). Adorno's language also serves as one reminder of the complex but close relationship between Frankfurt School critical theory and Judaeo-Christian ethics and eschatology; the founding members of the School were Jews (cf. Arens 1997: 223–24).

contours of recent research, where it will depend upon, differ from, or build further on that work. More significantly, it shows how little work has even attempted the task of relating Pauline ethics to the wider sphere of contemporary ethical and political debate. Where such work has been attempted, as, notably, by Boyarin, it raises questions that are taken as a fundamental contribution to the agenda for what follows.

The second chapter turns to the contemporary context, and to the debate between liberals and communitarians. These contrasting approaches, illustrated through a study of the discourse ethics of Jürgen Habermas and the ecclesial ethics of Stanley Hauerwas, along with the key questions arising from Boyarin's work, both shape the kinds of questions with which the exegetical studies are concerned and also present a set of issues and questions in relation to which Paul's thought may generate some valuable and pertinent reflections. The third chapter, by contrast, while still engaged in primarily theoretical construction, outlines some of the conceptual resources with which we can best approach Paul's letters and specifically the subject of Paul's ethics. That is to say, while ch. 2 outlines a contemporary debate which forms the main forum for our reflections it does not itself offer a conceptual framework with which to approach the ancient horizon: that is what ch. 3 seeks to provide.

The exegetical studies begin in ch. 4 with the theme of solidarity, where I argue that this is, though too often overlooked, the fundamental value in Pauline ethics and the foundation on which much else is built. Chapter 5 considers how this communal solidarity relates to the theme of distinction – conveyed through notions like purity, holiness, and so on – and how this can be understood in relation to group identity and boundaries. Also evident here, albeit ironically, is the fact that ethical values are, to at least a significant degree, shared with the wider world. Social interaction, moreover, is in a number of respects open. Chapter 6 focuses on the two longest and most important (and related) passages of moral argumentation in Paul's letters: 1 Cor. 8.1–11.1 and Rom. 14.1–15.13. These passages warrant careful attention as the principal examples of Paul's engaging in reflective moral argument, and also offer important insights into the ways in which he deals with differences of ethical conviction within the Christian communities. There are, indeed, significant parallels in the structure of Pauline and liberal thought here. Chapter 7 picks up a theme that emerges as important in the previous chapter, that of 'other-regard', a moral value that is explicitly undergirded by the paradigm of Christ's self-giving. A number of specific passages are treated here, in an attempt to show the christologically-defined contours of this other-regard and its contribution to the shape of Pauline ethics. Indeed, solidarity and other-regard, I conclude, form the two metanorms of Pauline ethics (§9.1.1). Chapter 8 turns to the neglected evidence concerning ethics and outsiders. While Paul's ethics doubtless has a strongly ecclesial focus, there are nonetheless important indications that he sees ethical knowledge and standards as shared in common. His oft-repeated exhortation to Christians to do good to all people, moreover, reflects a conviction that notions of what is good are widely shared. This material is relevant, of course, to considering whether, and in what ways, the liberal goal of a public moral consensus, a framework for social cohesion, is possible. Finally, the ninth chapter draws together the findings of the study in the form of brief theses, conclusions, and proposals. These concern the shape of Pauline ethics itself, Pauline ethics in relation to the liberal-communitarian debate, and possible models for the appropriation of Pauline ethics today.

Chapter 1

APPROACHES TO PAULINE ETHICS: FROM BULTMANN TO BOYARIN

Studies of Pauline ethics, and New Testament ethics more generally, have a considerable history, going back to the period when critical biblical study was developing in the nineteenth century. Only then, Victor Paul Furnish notes, 'did interpreters begin to focus on the "ethics" of Paul *per se* as a suitable topic for independent investigation' (Furnish 1968: 242). The earliest treatment of New Testament ethics noted by Furnish dates from 1798 (Immanuel Berger's *Versuch einer moralischen Einleitung ins Neuen Testament für Religionslehrer und denkende Christen*) and the first full-scale treatment of Paul's ethics from 1868 (H.Fr.Th.L. Ernesti's *Die Ethik des Apostels Paulus in ihren Grundzügen dargestellt*).[1] Other early landmark studies include the major study of *Neutestamentliche Ethik* by Hermann Jacoby, published in 1899, which devotes 165 pages specifically to Paul's ethics (Jacoby 1899: 241–406), and the two-volume work *Die Ethik des Apostels Paulus*, by Alfred Juncker (Juncker 1904, 1919). The early work of Paul Wernle (Wernle 1897) also played a significant role in generating scholarly discussion of Paul's ethics (cf. further below, on Bultmann). There have, of course, been many studies since, especially in German scholarship, in which major works on New Testament ethics have until recently been somewhat more frequent than in the English-speaking world.[2] Yet, until comparatively recently, New Testament ethics remained a somewhat sparsely populated research field. Furnish, writing in 1968,

---

1. These two works are known to me only from Furnish (and Furnish knows Berger only via Baur). Furnish (1968: 242–79) offers an excellent 'survey of nineteenth and twentieth-century interpretations of Paul's ethic', up to the mid-1960s, with full attention to early works in this period. By contrast, McDonald (1998: 1) mentions only Jacoby's study of 1899 (Jacoby 1899) as the starting point for studies of NT ethics; Chang's (1995) overview of German discussion of NT ethics concentrates on more recent publications and mentions little of the nineteenth-century work.

2. Examples of studies of NT ethics in German from the 1960s and 1970s include Schnackenburg 1962 (ET: 1965); Wendland 1970; Schelke 1970; Strecker 1972; on Pauline ethics specifically, Merk 1968; Halter 1977; Hasenstab 1977. The massive works of the Swiss scholar Ceslaus Spicq, published in French, on agape in the NT (3 vols, 1958–59) and on the moral theology of the NT (2 vols, 1970), also deserve mention. For a valuable survey of

could comment that '[o]nly a few major critical studies of biblical ethics have been published in the last several decades, and most of the exegetical work on which Christian ethicists are forced to depend is sadly inadequate' (1968: 7).

Paul's ethics in particular have been a neglected area of research, especially compared with other topics in Pauline studies. One example, noted by Brian Rosner (1995: 1), may suffice to illustrate this point: Hans Hübner's lengthy review of *Paulusforschung seit 1945*, published in 1987, devotes only a six-page excursus to Paul's ethics (Hübner 1987: 2802–08), compared with lengthy sections on the law, righteousness and justification (pp. 2668–721). However, one should also note (as Rosner does not) Hübner's comments on his treatment of Paul's ethics: he regards the topic as no independent theme but rather as implied throughout the previous discussions of law, righteousness, etc.[3] Hübner is indeed right to indicate that Paul's ethics do not constitute a discrete or clearly delimitable area of research, since so many other areas of discussion in the study of Paul necessarily impinge upon it, not least due to the close integration of theology and ethics in Paul (see below). A wide range of Pauline studies therefore needs to be taken into account in any attempt to determine an approach to Pauline ethics. Nonetheless, it still stands worthy of note that studies specifically devoted to Paul's ethics have been relatively few in number, and Furnish's 1968 monograph remains a landmark publication.[4]

During the last twenty years or so, however, the subject of New Testament ethics has received greater attention, particularly in the English-speaking world, and especially the USA. These studies have come from a range of perspectives, some of which will be more fully reviewed below. They have included studies aimed at elucidating the social context of early Christian ethics,[5] at exploring the parallels between New Testament ethics

---

literature on Pauline ethics from 1964 to 1994, see Willis 1996; on approaches to NT ethics in German scholarship, see Chang 1995; on biblical ethics more generally, see the recent annotated bibliography compiled by Amadon and Eklund 2001.

3. 'Das Thema "Ethik bei Paulus" ist kein eigenständiges Thema. Es ist im Grunde in all dem, was bereits ausgeführt wurde, impliziert' (Hübner 1987: 2802). One might also qualify Rosner's comment that Hübner's review 'accurately presents the field' (1995: 1): it is focused predominantly on the theological themes that have dominated German discussion of Paul, and makes very little mention of the socially orientated studies (admittedly only gaining momentum in the late 1970s and early 1980s) of Paul's practice and communities (the bibliography lists nothing by Edwin Judge, Wayne Meeks, Abraham Malherbe and Ronald Hock, for example, and only one of the series of influential studies by Gerd Theissen, later collected in Theissen 1979 and 1982). Hübner is also dismissive of Sanders's work (cf. p. 2655).

4. It is rightly praised as an important work by Hübner (1987: 2805) and Willis (1996: 307).

5. E.g., Meeks 1986, 1993; see further §1.5 below.

and contemporary Jewish or Graeco-Roman ethics,[6] at elucidating the content of New Testament ethics exegetically or in their historical development,[7] or at bridging the gap between New Testament studies and contemporary ethics.[8] The recent *magnum opus* by Richard Hays (1997a) stands as a representative mark of this heightened interest, and specifically of the concern to link New Testament ethics with contemporary ethical discussion. In the field of Pauline studies there has also been a number of recent books, dealing both with the general shape and motivations of Pauline ethics, and with particular aspects or topics within them, though nothing that would rival Furnish's book in breadth and comprehensive treatment of the subject.[9]

There are many wider societal factors which may help to explain the increased attention given to ethics generally, and thus to New Testament ethics specifically. There is perhaps a kind of belated Kantian influence on a move from metaphysics to morality, whereby some regard the practical field of ethics as more accessible to human investigation, compared with

---

6. E.g., focused on the Jewish traditions: Reinmuth 1985; Tomson 1990; Rosner 1994; Bockmuehl 2000; on the Graeco-Roman parallels: Malherbe 1987, 1989; Deming 1995, etc. See further §1.2-3 below.

7. E.g., Matera 1996, whose study of the ethical legacies of Jesus and Paul aims primarily to be a 'descriptive' work, focusing on various texts in turn, rather than seeking to trace a process of historical development from, say, the historical Jesus through Mark, Matthew, etc. (cf. Matera 1996: 8–9), *pace* McDonald (1998: 4), who writes that Matera's study 'largely followed conventional diachronic lines'. Matera simply treats each of the four Gospels in turn, followed by the Pauline letters treated individually, with a view to understanding their various perspectives on ethics, though he does outline some synthesizing conclusions at the end of his book (pp. 248–55). Cf. also Houlden 1975. Historically orientated studies, which treat NT ethics in a diachronic perspective beginning with the historical Jesus (the approach taken by most German studies) include Wendland 1970; Schnackenburg 1986, 1988; Schulz 1987; Schrage 1988. Schulz distinguishes, even in the undisputed Pauline letters, between an early Pauline and a later Pauline approach to ethics, while Marxsen (1989, 1993) distinguishes between 'developments' and 'false developments' in NT ethics (1989: 201–64; 1993: 228–309).

8. E.g., Deidun 1981; Ogletree 1983; Verhey 1984; Countryman 1988; Hays 1997a. A similar concern motivates Sanders 1975, though unlike these other studies, the burden of Sanders's argument is a negative one: that the NT's ethics, and specifically the ethics of Jesus and Paul, being profoundly shaped by an imminent eschatology, can be of little use in contemporary ethics. Mention should also be made of the recent attempt to read NT ethics from a particular, African-American, perspective in Blount 2001.

9. E.g., Cruz 1990; Sampley 1991; Hjort 2000, all of which deal, in different ways, with the shape and character of Pauline ethics, and the relation between theology and ethics in Paul. Söding 1995 studies the love-command in Paul; Barcley 1999 examines the (very few) 'Christ in you' expressions in Paul (Gal. 2.20; 4.19; Rom. 8.10; 2 Cor. 13.5; and Col. 1.27) in a study of 'Paul's theology and ethics', but has little to say on Paul's ethics; Watson 2000a is a study focused on Paul's sexual ethics. The collection of essays in Rosner 1995 presents a valuable collection of approaches to Pauline ethics through the twentieth century. For earlier works, see n. 2 above.

the speculative realms of doctrine. Marx's distinction between purely scholastic philosophy, which is essentially irrelevant and impotent, and thought which demonstrates its truth in practice, in changing the world – most famously expressed in his theses on Feuerbach – also influences a trend to focus on what we must do, rather than what we should believe: orthopraxy comes to be seen as more important than orthodoxy.[10] The much more recent development of liberation theology, which has learnt a good deal from Marx, of course, has also pressed our focus towards *action*, or praxis, which again brings questions of ethics to the fore. There is also the prominence of many specific ethical issues in the public domain, and the profile of ethics in educational curricula, that not only heightens interest in ethics as a subject but also – at least in some quarters – raises questions about the extent to which the Bible can shed light on such quandaries.[11] More critically, one may ask, with Alasdair MacIntyre (1985), whether the explosion of discussion and debate concerning ethical issues in fact reflects the collapse of a shared moral tradition, such that the common foundations for ethics no longer exist.

Yet despite the renewed attention devoted in recent years to New Testament and specifically Pauline ethics, the need for further work on Paul remains. This is partly due to the relative dearth of studies of Paul's ethics – as noted above, Furnish's 1968 book still stands as probably the most wide-ranging and systematic modern study. But it is also due to the specific ways in which contemporary studies have, and have not, approached the study of Paul's ethics. One of the things that has most clearly been lacking is studies which seek to bring Pauline ethics into conversation with contemporary approaches in the field of ethics, beyond as well as within the Christian tradition. Such a claim requires elucidation, of course, and in order to explain and to justify the approach taken in this study, as well as to locate it within current research, a selective review of the variety of contemporary approaches to Pauline ethics will be presented.

1.1 *Theology and Ethics: Indicative and Imperative*

As in so many areas of New Testament study, Rudolf Bultmann provided a crucial impetus to critical discussion of Paul's ethics and specifically to the understanding of the relationship between theology and ethics in Paul. In his essay of 1924, 'Das Problem der Ethik bei Paulus', Bultmann sought to understand the nature of the relationship between the indicative and the imperative in Paul, between the 'statements according to which the justified

10. See Marx 1969: 5–7; ET in Elster 1986.
11. Kettner (1992: 9) notes 'the spectacular boom' in 'applied' or 'practical' ethics, especially in the USA, in the previous decade or so.

person is free from sin, has died to sin' and 'those statements in which the fight against sin is urged, which also apply to the justified' (see esp. Rom. 6.1-7; Gal. 5.13-25; 1 Cor. 6.9-11).[12] In Paul, as Bultmann notes, these indicatives and imperatives 'are very closely tied together and form an antinomy', as concisely in Gal. 5.25 (Bultmann 1924: 123; 1995: 195). Earlier research, notably by Wernle (1897), had already drawn attention to this problem, but failed adequately to understand it.

Bultmann's answer to the problem stems from his conviction that justification enacts no empirical, visible change in a person, but is rather concerned with God's verdict on them, apprehended only through the eyes of faith.[13] Thus 'sin is not something empirically perceptible. Nor is righteousness. That means therefore that the identity of the justified person with the empirical person is *believed*.'[14] Furthermore, and put provocatively, '[f]or the believer, the moral demand has acquired *no new content*, and his moral conduct is distinguishable from that of others only in that it bears the character of obedience' (1924: 138; cf. 1995: 213). The relationship between the indicative and imperative in Paul, then, is *not* for Bultmann to be understood as the relationship between statements describing an actual, empirical transformation and statements which call for distinctive moral conduct, new moral ideals, in keeping with that transformation. Rather, both indicative and imperative express the viewpoint of faith; they relate to the existence of those who understand themselves to be justified. For such persons, the imperative indicates the character of their faith as obedience just as the indicative describes their righteous status as faith perceives it (cf. 1924: 139–40; 1995: 215–16). The imperatives do not, then, call for the believer to act in ways empirically distinguishable from those of other people, but indicate that the believer's action is to be understood *as obedience*. Thus, for Bultmann, indicative and imperative are closely intertwined:

> the indicative calls forth the imperative. The indicative gives expression to the new self-understanding of the believer, for the statement 'I am freed from sin' is not a dogmatic one, but an existential one ... the imperative reminds him that he is free from sin, provided that his will is

---

12. Bultmann 1924: 123. ET in Bultmann 1995: 195, though I have departed from that translation a little here. Hübner (1987: 2802) refers to Bultmann's essay as 'ein Markstein in der Forschung'.

13. 'Πίστις is ... the conviction that only through God's verdict is man considered justified' (Bultmann 1924: 135–36; 1995: 211). Bultmann thus swiftly dismisses the old debate about whether the justified person is only *considered* righteous or *is* actually righteous: 'Natürlich *ist* im Sinne des Paulus gerecht, wer von Gott als gerecht angesehen wird' (1924: 136 n. 1, emphasis original; cf. 1995: 211 n. 39).

14. Bultmann 1924: 136 (my translation here differs from that in 1995: 212, not least since the latter omits the sentence 'Ebensowenig ist es die δικαιοσύνη').

renewed in obedience to the commandment of God. (Bultmann 1960: 76–77)

Bultmann's solution to the problem of indicative and imperative, bearing the hallmarks of his essentially existentialist perspective, has not, of course, been universally accepted. But it did serve to direct attention to the importance of understanding the indicative and imperative as a key to understanding the relationship between theology and ethics in Paul. Some have implied a greater separation between the two than did Bultmann,[15] while others, notably Furnish, have developed the view of indicative and imperative as intrinsically interrelated and have consequently seen theology and ethics as inextricably intertwined in Paul.[16] Indeed, many studies of New Testament and Pauline ethics have stressed the extent to which Paul's ethics are rooted in his gospel, his ethical admonitions finding their basis and motivation in his convictions about the saving work of God in Christ.[17] Furnish goes so far as to make the indicative–imperative issue the central test of any study of Paul's ethics: 'no interpretation of the Pauline ethic can be judged successful which does not grapple with the problem of indicative and imperative in Paul's thought' (1968: 279).

Bultmann's claim that the moral demands Paul makes of the believer have 'no new content' – a claim that was indeed a focus for criticism[18] – also raises the important question as to the extent to which the substantive ethics Paul urges are parallel to those taught in his contemporary world, in Judaism or in Graeco-Roman moral traditions, or whether they are in any way distinctive.[19] Various aspects of these contemporary ethics have been energetically explored in recent studies (see below). It also raises the question as to whether Bultmann 'paid enough attention to the concrete ethical exhortations in the Pauline letters' which may 'require some modification of the judgment that for Paul the new life in Christ has no

---

15. E.g. in C.H. Dodd's distinction between *kerygma* and *didache* (see Dodd 1936, 1950; Parsons 1995: 218–21; Furnish 1968: 272–74). Dodd sees the Pauline epistles as characterized by a division into two parts, the first dealing with 'religious themes', the second with 'ethical precepts and admonitions'. He does not deny an organic link between the two, but does regard the divisions as 'pretty well marked' (Dodd 1950: 5). Yet he agrees that Christian ethics 'arise out of a response to the Gospel' (p. 10). For an overview of approaches to this issue, see Parsons 1995.

16. Cf. Furnish 1968: 13: 'The thesis which finally emerges from this investigation is that the apostle's ethical concerns are not secondary but radically integral to his basic theological convictions.'

17. E.g., Schnackenburg 1988: 14–26; Schrage 1988: 167–86; Hays 1997a: 16–36.

18. Cf. Furnish 1968: 264–65; Hübner 1987: 2803.

19. According to Bultmann: 'What is demanded of the justified is only what is good, pleasing and perfect, what one may name as virtuous and praiseworthy (Rom 12.2; Phil 4.8). The moral commandments of the Old Testament are valid just as are the catalogues of virtue and vice of the paraenetic tradition of hellenistic Judaism' (1924: 138; cf. 1995: 213–14).

new "content" as such' (Furnish 1968: 264). It was precisely the view that the Pauline (and indeed biblical) ethic required and generated no specific, concrete commands that was the target of Wolfgang Schrage's critique in his important monograph *Die konkreten Einzelgebote in der paulinischen Paränese* (1961). Schrage opens his book by noting that many scholars, Bultmann included, express the view that the moral demand of the New Testament can be reduced to, or focused in, the love-command, making other commands superfluous, as in the dictum attributed to Augustine, *Ama, et fac quod vis*.[20] Paul's view of the Christian as free from law and living in the Spirit led many exegetes to the conclusion that 'the point (*Sinn*) of the Pauline exhortations consisted precisely in making these and indeed *all* specific commandments superfluous' (Schrage 1961: 11, my emphasis).

Schrage succeeds in showing how specific commands and exhortations are integral to the Pauline ethic: while love is indeed, Schrage affirms, the highest and the fundamental norm,[21] Paul's ethic cannot simply be reduced to the command to love, but sets out in some detail '*what* love forbade and *what* love commanded' (p. 270). He also concludes, however, that Paul's ethics finds its distinctiveness not so much in the *Was* – much of which is indeed, as Bultmann supposed, derived from contemporary moral norms, Jewish and Gentile – but more in the *Wie*, and in the new sense and purpose (*Sinn*) which Paul provides (Schrage 1961: 200–209). There is essentially a continuity of ethical norms between Old and New Testaments, though the Old Testament law becomes valid for the Christian only as it first becomes the law of Christ (pp. 233–34, 237–38).

Schrage successfully refuted the view that there was essentially no concrete content to Pauline ethics worth elucidating, beyond the imperative to love (though it is still worth stressing that, in at least some letters, Paul's ethical instructions are strikingly general and 'under-developed' in terms of specific commands).[22] But he does not dispute the profound integration of theology and ethics in Paul and, like many other

20. See e.g. Bultmann 1966: 238–39 (with the quotation of Augustine at 239 n. 1): '*Was* der Mensch tun soll, ist durch den Hinweis auf die natürliche Selbst-liebe genügend gesagt. Die Frage: was ist Liebe? kann nur auf *eine* Weise beantwortet werden, nämlich durch das Tun der Liebe, das ein Sein in der Liebe ist ... Es gibt also keine christliche Ethik im Sinne einer einsichtigen Theorie über das, was der Christ zu tun und zu lassen hat.' Schrage notes that this dictum of Augustine's 'war von mir nicht zu verifizieren', except in the form *Dilige, et quod vis fac* (Schrage 1961: 9 n. 2).

21. The centrality of love, ἀγάπη, to the whole of the NT is also the subject of the massive treatment by Spicq (1958–59), who seeks to elaborate a NT theology based around this central theme. See also Furnish 1973; Deidun 1981: 104–226; Söding 1995.

22. Cf. Lategan 1990: 320, who notes 'the apparently underdeveloped nature of Paul's ethical statements [in Galatians] ... the relative scarcity of explicit ethical commands or directions'.

interpreters of Paul's ethics, begins his outline of Pauline ethics (in his major work on *The Ethics of the New Testament* [1988]) by examining their theological basis (Schrage 1988: 167–86).[23] He then sketches the 'nature and structure of the new life' (pp. 186–98) before finally considering the material criteria and concrete ethics Paul presents (pp. 198–239).

An important point to emerge from this approach to Pauline ethics is the close integration of theology and ethics in Paul; this basic insight is unlikely to be dislodged, despite the tendency among earlier scholars such as Martin Dibelius, C.H. Dodd and W.D. Davies to see Paul's ethics as based on traditional forms of early Christian paraenesis,[24] and more recent studies of the parallels between Paul's teaching and the ethical traditions of Judaism and Graeco-Roman philosophy (see §1.2-4 below). Certainly aspects of Paul's theological convictions, especially his Christology, provide a basis and motivation for ethics in crucial ways, as we shall see in more detail in subsequent chapters.[25] Yet, as Schrage's 1961 study shows, there are also distinctions to be made between the basis and motivation Paul provides for his ethics and the actual content of those ethics; in this latter respect, there may well be considerable overlap between Paul's ethics and those evident in other contemporary traditions (including, of course, Paul's own Judaism). These material overlaps are the main focus of the research reviewed in the following two sections, while the significance of the apparently shared ethical convictions will be of relevance later in this study.

The close integration of theology and ethics, and the specific conjunction of indicative and imperative, can, however, be understood and conceptualized in new and different ways, as outlined in ch. 3 below. There I draw on various social-scientific perspectives in order to provide a framework which makes better sense of these connections, and avoids the conundrum Bultmann presumed, that the Pauline indicatives and imperatives are self-contradictory, or at least paradoxical. This framework, moreover, enables Paul's ethics to be studied in ways which go beyond elucidating their internal logic and content on their own terms and in their own language. This is of significance for any attempt to begin to engage Pauline ethics in dialogue with other approaches to ethics, and to consider the contribution Pauline ethics might make to the public sphere, to plural communities and societies. While it is important for understanding the theological framework of Paul's ethics to attempt to

---

23. 'Paul so integrated his ethics into his theology that any presentation of the basis of Pauline ethics must perforce sketch an outline of Pauline theology' (Schrage 1988: 167). Cf. also n.17 above.

24. See e.g. Dibelius 1928: 18–19; Carrington 1940; Dodd 1950; Davies 1955: 111–46.

25. On the motivations for ethical action in Paul, see esp. Merk 1968; specifically on the christological motivations, Cruz 1990.

elucidate, say, the significance of eschatology or the relation between the indicative of justification and the imperative of obedience, it is also important to go beyond this, to theorize Pauline ethics in ways that cast them in terms which can transcend their own specific linguistic/ideological domain, if a conversation beyond the bounds of the Pauline thought-world is to begin.[26]

1.2 *Pauline Ethics as* Halakah

The issue of 'Paul and the (Jewish) Law' has been a prominent preoccupation of Pauline scholars for a long time.[27] In a nutshell, this is because Paul makes both (apparently) positive and (apparently) negative statements about the law, a reflection of the fact that he wishes to affirm that the law plays a role in God's saving purposes and is by no means opposed to them (cf. Gal. 3.21) but also insists that 'being righteoused' ($\delta\iota\kappa\alpha\iota\circ\hat{\upsilon}\sigma\theta\alpha\iota$)[28] comes not through the works of the law but $\delta\iota\grave{\alpha}/\grave{\epsilon}\kappa$ πίστεως Χριστοῦ (Gal. 2.16).[29] Exploring Paul's position on the law is crucial to assessing the extent to which there is continuity and/or discontinuity between Paul and Judaism, or, more specifically, between the pre- and post-conversion Paul.[30]

Of particular relevance to the understanding of Paul's ethics is the question as to whether Paul continues to regard the law as providing ethical guidance, and indeed whether his ethics are to a significant degree derived from scripture, specifically the Torah. Positive and negative

26. Another way of expressing this is to use the anthropological distinction between *emic* and *etic* perspectives, the former using language and terminology that is native, or internal, to a culture or community, the latter utilizing terminology drawn from a foreign or broader discourse, such as the technical language of social science. Both approaches have an important place: emic descriptions attempt to grasp a language or text on its own terms, to understand its own 'world', while etic analyses enable comparison and communication between otherwise distinct linguistic and cultural worlds.

27. For brief introductions, see Roetzel 1995; Horrell 2000a: 69–75, 82–95; Kopalski 2001. There is a massive literature devoted to this topic, to which these aforementioned works provide an initial orientation.

28. I here follow E.P. Sanders in using 'righteous' as a verb, a useful way of retaining visible links between the various Greek words of the *dik-* group (Sanders 1983: 6–10, 13–14 n. 18; 1991: 46; Horrell 2000a: 70–71).

29. Whether to translate πίστις Χριστοῦ as a subjective genitive ('the faith[fulness] of Christ') or objective genitive ('faith in Christ') is currently subject to much debate, which I do not need to enter here; see e.g. the essays in Johnson and Hay 1997: 35–92.

30. Whether the term 'conversion' should be used is controversial, though I think it is apposite. For brief discussion and further references, see Horrell 2000a: 26–27.

answers have been given to this question,[31] though most scholars present a nuanced answer rather than a straightforward yes or no, with the Torah indeed a formative influence, but reconfigured around Christology, centred in the love-command, and in some crucial respects no longer obligatory.[32] However, a number of recent authors have argued that Paul does indeed base his ethics on the Jewish scriptures, and on later Jewish traditions, to a greater extent than has generally been recognized. Brian Rosner, for example, examines a significant section of Pauline teaching, 1 Corinthians 5–7, and concludes that 'the Jewish Scriptures are a crucial and formative source for Paul's ethics' (Rosner 1994: 177).[33] While some of Rosner's suggested parallels and influences are less convincing than others, it is undeniable that Paul's thought, and his ethics, are shaped by the Jewish scriptures; what remains more open to debate is the extent to which other influences are also formative, and where, if at all, Paul's christologically focused ethic departs from the contours of Torah-obedience.

Largely complementary to studies such as Rosner's are recent works which have focused on the extent to which Paul's ethics run parallel to, and may be described as, Jewish *halakah*, developing the earlier claim of W.D. Davies that Paul's pattern of teaching was indebted to Jewish traditions and codes outlining ethics incumbent on all humanity, such as the Noachide commandments and the *derek 'eretz* literature (though Davies sees the words of Jesus as the *primary* source for Paul's ethical teaching and the 'basis for a kind of Christian Halakah' [Davies 1955: 144; see §1.4 below]).[34] Peter Tomson (1990), for example, argues that Paul is developing *halakah* for Gentiles, in ways which demonstrably fit within the context of rabbinic *halakoth*, and as such does not reject or repudiate the Jewish law. Similarly, Markus Bockmuehl (1995; 2000) proposes that Paul's ethics derive much of their substance from the traditions which related Jewish law to Gentiles, specifically the Noachide commandments which the rabbis saw as relevant to all humanity. Bockmuehl's argument is specifically about the substance of Pauline ethics; he makes the distinction between this and the '*theological* key to New Testament ethics', which

---

31. See, e.g., the contrasting essays of von Harnack and Holtz in Rosner 1995: 27–71 and Rosner's discussion on pp. 5–10. Lindemann 1986 argues the case that ethics for Paul is 'keinesfalls die Praktizierung der Tora' (p. 265) but derives rather from the character of life 'in Christ'.

32. Cf., e.g., Furnish 1968: 28–34; Schrage 1961: 228–38; 1988: 201–207.

33. Cf. also Finsterbusch 1996.

34. Davies 1955: 111–36. On the Noachide commandments (which Davies does not see as normative for Paul) see pp. 113–17. Davies concludes: 'While we may have been unable definitely to point to specific Jewish codes used by Paul and the other New Testament writers, we have shown that there was a tradition well defined and familiar within Judaism of ethical exhortation, which would and probably did supply precedents for the early Christian leaders in their work of moral education' (p. 135).

'should instead be sought in christology and the teaching and example of Jesus' (2000: 173).

Thus, according to this perspective, while Paul denies the law a soteriological function, he does not deny it an ethical function.[35] And the reason Paul does not urge circumcision and full observance of the food laws upon his converts is *not* because he has abandoned the law, in at least some respects, but rather because he is writing to *Gentiles*, to whom the whole law does not apply. Paul's view, Tomson suggests, was that 'Jews and gentiles should each stick to their respective ways of life' wherein 'gentiles kept their minimum set of "commandments of God" while Jewish Christians kept "the whole law"' (Tomson 1996: 267, 269). Paul himself thus possessed a 'double membership: of the group of those "respecting the law", the Jews, and of the body of Christ' (Tomson 1990: 281). Bockmuehl presents a similar argument: '[t]he apostle himself in 1 Corinthians 7:17ff makes clear that his "rule for all the churches" is for Jews to keep the Torah (indeed Gal. 5:3, too, may mean they are obliged to do so) and for Gentiles to keep what pertains to them' (Bockmuehl 2000: 170–71). Bockmuehl quotes Michael Wyschogrod with approval: 'The distinction that needs to be made, therefore, is not between the law before Christ and after Christ, but the law for Jews and for Gentiles' (p. 171).

This recent work is undoubtedly important in drawing attention to the parallels between Pauline teaching and biblical and post-biblical Jewish ethics, and in helping to show how some of the particular substantive foci of Pauline ethics – sexual immorality and idolatry, above all – derive from Paul's Judaism and specifically from the Jewish traditions of ethics for Gentiles (cf. also Segal 1990: 187–223). Yet there are also questions to be raised. First one may ask how sharply the distinction between the soteriological and ethical function of the law may be drawn – a crucial point for this perspective – particularly when both dimensions are arguably intertwined in the process of constructing and defining 'Christian' community and identity.[36] Allen Verhey seems closer to the mark in his comment that '[j]ustification by faith rather than by the works of the law establishes a *social reality* in which "there is no distinction" (Rom. 3:22;

35. See, e.g., Finsterbusch 1996: 15, 61, 63–64, 82–83, *et passim*, who argues, 'daß in Paulus' Augen die Thora universaler Maßstab für gerechtes Handeln ist, daß sie aber für Juden und Heiden nicht in gleichem Umfang gültig ist' (p. 15). 'Die Rechtfertigung aus Glauben setzt die ethische Funktion der Thora also nicht außer Kraft' (p. 83); Tomson 1996: 266; Bockmuehl 1998b: 787.

36. Cf. below §3.2; Horrell 2000b; Esler 1996, 1998.

10:12)' (Verhey 1984: 113, my emphasis).[37] Secondly, one may wonder whether this view can sustain a cogent exegesis of Paul's letters themselves. Paul describes himself in ways which seem clearly to express some distance between his current self-perception and his former life in Judaism (Gal. 1.13; Phil. 3.7-8), such that he is now no longer ὑπὸ νόμον (1 Cor. 9.20; cf. Gal. 2.17-21) and can describe himself as becoming on occasion ὡς Ἰουδαῖος (1 Cor. 9.20). He and Peter no longer live like Jews (Ἰουδαϊκῶς) but like Gentiles (ἐθνικῶς, Gal. 2.14). It is telling that Tomson must delete a number of these Pauline statements, on the basis of weak textual evidence, since they conflict with the picture of Paul he presents.[38] Being 'no longer under the law' would seem to imply an ethical as well as soteriological stance, not least when Paul declares his position on food as one in which all foods are clean, a stance which plainly goes against the requirements of the Jewish law (Rom. 14.20). True, he does not impose this stance on all members of the congregation, but it is, nonetheless, expressive of *his* current conviction and practice 'in the Lord Jesus' (Rom. 14.14; see further §6.2 below). Thirdly, the position presented by Tomson, Bockmuehl, and others seems to depend on the assumption that in his ethical teaching Paul is addressing only Gentiles. On a rather general level this must of course be affirmed: Paul's self-declared position is as apostle to the Gentiles (cf. Gal. 1.16; 2.7) and at least some of his congregations seem to be largely Gentile (cf. e.g. 1 Thess. 1.9; 1 Cor. 8.7; 12.3). Yet it is also clear that there were Jews among the congregations to which Paul writes (e.g. Acts 18.2-26; Rom. 16.3, 7, 11, 21, 23; 1 Cor. 1.1, 14; 7.18-19; 16.19),[39] and nowhere does Paul state that his ethical teaching applies only to Gentile converts, while Jewish Christians must obey the whole law.[40] Paul also claims for *all* those

---

37. Granted, there remain crucial questions about what this 'no distinction' means, and specifically whether and in what ways it permits or preserves difference, in this case differences in identity between Jew and Gentile. These issues are the subject of further discussion below, see esp. §4.5, §6.3.4-6.4.

38. See Tomson 1990: 276–79 (on 1 Cor. 9.20). The phrase μὴ ὢν αὐτὸς ὑπὸ νόμον is most likely to have been omitted through homoeoteleuton and most commentators accept the words, as well as the ὡς before Ἰουδαῖος (omitted only in F, G*, 6*, 326, 1729 pc), as original (see Fee 1987: 422 nn. 2–3; Metzger 1994: 493). The phrase καὶ οὐχὶ Ἰουδαϊκῶς in Gal. 2.14 is again most likely original (in some form or other: there are variations in the textual tradition). Following P^{46} in omitting it Tomson paraphrases the sentence thus: 'Before, you agreed to live and eat as a Jew together with the gentiles, and although some call that "living like a gentile", why do you now separate and wish to eat with them only if they become Jews?' (1990: 229–30). This seems to me quite clearly to alter the sense of what Paul actually writes.

39. On Jews among the Corinthian congregation, see further Horrell 1996: 91–92; Richardson 1986; in the Roman church, see Lampe 1987: 53–63; 1991a: 224–25.

40. *Pace* Bockmuehl (2000: 171, quoted above) neither 1 Cor. 7.19 nor Gal. 5.3 firmly supports this point: in the former text it is probably more plausible to take Paul's declaration that circumcision is 'nothing' as an indication that 'keeping the commandments of God', for all Christians, no longer refers to this requirement (cf. Rom. 13.8; Gal. 5.14; §7.3 below). And

in Christ – Gentiles as well as Jews, without distinction (cf. Rom. 3.22; 10.12; 1 Cor. 7.19; Gal. 5.6; 6.15) – the privileged identity descriptions which traditionally belong to what he calls 'Israel according to the flesh' (τὸν Ἰσραὴλ κατὰ σάρκα, 1 Cor. 10.18; cf. Rom. 9.3).[41] All who are in Christ are equally and without distinction descendants of Abraham (Gal. 3.6–4.6, 21-31; cf. Rom. 9.8; 2 Cor. 11.22), the 'people of God' (cf. Rom. 9.24-25; 2 Cor. 6.16), members of a 'redefined' Israel, an 'Israel according to the Spirit' (Ἰσραὴλ κατὰ πνεῦμα, cf. Gal. 4.29; Rom. 9.6-8; esp. Gal. 6.16).[42] Moreover, the social and ethical boundaries Paul draws imply not that his ethical teaching was for Jews and Gentiles to 'stick to their respective ways of life' (Tomson 1996: 267) but rather that the crucial distinction between insider and outsider, ἀδελφός and non-ἀδελφός, now relates to those who are, and are not, 'in the Lord' (ἐν κυρίῳ, 1 Cor. 7.39; cf. 5.11, further ch. 5 below).

The picture of Paul's ethics as assuming a framework in which Jewish Christians and Gentile Christians must accept different ethical obligations, the former following the whole Torah, the latter only that deemed applicable to them, and so as remaining in regard to ethics entirely within the bounds of Torah-loyal Judaism thus seems to me unconvincing. Nonetheless, in showing the extent to which Paul's ethics share much of their substance, as well as their ideological framing, with Jewish traditions, these studies make a fundamental contribution to our understanding.

1.3 *Pauline Ethics and Graeco-Roman Moral Philosophy*

A contrasting approach in recent studies of Paul is taken by those whose concern is to explore the parallels between Paul's teaching and that of contemporary Graeco-Roman philosophers, developing the viewpoint proposed by Martin Dibelius, 'that the "Pauline paraenesis" consists of materials appropriated from the Hellenistic world and then "Christia-

---

Gal. 5.3 serves as a warning to *Gentile* converts not to succumb to the temptation to undergo circumcision (5.1-6); Jewish Christians, like Paul, have died to the law and have no reason, according to Paul, to 'rebuild' that former position (Gal. 2.18-19; Rom. 7.1-6). See further Horrell 2000b: 336–39.

41. Paul also deems the scriptures and the patriarchs to be the heritage of this new community of Gentiles and Jews in Christ (Rom. 15.4; 1 Cor. 10.11; cf. Rom. 4.1). Nonetheless, he also remains acutely conscious of the existence of ethnic Israel, whose 'failure' to convert is a cause of real anguish (Romans 9–11). Paul believed that in the providential purposes of God this tension would be resolved – and soon! – when Israel's time of hardening and unbelief was ended and she finally came to be saved (Rom. 11.23–26).

42. Cf. Dahl 1950: 163; see further Horrell 2000b: 341–42. It is disputed whether Gal. 6.16 refers to the Church; for arguments in favour of this interpretation, see e.g. Dahl 1950; Barclay 1988: 98; Longenecker 1990: 298–99.

nized" by the apostle' (Furnish 1968: 260).[43] These studies are not specifically restricted to the subject of Paul's ethics, but they certainly impinge relevantly upon it. Hans Dieter Betz, for example, commenting on Gal. 5.25–6.10, makes the following provocative claim:

> Paul does not provide the Christian with a specifically Christian ethic. The Christian is addressed as an educated and responsible person. He is expected to do no more than what would be expected of any other educated person in the Hellenistic culture of the time. In a rather conspicuous way Paul conforms to the ethical thought of his contemporaries. (Betz 1979: 292)[44]

Betz's commentary on this section of Galatians constitutes in part an attempt to document this claim, with frequent citation of parallels in ancient philosophy and other contemporary sources. Yet it should also be noted that, while Betz does see Paul drawing on contemporary Hellenistic morality for various aspects of his moral instruction, he does not deny that Paul's ethics have a theological foundation, being based upon his kerygma of Christ crucified: 'Greek philosophical ethics could not provide a suitable foundation for Christian ethics'; yet 'Paul could use whatever material was in conformity with the kerygma upon which his ethics was to be based'.[45]

Two recent dissertations, both directed by Betz, also attempt, through detailed studies of particular passages, to document the extent of the parallels between the ideas expressed in Pauline teaching and in contemporary Graeco-Roman writings. The central claim of Will Deming's study is 'that Paul's discussion of marriage and celibacy [in 1 Corinthians 7] is best understood against the background of Stoic and Cynic discourse on these topics' (Deming 1995: 48). Like some of his Stoic

---

43. See Furnish 1968: 259–62 for an outline of Dibelius's views. In *Urchristentum und Kultur* (1928) Dibelius describes the problems which arose as the Christian movement grew in numbers, and spread among the better-off: questions about the regulation of family and household life, about the use of possessions, about relations with the state and so on became pressing. The Christians therefore looked to traditional material for ethical guidance. Yet the teaching of Jesus could not meet the demands arising in this context, 'denn diese Worte waren in viel einfachere Kulturverhältnisse hinein gesprochen. Regeln zur Ordnung des mannigfach verflochtenen hellenistischen Kulturlebens mußte man der hellenistischen Welt selbst entnehmen, soweit sie den Christen zugänglich war, also dem griechischen Judentum und der Popularphilosophie. Das ist in der Tat geschehen' (p. 18). Dibelius goes on to point to the Stoic origin of household ethics, but speaks of a 'Verchristlichung' of both the content and the form of such ethics as were taken over (p. 19).

44. Cf. also Meeks 1993: 20. For criticism of Betz's proposal here, see Hays 1987.

45. Betz 1989: 56, 58; cf. 67 (also Betz 1988). Betz sees a historical development through the Pauline letters, from 1 Thessalonians, through Galatians and 1–2 Corinthians, to Romans, in which Paul tries in various ways to establish a foundation for his ethics, reaching a mature position only in Rom. 12.1-2. I am not convinced, however, there is sufficient evidence in the texts to sketch these changes and revisions as Betz does.

and Cynic contemporaries, and influenced by their reflections on the subject, Deming suggests, Paul advised against marriage during a period of severe tribulation (cf. 1 Cor. 7.26). Mark Reasoner's study of Rom. 14.1–15.13 explores the evidence concerning vegetarianism, asceticism, observance of special days and so on in first-century Rome, concluding that 'everything in Rom. 14.1–15.13, including Paul's description of the food controversy and his advice for its resolution, fits with what we know of first-century Rome' (Reasoner 1999: 221).

Abraham Malherbe has also done much to illuminate the parallels between Paul's exhortations and those found in moral philosophers contemporary with him.[46] A wide range of popular philosophical traditions must be taken into account, because they all, like Paul, 'aimed at moral reformation' (Malherbe 1989: 5). Focusing particularly on Paul's letters to the Thessalonians, Malherbe comes to the firm conclusion 'that Paul was thoroughly familiar with the teaching, methods of operation, and style of argumentation of the philosophers of the period, all of which he adopted and adapted to his own purposes' (1989: 68; cf. 1987: 94, etc.). Similarly to Betz, Malherbe considers that what most distinguishes Paul's moral exhortation from that of the philosophers are the kinds of motivation, the religious or theological warrants, which Paul employs (1989: 60–61).[47]

By far the most ambitious recent attempt to interpret Paul's thought in the light of ancient moral philosophy is Troels Engberg-Pedersen's major study *Paul and the Stoics* (2000).[48] Engberg-Pedersen is explicitly concerned to go beyond Malherbe and others in finding parallels not merely between various 'particular, relatively minor *topoi*' in Stoic philosophy and in Paul, but with regard to a 'major pattern of thought' (p. 10) which exhibits in both the 'same basic structure' (p. 46, cf. p. 301). Moreover, he is less inclined than Malherbe 'to claim that Paul's thought remains different from that of the moral philosophers at crucial points' (p. 10). In other words, Engberg-Pedersen's claim is much more grand and far reaching: that a certain 'model' of anthropology and ethics can be seen to

---

46. See esp. Malherbe 1987, 1989; and the collection of texts in Malherbe 1986. Malherbe gives an extended *Forschungsbericht* concerning this area of study in Malherbe 1992. Malherbe considers a wide range of Graeco-Roman philosophical traditions, though the Cynic and Epicurean parallels are often found to be of particular significance. The importance of Cynic parallels to Paul and his churches is also stressed by Downing 1998. On the Epicurean parallels, particularly to Paul's strategy of 'adaptability', see esp. Glad 1995.

47. Malherbe speaks of the 'combination of philosophical moral tradition and Christian religious or theological warrant' (1989: 60).

48. Cf. for example the comment of Barclay 2001a: 233: 'one of the most significant and far-reaching treatments of Pauline thought since the Bultmann–Käsemann debates'. See also the major review essays resulting from a panel discussion of Engberg-Pedersen's book at the SBL annual meeting: Attridge 2002; Furnish 2002a; Gaca 2002; Stowers 2002; with response from Engberg-Pedersen 2002a.

underpin both Stoic and Pauline thought; a comparable and fundamental pattern underlies them both (pp. 33–44, etc.). Indeed, while Engberg-Pedersen is reluctant to speculate as to the 'possible roads of influence' (p. 301) it is clear that the direction of traffic is from Stoicism to Paul: it was the Stoics' attempt to articulate a better way of life 'that made Stoicism such an attractive repository of ideas for Paul' (p. 79). This basic (Stoic) pattern of thought with which Engberg-Pedersen elucidates Paul's thought is expressed in terms of a model, referred to as the I-X-S model, where an individual (I) moves by means of X to S: 'The experience of Christ (X) as seen in the Christ-event lifts the individual out of his or her individuality, leaves it behind and carries him or her to a state of communality (S) shared with all those who have undergone the same process ... the model for this process is to be found in Stoicism', *mutatis mutandis*, such as 'reason' in place of Christ (p. 294).[49]

There are a number of features of Engberg-Pedersen's rich treatment of Paul that will resonate with my own, notably his emphasis on the integration of theology and ethics in Paul (p. 295), via his treatment of Paul's letters as essentially paraenetic (p. 294), that is, as 'practical thought' (p. 50), orientated towards a form of life, indeed what Paul considered 'the best form of life' (p. 79). Also notable is his hermeneutical concern, to read Paul as a moral philosopher worth taking seriously, in ways which enable his thought to be considered as a 'real option' for us (see pp. 24–30, 303–304, etc.; cf. §1.6-7 below).[50] In this latter respect, Engberg-Pedersen presents an essentially Bultmannian focus, emphasizing the 'cognitive' dimension of Pauline thought, the appeal to a transformed self-understanding,[51] though one which avoids the individualism of Bultmann's existentialism through a strong emphasis on the communal location in which the convert, with their new identity, finds themselves. One may question whether the I-X-S model – essentially a model of conversion/identity-transformation – accommodates adequately all the key features of Pauline thought, and, conversely, whether other ancient or modern patterns of thought, with or without links to the Stoics, might also be deemed to 'fit' the (rather generalized) model.[52] One may also suggest that the differences between Paul and the Stoics, even on the model's own terms, are more far reaching than Engberg-Pedersen allows, for example, in the different roles played by Christ/God or by reason as the

---

49. See further Engberg-Pedersen 2000: 33–44. Cf. also the brief summary in Downing 2001: 278.

50. For critical discussion on this and other issues, see Martyn 2002 and Engberg-Pedersen 2002b.

51. See, e.g., the references to 'understanding' and 'self-understanding' on Engberg-Pedersen 2000: 168; on the importance of the 'cognitive' dimension, e.g., pp. 296–97.

52. A point well made by Gaca 2002.

transforming X, and (more crucially?) their function in constructing (real) forms of human solidarity and community.[53] A key difference from the current project, however, is simply that Engberg-Pedersen seeks to illuminate the structure and logic of Paul's thought by comparison with an ancient, Stoic, model, whereas my own study involves the attempt to bring Pauline ethics into conversation with contemporary ethics by comparing modern traditions of thought with Paul's.

It is undoubtedly the case that such research has considerably broadened our appreciation of the extent to which Paul's ethics display points of contact with various moral and philosophical traditions contemporary with him, even, if we follow Engberg-Pedersen, quite fundamental similarities in their pattern of thought.[54] In some cases, however, focusing on certain sources of parallels leads to a neglect of other important information. Just as Rosner, for example, in his desire to focus on the scriptural sources of Paul's teaching, minimizes the Graeco-Roman parallels in a treatment far too swift to be convincing (Rosner 1994: 29–33), so too some who have chosen to focus on the Graeco-Roman parallels may be criticized for ignoring or downplaying the parallels in Jewish sources.[55] When, for example, Malherbe discusses Paul's pastoral letter to the Thessalonians as a new literary creation, though with 'pagan predecessors' (1987: 68–69), it seems odd not to consider the diaspora letters in Jewish texts as a comparable phenomenon (cf. Jer. 29; Dan. 4.1, 37c [LXX]; 6.26 [LXX: Theod.]; 2 Macc. 1.1-9; *2 Bar* 78.2–86.1; note also Acts 15.23-29; James 1.1; 1 Pet. 1.1).[56] More significantly, one must surely question whether Engberg-Pedersen can hope to grasp the basic structure of Paul's thought in a treatment which, according to its own index, makes

53. Cf. the points raised by Barclay 2001a and Esler 2004 (esp. pp. 108–14).

54. Engberg-Pedersen elsewhere presses for a methodological preference in favour of similarity rather than difference, claiming that 'an adequate historical analysis must leave out the category of uniqueness' (2001: 2). Granted, uniqueness cannot be presumed on theological grounds, nor asserted without extensive historical comparison, but – without implying any theological judgment – good history must surely always appreciate uniqueness in all contexts and traditions of human thought and action: no two phenomena are ever actually the same, and to shelve any notion of uniqueness is to marginalize what may be crucial, perhaps from a misguided zeal to avoid theologically grounded privilege. As John Milbank writes, the early Church's 'surprising, unique features are precisely the reason why it made a historical difference, why we are still interested in it at all'. Milbank emphasizes that he is 'not making an apologetic point here, but only an historical one' (1990: 117; see further pp. 116–21). Cf. also Esler's (2004) stress on the differences between Paul's and the Stoics' moral vision.

55. E.g. Deming 1995: 142; Reasoner 1999: 128–38, 146–58. Reasoner's own evidence seems to point rather more strongly in the direction of Jewish concerns being central to the situation Paul addresses in Romans 14–15 than Reasoner allows.

56. See further Taatz 1991; Bauckham 1999: 11–28. Taatz examines the letters in 2 Maccabees, the letters of the Jeremiah–Baruch tradition, and the letters from Elephantine as context for understanding the Pauline letters.

not a single reference to an Old Testament or any other Jewish text (Engberg-Pedersen 2000).[57] Nonetheless, the essential insight of these studies, along with those outlined in the previous section, must be affirmed, despite disagreement over the relative weight of influence from Jewish and Graeco-Roman traditions: that at a number of points, the content of Paul's moral exhortation exhibits similarity with, and probably the influence of, contemporary Graeco-Roman as well as Jewish moral traditions. Nor is it to be denied, in contrast, that Paul gives to his ethical instruction a distinctively Christian, theological basis and motivation.[58] What remains open to debate is the *extent* to which this theological basis shapes and forms the character and content of Pauline ethics, or, put the other way round, the extent to which they reproduce what was morally commonplace or presume a model essentially derived from other ancient traditions.

1.4 *Pauline Ethics and the Teaching of Jesus*

A third area to which scholars have looked in their quest to understand the shape and content of Pauline ethics is the teaching of Jesus. Here the work of C.H. Dodd and W.D. Davies forms an influential landmark in early research. In his examination of Paul's phrase ἔννομος Χριστοῦ (1 Cor. 9.21; cf. Gal. 6.2), Dodd argued that this refers primarily to 'the precepts which Jesus Christ was believed to have given to his disciples, and which they handed down in the Church ... maxims which formed part of the tradition of the sayings of Jesus are treated as if they were in some sort elements of a new Torah'.[59] Davies, one of Dodd's (and David Daube's) students, developed this view much more emphatically in his examination of Paul in the context of rabbinic Judaism (Davies 1955). While Davies considered that Jewish ethical traditions had influenced Paul and the early Christians (cf. §1.2 above) he was clear 'that it was the words of Jesus Himself that formed Paul's primary source in his work as ethical διδάσκαλος' (p. 136). Following (though not entirely uncritically) Alfred Resch's study of the parallels between the synoptic gospels and the Pauline

---

57. Interpreting Paul 'beyond the Judaism/Hellenism divide' (Engberg-Pedersen 2001) should not mean ignoring Judaism!

58. Cf. already the conclusions of Schrage 1961: 200–209 (see §1.1 above). Note also the conclusions of Lategan 1990 (largely in dialogue with the work of Betz) on the question as to whether or not Paul presents a distinctively Christian ethic in Galatians: 'The answer is both no and yes ... no in the sense that in terms of content, he is neither introducing new concepts nor proposing a line of conduct that is in conflict with the conventional morality of the time ... yes in the sense that Paul develops a new understanding of what ethical responsibility entails' (p. 327).

59. Dodd 1968, quotations from pp. 147 and 145 respectively.

epistles (Resch 1904), Davies concluded that the words of Jesus 'permeate all his [sc. Paul's] ethical instructions' (p. 141); 'Paul is steeped in the mind and words of his Lord' (p. 140). Moreover, in examining the phrase 'the law of Christ', Davies suggests

> that Paul must have regarded Jesus in the light of a new Moses, and that he recognized in the words of Christ a νόμος τοῦ Χριστοῦ which formed for him the basis for a kind of Christian Halakah. When he used the phrase νόμος τοῦ Χριστοῦ he meant that the actual words of Jesus were for him a New Torah. (p. 144; cf. pp. 145, 147)

Davies also makes clear, however, that Paul did not focus only on the *words* of Jesus, but also on his person and character: 'when Paul had to impress certain ethical duties upon his converts he appealed to what Jesus essentially was and did' (p. 147; cf. p. 149).

This kind of 'maximalist' case for the influence of Jesus' teaching upon Paul's ethics has recently been reasserted by David Wenham (1995). Wenham's examination is not restricted to the topic of ethics, however, but much more generally argues for 'massive overlap' between the teaching of Jesus and Paul, with many echoes of Jesus' teaching detected in Paul's letters (p. 377). Moreover, 'the overall structure of Jesus' and Paul's theology is the same' (p. 399). Thus Paul can more fairly be described as a 'follower of Jesus' than as 'founder of Christianity'.

There are, however, strong reasons to question the case Davies and Wenham (in different ways) present. There has long been debate concerning the extent of Paul's interest in, and knowledge of, the historical Jesus and his teaching, with Davies and Wenham representing the maximalist case made earlier by Resch, and Bultmann, and more recently Nikolaus Walter and Frans Neirynck, the minimalist position.[60] Bultmann famously expressed the view that Paul's theology was a 'new structure' little influenced by the content and shape of Jesus' teaching and message:

> his [sc. Paul's] letters barely show traces of the influence of Palestinian tradition concerning the history and preaching of Jesus. All that is important to him in the story of Jesus is the fact that Jesus was born a Jew and lived under the Law (Gal. 4:4) and that he had been crucified … Paul's theology proper, with its theological, anthropological, and soteriological ideas, is not at all a recapitulation of Jesus' own preaching nor a further development of it … (Bultmann 1952: 188–89)

---

60. An overview of the early debate (from Baur to Bultmann) is given by Furnish 1989; for a brief survey of more recent debate, see Barclay 1993a. For concise overviews see also Furnish 1993; Dunn 1994. The terms maximalist and minimalist are used to contrast those who argue for a very widespread and evident influence of Jesus' teaching in Paul's letters (the maximalist case) and those who argue that there are only very few signs of such influence (the minimalist case).

Neirynck and Walter independently assess the evidence for the use of Jesus tradition in Paul's letters and come to similar and minimal conclusions:[61] 'In the Pauline epistles there are two instances of an explicit reference to a command of the Lord, in 1 Cor 7,10-11 and 9,14 ... Elsewhere in the Pauline letters there is no certain trace of a conscious use of sayings of Jesus' (Neirynck 1986: 320; cf. Walter 1989). To these two references are often added 1 Cor. 11.23-25 and 1 Thess. 4.15-17,[62] though Neirynck and Walter dispute the latter, on the grounds that the phrase ἐν λόγῳ κυρίου ('by a word of the Lord') might equally well refer to a prophetic saying communicated by the ascended Lord to Paul or some other Christian prophet (cf. 2 Cor. 12.9 [ὁ κύριος] εἴρηκέν μοι ...).[63] Furthermore, they regard 1 Cor. 11.23–25 as something of a special case. Walter points out that the passage is clearly available to Paul through being fixed in tradition (Walter 1989: 54–55). It 'stems from liturgical and ritual tradition and so is in a special position'.[64] Neirynck agrees with Walter: 'Since 1 Cor 11,23-25 is a quotation of a liturgical tradition, the command ordaining support for the apostles in 9,14 and the command of the Lord prohibiting divorce in 7,10-11 are the only explicit references to an actual saying of Jesus in 1 Corinthians' (Neirynck 1986: 277). Romans 14.14 may also be mentioned as a possible indication of Paul's knowledge of the Jesus tradition (πέπεισμαι ἐν κυρίῳ Ἰησοῦ ὅτι ...),[65] where there is a possible allusion to Mk 7.15 (//Mt. 15.11), used, significantly, in discussing an ethical issue (see §6.2 below), though it is by no means certain that πέπεισμαι ἐν κυρίῳ Ἰησοῦ should be taken as an explicit reference to Jesus' teaching (note, for example, the same phrase in Phil. 2.19: Ἐλπίζω δὲ ἐν κυρίῳ Ἰησοῦ Τιμόθεον ταχέως πέμψαι ὑμῖν).[66]

Whether or not one finds such minimalist conclusions entirely compelling, it is nonetheless widely agreed, and hardly to be disputed, that there are only very few places where Paul *explicitly* cites teaching which he attributes to Jesus (cf. Wenham 1995: 3–4). (It is important to

---

61. See Walter 1989: 80 n. 60 and Neirynck 1986: 321, where each refers, in conclusion, to the parallel work of the other; also Wedderburn 1989d: 117 n. 1.

62. See e.g. Sanders and Davies 1989: 323–30 with 352 n. 13; Neirynck 1986: 306–20; Goulder 1974: 144–47.

63. Neirynck 1986: 308–11; Walter 1989: 66–67; also Allison 1982: 26 n. 18; Dunn 1994: 161 n. 17. Richardson (1980) suggests (tentatively) that 1 Cor. 7.10 may be a word from the exalted Lord rather than from (earthly) Jesus tradition, but few have followed this view. This is one of the few places where there seems to be clear contact between Paul and the synoptic tradition.

64. Walter 1989: 60, see pp. 62–63 on 1 Cor. 11.23-25 and the question of Paul's knowledge of a passion narrative; also Wenham 1995: 4 n. 11.

65. Further possibilites are listed by Kim 1993: 475–80; Wenham 1995. Allison (1982: 2) also lists 1 Cor. 7.25 and 14.37 as references to '"Words of the Lord" in Paul's epistles'.

66. Cf. also Gal. 5.10; Phil. 1.14; 2.24; Walter 1989: 57; Neirynck 1986: 307–308.

note that this is a characteristic shared with virtually all the earliest Christian epistles.)[67] Thus, while one can certainly discuss possible echoes of the synoptic tradition in Paul,[68] and assess the extent of theological or ethical similarity between Jesus and Paul,[69] it is highly implausible to claim, as Davies does, that the words of Jesus formed Paul's primary source for ethical instruction. Resch's argument for a huge number of parallels is widely recognized as vastly overstated. Paul's letters are strikingly *lacking* in places where Paul appeals to Jesus' teaching when giving moral guidance: he does not make appeals based on 'what the Lord Jesus said'.[70] Davies's interpretation of the 'law of Christ' as a 'New Torah' is also highly unlikely, not least since the notion of a new Torah for the messianic age has been shown to be lacking in the Jewish sources.[71] What Paul does mean by the law of Christ will need to be discussed more fully in the course of our study (see §7.3). What we shall find as a fundamental influence on the shape and content of Paul's ethics is *not* the words and teaching of Jesus but rather the self-giving of Jesus Christ, which constitutes a principal moral paradigm (see ch. 7).

1.5 *Morals and Community: Pauline Ethics in Social Context*

One of the notable developments in New Testament studies since the 1970s has been the increased interest in social aspects of early Christianity and the pursuit of this interest through approaches which use a wide variety of resources – models, theories, typologies and so on – drawn from the social sciences, primarily sociology and anthropology.[72] This interest in social questions has long historical roots, as explored by Ralph Hochschild (1999), but (re)emerged in the 1970s after a period of neglect, revitalized by

67. See Thompson 1991: 36–76, who helpfully outlines the range of possible reasons for this lack of explicit citation.

68. To give just two examples, 1 Cor. 13.2 seems to echo Mt. 17.20, and Rom. 12.14-17 shows clear points of contact with Mt. 5.39-44//Lk. 6.27-36. The latter may indeed show that Paul draws here on early Christian paraenetic tradition, which may in turn be rooted in dominical teaching; see further §8.4. On the possible echoes in Romans 12–15 see further Thompson 1991.

69. On which see Wedderburn 1989c; Wenham 1995. Wedderburn helpfully points out that questions about similarity are not the same as questions about continuity, the latter implying direct links and historical connections (1989b: 13–14; cf. 1989c and 1989d).

70. Contrast Acts 20.35, though this is the only place in Acts where a 'saying' (supposedly) of Jesus is directly quoted, and for specific reasons (see Horrell 1997a: 598–99).

71. Schäfer 1974 assesses the evidence concerning the view of the Torah in the messianic age and reaches the conclusion, 'daß weder die Vorstellung einer neuen Torah noch die Erwartung einer völligen Aufhebung der Torah für das rabbinische Judentum charakteristisch ist' (p. 42; cf. p. 36). Cf. also Räisänen 1992: 225–51; Bockmuehl 2000: 14.

72. For overviews of this area of NT studies, see Horrell 1999, 2002a.

the possibilities offered by the expanding social sciences.[73] The development of so-called social-scientific approaches (cf. Horrell 1999) has led to a number of new perspectives on Pauline ethics.[74]

The early work of Gerd Theissen, for example, which has been so influential in this area of New Testament studies, was concerned not so much with Paul's ethics as with the social context of the Corinthian congregation, seeking to analyse the pattern of social stratification among the members of the church and to assess the impact of this social stratification upon various disputes and conflicts within the community (Theissen 1982).[75] Yet Theissen also sought to assess the character of Paul's response to these conflicts, and thus to describe the way in which Paul's teaching shaped the social relationships among members of the congregation. Hence his work attempts to grasp the kind of social ethic Paul developed.[76] Theissen describes this ethic as one of 'love patriarchalism', which 'takes social differences for granted, but ameliorates them through an obligation of respect and love, an obligation imposed upon those who are socially stronger. From the weak are required subordination, fidelity and esteem' (Theissen 1982: 107). This assessment of the character of Paul's ethic, derived in part from Ernst Troeltsch (1931: 69–89), may certainly be questioned,[77] but it valuably draws our attention to questions concerning the ways in which Pauline teaching impacts upon social relationships and attempts to shape them. These questions are important in any assessment of Paul's ethics.

In various ways, a number of other recent studies have explored the character of early Christian morality in its community, or more broadly social, context. Wayne Meeks, for example, has investigated the moral world of the first Christians (1986) and, adopting an ethnographic approach (Meeks 1993: 8–11), has sought to show how the process of forming communities and generating moral reflection proceeded in the first

---

73. On the reasons for the neglect and the reemergence of interest, see Barton 1992: 399–406; Theissen 1993: 1–29.

74. Stephen Barton, for example, speaks of the ways in which social-scientific criticism has 'revitalized' historical criticism, and suggests that it 'remains to be seen' whether this approach can also revitalize the study of New Testament theology and ethics. Barton mentions the work of Wayne Meeks and William Countryman (see below) as 'promising beginnings' in this latter regard (Barton 1997: 286; cf. also 1995).

75. Theissen's essays were originally published in the mid-1970s and first collected in book form in Theissen 1979. To locate Theissen's studies in the context of scholarly studies of the Corinthian church, see Adams and Horrell 2004.

76. Rosner (1995) therefore includes one of Theissen's essays in a section dealing with 'the social dimension of Pauline ethics', as well as essays (by Edwin Judge and Bruce Winter) which relate to 'the social context of Pauline ethics'.

77. See Horrell 1996 for criticism of the love patriarchalism thesis (esp. pp. 126–98). For the derivation of the idea of love patriarchalism from Troeltsch, see pp. 126–27.

two centuries of Christianity's existence.[78] For Meeks, making morals and making community are essentially one, indistinguishable process (1993: 5, 213), and Meeks's interest focuses not so much on 'ethics' as reflection on moral practice, but rather on morality itself, defined as 'a pervasive and, often, only partly conscious set of value-laden dispositions, inclinations, attitudes, and habits' (1993: 4). Meeks thus broadens the concerns of an enquiry into the ethics of the first Christians from a focus on rules or moral arguments to a consideration of the whole process of 'the moral formation of the early Christian communities' (1986: 13); the New Testament texts, Meeks suggests, 'had as their primary aim the shaping of the life of Christian communities' (1986: 12); they are instruments of 'moral formation' (Meeks 1996a: 317–18; cf. 2001: 136). Indeed, Meeks makes it clear that questions such as 'What does the New Testament teach on homosexuality (or other such topics)?' are 'historically naïve', since early Christian morality was a complex and diverse system 'that defies reduction to basic rules or underlying principles' (1993: ix). More provocatively put, '[t]here was not even ... any such thing as "New Testament ethics." What the ethnographer of early Christianity finds is only a record of experimentation, of trial and error, of tradition creatively misread and innovation craftily wedged into the cracks of custom' (1993: 216).

While Meeks intends his study as an essentially historical enquiry, and eschews any attempt to discern contemporary ethics from the 'ethics' found in the New Testament, he does elucidate a number of key theses which, he considers, follow from his study of early Christian morality (1993: 213–19). One is that 'a Christian moral community must be rooted in the past', and specifically must regard its roots in Judaism as a 'privileged dimension of its past' and indeed its present (pp. 214–15). However, Meeks is equally clear that the past cannot be replicated. Implicitly critical of the rhetoric of 'following the New Testament's teaching', or 'obeying the Bible', he stresses the danger of anachronism, maintains that there was no 'golden age' of early Christian ethics which contemporary Christians might emulate, and insists that 'faithfulness ought not to be confused with nostalgia' (p. 215). Instead, the diversity of early Christian ethics, and specifically the polyphonic ethics of Paul 'at his best', should teach us that 'Christian ethics must be polyphonic' (p. 216; cf. Meeks 1988). Again with a clear if implicit polemic against certain kinds of

---

78. This also involves for Meeks studying a range of early Christian documents, within and beyond the canon; for the historian there is no reason to privilege the canonical texts alone. A comparable approach is taken by McDonald 1998, who also explores the contexts and traditions within which early Christian morality was formed, and sees moral reflection as emerging from the ethos which faith communities translate into practice and articulate as teaching (cf. p. 10).

appeal to 'biblical' morality, Meeks insists that it is not 'moral certainty' but rather 'moral confidence' that we require (1993: 217).

Much more explicitly concerned to find ways to derive contemporary ethics from the New Testament, yet equally concerned to understand the New Testament's teaching in its social and cultural context is William Countryman (1988). For Countryman, it is vital to appreciate the profound cultural differences between the New Testament world and our own – by which Countryman means essentially the USA, his own context (1988: 143, 237, etc.).[79] Indeed the strangeness of the biblical text can serve an important theological purpose: 'to relativize the present, to rule out in advance the notion that things can be only as they are' (p. 238; cf. p. 4). Countryman's specific focus is on sexual ethics, but rather than seek simply to exegete the relevant texts, he argues that the New Testament's sexual ethics can only be understood in the context of codes of purity and of property, codes which vary from culture to culture (p. 4). Countryman's argument is that the New Testament writers do not insist on conformity to the external purity code; they imply rather 'the end of the ethic of physical purity' (p. 143). For Paul specifically, this is seen in his stance regarding Gentiles, whom he did not expect to adhere to the physical purity code (p. 117). New Testament sexual ethics are instead based on the property code, in which the fundamental sin is greed, taking the property of another (pp. 147–48).

These findings are then brought to bear on the task of outlining a contemporary sexual ethics (pp. 237–67). Since the New Testament writers do not insist on adherence to a purity code, neither should a contemporary Christian sexual ethic. 'Individual Christians may continue to observe the purity code of their culture, but they may not demand that other Christians do so' (p. 241). A sexual ethic can, however, base itself on the principle of sexual property, though a fundamental shift between the worlds of antiquity and western modernity needs to be recognized: in the former, 'sexual property belonged to the family through the agency of the male householder, in our own era it belongs to the individual' (p. 241). Thus a cardinal sin in the New Testament world was adultery, infringing the sexual property rights of the male householder to whom a woman belonged, whereas in our own day it is rape, taking another's sexual property without their consent (pp. 157–59, 247–50). Countryman also considers the types of 'goods' which sexual relationships are intended to convey and how these too change with time. For the New Testament

79. This concern to avoid anachronistic and ethnocentric interpretations, and to appreciate the differences between 'Mediterranean' culture and modern American (and Western European) culture, is fundamental to the work of the Context Group: see esp. Malina 1981; Rohrbaugh 1996; Neyrey 1990; Malina and Neyrey 1996, etc., and the discussion in Horrell 1999: 12–15.

writers, the capacity to engender children as heirs was a fundamental good of marriage (hence the prominent problem of the 'barren' wife). Now, different perceptions of the essential goods – companionship, mutual support, etc. – lead to different ethical consequences:

> the church ... may as easily bless homosexual as heterosexual unions, for the new definition of the goods making up sexual property, which has already come informally to prevail in our society, makes no distinction between the two. Two persons of the same sex cannot engender children and could not therefore have contracted a full-fledged marriage in the familial milieu of the New Testament itself; they are, however, fully capable of giving one another the interior goods demanded by marriage in our time. (p. 263)

Countryman's provocative book, with its radical conclusions,[80] will hardly convince all, and questions may be raised at the exegetical level (have purity concerns been excluded to the extent that Countryman asserts, e.g. in 1 Cor. 5–7 [cf. §5.2 below]?), as well as the theological and hermeneutical (are the underlying cultural principles concerning property and greed the best route to appropriating the New Testament's sexual ethics?). Nonetheless, it does demonstrate the potential for understanding the New Testament's ethical prescriptions in a broader framework and in their cultural context, and shows that appreciating the cultural gap between now and then need not imply the irrelevance of the Bible to contemporary ethical discussion.

A social-scientific approach such as that represented by Meeks, which treats the early Christian texts as community-forming documents, instruments of moral formation, will be of central importance in this study (see §3.1). However, in contrast to Meeks's studies, more space will be given to elucidating the theoretical framework within which to conceive of this process of moral formation, and also to outlining some key directions in contemporary ethical theory as a context in which to attempt a reading of Paul's ethics. While Meeks is highly cautious about attempts to use the Bible in contemporary ethics, I hope to show that making such links is of considerable value, and can be done in ways which avoid the naïve anachronism Meeks rightly opposes. Moreover, while Meeks focuses on early Christian 'morality' as an 'only partly conscious' set of values and habits (1993: 4), I intend to focus much more on Paul's letters as precisely conscious reflection on moral issues, indeed as a kind of moral philosophy (cf. §3.4). Paul does devote considerable energy to formulating moral arguments, and to trying to construct the kind of moral framework which

---

80. E.g.: 'the gospel allows no rule against the following, in and of themselves: masturbation, nonvaginal heterosexual intercourse, bestiality, polygamy, homosexual acts, or erotic art and literature' (Countryman 1988: 243).

can sustain the unity of the communities to which he writes. Thus, while following Meeks's focus away from a narrow conception of 'ethics' and towards the broader, community-forming dimensions of the texts, in contrast to Meeks, the reading of Pauline ethics in the context of contemporary ethical theory is intended to facilitate reflection on the contemporary potential of these first-century examples of moral reflection and formation.

1.6 *Appropriating Pauline Ethics*

As well as adopting approaches which attempt to understand early Christian ethics in their socio-historical and cultural context, Meeks, and especially Countryman, also give some space to considering the contemporary implications of their studies. Nonetheless, sustained reflection on how this contemporary appropriation might take place has been largely lacking.[81] In 1983 Thomas Ogletree opened his book on the use of the Bible in Christian ethics with the statement that '[i]n the past twenty-five years a troublesome gap has developed between biblical scholarship and studies in Christian ethics' (Ogletree 1983: xi). Twelve years later, in his 1995 presidential address to the Society of Biblical Literature, Leander Keck indicated that the situation had hardly changed: 'conversation between the subfield of New Testament ethics and Christian ethics is not flourishing' (Keck 1996: 4).[82] There have of course been various attempts to bridge the gap between biblical studies and contemporary ethics, Countryman's included (see above), but generally the comments of Ogletree and Keck are apposite, especially in certain respects.[83]

---

81.   This is a point also stressed by Burridge, forthcoming.

82.   Keck's response to this lack is to call for study to analyse the NT material in terms of 'reasons given for or against behavior – the warrants and sanctions – and then to develop a taxonomy of adduced reasons' (1996: 8).

83.   Note, however, specifically in relation to Paul, Hasenstab 1977; and Halter 1977. Hasenstab examines the various models with which Paul's ethics have been read and appropriated. His main aim is to develop not a model of Pauline ethics in the historical sense, but an 'Autonomie-Modell aus paulinischem Geist' (p. 25), for which he finds the notion of κλῆσις in Paul the most valuable resource (pp. 26, 316–17, etc.). His book thus represents one attempt to draw on Pauline ethics in developing contemporary models for moral theology, but the model Hasenstab seeks is one in which autonomy is the central and defining feature. Autonomy, however, seems remote from the central concerns and assumptions of Pauline ethics, with their thoroughly communal and corporate focus. (Cf. Verhey's comments on the idea of an 'autonomous' ethic as entirely incompatible with biblical ethics, though Verhey has in view an ethic with a stance of 'neutral rationality' rather than one based on a sense of personal autonomy [1984: 175–76].) Halter, through a lengthy study of Pauline passages dealing with baptism, and of the character of the existence of those baptized in Christ, seeks to

Ogletree's book itself represents an attempt precisely to bridge the gap its author laments. While a number of studies attempt to draw links between biblical ethics and contemporary *Christian* ethics, Ogletree's is one of very few works to engage more widely with various 'conceptions of the moral life in modern Western thought' in forming a framework with which to approach the understanding of biblical ethics. Ogletree looks at what he terms consequentialist, deontological, and perfectionist perspectives in contemporary ethics, and, noting weaknesses in each approach, seeks to unite 'their central elements into a single, complex theory' (Ogletree 1983: 34). When he turns to Paul (after chapters on Old Testament morality and the synoptic gospels) Ogletree begins by focusing on the 'motif' of justification by faith, which 'celebrates the acquittal of the guilty' and thus 'highlights what we have come to call the "indicative" of the gospel' (p. 138). The second dominant motif, that of 'dying and rising with Christ', to which Ogletree next turns, 'attests the change which the gospel effects in persons of faith' and thus 'highlights what we have come to call the "imperative" of the gospel' (p. 138; see pp. 146–52). This 'death-resurrection motif', Ogletree suggests, 'functions as a model of Christian self-giving which we are called to imitate ... Christ's dying and rising, particularly his dying, have normative significance for the moral life of the Christian' (p. 148). Specifically, the imitation to which the Christian is called implies 'a readiness to suffer for the sake of the gospel; humility and self-abasement before God; and self-giving, even self-subjection, to the neighbor' (p. 148; see pp. 148–50). Turning to the subject of 'cultural pluralism and the unity of faith' (pp. 152–68), Ogletree perceives as Paul's 'central preoccupation ... to devise concrete ways in which Jew and gentile, slave and free, male and female might enact in human community their oneness in Christ' (p. 152). In Paul's treatment of cultural forms as relative, provisionally valid but not determinative (p. 155), Ogletree sees important material for 'the imaginative development of social thought in a modern context of cultural pluralism ... The controlling image is that of a common life which embraces and even encourages plurality so long as that plurality does not violate the whole, but rather enriches it and builds it up' (pp. 158–59; cf. p. 171). Christ's 'humilation and exaltation ... model receptivity to fellow human beings in their strangeness and difference in order that new modes of community might be formed' (p. 158). In concluding the book, Ogletree points, among other things, to the importance of criticism and critical theory as means to establish critical

---

outline Pauline criteria for the characteristics (*proprium*) of Christian morality ('das Proprium der christlichen Moral, d.h. ... Identität und Besonderheit der christlichen Existenz und ihres Ethos' [1977: 455]). The large majority of the book, however, is taken up with discussion of the Pauline material. A concern to read Pauline ethics with a view to the contemporary renewal of moral theology also characterizes the approach of Deidun 1981.

distance from dominant social institutions, but insists also that criticism 'remains abstract and empty unless it is funded by concrete experiences of social alternatives', which the fellowship of the church should provide (p. 185). Ogletree also raises the questions as to whether, and how, the 'eschatological ethic' that the New Testament represents can 'concern itself directly with the well-being of the larger society' (p. 187). He proposes criteria for Christian social involvement (pp. 189–90), underlying which is the claim 'that a Christian social ethic must proceed not on the basis of explicit New Testament commentary on economic and political institutions, but by analogy to developments within the early Christian communities themselves' (p. 192).

Ogletree's book, and specifically the chapter on Paul, contains many suggestive insights which will be seen to resonate with the central themes and arguments of this book. His attempt to fuse major traditions of ethical theory into one 'single, complex theory' (p. 34) is, however, probably overambitious, and, moreover, does not allow one to consider whether and in what ways the biblical traditions might resonate more with certain approaches rather than others, or might be suggestive in terms of developing a critique of one approach or other. His treatment of Paul is of course relatively brief, leaving much more to be done by way of detailed exegesis.

Allen Verhey's (1984) study of ethics in the New Testament is likewise concerned not only to outline the ethics of the various New Testament texts – though Verhey does that at some length, beginning with the ethic of Jesus (pp. 6–152) – but also to consider how these texts may be used in Christian ethics. In contrast to Ogletree, however, Verhey's focus in this latter regard is on how scripture should be used and regarded as an authoritative source for Christian ethics. He gives only a little attention to 'other sources of moral guidance', including various traditions of ethical theory (pp. 166–68, 187–94). In this focus on how the New Testament's ethics can be read and appropriated as scripture in the life of the church, with scripture as the final and ultimate authority, Verhey's approach is very close to that of Richard Hays (1997a). Just as Verhey insists that judgments about the message of scripture 'must be fashioned and exercised only in the midst of reverently listening to *the whole canon within the believing community*' (Verhey 1984: 168–69) and aims to contribute to 'the church's task of continually rediscovering and recovering a manner of life worthy of its story and its scripture' (pp. 186–87), so too Hays makes clear that his intended audience consists primarily of 'readers who stand within a community whose identity is constituted by its confession that the New Testament is normative' (Hays 1997a: 10); the book is an invitation to a '*critical, reflective conversation in which we stand together under the judgment and guidance of scripture*' (p. xi).

Since Hays's book represents the most significant and wide-ranging recent study of New Testament ethics, it is appropriate to devote some space to outlining its contents and considering pertinent criticisms, not least in order to make clear where this project distinguishes itself from Hays's important work.

Hays's concern is to do much more than to outline the ethics of the various New Testament texts; the majority of the book is devoted to considering how the 'witness' of these diverse texts might be synthesized, interpreted, and applied today. But the first task to be attempted, according to Hays, is a 'descriptive' one, which consists, fundamentally, of 'listening' to the diverse voices of the New Testament: 'Our first responsibility as interpreters is to listen to the individual witnesses' (p. 188). The survey of New Testament texts, which begins with Paul and ends with Revelation (pp. 13–185), is 'governed by a rigorous intent to let the individual texts have their say, to allow the distinctive voice of each to be heard' (p. 187). (This survey is, however, selective: as Bockmuehl notes [1997: 86], 'Hebrews and 1 Peter are notably absent'.)

Next Hays considers how these diverse voices might be synthesized, in order to allow a coherent moral vision to emerge. While insisting that the diversity within the texts must not be artificially harmonized, and arguing against 'love' and 'liberation' as adequate 'focal images' to unify the New Testament's ethical message, Hays proposes three such images as the most adequate to guide a synthetic reading: community, cross, and new creation (1997a: 187–205). These serve as *'lenses* that bring our reading of the canonical texts into sharper focus as we seek to discern what is central or fundamental in the ethical vision of the New Testament as a whole' (p. 200).

The third major section of the book is devoted to what Hays calls 'the hermeneutical task', and appraises five diverse ways in which scripture is used in ethics, in the work of Reinhold Niebuhr, Karl Barth, John Howard Yoder, Stanley Hauerwas, and Elisabeth Schüssler Fiorenza, concluding with some normative proposals on how we should use the texts (pp. 207–312). The work of each of these representative figures is assessed by examining their modes of appeal to scripture, their use of 'other modes of authority' (tradition, reason, and experience), and the concrete communal embodiment that has, or might, result from their particular version of the moral vision. Hays poses 'diagnostic questions' to each of these interpreters, asking how they measure up in each of the four stages of the task of interpretation, which correspond to the major sections of the book: descriptive (exegetical engagement), synthetic (selective or comprehensive approach), hermeneutical (modes of appeal and appeals to other sources of authority), and pragmatic (embodiment in community) (see pp. 212–13).

Finally, Hays himself turns to the 'pragmatic task', and examines a number of 'test cases' in the attempt to discern what 'living under the word' might mean today (pp. 313–470): violence, divorce and remarriage, homosexuality, anti-Judaism and ethnic conflict, abortion, and, more briefly, sharing possessions, which slightly oddly appears as a kind of mini-chapter within the conclusion. In each of these cases, Hays proceeds through his four stages of interpretation: reading the texts, attempting a synthesis, hermeneutics, and practical application ('living the text'). His conclusions are clear and forthright, for example, on the rejection of violence, on the value and intended permanence of marriage, though with divorce and remarriage allowed in certain situations, and on the principle of 'sexual abstinence' for homosexuals unable 'to change their orientation and enter a heterosexual marriage relationship' (p. 401).[84]

Hays's major book has, unsurprisingly, received a number of major reviews, and the reviewers raise many significant questions alongside their generally warm appreciation of the book's merits.[85] Some of these questions, while important, are not highly pertinent to the current project, for obvious reasons, such as Richard Burridge's question as to whether Hays makes Paul (rather than Jesus) too central to his description of the New Testament's ethics, deriving his focal images – community, cross and new creation – primarily from Paul's letters (Burridge 1998).[86] Burridge also questions Hays's dismissal of love and liberation as possible lenses for

---

84. On this controversial issue, while Hays is clear in insisting that homosexuality (*sic*) should not be singled out as a 'special sin', when the New Testament gives far greater grounds for the condemnation of greed, materialism or violence (Hays 1997a: 400, 403), he is surprisingly forthright in regarding homosexuality as analogous to a 'disease' (p. 398) and in identifying homosexuality per se, rather than any particular acts, as sinful ('homosexuality as a special sin' [p. 403; cf. p. 400]). For criticism of Hays's approach to this issue, see Martin 1995b.

85. Significant reviews include those by Bockmuehl 1997; Burridge 1998; Gundry-Volf 1999; Martin 1998a; and Watson 1997. Martin's review is excessively negative – the opening line runs: 'Richard Hays's most recent book is a disappointment' – but raises a number of important issues. Cranfield (1998: 167–75) also raises important questions, including that concerning Hays's neglect of the theme of the Christian's political responsibility. This omission reflects a wider tendency on Hays's part (following Hauerwas and others) to treat the church as in contrast to the world and to give too little consideration to the ways in which Christians might share common ground in ethics with other members of their wider civic communities. These issues will attain greater significance through the course of this study.

86. As noted above, Hays's survey begins with Paul and moves through the later Paulines, the four Gospels (and Acts), to conclude with Revelation. The prioritization of Paul is justified partly on grounds of chronological order and partly on the basis that 'Paul offers the most extensive and explicit wrestling with ethical issues' (1997a: 14). Reasons are (later) given why the historical Jesus should not be a key focus (pp. 158–68). Yet given that Hays is not interested in 'developmental history' (p. 14) it is certainly a pertinent question whether the choice of order affects or reflects a deeper prioritization.

synthesis. Indeed, the case for rejecting either of them is not made strongly.[87] Regarding love, Hays points out, for example, that it is not mentioned in the book of Acts (Hays 1997a: 201). True enough, if one searches only for words, but on that basis one should also observe that the words for 'cross' and 'crucify' ($\sigma\tau\alpha\nu\rho\dot{o}\varsigma/\sigma\tau\alpha\nu\rho\dot{o}\omega$) are absent from Romans, 1 and 2 Thessalonians, the Pastoral Epistles, Petrine Epistles, and Johannine Epistles.[88] But just as a focus on Jesus' death is certainly prominent in Romans, to take only the most obvious Pauline example, so are depictions of the practice of love present in Acts (e.g. 2.44-45; 4.32-35; 6.1; 7.60; etc.). Hays also objects that love is too vague and abstract, too easily 'a cover for all manner of vapid self-indulgence' (p. 202), to serve as a focal image. Again true enough: love needs definition and content, which it acquires for Christians in the paradigmatic self-giving of Jesus (cf. p. 202), but so does 'cross', which has served as a symbol for conquering violence as well as for non-violent self-giving. No symbol is univocal or unambiguous in meaning.[89] Regarding liberation, central to the work of Fiorenza (1983) and more recently Brian Blount (2001), Hays considers it to have 'a broader base of textual support than does love' but as 'unable to bring the full spectrum of New Testament witnesses into focus ... the image ... actually stands in severe tension with the ethic of the pastoral Epistles' (1997a: 203). But since Hays himself insists that forced harmonization of the diverse New Testament witnesses must not be undertaken, and indeed suggests (citing the contrasting views of the state in Romans 13 and Revelation 13) that in certain cases one will have to choose one perspective over another (p. 190), it could still be suggested that liberation should be made central, *on theological grounds*, even if this liberative focus stands in tension with certain New Testament texts.[90]

One of the points on which Dale Martin criticizes Hays concerns his repeated references to 'listening' to the New Testament, as if the latter were an 'agent' who 'speaks', independent of the interpreter (Martin 1998a: 358). While Hays makes some acknowledgment of the fact that hermeneutical concerns are interwoven with exegesis from the start (Hays 1997a: 7–8), the structure of his presentation, together with the frequent references to listening to the texts' voices, does indeed veil the extent to which the interpreter is throughout active in the construction of meaning, making hermeneutical decisions as to how to read, how to select

---

87. Hays makes no mention of a number of major studies of agape as central to NT and specifically Pauline ethics, especially Spicq 1958–59; Furnish 1973; also Deidun 1981: 104–226; and (too recent for Hays to take account of) Söding 1995.

88. Though note the use of $\sigma\nu\sigma\tau\alpha\nu\rho\dot{o}\omega$ in Rom. 6.6 (and Gal. 2.19).

89. I am grateful to Richard Burridge for discussion on this point.

90. Cf. further Watson 1994: 231–36, where Watson discusses how 'a critique of aspects of the biblical text can be justified on inner-biblical, theological grounds' (p. 231).

and expound various features and themes of the text.[91] The text by itself is mute. Hays's stance has serious and pernicious consequences, according to Martin, especially when combined with the presentation of his interpretative method as a means adequately to synthesize and apply the New Testament's ethics:

> Hays does not seem to recognize that his method is not what engenders the results. In each case a different conclusion would result from a slight tweaking here or there of the different factors in interpretation: a bit more scripture here, a bit more tradition there; a bit less 'reason' here, a bit less 'experience' there ... neither the *text* nor the *method* renders the conclusions. *Hays* renders the conclusions. (Martin 1998a: 359)

Furthermore, Martin suggests, when Hays appeals to the cross 'to insist that teenage girls must reject abortion (pp. 453, 460), that gay people must reject physical intimacy (pp. 402–3), and that peasants must reject armed struggle against a fascist regime (pp. 338–43)', he is precisely contradicting his own principle that 'the cross should not be used by those who hold power in order to ensure the acquiescent suffering of the powerless' (Martin 1998a: 359; cf. Hays 1997a: 197). Thus Hays's arguments constitute an attempt to mask 'his own interpretive agency behind the mythological agency of the "text itself"', one version of 'the tendency of many to hide their own oppression of others behind the Bible' (Martin 1998a: 359–60).

This criticism gains added force from the case set out in Wayne Meeks's (1996b) essay on the use of the Bible in '[t]he proslavery arguments of eighteenth and nineteenth century America'. This is an instance, Meeks suggests, where 'an honest and historically sensitive reading of the New Testament appears to support practices or institutions that Christians now find morally abominable' (p. 232). To be sure, Meeks's point is different from Martin's: while Martin criticizes Hays's appeal to the Bible as a strategy which cloaks his own (ab)use of interpretative and oppressive power, Meeks raises the question about the 'morality' of the biblical material itself. If it is true, as Meeks suggests, that the proslavery lobby had the better exegetical arguments on their side, and that 'critical study appears to confirm their most fundamental position',[92] then it is difficult 'to state clearly why the proslavery readers of the Bible were wrong'

---

91. I would not want to suggest, however, that this created meaning is an arbitrary construction on the part of the reader: the text limits what is possible as a reading which does not do violence to the text.

92. Meeks describes that position as follows: 'the New Testament contains passages that do not merely recommend subjection by wives, children, and slaves to their husbands, parents, and masters. In addition those passages signal acceptance of an organic construction of society for which such subjection is essential' (Meeks 1996b: 245).

(p. 245). Indeed, Meeks outlines a range of solutions to this moral dilemma and finds them all wanting,[93] though he concludes by suggesting a 'rule of thumb' for 'ethical use of the Bible': 'to ensure that among the voices interpreting the tradition are those of the ones who have experienced harm from that tradition' (pp. 252–53). Though he does not develop the point, Meeks clearly implies that those who support 'the subordination of women and the condemnation of same-sex unions – arguments for which are often strikingly analogous to those used by the proslavery apologists' – are making the same moral error as the proslavery exegetes (p. 251; cf. p. 246 with n. 28).

The points raised by Martin and by Meeks highlight some of the difficulties in attempts to derive contemporary ethics from the New Testament. Meeks illustrates how ambiguous is the New Testament's contribution to moral debate, while Martin shows the need for a consideration of the issues of power bound up with making ethical injunctions, for an approach which demonstrates awareness of the extent to which the interpreter constructs meaning in their own reading context, and for a more theoretically engaged approach. This leads to a final point of criticism regarding Hays.

While Hays engages in a detailed assessment of five approaches to the use of scripture in ethics, this assessment is limited to a consideration of precisely that: how scripture is used. Apart from the consideration of how 'other modes of authority' are deployed – namely, tradition, reason and experience – there is rather little engagement with the theoretical foundations, the ethical theory, which underpins each approach.[94] (And, indeed, three of the five authors, Barth, Yoder and Hauerwas, have rather close similarities and connections in this regard.)[95] This may be illustrated in the case of Hauerwas. Hays offers a brief introduction to Hauerwas's 'approach to theological ethics' (pp. 254–58) and some sharp and telling criticisms both of Hauerwas's failure to pursue any rigorous exegesis (cf. pp. 258–60) and of the ways in which Hauerwas's appeal to the faithful

---

93. Including Hays's approach, at that time 'forthcoming', which is described as a version of the 'seed growing secretly' strategy, wherein 'the egalitarian implications of the gospel are planted like a mustard seed in the soil of the early Christian communities'. Meeks notes various difficulties with this approach, the most obvious that, 'if the effects of the egalitarian gospel were invisible for so very many centuries, it cannot have had much force to begin with' (Meeks 1996b: 249–50 with n. 34).

94. This is congruent with, though more specific than, Martin's rather sweeping criticism of Hays for ignoring 'the most relevant philosophy, theology, and critical theory' (Martin 1998a: 358).

95. As Hays notes (1997a: 239), Yoder studied under Barth and published a book on Barth and the problem of war; Hauerwas is also indebted to Barth (cf. p. 254; Hauerwas 2001) and often comments on his indebtedness to the work of Yoder (as Hays also notes [1997a: 254]; see e.g. Hauerwas's foreword to Carter 2001).

Christian community as the only place where scripture can rightly be interpreted undermines his own hermeneutical position.[96] Yet the theoretical basis for the kind of communitarian tradition that Hauerwas represents is scarcely described; Alasdair MacIntyre, for example, whose work is so influential on the position Hauerwas adopts, receives not a single mention in this section (and only one in the whole book).[97] Consequently, and this is the important point, the reader hardly sees how close Hays's interpretative and theoretical perspective is in key respects to that of Hauerwas, despite the trenchant criticisms Hays mentions;[98] the particular kind of ethical theory – a Hauerwas-like ecclesial ethics (see ch. 2 below) – that underpins Hays's approach remains more implicit than explicit. Despite the language of 'listening' first to the texts, the reading throughout is conducted within this theoretical framework.[99] This means (as, for different reasons, with Ogletree's amalgamation of ethical theories into a single approach) that Hays does not show how or why the New Testament's ethics might resonate with different approaches to ethical theory, nor consider whether the New Testament might help to generate critical reflections in such a theoretical debate. I hope that the introduction of two significant strands of recent debate in ethics in this book will go some way to illustrating the benefits of this theoretical engagement.

96. See Hays 1997a: 264–66. Hays notes Hauerwas's membership of the United Methodist Church in the USA, which Hays describes as 'a large, pluralistic, bureaucratic organization that champions precisely the values of liberal individualism that Hauerwas decries'. As a church divided from Rome, on Hauerwas's own terms, it lacks 'the ability to use faithfully Scripture for the whole church'. 'All this would seem to mean, according to Hauerwas's own standards, that he himself should be incapable of interpreting Scripture rightly, since he does not participate in a community capable of manifesting and nurturing the necessary virtues' (p. 265).

97. Hays 1997a: 213 n. 8, where Hays mentions approvingly MacIntyre's argument that reason and rationality are tradition-bound, precisely a key point for Hauerwas and a point at issue in the debate with 'liberal' ethicists (see ch. 2 below).

98. For just one example, see Hays 1997a: 310 (cf. also p. 295): 'The New Testament is fundamentally the *story* of God's redemptive action; thus, the paradigmatic mode has theological primacy, and narrative texts are fundamental resources for normative ethics.' On Hauerwas, see ch. 2 below.

99. Thus it seems to me that Esler's critique of Hays's approach (Esler 2003a), in the context of an appeal for a more Aristotelian, virtue-focused approach, misses the essential orientation of Hays's project; see below §3.4 with n. 25.

1.7 *Paul beyond the Church: Political Ethics and Cultural Criticism*

Another aim of the current study is to engage in a reading of Paul's ethics that looks beyond the context of the church's use of scripture to consider the contribution of Pauline ethics to our thinking about public morality in contemporary, plural societies. As we have seen, the studies that have explicitly considered the connections between Pauline ethics and contemporary ethics – and there have not been a great many of these – have almost entirely focused on the subject of Christian ethics, and specifically on the use of the Bible in ethics.[100]

In regard to this desire to read Paul 'beyond the church', there is, however, one recent study of Paul which deserves our consideration since, though it is not explicitly a study of Paul's ethics as such, it constitutes an attempt to assess the political and cultural implications of Paul's thought, beyond the context of the Christian community: Daniel Boyarin's *A Radical Jew: Paul and the Politics of Identity* (1994).[101] Boyarin explicitly aims 'to read Paul through the kaleidoscope of contemporary critical and cultural concerns', noting the similarity of his approach with that of Elizabeth Castelli, in her *Imitating Paul* (Boyarin 1994: 12; Castelli 1991). He eschews the model of 'seeing Paul as a text and my task as that of a philologist', choosing instead to 'see us engaged across the centuries in a common enterprise of cultural criticism' (Boyarin 1994: 3–4). This involves considering how what Paul says constitutes '*an ethical challenge*' (p. 3, my emphasis).

Focusing throughout primarily on Paul's letter to the Galatians, Gal. 3.28 in particular presents for Boyarin a crucial question:

> When Paul says, There is no Jew or Greek, no male and female in Christ, he is raising an issue with which we all struggle. Are the specificities of human identity, the differences, of value, or are they only an obstacle in the striving for justice and liberation? (p. 3)

---

100. Another recent example is the study of Hjort 2000, which investigates Paul's ethics through a study of Rom. 6.1-14; 12.1-2; and Gal. 5.13-26, and then compares Paul's approach with that of Emil Brunner in an attempt to foster dialogue between NT studies and systematic theology. Hjort's study, however, is restricted to these few passages deemed to be fundamental to understanding the foundations of Paul's ethics, and so does not consider passages where Paul engages at length in ethical argument (Romans 14–15; 1 Corinthians 8–10, etc.). She sees the indicative, specifically God's saving act in Christ, as necessarily prior to the ethical imperative – this is 'the irreversible sequence' – and so sees in Paul (and in Brunner) 'a *consecutive ethic of gratitude*' (p. 185).

101. It is relevant to note in this context that Boyarin mentions particularly, and with great appreciation, Hays's generous input to his thinking on Paul, their disagreements notwithstanding (Boyarin 1994: ix–x).

With Gal. 3.28 thus acquiring a central place in his interpretation of Paul, Boyarin sees at the foundation of Paul's theology a desire to unite all people as One in Christ, in whom the distinctions between sexes, classes, and races become insignificant. Paul's impulse is towards the formation of a non-differentiated, non-hierarchical humanity. This laudable concern offers an important contribution towards the construction of communities in which there is social concern for all, human solidarity, and so on. Yet it implicitly requires the eradication of all human cultural specificities, and since there is no such thing as cultural unspecificity this actually means, ultimately, 'as it has meant in this history of European cultural imperialism', the merging of all people into the dominant culture (p. 8). Paul was 'a passionate striver for human liberation and equality', though 'this very passion for equality led Paul, for various cultural reasons, to equate equality with sameness'. Consequently, despite 'the goodness of his intentions, his social thought was therefore deeply flawed' (p. 9). What in Paul is generally seen as tolerance actually deprives people of the right to be different, reducing what is culturally essential to a matter of taste (p. 32), and dissolving all people into a single essence in which cultural practice is irrelevant and only faith in Christ is significant (p. 10). By contrast, the positive and counterbalancing strength of rabbinic Judaism is that it recognizes its own call to be distinctive yet does not envisage the incorporation of all humanity into its own particular identity; thus it envisages space for difference in ways which Paul does not. Yet, this too has its negative side:

> Jewish difference with its concomitant nearly exclusive emphasis on caring for other Jews – even when Jews are powerless and dominated – can become an ugly lack of caring for the fate of others and thus another form of racism, logically opposed to the first [sc. the coercion to conform] but equally as dangerous. The insistence on *difference* can produce an *indifference* (or worse) toward Others. (p. 235)

Thus the key 'theme' of the book 'is that the claims of difference and the desire for universality are both – contradictorily – necessary; both are equally problematic' (p. 10). Paul epitomizes the drive towards universality, rabbinic Judaism the importance of ethnic difference. Hence, '[t]he genius of Christianity is its concern for all of the peoples of the world; the genius of rabbinic Judaism is its ability to leave other people alone' (p. 232).

Boyarin's appreciation of positive and negative aspects to both Paulinism and rabbinic Judaism leads him to seek to formulate a hopeful solution in the form of a dialectic. 'A dialectic which would utilise each as antithesis to the other, correcting in the "Christian" system its tendencies toward a coercive universalism and in the "Jewish" system its tendencies toward contemptuous neglect for human solidarity might lead beyond both toward a better social system' (p. 235). 'Somewhere in the dialectic a synthesis must be found, one that will allow for stubborn hanging on to ethnic, cultural specificity but in a context of deeply felt and enacted human solidarity' (p. 257).

Boyarin proposes a notion of 'diasporizing identity' as the best model for synthesizing this dialectic. 'Diaspora can teach us that it is possible for a people to maintain its distinctive culture, its difference, without controlling land, a fortiori without controlling other people or developing a need to dispossess them of their lands' (p. 259). With a diasporic consciousness it is possible for a people to find a way of preserving their cultural identity while simultaneously living among their fellow, different, human beings without either denying or seeking to alter their important differences.

Boyarin's stimulating and provocative study raises important questions for any attempt to appropriate Paul's thought today, or, at least, any attempt which is concerned about the impact of that thought beyond the boundaries of the Christian confession, on the diverse religious and cultural communities of a plural world. While many specific points in Boyarin's interpretation of Paul can be questioned, by engaging Pauline thought in terms related to contemporary political and cultural concerns, Boyarin highlights fundamental ethical questions which should not be ignored. What contribution does Paul have to offer to the central moral task of engendering and maintaining human solidarity while at the same time sustaining and protecting difference and diversity? Are Boyarin and Castelli (whom Boyarin echoes on this point) right to maintain that Paul's vision is essentially one in which human solidarity is constructed only on the basis of a coerced sameness, a unity 'in Christ', which eradicates cultural, ethnic, and religious difference?[102]

In his appreciative yet critical review essay, Tom Wright strikingly if unintentionally vindicates Boyarin's thesis, at exactly the point where he intends to confront it. Concerning Boyarin's suggestion that the logic of Paul's gospel constitutes a drive to sameness, to an artificial and oppressive Oneness, Wright writes:

> But there is, nonetheless, a very much differentiated and yet still unified Christian family today. The white European male is very much the exception rather than the rule, among millions of Christians in the contemporary world. And, if I read Paul aright, he would rejoice in African Christians being African Christians, not European clones; in female Christians being female Christians, not pseudo-males; and, yes,

---

102. Cf. Castelli 1991: 22: 'if imitation and the drive toward sameness are exhorted and celebrated, then difference is perceived as problematic, dangerous, threatening ... the prescription of sameness implies the repression of difference.' See further pp. 134–36, etc.

in Jewish Christians being Jewish Christians, not in the sense that they form a group apart, a cut above all others, but because 'if their casting away means reconciliation for the world, what will their acceptance mean if not life from the dead?'. (Rom. 11.15) (Wright 1995: 22)

The ringing repetition of the word *Christian* illustrates precisely Boyarin's point that the 'tolerance' of difference in Pauline thought exists only in conjunction with an essential Oneness in Christ. Cultural difference is tolerated, but only insofar as it is a matter of *in*difference, which in fact undercuts the integrity of such differences. Indeed, Boyarin already makes clear in the book that Wright's riposte has missed its mark, 'since the question for me is *not* the relative statuses of Jewish and gentile Christians but the statuses of those – Jews and others – who choose not to be Christians' (p. 9).[103]

Boyarin thus helps to set the agenda for this study in significant ways. Like Ogletree, though with a less sanguine appraisal of Paul in this regard, Boyarin raises the question as to how Paul's thought might contribute to our thinking about issues of pluralism, tolerance, and difference, beyond, as well as within, the Christian community. Again like Ogletree, however, Boyarin does not provide detailed consideration of crucial Pauline passages relevant to this theme. With his focus on the letter to the Galatians, crucial Pauline arguments in, for example, Romans 14–15 and 1 Corinthians 8–10 receive little attention. Equally important is Boyarin's appreciation of the need for forms of 'deeply felt and enacted human solidarity' (p. 257), though Boyarin has little to say on how this solidarity might be nurtured. Again, there is need for further consideration of the ways in which Paul specifically sought to engender solidarity, and what the contemporary value of this might be. But what Boyarin does do is to place a fundamental question of political ethics firmly on the table: how did Paul – and how might we – conceive of human communities as places of solidarity and difference?

---

103. Cf. also Campbell 1991, whose study of Paul, and primarily of his letter to the Romans, is motivated (similarly to Boyarin) by current concerns about cultural diversity and pluralism (cf. p. iii) and specifically about Jewish-Christian relations. Campbell is much more optimistic than Boyarin about Paul's support for pluralism, but his focus is on pluralism *within* the early Christian churches (see esp. pp. 98–121) and so, like Wright, he does not really consider the issues Boyarin presses. Nonetheless, Campbell is certainly concerned to highlight the importance for Paul of Christianity's continuing Jewish roots, Paul's stress (in Romans 9–11) on 'the positive continuity ... of the people of God in history' (p. 52), and thus to call for 'a positive appreciation of Christianity's continuing debt to Judaism, and for an end to all implicit anti-Judaism within Christianity' (p. 77).

1.8 *Conclusion*

There is, then, a wide variety of approaches to the study of Pauline ethics, sometimes complementary, sometimes opposed, sometimes simply different. Besides simply sketching the state of play, as it were, the preceding survey also begins to generate the agenda for the following study, and to indicate how it connects with, departs or differs from, the approaches and findings of contemporary scholarship. The widespread acknowledgment of the integration of theology and ethics in Paul is affirmed here, though understood and expressed in terms of a different theoretical and conceptual framework (see ch. 3). This framework shares a basic orientation in common with those recent approaches which have studied Paul's ethics not so much as rules or injunctions, separable from other aspects of his world-view, but rather as part and parcel of a community-forming discourse (§1.5).

In terms of the historical sources of Paul's ethics, it will become clear that the following study is not an attempt to explore or identify these sources, whether in Judaism, Graeco-Roman philosophy, or Jesus' teaching, though the findings of studies in these areas, critically assessed, will be of some significance in what follows (e.g. §5.5). Although recent studies have shed much new light on the specific traditions to which Paul is indebted, a balanced overall assessment would seem to remain pretty much in line with that enunciated by Furnish several decades ago: Paul's 'concrete ethical teaching ... shares many of the formal and material characteristics of the ethical literature and traditions of the Hellenistic world at large. Paul does not hesitate to employ current forms, concepts, and standards, even secular ones, already familiar to his readers' (1968: 65). Furnish identifies the Old Testament and 'the words of the Lord' as having 'a special priority' (I would want to qualify the 'priority' of the latter, however; cf. §7.2), but suggests that '[b]eyond these, however, important parallels may also be discerned between his ethical instruction and that of the rabbis, the Jewish apocalypticists, and the Hellenistic popular philosophers' (p. 65). Neither Paul's 'Jewishness' nor his 'Hellenism' should be 'one-sidedly' emphasized (p. 66).[104] Moreover, it is crucial also to stress, for Furnish, that 'Paul is an apostle, and it is in the perspective of the whole redemptive event of Christ that this apostle frames his ethical convictions' (p. 67). Indeed, despite disagreements and differences of focus and emphasis, at a general level there may be said to

---

104. Recent work has shown that these two categories, and the clear distinction which they imply, should be significantly deconstructed (see the essays in Engberg-Pedersen 2001). Nonetheless, as seen above (§1.2-3) work on the sources of Pauline ethics often focuses on either the Jewish or the Graeco-Roman background.

be a broad consensus, from Bultmann onwards, that the substance of Paul's ethical teaching shares much in common with moral traditions current in his world, and that the distinctiveness of Paul's ethics lies primarily in the theological/christological framework into which he places, reframes, and shapes these ethics and with which he provides them warrant and motivation.[105]

The preceding survey also illustrates how little previous work has attempted what is here taken as a central task: that of engaging Pauline thought with contemporary ethical theory. Indeed, almost all of the studies which are concerned with contemporary appropriation focus specifically on the subject of Christian ethics, on the ways in which Pauline ethics *as scripture* can be appropriated by the church. The general lack of wider engagement is what makes Boyarin's book so significant. Indeed, it will be clear, not least from the title, how far Boyarin's striking book influences the agenda for this study of Paul's ethics. 'Solidarity and difference' encapsulates in a nutshell the central ethical issue to which Boyarin draws attention. To define the key question in these terms is, of course, to cast it in terms relevant to social, political, and public ethics, to the subject of the nature and formation of human communities. It is also, and deliberately, to cast it in terms which have wider meaning than those specific to the religious discourse of Pauline Christianity. This may indeed imply a reading of Paul's thought which goes beyond and even against its original intentions (cf. §9.3). But that is essential to the process of engaging Paul's ethics in new and wider contexts, and specifically in a conversation with contemporary ethical theory. The task of the next chapter is to outline that contemporary debate, and so to sketch the context in which our reading of Paul will take place.

---

105. Cf. Bultmann 1924: 138; Schrage 1961: 200–209; Verhey 1984: 112, 121; et al.

Chapter 2

LIBERALS AND COMMUNITARIANS: CONTRASTING APPROACHES IN CONTEMPORARY ETHICAL THEORY

The purpose of this chapter is to sketch two contrasting approaches in current ethical theory in order to establish a contemporary context in which to read Paul's ethics. The outline of contemporary theories is not intended to provide a model with which we shall then interpret Paul. Rather, it is intended to highlight the kinds of issues that are at stake in this contemporary theoretical debate, in order that we may then engage in a reading of Pauline ethics which attends to these kinds of questions and thus helps to generate our own thought in relation to this debate (cf. Introduction above).

The liberal-communitarian debate has been described as 'the central debate in Anglo-American political theory during the 1980s'.[1] This comment indicates two reasons why I have chosen it as the focus of attention. The first is quite simply its importance as a major area of debate, and specifically a debate between proponents of fundamentally contrasting approaches to ethics. The second reason, however, relates to my desire, explained towards the end of the previous chapter, to focus on Paul's ethics as *political* ethics, by which I mean ethics concerned with the bases for and regulation of community or public life. My interest, like that of both the major figures considered in this chapter, is not primarily in resolving specific ethical dilemmas or quandaries. Rather, it is in ethics conceived as reflection on the ways in which human sociality should rightly be sustained and practised. It is within such a conception of ethics that Boyarin's questions – about the nurturing of human solidarity and the valuing of difference – can properly be considered.

The plan for this chapter is as follows: after outlining several important caveats I sketch the essential differences between a liberal and a

---

1. Susan Moller Okin, quoted in Bell 1993: 2; cf. pp. 27–28. Cf. also the comments of Mulhall and Swift (1996: xii): 'These debates [those "grouped together under the label of the communitarian critique of liberalism"] became central to the discipline [of political theory] during the 1980s and continue, in one way or another, to inform a great deal of contemporary theory.' Considering the moral basis for liberal society in light of communitarian critiques is also a major concern of Plant 2001.

communitarian approach, and introduce briefly the two key figures on whom the chapter will concentrate. In the first major section I then outline the programme of discourse ethics as proposed by Jürgen Habermas. Following that the focus shifts to the ecclesial ethics developed by Stanley Hauerwas. After the presentation of the approach taken by each of these writers, I briefly consider major criticisms of each approach and areas in which there seems to be overlap or (at least the scope for) agreement.

Before proceeding further, it is important to set out a few caveats which should qualify all that follows in this chapter. First, while I will shortly outline the basic contours of both a liberal and a communitarian approach, it should be stressed that there is no standard or agreed 'liberal' or 'communitarian' viewpoint: 'there are different kinds of both liberalism and communitarianism' (Mulhall and Swift 1996: 1).[2] Furthermore, while the label 'liberal' is self-consciously adopted by at least some key figures on that side of the debate (as evident, for example, in the title of John Rawls's *Political Liberalism* [1993]), most of the writers regarded as representing the communitarian side of the discussion do not adopt or even accept the label (see Bell 1993: 4 with 17 n. 4). The latter are united, to at least a degree, in their critical stance towards contemporary liberalism, but beyond that can hardly be taken to represent a singular, common stance. While there is enough common ground on each side for the debate to be justifiably cast in terms of a liberal-communitarian distinction, the diversity of viewpoints requires a strategy like that adopted here, where I focus on specific figures rather than on some amalgam of perspectives. However, this chosen focus also requires another caveat: neither Habermas nor Hauerwas would necessarily leap to mind as the most obvious representative of either side of the debate. Habermas is generally identified with the critical social theory tradition of the Frankfurt School, and as a political philosopher and social theorist broadly on the political left.[3] The label 'liberal' in this context refers, then, not to a position on the left–right political spectrum – still less to the kind of neo-liberalism that stands for

2. Cf. also Fergusson 1997a: 32; Frazer and Lacey 1993: 42–43, 101–104, 167. Specifically on the communitarian viewpoint, Walter Reese-Schäfer comments, 'daß die kommunitaristischen Autoren keine einheitliche und kohärente Gruppe, sondern ein breites Spektrum bilden' (2001 col. 1532).

3. Frazer and Lacey (1993: 107) even label him 'a kind of communitarian', though this is done on the basis of his interest in an 'ideal speech community' and therefore too easily presumes that an interest in community is sufficient to define an approach as broadly communitarian. In the following sentence they note that Habermas's position has been compared with that of (the undoubtedly 'liberal') Rawls. Moreover, Habermas's self-declared location firmly in the Kantian tradition, together with his critical responses to the work of Alasdair MacIntyre and other communitarian critics, *inter alia* place his work in at least some crucial respects in the 'liberal' camp. Benhabib (1992: vii) locates discourse ethics 'somewhere between liberalism and communitarianism, Kantian universalism and Hegelian Sittlichkeit';

market liberalization and deregulation – but rather to the philosophical standpoint that underpins a certain set of convictions about the possibilities and bases for a public moral (and legal) framework (see below). In this sense, although Rawls dominates Anglo-American discussions of liberalism, Arne Rasmusson is right to identify Habermas, along with Rawls, as 'the two leading liberal theorists' (1994: 269).[4] In contrast, Hauerwas regards his work as a specifically theological enterprise rather than one to be identified as a particular kind of political philosophy or ethics, and has himself rejected the communitarian label (Hauerwas 1994: 156–63). Nevertheless, he does accept the accuracy of his being broadly aligned with the communitarian movement, noting that 'I generally share their historicist starting point as well as their more communitarian and antiliberal political and social theory' (Hauerwas 1987: 92; cf. Quirk 1987: 78–79). And in the context of a study of Paul's ethics there is much to be said for considering a communitarian-type ethicist who represents a specifically theological-ecclesial tradition. There are, then, as will become still clearer in what follows, good reasons to chose these two figures as representatives of contrasting 'liberal' and 'communitarian' approaches to ethics.

My final preliminary caveat concerns what this chapter can and cannot be. The liberal-communitarian debate involves complex and detailed discussion of many viewpoints and arguments in political theory. And each of the figures on whom I focus, Habermas and Hauerwas, has produced a very substantial and varied œuvre which is (especially in the case of Habermas) itself the subject of much detailed secondary discussion. For both of these reasons, this single chapter cannot possibly do justice to the detail and nuance of either the wider theoretical debate or the work of the two chosen authors. Those who wish for more detailed discussion should consult the various book-length treatments that are available.[5] What this chapter does aim to do is to present the two contrasting approaches in such a way that their main contrasts can be seen, the main issues at stake

nonetheless Habermas is clear that his project stands in the Kantian tradition, though reformulated in such a way that Hegel's critique of Kant is no longer telling (Habermas 1990: 195–215).

4. See further Rasmusson 1994: 249–52 on liberalism as the 'principal ideology of modernity' and on the various uses and understandings of the term in the US and Europe. On Habermas as a key proponent of liberal theory see pp. 269–71 and §2.2 below.

5. On the liberal-communitarian debate, see esp. Mulhall and Swift 1996; Bell 1993; Frazer and Lacey 1993. On this debate as related specifically to theological ethics, see Fergusson 1997a, 1998. Important works by (and about) Habermas and Hauerwas will be mentioned in the sections that follow, but for key secondary treatments see the following: on discourse ethics, Benhabib and Dallmayr 1990; Apel and Kettner 1992; Rehg 1994; on Hauerwas's theological ethics, Nation and Wells 2000; Wells 1998.

clarified, and the stage set for a reading of Paul in the context of this contemporary debate.

2.1 *The Liberal–Communitarian Debate*

Before proceeding to a consideration of the specific approaches offered by Habermas and Hauerwas, a brief sketch of the key elements of a liberal and a communitarian approach may be helpful. Broadly speaking, liberals – or at least, one major tradition within liberalism – emphasize the possibility of a rational basis for an agreed public morality and system of justice, within which individuals can pursue their own freely chosen visions of the good, visions which vary according to identity, religion, culture, and so on. What liberals believe is possible, and seek to articulate, therefore, is a moral basis for the public sphere, for society, with a rational, universally justifiable grounding which transcends the specific values and goods of particular traditions. In this quest for a universally valid basis for ethics, liberalism stands in the Kantian tradition.[6] Liberalism places considerable value on the individual's liberty, specifically liberty to choose rather than be compelled to adopt a particular vision of the good life, of what is 'good' for them, hence freedom of religion, of speech, and so on. But these diverse and freely chosen individual projects have to be pursued under the umbrella of a public framework of justice, which regulates conflicts of interests, conflicts over resources, and so on. And one of the tasks of liberal theory is to show that all people should, indeed would (under certain conditions of insight and understanding), accept and agree to liberal principles of justice as the best means for regulating public life. Thus, liberalism (again following Kant) is primarily a deontological ethic which prioritizes the right over the good. What this shorthand ethics terminology means is that in the realm of interpersonal regulation, in the public arena, what takes priority is the duty (Gk: *deon*) one has to act justly, as opposed to teleologically, with action orientated towards some vision of the good as its outcome, the principles of (public) justice being separable from the vision of the good inherent in particular traditions and individual life-projects.[7] Whether the state should therefore be entirely 'neutral' with regard to the various visions of the good life chosen by its citizens is a point of debate within liberalism. A 'neutral' state, as Daniel Bell summarizes,

---

6. The extent to which liberalism presumes, or seeks to offer, a *universal* basis for ethics is, however, open to variety and debate, with the later Rawls, for example, retreating from a strongly universalist conception of political liberalism. For discussion, see Mulhall and Swift 1996: 20–21, 205–13.

7. For further discussion of the themes of deontology, the right and the good, in particular relation to discourse ethics and communitarianism, see Benhabib 1992: 38–46, 71–76; on the

'should provide a fair framework for individuals to seek the good in their own way, but it acts unjustly when it presumes to say what is valuable in life, thus restricting people's capacity for self-determination' (Bell 1993: 4). As Stephen Mulhall and Adam Swift point out, however, the liberal state is in reality certainly not neutral in all respects, either with regard to the kinds of life and action it treats as compatible with 'justice', or, indeed, with regard to the kinds of good life that are regarded as more and less valuable (taxing gambling and subsidizing opera for example, as Mulhall and Swift note, is precisely a means by which the state expresses convictions as to the relative merits of ways of life). More fundamentally, it may be suggested, liberalism's 'pretensions to neutrality' may be seen to conceal a clear preference in terms of what is and is not truly good: '[i]nstead of eschewing judgments about what makes a life valuable, liberalism consists essentially of the claim that a good life is one which has been freely or autonomously chosen by the person living it' (Mulhall and Swift 1996: 32).

Communitarianism, as commentators on the debate show, is best understood, at least initially, as a critique of various aspects of the liberal position.[8] One major area of critique concerns the liberal conception of the self. Bell refers, for example, to the claim that 'liberalism rests on an overly individualistic conception of the self' (1993: 4). More revealing than the label 'individualistic' as a description of the liberal notion of the self, I think, is the term 'unencumbered'.[9] In other words, with its focus on the prospects for demonstrating a rational and universal basis for public morality, and its focus on freedom of choice, liberalism – so communitarians argue – fails to do justice to the extent to which human beings are, in terms of their identity, moral values, and so on, formed by their social context and the traditions of their communities of nurture and attachment. The liberal view

> seems to presuppose that we are indeed individuals capable freely of forming, and changing, our own views about how we should live our lives ... But is this true to our moral experience? Can we really step back from the particular values that we have and change them for new ones, or are we rather made the very people that we are by the values

separation of the right and the good in liberalism, and the relation of that distinction to the notion of state neutrality, see Mulhall and Swift 1996: 29–33. More generally on Kantian ethics, see O'Neill 1991 and on deontological ethics, Davis 1991.

8. In what follows I am indebted to the presentations by Mulhall and Swift 1996: 10–33; Bell 1993: 4–8; and also Benhabib 1992, esp. chs 1–2. See also the brief overviews by Reese-Schäfer 2001 and Schoberth 2001.

9. Benhabib refers to 'the communitarian critique of liberal visions of the "unencumbered self"' (1992: 3, cf. 71–76). Mulhall and Swift (1996: 13) label this theme in the communitarian critique 'asocial individualism'.

that we endorse, so that such detachment is impossible? (Mulhall and
Swift 1996: 11)

Indeed, the communitarian perspective suggests not only that the liberal
view is implausible but also that in its valuation of reflective choice it
devalues the moral intuitions and commitments that derive from our
(subconscious) self-formation. Bell argues that many of our best actions
and deepest commitments are *not* self-consciously chosen, but are not for
that reason less morally praiseworthy (cf. Bell 1993: 5–6).

Linked with the communitarian emphasis on the person as embedded in
their social or community context is the claim that liberalism insufficiently
values '[c]onceptions of the good that are more strongly communal in
content' (Mulhall and Swift 1996: 15), devaluing the community ties and
contexts that make us who we are. The positive claim may be expressed as
a 'need to experience our lives as bound up with the good of the
communities out of which our identity has been constituted' (Bell 1993: 14;
cf. pp. 11–14).

A further theme in the communitarian critique concerns liberalism's
'universalism'.[10] That is to say, in its attempt to provide a rational basis for
public morality, liberal theory not only envisages people as able to abstract
themselves from the particularities of their social formation but also
appears (in at least some of its forms) to regard its own conclusions as of
universal validity. This universalizing claim may be criticized in a number
of ways. It assumes, first, that human rationality is, in at least certain key
respects, cross-culturally and historically stable; liberalism may therefore
be accused of giving insufficient attention to the diversity of cultures and
their forms of rationality, to the different values and moral norms which
various cultures treasure. Put another way, the form of liberalism's
universal claims may be argued to represent, in actual fact, an ethnocentric
(and even imperialistic) universalizing of moral intuitions that are (merely)
specific values of modern Western culture.[11] Moreover, what liberalism
denies, according to Alasdair MacIntyre (1985), one of the so-called
communitarian critics, is that it is only from within a particular tradition
that we find resources to approach, let alone resolve, questions of morality.
'The Enlightment [liberal] project of seeking to establish morality on
grounds independent of the claims of a tradition is therefore doomed from
the outset' (Fergusson 1997a: 34).[12] MacIntyre therefore champions a form

10.   On this theme, see Bell 1993: 6–7; Mulhall and Swift 1996: 18–21.
11.   Cf. Habermas 1990: 76, where he voices this 'skeptic's' objection; for his response see
pp. 82–98 and below.
12.   Cf. also Horton and Mendus 1994b: 3; MacIntyre 1994: 295. In work subsequent to
After Virtue (1981, [2]1985), it should be noted, MacIntyre describes liberalism as itself a
particular tradition: 'what began as an attempt to found morality upon tradition-independent

of 'tradition-constituted enquiry', finding in Aquinas's synthesis of Aristotelian ethics and Augustinian theology the most adequate tradition with which to work.[13]

This brief sketch of some outline features of the liberal and the communitarian approach begins to set the contours for the discussion that follows. It will, moreover, enable us to be alert to the ways in which our two chosen authors do, and do not, reflect an essentially 'liberal' or 'communitarian' perspective.

2.2 *Jürgen Habermas's Discourse Ethics*

Jürgen Habermas, born in 1929, has become one of the most discussed contemporary philosophers, certainly in Germany, but also worldwide.[14] In Germany he is among the most prominent public intellectuals, a mentor to the current generation of Social Democrat/Green politicians, especially Joschka Fischer.[15] Habermas's early academic life was spent as a member of the post-war Frankfurt School, under Theodor Adorno and Max Horkheimer, though the directions in which his work developed led to a departure from the positions promoted by these theorists (see White 1995b: 5). Habermas is thus essentially to be identified as a political philosopher in the tradition of critical social theory, a tradition which, indebted to Marx, seeks both to analyse contemporary society and also to subject it to an emancipatory critique – though it is debated how far Habermas retains these critical perspectives (see n. 18 below).[16] Habermas's writings, while developing a strong critique of contemporary

principles which any human beings could accept insofar as they were rational, ended with the creation and perpetuation of one more moral tradition' (Mulhall and Swift 1996: 98; cf. MacIntyre 1988: 326–48, esp. 345–46).

13. Cf. Horton and Mendus 1994b: 3–4; MacIntyre 1985: 278. MacIntyre's position is similar to, and profoundly influential upon, Hauerwas's: see §2.3 below.

14. Cf. e.g., Arens 1989b: 9: 'Jürgen Habermas ist in den letzten Jahren weltweit zum meistdiskutierten deutschsprachigen Philosophen der Gegenwart geworden'; Fiorenza 1992a: 1; Bronner 1994: 9, 283–84 ('unquestionably, the most encyclopedic and prolific thinker of the postwar period', p. 283). For introductions to Habermas's work see Reese-Schäfer 1991; Horster 1984, 1990; White 1988.

15. See Müller 2001, who describes Habermas in 'the unofficial role of philosopher-king to the Social Democrat/Green government in Berlin' (p. 44). One might compare Anthony Giddens's position as one of the acknowledged gurus of Blair's New Labour in the UK.

16. On the character of critical social theory, as developed in the Frankfurt School and by Habermas, as not only analytical but also 'normative' – that is, as contributing to the transformation of the world and the construction of more human societies – see Benhabib 1986.

capitalist modernity,[17] also reflect a commitment to the principles of liberal democracy, and to justifying these principles within a critical social theory, leading Stephen Bronner to characterize him as '*the* great exponent of political liberalism in Germany' (Bronner 1994: 284).[18] Indeed, Habermas's approach to political ethics is often compared with that of John Rawls, among others,[19] and Habermas himself regards his own and Rawls's approaches as sharing a family likeness.[20] While Rawls is often (and justifiably) taken as a key representative of modern political liberalism,[21] there are good reasons to focus on Habermas. Not only is he among the most influential of contemporary political philosophers but he also brings, of course, a continental European perspective that broadens our focus beyond the often linguistically parochial Anglo-American discussion: it is not insignificant to recall that it is in Rasmusson's study – written in Sweden – that Rawls and Habermas are together described as 'the two leading liberal theorists' (1994: 269). More significantly, Habermas may be argued to have articulated, in his discourse ethics, the most cogent account of a universal and rational basis for the testing of ethical norms in the public sphere, based upon the general presuppositions of human argumentation (see below), an account which warrants careful attention. His reformulation of a Kantian-type ethic, moreover, also brings from critical theory an emancipatory and eschatological focus in which the ideal to which human communication (counter-factually) points consists in a form of egalitarian solidarity. The pertinence of these commitments to the issues raised by Boyarin (see §1.7) and to the conversation with Paul's ethics will become apparent.

17. For example, in his theorization of the 'system' and the 'lifeworld' – the former the administrative and commercial areas of modern society ordered by money and power, the latter the world of shared meanings and social interaction – Habermas sees in modern capitalism the creeping colonialization of the latter by the former, and also the technocratization of decisions from which judgments of value are increasingly excluded. Cf. Fiorenza 1992b: 67–72.

18. Bronner later states: 'Habermas is a brilliant theorist of liberal democracy. But whether his democratic standpoint any longer offers anything more radical, let alone, socialist is questionable and to that extent a certain undermining of the critical character of critical theory has taken place' (1994: 285). Thus Bronner (and cf. also Pleasants 1998) questions the extent to which Habermas really retains the 'critical' intention of critical social theory.

19. See e.g. Reese-Schäfer 1991: 54; Benhabib 1992: 24; Moon 1995; Habermas 1990: 43.

20. In an article exchange on Rawls's *Political Liberalism*, Habermas writes: 'Because I admire this project, share its intentions, and regard its essential results as correct, the dissent I express here will remain within the bounds of a familial dispute. My doubts are limited to whether Rawls always brings to bear against his critics his important normative convictions in their most compelling form' (Habermas 1995: 110). Cf. also Habermas 1990: 43, 66–67. For Rawls's reply, see Rawls 1995.

21. E.g. in Mulhall and Swift 1996: 1–9, etc.; Bell 1993: 2–4; Frazer and Lacey 1993: 43, *et passim*.

As a moral theorist Habermas stands clearly and explicitly in the Kantian tradition and thus develops a deontological ethic which prioritizes the right – public questions of justice – over the good – the various goals and values for which various individuals and traditions aim.[22] Indeed, the concern of discourse ethics is with the ways in which conflicts of interests, of convictions, and so on, can be justly resolved; or, put more specifically, with the kind of public ethics which can test the validity of the various norms generated by the different traditions coexisting in a plural society. This can be illustrated through the distinct meanings Habermas gives to the terms 'ethics' (*Ethik*) and 'morality' (*Moralität*) (see Habermas 1993: 1–8; 1991: 100–108). Habermas distinguishes three possible levels at which practical reason may be exercised in relation to the question 'What should I do?' (1993: 8). The first level is simply pragmatic: decisions about whether to fix my bike or dig the garden, to travel to Denmark or to Norway, are not in the first instance – though they may quickly involve – ethical or moral decisions. The second is the ethical level, wherein the questions faced are bound up with the individual's sense of the good (as opposed to what is merely possible or expedient) and with their sense of identity (Habermas 1993: 4; 1991: 103). The third level, however, that of morality, concerns the question 'What should I do?' when 'my actions affect the interests of others and lead to conflicts that should be regulated in an impartial manner, that is, from the moral (*moralisch*) point of view' (Habermas 1993: 5; 1991: 105). These conflicts that disrupt our orderly coexistence require a concern 'with the justification and application of norms that stipulate reciprocal rights and duties' (1993: 9; 1991: 109). In the light of this distinction, which he worked out only in a lecture given in 1988, Habermas explains that his theory of discourse ethics should really be termed a 'discourse theory of morality' (*Diskurstheorie der Moral*) (1993: vii; 1991: 7). But since the term 'discourse ethics' had already become established, Habermas retains it.[23]

Setting his face against the fashions of postmodern, relativist, and communitarian ethics, and against 'ethical skepticism in all its forms or guises' (Dallmayr 1990: 3), Habermas seeks to elucidate a universally valid basis for morality, in the Kantian tradition, which transcends the particular convictions of specific ethical traditions (cf. Habermas 1990:

---

22. Cf., e.g., Habermas 1990: 180, 195; McCarthy 1990: vii–viii; Gebauer 1993: 46.

23. It is important to note that this distinction is almost diametrically opposite to that drawn by Wayne Meeks, and followed by other New Testament scholars, on which see further §3.5 below (Meeks 1993: 4; followed by McDonald 1998: 5–6). Others simply use the terms as equivalents. Frank Matera, for example, is candid: 'Throughout this work I use the adjectives "moral" and "ethical" interchangeably' (Matera 1996: 259 n. 1). Cf. also the use of both terms in the full title of Hays 1997a.

197–98).[24] Where Habermas differs decisively from Kant is in insisting, in view of developments in philosophy since Kant, especially the so-called 'linguistic turn', that rational moral imperatives cannot derive from the monological reflections of the individual – as might be taken to be implied in Kant's formulation of the categorical imperative[25] – but must rather arise from the communicative interaction of human subjects located (necessarily) in a social-linguistic context.[26] From the perspective worked out in great detail in Habermas's *Theory of Communicative Action* (1981; ET 1984, 1987), rationality, or reason, is embedded 'in *language* in general, and in *communication* in particular' (Giddens 1987: 227). The key move enabling Habermas to work towards a reformulation of a universal 'categorical imperative' is the focus on the nature of language and human communication itself, and more specifically on 'the universal pragmatic presuppositions of argumentation' – '*die allgemeine pragmatische Voraussetzungen von Argumentation*' (Habermas 1991: 32).[27] This sphere of communicative action is the context in which human beings are located, yet it is at its most general a context *universally* shared by all competent human subjects.[28]

According to Habermas, to engage in communication through language itself unavoidably implies certain presumptions. Implicit in the very fact of

24.   Cf. also De Angelis 1999: 6–8, 117–20: 'Ziel ist die Rekonstruktion universaler Grundlagen von Rationalität überhaupt, welche der Abspaltung und schließlich der Gefährdung der Vernunftproblematik durch die Berufung auf die irreduzible Vielfalt von historischen und kulturverschiedenen Rationalitätskonzepten entgegentreten soll' (p. 6).

25.   '[H]andle nur nach derjenigen Maxime, durch die du zugleich wollen kannst, daß sie ein allgemenes Gesetz werde' (Kant 1911: 421). O'Neill gives an English version of the imperative: 'Act only on the maxim through which you can at the same time will that it be a universal law' (O'Neill 1991: 177).

26.   Habermas 1990: 203: 'discourse ethics rejects the monological approach of Kant, who assumed that the individual tests his maxims of action *foro interno* or, as Husserl put it, in the loneliness of his soul'. Cf. pp. 24, 26–28, 50, 61, 67, 131, 199; Cronin 1993: xii, xxii; Honneth 1995: 295–96.

27.   The central focus and basis for discourse ethics are therefore well described in, for example, the following summary comments: '"Diskursethik" bezeichnet ein Begründungs-programm normativer philosophischer Moraltheorie, das die kommunikative Vernunft als die einzige Quelle auszeichnet, die unter den wertpluralistischen und rationalitätsskeptischen Bedingungen der Modern eine rational definitive Rechtfertigung allgemeinverbindlicher moralischer Verpflichtungen gestattet' (Apel and Kettner 1992: 7); discourse ethics's concern is 'a concern indissolubly connected with language and communication. Moreover, normative yardsticks or principles from this vantage are not simply the contingent outcome of communicative exchanges but are seen as premises or preconditions of intelligible language and communication as such' (Dallmayr 1990: 2; pp. 1–3 give a good orientation to discourse ethics in the wider context of ethical theory).

28.   Thus Habermas does not envisage the human subject as unsituated and without context, but 'plädiert vielmehr für einen Begriff universeller *und dennoch situierter* Vernunft' (De Angelis 1999: 7, my emphasis).

human communication is a principle of universal rationality that cannot be denied without falling into a performative contradiction.[29] One presupposition is that communication is possible, though not unproblematic or undistorted, and that understanding can (only) be achieved through *participation* in communication.[30] Second, assuming that if I believe I *ought* to do something that means that I *have good reasons* for doing it (Habermas 1990: 49), then it follows that I could, at least in theory, present reasons for my moral convictions and actions. Further, I could (again at least in principle) be persuaded by better reasons to believe and act otherwise. Implicit in this communicative and persuasive character of linguistic argumentation is the 'eschatological' notion of an ideal speech situation, or (following Karl-Otto Apel) an ideal community of communication (*die ideale Kommunikationsgemeinschaft*),[31] namely, the situation in which all that distorts communication – money, power, forms of violent or covert coercion, etc. – is absent and all that can persuade is what Habermas calls 'the unforced force (*der zwanglose Zwang*) of the better argument' (1993: 23; 1991: 123).[32] In other words, inherent in the very character of language and communication, according to Habermas, is the drive towards discursive persuasion based on nothing other than the force of argument itself.

The discourse ethics which Habermas formulates on the basis of these arguments about the nature of communication is not intended itself to supply substantive moral norms, which arise instead from existing horizons of values, ethical traditions, and visions of the good life, etc. What discourse ethics does intend to supply is a procedure of validation, by which norms can be declared as valid (or not).[33] Moral dilemmas cannot justly be resolved by appealing to an authoritative tradition. It is only from

29. On which see e.g. Habermas 1990: 80–82; Apel 1990: 43, 46–47. Apel and Habermas disagree, however, as to whether this notion provides an ultimate justification (*Letztbegründung*) for discourse ethics, with Apel inclining towards this stronger claim, and Habermas supporting it only in a weaker sense (see Reese-Schäfer 1991: 58–59; Habermas 1990: 44).

30. Habermas 1990: 24, 26–28, 50, etc.

31. See Habermas 1990: 88, 202; 1993: 56–57, 163–65; Apel 1990; 1992: 17. On the parallels with Christian eschatology, see Adams 1996. For critique of this concept in Habermas's work, see De Angelis 1999: 67–94.

32. Here is one difference from Rawls, whose attempt to articulate a system which ensures impartial consideration of all involves the idea of an 'original position' in which subjects are placed under the constraints of a 'veil of ignorance' (see Rawls 2001: 14–18; Mulhall and Swift 1996: 3–9).

33. See Ferrera 1985: 51; Habermas 1990: 105–109, 122: 'Discourse ethics does not set up substantive orientations. Instead it establishes a *procedure* based on presuppositions and designed to guarantee the impartiality of the process of judging' (p. 122). 'Facts and norms that had previously gone unquestioned can now be true or false, valid or invalid' (p. 107).

real discourse among *participants*, according to Habermas, that valid norms of action can be discerned and agreed.[34] What is universalizable is a *procedure* of moral argumentation by which *valid* norms may be determined (Habermas 1990: 68, cf. pp. 14, 19, 86). Indeed, Habermas argues, 'every argumentation, regardless of the context in which it occurs, rests on the pragmatic presuppositions from whose propositional content the principle of universalism (U) can be derived' (Habermas 1990: 82). Habermas's formulation of this principle of universalization (*Universalisierungsgrundsatz*), the first main step towards formulating a discourse ethics, takes its bearings from Kant's categorical imperative, 'so conceived as to exclude as invalid any norm that could not meet with the qualified assent of all who are or might be affected by it' (Habermas 1990: 63).

> Thus, every valid norm has to fulfill the following condition:
> (U) All affected can accept the consequences and the side effects its *general* observance can be anticipated to have for the satisfaction of *everyone's* interests (and these consequences are preferred to those of known alternative possibilities for regulation). (Habermas 1990: 65)[35]

Habermas's key claim, in terms of justifying the universal applicability of this principle, is that this principle 'is implied by the presuppositions of argumentation in general':

> Every person who accepts the universal and necessary communicative presuppositions of argumentative speech and who knows what it means to justify a norm of action implicitly presupposes as valid the principle of universalization, whether in the form I gave it or in an equivalent form. (Habermas 1990: 86)

If U, then, can be derived from 'the universal pragmatic presuppositions of argumentation' (Habermas 1991: 32) – a central claim of Habermas's discourse ethics – then the basic principle of such an ethics can be concisely formulated. This principle (the *diskursethische Grundsatz*), which contains 'the distinctive idea of an ethics of discourse', Habermas gives as follows:

---

34. Habermas 1990: 50, 93–94, 103, 122, 211; Cronin 1993: xxiv; Rogerson 1995: 19.

35. The original German runs as follows: 'So muß jede gültige Norm der Bedingung genügen, – daß die Folgen und Nebenwirkungen, die sich jeweils aus ihrer *allgemeinen* Befolgung für die Befriedigung der Interessen eines *jeden* Einzelnen (voraussichtlich) ergeben, von *allen* Betroffenen akzeptiert (und den Auswirkungen der bekannten alternativen Regelungsmöglichkeiten vorgezogen) werden können' (Habermas 1983: 75–76). It is worth nothing the emphasis Habermas places on '*all* affected' and the stress on '*every* single individual' ('eines *jeden* Einzelnen' is perhaps rather weakly conveyed in the translation 'everyone's'). In the similar (re)statement in Habermas 1991: 32, it is significant to note the addition of 'zwanglos': 'von *allen* Betroffenen zwanglos akzeptiert werden können'.

(D) Only those norms can claim to be valid that meet (or could meet) with the approval of all affected in their capacity as participants in a practical discourse. (Habermas 1990: 66)[36]

Like Kant's categorical imperative, Habermas's formulation of the basic principles of discourse ethics is clearly founded on the conviction that a valid moral norm has to be one that *all* could accept, the key difference between Kant and Habermas being that while the former expresses the universal imperative in terms oriented to the individual's moral reflection, the latter insists that such norms could only emerge through real discourse among affected participants.[37] Conceivably valid norms must take account of the interests of all; norms of action which represent class-based or sectional group interests would fail the universalization test. Moreover, the emphasis on argumentation as the process by which norms are discerned is founded on the conviction that norms are only valid if they are arrived at without coercion or 'the possibility of repression, be it ever so subtle or covert' (1990: 89). Argumentation is only validly such if it is free from domination, if 'all concerned in principle take part, freely and equally, in a cooperative search for truth, where nothing coerces except the force of the better argument' (1990: 198). Ideological, power- or interest-based distortions would invalidate any consensus on norms.

The apparent goal of discourse ethics, that all affected participants reach consensus through an argumentative discourse free from coercion and distortion, forming something like an ideal community of communication, is, of course, easily criticized as utopian. Habermas, however, maintains that although the ideal speech situation is indeed held up as a 'counter-factual' ideal, its conditions are at least partially realized and recognized implicitly in real human discourse (1993: 56–58). Karl-Otto Apel, with whom Habermas shares the main outlines of an approach to discourse ethics,[38] suggests, in this vein, that *everyone* who engages in argument, even in serious and responsible communication, 'must *anticipate* as an *ideal state of affairs* and assume as fulfilled in a certain manner, counter-factually, the conditions of an ideal community of communication or an ideal speech situation' (Apel 1990: 46). Seyla Benhabib, a persuasive though not uncritical interpreter of Habermas and proponent of discourse ethics, makes a similar point: 'To argue that the counterfactual ideals of

---

36.   The German here translated runs: 'Der Diskursethik zufolge darf eine Norm nur dann Geltung beanspruchen, wenn alle von ihr möglicherweise Betroffenen als *Teilnehmer eines praktischen Diskurses* Einverständnis darüber erzielen (bzw. erzielen würden)' (Habermas 1983: 76). Cf. a similar (re)statement in Habermas 1991: 32.

37.   Universal applicability is a key principle in the formulation of Kant's ethics: 'the thought is that nothing could be a moral principle which cannot be a principle for all' (O'Neill 1991: 177).

38.   See e.g. Habermas 1990: 43; 1993: 19; Apel 1990.

reciprocity, equality and the "gentle force of reason" are implicit in the very structures of communicative action is to argue that the "moral point of view" articulates more precisely those implicit structures of speech and action within which human life unfolds' (1992: 52). In other words, to participate in speech, or argument at all, I must presume that, to at least some extent, and even sometimes counterfactually, I can be understood and understand, and that what should *alone* be persuasive is the content of my (and others') communication – and in these presuppositions are implied certain *moral* values (see below). Apel draws a further distinction between discourse ethics's ideal community of communication and utopic visions:

> ethics, like utopia, commences from an *ideal* that is distinguished from existing reality; but it does not anticipate the ideal through the conception of an empirically possible alternative or counterworld; rather it views the ideal merely as a *regulative idea*, whose approxima- tion to the conditions of reality ... can indeed be striven for but never be completely assumed to be realizable. (Apel 1990: 46)

This ideal, with its vision of democratization, participation, and non- distorted (by power, money, etc.) communication, is thus both presumed but unrealized in real human argumentation, and can serve as a regulative principle in political life (Apel 1990: 54–55). Here the critical and emancipatory commitments of discourse ethics, and critical theory more generally, are evident. As an ideal which 'anticipates' what does not exist, except partially and imperfectly, yet which draws real and imperfectly structured discourse towards its goal, the ideal speech situation may be suggested to have significant parallels with Christian notions of hope and eschatology (Adams 1996). Benhabib, in her critical discussion of Habermas's formal principle of universalizability, suggests that this principle, rightly interpreted, 'involves the utopian projection of a way of life in which respect and reciprocity reign' (Benhabib 1992: 38). Indeed, she proposes shifting the emphasis of discourse or communicative ethics away from the ideal of rational agreement and towards 'sustaining those normative practices and moral relationships within which reasoned agreement *as a way of life* can flourish and continue' (p. 38). In her view, the process of dialogue and the furthering of mutual understanding are more important than consensus itself (p. 52).[39]

When Habermas asks about the 'moral intuitions' that discourse ethics conceptualizes (*bringt ... auf den Begriff*) he recognizes the need to consider how a *procedural* account of the moral point of view can give an

---

39.   Cf. also De Angelis 1999: 182, who suggests, in view of the fact that solutions that are equally in the interests of all are unlikely, that discourse ethics needs to give more attention to compromise as well as consensus.

adequate account of *substantive* moral intuitions (Habermas 1990: 199; 1991: 14). 'Every morality', Habermas suggests, 'revolves around equality of respect (*Gleichbehandlung*), solidarity, and the common good (*allgemeines Wohl*)' (1990: 201; 1991: 17), given the requirement simultaneously to protect both the individual and the well-being of the community to which they belong, 'the web of intersubjective relations of mutual recognition by which these individuals survive as members of a community': morality 'cannot protect the one without the other' (1990: 200; 1991: 16). 'To these two aspects correspond the principles of justice and solidarity' where the first principle 'postulates equal respect and equal rights for the individual whereas the second postulates empathy and concern for the well-being of one's neighbour' (1990: 200; 1991: 16; cf. 1993: 1, 67–68, 154). The crucial argument Habermas then makes is that these moral principles are fundamental ideas which can be traced back to the conditions of symmetry and expectations of reciprocity basic to communicative action, that is to say, that they are already implicit in the presuppositions of human communication, can be discerned in everyday practices orientated to understanding.[40]

Benhabib also elaborates similar principles as the 'strong ethical assumptions' entailed by the 'presuppositions of argumentative speech': the first principle she calls that of 'universal moral respect' – 'that we recognise the right of all beings capable of speech and action to be participants in the moral conversation'; and the second, that of 'egalitarian reciprocity' – 'that within such conversations each has the same symmetrical rights to various speech acts, to initiate new topics, to ask for reflection about the presuppositions of the conversation, etc.' (Benhabib 1992: 29, cf. pp. 105, 110). Benhabib's point is to illustrate that while Habermas sees discourse ethics as providing only a *procedure* for the justification of valid moral norms, substantive 'metanorms' are in fact implicit in its formulation, a point Habermas seems also to support (see above).[41]

---

40. I am here paraphrasing Habermas 1991: 17, since the English translation (in Habermas 1990: 201) seems to me slightly to obscure the point by rendering *zurückführen* as 'be reduced to': 'Fundamental ideas like these can be reduced to the relations ... presupposed in communicative action'; though the following sentence makes it somewhat clearer: 'the common core of all kinds of morality can be traced back to ...' The point is not so much that these moral intuitions can be 'reduced' to the presuppositions of communicative action, but rather that they are already to be found in these very presuppositions. The crucial passage in Habermas runs as follows: 'Alle Moralen kreisen um Gleichbehandlung, Solidarität und allgemeines Wohl; das sind aber Vorstellungen, die sich auf die Symmetriebedingungen und Reziprozitätserwartungen des kommunikativen Handelns zurückführen, d.h. in den wechselseitigen Zuschreibungen und gemeinsam Unterstellungen einer verständigungs-orientierten Alltagspraxis auffinden lassen' (1991: 17).

41. Cf. Taylor 1989: 88, who accuses Habermas, and others, of 'a strange pragmatic contradiction, whereby the very goods which move them push them to deny or denature all

Benhabib is clear and candid about the fact that these 'metanorms of communicative ethics', 'often embodied in the constitutions of liberal democracies', imply substantive limits on the extent to which the 'specific norms' of varied traditions can be pursued within such a universal moral framework: 'where there is a clash between the metanorms of communicative ethics and the specific norms of a moral way of life, the latter must be subordinated to the former' (Benhabib 1992: 45). While communicative ethics encourages 'plurality, tolerance and diversity' (p. 44), it does so within the firmly circumscribed limits of its tradition-transcendent norms.

Finally, it should be noted that Habermas (and Benhabib, and others) regard discourse ethics as a postconventional and posttraditional form of morality that, in Habermas's words, 'has detached itself from the religious and metaphysical contexts from which it arose' (1993: 39). Only so can it offer rationally grounded and universally applicable principles, since 'convincing reasons can no longer appeal to the authority of unquestioned traditions' (p. 151). Benhabib is again explicit about the kind of culture that discourse ethics both presumes and privileges: a 'secular, universalist, reflexive culture in which debate, articulation and contention about value questions as well as conceptions of justice and the good have become a way of life' (1992: 42). At least in the public sphere, Habermas maintains, the moral values formerly justified on the basis of authoritative religious traditions must (and can) now only be justified through rational, consensus-seeking discourse: the task of philosophy is to translate religious language into the language of public reason (cf. Habermas 2002: 162–63).[42] While Habermas acknowledges that the central moral values of modern liberalism cannot be understood apart from their Judaeo-Christian origins (cf. 2002: 147–49, 154–55, 160, etc.), he contends that they cannot continue to be justified on this religious basis: 'from religions truths, after the religious world views have collapsed, nothing more and nothing other than the secular principles of a universalist ethics of responsibility can be salvaged, and this means: can be accepted for good reasons, on the basis of insight'.[43] In dialogue with theologians, Habermas later concedes that he perhaps too quickly affirmed this position, given that '[t]he process of a critical appropriation of the essential contents of religious tradition is still

such goods' – that is, the strong 'moral ideals' which drive their thinking. For discussion on this point, see also Rawls 1995: 173–78, who also insists that Habermas's ethic is substantive as well as procedural.

42. See Arens 1989b: 11–17, for an outline of Habermas's position on religion. Adams also concisely summarizes Habermas's view: 'The structure of argument in a pluralistic world substitutes for theology, and the latter has no role to play in contemporary moral debate' (Adams 2003: 75).

43. Habermas 1992: 237, here quoting from an earlier (1985) work of his, which he proceeds somewhat to qualify, as indicated in what follows above.

underway and the outcome is difficult to predict'. Indeed, the question as to whether this will be the route of historical development 'has to *remain open* from the point of view of the social scientist who proceeds reconstructively and who is careful not simply to project developing trends forward in a straight line' (Habermas 1992: 237; cf. 2002: 162–63). Nonetheless, this is clearly the nub of Habermas's own view, and one which underpins the role he regards discourse ethics as filling, with its translation of religiously grounded ethics into an ethics grounded in rational argumentation.[44]

2.3 *Stanley Hauerwas's Ecclesial Ethics*

It is not difficult to see why Stanley Hauerwas should be chosen to provide a contrasting perspective to the one outlined immediately above: Hauerwas's work is clearly and polemically opposed to the 'false universalism of liberalism' (Hauerwas 1999: 16) and to any notion that liberal political democracy represents a kind of social order that Christians should seek to legitimate and sustain.[45] Indeed, Samuel Wells comments that '[s]ometimes it appears that Hauerwas spends so much time demolishing the presuppositions of Christians who may be tempted to seek common cause with liberal democracies, that there is little time left for constructive proposals' (Wells 1998: 89). For Hauerwas, political liberalism, far from being a regime in which Christian values are well embodied and under which Christians can 'freely' practise their religion, involves the acceptance of a framework in which religion is privatized, in which belief in God is acceptable only as something which fundamentally 'does not matter',[46] and in which 'the desires and habits of those who claim to be Christian' are shaped not by the Church but by the tenets and practices of

44. This has not, however, prevented theologians from taking considerable interest in Habermas's work; for examples see Browning and Fiorenza 1992; Arens 1989a, 1991; Höhn 1985; Knapp 1993. Also notable is the interest in developing a conversation between discourse ethics and South American liberation ethics (e.g. Fornet-Betancourt 1992). Habermas has occasionally responded to the theologians' discussion, e.g. Habermas 1992, 1997; these and other essays on religion are now collected in Habermas 2002.

45. 'Christians would be ill advised to try to rescue the liberal project either in its epistemological or its political form' (Hauerwas 1999: 35, *et cf. passim*); 'Christians have no stake in Western civilisation nor should we try to rescue the epistemological or political forms of liberalism ... The reason Christians should not underwrite the epistemology and politics of liberalism is very simple: they are not true' (Hauerwas 2000: 325). Such quotations could easily be multiplied.

46. 'Christians in modernity have lost the ability to answer questions about the truthfulness of what we believe because we have accepted beliefs about the world that presuppose that God does not matter' (Hauerwas 2001: 231); 'modernity as well as

liberalism itself (Hauerwas 1999: 8). What Hauerwas is essentially concerned to do, in his own terms, is to call the Church to be faithful, to be the Church and not the world, that is, to live as a community whose practices and ethics are shaped by its own particular, true, story, and to narrate the world 'on our terms rather than the world's terms' (1999: 8; cf. Wells 1998: 1). To begin to understand the reasons for Hauerwas's stance, and the ways in which he articulates it, as well as to assess the degree to which he fits under the communitarian banner, it is necessary to outline the key features of his approach to ethics.

'Stanley Hauerwas was born in 1940 in Texas, the son of a bricklayer' (Wells 1998: 1). As we shall see, recording such biographical details is not, from Hauerwas's perspective, irrelevant to understanding his position on ethics. A prolific author, he has become one of the most prominent contemporary figues in Christian ethics – 'perhaps North America's most important theological ethicist' (Berkman 2001: 3) – though to define his field as 'ethics' would not meet entirely with Hauerwas's approval, for reasons which will become clear.[47] Hauerwas has always, and explicitly, eschewed the writing of systematic 'big books', choosing the 'occasional essay' as his favoured mode of argument; most of his books are collections of essays.[48] An excellent systematic analysis of Hauerwas's work is provided by Samuel Wells (1998), whose key headings I shall follow below, though Wells's survey is also meant to present the story of Hauerwas's developing approach.[49] (In this very compressed treatment, I shall not be concerned to trace such development, but aim only to give an overall impression that is true to Hauerwas's position.)

postmodernity but names the development of social orders that presume that God does not exist or even if God exists we must live as if God does not matter' (Hauerwas 1999: 8; cf. also 1998a: 43).

47. An extensive collection of Hauerwas's writings is now available in Berkman and Cartwright 2001 (and see pp. 673–98 for an annotated bibliography); for details of Hauerwas's works to 1997 see Wells 1998: 181–95.

48. Cf. Hauerwas 2000: 320; Wells 1998: 1; Cavanaugh 2001: 31. In what perhaps comes closest to being such a 'big book', *With the Grain of the Universe*, Hauerwas writes: 'if this book is different than my past work, I hope the difference is simply that here I make clear why I do not think theologians, particularly in our day, can or should write "big books" that "pull it all together". Any theology that threatens to become a position more determinative than the Christian practice of prayer betrays its subject' (2001: 10).

49. Note Hauerwas's preface to the book (Wells 1998: x–xii), in which he states that 'Wells has certainly provided a wonderfully fair account of what I hope I have said' (p. x). Elsewhere he states that 'Wells is one of those wonderful readers who understands me better than I understand myself' (1997: 237 n. 17).

2.3.1 *From quandary to character*

Hauerwas observes, critically, that contemporary ethics is focused on exploring – and hopefully even resolving – the various 'moral quandaries' that beset contemporary people.[50] The focus on quandaries correlates with a 'decisionism' which places the making of ethical decisions at the forefront of ethical inquiry (cf. Wells 1998: 16–18). Hauerwas is critical of such a conception of ethics in that it presumes the modern, Kantian, notion of disembodied, rational, reflection, and creates the possibility for such a distinctly conceived subject as 'ethics', wherein 'ethics' becomes (supposedly) detached from particular traditions and from tradition-constituted selves (cf. Hauerwas 1999: 27–31). Like Alasdair MacIntyre, one of the more important influences on Hauerwas,[51] Hauerwas turns instead to the Aristotelian focus on character and virtue: the centre of moral reflection becomes not moral decisions but moral people, people of character, not moral choices but moral habits (cf. Wells 1998: 17, 20; Hauerwas 1975).[52] Indeed, key features of Aristotle's approach to ethics are central too to Hauerwas's: that ethics is social and political, that ethics is teleological, that is, aimed at the good, and that goodness of character has to be developed through practice.[53] What Christians are called to *be* is more fundamental than any ethic, or ethical position, they might *have*: they 'must, above all, be a people of virtue – not simply any virtue, but the virtues necessary for remembering and telling the story of a crucified savior' (Hauerwas 1983: 103). A key question for any moral tradition, then, is whether it can produce people of good character, and Hauerwas's criticism of liberalism is, in part, that it lacks the resources to do this.

2.3.2 *From character to story*

Also key to Hauerwas's approach to ethics is the category of story, or narrative, another feature of his approach shared with MacIntyre, as well

---

50. See e.g. Hauerwas 1983: 4; 1999: 29; Wells 1998: 13–39.

51. See esp. MacIntyre 1985. Note Hauerwas's comments in 1983: xiii; 1999: 20, 192–93; 2001: 10, 18–26; Hauerwas and Pinches 1997: vii; also Wells 1998: 31–33. As well as Aristotle, Aquinas also becomes a key figure for both Hauerwas and MacIntyre.

52. For example, in the introduction to the third edition (1994) of *Character and the Christian Life* (Hauerwas 1975), Hauerwas comments: 'I continue to think that the analysis of the relation of action and agency I provided ... places the burden of proof on those who would abstractly treat "dilemmas" apart from questions of virtue and character' (p. xxiii).

53. Cf. Ross 1949: 187–92; and esp. Hauerwas and Pinches 1997. Autobiography is also relevant here, as Cavanaugh (2001: 18) points out: 'Long before he laid eyes on the *Nicomachean Ethics*, the Aristotelian theme of formation as a craft through apprenticeship to a master was hammered into his [sc. Hauerwas's] soul on the job at his father's side'.

as with other theologians, notably those of the 'Yale School' of postliberal theology.[54] The importance of story for Hauerwas is perhaps most clearly shown in his essay entitled 'A Story-Formed Community', in which he begins by setting out 'ten theses toward the reform of Christian social ethics' (Hauerwas 1981: 9–12).[55] The first thesis refers to 'the narrative structure of Christian convictions', while the second asserts that 'every social ethic involves a narrative ... The form and substance of a community is narrative dependent and therefore what counts as "social ethics" is a correlative of the content of that narrative' (pp. 9–10). Hauerwas then illustrates these convictions through a reading of the novel *Watership Down*, in which he shows how the various rabbit communities depicted there are formed and structured by their different narratives about the character of rabbit existence.

This is, in part, why it is relevant for Hauerwas to mention that he is a Texan. An apparently anecdotal piece of personal information exemplifies a critique of the liberal notion of the 'unencumbered self' by indicating that Hauerwas's position, indeed his identity, cannot be understood apart from the stories and traditions that have made him who he is.[56] The notion of a rational, reflective, self that can adopt a 'view from nowhere', can choose its own identity, is a (liberal) delusion. Like MacIntyre, Hauerwas regards as illusory (and perniciously deceptive) the idea that there could ever be tradition-independent enquiry.

> Ironically, the most coercive aspect of the liberal account of the world is that we are free to make up our own story. The story that liberalism teaches us is that we have no story, and as a result we fail to notice how deeply that story determines our lives. (Hauerwas 1981: 84)[57]

54.   Cf. MacIntyre 1985: 121–30, 144–45, etc. On the similarities between Hauerwas's approach and the Yale theologians Hans Frei and George Lindbeck, see Wells 1998: 53–60. Cf. also Harink 2003. Hauerwas also shares this focus on narrative with John Milbank, whose *Theology and Social Theory* (1990) articulates a theoretical position closely in harmony with Hauerwas's own (see further below).

55.   The emphasis on story as fundamental to Hauerwas's approach is equally evident in *With the Grain of the Universe* (2001), where Hauerwas essentially presents a storied argument, and echoes Milbank's argument that '"narrating", exactly because narration is the "science" of the particular, is a more basic category than either explanation or understanding' (p. 206; cf. Milbank 1990: 266–67; Hauerwas 2001: 21–22, 205–206).

56.   'Because I was raised Texan ... I knew I was never free to be "modern" and "self-creating". I would always be, for better or worse, Texan. It was my first lesson in particularity; as some would put it, being Texan made me realise early that the foundationalist epistemologies of the Enlightenment had to be wrong ... I prefer simply to have a Texan epistemology' (Hauerwas 1990: 214). See further Albrecht 1995: 29–32; Nation 2000: 22.

57.   The 'story that we have no story' nicely encapsulates a certain ambivalence in the treatment of liberalism, which may perhaps be paralleled with MacIntyre's treatment: the critique of post-Enlightenment morality, especially in *After Virtue* (1985), is that it constitutes

More prosaically put, liberalism both insists that people's traditions and stories 'do not matter', that they can and must be set aside insofar as they are trumped by the tradition-transcendent values of liberal democracy, and also masks in universal claims to rationality its own identity as a particular story about the character of human community.

2.3.3 *From story to community*

For Hauerwas the importance of the emphasis on story, or tradition, is not primarily to show how an individual's self-identity is formed but rather to indicate how communities are constituted. Hauerwas quotes Joseph Blenkinsopp with approval: 'without the tradition there is no shared memory and therefore no community' (Hauerwas 1981: 53). Communities are formed by traditions or, more specifically, by the practices in which traditions and stories are embodied and reproduced. It is belonging to a community which shapes a person's character and habits. And Hauerwas's critique of liberalism is not so much that it neglects community, or fails to shape people's character, but rather concerns the ways in which it does this. Precisely his challenge to Christians is that they have allowed their habits to be formed by the narrative of liberalism rather than that of Christianity, and that these habits include, *inter alia*, the presumption that religion is merely a private matter, that economic acquisition is essential for societal wellbeing, and that nation-states are the only communities of belonging and allegiance for which one might justifiably be called to die (and to kill).[58]

2.3.4 *From community to the church*

Despite the more general theoretical statements of some of Hauerwas's 'ten theses', mentioned briefly above – 'that every social ethic involves a narrative', and so on – it is clear (and particularly as Hauerwas's work progresses) that his focus is not on such general theoretical claims, but on particular claims about the truthfulness of the Christian story and on the ways in which this story should shape the practices of the particular community called the Church (cf. Wells 1998: 52). This begins to show why

---

an attempt to construct a universal, rational basis for ethics, independent of a particular tradition or narrative, but lacks coherence since it is actually a morality based only on the fragmented ruins of older traditions; but later (e.g. MacIntyre 1988: 345–46) liberalism itself is regarded as (having become) a tradition (cf. n. 12 above). Hauerwas's approach may again be paralleled also with Milbank's, in which Christianity's task is to 'outnarrate' its secular usurpers (Milbank 1990: 330).

58. Cf., e.g., Hauerwas 1998a: 219–26; 1999: 23–44.

Hauerwas is, and at the same time is not – and does not want to be labelled – a communitarian. Certainly he echoes some of the key themes of communitarianism: a rejection of the liberal notions of universal rationality and of the 'unencumbered self'. He also shares with communitarians, especially Alasdair MacIntyre, a focus on narrative as the basis for the formation of identity and community, and the conviction that only from within a tradition can one talk coherently about morality and specifically moral virtues, virtues engendered by the practices of tradition-constituted communities. Thus he can suggest, for example, that 'modern liberal societies lack the means to generate an intelligible account of justice' (1999: 68). The 'liberal world', in Hauerwas's view, 'is beginning to come apart', 'having finally undermined the moral capital on which it depended but for which it equally could not account on its own terms' (pp. 31, 43). However, as David Fergusson points out, Hauerwas 'does not wish his ethics to be sustained by the philosophical arguments for communitarianism, but rather by more exclusive theological considerations' (Fergusson 1998: 183 n. 1).

Hauerwas's central claims are not about virtue or narrative or community per se but about the truthfulness of the Christian story of God, God's saving action in the cross of Christ, and the embodiment of this salvation in the 'politics called church'.[59] From these central convictions follows Hauerwas's call for the Church to be the Church: 'the primary social task of the church is to be itself' (Hauerwas 1981: 10; cf. 1983: 99). As such, the Church stands as a 'political alternative', as 'that community constituted by practices by which all other politics are to be judged ... an alternative politics to the politics that so dominate our lives' (Hauerwas 1999: 35, 6). This is why Rasmusson can aptly describe Hauerwas's project as 'theological politics' in contrast to 'political theology', where the latter envisages the theological task as one of mediating the Christian message to the modern world (Rasmusson 1994). For Hauerwas, as Rasmusson remarks, 'it is the politics of the church and not the politics of the world that forms the primary context' (p. 377). The politics of the Church is determined by the character of God, seen in Jesus Christ, and thus fundamentally has the character of peaceable non-violence – on this theme in particular, so central to Hauerwas's writing, the

---

59. Hauerwas 2001: 17; cf. 1998a: 37–59. In the latter essay, in response to a comment of Nigel Biggar's that despite God's fundamental centrality 'God was ... curiously missing from my work', Hauerwas responds that '[o]ver the years I have tried to write about Christian ethics in a manner that would render Christian life unintelligible if God – in particular, the God of Jesus Christ – did not exist' (pp. 37–38) For a useful summary of Hauerwas's key proposals, see Wells 1998: 126–30. These begin with belief in the 'holy God', whose character is revealed in the 'holy story' and imitated by the 'holy people' who form the Church.

influence of John Howard Yoder is especially strong.[60] Here again we find not only a stark condemnation of a church which has, in Hauerwas's view, been so massively faithless in its accommodation to the violence of war but also a sharp critique of post-Enlightenment liberalism:

> The whole point, after all, of the philosophical and political developments since the Enlightenment is to create people incapable of killing other people in the name of God. Ironically, since the Enlightenment's triumph, people no longer kill one another in the name of God but in the names of nation-states ... the political achievement of the Enlightenment has been to create people who believe it necessary to kill others in the interest of something called 'the nation,' which is allegedly protecting and ensuring their freedom as individuals. (Hauerwas 1999: 33)

And this brings us to the context in which Hauerwas writes, and which is fundamental to understanding him: the USA and specifically the traditions of Christian social ethics in America.[61] According to Hauerwas, with the particular nature of American self-understanding and the 'social gospel' direction in which key figures in theology turned, the presumption became 'that the subject of Christian ethics in America is America' (Hauerwas 1998b: 65). In other words, not only was the theological task seen as 'crafting an account of liberal Christianity acceptable to a liberal culture and politics' (Hauerwas 2001: 88, describing the 'animating center' of Reinhold Niebuhr's work) but also the ethical task was perceived in terms of 'sustaining as well as shaping the ethos of America' (Hauerwas 1998b: 70). It is against such a background that the fiery polemic of Hauerwas's work is to be read: the Church is not, and never will be, contiguous with the 'world', nor with the specific part of the world called America, and to do Christian ethics as if American society were the political community to be addressed is to fail to see both the nature of the Church as an alternative (trans-national) politics and also the extent to which the liberal ideology of democratic nation-states actually determines the way Christians live. This is why the point about nation-states (rather than the Church) commanding a supreme loyalty – to kill or be killed for – is for Hauerwas so crucial. His contrary vision is of the peaceable kingdom, a salvation embodied in the political alternative called the Church. For Christians to begin to rediscover their ability to be this alternative, they need to be nurtured and formed by the Christian story of God, whose truth they discover and

---

60. See Wells 1998: 90–125. Wells comments: 'The single characteristic that summarizes the journey from community to the Church is nonviolence. This is the last of Hauerwas' key themes to emerge – after virtue, character, narrative, truthfulness and community – but it becomes the theme that underpins all the others' (p. 124).

61. Cf. Hauerwas 1998b; 1999: 69–92; Wells 1998: 3–10; 2002: 81.

whose character they imitate, as they together 'develop the particular *habits* and *practices* modelled on [the Church's] understanding of *virtue* ... one needs to practise with experts if one is to become a Christian disciple' (Wells 1998: 129).[62]

> The church is where the stories of Israel and Jesus are told, enacted, and heard, and it is our conviction that there is literally nothing more important we can do. But the telling of that story requires that we be a particular kind of people if we and the world are to hear the story truthfully. That means that the church must never cease from being a community of peace and truth in a world of mendacity and fear. (Hauerwas 1983: 99–100)

2.4 *Critical Reactions*

It should already be clear, from the sketch of the liberal-communitarian debate above and from the extent to which Habermas's discourse ethics and Hauerwas's ecclesial ethics represent contrasting opposites, that critical reactions to each set of proposals could take the form of essentially reiterating the alternative perspective. I shall, however, limit what could be an exercise in repetition and focus instead, albeit cursorily, on key criticisms of each approach. It will not be a surprise to learn that each perspective has been subjected to both sharp and sympathetic critique.[63] More significant to note, perhaps, is the feminist critique that has been brought to bear on both sides of the liberal-communitarian debate and specifically on both discourse ethics and Hauerwas's ecclesial ethics.

It is, of course, an obvious question to ask whether Habermas's attempt to provide a universal grounding for ethics is, as Richard Gebauer argues, doomed, and the project of critical theory with it, like a supertanker sinking 'in a sea of historical contingencies' (Gebauer 1993: 189). Habermas clearly considers that he has found in the universal presuppositions of argumentative speech just such a basis for the validation of ethical norms, but a critic may query whether the resulting programme does

---

62. Cf. Hauerwas 2001: 174, where it becomes clear why Barth is the hero of the story Hauerwas tells in this book: Barth's *Church Dogmatics* is seen as 'a manual designed to train Christians that the habits of our speech must be disciplined by the God found in Jesus Christ ... this training, which requires both intellectual and moral transformation, enables Christians to see the world as it is, and not as it appears'. Barth was 'engaged in a massive attempt to overturn the epistemological prejudices of modernity' (p. 190).

63. E.g., for a sharp critique of Habermas's discourse ethics, see Gebauer 1993, for sympathetic, 'internal' critique, see Benhabib 1992; a polemical criticism of Hauerwas is developed by Albrecht 1995, 1997, and a sympathetic critique which seeks to strengthen and supplement Hauerwas's work by Wells 1998.

justice to the culturally diverse and tradition-specific forms of human rationality, and, indeed, whether Habermas is simply too optimistic about the moral potential of a posttraditional rationality. The focus on real participation in discourse as the means to validate norms also raises questions about how those unable 'really' to participate in argumentation – those with serious mental handicap, or who lack communicative ability, for example – are able to bring their interests and perspective to the table, so to speak.[64] And Habermas's discourse theory of morality seems, on its own terms, unable to give any substantial grounding to environmental or ecological ethics, since its concern is with the moral regulation of human conflicts of interest: 'Human responsibility for plants and for the preservation of whole species cannot be derived from duties of interaction, and thus cannot be *morally* justified. Nevertheless ... there are good *ethical reasons* that speak in favor of the protection of plants and species' (Habermas 1993: 111; see pp. 105–11).[65] More fundamentally still – and here I echo both the communitarian critique of liberalism generally and Hauerwas's ethics particularly – one may question whether moral norms can or should be based on 'reasons', or whether in fact they derive from a narrative account of our identity, history, and purpose, or are embedded (and rightly so) in our unconscious, unreflected habits and inclinations.

Indeed, one key area in the feminist critique of liberal political theory concerns the liberal focus on rationality. Specifically, feminists voice the suspicion that the 'impartial' moral reasoner may actually be a biased, 'disembodied', male construct, insufficiently incorporating the emotive, affective, embodied, contextual aspects which women have been found to prioritize in moral decision-making more than men (see Frazer and Lacey 1993: 61–64). While Habermas does not exactly present the 'liberal' view of the disembodied or unencumbered self, not least since his difference from Kant lies in specifying that the individual does not make moral decisions in reflective isolation but only as situated in communicative contexts, he may nonetheless be said to presume a certain model of ungendered (but implicitly male) moral rationality, and his indebtedness to Lawrence Kohlberg's theory of stages of moral development – itself subjected to feminist critique for its orientation towards 'justice and rights', prominent especially in male subjects, rather than the contextualized empathy for the

---

64. There is perhaps a relevant qualification in Habermas's (D) principle (see above), that norms can only be valid if they meet – 'or *could* meet' (my emphasis) – with the approval of all affected. But, if applied to the cases mentioned above and considered in terms of what certain people *would* accept, how far does this compromise the insistence that only through real participation in a discourse of all affected can norms be tested and validated?

65. The distinction between moral and ethical needs to be understood here on Habermas's terms, as explained above (p. 55).

concrete other more strongly evident among women – suggests that this critique may be telling.[66]

Another important area in the feminist critique of liberalism generally and of discourse ethics in particular concerns the distinction between the right and the good, the public and the private, and the priority placed in each case on the former.[67] For feminists, the focus on public justice carries the danger of giving insufficient attention to, or leaving out of view altogether, crucial contexts in which women often suffer abuse and oppression, namely, those of the home and family. Benhabib makes the bold claim that '[a]ll struggles against oppression in the modern world begin by redefining what had previously been considered "private", non-public and non-political issues as matters of public concern, as issues of justice, as sites of power which need discursive legitimation' (Benhabib 1992: 100; cf. p. 109).

Discourse ethics has also been criticized for its lack of concrete applicability, specifically its inability to deal with conflicts between people who subscribe to different sets of values (Ferrera 1985). This point may be broadened and reframed in terms of the questions directed to discourse ethics from the perspective of the communitarian (and specifically Hauerwasian) critique of liberalism. Discourse ethics attempts essentially to provide a procedure for the validation of norms, but does not, at least on its own terms, generate specific moral norms; thus it depends on other forms of life, ethical traditions, and so on, for these substantive matters – they must meet 'halfway', so to speak (cf. Habermas 1990: 109). The questions then are as follows: does liberal democracy actually protect and sustain the 'forms of life' on which it depends for the generation of 'moral capital', or does it, as Hauerwas argues, undermine the moral resources on which it is dependent but for which it cannot itself account (Hauerwas 1999: 43)?[68] Specifically, as Hauerwas suggests, liberalism may be argued to undermine these forms of life by relativizing and thus denying the truth of

---

66. See further Benhabib 1992: 148–77, on the Kohlberg–Gilligan debate; and Habermas 1990: 33–41, 119–33, 172–88; 1991: 49–76; 1993: 113–32, on Kohlberg. The point of the critique is, at least in part, to query the value of Kohlberg's finding that men are more likely to reach stages four and five of moral reasoning, since the definitions favour a particular kind of moral reasoning. Nonetheless, Habermas maintains that Gilligan's and Benhabib's concerns can be accommodated within his discourse ethics (1993: 153–54). Giddens notes that a 'critical critic' of Habermas might well question his use of Piaget and Kohlberg – whose findings fit well with his theories – rather than, say, Lévi-Strauss (Giddens 1987: 247–49). In seeking empirical support for his theory, Giddens asks, has Habermas not rather conveniently chosen the work that happens to fit in well?

67. For this critique of liberalism generally, see Frazer and Lacey 1993: 64–66, 72–76; as related specifically to discourse ethics, see Benhabib 1992: 38–39, 107–13, 170, etc.

68. Cf. Hauerwas 1994: 109 n. 9: 'Liberalism as a politics and morality has been made possible by its continued reliance on forms of life it could not account for within its own

the 'stories' on which such moral capital depends – they are simply a matter of choice or personal preference – and also (and more subtly) by coercively making its own 'story' the determinative one. Since Habermas sees justice and solidarity as fundamental to his own, and any, account of morality, it may be questioned, for example, whether liberalism has 'the means to generate an intelligible account of justice' since any such account could only be 'tradition-dependent' (Hauerwas 1999: 68, 49): does Habermas's deontological, justice-focused morality provide the basis for a sufficiently 'thick' notion of justice, and does it provide any answer to the fundamental question of why one should in any case be just?[69] The liberal notion of the social contract may seem a somewhat 'thin' basis on which to expect people to accept the duty to act justly,[70] especially in contrast with the more Aristotelian notion of justice as a virtue, defined in a tradition-specific way, which can be developed in people's characters through justice-embodying practices. Moreover, there is a strong case to be considered that modern liberal democracies actually erode the sense of the common good, the civic virtues, the bases of human community, leading instead to 'the relentless atomization and commodification of all human needs and of human beings themselves' (Albrecht 1995: 141; cf. also pp. 18–19; Bell 1993). There is of course room for dispute as to how far the pessimistic 'crisis and moral decline' analysis of modern liberal democracies is compelling – after all, if myths of progress carry dangers, myths of crisis and decline are equally open to question – but the diagnosis is compelling enough, I think, to be taken very seriously. Moreover, while Habermas himself is by no means uncritical of the operations of contemporary capitalism it is unclear whether his deontological, formal-procedural ethic can contribute substantially to the re-education of desires and virtues necessary for the creation of a society in which the values of justice and solidarity are more fully embodied.

Criticisms of Hauerwas are, of course, of a completely different kind.[71] One area of criticism concerns what may be seen as fideism in Hauerwas's work: Hauerwas insists that the Christian story is true but cannot, or at

presuppositions. There is nothing wrong about it having done so except the power of liberal practices has increasingly undermined just those forms of life for which it could not account – such as why we have children.'

69. The language of thick and thin in this context is derived from Fiorenza (1992b: 82–83), who in turn is drawing on Rawls.

70. Cf., e.g., De Angelis 1999: 182–89, who proposes a Hobbesian social contract approach as a useful supplement to Habermas's discourse ethics, in view of the challenge of the question, 'warum moralisch sein?' She argues that Habermas's approach needs to make more plausible the necessity to enter discourse as the means to resolve moral disputes and validate moral norms.

71. Five principal themes of critique are helpfully summarized by Wells (1998: 130–32).

least does not, provide reasons why anyone should find it to be so (see Wells 1998: 77–89, 130). This is, of course, essentially because of his rejection of foundationalism: there can be no appeal to universal 'reasons' external to the tradition because there can be no tradition-transcendent, objective rationality (the Enlightenment myth). The character of Christian testimony, to the Church and the world, can only be that of witness (cf. Hauerwas 2001: 193–204, etc.). Hauerwas is prepared, however, to appeal to a pragmatic test of the truth of Christianity, namely, its ability to produce people of moral character.[72] This is, however, a precarious claim, since the Christian tradition has 'produced' a fair mix of villains and hero(in)es, and other traditions too have produced their noble, virtuous characters, even in the terms in which Hauerwas's tradition defines such virtue (Gandhi being one obvious example). And to appeal as Wells does to the story of a Christian community which acted virtuously, its members displaying right moral habits through being shaped by tradition and practice, to show that 'what Hauerwas commends can be done, has been done, and does produce people of virtue' (Wells 1998: 140; see pp. 134–40) invites the kind of counter-example that Duncan Forrester presents (Forrester 2000). Forrester reflects on the likely character of the small congregation that met in the little church just outside the perimeter fence of Dachau: 'In all probability it was just a quiet little congregation meeting in a much loved building as if nothing unusual was happening behind the wire close by' (p. 194). Thus it raises awkward questions for Hauerwas's conception of the Church as an 'alternative politics', a 'social ethic'. By contrast, Forrester considers the practices of those interred in the prison camp, 'where there was to be found from time to time a virtually sacramental sharing of bread, which expressed just that basic human solidarity that the Nazis were determined to destroy' (p. 200). This comparison culminates in an 'empirical refutation' of the depiction of the Church in Hauerwas's writings: 'that church [at Dachau] is not like the Church of which Hauerwas speaks, and paradoxically the virtues that he sees as central to the Christian community are exemplified in costly ways within the camp, far from the orbit of the church' (p. 206). Hauerwas agrees with a central impliction of this, that the Church as he describes it – which critics often see as an ideal remote from the empirical realities of actually existing churches (cf. Fergusson 1998: 66) – is a 'task' rather than a status (Hauerwas 2000: 326). It is easy to state that the immoral Christian people and communities have simply been unfaithful to their calling. But

---

72. For example, discussing Dorothy Day, the co-founder of 'Homes of Hospitality' and the *Catholic Worker*, Hauerwas writes: 'For those inclined to so dismiss my argument, I have no decisive response other than to ask if they represent practices that can produce a Dorothy Day' (2001: 231).

the admission that the vision is a calling and not a reality diminishes the force of Hauerwas's claim that the truth of Christianity is demonstrated in the people it produces.

The fact that the real Church is generally rather unlike the Church Hauerwas envisages also raises a further question, related to the theme of fideism. If, as Hauerwas insists, his (and other Christians') moral character is formed by participation in a community which celebrates and embodies the true story of God, then where does he find the critical purchase to argue that the Church's reading of its tradition – on crucial issues like pacifism versus just war – has been unfaithful and misguided? This point may be sharpened through a focus on Hauerwas's treatment of scripture. It is not, on Hauerwas's view, simply through reading the Bible that Christians are to discover their ethical priorities.[73] Discerning the message aright depends on there being 'a community capable of hearing the story of God we find in the scripture and living in a manner that is faithful to that story' (Hauerwas 1981: 1). As Hays puts it, summarizing Hauerwas's view, '[o]nly a community already formed by the story of the kingdom of God can begin to read scripture rightly' (Hays 1997a: 255). An example of this reading theory is found in Hauerwas's sermon on the Sermon on the Mount: 'put as contentiously as I can, you cannot rightly read the Sermon on the Mount unless you are a pacifist ... The Sermon does not generate an ethic of nonviolence, but rather a community of nonviolence is necessary if the Sermon is to be read rightly' (Hauerwas 1993: 64, 72; also quoted in Hays 1997a: 259). But since the Christian community on the whole, including the particular denomination of which Hauerwas is a member, has not adopted a pacifist stance, whence then does Hauerwas acquire the ability to read the Sermon 'rightly'? And whence, in the first place, would the Christian community ever be led to a pacifist stance? 'Thus, in the end', Hays concludes, 'Hauerwas's hermeneutical position comes unravelled' (Hays 1997a: 265). Hauerwas's reading strategy, which simply rules other interpretations out of court, also raises crucial questions about his treatment of diversity within the Christian tradition and communities, connected with issues of power (see below).

Another of the prominent criticisms of Hauerwas is that his work represents a 'sectarian' view of the Church's relationship to society.[74] Insofar as this criticism presumes Hauerwas's stance to be one in which the

---

73. Note, for example, the 'primary contention' of *Unleashing the Scripture* (Hauerwas 1993): '*The Bible is not and should not be accessible to merely anyone, but rather it should only be made available to those who have undergone the hard discipline of existing as part of God's people*' (p. 9, italics original). 'No task is more important than for the Church to take the Bible out of the hands of individual Christians in North America' (p. 15). Cf. also Hays 1997a: 255.

74. See, e.g., Miscamble 1987; Quirk 1987; Hauerwas 1987 for discussion; further Biggar 2000; Fergusson 1997b; 1998: 64–67.

Church is simply removed from society and from its 'life and death policy issues' (Miscamble 1987: 73) it is largely misguided: Hauerwas is concerned not with the withdrawal of the Church from the world but with what it means for the Church to be the Church, in and for the world.[75] His plea is for the Church to be shaped in its thought and practice not by the 'world's story' but by its own tradition; Christian engagement in political and social issues should be done from a Christian standpoint. Indeed, Hauerwas turns the criticism on its head, maintaining that his view of the Church as a universal society stands 'against the sectarian character of the nation-state' (Hauerwas 1987: 88). Nonetheless, there remain issues to be addressed, stemming from what Fergusson refers to as Hauerwas's 'over-concentration on the distinctiveness of the church' (Fergusson 1997b: 244; cf. 1998: 67).

With his stark polemic against liberalism Hauerwas effectively denies, and certainly shows little interest in, the extent to which moral insights and convictions may be shared among traditions, and with liberalism specifically. He does not give much consideration to the ways in which Christians, who invariably inhabit various 'communities' (of profession, locality, family, etc.) as well as the Church community, may seek 'common cause' with others (Fergusson 1997a: 46; 1997b: 248).[76] Nor does he seek to explore the ways in which Christians might cooperate with others to build the kind of 'moral consensus which alone can sustain a pluralist culture' (Fergusson 1998: 75). Indeed, insofar as he makes policy recommenda-tions, such as his plea for universities which are 'recognizably Christian' rather than 'shaped by the practices and knowledge required by a democratic social order' (2001: 232; see pp. 231–40), they would seem to foster forms of Christian separatism and thus to strengthen divisions and mistrust in society. The welcome for the stranger which Hauerwas sees as a basic Christian virtue is unlikely to be nurtured without real and intimate encounter with 'strangers', still less the wider goal of transcending precisely the perception of the Other as Stranger. Neither does Hauerwas do justice to the extent to which 'it is largely from liberalism that Christianity has learnt some of the (more liberal) political implications of its "story"', nor,

---

75. Cf. Hauerwas 1983: 99–102; Wells 1998: 99. Hauerwas seeks 'to position the church in a manner such that the church can serve society imaginatively by not being captured by societal options or corresponding governmental policy' (Hauerwas 1987: 90).

76. Fergusson elsewhere comments on Hauerwas's tendency 'to depict secular arguments in the worst possible light. While not only unfair on much that is sane and decent outwith the church, this characterisation of an alternative position renders allies as foes and hinders the process of making common cause' (1998: 73). For example, Hauerwas does 'not know why people who are not Christians have children', and sees no reason to investigate (1981: 210–11); but he is able to assert that '[f]rom the world's perspective the birth of a child represents but another drain on our material and psychological resources' (p. 228). Cf. §9.2.3 n. 6 below.

indeed, to the flip side of the same coin, that 'there are considerable respects in which liberalism is rooted in Christianity'. Thus, Hauerwas's 'sharp distinction between liberalism and Christianity ... is not sustainable' (Biggar 2000: 159). Hauerwas's inclination to deny that Christians owe anything to 'liberal' explanations or values may be illustrated with some of his statements on subjects such as women and slavery. For example, he writes, 'I do not share many feminist views of justice for the simple reason that they assume egalitarian and distributivist notions of justice so characteristic of liberal political theory' (1997: 235; cf. 2000: 328). Or on slavery: 'The problem with slavery is not that it violates "the inherent dignity of our humanity," but that as a people we have found that we cannot worship together at the table of the Lord if one claims an ownership over others that only God has the right to claim' (1981: 106). What is clear here is the attempt to derive an argument against slavery from the practices of the Christian community and not from so-called liberal principles. Yet Hauerwas's conviction that the Christian tradition has the resources to locate and correct 'perversions' such as the oppression of women and slaves (1997: 236) has a fair weight of history against it (cf. further Meeks 1996b). It seems entirely likely that a Christian community committed only to living out its own story, deaf to the anti-slavery movement, the women's movement, the environmental movement, and so on, would continue to practise the forms of oppression and neglect that have so characterized its history.[77]

This critique of Hauerwas may here be linked with a more general liberal criticism of communitarianism, namely, the tendency at least implicitly to support a conservative and authoritarian position (cf. Frazer and Lacey 1993: 130–62; Fergusson 1997a: 39).[78] The appeal for a form of community shaped by tradition and nurturing virtue by its practices may both ignore the diversity that does exist (and always has existed) in the telling and practising of the tradition, and also mask the fact that 'the' tradition is established and maintained by the powerful, through the marginalizing and silencing of other voices (cf. esp. Albrecht 1995). The communitarian argument, directed against liberal individualism – that moral virtue can only be engendered through our participation in the communities which constitute our identity, and that such tradition-constituted communities can shape our (subconscious) habits such that we cultivate moral character

77. I would not wish to deny that these 'liberal' movements also owe something, in various ways, to Christianity, although they also raise critical concerns against the tradition. But precisely this rather complex interplay is that to which Hauerwas fails to do justice.

78. This criticism forms a starting point for Porter's (1993) analysis of MacIntyre's work, in which she defends his approach from the criticism of authoritarianism, by showing how it presupposes and fosters 'the classical liberal virtues of tolerance and openness to pluralism' (p. 516).

(cf. e.g. Bell 1993: 13–14) – can be subjected to a compelling critique: it is precisely (and only) through the (liberal) value of reflective questioning, even of our most 'constitutive attachments', and the consequent freedom to choose to reject them, that the opportunity for liberation from forms of oppression becomes available.[79]

The fact that Hauerwas's presentation of the Christian story and its implications represents a particular perspective and a specific (male) 'location' is also well brought-out by feminist critics. For all his powerful calling of the Church to a stance of nonviolence, it seems that the violence Hauerwas means to define is primarily the violence of war: he does not attend to the forms of violence frequently encountered by women in domestic contexts nor to the violence of oppression (Albrecht 1995: 124, 136, 156, etc.; Woodhead 2000: 171–76). Hauerwas's tendency to use 'homogenising discourse' not only about the Church, but also the world (Woodhead 2000: 183), can thus be criticized both as a (male) strategy of power and also as a denial of the (always contested) plurality within the Christian tradition(s) and communities.[80] Hauerwas's argument that the heart of the Church's witness is to be located in a stance of nonviolence is precisely that: Hauerwas's argument. It is Hauerwas's reading of the implications of the Christian story and tradition, and it is a reading that many Christians through the ages have disputed. Leaving the merits of Hauerwas's case aside, his approach implies that sharing a tradition-based identity in Christian community provides coherent moral guidance –if only Christians would stop being formed by liberalism's story. The reality of Christian plurality and dispute implies not only that the tradition is open

---

79.   This feminist case is powerfully presented by Will Kymlicka, in his critical response to Daniel Bell (in Bell 1993: 208–21): 'What we need is a conception of the self that recognizes that we have constitutive attachments, and that they are damaging to give up, but that these attachments can themselves be damaging, and hence that we must be free to question and possibly reject them even when they don't "break down"' (p. 210). Kymlicka also exposes the oppressive potential of the kind of governmental measures Bell commends to further the communitarian agenda (pp. 215–19), which perhaps in part explains why MacIntyre is insistent that he does not see the nation-state as a 'community' nor does he seek government implementation of any communitarian programme. Only small-scale, local communities, on MacIntyre's view, have a hope of being the kind of virtue-nurturing communities he has in mind (though small-scale communities can be equally oppressive, of course!) (see MacIntyre 1994: 302–303; 1985: 263).

80.   Cf. Albrecht 1995: 'Hauerwas seems not to recognise the reality of relationships of domination with "the Christian narrative" and its tradition, nor the multiplicity of voices, nor the silencing throughout history of many Christians' stories [p. 101] ... Hauerwas describes the Christian church as a community shaped by a unified discourse that sustains unchanging values and behaviors. I argue that such a vision functions, and has always functioned, not to honor the skills of masters, but to mask domination by masters' (p. 148); also Albrecht 1997: 225–26.

to various readings but also that claims to interpret it rightly are always tied up with claims to power.

2.5 *Common Ground?*

Just as Habermas's and Hauerwas's approaches may be presented as contrasting opposites, so too the respective criticisms in some respects balance each other. While Habermas's discourse ethics may legitimately be questioned insofar as it presupposes a universal conception of human rationality, Hauerwas may be criticized for implying too great a degree of incommensurability and distinction between traditions, specifically between liberalism and Christianity. Even to raise the question about common ground between them may seem pointless,[81] especially since the sources of authority to which each appeals are fundamentally different.[82]

Yet we may perhaps move towards at least a degree of compatibility between the approaches if we contrast their aims. Hauerwas's overriding concern is to spell out *for the Church* what the Christian tradition should mean in practice, calling in effect for Christians to be shaped by their own story and not that of liberal democracy and thus to be faithful witnesses. In doing so, he does not take his task to be one of reflecting on what kind of moral framework might be necessary for various groups and traditions (including those that Christians represent) to negotiate their claims and counterclaims in the public sphere. This is presumably because the very idea of such a tradition-transcendent framework is one Hauerwas regards as impossible and illusory. Nonetheless, it is significant that he does not see as a pressing task articulating how his own tradition might narrate the public space so as to foster a generous and humble encounter with the Other(s) of other traditions, nor exploring how different traditions might discern common ground. What may be seen as the primary moral challenge for political ethics – creating sufficient consensus for people of

81. This is perhaps especially so since Habermas and Hauerwas are not (and are never likely to be) engaged in direct debate. In the field of political theory, however, the debates between liberals and communitarians have had an impact, particularly on the ways in which liberal theory has been reframed and revised, especially by Rawls, leading Bell to speak of 'the communitarianization of liberalism' (Bell 1993: 8; further Mulhall and Swift 1996: 191–222). Fergusson also explores these moves towards convergence, which are influential on his own mediating position (1997a, 1998).

82. For Hauerwas, authority lies with God, whose story is known through the witnesses of scripture and Christian tradition; for Habermas, the only convincing 'authority' in posttraditional and postmetaphysical thought can be the consensus wrought through discourse, shaped by the universal presuppositions of human argumentation.

different traditions, cultures, and religions to live peaceably together – is not the challenge Hauerwas wishes to address.[83]

Habermas's key concern, in contrast, is precisely to theorize the kind of morality necessary for the regulation of the public space in which conflicts of interest and conviction, often arising from commitments to different ways of life, must be resolved. He recognizes that specific traditions and forms of life are crucial for people's identity and ethical convictions, but equally insists that tradition-specific justifications cannot suffice to validate a norm in the public sphere of modern, plural, secular societies.

To some degree, then, we may place Habermas and Hauerwas side by side simply by observing that the tasks they see as their priority are utterly different: one seeks to elaborate the implications of a specific tradition, such that adherents of that tradition might properly bring that perspective to bear on public life; the other seeks to outline the kind of public discourse needed for this and other perspectives to be fairly subjected to discussion in the public sphere. Habermas's concern is less with the generation of moral norms and more with their rational testing for universal validity. It is also notable that, in pursuing these different tasks, each of them avoids a focus on 'quandaries', though for very different reasons. For Habermas this is because his task as moral philosopher is not to formulate substantive norms but to outline procedures for their discursive validation; for Hauerwas this is because his concern is to challenge the very presumptions that underpin the formulation of such quandaries, rather than to accept them in the terms given. We may go on, however, and ask whether this kind of 'different aims' complementarity might extend further.

For example, despite his forthright, passionate, and polemical championing of a particular vision of what a faithful Christian ethic should look like, Hauerwas is clear – not least through his insistence that nonviolence is at the heart of such an ethic – that such a vision is never to be imposed by coercion. The 'hallmark' of a Christian community, 'formed on trust rather than distrust', 'is its refusal to resort to violence to secure its own existence or to insure internal obedience. For as a community convinced of the truth, we refuse to trust any other power to compel than the truth itself' (Hauerwas 1981: 85). Though framed in different terms, this is of course very similar to Habermas's insistence that valid norms can be ascertained only through noncoercive, nonviolent argumentation, where nothing compels except 'the unforced force of the better argument' (Habermas

83. Cf. Plant (2001: 140–41), who sees Hauerwas's view as a 'bleak' alternative, 'namely, that modern society is an arena of competing and incommensurable narratives with no overall moral resources to bind society together' (p. 141). Interestingly, Plant concludes his book with Habermas, whose work suggests 'the possibility of dialogue between persons situated in moral and religious traditions ... [People share] a common world of meaning and dialogue seems perfectly possible and, indeed, a central human imperative' (p. 359).

1993: 23). There is, then, some common ground in the agreed mode in which ethical conflicts are to be explored and resolved – notwithstanding a clear difference regarding the sources of authority to which argument may appeal (cf. n. 82 above). Furthermore, if Christian articulation of moral claims in encounter with other traditions is also to follow this nonviolent, noncoercive pattern, as for Hauerwas it surely must, then we might well find in Habermas's work valuable reflection on the kind of discursive morality necessary for the fostering of such peaceful debate between (as well as within) traditions, even if Hauerwas eschews such reflection. Fergusson also makes the point, discussing MacIntyre's work, that (according to MacIntyre) a viable tradition flourishes through ongoing internal and external debate, such that 'the peaceful coexistence of rival traditions which can debate and argue their most fundamental differences' is a requirement for such flourishing and progress. This of course implies 'a polity in which different traditions are tolerated and brought together in dialogue' (Fergusson 1998: 126). So, Fergusson concludes, summarizing the argument of Jean Porter (1993), 'if a tradition survives and prospers by engagement with its rivals, then a condition of tradition-constituted inquiry must be the maintenance of tolerance, pluralism, and openness to change within our societies. And these, of course, are amongst the central values of liberalism' (Fergusson 1998: 127).[84] Hauerwas's strident and polemical critique of liberalism, it might be suggested, can find space for its articulation precisely in the academic and political context of liberalism, where radical (nonviolent) disagreement and dissent are tolerated and protected under the banner of free speech. So again we are led to discern a more complex and overlapping relationship between liberalism and communitarianism than Hauerwas's stark polemic suggests.

All this – the starkly different perspectives themselves, the points for and against each approach, and their complementary and even overlapping aspects – sets a contemporary scene for our reading of Paul. Clearly, some kinds of questions we might conceivably pursue in such a reading would simply and rapidly indicate the vast difference between contemporary moral philosophy and Paul's ethics; one hardly needs to engage in a detailed study to show that Paul's ethics are not based on a posttraditional, postmetaphysical appeal to a universal rationality grounded in the pragmatic presuppositions of human communication. A basic similarity with an ecclesial ethic is, of course, more readily apparent. But other questions may prove more fruitful: What emerge as the 'metanorms' of

---

84. See Porter 1993: 516, 523, 526–30. E.g.: 'I want to suggest that when MacIntyre's theory of rationality is read in the context of the tradition of late liberalism that he himself inhabits, it becomes apparent that he both presupposes and fosters the virtues of tolerance, respect for pluralism, and openness to revision and change that are constitutive of that way of life' (p. 523).

Pauline ethics, and might these resonate with liberal as well as ecclesial moral values? How does Paul conceive of the distinctive identity of the Christian community, and how does this relate to the possibilities for the wider sharing of ethical values? Does Paul make any appeal to a universal rationality on the basis of which ethical values can be expected to be shared by all humankind, or show any indications that such a moral consensus is attainable? How, if at all, does Paul treat differences (of ethical conviction) within the community, and what kind of moral arguments does he use when faced with such diversity – and does the substance and structure of his arguments suggest points of contact with liberalism, as well as (perhaps) critical considerations for an ecclesial ethics? And the over-arching question: What might the shape and structure of Pauline ethics suggest by way of critical and constructive conclusions in relation to issues raised in the liberal-communitarian debate? Various aspects of these and other questions are treated in what follows, especially in the reflections at the end of each chapter, but it is only in conclusion (ch. 9) that they are systematically brought together.

Chapter 3

READING PAUL: MYTH, RITUAL, IDENTITY AND ETHICS

The previous chapter outlined two very different approaches in recent ethical theory, in order to provide a contemporary context with which to engage, in our thinking with (though also beyond, and against) Paul. As I made clear there, however, the outline of this theoretical debate does not itself provide a conceptual framework for reading Paul's ethics, does not provide theoretical tools to guide our handling of his texts. That is the purpose of this (far shorter) chapter, which brings us much closer to Paul in the sense of setting out a conceptual framework for understanding what Paul's texts are, what they are doing, and how we should conceive of 'ethics' within them. This conceptual framework, derived from a range of social-scientific resources, uses general, 'etic' terms which cast Pauline ethics into the kinds of categories with which other traditions and materials could also be described (cf. §1.1, n. 26 above); but at the same time the framework is intended specifically to 'fit' the Pauline material – the concepts are outlined with this material particularly in view, and are not simply elements of a general theory or model.

3.1 *Symbolic Universe, Story and Myth*

Since the early 1970s, when social-scientific perspectives began to be energetically explored by New Testament scholars, the work of Peter Berger and Thomas Luckmann has been among the most widely used theoretical resources from the social sciences, specifically the sociology of knowledge.[1] In their classic theoretical treatise *The Social Construction of Reality*, Berger and Luckmann (1966) set out to examine the ways in which what is generally taken for granted as 'the way things are', what passes for knowledge in society, is a human product, a constructed creation.[2] This

---

1. For a survey of the influence of Peter Berger's work on New Testament studies, see Horrell 2001a; on the development of social-scientific approaches more generally cf. §1.5 above.

2. For more detailed summary and critique of Berger and Luckmann's work, and its application to NT studies, see Horrell 1993; 1996: 39–45.

socially constructed world gives order and meaning to human life, thus meeting the basic human need for *meaning*, in the face of the ever-present threat of chaos, anomie, and death (cf. Berger 1967: 52–80; 1974; Wuthnow 1986: 126, 136, etc.). '*All* societies are constructions in the face of chaos' (Berger and Luckmann 1966: 121).

Every such social construction of reality, according to Berger and Luckmann, requires legitimation, 'ways by which it can be "explained" and justified' (Berger and Luckmann 1966: 79; see pp. 110–46). At the most comprehensive level, this is provided by what Berger and Luckmann call a 'symbolic universe', that is, a body of 'theoretical tradition' that 'encompasses the institutional order in a symbolic totality' (Berger and Luckmann 1966: 113; see pp. 113–22). Symbolic universes 'are sheltering canopies over the institutional order as well as over individual biography. They also provide the delimitation of social reality; that is, they set the limits of what is relevant in terms of social interaction' (Berger and Luckmann 1966: 120). It is in these terms that Berger conceives of religion, as a 'sacred canopy' which provides meaning and legitimates a social order (Berger 1967).[3]

This kind of perspective is of considerable value for a study of Pauline ethics, or indeed of any New Testament text or tradition, for a number of reasons.[4] First, unlike some reductionistic social-scientific approaches which see religious ideas as merely reflections of specific socio-economic relationships, Berger and Luckmann take the constructed cosmos of meaning with great seriousness as a (perhaps *the*) central human achievement in the making of society.[5] Second, Berger's approach to religion highlights that fact that the 'body of tradition', the subject matter of systematic theology, shapes and orders human life for those living under its 'canopy'. It not only creates a framework of meaning and significance, but also determines the boundaries of right and wrong, structures human relationships and actions. From this perspective there is an inextricable connection between theological ideas and social practice. This clearly, and importantly, blurs the distinctions often drawn between theology and ethics, doctrine and practice, not least in the Pauline letters. Once the whole body of material is seen as a community-forming, meaning-giving and praxis-shaping 'symbolic universe' then such distinctions become

---

3. In Berger 1967 the theoretical framework from Berger and Luckmann 1966 is applied specifically to religion. The US title, *The Sacred Canopy*, was rather more revealing of the perspective taken than the UK one, *The Social Reality of Religion*.

4. See further Horrell 2001a: 146–48.

5. This raises, of course, theological questions about the possible 'truth' of what is essentially regarded as a human projection. For Berger's own response to these issues, see Berger 1967: 179–88; 1969, and further discussion in Cairns 1974; Gill 1974; 1975: 29–34; 1977: 16–22; Woodhead, Heelas and Martin 2001.

somewhat (though not entirely) artificial. Thus, for example, Raymond Pickett (1997), drawing on Berger and Luckmann's work in his study of Paul's presentation of Jesus' death in the Corinthian letters, regards the central symbol of the cross not solely as a theological or doctrinal topic, but rather as a symbol on which Paul draws to shape the praxis of the Corinthian community (cf. p. 29). Describing his project as an exercise in 'sociological exegesis' (p. 34), Pickett emphasizes that his concern is to move beyond social and historical description to an analysis of the 'social impact' that 'a text, or symbol within the text, was designed to have in the realm of social interaction' (p. 35).

However, the term symbolic universe (or symbolic order) can imply too static and fixed a conception of the social order and its legitimating 'canopy'.[6] Moreover, this sacred canopy often, and certainly in the case of Paul and early Christianity, has a narrative character: it is not simply a galaxy of symbols and beliefs, arranged in an overarching sky, but rather a story with some sense of temporal extension and direction. Paul's texts are not, of course, narrative in form, and the (few) narratives explicitly recounted within them are mostly those of Paul's own experiences (esp. Gal. 1.13–2.14; cf. also 2 Cor. 11.22–12.11; Barclay 2002). Nonetheless, it can be shown that a narrative underpins Paul's 'theologizing': the story of God's saving act in Jesus Christ.[7] Before developing this point, I want to make the claim more precise and to suggest that Paul's letters are shaped and informed by a 'myth'.

The term 'myth', of course, conjours up a range of allusions, not least the popular connotation of a myth as essentially a lie. In the study of religion, however, the term myth has been more positively used to refer to a means by which (a) 'truth' is conveyed.[8] Nonetheless, its application to the New Testament's theology may be regarded with some suspicion,[9] and its positive retrieval requires an emergence from the shadow cast by Bultmann's hermeneutical programme of demythologization (see Bultmann 1985: 1–43, 95–130). For Bultmann, the New Testament's message was cloaked in the mythological language and presuppositions of the first-

---

6. Cf. the criticisms of Berger and Luckmann's project outlined in Horrell 1993; 1996: 41–45; 2001a: 148–51.

7. See esp. Hays 1983. For critical assessment of this narrative approach to Paul, see Longenecker 2002 and the response by Hays 2004.

8. Cf. Doniger 1998: 2–3, who shows that this ambiguity goes back to Plato, and astutely comments that '[w]hat makes this ambiguity possible is that a myth is above all a story that is *believed*, believed to be true' (p. 2).

9. It is revealing, for example, that even in a work which seeks to take symbol, metaphor and myth seriously and positively in Christian theology, Paul Avis can write: 'If there is myth in the New Testament – and some of us are troubled by the thought – let us prepare the appropriate tools to interpret it. If there is myth in the creed and Christian doctrine ... let us make a rigorous attempt to deal with it constructively' (Avis 1999: 123).

century world, and was thus simply no longer believable to modern people. What was required was to demythologize the *kerygma*, such that its essential existential challenge could be recovered. However, in a context in which the categories of narrative and myth have been reappropriated, and applied even to the very modern arenas of science, politics, culture, and so on,[10] it should be clear that the problems Bultmann identifies could not be overcome by demythologization, but only by a process of *re*mythologization, a process which, in fact, the history of Christian theology represents, as the story of the faith is constantly retold and reconfigured in the light of changing contexts and challenges.

In a recent treatment of the topic of myth, Wendy Doniger (1998) describes myths as 'one discrete subdivision of the broader category of "story"' (p. 1). Similarly, Gerd Theissen, outlining a framework for the interpretation of primitive Christian religion, states that '[m]*yths* explain in narrative form what fundamentally determines the world and life' (Theissen 1999: 3). Doniger's description continues:

> a myth is above all a story that is *believed*, believed to be true ... a story that is sacred to and shared by a group of people who find their most important meanings in it; it is a story believed to have been composed in the past about an event in the past, or, more rarely, in the future, an event that continues to have meaning in the present because it is remembered ... a myth is not bounded by a single text ... (which I would call a text or a telling) but [refers] to the narrative that underlies the whole series of tellings, encompassing them all. (Doniger 1998: 2–3)

In this sense it is entirely appropriate to conceive of Paul's letters as texts which depend on, echo, reproduce, and reshape, the early Christian myth(s). To be sure, the myth Paul believes finds its central focus not in primaeval events (though these are there within it) but in rather recent ones, in the death and resurrection of Christ. But even these recent events are received and regarded by Paul as a tradition, attested by a range of witnesses and passed onto him, and now shared by a group who certainly find their most important meanings in it (1 Cor. 11.2, 23; 15.1-8).[11] And the recent Christ-event provides the central viewpoint from which the distant

10. Cf. for example, the discussion of capitalism, Marxism, etc., in narrative terms in Milbank 1990, where the challenge for Christianity is to 'outnarrate' these other stories about the world; the narrative terms applied to liberalism, as well as Christianity, in Hauerwas's work (see §2.3 above); and the analysis of American culture and politics in terms of the myth of the superhero in Lawrence and Jewett 2002. Lawrence and Jewett, while calling for a thoroughly critical analysis of this 'monomyth' and its implications, do not propose that such myth should be abandoned but rather 'temperately reshaped'; echoing A.N. Whitehead, the 'fearlessness of revision' should be combined with 'a reverence for symbols' (p. 361).

11. Cf. Doniger 1998: 135, where she is dealing with the question of finding women's voices even in 'men's texts': 'The author of a myth is a tradition, not just one human male; and

past is renarrated (1 Cor. 10.1-11) and the basis for the vision of a (near) future consummation. Moreover, like many religious myths, Paul's myths feature divine and divine-human characters, acting in response to the perennial problems of human wickedness and mortality.

The centre of the myth which Paul's letters reflect is undoubtedly the Christ-event, that is the descending, dying, and rising of Jesus Christ, which represents the saving action of God in which believers participate.[12] This central key clearly has a 'vertical' dimension (cf. Campbell 2002) – descending and ascending – but it also has a horizontal dimension, a temporal extension: in the fullness of time, after the period of the law, God sent forth his son (Gal. 4.3-5), who died, rose, and will return again (1 Thess. 4.14-17).[13] Thus, while Paul perceives the Christ-event as for him an 'apocalyptic' event, which has disrupted and re-oriented his very self (Gal. 2.19-20), and while this Christ-event requires a recasting of the stories Paul had previously held true, it is not simply a 'punctiliar' event but rather one which Paul casts within a narrative framework.[14]

Although the centre of Paul's myth is the Christ-story, it begins, chronologically ordered, with God's creation and the 'fall' of Adam, the archetypal and representative human figure, typologically compared and contrasted with Christ (Rom. 5.12-21), through whom sin entered the world. Abraham is also a crucial figure, not only as a paradigm of faith (Rom. 4.1-25) but also as the recipient of God's promise to bless all the nations in him (Gen. 12.3). For it is this promise Paul sees fulfilled in Christ, the singular 'seed' of Abraham (Gal. 3.16). In the time between the promise to Abraham and the coming of Christ God gave the Law (Gal. 3.17-25; cf. Rom. 5.20), the intentions of which Paul (or at least Pauline scholars) struggle(s) to articulate coherently, in the light of the new conviction that Christ is τέλος νόμου – the end or goal of the Law (Rom. 10.4). The coming, dying, and rising of Christ, sent by God as a human

---

traditions have women in them too.' This point can be nicely illustrated with reference to the stories about the resurrection of Jesus, in which women certainly feature prominently, even if Paul omits them from his list of witnesses (1 Cor. 15.5-8; cf. Mk 16.1-8 and pars).

12.   Cf. Rom. 8.3-4; 1 Cor. 15.3-4; Gal. 4.4-6; Phil. 2.6-11, etc. This 'story of Christ' is the central focus in Hays 1983. Despite the central prominence of the Christ-event, J.C. Beker has rightly drawn attention to the theocentricity of Paul's thought: it is God who sent Christ, raised him from death, and will ultimately be 'all in all' (1 Cor. 15.28; Beker 1980: 362–67).

13.   Cf. Hays 1983: 267 n. 1, whose reading of Paul, contra the punctiliar emphasis of Bultmann (and later Martyn), 'emphasises that the salvation event has temporal extension and shape; the event of the cross has meaning not as an isolated event but as an event within a story'. Contrast Martyn 1997a: 347–48, 389, etc.

14.   In this paragraph I echo a number of the points under discussion in Longenecker 2002, reiterating very briefly my own position as articulated more fully there in response to John Barclay's essay and with references to relevant literature: see Barclay 2002; Horrell 2002c; Watson 2002.

being to die on the cross for the sins of humanity, mark the decisive fulfilment of God's saving purposes, and mark the boundary between the end of the old age and the beginning of the new (1 Cor. 10.11). As J.C. Beker puts it: 'the Christ-event is the turning-point in time that announces the end of time' (Beker 1980: 362). God's raising of Christ from death and his exalting him as Lord indicate not only God's decisive if yet to be completed victory over hostile powers (1 Cor. 15.12-28) but also the possibility for those who come to live 'in Christ', who die to their old life and begin anew, to share in this promise of resurrection and life (Rom. 6.1-5). Adoption into this new family is confirmed by the Spirit, given to all who believe (Rom. 8.9-17; Gal. 4.6), and who also empowers those in Christ to 'walk in newness of life' (Rom. 6.4; 8.1-8), to live as holy people, in accordance with God's will (1 Thess. 4.3). In the present time, those in Christ look forward expectantly to the time when their salvation will finally be fully realized. The completion of the process of salvation is near, when the mysterious plan of God, which somehow encompasses all people and all creation, will finally come to fruition (Rom. 8.21; 11.32) and when believers will live with the Lord forever (1 Thess. 4.17).[15] The various elements of this story provide the theological basis and motivational framework for Pauline ethics, as many have noted; Schrage, for example, considers in turn the christological, sacramental, pneumatological, and eschatological bases (1988: 172–86).

Such a bare outline of the central myth of Pauline thought naturally raises a host of questions; Paul's letters are subject to such extensive exegetical discussion that each of the themes mentioned above could be nuanced or contested in a variety of ways. One question of particular pertinence, not least since it is relevant to much of what follows in this book, concerns the situational specificity of Paul's various letters. Given the long-recognized degree to which Paul's letters (including Romans)[16] address particular and diverse situations, and vary in their content and emphases, one may question any presentation of Paul's thought which simply amalgamates this material into a single story, myth, or 'theology'. A concern to do justice to the individual texts can be taken to require an engagement with each on its own terms alone, such that one analyses the distinctive theology, or ethics, of Romans, 1 Corinthians, Galatians, and

---

15. For this brief sketch, and elaboration of the key themes within it, see Horrell 2000a: 54–81.

16. Romans has long been regarded as a systematic compendium of Paul's theology, or as his 'last will and testament' (Bornkamm 1991), but recent study has increasingly affirmed the situational character of the letter, its composition and contents being related both to the situation in Rome and to Paul's own circumstances and plans (see esp. Wedderburn 1988; Donfried 1991).

so on.[17] That will not be the approach I take in this book, and this therefore requires at least a brief justification.

Certainly any reading of Paul's letters must take due account of the specific literary and situational character of each text. The concerns, emphases, and language vary widely, indicating at least in part the very different audiences and 'problems' Paul is addressing. To give just one clear example, the theme of 'wisdom' is prominent in the opening chapters of 1 Corinthians – most likely reflecting the language and concerns of some at Corinth – but appears only infrequently elsewhere, and not at all in Galatians, Philippians, or 1 Thessalonians.[18] Other comparable instances could easily be given. Moreover, recent studies have shown that one should reckon with a degree of variation among the Pauline letters at a more general theological level, correlated with the varied social character and location of the different congregations (Barclay 1992; Adams 2000). Edward Adams, for example, shows how the portrayal of 'the world' varies significantly between 1 Corinthians and Romans, and explains this variation plausibly on the basis of the different character of the congregations Paul is addressing in each letter (Adams 2000). A contextually sensitive treatment of any passage from the Pauline corpus is therefore imperative. However, an appropriate level of sensitivity to literary and social context, and to the variety among the letters, should not be raised to the point whereby it excludes any possibility of talking generally of Paul's theology, ethics, or whatever. When this happens, scholars have become so focused on identifying differences that they are no longer able to operate in a more synthetic mode. After all, many of the same elements of Christian mythology appear throughout Paul's letters, albeit with various distinctive emphases and omissions; comparable exhortations and ethical imperatives occur in different letters; and Paul uses similar forms of moral argument and motivation in addressing different situations. To sketch an overall picture, with due attention to the variety of detail, should be neither impossible nor implausible. (The same applies, *mutatis mutandis*, to treatments of early Christianity as a whole; cf. Theissen 1999).

17. This is the approach to Paul's ethics taken by Matera 1996, though he offers some synthesizing conclusions at the end of the book (pp. 248–55). Schulz (1987) divides Paul's ethics (in the undisputed letters) into an 'early phase' and a 'late phase', though only 1 Thessalonians counts as a witness of the early phase. Broader approaches to Paul along these lines include Becker 1989; Roetzel 1998; and the series of volumes produced by the SBL seminar group focused on the theme of Pauline theology (Bassler 1991; Hay 1993; Hay and Johnson 1995; Johnson and Hay 1997).

18. The words σοφός and σοφία appear 29 times in 1 Corinthians, mostly in chs 1–3, and elsewhere in the undisputed Pauline letters only in Romans (5 times) and 2 Corinthians (once).

Another of Doniger's key points about myth is that, contrary to some views, myths are not apolitical. On the contrary, myths are used to construct and to legitimate patterns of social organization. This does not mean, however, that a myth implies one, stable, political stance. 'Different tellings of the same myth may make explicit different political agendas embedded in it. Ancient myths have always been recycled for various, opposed political purposes' (Doniger 1998: 101). It does mean that if our concern is with Paul's ethics as political ethics, as discourse bound up with the process of community-formation, then our inquiry cannot focus only on the explicitly exhortatory sections of Paul's letters, but must consider how the myth itself is used to form and structure community.

3.2 *Ritual and Practice*

Myth in general, as a religious story believed to be true, and Paul's mythology in particular, is not preserved simply through telling, in either oral or literary form. The stories which contain the 'most important meanings' for Paul and the early Christians are also enacted, performed, in ritual. Indeed, it is not least through such performance that myth exercises its community-forming power.

Bruce Malina and Jerome Neyrey, drawing on the work of the anthropologist Victor Turner, have proposed a series of criteria to classify two distinct kinds of ritual activity (Malina 1986: 139–43; Neyrey 1990: 75–81). Adopting the term 'rite' as the overall label for such activity, they distinguish between 'ritual' and 'ceremony'. Not all of their criteria are equally compelling, certainly in relation to the Pauline texts: the distinction between 'professionals' (who preside over rituals) and 'officials' (who preside over ceremonies), for example, cannot be meaningfully applied. But the identification of a 'ritual' as an essentially boundary-crossing, status-transforming/reversing activity, practised irregularly when 'needed', as opposed to a 'ceremony', which confirms roles and status and is practised according to a regular, planned calendar, valuably draws attention to the different kinds of things that such activity *does*. It takes only a little thought to classify the two major 'rites' of early Christianity, baptism and Lord's supper (see §4.1), as ritual and ceremony respectively. I prefer, however, to retain the term 'ritual' as the overall label for all such activity, and to use 'rite' (rather than 'ritual') and 'ceremony' when necessary to distinguish the two main types of such activity.[19]

---

19. In fact Malina and Neyrey are not entirely consistent in their use of these terms, and present the schema I follow here in Malina and Neyrey 1988: 9: '*Ritual* is behavior concerning

A focus on ritual activity helps to remind us that early Christian faith was practised and performed as well as 'believed'. Our much more modern focus on the cognitive dimensions of (often privatized) religious faith can lead to an anachronistic treatment of texts like Paul's letters as primarily documents outlining, correcting, and instructing their recipients about the content of what they are to believe, with certain sections (the 'ethical' sections) concerned with the consequent practical instruction. Clearly the Pauline letters are about what their recipients should believe, but to describe them in these terms is reductionistic. We should also be concerned to ask about the various kinds of 'doing' that are intrinsically tied up with the promulgation of the early Christian myth. This means asking how the story of the faith was enacted and embodied in ritual activity, and so on, and also asking, with Wayne Meeks, not only about what each Pauline text 'says, but what it does' (Meeks 1983: 7). That is to say, these texts are intended not only to inform, or to convey content, but also quite clearly to persuade, and to shape the social practice of those to whom they are directed.

A social-scientific approach therefore provides ways to conceptualize the Pauline material that takes us beyond describing it as either theology or ethics, and challenges the sharp distinction between the two. From the perspective outlined here, we should view the Pauline material as a development of a body of tradition, based on a specific narrative myth, which gave meaning and order to the lives of those who 'inhabited' it. This mythology is enacted in ritual performance and shapes the lives of its adherents.

3.3 *Identity, World-View and Ethos*

This rather general interpretative framework can be further sharpened with the introduction of additional categories. The first is that of identity. Identity has become something of a buzz-word in recent social science and in studies of early Christianity. Yet the apparently simple notion proves to be somewhat slippery to define and use. This is largely because a person's identity comprises a multiplicity of factors, or even a multiplicity of identities, not all of which are relevant, or salient, in every situation. In dealing with early 'Christian' identity,[20] we are dealing with *social* as

---

the lines that make up the purity or societal system. Line crossings are called *rites*, while the celebration of lines and of those within is called a *ceremony*.' See further Horrell 1999: 39 n. 1, 233–34.

20. The word 'Christian' is, of course, never used by Paul, and appears only three times in the NT (Acts 11.26; 26.28; 1 Pet. 4.16). Moreover, its use in relation to the early period can imply the anachronistic assumption that the members of the earliest churches belonged to an

opposed to personal identity; that is to say, with identity based on belonging to a particular and defined *group*.[21] Henri Tajfel's definition of social identity makes this clear:

> social identity [is] ... that *part* of an individual's self-concept which derives from his knowledge of his membership of a social group (or groups) together with the value and emotional significance attached to that membership ... however rich and complex may be the individuals' view of themselves in relation to the surrounding world, social and physical, *some* aspects of that view are contributed by the membership of certain social groups or categories. Some of these memberships are more salient than others; and some may vary in salience in time and as a function of a variety of social situations. (Tajfel 1981: 255)

The social identity theory developed by Tajfel and his followers can therefore be helpful for understanding the development of Christian identity, as Philip Esler has shown, in a series of detailed studies applying these ideas to various New Testament texts, notably Galatians and Romans (Esler 1998; 2003b; cf. also Horrell 2002b). Specifically, as Esler has shown, a focus on the letters as identity-forming documents again cuts across the traditional distinction between theology and ethics (cf. Esler 1996; 1998: 45, 229, etc.). The identity of a group, according to social identity theory, has cognitive, emotional, and evaluative dimensions, and is further defined by 'norms' that stipulate 'a range of acceptable (and unacceptable) attitudes and behaviors' for members of the group (Esler 2003a: 54, quoting Rupert Brown). Moreover, distinctions drawn between ingroup and outgroup members serve to enhance a *positive* – and necessarily comparative – sense of group identity (see further §5.2 below).

Identity encompasses both belief and behaviour, or, to pick up the terms suggested by anthropologist Clifford Geertz, 'world-view' and 'ethos' (Geertz 1973; cf. also Keck 1974).[22] Geertz's terms clearly correlate, at least

---

institutionalized movement with a defined and distinct (religious) identity. Thus Esler has argued for its replacement with 'Christ-followers' (Esler 1998: 3, 44, etc.). However, while we must be aware of the anachronism that can be sustained by a failure to recognize the shifting nuances of a term over time (a general linguistic problem not restricted to this word), 'Christian' seems the best term available: it does, after all, originate in the NT period, while Esler's term 'Christ-followers' is a modern neologism. The best Pauline appellation would probably be to refer to a Christian as an 'in-Christ' (cf. 2 Cor. 12.2, etc.), but that clumsy term is functionally equivalent to 'Christian'.

21. Tajfel and Turner define a group as follows: 'a collection of individuals who perceive themselves to be members of the same social category, share some emotional involvement in this common definition of themselves, and achieve some degree of social consensus about the evaluation of their group and of their membership in it' (quoted in Turner and Bourhis 1996: 30).

22. For an interesting attempt to correlate ethos and identity in a study of the Pauline communities, see Wolter 1997.

on a broad level, with the distinction between theology and ethics; they remind us that, even within a social-scientific framework, these two categories, however labelled, should not be collapsed altogether. A people's world-view 'is their picture of the way things in sheer actuality are, their concept of nature, of self, of society. It contains their most comprehensive ideas of order'. 'A people's ethos', in contrast, 'is the tone, character, and quality of their life, its moral and aesthetic style and mood; it is the underlying attitude toward themselves and their world that life reflects' (Geertz 1973: 127). A narrative myth which presents and constructs a specific symbolic universe, and which undergirds the identity of a particular social group, both establishes a view of the way the world is and shapes the moral values and practices of its adherents. However, Geertz also insists that world-view and ethos are thoroughly enmeshed and synthesized in religion and culture, particularly as they are embodied in ritual: 'meanings can only be "stored" in symbols ... Such religious symbols, dramatized in rituals or related in myths, are felt somehow to sum up, for those for whom they are resonant, what is known about the way the world is, the quality of the emotional life it supports, and the way one ought to behave while in it'. Geertz therefore refers to the 'tendency to synthesize world-view and ethos at some level' (p. 127) simply because 'there is conceived to be a simple and fundamental congruence ... between the approved style of life and the assumed structure of reality' (p. 129).

Both the focus on identity and Geertz's approach to world-view and ethos provide new ways of conceptualizing, and resolving, the famous antinomy between indicative and imperative in Paul, which, we recall, was seen by Furnish as a fundamental crux in the interpretation of Paul's ethics (Furnish 1968: 279; §1.1 above). Most New Testament interpreters have tried to understand this apparent paradox specifically in terms of Paul's theological convictions, relating it to such themes as justification, eschatology, and so on, and have given the impression that this is an issue which arises from the particular character of Paul's theological ethics. While there are certainly specific factors in Paul's belief-system that create an impetus towards this indicative–imperative antinomy – not least his inaugurated eschatology: 'you are now what you are still to become' – its apparently paradoxical character appears less so from this social-scientific perspective.

At a general level, for example, Geertz speaks, as we have seen, of the synthesis of world-view and ethos on the basis of the assumed congruence between the 'structure of reality' (indicative) and 'the approved style of life' (imperative). 'Is' and 'ought' are thus related together: 'The powerfully coercive "ought" is felt to grow out of a comprehensive factual "is," and in such a way religion grounds the most specific requirements of human action in the most general contexts of human existence' (Geertz 1973: 126). This is, of course, an observation derived from the study of diverse (and non-Christian) religious cultures, and indicates that the intimate relation of indicative and imperative is hardly a uniquely Pauline phenomenon. The more specifically paradoxical form of the Pauline indicative–imperative expressions – you are X, so be X – can be well understood in relation to social identity theory. They appear 'self-contradictory' (Bultmann 1995: 195) when they are regarded as comparable with treatments of actual fact, or biological identity, when to urge someone to 'be what they are' is nonsensical. However, as expressions related to a mythologically under-girded, socially constructed identity – an identity which is always, at least potentially, vulnerable, fragile and malleable – they are not paradoxical but rather indications (tacit and implicit to be sure) that this identity is constructed not given, produced and reproduced not fixed. Since social identity is constantly in process, as it were, reinforced or transformed over time, then there is certainly a clear logic in urging someone to be who they are, to act in ways congruent with their (current group) identity, particularly when there is perceived to be some threat to the viability of the group's identity, or to its boundaries or integrity. People may, of course, choose to leave the group, or redefine its basis and criteria for membership in ways which a leader regards as 'beyond the pale', as compromising the very identity of the group (cf. Gal. 3.1-5 with 5.25). Alternatively, someone's conduct may be so contrary to the norms of the group that s/he will be deemed no longer to share the common group identity, and will be recategorized as an outsider (1 Cor. 5.11-13; see §5.3 below).

The apparently paradoxical nature of the Pauline indicative–imperative formulations can, then, be resolved when the indicatives in question are seen not as statements which can be held to be either 'true' or not but as identity-descriptors and group norms which need to be constantly affirmed. For example, the sentence in Gal. 5.25 which Bultmann saw as a classic and concise expression of the Pauline antinomy (Bultmann 1924: 123) appears paradoxical when interpreted as implying, 'we are in actual fact people who live by the spirit, so we should live by the spirit'. If we expressed its meaning in the following way, however, its intentions seem no longer paradoxical: 'we are defined or identified as the people who live by the spirit – this is one of our positive identity-descriptors – therefore we must continually affirm and reinforce this facet of our group identity'.[23]

---

23. On the Spirit as a positive badge of group identity see Esler 1998: 208 (cf. also pp. 184, 203–204). Wolter (1997: 444) also questions the traditional formulations of the indicative–imperative issue on the basis of his study of ethos and identity. However, I am not sure that his proposal that 'faith' provides the boundary-defining 'ethos' of the Pauline communities, such that patterns of action can (within limits) be flexible and diverse, specifically illuminates the indicative–imperative relationship.

The same could be said of other such themes which Paul expresses in both indicative and imperative forms (cf. e.g. Rom. 6.1-14).

3.4 *Ethics and Morality*

Do these conceptions of identity, world-view, and ethos further imply, as Philip Esler has recently argued, that we should desist from 'endlessly reiterating labels like "ethics"' when they are not appropriate to the texts we are studying (Esler 2003a: 53, cf. p. 61)? Esler's argument, briefly, is that 'in the modern world "ethics" largely refers to the systematic formulation of rules for good conduct by individuals', a concern which is hardly that of the New Testament material (p. 52). Instead, Esler argues for an approach to the Pauline material based on a combination of the ancient, Aristotelian approach to the virtues and the good life and the modern approach of social identity theory, in which 'norms', rather than 'ethics', are the focus. Norms, Esler suggests, 'constitute frames of reference, or signposts, through which the world can be interpreted'; they 'bring a measure of order and predictability' and are 'necessary for the maintenance and enhancement of the identity of [the] group'. 'Norms in this sense are considerably wider than the "ethics" that is regularly discovered in passages like Romans 12:1–15:13 in scholarly discussion at present' (p. 55). In a broadly comparable way, Wayne Meeks, also adopting an Aristotelian approach (Meeks 1993: 7–8), chooses to focus not on New Testament 'ethics' but on early Christian 'morality' (pp. 3–5). Meeks takes 'ethics' to signify 'a reflective, second-order activity; it is morality rendered self-conscious'. 'Morality', by contrast, 'names a dimension of life, a pervasive and, often, only partly conscious set of value-laden dispositions, inclinations, attitudes and habits' (p. 4). His focus, then, is not on the ethical reflection in early Christian texts – not least because these texts reveal, for Meeks, no coherent and systematic ethics, but only a rather diverse 'record of experimentation' (p. 216; cf. §1.5 above) – but rather on the process of 'moral formation' which they record, a process that is itself 'inextricable from the process by which distinctive communities were taking shape' (p. 5). Ian McDonald follows Meeks in this focus on 'morality' and community, adding 'ethos' as an equally important term. Ethos, for McDonald, indicates 'the distinctive character or spirit of a community, people, or culture ... moral exhortation is primarily designed to reinforce ethos' (McDonald 1998: 6).[24]

---

24. Cf. also the definition of ethos offered by Wolter 1997: 430–31: a 'Kanon von habitualisierten Handlungen, der innerhalb eines sozialen Systems in Geltung steht. Diese

These new approaches, as I have already indicated (§1.5), do bring important perspectives to the study of New Testament ethics, making clear that the moral formation of the early Christian communities is a much broader process than is implied by a focus on the 'ethics' contained in (say) certain sections of Paul's letters, and that this process is intrinsically tied up with the formation of group-identity and community. Nevertheless, there are also good reasons to reject the argument against the use of the word 'ethics' in such a study, particularly in the strong form presented by Esler.[25]

First, while some approaches to ethics focus on 'the systematic formulation of rules for good conduct by individuals', and while deontological and utilitarian ethics have indeed been prominent in modern discussion (Esler 2003a: 52; cf. p. 55), this cannot be taken as a description of the discipline of ethics *in toto*. Nor is contemporary ethics rightly dismissed as 'largely absorbed with individual human agents' (p. 52). Indeed, the Aristotelian approach which Esler favours is, of course (as Esler recognizes), an influential and prominent tradition in the contemporary field of ethics. And even Habermas's more Kantian, deontological approach can hardly be said to focus on 'rules for the individual' (cf. §2.2). It is unnecessary and inconsistent first to define 'ethics' narrowly – as describing a particular approach with which one disagrees – and then to argue for the rejection of the term and for the adoption of an equally influential approach to ethics. Why cede use of the term to one's opponents? Aristotelian virtues and Tajfelian identity-defining norms are still rightly part of the field of ethics, appropriately defined.

Second, there is, even in Meeks's sense, *ethics* in the Pauline letters. Paul self-consciously addresses a range of 'problems' and issues in the communities, grounding his exhortation in the central symbols and stories of the tradition, and giving guidance as to what should and should not be done. Paul's morality is 'self-conscious' and reflective, in its community-

---

Handlungen werden von einem überindividuellen Konsens getragen und sind so eindeutig, daß sie reproduziert werden können und nicht mehr durch aktuelle ethische Entscheidungen generiert werden müssen'.

25. Esler's criticism of Hays (1997a) is also wide of the mark: Hays's book is described as 'mainly preoccupied with determining the criteria for right or wrong action, an interest parallel to the focus upon deontological or utilitarian approaches to this subject which held the field prior to the renewal of an interest in Aristotelian approaches to a good life' (Esler 2003a: 57). Hays certainly seeks to apply his readings of NT ethics to a range of moral problems, and is forthright in outlining substantive conclusions, and he may be criticized for the lack of engagement with ethical theory (see §1.6 above). But Esler's criticism overlooks the Aristotelian/Hauerwasian focus throughout Hays's book on the NT as a collection of texts meant to form the character of the Christian community. 'Criteria for right or wrong action', in a deontological or utilitarian sense, are hardly its preoccupation.

shaping aims, its articulation of moral norms and practices, and its motivational structure.

A further question arises from the rather different use to which Habermas puts the terms ethics and morality (see §2.2). Questions of 'ethics', for Habermas, concern matters bound up with a person's sense of the good and of identity (precisely Esler's two foci), whereas questions of 'morality' become involved when conflicts arise because of clashing interests or convictions. On this definition too, we could suggest that Paul is involved in moral, as well as ethical, reflection: his exhortation is in some cases precisely directed to the peaceful ordering of situations in which differences of conviction and practice lead to conflict (see ch. 6).

How then should we employ these various terms? I shall not pretend in what follows in this book to make clear and rigorous distinctions between ethos, ethics, and morality; their general usage is too diverse and their meanings too overlapping (especially as regards the latter two terms) for this to be achieved. Nonetheless, I shall conceive of these terms broadly as follows, and will indicate these specific meanings explicitly when they are especially pertinent to the discussion. *Ethos* will be used to refer to the general, and often implicit, sense of the kind of 'tone, character and quality of life' (cf. Geertz 1973: 127) which shapes (or which Paul wishes to shape) the communities to which Paul writes. General and implicit though it may be, the 'ethos' of a community nonetheless fundamentally shapes social interaction and a sense of identity. This word thus does a job pretty much equivalent to 'morality' in Meeks's usage, such that morality can usefully be saved to designate something different. *Ethics* will be used to refer to the discourse in which Paul addresses issues and problems, and articulates a response to them, giving reasons why certain patterns of conduct are right or wrong, and motivations for acting rightly. Paul's argumentation will be regarded as specifically concerned with *moral* questions, in Habermas's sense, when it can be seen to be orientated to the ordering of situations of conflict and ethical disagreement. But all of these aspects of ethos, ethics, and morality are, I would argue, legitimately included (and intimately bound together) under the auspices of a study of 'Pauline ethics'.

3.5 *Conclusion*

We have, then, reached the point where we have in place a certain critical and conceptual framework for reading Paul's texts; we now know what we mean by 'Pauline ethics', or at least, what is included under that heading. Paul's letters are to be seen as reflecting, and contributing to, a narrative myth which constructs a particular symbolic universe, giving meaning and order to the lives of those who inhabit it. This myth, enacted in ritual, is an identity- and community-forming narrative which shapes both the world-view (the 'is') and the ethos (the 'ought') of its adherents. Clearly it is the 'ethos', the 'ought', that is the particular concern of a study of Paul's ethics. Paul's letters do not, however, only imply a particular kind of shaping of the community and its ethos, they also contain explicit and self-conscious argumentation on questions of conduct and attempts to articulate ways to resolve conflict and disagreement. They are, therefore, rightly seen as instances of ethical and moral reflection.

This broad framework of interpretation suggests that, at least at a general level, everything in Paul's letters is potentially relevant to a consideration of his 'ethics'. If the myth itself – the central story and its symbols and ideas – shapes the ethos and social practice of the community, then our inquiry cannot be limited only to certain explicitly paraenetic sections of the texts. Nonetheless, partly through the distinction between world-view and ethos, but more sharply still through the focus on ethics and morality, certain passages will call for more detailed attention. These are, of course, the places where Paul is explicitly addressing concrete issues of conduct and practice, or seeking to resolve issues of conflict and dispute.

One final set of questions should also be addressed. Does the framework outlined in this chapter, where Pauline ethics are conceived of as enmeshed within a narrative myth that shapes the ethos of particular communities, not immediately imply that the 'theoretical' basis of Paul's ethics is more like Hauerwas's than Habermas's? And does this not then render the comparison set up in ch. 2 irrelevant? The answer to the first question is indeed yes. It is pretty clear at a basic level – though the detail remains to be examined – that Paul's ethics have a tradition-specific, 'metaphysical' basis, rather than a postmetaphysical, posttraditional form grounded in the universal presuppositions of human argumentation. But the answer to the second question is no. First, because the point of sketching the liberal-communitarian debate, as I have already made clear, is not primarily to enable us to classify Paul as one type of thinker or the other, but rather to sketch a contemporary debate as a context for our reading of Paul and in relation to which our reading may generate fruitful reflections. Secondly, because the bald assertion that Paul's approach to ethics is more like Hauerwas's than Habermas's leaves unexamined the interesting questions about the ways in which Paul's moral thought might parallel, critique and/ or affirm the different kinds of approach we find in both Hauerwas and Habermas, and might be taken up and developed in our own moral reflection.

Chapter 4

THE CONSTRUCTION OF COMMUNITY: CORPORATE SOLIDARITY IN CHRIST

The agenda which emerged in ch. 1, and specifically from Boyarin's treatment of 'Paul and the politics of identity', leads us first to a consideration of questions concerning 'solidarity', that is, a sense of corporate bound-togetherness.[1] In what ways, picking up the terminology outlined in ch. 3, does Paul draw on the early Christian myth, and promote its embodiment in ritual, to foster forms of solidarity and to construct a particular kind of community-ethos? And how might this relate to the kinds of issues raised in the debate surveyed in ch. 2? Does solidarity emerge as a particular concern of this particular tradition of morality, and in what specific forms? How are Paul's appeals for solidarity grounded?

The central argument of this chapter is that the first and most fundamental moral value, a metanorm,[2] in Pauline ethics is that of corporate solidarity, a form of human solidarity with egalitarian impulses.[3]

---

1. Cf. *OED*, 2941, which defines solidarity as 'unity or accordance of feeling, action, etc. ... mutual support or cohesiveness within a group'. This term, as used also by Boyarin (see §1.7), seems to me the most apposite one to employ here, though I recognize it has a range of nuances in different contexts. What is important, of course, is to investigate what kind of 'solidarity', if any, Paul seems to envisage and promote.

2. Cf. Benhabib 1992: 45; above §2.2 and §9.1.1 below. Following Benhabib, I regard a metanorm as one which determines the moral framework within which other norms, values and customs can be articulated and practised.

3. *OED*, 788, defines 'egalitarian' as that which 'asserts the equality of all humankind ... the principle of equal treatment for all persons'. Scott Bartchy (1999) and John Elliott (2003) have objected to the application of this label to the early Christian movement, stressing instead its family-oriented, kinship character (cf. also Clarke 2004; §4.2 below). For Bartchy the language of egalitarianism belongs within the sphere of politics, whereas sibling language belongs in the sphere of kinship. But given the use of kinship language in a variety of social and political settings (e.g. between a king and a hoped-for ally; Josephus, *Ant.* 13.45) this distinction seems hard to sustain (see further Horrell 2001b: 296–97 and 303 n. 42). Much of Elliott's critique can be avoided by distinguishing between the (limited) claim that the tradition contains egalitarian impulses and the proposal that the early Christian communities actually were egalitarian (a distinction missing in e.g. Atkins 1991). In this way, *pace* Elliott (2003: 188–89), it is not self-contradictory to imagine communities with both egalitarian and hierarchical tendencies, even if the two concepts are theoretically 'mutually exclusive' (cf.

That is to say, a primary goal of Paul's discourse is to engender communal solidarity, and to attempt to restore and strengthen it in the face of conflict and division. This primary norm emerges clearly when we adopt the kind of interpretative perspective outlined in the previous chapter, looking not only at the specifically 'ethical' sections of Paul's letters but also more broadly at the kind of community-ethos which the texts engender. This claim about the centrality of solidarity among the norms of Pauline ethics is not intended as a comparative claim – that Paul is *more* interested in generating human solidarity than other ancient moralists, or whatever – since assessing such comparisons is, as I have already made clear in ch. 1, not my main aim. It is a claim, however, which suggests a rather different view of the priorities of Paul's ethics than that which is often presented, and which will be of importance for our reflections on their significance and possible contribution in the context of contemporary debate (see §4.6; ch. 9).

Allen Verhey, for example, sees freedom, followed by love, as the most fundamental of Paul's ethical values (Verhey 1984: 107–108); Gerd Theissen lists love of neighbour and renunciation of status as the two basic values of early Christian ethics (Theissen 1999: 63–80).[4] Wolfgang Schrage mentions 'the ethics and praxis of Christian solidarity' in his discussion of Pauline ethics (1988: 234) but the theme does not receive distinct or significant treatment. Frank Matera suggests that '[o]ne of the most overlooked aspects of the New Testament's ethical teaching is its communal dimension', but this is perceived in terms of the need to realize that Paul's instruction is *addressed* to 'communities of believers' (1996: 250). Matera's comment, like those of others, reflects a perspective in which Paul's ethics are (at least implicitly) defined as the kind of instruction Paul gives *to* (already existing) 'communities of believers', thus neglecting the broader, but also logically prior and morally fundamental, questions about the ways in which Paul's discourse forms a community-ethos in the first place.[5] Richard Hays, as we have seen, (rightly) stresses the community-oriented, community-forming, character of Pauline ethics, and indeed of New Testament ethics generally, but gives

further Schmeller 1995; Sandnes 1997). Elliott is right, however, to stress that in texts like Gal. 3.28 and 1 Cor. 12.13 the central concern is not so much equality as 'oneness and unity' (2003: 182).

4. These two basic values can be seen as different aspects of what I term 'other-regard' (see ch. 7; also §9.1.1) and to a large extent depend on a prior valuation of corporate solidarity – which love for one another and renunciation of status help to sustain.

5. Among earlier studies, however, Dodd 1950 is notable for the attention given to 'the pervasive sense of the organic nature of the community' as a 'second outstanding feature of the ethical teaching of the early church' (after eschatology, and followed by the imitation of Christ) (p. 32; see pp. 32–39).

only brief consideration to the ways in which solidarity in community is specifically generated by Paul (cf. Hays 1997a: 32–36). In this chapter I want to substantiate the claim *that* Pauline ethics has corporate solidarity as its key moral norm precisely through an examination of *how* that solidarity is generated.

4.1 *Ritual and Solidarity: Baptism and Lord's Supper*

We may best begin with the two 'major ritual complexes' (Meeks 1983: 150) of early Christianity: baptism and Lord's supper,[6] since these constitute the most significant forms of repeated performance through which early Christian faith was enacted, made visible as well as audible.[7] In terms of forming 'world-view' and 'ethos', then, these activities play a key role. In the case of baptism, of course, the ritual also constitutes the rite of entry into the community, such that the character and interpretation of baptism should be an important indicator of the kind of ethos Paul sought to instill. The Lord's supper, the central act of early Christian worship, celebrated regularly, probably weekly,[8] forms an equally significant focal point for those who are members of the community.[9]

More incidentally, baptism and Lord's supper also illustrate well the need not to overpress the individuality of the Pauline texts and churches (cf. §3.1). Certainly there are important contextual considerations to be borne in mind: whether Paul's understanding of baptism develops over time or varies according to context, such that the view of Romans 6 should not be assumed as self-evident for the time of 1 Thessalonians (cf. Schulz 1987: 317); the possible diversity of early Christian baptismal traditions (Acts 19.1-7, for example, suggests that some such diversity endured at least for a time); and, in relation to the Lord's supper, questions as to the ubiquity and/or diversity of practice in regard to this common meal (cf.

---

6. There are of course various terms one might use to refer to this ritual, but since 'Lord's supper' is a recognized translation of the phrase Paul uses in 1 Cor. 11.20 (κυριακὸν δεῖπνον) it seems the obvious choice (cf. NRSV, etc.; Lutherbibel, 1985 ['das Abendmahl des Herrn']; Thiselton 2000: 863–64).

7. For a recent overview of the NT materials on these two rituals, see Hahn 2002: 507–64. Hahn comments as follows on their centrality: 'Die christliche Taufe ist von Pfingsten an allgemein praktiziert worden und wird im Urchristentum überall vorausgesetzt' (p. 509), while the Lord's supper became 'das Zentrum des urchristlichen Gottesdienstes' (p. 533).

8. Cf. 1 Cor. 16.2, though it is disputed whether this indicates the regularity and time of congregational meetings. Cf., e.g., the arguments in favour of Sunday as the day of regular Christian meeting in NT times in Llewelyn 2001 and the critique by Young 2003.

9. For a more detailed study of these two rituals, in relation to the Corinthian community, see Horrell 1996: 80–88, 102–105, 150–55; more generally in relation to the Pauline churches, Meeks 1983: 140–63; MacDonald 1988: 61–71.

Marshall 1980: 107–40). Nonetheless, despite the paucity of Pauline references to these ritual practices (see below), most scholars do not incline to deny that baptism and Lord's supper were commonly practised throughout the Pauline/early Christian churches, not least since the texts we do have seem to imply that such practice can be presumed and that traditions for its interpretation were shared.

4.1.1 *Baptism*

In the terminology outlined above (§3.2) baptism is a specific type of ritual, a *rite*, which has to do with boundary-crossing and status-transformation. It is the rite of initiation (see esp. Meeks 1983: 150–57). The presumption that baptism was generally practised, and specifically performed 'in the name of (the Lord) Jesus (Christ)', is clear in Paul's sharp critique of the Corinthians' factionalism: 'were you baptised in the name of Paul (εἰς τὸ ὄνομα Παύλου)?' (1 Cor. 1.13).[10] And the Corinthians' participation in both the rituals of baptism and Lord's supper is also presumed by the striking illustration in 1 Cor. 10.1-4. Nonetheless, explicit references to the form and character of the rite are relatively scarce; the three most important texts in Paul's letters are Rom. 6.1-14; 1 Cor. 12.12-13; and Gal. 3.26-29, where in each case baptism is explicitly in view.[11] These texts, especially Romans 6, have been the subject of extensive exegetical attention and only points relevant to the present enquiry can be touched upon here.[12]

Romans 6 is the logical text with which to begin, since here we see how the central events of the Christian myth – the death, burial and resurrection of Christ (cf. 1 Cor. 15.3-4) – are reenacted in the rite of baptism; the myth gives the ritual its key meaning and the ritual at the same time reinforces the prominence of this central drama of the faith. Baptism is the act in which believers *participate* in these events 'with'

10. The precise formula is harder to ascertain: in the Pauline letters, 1 Cor. 1.13 might imply a simple formula, 'in the name of Jesus', while the longer form is found in 1 Cor. 6.11 ('in the name of the Lord Jesus Christ'), which may also allude to baptism. Acts has both 'in the name of the Lord Jesus' (Acts 8.16; 19.5) and 'in the name of Jesus Christ' (Acts 10.48). For further discussion, see Hartman 1992: 39–46.

11. These three texts are the focus of attention in Fape's recent study of Paul's concept of baptism (1999). Hartman (1992: 53–81) also includes 1 Cor. 1.12-17; and 6.11 (cf. above note). Dunn's argument that Rom. 6.1-14; Gal. 3.26-27; and 1 Cor. 12.13 contain 'metaphors' which point to the spiritual realities of conversion-initiation and Spirit-baptism, not the rite of water-baptism itself, seems to me unlikely, pressing a distinction between 'outward rite' and 'spiritual reality' which Paul does not make in these texts (Dunn 1970: 109, 129, 142, etc.).

12. In addition to the works cited in the previous note, see Frankemölle 1970 on baptism in Romans 6, and on the background and context, Wedderburn 1987.

Christ;[13] it constitutes an incorporation into the Christ-event, such that the death of Christ and his burial (symbolized by immersion under the water)[14] become the Christian's own death and burial too (Rom. 6.3-4). Participation in resurrection, though often seen by an earlier generation of scholars as already implicit here – 'dying and rising with Christ'[15] – remains a future hope (6.5, 8), though one which can be confidently held precisely on the basis of the Christian's participation in Christ's death (6.4-5). The present post-baptismal reality certainly constitutes, for Paul, a 'walking in newness of life' (6.4; cf. 2 Cor. 5.17), but one which is empowered by the Spirit and characterized by a sense of travail and yearning for the arrival of the future hope (Rom. 8.18-39; cf. 1 Cor. 15.12-19). The point of this passage in Romans is to demonstrate why Christians should not, cannot indeed, 'continue in sin' (6.1): they have quite simply 'died' to sin and now live for God 'in Christ' (6.2, 6, 11). Put in more sociological terms, baptism symbolises the convert's transition, via 'death', from one world to another, a 'separation ... from the outside world' and an 'integration ... into another world' (Meeks 1983: 156).[16] Paul recognizes, however, despite his strikingly realistic language about having died and been buried with Christ, that this is something other than a literally factual change, since he urges his readers to 'count themselves dead to sin and alive to God' (6.11), and instructs them to live appropriately (6.12-14; cf. 8.1-17). As I suggested above (§3.3), this juxtaposition of indicative and imperative is best understood as related to the construction of an always vulnerable social identity: the indicative describes the new identity of group members, an identity constructed via the rituals in which the central myth is embodied; the imperative urges them to continue to make this designation of central and defining importance for identity and practice.

Despite the uniqueness of Romans 6 there are indications that its perspective was more widely known, even 'traditional' (Wedderburn 1987: 37–69; Hartman 1992: 82–93). The description of baptism's significance opens with the rhetorical question, 'Do you not know ...' ($\dot{\eta}$ ἀγνοεῖτε ...

---

13. Note the various words which begin with the preposition συν-, used in Rom. 6.4-6 to describe what has happened in baptism: συνετάφημεν ... σύμφυτοι ... συνεσταυρώθη; cf. also Gal. 2.19.

14. Cf. Mt. 3.16; Mk 1.10; Meeks 1983: 150–51.

15. See, e.g., Tannehill 1967; Hunter 1961: 66, 70, 135. This view has recently been restated, in a nuanced argument, by Catchpole 2004. For arguments against this 'realized resurrection' interpretation, see esp. Wedderburn 1987: 1–89; Sanders 1977: 449–50, 468.

16. Schulz 1987: 317–18, while insisting that the later Romans 6 should not guide the interpretation of 1 Thessalonians, nonetheless sees echoes of the ritual of baptism in this early letter, specifically in terms of the transfer from darkness to light (1 Thess. 5.4-5). Thus he suggests: 'Schon der frühe Paulus kennt also die sakramentale Begründung (5,4f) der Ethik (5,6-8)' (p. 318).

6.3). While this might be seen as a 'polite teacher's way of passing on new knowledge' (Dunn 1970: 144 n. 17) it seems more likely to imply Paul's perception that such an understanding of baptism was shared and known (cf. Wedderburn 1987: 40–43).[17] Moreover, the idea of the Christian's participation in Christ's death is clearly reflected elsewhere (2 Cor. 5.14; Gal. 2.19-20).

While Romans 6 focuses, in a sense, on the transition that occurs through the rite of baptism, the other key texts show more clearly something of the kind of new social reality that baptism is seen to establish.[18] There may be some uncertainty about the degree to which the perspective of Romans 6 was traditional and widespread, but there can be little doubt that the formulations in 1 Cor. 12.13 and Gal. 3.27-28 reflect early Christian baptismal tradition. A number of early Christian texts reflect a similar tradition in referring to the ways in which various kinds of opposites become united as one;[19] and the conviction that Paul is drawing on such a tradition in these two texts is strengthened by the observation that the pairs he cites in each case are not all of particular relevance to their epistolary contexts[20] and that the block of text in Galatians seems to be marked out from its surrounding verses by the change from first person to second person plural forms.[21]

These two Pauline texts do of course differ from one another, in ways that reflect the orientation of each to its specific epistolary context. In Gal. 3.26-29, there is an emphasis on the motif of sonship (Hahn 2002: 516), connected with the wider argument that those in Christ are sons and heirs of God, inheritors of the promise made to Abraham's 'seed', who is Christ (Gal. 3.6-9, 15-19). In 1 Cor. 12.12-13, where Paul is dealing with questions about 'spiritual gifts' (τὰ πνευματικά, 12.1; 14.1), and addressing a situation

17. Dunn later moves rather closer to the latter view, accepting that Paul is probably 'appealing to something familiar' (1988: 308).

18. Cf. Hahn 2002: 512, who notes the two aspects especially characteristic of Paul's view of baptism: participation in the death and resurrection of Christ, and ecclesiological relevance.

19. Also in the Pauline tradition, see Col. 3.10-11 and cf. also Rom. 10.12; 12.5; 1 Cor. 10.17. A number of texts repeat a tradition about male and female becoming one, a tradition Dennis MacDonald (1987: 17–63, etc.) argues goes back to a dominical saying recorded (according to Clement of Alexandria, *Strom.* 3.13) in the *Gospel of the Egyptians*; cf. also *2 Clem.* 12.2-5; *Gos. Thom.* 114. See further Meeks 1974; Betz 1979: 182–94; Paulsen 1980: 78–85.

20. In Galatians, only the pair Jew/Greek has particular pertinence to Paul's argument, and in 1 Cor. 12.13 neither pair quoted is especially relevant to Paul's argument about the unity-in-diversity of the body, which focuses on the diverse spiritual gifts given to the members.

21. The change from first to second person occurs betwen Gal. 3.25 and 26, with the return to first person forms taking place between 3.29 and 4.3. Cf. Betz 1979: 185 with n. 29, 204.

where some gifts (and hence people) are rated more highly than others (12.1-11; 14.1-40), the motifs of the body and the Spirit are prominent (see further §4.4). The similarities of theme and content are, however, striking, and may best be summarized in the phrase 'many into one'.[22] Both passages list comparable pairs of opposites: Jew/Greek, slave/free. The pair male/female which concludes the list in Gal. 3.28 is missing from the list in 1 Cor. 12.13, and Hans Dieter Betz regards it as 'a secondary addition to an earlier version of the saying' (Betz 1979: 182). However, there seem stronger arguments for regarding it as included in the earliest forms of the tradition.[23] As Scott Bartchy points out, the threefold pairing of the Galatians formula can be seen to underlie the pattern of thought in 1 Corinthians 7 (Bartchy 1973: 162–65), while the omission of male/female from the formula in 1 Corinthians 12 seems likely to be explicable on the grounds of Paul's awareness of its potentially radical implications. Given the gender issues he felt moved to address at Corinth, dropping the reference to baptism's transcendance of the male/female distinction may well have seemed (to Paul, at least) a sensible and pragmatic strategy. Indeed, the 1 Corinthians formulation is overall less overtly radical than its equivalent in Galatians: in 1 Cor. 12.13 many diverse groups – '*whether* Jews *or* Greeks, slaves or free (εἴτε ... εἴτε, κτλ.)' – are said to have become one body in Christ, while Gal. 3.28 actually declares that 'there is neither[24] Jew nor Greek, neither slave nor free, neither male and female (οὐκ ἔνι ... οὐδέ, κτλ.)'.[25] In both cases, of course, crucial questions remain as to whether the message of baptismal unification implies that these previous distinctions have been entirely *erased* so as, effectively, no longer to exist, or whether they are instead *relativized* in some way, or simply *encompassed* within a new and wider sphere of belonging. Whichever is the case, some form of egalitarian impulse also seems apparent in this strong stress upon becoming one, *without distinction*.[26] These questions, however, will occupy our attention below (§4.5-6; §6.4); for now what is important to note is the

---

22. See further Witherington 1981: 596–97; Meeks 1974.

23. If MacDonald 1987 is right, then the idea of male-female union is the earliest element of the tradition (see n. 19 above), though this remains uncertain, not least in view of the prominence of the Jew/Gentile question for the earliest Church, which would suggest that this pair would be of primary significance, as it is for Paul.

24. οὐκ ἔνι stands for οὐκ ἔνεστιν, 'there is not', as noted, e.g., by Betz 1979: 190; Mußner 1988: 264 n. 91.

25. The switch from οὐδέ to καί in this last pairing reflects the influence of Gen. 1.27 (LXX): ἄρσεν καὶ θῆλυ ἐποίησεν αὐτούς.

26. Cf. further Strecker 1999: 354–58: Gal. 3.28 'artikuliert eine in der Taufe umgesetzte Auflösung der Differenzen der Sozialstruktur, die über das rituelle Handeln hinaus den Alltag neu qualifiziert und ihn mit universalistischen und egalitären Communitaswerten tränkt' (p. 358). See further pp. 358–407, where Strecker explores this sense of 'ethnic', 'social' and 'sexual' communitas, and n. 96 below.

prominent theme of unification: *baptism constructs a new form of human solidarity which transcends the lines of previous distinctions.* Diverse groups are all made 'one'; both texts emphasize this through their forceful repetition of πάντες as well as their explicit declarations of this 'oneness'.[27] And the 1 Corinthians text expresses this oneness literally in terms of a *corporate* solidarity, with its declaration, developed in the following verses (on which see §4.4 below), that the 'many' who were baptized now form one *body* (ἐν σῶμα). That these proclamations of oneness and corporeity are meant to imply a form of communal solidarity, and not merely a oneness in terms of sharing equally in the same salvation, will become increasingly clear as we study further aspects of this construction of community through the rest of this chapter.

4.1.2 *Lord's supper*

While baptism may be defined as a *rite* of initiation concerned with boundary-crossing and status-transformation, the Lord's supper is clearly a *ceremony*, practised regularly, which confirms and celebrates the status and identity of community members. Here the paucity of relevant Pauline material is even greater than in connection with baptism; only two passages in 1 Corinthians (10.16-17 and 11.17-34) give any direct indication as to how the supper was celebrated in early Christianity (cf. Marshall 1980: 16).[28] Were it not for the Corinthians' 'errors' in connection with this ritual, we would never have known how much they already knew about the traditions associated with this ceremony, nor that they practised it regularly. But the fact that the Corinthians' knowledge and practice is only 'accidentally' revealed, together with the indications that the traditions of which Paul reminds them were indeed shared traditions rather than new instruction, adds weight to the general presumption that this ritual was widely and commonly practised in the early Christian churches.

Just as Romans 6 shows how baptism enacts and gains its meaning from the central drama of the early Christian myth, so 1 Cor. 11.23-26 indicates that the Lord's supper similarly reenacts and derives its significance from

---

27. For πάντες see 1 Cor. 12.13 (twice, plus πάντα in v. 12); Gal. 3.26, 28. The central positive declaration in Gal. 3.28 is that 'you are all one (εἷς) in Christ Jesus'; 1 Cor. 12.12-13 uses one (ἕν) four times, three in relation to the oneness of the body (σῶμα), one with reference to the Spirit. The use of the masculine form in Gal. 3.28 probably reflects Paul's view that the 'new unity' is 'fundamentally and irreducibly identified with Christ himself' (Martyn 1997a: 377; cf. Mußner 1988: 264–65; Eph. 2.15).

28. Marshall also provides a valuable survey of the other NT evidence, on both the character of the Last Supper and the possible NT references to eucharistic celebrations in the early churches.

the story of Christ's self-giving death and (implicitly) his resurrection and the consequent hope of his return (11.26). Paul reminds the Corinthians of the narrative which gives meaning to the common meal they celebrate,[29] indicating that this is tradition which he both received ($\pi\alpha\rho\acute{\epsilon}\lambda\alpha\beta\text{o}\nu$) and passed on ($\pi\alpha\rho\acute{\epsilon}\delta\omega\kappa\alpha$).[30] The similarity of vv. 23-25 with the synoptic gospel accounts of the Last Supper, especially the Lukan text, shows that this tradition was widely known and shared, albeit in slightly varying forms.[31] The meal, and specifically its bread and cup, are a remembrance ($\dot{\alpha}\nu\acute{\alpha}\mu\nu\eta\sigma\iota\varsigma$) of Jesus' giving of his body and blood for the sake of his followers ($\dot{\upsilon}\pi\grave{\epsilon}\rho$ $\dot{\upsilon}\mu\hat{\omega}\nu$) (11.24-25). The probably Pauline addition to the tradition, v. 26, shows that the meal functions not only as a remembrance, looking back to Christ's death, but also as a proclamation of this death which points forward to the time when he will return ($\check{\alpha}\chi\rho\iota$ $\text{o}\hat{\upsilon}$ $\check{\epsilon}\lambda\theta\eta$). Thus, as with baptism, the central story of the Christian myth is encapsulated in this ritual practice.

Again as is the case with baptism, the texts also indicate something of the way in which this ritual constructs a particular community-ethos. Most revealing here is 1 Cor. 10.16-17, which Gunther Bornkamm describes as 'the only authentic commentary in the New Testament itself on the words of institution' (Bornkamm 1969: 139). In illustrating why the Corinthians should avoid participation in pagan sacrificial meals (see §6.1), Paul declares that sharing in the cup and the bread of the Lord's supper establishes a $\kappa\text{o}\iota\nu\omega\nu\acute{\iota}\alpha$ – a participation together[32] – in the blood and body of Christ (10.16). More specifically, and in terms highly reminiscent of the 'many into one' baptismal declaration, the 'one bread' shared at the supper is taken to demonstrate that 'we many are one body' ($\check{\epsilon}\nu$ $\sigma\hat{\omega}\mu\alpha$ $\text{o}\acute{\iota}$ $\pi\text{o}\lambda\lambda\text{o}\acute{\iota}$ $\acute{\epsilon}\sigma\mu\epsilon\nu$, 10.17). As Paul Gardner has noted, the fact that Paul can present this material as an illustration to support an argument against becoming 'participants with demons' ($\kappa\text{o}\iota\nu\omega\nu\text{o}\grave{\upsilon}\varsigma$ $\tau\hat{\omega}\nu$ $\delta\alpha\iota\mu\text{o}\nu\acute{\iota}\omega\nu$, 10.20) suggests that

---

29. It is generally accepted that the celebration comprises, or at least takes place within the context of, a proper meal (see, e.g., Theissen 1982: 145–74; Lampe 1991b: 183; Schrage 1999: 26–27; Thiselton 2000: 848–99). Justin Meggitt's attempt to argue to the contrary, and to suggest a distinction at this early stage between love-feasts (meals) and eucharist (sharing only of bread and wine, not a proper meal) seems to me unconvincing, assuming the distinction that needs to be proven (Meggitt 1998: 189–93).

30. Cf. 1 Cor. 11.2; 15.3; on the language for the passing on of tradition here, see Ellis 1986: 481; Tomson 1990: 145–46.

31. For detailed discussion see, e.g., Marshall 1980: 40–56, with tables 2 and 3; Jeremias 1960: 132–95.

32. It is difficult to convey the sense of the term $\kappa\text{o}\iota\nu\omega\nu\acute{\iota}\alpha$ in a single-word translation (cf. BDAG, 552–53: 'close association involving mutual interests and sharing ... fellowship ... participation', etc.). To use somewhat overworn metaphors, the 'sharing' in view here has both 'vertical' and 'horizontal' dimensions, inextricably intertwined, as Paul's further discussion in 1 Cor. 11.17-34 makes plain (see below).

this interpretation of the supper's significance was also traditional and known, at least in the churches among which Paul worked (cf. Gardner 1994: 161–65, 167, 171, 183). Indeed, the reasons for Paul's sharp criticism of the Corinthians' current practice (11.17-34) can most clearly be understood in relation to this 'many into one' tradition (cf. Horrell 1995a).

Whatever the details of the social situation at Corinth,[33] it is clear that there are divisions (σχίσματα) among the congregation during this commensual celebration (11.18). Some 'get on with eating their own supper' while others go hungry; Paul clearly contrasts the overindulgence of some with the lack experienced by others (11.21).[34] The behaviour of those who overindulge, when they could eat and drink 'at home' (ἐν οἴκῳ, 11.34, cf. v. 22), is seen by Paul to represent a despising of the ἐκκλησία and as bringing shame on 'the have-nots'.[35] The tradition which Paul proceeds to cite, reminding the Corinthians of the Lord's supper narrative, does not directly address these problems, nor make clear precisely why the Corinthian practice should be such as to compromise the very identity of the ritual (cf. 11.20). It does, however, remind the community of the narrative which gives the meal its meaning, with its focus on the death of Christ, and so, at least implicitly, raises the question as to whether their conduct towards one another reflects the pattern of Christ's self-giving death for others (Lampe 1991b: 211; cf. pp. 208–13; Engberg-Pedersen 1993: 115).

33. The view most fully articulated by Gerd Theissen (1982: 145–74), that the conflict is between richer and poorer, or higher and lower class, members of the congregation, is very widely held (see, e.g., Fee 1987: 531–45; Lampe 1991b: 192; Horrell 1996: 104–105; Winter 2001: 158; etc.). It has, however, been challenged by Justin Meggitt (1998: 118–22), who does not consider that the evidence is sufficient to support this view (for Theissen's reaffirmation of his interpretation, see Theissen 2003a: 377–81).

34. Overindulgence generally, as well as specifically drunkenness, seems to be the intended implication of μεθύει in contrast to πεινᾷ (v. 21). For detailed discussion of the possible background implied by this verse, see esp. Theissen 1982: 147–59; Lampe 1991b; Winter 2001: 142–58.

35. The phrase τοὺς μὴ ἔχοντας (v. 22b) has often been taken in an absolute sense, 'the have-nots' (e.g. Klauck 1982: 293; Meeks 1983: 68; Theissen 2003a: 378–79). Meggitt has recently argued that such an absolute use (i.e. lacking a specified or implied object) is unlikely, and that it is specifically the bread and wine of the eucharist that these people 'do not have' (Meggitt 1998: 119–20). However, the more obvious candidate for an implied object would seem to be οἰκίας, mentioned in the previous clause (v. 22a), as already noted by Meeks (1983: 68). This would then indicate that some members of the congregation either lacked connections with a 'household', as Bruce Winter has suggested (Winter 1994: 203), or perhaps were more literally destitute, lacking any dwelling place. Is it implausible that some such destitutes were welcomed as part of the Corinthian gathering? This would then suggest some degree of socio-economic disparity within the congregation, *pace* Meggitt. (On the wider debate concerning the socio-economic level of the Pauline Christians, see recently Meggitt 1998, 2001; Martin 2001a; Theissen 2001, 2003a; Holmberg 2004; Friesen 2004.)

Paul's more specific and concluding instructions (ὥστε ...) follow this reminder of tradition. The way in which some of the Corinthians currently practise this ceremony is ἀναξίως, done 'in an unworthy manner', such as makes them 'liable' (ἔνοχος) for the body and blood of the Lord (11.27). That is to say, what Paul labels as 'unworthy' here is not so much the individual's stance towards the elements of bread and wine, but rather the nature of their conduct in relation to others at the supper.[36] Their misconduct brings sickness and even death, signs of the Lord's judgment (11.30-32). What is required is that each person 'test' themselves (δοκιμαζέτω) and eat and drink in a way that avoids the failure implicit in 'not discerning the body' (μὴ διακρίνων τὸ σῶμα). This last phrase is notoriously ambiguous: to what should 'body' be taken to refer, to Christ's body given in death, to the bread as that body, or to the congregation?[37]

The various possibilities cannot be neatly separated, since to some degree all are probably implicit in the phrase.[38] Nonetheless, there are good reasons to suggest that a focus on the community as the body should be found here (cf. Fee 1987: 563–64). If Paul had meant to refer primarily to the elements of the supper, the bread and the wine, and their representation of Christ's self-giving death, then it seems odd that he wrote only τὸ σῶμα, given that in the previous lines he has constantly repeated references to both elements ('eats the bread or drinks the cup ... the body and blood of the Lord ... eat of the bread and drink of the cup ... who eats and drinks ... eats and drinks', vv. 27–29).[39] The disjunction marked by the singular reference to 'the body' suggests that the discernment called for is the recognition of the community as the body, which recalls, of course, precisely what 10.17 has told us the common consumption of the bread represents. This is why the Corinthian divisions, the indulgence of some and the neglect of others, represent an abuse so crucial as to render their gathering no longer really the supper at all (11.20): their meal fails to be an enactment of oneness, of corporate solidarity, and instead demonstrates a despising of the fundamental

---

36. Cf. Klauck 1982: 324; also Lampe 1991b: 209–12; Fee 1987: 559–61, esp. n. 10.

37. See, e.g., Barrett 1971: 273–75; Thiselton 2000: 891–94, for discussion of the possibilities.

38. Cf. Hahn 2002: 547, who suggests that Paul deliberately formulated the phrase indefinitely, 'da der hier gemeinte „Leib" sowohl der für uns in den Tod gegebene und in den Gaben des Mahls uns dargereichte Leib Jesu Christi ist als auch der durch ihn konstituierte Leib der Gemeinde'.

39. *Pace* Barrett 1971: 275. Engberg-Pedersen's suggestion that 'body' here refers to 'the bread and the wine' together, the whole thing one eats and drinks, also seems unlikely given Paul's tendency to refer to both elements and to link the body specifically with the bread (Engberg-Pedersen 1993: 121–22).

character of the ἐκκλησία.[40] Hence Paul's final advice that they 'wait for' (or 'welcome and accept') one another.[41] So it becomes evident that just as baptism constructs a new social reality, a solidarity which transcends former distinctions, so the Lord's supper is meant to confirm and consolidate that solidarity, demonstrating through the concrete sharing of a meal that many have become one body in Christ. Again, some level of egalitarian impulse is probably implicit in the vision of all sharing equally in the common meal.[42] To be sure, again an important question remains, in terms of the actual impact of this on social relationships: how far does Paul compromise the character of this solidarity with his advice that those who are hungry should eat at home (11.34, 22; cf. Theissen 1982: 163–64; §4.5 below)?

Nevertheless, what should be stressed at this point is the theme that emerges prominently in connection with both of the foundational Christian rituals. Early Christian tradition, shared by Paul, saw the key social achievement of these community-forming actions to consist in the bringing together of many people into one body, the construction of a new form of corporate solidarity. Both rituals, baptism and Lord's supper, at least as Paul interprets them, communicate and reinforce a world-view in which the death and resurrection of Christ are the central events in a cosmic story – these events give meaning to the world, providing the fundamental hermeneutical orientation by which it is to be understood – and at the same time convey as the central theme of the Christian ethos the notion of a solidarity in Christ which transcends former distinctions.

4.2 *A Community of* Adelphoi: *Identity and Ethos*

Indications of the kind of ethos Paul intends the congregations to have may also be gained from a consideration of the terms with which their identity is described. These terms are, of course, many and diverse, and a considerable number of them reflect Paul's claiming for these believers in Christ the privileged identity descriptors that traditionally belong to Israel: they are, for example, Abraham's descendants (Gal. 3.6–4.6, 21-31),

40. Cf. also Schrage 1999: 26: 'Die paulinische Kritik richtet sich nicht gegen das Übermaß an Essen und Trinken als solches, sondern gegen die fehlende κοινωνία in Form der Lieb- und Rücksichtlosigkeit gegenüber den Habenichtsen.'

41. For discussion as to whether ἐκδέχεσθε should be taken in a temporal sense or in the relational sense of acceptance, see Schrage 1999: 56; Thiselton 2000: 898–99, both of whom favour the temporal meaning.

42. Cf. Engberg-Pedersen 1993: 110–11, who argues that Paul expects the food and drink to be shared out equally; Strecker 1999: 313–35. The idea that meals might be occasions for a demonstration of equality is by no means unique to Paul; cf., e.g., Lucian, *Saturnalia* 22, 32; Xenophon, *Mem.* 3.14.1; Plutarch, *Mor.* 226E–227A.

inheritors of God's promise to Isaac (Gal. 4.28), the circumcision (Phil. 3.3), and so on (cf. §1.2 above). Some of these terms, as in their Jewish setting, specifically reflect an identity construed in terms of distinction and separation from the world, most notably and frequently the label ἅγιοι (contrasted with 'the world' in 1 Cor. 6.2), a theme that will occupy our attention in the next chapter.[43] The designation of Christians as 'those who believe' (οἱ πιστεύοντες), another Pauline appellation (1 Thess. 1.7, 2.10), indicates the central role that 'having faith' plays in defining the identity of those who belong to this movement (cf. Wolter 1997).[44] Relevantly for our concerns, many of these terms also describe this identity in *corporate* terms (e.g. 1 Cor. 3.9, 16). There is one term, however, that warrants somewhat fuller investigation here: the description of believers as ἀδελφοί.[45]

The prima facie importance of this particular identity descriptor is indicated by the fact, rightly noted by Robert Banks, that it is – despite its relative neglect in New Testament studies[46] – 'far and away Paul's favorite way of referring to the members of the communities to whom he is writing' (Banks 1994: 50–51). This kinship term is by no means unique to Paul – Matthew, for example, also uses it quite frequently (e.g. Mt. 5.22-24, 47; 7.3-5; 18.15, 21, 35; 23.8) – but it is particularly common in Paul's own letters, notably more so than in the deutero-Pauline and Pastoral letters (see Horrell 2001b). Paul uses ἀδελφοί (and, less frequently, singular equivalents, masculine and feminine) to refer to Christian believers 112 times in the seven authentic letters. This compares with 25 such uses of ἅγιος/ἅγιοι[47] and perhaps 15 of οἱ πιστεύοντες (or near equivalents).[48] The

43. E.g., Rom. 1.7; 1 Cor. 1.2; 2 Cor. 1.1; Phil. 1.1; Phlm. 5, and frequently elsewhere. See further §5.1 with n. 4 below.

44. However, I am less convinced that 'faith' per se can be regarded as that which defines the ethos and identity of the Pauline communities, as Wolter argues, since without specific practices and actions to indicate what this particular 'faith' implies the concept is too cognitive and general to form ethos and identity.

45. In the following section I summarize some of the material in Horrell 2001b.

46. Cf. the comments of Bartchy 1999: 69–70; Aasgaard 2002: 516–18. The more theological images of 'new creation', 'body of Christ', etc., tend to dominate studies of Paul's ecclesiology (e.g. in Doohan 1989). For notable studies of the sibling imagery in Paul see Schäfer 1989; Aasgaard 1997, 1998, 2002; Bartchy 1999; and more broadly on the family imagery in Paul, Allmen 1981.

47. There are also other relevant occurrences, such as in Rom. 12.1; 1 Thess. 4.4; 5.26, as well as many references to the Holy Spirit, so the notion of holiness as a defining characteristic of the Christian movement is more widespread in Paul's letters than these 25 references alone, though, with a grand total of 50 uses, nowhere near as common as ἀδελφός.

48. It is difficult to decide which uses of πιστεύω should rightly be regarded as identity descriptors. Some clearly are (e.g. 1 Thess. 1.7; 2.10) while others clearly are not (e.g. 1 Cor. 11.18). I have cast my net reasonably broadly, including, for example, Rom. 9.33 and 10.11, but excluding Rom. 10.9 and 1 Cor. 13.2. As with holiness, the sense that having faith is key to early Christian identity is clear and widespread, but even if we were to include every use of the

frequency of occurrences of ἀδελφός-language does vary somewhat even among the genuine Pauline letters, in ways that a contextual analysis of each might well illuminate, but the relative consistency of appearance warrants its treatment as a common theme of Pauline discourse.[49]

The term ἀδελφός is, of course, widely used in the ancient world, primarily to signify a blood brother (or sister, with ἀδελφή) but also in relation to various other bonds and relationships where a sibling-like interaction is presumed or sought.[50] The frequent use in the Hebrew Bible and later Jewish literature of the Hebrew אח or the Greek ἀδελφός to denote kinsfolk and fellow Israelites provides a direct source for the early Christian usage.[51] Thus, in its varied contexts, whether related to immediate family, extended kin, or metaphorically kin-like relations, the term indicates the existence of, or the desire for, a sibling-like bond between the parties involved. Such a bond, insofar as it is expressed by the designation ἀδελφός, is depicted as essentially an egalitarian one:[52] ἀδελφοί are ranked together on the same level.[53] Of course, reality is such that various factors compromise and render impossible full equality; but the

verb in the seven letters their number would only reach 42, well short of half the number of occurrences of ἀδελφός. Also relevant, of course, as the negative counterpart, is the designation ἄπιστος, which appears in 1 Cor. 6.6; 7.12-15 (five times); 10.27; 14.22-24 (four times); 2 Cor. 4.4; 6.14-15. Πιστός is used to designate a believer only in 2 Cor. 6.15.

49. See the table of appearances in Horrell 2001b: 311; cf. also Allmen 1981: xxvii, with discussion on pp. 156–65. For example it is notable that the highest incidence of sibling language is found in 1 Thessalonians, a community with which Paul is on good terms (1 Thess. 1.2-10; 4.9-12) and the lowest in 2 Corinthians, where the relationship between Paul and the Corinthians has been highly strained.

50. For detail on the range of ancient uses, see Horrell 2001b: 296–97; Aasgaard 1998: 119–27; Schelke 1954; LSJ, 20.

51. Cf. von Soden, *TDNT* 1: 145: 'There can be little doubt, however, that ἀδελφός is one of the titles of the people of Israel taken over by the Christian community.' E.g., Gen. 13.8; Exod. 2.11; Lev. 25.35-36; Deut. 15.7, 9, 11-12; 22.1-4; 2 Macc. 1.1; Philo, *Virt.* 82; Josephus, *War* 2.122 (on the Essenes); 1QS 6.10, 22; CD 6.20; 7.2; further Str-B 1: 276; Ringgren, *TDOT* 1: 188–93.

52. See n. 3 above for possible objections to the use of this term, and esp. Clarke 2004 (cf. further n. 55 below). Sandnes 1997 examines the 'brotherhood' and 'household/family' language in early Christianity, seeing the former as implying an egalitarian structure, the latter a hierarchical one. He inverts the argument of Fiorenza and others, suggesting that 'egalitarian structures are emerging within patriarchal household structures' (p. 162). On 'brotherhood' (*Bruderschaft*) as implying an egalitarian pattern of relationships, see also Schäfer 1989, for whom the 'Bruder-Titel signalisiert Egalität' (p. 37; cf. p. 444), though Schäfer downplays the evidence concerning the exercise of power and authority and overstresses the extent to which 'brotherly' equality characterized the Pauline congregations (e.g. pp. 335, 369–85, 407–18, etc.).

53. There were of course various ways in which sisters were not equal to brothers, not least in terms of social status, power, inheritance, etc. I think it is clear that Paul intends the address ἀδελφοί to include both women and men (*pace* Fatum 1997), and designates them all

drive towards equality is nonetheless an impulse which the ἀδελφός label implies.[54] Moreover, a sense of hierarchy or superiority may be conveyed in the same contexts through other adjectives (older, younger, etc.) or labels (Paul is, for example, both brother and father, the latter implying a position of authority and superiority: 1 Cor. 4.14-15).[55] More specifically, as Reidar Aasgaard (2002) has suggested, in using the term ἀδελφός Paul evokes a set of common ideas about what it meant to be a sibling, implying that these ideas were to characterize relationships among Christians too. Aasgaard summarizes these 'common ideas', pointing to the expectation that siblings would 'love one another and ... show each other tolerance ... be generous towards each other ... and forgiving'. They were also expected to uphold the honour and harmony of the family (Aasgaard 2002: 519; further 1998: 41–127). The Christians' identity as ἀδελφοί, while presuming these wider cultural norms, is specifically grounded, once again, in the Christian myth: all are siblings because they have been adopted as 'sons' by God the Father, an adoption made possible by the redemptive act of their brother, Christ (Rom. 8.29; cf. Rom. 8.14-17; Gal. 4.5-6).[56]

Aasgaard's key point, which I find persuasive, is that Paul's labelling of Christians as ἀδελφοί implies a 'role-ethics', a set of expectations as to how behaviour and relationships should be structured which follow from a certain role-designation (cf. also Horrell 2001b). In view of the frequency of the sibling label in Paul, Aasgaard rightly suggests that the ethical implications of this particular role-identity have been far too much neglected in studies of Pauline ethics (Aasgaard 2002: 513–15), partly, at least, because, as I have also argued, studies of 'ethics' in Paul have been

as υἱοὶ θεοῦ (and thus equally inheritors; Gal. 3.26). Discerning the degree to which Paul implies a sense of gender equality is, however, a more complex issue; the evidence suggests an ambivalent or compromised stance, on which see briefly §4.5 below; Fiorenza 1983, etc.

54. Cf. Plutarch, *Mor.* 484B–486D, esp. 484C-D: 'all manner of inequality is dangerous as likely to foster brothers' quarrels, and though it is impossible for them to be equal and on the same footing in all respects (for on the one hand our natures at the very beginning make an unequal apportionment, and then later on our varying fortunes beget envies and jealousies, the most shameful diseases and baneful plagues, ruinous not only for private houses, but for whole states as well); against these inequalities we must be on our guard and must cure them, if they arise.' Plutarch discusses how to deal with the tensions and problems arising between inferior and superior brothers. See further Aasgaard 1997 for the comparison between Paul and Plutarch on this topic; Clarke 2004.

55. Similarly, the papyri to which Andrew Clarke (2004) draws attention, in which, e.g., an elder brother is addressed as κύριέ μου ἀδελφέ, do not undermine the claim that the term ἀδελφός itself, *unqualified* by other terms, implies a relationship of equal standing. Other words are needed to show when and how some sense of higher or lower ranking is implied. Clarke is right, however, that the sense of familial affection implied by the appellation does not require a relationship of equality.

56. *Pace* Aasgaard (1998: 151–64), who minimizes the theological and christological bases for Paul's view of Christians as siblings, notably in discussion of Rom. 8.29.

conceived too narrowly and have therefore neglected some of the most fundamental ways in which Paul seeks to shape the character and ethos of the Christian community.

That Paul understands this identity-designation to have moral implications, and does not merely reproduce it as a common Christian appellation, can be clearly seen when we note the passages where the term appears with particular frequency. Unsurprisingly, many of the Pauline uses appear simply as a typical form of address, though that does not make them any less significant in terms of reinforcing particular role-expectations (e.g. Rom. 1.13; 11.25; 15.30; 1 Cor. 1.10; 1 Thess. 5.14, etc.).[57] But in a number of texts the sibling language is used with an apparently deliberate and repeated emphasis to impress an ethical demand. The most notable examples are Rom. 14.10-21 (where there are five occurrences), 1 Cor. 6.5-8 (four occurrences), and 1 Cor. 8.11-13 (four occurrences).[58] Philemon 16 is also worthy of particular attention.

In Romans 14 and 1 Corinthians 8 – both important passages which we shall consider in more depth in ch. 6 – Paul is addressing situations where there is some kind of conflict between groups of 'strong' and 'weak' Christian believers, who take different stances with regard to certain practices relating to food. The identification of the 'other' as an ἀδελφός, specifically an ἀδελφός for whom Christ died (1 Cor. 8.11; Rom. 14.15), presses the case for an 'other-regarding' moral concern congruent with this shared identity (see further ch. 7). The force of the case is sharpened both by using singular forms and personal pronouns and with the specifically christological link (see 1 Cor. 8.11-13; Rom. 14.10-21; 1 Cor. 6.5-6; 1 Thess. 4.6). And in 1 Cor. 6.5-8 it is the other's identity as ἀδελφός that serves to indicate what a 'complete defeat', what a denial of this identity, it is when brother takes brother to court. It would be better to suffer wrong and injury than to inflict it on an ἀδελφός (6.7-8) – a general moral principle sharpened with specifically christological resonances (see ch. 7).[59] In Philemon 16 the ἀδελφός-language is used to redefine the relationship between owner and slave, and not only in 'spiritual' terms: Onesimos is to be received 'no longer as a slave but more than a slave, a beloved brother (ἀδελφὸν ἀγαπητόν), both in the flesh and in the Lord (καὶ ἐν σαρκὶ καὶ ἐν κυρίῳ)'. Once again we face the question as to what difference this makes in practical terms, but will defer this point until a later section (§4.5); what is

---

57. For a comprehensive study see Schäfer 1989: 330–52.

58. Cf. the detailed discussion in Aasgaard 1998: 129–332; 2002: 522–24, 526–28; Horrell 2001b: 300–302. Other passages could of course be mentioned, such as 1 Cor. 7.12-15 and 1 Thess. 4.6.

59. The principle that it is better to suffer wrong than to do wrong is expressed, e.g., by Plato, *Gorgias* 509C; Epictetus, *Diss.* 4.5.10, as noted by a number of commentators, e.g., Conzelmann 1975: 106; Barrett 1971: 139.

clear as a minimum is Paul's conviction that denoting their relationship in terms of one between siblings is meant to give it a new character, implicitly defined in terms of the ἀδελφός-role.

The ἀδελφός-language, then, apart from its frequent use as a standard form of address, is deliberately used as part of an appeal for mutual regard, for an 'other-regarding' morality, and specifically (in Rom. 14 and 1 Cor. 8) a concern for the weaker sibling. In Scott Bartchy's words, through his use of ἀδελφός-language Paul's 'readers were challenged to practice the general reciprocity and mutual support that characterized the relations among siblings at their best' (Bartchy 1999: 77). This other-regarding morality and its christological foundations will be our concern in a subsequent chapter (ch. 7). For now it is most relevant to note that underlying this morality, and essential to it, is a notion of familial solidarity that is implied in the designation of the community members as ἀδελφοί. Onesimos and Philemon are redefined as ἀδελφοί, a designation that implies a kind of equal-regard, and that (in some sense) supervenes over their (former) relationship as owner and slave. The reason why believers should show a generous concern for one another is precisely because the other is an ἀδελφός and as such belongs with them to the same family group. The mutual love that should characterize the congregations is the love of siblings, a φιλαδελφία (Rom. 12.10; 1 Thess. 4.9). This solidarity, we should note, is explicitly seen to reach beyond the confines of the local congregation to encompass believers elsewhere, who also share this family identity (1 Thess. 4.10). The practical forms of solidarity – such as sharing material goods – operate not only on the local level (though certainly there: Gal. 6.6) but also throughout the Christian movement, notably through the practice of the virtue of hospitality and the support offered to travelling leaders (Rom. 12.13; cf., e.g., Rom. 15.24; 16.2, 23; 1 Cor. 16.6, 11; Phlm. 22).[60] Inter-church solidarity is shown most clearly and concretely in Paul's collection project, which will be dealt with more fully in a subsequent chapter (§7.4). Here, as Justin Meggitt (1998: 158–61) has suggested, we see a form of mutualism between early Christian congregations (cf. Rom. 15.27; 2 Cor. 8.14; further §7.4). The family solidarity extends, then, to the realm of material goods and beyond the local community.

---

60. On the verb προπέμπω ('to send [someone] on [their] way', used in Rom. 15.24; 1 Cor. 16.6, 11; 2 Cor. 1.16) as meaning 'to equip somebody for the continuation of a journey', i.e., with material support, see Holmberg 1978: 89.

4.3 *Appeals for Unity in the Face of Division*

Further indications of the priority given to fostering a form of corporate solidarity may be found in Paul's appeals for unity in the face of division. Here the most important text is of course the opening four chapters of 1 Corinthians, though other texts are also relevant as illustrations of this concern for unity and of its particular character (cf. Hahn 1996). Margaret Mitchell (1991), in an exegetical and rhetorical analysis of 1 Corinthians, has persuasively highlighted the appeal for a restoration of unity in the face of factionalism as the key aim of 1 Corinthians 1–4, if not of the whole letter.[61] '1 Corinthians', Mitchell proposes, 'is throughout an argument for ecclesial unity, as centred in the πρόθεσις, or thesis statement of the argument, in 1:10' (1991: 1). Here Paul appeals (παρακαλῶ) to the Corinthians, reminding them of their shared identity as ἀδελφοί and grounding his appeal in 'the name of the Lord Jesus Christ',[62] 'that they may all say the same thing, that there may be no divisions (σχίσματα) among them, but that they may be "knitted together again" [Thiselton 2000: 115] in the same mind and the same opinion' (1 Cor. 1.10). Precisely what kind of divisions were evident at Corinth, and what their cause was, has been much debated among scholars, ever since F.C. Baur's epoch-making article of 1831 (Baur 1831).[63] But rather than seek to understand the divisions on the basis of theological or doctrinal differences (so Baur), or to deny that they are really divisions at all (so Munck 1959: 135–67), the most promising approaches focus on the fact of division as itself the problem Paul perceives. Laurence Welborn (1987) has, for example, suggested that the most illuminating background to Paul's discussion lies in the factionalism and rivalry of ancient politics, thus comparing Paul's appeal with political appeals to restore harmony and concord (cf. also Mitchell 1991). Paul certainly gives little hint of any doctrinal issues at stake here – except insofar as a christologically grounded unity is itself, of course, a 'doctrinal' issue – indicating instead that he regards the Corinthians' jealous rivalry (1 Cor. 3.3) as founded on claims to wisdom, power and status reflective of the values of 'this world', 'this present age'

---

61. I am less convinced that *all* of the sections of the letter (e.g. 11.2-16, etc.) can plausibly be seen as a series of 'proofs' in relation to this single argument; here Mitchell seems to me to press the formal rhetorical analysis too far.

62. Thiselton (2000) rightly notes that Paul's naming of Christ 'provides the ground for the request or plea' (p. 112) and that the identification of the believers as ἀδελφοί here and in 1 Cor. 1.11, far from being merely conventional, indicates the inappropriateness of divisions and points to the mutual loyalty and respect which should characterize a family (p. 114).

63. On the various attempts to understand the character of the Corinthian divisions, and the history of debate, see Adams and Horrell 2004.

(1 Cor. 1.20; 2.6, etc.);[64] Meeks writes of a 'kind of competitive jostling for status and esteem' among the Corinthians (1993: 63).

The unity which the Corinthians share by virtue of their baptism, the ritual which has made them Christ's one body, already indicates why division is so inconceivable: 'Has Christ been divided up ($\mu\epsilon\mu\acute{\epsilon}\rho\iota\sigma\tau\alpha\iota$)?' (1 Cor. 1.13). Paul's more developed answer to the current problems begins, however, with 'the word of the cross' (1.18-25), the word which indicates God's decisive rejection of 'worldly wisdom' and status, a rejection mirrored in the calling of a community comprised largely of the nobodies ($\tau\grave{\alpha}$ $\mu\grave{\eta}$ $\ddot{o}\nu\tau\alpha$, 1.26-28) and in a message announced with fear and inarticulateness (2.1-5). The way to bring such a divided community to a state of unity in which harmony and agreement may be sought, then, is for Paul not through sustaining the kind of 'worldly' order which he considers the Corinthian 'wise' to represent. It is rather through overturning and negating the value system upon which such an order is constructed: God's election of the nobodies is repeatedly and forcefully presented as just such a reversal, the intention of which is explicitly to shame the wise and bring to nothing the 'somebodies' ($\tau\grave{\alpha}$ $\ddot{o}\nu\tau\alpha$, 1.26-28; see Horrell 1996: 132–37). In place of this old order is presented a vision of the community as a corporate entity in which boasting in oneself over against others is inappropriate (1.29). Even the apostolic leaders are portrayed merely as servants, labourers, co-workers in the task of constructing God's building, his temple even, which the Corinthians together comprise (3.5-23). The images which pile up in ch. 3 all describe the community as a corporate entity which belongs to God: God's field, God's building, God's temple (3.9, 16).[65] As such, it is not a case of the Corinthians 'belonging' to particular apostles, as has begun to be expressed in the divisive and competitive slogans, 'I am of Paul, but I am of Apollos, etc.' (1.12, cf. 3.4, 22). Rather, as God's corporate new community, the temple in which the Spirit dwells (3.16-17), all the apostles, indeed everything present and future, belong to the Corinthians, who belong to Christ, and Christ to God (3.22-23; cf. Furnish 1990).

The major section from 1.10 to 4.21 closes as it began with an explicit appeal ($\pi\alpha\rho\alpha\kappa\alpha\lambda\hat{\omega}$, 4.16). The opening appeal made clear Paul's aim to restore unity and agreement. Ridding the community of the factiousness caused by competitive claims to wisdom requires a negation of the very basis of those claims, and Paul has spent the opening chapters of the letter showing what kind of structural change is necessary for true unity and agreement to become possible: the worldly order of wisdom and power must

---

64. See further the list of contrasts presented by Clarke 1993: 101–102.
65. On the images of the building and the temple, see Vielhauer 1940 and Lanci 1997 respectively.

be overturned, as indeed it has been in the cross. However, this reversal does not simply introduce a mirror image of its predecessor but instead undergirds a new kind of corporeity. Paul's second appeal, addressed especially to those who are 'puffed up' (4.18), is that they imitate him (μιμηταί μου γίνεσθε). Given what has preceded in 4.8-13 – the list of apostolic hardships, to the point of becoming the 'scum of the earth'[66] – this imitation must consist in imitating Paul's debased and humiliated lifestyle (see further Martin 1990: 117–35; Horrell 1996: 199–204). This rather concrete and shocking social transformation is what it means for those who are wise in this age to become fools (1 Cor. 3.18), but this is a prerequisite for the replacement of competitive sophistry with corporate solidarity.

There is, of course, a certain irony underlying all this, which comes rather menacingly to the surface in 4.18-21. At the same time as Paul is denouncing claims to worldly wisdom, extolling God's choice of the nobodies, and depicting the believers at Corinth as a corporate community whose servants the apostles are, he insists that he is the bearer of true wisdom, though the Corinthians are too immature and worldly to receive it (2.6-7; 3.1-3). All the Corinthians, and Paul himself, may be ἀδελφοί, bound together with a familial and corporate solidarity in Christ; but Paul is the only 'brother' who is also their father and as such able to admonish them as his children and to threaten them with physical punishment if they do not comply (4.14-15, 21; cf. Lassen 1991). Paul is strikingly explicit about the fact that this is a matter of *power* (1 Cor. 4.19-20, note δύναμις twice). It is, then, abundantly clear that his call to imitation, and the wider passage of admonition within which it is set, constitutes a 'discourse of power', as Elizabeth Castelli (1991) and Sandra Hack Polaski (1999) have suggested.

While it is certainly important to identify such uses of power, this revelation should not itself be taken to constitute a critique, not least since forms of power are woven into all human relations and interactions. More crucial, though complex, are questions about what Paul seeks to use power to do, and how. Here at least it seems that Paul's concern is to assert his own power in seeking to disempower the powerful and puffed up (οἱ δυνατοί ... οἱ πεφυσιωμένοι), to reverse the valuations of the wise and powerful and the despised nobodies, in order to construct a community in which solidarity can thus be established (see further §4.4 below). There is here what we may perhaps call the irony of power – an irony prevalent in much political practice[67] – whereby the attempt to foster a communal solidarity is executed from a position of (claimed) superior authority. Also

---

66. On the phrase ὡς περικαθάρματα τοῦ κόσμου ἐγενήθημεν, πάντων περίψημα ἕως ἄρτι (1 Cor. 4.13) see Horrell 1996: 202; Thiselton 2000: 364–65.

67. Benhabib (1992: 37), for example, notes the contradiction expressed in Rousseau's dictum, 'on les forcera d'être libre'.

important to consider is the relationship between the degree of diversity and self-determination Paul appears to countenance and the values and practices about which he will tolerate no dissent. Clearly, the need for unity – expressive of a certain kind of corporate solidarity – is one such non-negotiable. In this 'intolerant' framework for tolerance, as will be discussed later (§6.4), there are interesting parallels between Pauline and liberal ethics.

Paul's attempt to restore unity and to foster solidarity raises another question: does his appeal for agreement and univocity (1.10) imply a drive towards sameness, as Castelli (1991) has argued in relation to the theme of imitation? Certain aspects of this question must also be deferred, since they will be treated in a later chapter (ch. 6), though the outline of that later discussion may be anticipated here insofar as it relates to 1 Cor. 1.10. Here, 'speaking the same thing' (τὸ αὐτὸ λέγητε) and sharing the same mind (ἐν τῷ αὐτῷ νοΐ) and the same disposition (ἐν τῇ αὐτῇ γνώμῃ) do not need to imply a complete or blanket 'sameness', an unvaried conformity, but rather the kind of unanimity and shared outlook which provide the basis for solidarity, within which a circumscribed diversity may be sustained (see further chs 6, 9). Questions about sameness and difference may, however, begin to be addressed through a consideration of Paul's language about the community as a body, to which I turn in the next section.

First, however, I want to comment briefly on some of the other places where an appeal for unity or agreement is apparent (or implicit). The appeal of 1 Cor. 1.10 certainly reappears elsewhere, in ways which indicate its character as an established theme of Pauline paraenesis. Romans 12.16, while missing the polemical edge directed at the Corinthian 'wise', concisely encapsulates not only the appeal for a common mind (τὸ αὐτὸ εἰς ἀλλήλους φρονοῦντες) but also the need for sober self-assessment and association with the humble. The appeal – τὸ αὐτὸ φρονεῖν – appears again in Rom. 15.5; 2 Cor. 13.11; Phil. 2.2; and 4.2, the last case constituting an appeal for reconciliation between Euodia and Syntyche, the others all directed towards congregations. Indeed, while the Philippian church does not seem to face the degree of disunity evident at Corinth, Paul's concern to foster there a loving unity of heart and mind is clear (cf. Bockmuehl 1998a: 108; Phil. 2.1-4); the same could be said for Romans (see §6.2). Broadly comparable too is Paul's appeal for reconciliation in 2 Corinthians, where the particular concern is the strained relationships between him and the community. The explicit appeal may be for reconciliation with God (2 Cor. 5.20) but it is clear that this correlates with an appeal to restore relations fully with Paul (2 Cor. 7.2).

A rather different kind of response to disagreement seems to be evident in Galatians, where instead of pleas for reconciliation and harmony of purpose we find angry denunciations of those who dare to preach 'another gospel' (Gal. 1.6-9). Does this vehement and inflexible stance stand in contradiction to the appeals for unity elsewhere? The situation in Galatia and before it at Antioch, like that at Corinth, is the subject of a wide diversity of competing scholarly reconstructions. Nevertheless, we can be reasonably confident in asserting that the issue in Galatians concerns the place of the Jewish law in the Christian community, and specifically the extent to which Gentile converts are obliged to follow prescriptions concerning the boundary-marking 'works of the law' in order to count themselves as fully and properly inheritors of the promise to Abraham, members of the community of God's people (cf. e.g. Dunn 1990: 183–264). The so-called 'incident at Antioch' (Gal. 2.11-14; Dunn 1990: 129–82) is evidently seen by Paul as a manifestation of essentially the same issues, such that what he reports to the Galatians as his response to that incident constitutes also his main 'thesis' in Galatians (Gal. 2.15-21).[68] While the details of the incident are uncertain and much disputed, it is clear, at least insofar as we trust Paul's report, our only source, that the Jewish believers at Antioch, led by Peter, and under pressure from people who came from Jerusalem representing James, withdrew from table-fellowship with Gentile believers, such that the participation of all in one common meal, presumably the Lord's supper, came at least temporarily to an end. The reason for this withdrawal was probably some version of the view either that the Gentile Christians were insufficiently observant of the necessary food regulations, or that the Jewish Christians could not be sure in such a context that they were not sinning in partaking of food and wine shared in intimate commensality with Gentiles.[69] Thus, from Paul's viewpoint, this withdrawal constitutes a demand, if congregational fellowship and unity are to be restored, that the Gentiles ἰουδαΐζειν – 'adopt Jewish customs or live like a Jew' (Gal. 2.14).[70] For Paul this demand is a denial of the truth of the gospel, that both Jewish and Gentile Christians attain their status as members of the community only on the basis of their incorporation into Christ. Personalizing the argument, Paul explains that he has 'died to the law' and 'been crucified with Christ', such that his life is now Christ's life in him (Gal. 2.19-20). Paul's vehemence in Galatians reflects his conviction

68. See Betz 1975; 1979: 16–25, and esp. p. 114; also Witherington 1998: 35, 169–96.

69. For significant discussions of this incident and its background, see Dunn 1990: 129–82; Sanders 1990; Esler 1998: 93–116; Holmberg 1998; Bockmuehl 2000: 49–83. Holmberg and Esler argue for a greater degree of Jewish separatism at meals than do Dunn, Sanders and Bockmuehl.

70. For this rendering of ἰουδαΐζειν see Barclay 1988: 36 n. 1; cf. BDAG, 478; Dunn 1990: 149–50. Richard Longenecker's 'to become a Jew' is too strong (Longenecker 1990: 78). That the verb itself does not necessarily imply full conversion to Judaism is implied by Josephus' report of Metilius' promise καὶ μέχρι περιτομῆς ἰουδαΐσειν (*War* 2.454; cf. 2.463). Cf. also Esth. 8.17 (LXX): καὶ πολλοὶ τῶν ἐθνῶν περιετέμοντο καὶ ἰουδάιζον διὰ τὸν φόβον τῶν Ἰουδαίων; Ignatius, *Magn.* 10.3; Plutarch, *Cicero* 7.5.

that the solidarity of Jew and Gentile in this new community (cf. Gal. 3.26-28) is founded on being in Christ, and on Christ alone.[71] An attempt to reintroduce the Jewish law as the basis for communal solidarity and belonging is regarded by Paul as annulling the value and truth of the message about Christ (Gal. 2.21, etc.). What the Galatian letter forcefully indicates then, is that Paul's appeals for unity and harmony, as 1 Corinthians also makes clear (1.13), are not for unity per se, but unity in Christ, where being in Christ provides the basis and ground of human solidarity. In short, the theme of corporate solidarity is equally fundamental in 1 Corinthians and Galatians, though stressed in different ways: in 1 Corinthians it is *solidarity* in Christ; in Galatians, solidarity *in Christ*. The implications of this stance, already identified as a crucial point in Boyarin's study (see §1.7), will be subject to further attention in subsequent sections (§6.4; §9.1).

4.4 *The Body: Whole and Parts*

In our consideration of the rituals of baptism and Lord's supper we have already seen that the notion that Christians form one body is important to the sense of solidarity Paul seeks to engender. The image of the body is, of course, an obvious though nonetheless profound and compelling image with which to undergird a notion of corporate unity, one which at the same time equally underscores the need for difference and diversity.

There are two significant texts where Paul presents the notion of the community as a body to engender the idea of a diversity-in-unity, or solidarity and difference: Rom. 12.4-8; and 1 Cor. 12.12-31.[72] Romans 12 is undoubtedly the later of these two texts, and probably represents in summary form the kind of ideas developed at more length in 1 Corinthians, there specifically orientated to the 'problems' in the Corinthian community.[73] In both texts the central idea is that of 'many

---

71. Cf. Hays 1997a: 32: 'His [sc. Paul's] passionate response to Cephas at Antioch (Gal. 2:11-21) sprang from his urgent conviction that Jews and Gentiles must be one in Christ, not separated by social barriers.' It should perhaps be emphasized that the stress falls on the 'in Christ' rather than the 'social barriers', which could, after all, have been overcome in other ways, namely, by an 'acceptable' level of Torah observance on the part of both Jewish and Gentile converts.

72. The idea of the believer as a member of Christ's body is also explicit in 1 Cor. 6.15, but here the concern is not with community solidarity as such but the competing unions between Christ and a πόρνη; on this passage and its wider context, see §5.3.

73. The references to the collection in 1 Cor. 16.1-4; 2 Corinthians 8–9; and Rom. 15.25-28 enable a relative chronology of these Pauline letters to be established (cf. Lüdemann 1984). On Rom. 12.4-8 as assuming the earlier material in 1 Corinthians 12, see e.g. Wilckens 1982: 13, though he follows Cranfield (1979: 617) in stressing that the idea of the community members

and one', parts and whole. Unlike the baptismal and eucharistic traditions, which emphasize only the unity or oneness of the community, here the body image is clearly intended to emphasize both sides of this dualism: one body, many members – each with a different task or gift, but equally part of the whole (Rom. 12.4-5; 1 Cor. 12.12-14). In Romans the body image itself is not further developed, but is followed by a list of the different kinds of gifts (χαρίσματα) which constitute the varied work (πρᾶξις) of each member of the body (vv. 6–8). The image is presented at greater length in 1 Corinthians, where the particular concern is with things of the spirit (πνευματικά), especially with tongue-speakers who consider themselves more spiritual than others who do not practise this ecstatic speech.[74] The body image serves Paul well as a basis not only for asserting that all these diverse people belong together in the same body, but also for insisting that the diverse gifts (χαρίσματα) are given by one and the same Spirit (12.4-11, 28-30).

Paul's use of the body image in this way, and specifically his insistence that a functioning body needs diverse parts (1 Cor. 12.15-20), at least at one level counts against the idea that his discourse constitutes 'a call to sameness with its implicit indictment of difference' (Castelli 1991: 116). There remain, of course, questions about the extent to which the 'legitimate' differences depend on a more fundamental sameness, as Boyarin has suggested (see chs 6, 9). Nevertheless, the way Paul employs this image reminds us of the need to distinguish and not equate solidarity and sameness.

Further indications of the kind of community-ethos Paul intends this image to foster emerge more clearly when his depiction of the communal body is compared with other ancient uses. The body image was indeed well known and widely used in Paul's time as an analogy of the social and political body, in some cases simply to express the idea that individuals were part of a wider social whole (e.g. Seneca, *Ep.* 95.52),[75] sometimes to depict an ideal and balanced form of social organization (Plato, *Pol.* 5.462C-D),[76] and most famously as a form of ideology which legitimated the status quo and the position of the ruling classes, as in the classic tale

---

as the body of Christ (as opposed to being one body *in* Christ) is not explicitly evident in Romans 12. This point is also important for Lindemann (1995), who argues that Paul uses the image of the body and its members in a way similar to its use in some traditions of ancient political philosophy (p. 153; see also n. 78 below): the fact that the community is 'the body *of Christ*' – an expression, Lindemann stresses, which does not appear until 1 Cor. 12.27 – does not materially affect its depiction.

74. On this passage in 1 Corinthians, see further Horrell 1996: 176–84.
75. Cf. also Seneca, *De Ira* 2.31.7.
76. Cf. also Aristotle, *Pol.* 5.1302b 35-37; Lindemann 1995: 145.

recounted by Livy (*History* 2.32):[77] sent to quell dissension against the ruling class among the Roman plebs, Menenius Agrippa compares the lower classes to the limbs of the body who might, like the plebs, object to labouring to provide nourishment for the apparently idle belly (the ruling class). Yet the result would be sickness and death for the whole body, since the stomach provides, as well as receives, nourishment. The analogy apparently proved convincing and harmony was restored. 'Naturally', Dale Martin quips, 'everyone lives happily ever after' (Martin 1995a: 93).

Against the background of the widespread use 'to solidify an unquestioned status hierarchy' (Martin 1995a: 94), Paul's use of the imagery is notable.[78] After outlining the basic point about unity and diversity (1 Cor. 12.12-14) Paul illustrates this with reference to parts of the body: foot and hand, eye and ear (12.15-20). The fact that Paul chooses pairs of parts which 'carry on comparable functions in the body' suggests, as Gordon Fee rightly notes, that Paul is not here concerned with questions of inferiority and superiority among the various parts of the body (Fee 1987: 610-11). But the interest shifts in the following section (12.21-26), where the parts chosen to illustrate the point have a more clearly hierarchical relationship to one another: eye to hand, head to feet. As Martin has argued, Paul's rhetoric here questions rather than reinforces this 'natural' hierarchy (1995a: 94). The (supposedly) weak and dishonourable parts are only *apparently* so (δοκοῦντα ... δοκοῦμεν, vv. 22-23), and are in fact more necessary, more respectable, more to be honoured than the apparently respectable parts (vv. 22-24). This cumulative emphasis reaches its rhetorical climax in the theological assertion that this work of arranging the body so as to reverse the apparent values of importance and honour – 'giving greater honour to the ones who lack' – is the work of God (v. 24, cf. v. 18). Paul's rhetoric, Martin suggests, 'pushes for an actual reversal of the normal, "this-worldly" attribution of honor and status. The lower is made higher, and the higher lower' (1995a: 96).

This theme of reversal recalls the earlier chapters of the letter (see §4.3), as also does the way in which Paul describes the *purpose* of this divine redistribution of honour and status. Just as 1 Cor. 1.10 presented the appeal 'that there be no divisions (σχίσματα) among you' but instead an agreement and unity of speech and purpose, so 12.25 explains the purpose of God's (re)arrangement of the body as a way to ensure 'that there be no division (σχίσμα) in the body but that the members may show the same care for one

---

77. Cf. also Plutarch, *Coriolanus* 6.1-4; Dio Cassius, *Frag.* 4.17; Dionysius of Halicarnassus 6.83.1-88.4. On the uses of the analogy as a form of conservative political ideology, see Martin 1991: 563–66 (=1995a: 92–94); Lindemann 1995: 142–44; more broadly Martin 1995a: 3–136.

78. Paul's depiction of the body is much closer to what Lindemann (1995: 153) describes as the 'democratic' version of the image, as found in Plato and Aristotle.

another (τὸ αὐτὸ ὑπὲρ ἀλλήλων μεριμνῶσιν)'. Their solidarity as members of the one body should make itself evident in forms of mutual empathy, suffering and rejoicing with one another (12.26).[79] Here then, while insisting on the need for diversity and difference among the members Paul also mounts a powerful appeal for solidarity and mutual regard, based on what we might label the value of 'equal regard' (τὸ αὐτὸ κτλ.) or (following Benhabib) an 'egalitarian reciprocity' (Benhabib 1992: 29; §2.2) – that is to say, that every member is worthy of the same degree of value and care.

What Paul's use of the body image reveals then, in the context of his confrontation with those among the Corinthians who consider themselves especially 'spiritual', is his intention to engender not merely a form of corporate solidarity, but specifically – as in 1 Cor. 1.10–4.21 – a form of solidarity constructed through reversing the conventional positions of high and low, wise and foolish, honourable and dishonourable, and fostering instead a mutual and egalitarian other-regard. But another similarity with 1 Corinthians 1–4 should also be noted. There, while calling his fellow siblings to restored unity, through the message of God's reversal of the hierarchy of worldly wisdom, Paul backed up his message with the father's threat of force (4.16-21). Here, while reversing conventional expectations of status and honour to construct a community characterized by equal-regard and mutual care, Paul also insists that God has indeed instituted a hierarchy in the body of Christ, and that he as an apostle is at the top of it (12.28). Once again we encounter the 'irony of power': Paul's appeal for corporate solidarity and mutual regard is made from a position of presumed authority.

4.5 *Solidarity in Practice: What Difference Does It Make?*

Galatians 3.28 may sometimes be acclaimed as the 'Magna Carta' of human equality and emancipation[80] but, as we have seen, questions arise as to what kind of difference, if any, the new solidarity as one body in Christ is supposed to make to the social relationships and relative positions of the various groups now united. Similarly with the Lord's supper, there are questions about the practical impact of this corporate solidarity, given Paul's instruction to the overindulgent to eat at home. Commentators have struggled to elucidate the implications of the baptismal declaration in non-self-contradictory ways: Ernest de Witt Burton insists, oxymoronically, that Gal. 3.28 'has nothing directly to do with the merging of nationalities

---

79. Plato comments similarly that in the well-governed πόλις, pain or pleasure, good or evil, experienced by any individual member will be shared by the whole community, comparing the city-community with a human body (*Pol.* 5.462A-E).

80. Cf. Witherington 1981: 593 with authors cited in n. 1.

or the abolition of slavery' though one feasible construal of its meaning is that 'whether you be Jew or Gentile, slave or master, man or woman, all these distinctions vanish'. To be sure, this potentially radical erasure of difference is immediately qualified and dissipated into the anodyne formulation 'there is no respect of persons with God', but even Burton is equally clear that the principle had 'indirect (*sic!*) social significance' (Burton 1921: 206–207).

It is striking how frequently studies of Paul, insofar as they have taken up these political questions at all, press a case for Paul as either liberator or oppressor, proto-feminist or spokesman for patriarchy. Thus Robin Scroggs can laud Paul as 'the only certain and consistent spokesman for the liberation and equality of women in the New Testament' (Scroggs 1972: 283); Neil Elliott can acclaim him as 'the apostle of liberation' (Elliott 1994: 230), arguing 'that Paul himself is far more an advocate of human liberation than the inherited theological tradition has led us to think' (p. 23).[81] On the other hand, Antoinette Wire can depict Paul as the consistent opponent of the Corinthian women prophets, the one who seeks to silence their voices (Wire 1990), while for Castelli (1991), as we have seen, Paul's discourse of power is essentially a coercive means to inscribe sameness. Yet neither side of a simple 'dichotomy' between 'oppressor' and 'liberator' does justice to the texts, which, as Margaret Mitchell rightly notes, require 'more complex, mixed, and nuanced portraits of one who offers no simple social legacy' (Mitchell 1996: 547, on Elliott 1994).[82]

While I cannot here offer a detailed study of all the relevant topics, many of which have been the subject of lengthy studies,[83] it is important briefly to consider what the evidence suggests about the extent to which the corporate solidarity in Christ has practical social consequences. Again, neither side of a simple dichotomy – 'all change' or 'no change' – does justice to the material. It is certainly inadequate to reduce the solidarity and unity achieved in baptism and celebrated in the Lord's supper to a matter of equal access to salvation, or standing in the eyes of God.[84] In the

81. Cf. also, e.g., Horsley 1998; Callaghan 2000, who describes 'Paul's *ekklēsia* in 1 Corinthians' as 'an emancipatory project ... Paul directs the community of addressees in emancipatory theory and practice' (p. 216).

82. Cf. also the comments on feminist approaches to Paul by Kittredge 2000. On slavery note the response of Stowers 1998 (to Horsley 1998), e.g.: 'Horsley tends to write as if there were only two positions: staunch social conservatives who find a conservative Paul and social progressives who find a socially progressive Paul' (p. 295). A cautious picture of Paul (and specifically his ethics) as liberating – sometimes – is given by Blount 2001: 119–57.

83. A few examples include: on the Jew/Gentile identity distinction, Boyarin 1994; Barclay 1996a, 1996b; on slave and free, Bartchy 1973; Gayer 1976; Horsley 1998; Braxton 2000; on male and female, Fiorenza 1983; Witherington 1988.

84. Cf. also Witherington 1981: 593 with n. 2, 601–602.

terms used above (§4.1.1), I suggest that corporate solidarity in Christ implies, for Paul, neither the *erasure* of previous distinctions nor merely their *encompassing* within a new sphere of belonging, but rather their *relativization* or revaluation, with real social implications.[85]

These issues will reappear, with particular reference to the questions Boyarin raises about Paul's eradication of Jewish cultural difference, in ch. 6. For now, an initial indication of Paul's stance can be derived from 1 Cor. 7.17-24, where, in the context of a discussion about relations between men and women, Paul illustrates his point with reference to circumcised and uncircumcised, slave and free, thus bringing together again the three pairs from Gal. 3.28 (so Bartchy 1973: 162–65). Referring first to circumcised and uncircumcised, Paul insists that people should neither remove nor seek the marks of circumcision: these markers of identity remain as they are, just as elsewhere where Paul indicates his continued sense of his own and others' identity as Jew or Gentile (Rom. 9.3; 2 Cor. 11.22; Gal. 2.14-15). Yet these marks of identity are now 'nothing' (οὐδέν) – a declaration repeated almost verbatim in Gal. 5.6; and 6.15 – since their significance has been transcended by a new mode of belonging, being in Christ, in which Jew and Gentile together constitute a 'new creation' (Gal. 6.15; see Horrell 2000b: 337–39). This relativizes Jewish identity insofar as it redraws the essential boundary between insider and outsider around those in Christ, without requiring that all insiders adopt or accept Jewish identity-defining practices: specifically Jewish patterns of conduct can be preserved and valued (Rom. 14.1– 15.13) except where they threaten the unity of the new community (Gal. 2.11-21). (See further §6.2.)

As far as slave and free are concerned, again social status need not be changed and is insignificant, at least in theory, insofar as it affects participation and role within the community (μή σοι μελέτω, 1 Cor. 7.21).[86] Indeed, 'worldly' statuses are reversed, revalued, from the Christian perspective (cf. Martin 1990: 65–66): the slave is Christ's freedperson, the freeperson is Christ's slave; all have one (new) owner, having been bought by God for a price (7.22-23; cf. 6.20). Nonetheless, Paul states the exception that slaves should take the opportunity of freedom if it becomes

---

85. Cf. Dunn 1993: 207, who suggests that the distinctions referred to in Gal. 3.28 had not been 'removed' but rather 'relativized'. It is a more open question whether the original formulation of the baptismal tradition was intended to express a more profound reunification (cf. Meeks 1974). But the ways in which Paul proceeds elsewhere to deal with relations between Jew and Greek, slave and free, male and female, gives some indication of what he (for better or worse) took to be the social implications of the declaration.

86. But for some of the practical barriers to participation, see Glancy 1998.

available.[87] The general exhortation to 'remain in your calling' – where 'calling' (κλῆσις) may well refer to God's call to life in Christ rather than to social position as a 'vocation' (so Bartchy 1973: 132–59) – does not, then, preclude change in the case of slaves. Nor, while it constitutes the essence of Paul's advice to married and single alike (i.e. don't change that status through either divorce or marriage), does it prohibit changes in marital status too (note the exceptions to the general advice to remain as you are stated in 1 Cor. 7.5, 9, 11, 15, 28, 36, 39). The case of Onesimos also illustrates the case for the revaluation and relativization of social status. Onesimos and Philemon remain owner and slave; or at least if Paul means to request Onesimos' manumission he does so obliquely and does not thereby imply any general programme of universal emancipation.[88] Yet he is also clear that the relationship between the two is henceforth to be defined differently: they are now ἀδελφοί.[89] That this is meant to imply some real change in the character of their relationship is emphasized explicitly by the striking insistence that this brotherhood pertains not only in the Lord (ἐν κυρίῳ) but also in the flesh (ἐν σαρκί) (Phlm. 16), as well as by the instruction that Onesimos is to be welcomed as if he were Paul and any wrong he has done reckoned to Paul's account instead (vv. 17–18). Craig de Vos (2001) suggests that the redefinition of their relationship as now one between ἀδελφοί, with all that that implied, requires a much more radical change than would manumission per se, given that the latter need not fundamentally alter the relationship between master/patron and slave/client. Certainly we cannot suppose that the social relationship between Philemon and Onesimos was to remain unchanged following Onesimos' conversion, yet neither are their identities as master and slave altogether erased.

Paul's interpretation of the implications of 'neither male and female' again indicates a certain qualified acceptance of the principle that distinctions are transcended through unification in Christ.[90] The distinction is neither entirely erased, nor left untouched, by incorporation into the

---

87. This statement depends, of course, on a particular interpretation of the notoriously ambiguous 1 Cor. 7.21b. For arguments in favour of the 'take freedom' interpretation and references to further discussion, see Horrell 1996: 162–66, and on the whole passage, pp. 158–67, also, more recently, Horsley 1998: 182–87.

88. Sara Winter (1987), for example, has argued that Paul does request Onesimos' manumission. Barclay 1991 stresses the reasons for the ambiguity of Paul's position.

89. On the implications of this, see also Petersen 1985: 266–70, 288–89. Callaghan rightly notes that 'fraternal love is a leitmotiv of the epistle' (1997: 49); less convincing is his argument that Onesimos was not actually a slave (see pp. 4–19, 44, 47, 69, etc.).

90. Thus Fiorenza (1983: 236) rightly characterizes 'Paul's impact on women's leadership in the Christian missionary movement' as 'double-edged'. 'On the one hand he affirms Christian equality and freedom ... On the other hand, he subordinates women's behaviour in marriage and in the worship assembly to the interests of Christian mission.'

body of Christ. That the baptismal declaration has some tangible social expression is evident in Paul's mention and acceptance of women leaders and co-workers (Rom. 16.1-16; Phil. 4.2-3), and in his balanced statements concerning the mutual responsibilities of husbands and wives (1 Corinthians 7).[91] Yet 1 Cor. 11.2-16 indicates that Paul felt the need to reaffirm a distinction between the sexes, to be marked in worship by different head attire, and that he did so on the basis of a created and hierarchical order (11.3-9).[92] Even there he counterbalances this 'order' with the affirmation that man and woman are interdependent 'in the Lord' (11.11-12),[93] but he clearly could not countenance a situation in which the identity-distinction between men and women was erased and no longer evidently marked.[94]

This nuanced, or one might say compromised, position regarding the social consequences of the new solidarity announced in baptism and celebrated in the Lord's supper, can also be seen in Paul's response to the Corinthians' eucharistic practice: the celebration itself must be a proper rather than merely symbolic meal, devoid of distinctions and divisions;[95] yet those who currently overindulge should satisfy their hunger 'at home' (1 Cor. 11.34). In other words, the ecclesial space in which the celebration occurs is one in which the implications of corporate solidarity in Christ should be evident, but life 'in the world' also continues, and slaves and masters, those higher or lower on the social scale, continue to have different opportunities and resources. This ecclesial space, it should be stressed, is not only a matter of soteriology, of equal access to salvation before God, but is also a social, political space, a space in which the social relationships and interactions of community members are newly conceived and restructured in the light of the world-view and ethos generated by the

---

91.   Note the parallel and reciprocal address to both men and women in 1 Cor. 7.2, 3, 4, 8, 10-11, 12-13, 14, 15, 16, 28, 32-34. Meeks (1974: 199) remarks on the number of almost 'monotonously parallel statements' here. On the wider questions of women's leadership and participation in the Pauline churches, see further Fiorenza 1990, 1983; Thurston 1998: 30–61.

92.   See the more detailed discussion in Horrell 1996: 168–76. Among those who argue that Paul is seeking here to reinforce the created distinction between male and female are Murphy-O'Connor 1980: 490; Fee 1987: 497–98; Jervis 1993 (esp. pp. 235–38).

93.   Watson 2000b (cf. also 2000a: 40–89) makes the statement of interdependence in 1 Cor. 11.11-12 central to the passage, arguing that the hierarchical and subordinationist language in vv. 3 and 7-9 actually plays a less significant role in determining the practice Paul commends. Nonetheless, Paul does begin his argument with the assertions of vv. 3-9, such that vv. 11-12 appear as a complementary and subsequent qualification rather than the central principle of the entire section.

94.   I omit treatment of 14.34-35, which seems to me most likely an interpolation; see Horrell 1996: 184–95.

95.   Cf. nn. 29 and 42 above, and esp. Lampe 1991b: 203–205; Engberg-Pedersen 1993: 110–11.

Christian myth; however, neither is the ἐκκλησία (yet) a space which encompasses the whole of life.[96] Corporate solidarity in Christ does not leave the sphere of everyday life untouched but neither does it entirely revolutionize it: Jews and Greeks, slaves and free, men and women, share intimate and commensual fellowship and are bound together with an egalitarian and familial identity as ἀδελφοί; but at the same time they continue to bear their existing identity, with its implications for the structuring of everyday life only some of which are transformed or negated in the light of the newly created solidarity. In part this may be connected with Paul's eschatology: for now, life in 'this present evil age' (Gal. 1.4) goes on, even if those who live in the world should do so as if they do so no longer (ὡς μή, 1 Cor. 7.30-31). But it is not clear that even in the eschatological fulfilment does Paul expect these identity distinctions to disappear: there is no hint (leaving aside Gal. 3.28) that Paul envisages a day when male and female will become merged into one androgynous (or male) identity, unlike the tradition recorded by Clement of Alexandria, among others (see n. 19 above). Nonetheless, whether or not Paul entirely accepts them, the impulses expressed in the baptismal declaration, the Lord's supper, the identification of believers as ἀδελφοί, and so on, provide the basis for a certain 'pull' towards an incorporationist egalitarianism within the tradition, notwithstanding other contrary forces and tendencies (see further below).

4.6 *Conclusion*

The thesis that the first and most fundamental moral norm in Pauline ethics is that of corporate solidarity is now hopefully well established: we have seen how this sense of solidarity, of many becoming one body, is prominent in various ways in the practices and discourse Paul describes and presents.[97] The various aspects we have examined can justifiably be claimed to have a central and fundamental role in constructing the ethos of the Christian community: baptism and Lord's supper are *the* two major

---

96. Another fruitful way to explore this tension is found in Strecker's (1999) application of Victor Turner's theory of liminality and communitas to the Pauline texts: 'Communitas ist die soziale Ausformung von' Liminalität. Sie begegnet nach Turner nicht nur in rituellen Schwellenphasen, sondern kann über das Ritual hinaus in die sozialen Strukturen einer Gruppe bzw. einer Gesellschaft hineinwirken, sie mit anti-strukturellen, egalitären Idealen durchsetzen und so transformieren' (p. 300). Thus the values of communitas (including a sense of *Egalität*) 'impregnate' everyday life and social structure (cf. p. 450: 'die über den rituellen Rahmen hinausgehende Imprägnierung des Alltags mit Communitaswerten'; similarly, p. 358). Cf. also MacDonald 1988: 61–71.

97. Cf. also the conclusion of Schmeller 1995: 95: that the ethos of the Pauline communities is 'von einer solidarischen Gruppenidentität geprägt'.

rituals of early Christianity; the designation ἀδελφοί is the most frequent appellation used in Paul's letters; appeals for unity are well established in Pauline paraenesis and are especially prominent when problems of division loom. Moreover, it is clear that this corporate solidarity is intended to convey moral implications, as we can see, for example, when Paul stresses the other's identity as ἀδελφός in order to press an ethical demand, or in the ways in which he opposes division and seeks to construct a new unity through the reversal of conventional hierarchies, the transcendance of former distinctions, and the establishment of mutual and equal other-regard. Yet it is notable that these facets and themes receive little attention in studies of Pauline ethics. We have already mentioned the lack of interest in ἀδελφός-language. Baptism and Lord's supper may be treated, as by Schrage, as the 'sacramental basis' for Pauline ethics, linked with the christological basis (Schrage 1988: 174–77), but this is often done without any focus on the moral significance of the kind of social achievement that baptism and Lord's supper represent in their construction of a boundary-transcending corporate solidarity.[98]

I have also claimed that this form of human solidarity contains egalitarian impulses. These are evident in the declaration of the transcendance of distinctions in baptism (although this does not, at least in Paul's view, imply the erasure of all such distinctions); in the unity expressed through sharing a common meal; in the emphasis on the fact that many have become one body, specifically through the reversal of existing hierarchies; in the appeal for an equality of regard and care among all the members of the body (1 Cor. 12.25); and in the predominant designation of all community members as ἀδελφοί.[99] Yet at the same time it must be stressed that these are *impulses*.[100] As such they are important factors within the tradition, which exert a certain moral and community-shaping force, but their presence does not imply that the churches to which Paul wrote were in fact egalitarian communities.[101] Nor should other impulses and modifications be ignored: Paul himself modifies the impulse with regard to male and female, by insisting on created difference and its

---

98. Cf. Blount 2001: 123–25, etc., who emphasizes the 'boundary-breaking' character of Paul's ethics.

99. Cf. Schmeller 1995: 'Die Gemeinden entwickelten einen hohen Grad von Einheit und Gleichwertigkeit, die allerdings fortwährend gefährdet waren' (p. 92). In the case of both the Pauline communities and the Graeco-Roman associations, though more strongly in the former, Schmeller argues, 'gehörte eine grundsätzliche Gleichwertigkeit ihrer Mitglieder zur Identität der Gruppe' (p. 94).

100. Cf. Schäfer's suggestion that 'der Begriff "Bruderschaft" eine Tendenz zur Egalität anzeigt' (1989: 444); and Strecker's mention of 'egalitären Züge' (and also 'konservativen' ones) in the Pauline corpus (1999: 300, 303, 358, 407, *et passim*; see pp. 300–452).

101. Cf. further Elliott 2003, on which see also n. 3 above; Horrell 1996: 124–25.

implications in ecclesial worship (1 Cor. 11.2-16); and alongside the identification of himself and others as equally ranked ἀδελφοί he also presents and reinforces the view of himself as authoritative leader, apostle and founding-father.

So the degree to which the corporate solidarity constructed in Christ implies equality and the transcendance of previous distinctions is limited, though significant. The egalitarian impulses are tempered by other tendencies and realities, and the 'former' identity-distinctions, while certainly subject to revaluation and relativization in light of the new solidarity in Christ, are not simply erased. And, as Elliott (2003: 182) rightly insists, the fundamental concern is not with equality per se, but with oneness and unity, created by incorporation into Christ. The extent to which solidarity in Christ transforms social relationships is also limited by the ongoing realities of life in the world, alongside life ἐν ἐκκλησίᾳ. The boundary between the two cannot clearly or easily be drawn, for in one sense the ecclesial realities impinge on the whole of life, but the newly established ecclesial realities do not transform all aspects of social location and interaction. Nonetheless, despite the ambivalence and ambiguities regarding the practical implications, it is clear enough that corporate solidarity, based on a vision of incorporation into Christ, many becoming one, is a basic metanorm in Pauline ethics, an essential foundation for the other aspects of Paul's ethical instruction.

We might find in this some vindication of Habermas's argument that all moralities revolve around 'equality of respect, solidarity, and the common good' and thus express a 'common core' of moral intuitions which are implicit in the very presuppositions of all communicative action (1990: 201; §2.2 above). Also comparable, though conceived of in very different ways, is the aim to reach a consensus, for all to have 'the same mind' (§4.3), a form of unity which for neither Paul nor Habermas implies uniformity or sameness. Furthermore, the specific form of solidarity Paul seeks to foster – a form based on the idea of incorporating diverse groups into a new unity (in Christ), where all are siblings (ἀδελφοί) and thus warrant the same care and respect – bears closer comparison with the liberal democratic values of equality and fraternity.[102] It remains to be seen whether Paul demonstrates the kind of 'tolerance' which permits a circumscribed pluralism, and thus suggests another point of comparison with liberal values (see ch. 6). Clearly it would be anachronistic to claim Paul as some kind of first-century anticipation of the French Revolution; but it is equally implausible to deny the similarities (which might reflect, in some part, the

---

102.   The third member of the famous triad, freedom, though sometimes claimed as a (or even *the*) fundamental value of Pauline ethics (e.g. Verhey 1984: 107–108), is, I think, less determinative for Paul's *ethics* than is often supposed; see §6.3.2 below.

Wirkungsgeschichte of these early Christian traditions).[103] Hauerwas's polemic against such liberal ideals, in contrast, would seem to under-estimate precisely these (admittedly partial) similarities. Nonetheless, it is equally clear that Paul's approach to community-construction is essentially akin to Hauerwas's communitarian-type ethics: even where ideas and images are shared with the wider world (the sibling-role, the image of the body, etc.) they acquire their significance and meaning only through their incorporation into the particular story which gives this community its identity and ethos. The basis for solidarity, for the construction of community, as the central Christian rituals show, is found in Paul's Christology: as believers make the story of Christ their own, participating in his death and new life, so they leave behind the old world, and become members of one body, in Christ.

---

103. *Pace* Elliott 2003: 205: 'However much we moderns and heirs of the American and French revolutions cherish the hard won prize of political and legal (and in some domains economic and social) equality, we must as honest historians acknowledge that this is a development of the modern era and not to be found in the societies and even mentalities of antiquity.' And that includes the 'material traces or literary record of the nascent Jesus movement'.

Chapter 5

PURITY, BOUNDARIES AND IDENTITY: THE RHETORIC OF DISTINCTION

The solidarity Paul seeks to generate in the communities to which he writes is the solidarity of a particular community, depicted as a pure and holy community standing in sharp distinction from the evil world in which it is located. Solidarity in Christ is what 'we' share, and this distinguishes 'us' from 'them'. The purpose of this chapter is to explore this sense of distinction and separation from the world, and to consider the ways in which this rhetoric of holiness constructs a sense of distinct group identity, drawing an ideological boundary between community and world. Paul's sexual ethics, developed most fully in 1 Corinthians 5–7, will be a particular focus, as will his strictures against idolatry, and the ways in which the theme of union with Christ appears again in relation to the specific concerns of this chapter.[1] We shall also consider how this sense of distinct identity correlates with patterns of external social interaction, insofar as these appear to be permitted or proscribed by Paul. This focus on the language of purity and separation will also be counterbalanced by a brief consideration of the extent to which ethical values are – contrary to what the rhetoric of distinction might imply – shared with the wider world. The implications of what emerges for our understanding of Pauline ethics in the context of contemporary debate will be assessed, though these implications will be further considered at a later point in the study (ch. 9).

5.1 *The Language of Distinction*

The obvious place to begin a consideration of the language of distinction is with the theme of holiness. Paul's frequent designation of Christian converts as ἅγιοι (holy ones) indicates that they are to regard themselves as

---

1. Some of the material in this and the following chapter was originally presented as a seminar paper at the research seminar on 'Idolatry', Department of Theology, University of Durham, May 2002; for publication details see Horrell forthcoming.

set apart and devoted to their God.[2] The use of the adjective ἅγιος to denote something sacred to the gods is found in Greek literature from the fifth century onwards,[3] though much more frequent, and influential on Paul, is of course the use of holiness language in the Jewish scriptures, especially in the priestly traditions.[4] In 1 Thessalonians, Paul's earliest letter, in a short section of what is often thought to be 'traditional' ethical instruction (1 Thess. 4.3-8),[5] this sense of holiness as distinction emerges clearly: the noun ἁγιασμός appears three times (4.3, 4, 7: half of its occurrences in Paul are here).[6] This ἁγιασμός stands in contrast to the sexual immorality which characterizes those outside, 'the Gentiles (τὰ ἔθνη) who do not know God' (4.5).[7] Unlike these Gentiles, who act on the basis of 'lustful desire' (4.5), Christians are 'to learn how to control their own vessel in holiness and honour' (4.4). The precise meaning of this latter phrase is much debated and notoriously ambiguous, particularly concerning the intended referent of σκεῦος (vessel), which might refer either to a wife (as in 1 Pet. 3.7) or to the man's own body, specifically his sexual organ, the penis. Linked with this, and also much discussed, is the meaning of κτᾶσθαι, which might be rendered 'possess', 'control', or 'acquire', depending in part on the sense given to σκεῦος.[8] But the contrast between lustful licentiousness (outside the community) and holy self-control (inside) is plain.

2. Twenty-five times: e.g. Rom. 1.7; 1 Cor. 1.2; 2 Cor. 1.1. This designation is, however, considerably less frequent than ἀδελφοί; cf. above §4.2 with nn. 46–49.

3. BDAG, 10, citing e.g. Herodotus 2.41, 44 (cf. also LSJ, 9; O. Proktsch, *TWNT* 1: 87–88).

4. Cf. Exod. 22.30; Lev. 11.44-45; 19.2; Num. 15.40; Ezra 8.28; *4 Ezra* 8.57 (LXX); Tob. 8.15 (LXX), etc. For overviews of the OT and NT material respectively, see D.P. Wright, *ABD* 3: 237–49, R. Hodgson, *ABD* 3: 249–54. Hodgson notes the particular prominence of holiness language in the LXX, compared with its rather infrequent use in other non-Jewish or Christian Greek literature: 'It is in the LXX, in fact, that *hagios* developed luxuriantly (ca. 700 occurrences), spawning a full family of cognates.'

5. Cf., e.g., Meeks 1993: 142, who refers to 'the traditional rules of marriage of which Paul reminds the converts in Thessalonica'; Holtz 1986: 150–51. Certainly Paul indicates that he is reminding the Thessalonians of previous instruction (see 1 Thess. 4.1, 2, 6, 11; Yarbrough 1985: 65–66), and this concise reminder seems to have little specific connection with problems or issues facing the Thessalonian churches at the time Paul writes (though for discussion of the various possibilities and suggestions, see Malherbe 2000: 235–37).

6. See also Rom. 6.19, 22; 1 Cor. 1.30.

7. Cf. the parallel in Jer. 10.25: 'the nations (הגוים/ἔθνη) that do not know you'. Cf. also Gal. 4.8-9 for the view of Gentile converts as those who previously did not know God.

8. Cf. Malherbe 2000: 226: 'This is one of the most disputed texts in the entire letter.' For a strong argument in favour of a reference to the male sexual organ, on the basis (partly) of the use of כלי in 4Q416, see Elgvin 1997. Holtz 1986: 156–58 and Malherbe 2000: 224–29 favour a reference to a wife.

A similar sense of distinction in contrast to 'the Gentiles' is found in references to the turning away from idolatry that denotes (Gentile) conversion to Christianity. The Thessalonians' conversion is concisely described as a 'turning to God from idols' (1 Thess. 1.9) while the Corinthians are similarly reminded that when they were Gentiles (ἔθνη) they 'were enticed and led astray to dumb idols' (1 Cor. 12.2). The incompatibility of the 'temple of God' and 'idols' is forcefully stressed in 2 Cor. 6.16. And idolatry is clearly a key theme in the story of humanity's turn from God as depicted at length in the opening chapter of Romans (Rom. 1.19-32; note e.g. v. 23).[9]

There are countless other texts where one can find a sense of distinction between sanctified Christians and the immoral world being sharply drawn. Some of these, as we have just seen, represent the distinction in relation to specific themes – sexual immorality and idolatry – others sketch a more general contrast between insiders and outsiders, such as the stark distinction implied in the description of the Thessalonians as 'children of the light and of the day, not of the night or of darkness' (1 Thess. 5.5; cf. also Phil. 2.15); the Thessalonian converts have escaped the wrath to come (1.10; 5.9), unlike those who continue in ignorance of the one true God (cf. also 1 Cor. 1.18). Much of this material is focused on the *transition* which converts have made in leaving one world behind and becoming part of another (cf. §4.1.1 above). The references to holiness in Romans 6, for example, come in the context of a passage that depicts the new life in Christ as a transfer of ownership, from slavery to sin, impurity and lawlessness, to slavery to God, which brings righteousness and ἁγιασμός (6.15-23; cf. 1 Cor. 6.20; 7.23). Particularly extensive depictions of these contrasting realms may be seen in the so-called catalogues of vices and virtues that appear at a number of places in Paul's letters (on these catalogues see further §5.5 below). 1 Cor. 6.9-11, for example, contains a lengthy list of the kinds of sinful people who will not inherit the kingdom of God, with a prominent focus (again) on sins of sexual immorality and idolatry, followed by the affirmation that although some of the Corinthians were previously such people, now they have been 'washed, sanctified, justified, in the name of the Lord Jesus Christ and in the Spirit of our God' (v. 11, almost certainly recalling the imagery of baptism). Similarly in Galatians, in the context of an exhortation to live by the Spirit (Gal. 5.16), Paul provides lengthy lists of the vices that characterize 'the works of the flesh (σάρξ)' and the virtues that constitute 'the fruit of the

---

9. Nineteen of the 32 NT uses of words from the εἰδωλ- word-group are in the seven undisputed letters of Paul, mostly clustered in 1 Corinthians 8–10. This word-group does not, however, specifically feature in Rom. 1.19-32, though idols and idolatry are clearly a theme here.

Spirit ($\pi\nu\epsilon\hat{\upsilon}\mu\alpha$)' (Gal. 5.19-23). This language serves as both description and exhortation, both indicative and imperative (cf. Gal. 5.25): it is intended both to describe the character of this community of converts, in contrast to the immoral world from which they have been rescued, and to exhort and to warn them to make sure that their conduct matches this strong description; thus it both affirms and reinforces their new social identity (cf. §3.3).

In his focus on sexual immorality and idolatry, and in his depiction of the immorality of the Gentile world in general, as has long been recognized, Paul echoes themes familiar from Jewish literature.[10] Idolatry, worshipping other gods, is not only a characteristic of the nations who are ignorant of the true God (cf. 2 Kgs 17.24-28; Ps. 79.6; Isa. 44.9-20; Jer. 10.25), but also a most heinous sin into which the people of Israel may disastrously be tempted, as paradigmatically in the story of the golden calf (Exod. 32.1-35). And sexual immorality is frequently linked with idolatry, as a symptom is linked with a cause, an equally disastrous consequence of turning from right devotion to God. This link may have been suggested, for example, in the description of the Israelites' behaviour at the sacrifice before the calf: 'the people sat down to eat and drink, and rose up to revel ($\pi\alpha\acute{\iota}\zeta\epsilon\iota\nu$, לְצַחֵק)' (Exod. 32.6).[11] Certainly Paul draws this link when he cites this verse as part of a warning to the Corinthians not to do like their forefathers (1 Cor. 10.1), not to be idolators ($\mu\eta\delta\grave{\epsilon}$ $\epsilon\grave{\iota}\delta\omega\lambda\omega\lambda\acute{\alpha}\tau\rho\alpha\iota$ $\gamma\acute{\iota}\nu\epsilon\sigma\theta\epsilon$, 10.7) and not to commit sexual immorality ($\mu\eta\delta\grave{\epsilon}$ $\pi\rho\nu\epsilon\acute{\upsilon}\omega\mu\epsilon\nu$, 10.8).[12]

Paul's dependence on Jewish tradition in this regard is probably clearest in the opening of the first main section of Romans (1.19-32), where the critique of Gentile depravity closely parallels similar material in the Wisdom of Solomon, a text dated somewhere between 150BCE and 50CE (Wis. 13–15). Like Paul, the author of Wisdom graphically depicts the foolishness of those who are ignorant of God, and worship instead human-made objects,

---

10. As Yarbrough (1985: 7) notes, Paul's language in 1 Thess. 4.4 ('the Gentiles who do not know God') 'belongs to the language of the Hebrew Bible, where it draws attention to the distinction between Israel and all the other nations of the world'. Yarbrough specifically mentions (p. 7 n. 2) the frequent distinction drawn between 'the Gentiles' ($\tau\alpha$ $\check{\epsilon}\theta\nu\eta$/הגוים) and 'the people of God' ($\acute{o}\lambda\alpha\acute{o}\varsigma$/העם), on which see further G. Bertram and K.L. Schmidt, *TWNT* 2: 362–70. Schmidt notes that the majority of NT uses, like the OT גוים, constitute a 'terminus technicus ... mit dem die Heiden im Gegensatz zu den Juden oder auch im Gegensatz zu den Christen bezeichnet werden' (p. 367). For the juxtaposition of $\lambda\alpha\acute{o}\varsigma$ and $\check{\epsilon}\theta\nu\eta$ in Paul, see esp. the OT citations in Rom. 15.10-11.

11. On the ways in which the rabbis and other Jewish exegetes understood this verse, particularly in terms of taking the verb צחק/$\pi\alpha\acute{\iota}\zeta\epsilon\iota\nu$ to imply a range of sins (including sexual immorality), see Meeks 1982: 67–71.

12. Paul also here draws on Num. 25.1-9, as well as Exodus 32. See further Meeks 1982; Collier 1994, who suggests that Numbers 11 is the main text on which Paul depends here.

and thus are led into all forms of wickedness and sin.[13] Here too we find the conviction that 'the idea of making idols was the beginning of sexual immorality (ἀρχὴ γὰρ πορνείας ἐπίνοια εἰδώλων)' (Wis. 14.12); indeed idolatry is the source and root of all evil (14.27). Paul also echoes this stereotypical Jewish view of the Gentile world in his passing reference to 'Gentile sinners' (ἐξ ἐθνῶν ἁμαρτωλοί), in contrast to those who are 'by nature Jews' (φύσει Ἰουδαῖοι, Gal. 2.15), even though here in Galatians this distinction is echoed only to be immediately problematized.[14] Thus John Barclay observes that

> Paul's perspective on the world ... operates in line with the traditional Scriptural excoriation of Gentiles ... Paul's most common construction of his world is in terms of the simple biblical division between Jews and 'the nations' ... he retains to the end of his life the assumption that the non-Jewish world is a cess-pit of godlessness and vice. (Barclay 1995: 107)

Despite the variation among Paul's letters, this is a perspective that occurs throughout. However, it should not be one-sidedly stressed, to the exclusion of other Pauline perspectives on the world and on outsiders: it needs to be interpreted in conjunction with the evidence indicating the extent of open social interaction and shared ethical values (§5.4–5.5 below) and in the light of the positive concern for, and depictions of, outsiders (see ch. 8).

The language of separation and distinction, with its stark contrasts between 'us' and 'them', light and dark, has also been linked more specifically with sectarian groups in both the modern and the ancient worlds. Thus the Qumran texts form an obvious point of comparison, notably in their strong distinction between insiders and outsiders, between 'the sons of light' and 'the sons of darkness' (1QS 1.9-10; cf. 3.20-21, etc.).[15] Many authors have also drawn on contemporary models of religious sects in order to illuminate the social context and experience which this language represents.[16] Most pertinent, however, for our present concerns, is a consideration of this language in terms of its role in the construction of *identity* (cf. §3.3).

---

13. Paul is, however, more specific about the sexual sins that follow from this failure to acknowledge God and consequent idolatry: cf. Rom. 1.26-27; Wis. 14.24-26.

14. Cf. Longenecker 1996: 81, who refers to Paul's use of 'stereotypical depictions of insiders and outsiders to the covenant – stereotypes common in much of Jewish literature of the time but soon to be disqualified by Paul'. See also Barclay 1988: 77 n. 7, who cites, *inter alia*, Ps. 9.18 (LXX); *Pss. Sol.* 2.1–2; 17.25; *Jub.* 23.23-24; 24.28 (and cf. 22.16); *4 Ezra* 3.28-36; Mt. 5.47 with Lk. 6.32; Mt. 26.45 with Lk. 18.32. Note also Tob. 13.8 (LXX).

15. See, e.g., Watson 1986: 41–43; Esler 1994: 70–91.

16. The first detailed treatment was by Scroggs 1975; for further references see Horrell 1999: 69–70, 91.

5.2 *Distinction and Positive Group Identity*

I have already suggested that one important aspect of a framework for understanding Paul's ethics is that of identity, specifically social identity as studied in social identity theory (§3.3). Fundamental to social identity theory were the discoveries of the early experiments carried out by Muzafer Sherif in the 1950s. These showed that simply categorizing people into groups led to an increase of positive bonds within the group and, in some situations, to hostility towards those outside the group (Sherif 1956; Turner 1996: 14–16; Esler 1998: 42). Since there were no factors other than membership of the group itself which distinguished insiders from outsiders, these experiments showed that merely the sense of belonging to a certain group can engender certain attitudes towards those categorized as insiders or outsiders. Henri Tajfel's research led to the formulation of two principles to describe this process of categorization, 'accentuation and assimilation: people tend to exaggerate the differences between categories and simultaneously minimise the differences within categories' (Brown 1996: 170). Group members are described in ways which sharpen the similarities they share, while heightening their distinction from outsiders. This categorization process thus leads to what is known as 'stereotyping', whether positive (of group members) or negative (of outsiders) (see Hogg and Abrams 1988: 68–78).

The social identity theory developed by Tajfel and his followers further proposed that it was 'a psychological requirement that groups provide their members with a positive social identity and that positive aspects of social identity were inherently comparative in nature, deriving from evaluative comparisons between social groups' (Turner 1996: 16; cf. Brown 1996: 179). While individuals may seek to enhance their social identity and status by leaving one group and joining another, this strategy is not possible in certain situations, and in any case, those intrinsically committed to a certain group, or who exercise leadership within it, will rather seek to enhance the positive identity of their own group vis-à-vis the outgroup(s) (cf. Esler 1998: 49–55).

From this perspective, the language of distinction, as I have called it, may be understood as an attempt to reinforce a strong sense of positive group identity, and to strengthen the sense of distinction in terms of a boundary between insiders and outsiders. Indeed, without drawing on social identity theory as such, this is how Larry Yarbrough (1985) interprets the treatment of marriage and sexual morality in Paul and in Jewish moral traditions: the references to Gentile immorality (cf. 1 Thess. 4.4) claim moral superiority for the in-group and serve to distinguish the group from the rest of the world.[17] The fact that such stark depictions of the contrasts between insiders and outsiders are often found in groups which may be described as sects may readily be explained on the basis that such groups are generally new, small, minority groups, whose membership is based on voluntary commitment rather than birth and inheritance, and whose status and existence is often fragile and vulnerable. Other forms of ethnic identity can also come under threat from powerful external cultural forces, whether that power comes from violent oppression or from the attractions of cultural alternatives.[18] In all these situations, then, when identity is especially fragile, there is evidently a particular need to reinforce a strong sense of positive group identity and (thus) to assure group members that their membership of the group is to be highly valued, and not compromised.

In terms of the boundary- and identity-distinction between Christians and Gentiles, as we have seen, Paul draws on the typically Jewish distinction between on the one hand the idolatry, sexual immorality and other sins which characterize 'the nations', and on the other the holiness and devotion to the one true God which characterize insiders. What Paul does, however, is to redraw the boundary around the people of God, those 'inside' the group, such that it now encompasses all who are in Christ, both Jews and Gentiles. Being in Christ, as we have already seen (ch. 4), is the basis for the solidarity of this new community. Thus, as Barclay remarks, 'Paul's success in winning Gentile converts does not cause him to redraw his conceptual map of the world, simply to move the chosen few among the Gentiles into the territory traditionally ascribed to Jews' (1996a: 388). As we have already had cause to note (§1.2; §4.2), Paul describes the (positive) identity of the Christian converts in thoroughly Jewish terms.

More complicated to assess, therefore, is the way in which Paul draws the boundary between the Christian community and Israel. That he draws such a boundary is clear enough, for example, in 1 Cor. 1.22-23; and 10.32, two texts where we find a proto-sociological designation of Christians as a distinct group, distinguished from Jews on the one hand and Greeks on the other. In essence, as Philip Esler (1998) has shown in a reading of Galatians informed by social identity theory, Paul claims for his converts the positive identity descriptors traditionally ascribed to Israel, notably 'righteousness' (see Esler 1998: 141–77), and claims that the gospel of Christ enables this positive identity to be attained in a way which was impossible under the old order. Thus, without Christ, Jews as well as

---

17. Cf. also Martin 1995a: 169: 'The condemnation of porneia in Jewish circles was a way of solidifying the boundary between the chosen people and everyone else with their idols and loose morals: porneia was something "they" did.'

18. As, of course, in the various attempts of Jews to negotiate a relationship with the forces – both of violence and of cultural attraction – of Hellenism (see esp. Barclay 1996a).

Gentiles, those who have the law and those without the law, are enslaved under the power of sin and stand guilty before God, despite the zeal which the Jews show for righteousness (Rom. 1.18–3.20; 10.1-13). In Christ, however, and empowered by the Spirit, Christians are able to be the kind of righteous, holy people which the law indicates as required by God but lacks the power to create (Rom. 8.3-4). Paul promotes an essentially Jewish view of what positive group identity entails – though this requires some spiritualizing and occasionally convoluted biblical exegesis, for example, in relation to circumcision (Rom. 2.28-29; Gal. 3.16) – but effectively claims that only Christians are truly able to *be* such people (cf. e.g. Gal. 3.1-5; 3.29–4.7; 4.21-31; Phil. 3.3, etc.).

The use of such language of distinction to denote positive group identity raises further questions concerning the ways in which this distinct identity is actually 'marked', both in ideological and in practical terms, and how this relates to ethical instruction. In other words, how does Paul consider that Christian converts are to show that they are holy, that they have transferred out of the world of idolatry and immorality and are under new ownership, under the lordship of Christ? To answer these questions we shall turn to some resources from the field of anthropology and examine in particular Paul's treatment of sexual ethics and idolatry in 1 Corinthians.

5.3 *Boundaries and the Body: Sexual Ethics and Idolatry*

In a now classic treatment of the subject of ethnic groups and boundaries, anthropologist Frederik Barth insisted, on the basis of a wide range of empirical studies, that ethnic identities and distinctions

> do not depend on an absence of mobility, contact and information but do entail social processes of exclusion and incorporation whereby discrete categories are maintained *despite* changing participation and membership in the course of individual life histories ... ethnic distinctions do not depend on an absence of social interation and acceptance ... cultural differences can persist despite inter-ethnic contact and interdependence. (Barth 1969: 9–10)

The main problem with previous studies of ethnicity, Barth argued, was that they had presumed that ethnic identity was sustained by the *isolation* which followed from 'racial difference, cultural difference, social separa- tion and language barriers, spontaneous and organized enmity' (p. 11). Barth's key move in shifting attention to the question of boundary- maintenance was to argue that only 'some cultural features are used by the actors as signals and emblems of differences, others are ignored, and in some relationships radical differences are played down and denied' (p. 14). In other words, just as (in certain situations) certain aspects of a person's complex identity can be(come) salient, or not, so too the maintenance of distinct identity does not depend on distinctiveness or, still less, isolation in all aspects of social life, but only in those areas taken as definitive of identity and difference. Maintenance of a group boundary requires 'not only criteria and signals for identification, but also a structuring of interaction which allows the persistence of cultural differences' (p. 16). Barth divides these key indicators of distinction into two main types: 'overt signals or signs' (dress, language, etc.) and 'basic value orientations' ('standards of morality', etc., p. 14).

Barth's ideas cannot, of course, simply be applied as a whole to the Pauline letters and the early Christian groups. These groups are not exactly 'ethnic' groups in the usual sense, not being 'largely biologically self-perpetuating' (Barth 1969: 10), but rather comprise members from diverse ethnic backgrounds, who retain a sense of their original ethnic identity (in Paul's case, see Rom. 9.3; 2 Cor. 11.22; Gal. 2.15). Moreover, in these newly formed groups, a sense of 'Christian' identity is only in the process of developing and taking shape (see Horrell 2002b). Nonetheless, Barth's ideas are relevant insofar as the early Christian groups are ones in which being 'in Christ', being a member of this group, is taken (at least by Paul) to denote one's 'basic, most general, identity' (Barth 1969: 13). This category of belonging is so fundamental that it defines the boundary between insider and outsider (cf. 1 Cor. 7.39) and relativizes other distinctions, like that between circumcised and uncircumcised, such that they can be described as 'nothing' (1 Cor. 7.19; Gal. 5.6).

What then are the 'overt signals' or 'basic value orientations' which Paul deems essential to the distinct identity of the Christian group? I shall seek to answer this question in a somewhat roundabout way, by looking at the ways in which Paul addresses issues of sexual morality and idolatry in 1 Corinthians before drawing out pertinent conclusions.

Paul's most detailed discourse on sex and sexual ethics is in 1 Corinthians 5–7, three chapters connected together by a concern with πορνεία, sexual immorality (5.1; 6.13, 18; 7.2) and where Paul develops in more detail the instruction concisely expressed in 1 Thess. 4.3-8 (ἀπέχεσθαι ὑμᾶς ἀπὸ τῆς πορνείας, κτλ.) (cf. Yarbrough 1985: 89–90).[19] Chapter 5 of 1 Corinthians deals with a case of incest which Paul finds outrageous: a man from within the congregation 'has' (ἔχειν) his father's wife, that is, has an ongoing relationship (of marriage or concubinage) with his step-mother.[20]

---

19. I have learned much from the dissertation of Alistair May (2001), which explores the ways in which Paul's sexual ethics in 1 Corinthians 5–7 contributes to the formation of early Christian identity. I cite this work with reference to chapter and section (rather than page) numbers, since it has been accessible to me on a CD kindly supplied by the author.

20. Most commentators agree that the present tense of ἔχειν implies an ongoing relationship, and that the phrase γυναῖκα τοῦ πατρός designates the stepmother (rather than

Paul's level of shock and concern is indicated in this opening verse, with his report that this behaviour is a matter of public knowledge and hence affects the standing and reputation of the group ($\dot{\alpha}$κούεται),[21] and his declaration that such immorality is 'not [tolerated] even among the Gentiles'.[22] It is indeed the case that such a sexual relationship was proscribed in both Jewish and Roman law[23] (a point to which we shall return in §5.5), though Paul's concern is not to appeal to shared ethical norms but rather to sharpen the sense of shame the congregation ought to feel: you are meant to be a holy people in the midst of an immoral world, but here among you is a form of behaviour not tolerated even among the Gentiles!

As Alistair May has persuasively and incisively shown (May 2001: ch. 4), Paul does not deal with this scandal in terms of an immoral *act*, but rather in terms which connect much more with issues of identity, with the offender as an immoral *person*, a πόρνος. (Indeed, it is noteworthy, as May observes, that the so-called vice-catalogues in 5.10; 5.11; and 6.9-11 list types of sinful people not actual vices themselves.) His action is such as to (re)define him as a πόρνος and not an $\dot{\alpha}$δελφός (cf. 5.11). 'The one who has done this' (5.2) is in the midst of the community when he should be outside, since by definition πόρνοι belong in the world (cf. 5.9-10) and not in the church. In terms of his identity, therefore, as revealed by his actions, he is misplaced. In Mary Douglas's terms he is 'dirt', matter which is out of place and thus disruptive of the right ordering of experience and the world (Douglas 1966: 2). Paul's explicit concern, moreover, is not with what we might call 'individual ethics', but rather with the effect of such a misplaced person on the identity and purity of the group. Drawing clearly on the language and imagery of the Jewish scriptures (see esp. Rosner 1994: 61–93), he describes the presence of the offender as 'old leaven' which leavens

---

natural mother), as in Lev. 18.8 (note the distinction drawn there between vv. 7 and 8). Whether the relationship was one of marriage or something less formal is uncertain. See e.g. Conzelmann 1975: 96; Schrage 1991: 369; Thiselton 2000: 386; May 2001 §4.2.3.

21.   Note here the distinction between the more private 'hearing' implied in $\dot{\alpha}$κούω (1 Cor. 11.18; cf. 1.11) and the passive $\dot{\alpha}$κούεται. On this point see esp. May 2001 §4.2.1.

22.   A verb needs to be supplied here: the suggestions include 'not found' (NRSV; cf. Schrage 1991: 367, 369, 'nicht … vorkommt'), 'unheard of' (Conzelmann 1975: 94) and 'not tolerated' (Thiselton 2000: 385). Neither of the former two suggestions would reflect the true situation, objectively, since cases of such incest were both known and reported 'among the Gentiles' (see e.g. Cicero, *Pro Cluentio* 5–6 [§§11-17]; Martial, *Epig.* 4.16; further May 2001 §4.2.3; Thiselton 2000: 385–86), making 'tolerated' an attractive suggestion. Nonetheless, Paul's rhetorical point is more important here than any objective reporting of what is actually the case in the Gentile world.

23.   Cf., e.g., Héring 1962: 34, who mentions Lev. 18.8 and Gaius, *Inst.* 1.63; Fee 1987: 200–201; South 1992: 29–30; Thiselton 2000: 385–86, with further primary and secondary sources mentioned there.

the whole lump (5.6-7), quoting a proverbial saying which he also repeats verbatim in Gal. 5.9: 'a little leaven leavens the whole lump (of dough)' (μικρὰ ζύμη ὅλον τὸ φύραμα ζυμοῖ). As May rightly insists, following Mitton (1973), and despite many modern translations (e.g. NRSV, NIV), ζύμη should be rendered 'leaven', not 'yeast', and understood to refer specifically to the character of the former.[24] Leaven comprises a portion of previously made dough which enables the raising effect of yeast to be reproduced through the incorporation of a piece of the old dough into a new batch. At the same time as this was a useful technique it was also risky, since any impurities or pollutants in the leaven would be transferred into the new dough, where they would come to permeate and infect the whole (Mitton 1973: 339–40). The Israelites' feast of unleavened bread thus served, at one level, periodically to start afresh and thus avoid the risk of contamination (Exod. 12.15-20). This explains why in the New Testament 'leaven is used symbolically to symbolize [*sic*] an evil influence which spreads like an infection' (Mitton 1973: 342). The intimate connection between the festival of the Passover lamb and the period of eating unleavened bread (see Exodus 12; cf. e.g. Mk 14.1, 12) explains the link Paul draws here, between the imagery of the pure unleavened lump which the community is meant to be and the sacrifice of Christ as the Passover which marks and enables the beginning of this period of new life and purity (1 Cor. 5.7-8). It is the identity and purity of the community with which Paul is fundamentally concerned and with the offender insofar as he pollutes the whole.[25]

Paul's verdict on the offender is implicit in the imagery with which he describes the person and his effect upon the community. Old leaven, a pollutant in the lump, must be cast away, put outside; πόρνοι belong in the world, not in the church. Thus, the offender must go where he belongs, be expelled from the community (5.2, 5, 13). Paul's citation of Deut. 17.7 as the final summary verdict expresses this concisely, and was perhaps chosen at least partly on the basis of a word-play between πόρνος and πονηρός (so Zaas 1984; see further Rosner 1994: 61–93). What exactly Paul means to imply in condemning the man to be 'handed over to Satan for the destruction of the flesh, so that his spirit may be saved on the day of the Lord' (1 Cor. 5.5) is obscure and much disputed. Does this imply, as Ernst

---

24. May 2001 §4.3.2. Cf. also Thiselton 2000: 401.

25. Countryman's (1988: 109, 197–202, 213, etc.) claim that Paul formulates sexual ethics on the basis of property rules, and not on the basis of purity, founders on this passage. Cf. Martin 1995a: 168: 'Paul's primary concern in this passage is the purity of the church, the body of Christ, and his anxieties center on the man as a potentially [should we not say: actually?] polluting agent within Christ's body, an agent whose presence threatens to pollute the entire body.' Body language is of course not explicit here in 1 Corinthians 5, though it becomes prominent in 6.12-20, on which see below.

Käsemann suggested, a death sentence on the offender (1969: 71)?[26] Or does it refer only to his 'exclusion from the fellowship of the Christian community' (South 1993: 544), with an expression of hope for his conversion, which would involve a more metaphorical destruction of the flesh (so May 2001 §4.4.2)?[27] However ominous the pronouncement, it is clearly also imbued with some kind of hope for the man's eventual salvation, even though the necessary precursor to this is a negative judgment. As May suggests, it may be that being placed where his identity locates him – as a πόρνος in the world – is seen by Paul as the essential precondition for any subsequent move to conversion or salvation.

The section which follows, 6.1-11, seems to deal with a different issue, cases of litigation in which community members take one another to court. It is possible, though no more than this, that cases concerning sexual relationships or marital disputes were in view, such that a topical link with the surrounding texts remains (Richardson 1983). (Also notable is the treatment of the same theme in 1 Thess. 4.6, again in the context of instruction on avoiding πορνεία.) A distinction between the community and the world is again both presumed and reinforced here: believers are ἅγιοι and those judging them are, like those among whom they live in the world, ἄδικοι. The list of wicked persons who will not inherit the kingdom, with which the passage concludes (6.9-11), shows that the theme of πορνεία is not far from Paul's mind (πόρνοι head the list here, as in 5.10 and 11) and reinforces the sense of distinction between insiders and outsiders.

In 6.12-20 Paul returns explicitly to the theme of sexual immorality.[28] Particularly notable here is the stress on the body (τὸ σῶμα), which is, Paul declares, in a statement of principle we shall later explore, not for πορνεία but for the Lord (τῷ κυρίῳ, 6.13). Just as Paul's focus in 5.1-13 was with a man who identified himself as a πόρνος through his union with his step-mother – herself probably an outsider rather than a Christian[29] – so here his focus is on the danger constituted by the possibility of Christian men

26. For other scholars who have proposed this view, often combining it with a view of Paul's pronouncement as a curse, see South 1993, who criticizes this view. For South's own proposals, see in more detail South 1992: 23–88.

27. For further discussion of the possibilities, see Thiselton 2000: 395–400.

28. Whether Paul here confronts a real (so, e.g., Fee 1987: 20) or hypothetical (so Hurd 1965: 86–89) situation among the Christians at Corinth is not particularly relevant to an assessment of the nature of the arguments Paul uses.

29. So, e.g., Lindemann 2000: 124: 'Mit großer Wahrscheinlichkeit ist die Frau nicht Mitglied der christlichen Gemeinde; jedenfalls geht es im folgenden ausschließlich um den Mann.'

uniting themselves with immoral women, outside the community.[30] The notion of union with Christ is the foundation on which Paul builds his instruction here: believers' bodies are members of Christ, limbs and organs of his body,[31] and the fact of this union rules out union with a πόρνη ('a woman who engages in improper sexual relations').[32] 'Shall I make the members of Christ members of a πόρνη' (ἄρας οὖν τὰ μέλη τοῦ Χριστοῦ ποιήσω πόρνης μέλη, 6.15)? Paul's formulation here is, as Renate Kirchhoff points out (1994: 113), oxymoronic and hence a forceful demonstration of his point: parts of Christ's body simply cannot at the same time be parts of a πόρνη's body – μὴ γένοιτο! Sexual union with a πόρνη would equate to becoming one body, since scripture describes the union of man and woman as creating one flesh (6.16, quoting Gen. 2.24). But those in the community are already one body in and with Christ (1 Cor. 12.12-27, see further ch. 4 above), a union Paul could hardly describe as equally fleshly, given his negative evaluation of σάρξ, but one which he here labels 'one spirit' (ἐν πνεῦμα, 6.17). This does not mean, at least in this case, that unions of flesh and unions of spirit have nothing to do with each other – otherwise Paul's argument would carry no force. On the contrary, both constitute a form of bodily oneness which renders union with Christ and with a πόρνη mutually incompatible; the argument is cast in terms of two competing, incompatible unions. Thus, since πορνεία is a sin against one's own body – allowing it to be polluted by union with a sexually immoral woman – it is especially to be shunned (6.18). That Paul's concerns here are wider than those of 'individual morality' is suggested by his concluding comments, which seem to suggest that the individual and the communal body are not entirely separable categories (see further Martin 1995a). The Corinthians

30.   On this passage as concerned with the construction of *male* identity, see Moxnes 2003, though as Riches (2003) points out in his response to Moxnes that does not mean Paul's constant concern is only with male identity. Kirchhoff (1994) also makes clear that Paul's instruction here is directed to men.

31.   If the word 'member' is used to translate μέλος here, we should stress that it is meant not in the rather weak English sense of being, say, a member of a club, but rather in the sense of being physically a part, limb, organ, or member of a body (cf. BDAG, 628; Thiselton 2000: 465).

32.   Cf. Kirchhoff 1994: 16–68, who explores the meaning of πόρνη in Jewish and Graeco-Roman literature, concluding that it should be taken to include, but not be restricted specifically to, prostitutes. The correct meaning of the term, she argues, is 'eine Frau, die regelwidrige Sexualkontakte unterhält' (p. 68; cf. pp. 34–37, 67–68). There is no appropriate one-word translation, therefore, in German (or in English), so, like Kirchhoff, I incline simply to repeat the Greek word. Cf. also May 2001 §6.7.2: 'Thus πόρνη is a pejorative term that includes primarily the prostitute, but also implicitly any women who can be stereotypically denoted by sexual vice.'

are reminded that their (plural) body (singular) – τὸ σῶμα ὑμῶν[33] – is a temple of the holy Spirit, a designation applied to the community as a whole in 1 Cor. 3.16.[34] They have collectively and individually come under the ownership of God and hence should glorify God in their body (again singular) – τῷ σώματι ὑμῶν (6.19-20).[35] So the concern that the body which is a part of Christ's body should not become united with another, immoral, body is not only a principle for individual sexual ethics. Rather, as Dale Martin has stressed, it is a reflection of concern lest the corporate body of Christ be polluted by the sexual penetration that crosses the boundary between this 'holy' body and the cosmos, the (immoral) world (Martin 1995a: 176-79).[36]

Paul's argument that sex makes two people one body but that Christians are already one body in and with Christ could provide a theological rationale for the avoidance of sex altogether (cf. May 2001 §6.5.2b). If the body is for the Lord (6.13) then should one not avoid or withdraw from any potentially competing unions of the body? As 1 Corinthians 7 makes clear, Paul does not want the logic of his position pushed that far, although his leaning towards asceticism is stronger than many exegetes allow:[37] the unmarried or celibate woman can be holy in body and in spirit in a way that the married cannot (7.34). In ch. 7 Paul turns explicitly to the matters raised by the Corinthians in their letter to him (7.1a). Many commentators accept the view, reflected also in modern Bible translations (e.g. NRSV), that the remainder of this verse is to be identified as a quotation of the Corinthians' opinion: 'it is good for a man not to touch a woman'.[38] However, while it is difficult to be confident about such an identification, it is at least apparent from the text that Paul's opinions, as expressed

---

33. Some scribes evidently found the singular form odd here, and substituted the plural σώματα. The plural form is used in 6.15: τὰ σώματα ὑμῶν μέλη Χριστοῦ ἐστιν.

34. Here, *pace* Countryman (1988: 109, 202–204), both property and purity concerns are evident as bases for sexual ethics.

35. One cannot put too much stress on the use of the singular noun with a plural possessive here, as similar constructions occur elsewhere in Paul: e.g., 1 Cor. 8.12 (αὐτῶν τὴν συνείδησιν); Phil. 3.21 (τὸ σῶμα τῆς ταπεινώσεως ἡμῶν), though here we might similarly discuss whether the individual/communal distinction is blurred.

36. *Pace* May 2001 §6.3.2a, who sees Paul's response here as 'individualistic ... to do with the believer and his relationship to Christ'. Also unconvincing is Kirchhoff's suggestion that σῶμα here 'steht metonymisch für die angesprochene Christen und benennt sie nach ihrer Pflicht' (1994: 143; cf. p. 138: 'Σῶμα in 1 Kor 6,12-20 ist ein Verpflichtungsname').

37. Cf., e.g., Phipps 1982; Moiser 1983; Scroggs 1972: 295–96. But for arguments in favour of seeing Paul as the ascetic, rather than the Corinthians, see May 2001 ch. 9; on Paul's asceticism, see also Martin 1995a: 209–12; Sanders 1991: 106–107; Pagels 1974: 542. And on Paul's view of marriage as a means of containing desire, Martin 1997a.

38. E.g., Rosner 1994: 151; Martin 1995a: 205; Schrage 1995: 53; Thiselton 2000: 498, and many others.

throughout the chapter, are pretty much consonant with that opening statement, although it is qualified in various ways ('yes, but ...').[39] Paul's preference for the single state is clear (7.8-9, 28, 36, 39-40), as is his desire that all should be like him in this regard, that is, unmarried (7.7-8), though he recognizes that all do not have this gift. Marriage is therefore permitted – it is no sin (7.6) – but remaining unmarried is 'better' (7.36-38). Unmarried people can be single-mindedly devoted to the Lord in a way that the married cannot (7.32-35). Marriage, with its sexual relations, is essentially perceived as a way of avoiding πορνεία (7.2) for those lacking sufficient self-control (7.9, 36); Paul allows it as a concession,[40] as in fact he allows many concessions to his general advice throughout this chapter (cf. 7.5, 9, 11, 15, 28, 36, 39). This preference for singleness is clearly shaped by Paul's sense of the 'present crisis', the nearness of the End which relativizes all worldly commitments and activities (7.26, 29-31).[41] Indeed, this sense of an impending end leads Paul almost to nullify the main theme of his instruction in this chapter – 'do not seek a change in status' (Fee 1987: 268) – when he exclaims that 'from now on, even those who have wives should be as if they had none' (7.29).

Yet the consistent practical advice through this chapter is to 'remain as you are', concisely summarized (from the male point of view) with regard to marriage in 7.27: 'Are you bound to a wife? Do not seek release. Are you free from a wife? Do not seek a wife.' The Corinthians should not conclude that the logic of union with Christ is withdrawal from existing social and sexual relationships (cf. the illustration of this principle in 7.17-24). While the conviction that it is best to remain unmarried is perhaps

39. See May 2001 ch. 9 for an argument that this phrase is Paul's and not the Corinthians'.

40. This last point depends on taking the concession of v. 6 to refer to the permission to be married and to have sex, i.e. to the whole of vv. 2–5 (so, e.g., Martin 1995a: 209–10) rather than to a permission to take periods of abstinence from sex, i.e. to v. 5 (so, e.g., Rosner 1994: 151–52). The expression of Paul's desire that all might be as he is, that is, unmarried, in v. 7, along with his clearly expressed preference for that state, adds weight to the former view; this was evidently the reading of the text presumed by those scribes who wrote θέλω γάρ, as opposed to θέλω δέ, in v. 7, though this might represent an ascetic tendency in the textual tradition (so Rosner 1994: 152).

41. Bruce Winter has suggested that the 'present crisis' likely refers to the distress caused by grain shortages in Corinth, of which there is evidence during the period when 1 Corinthians was written (Winter 2001: 215–68). While this is certainly possible (though speculative, especially in terms of its impact on the whole chapter), it is clear that Paul interprets this crisis in the context of an eschatological framework (perhaps as a part of the woes before the End) which is what drives his reflections on marriage. An interesting parallel in *3 Macc.* 1.16-19 is noted by Yarbrough 1985: 103 n. 38: here the crisis represented by Antiochus IV's desecration of the Temple (described as ἡ ἐνεστῶσα ἀνάγκη in recension q) leads to women abandoning their plans to marry.

driven by Paul's sense of the value of undivided devotion to Christ, even union with him, and by the sense of eschatological foreclosure, the conviction that the married should remain married is undergirded by the teaching of Jesus (7.10-11). This is, indeed, the only place where Paul draws explicitly on the teaching of Jesus to provide and justify an ethical ruling (παραγγέλλω, 7.10; on 1 Cor. 9.14 and Rom. 14.14 see below, §7.2 and §6.2, respectively).

Here in 1 Cor. 7.10-11 Paul reproduces what he regards as Jesus tradition in a concise manner. He seems to regard the Lord's word on divorce as carrying the kind of authority which makes the addition of supporting arguments (such as he adds in vv. 12–16) unnecessary (cf. Catchpole 1975: 105–106; Allison 1982: 3). Furthermore, although there is little language shared by both Paul's instruction and the relevant synoptic accounts, the content of the teaching is very similar (see Dungan 1971: 97–99). While arguments about the form and content of Jesus' original teaching remain, it can reasonably be maintained that Jesus' teaching on divorce contained essentially two elements. First, an affirmation (setting Genesis against Deuteronomy) that the Creator's intention is that the marriage bond should be a permanent union between husband and wife (Mt. 19.3-6; Mk 10.2-9). Second, in more practical terms, that remarriage after divorce (or divorce in order to remarry; Nolland 1995: 31-35) constitutes adultery (Mt. 5.31-32; 19.9; Mk 10.10-12; Lk. 16.18).[42] Paul uses different language – he does not mention adultery, and his instruction is focused more upon the woman – but the instruction is basically the same (certainly in 7.10-11): do not divorce, but if you do, remain unmarried.

Paul evidently regards the problems raised by 'mixed marriages', where one partner is not a Christian, as outside the scope of Jesus' own pronouncement (7.12). Nonetheless, the advice he gives is in effect very close in substance to the instruction in vv. 10-11: namely, do not divorce (vv. 12-13). The key difference is that if divorce occurs at the unbeliever's initiative it should be accepted – the Christian 'is not bound' (οὐ δεδούλωται) in such circumstances.[43] Particularly interesting are the reasons

---

42. Sanders and Davies (1989: 328) suggest that Jesus' original teaching was most likely 'a complete denial of divorce'. However, the existence of the saying specifying remarriage as adultery in both a Mark and a Q form makes its claim to authenticity strong; cf. Catchpole 1975: 111–13; Hooker 1991: 237; Nolland 1995: 25–35.

43. It is debated whether this statement is intended to permit remarriage (and thus goes against the Lord's teaching) or not. Its primary meaning would seem to be that the believer is not bound to maintain the marriage. Dungan (1971: 97–99) doubts that Paul's intention was to allow remarriage. Catchpole and Fee doubt whether Paul addresses the question here at all: 'this is not to say that Paul *disallows* remarriage in such cases; he simply does not speak to it at all' (Fee 1987: 303; cf. Catchpole 1975: 109 n. 2). While the permission might well extend to allowing a subsequent marriage, Paul would hardly have recommended such a course: even in

Paul gives for remaining in such a marriage: the unbelieving spouse is made holy (ἡγίασται) by the believer; hence the children of such a marriage are also holy (ἅγια) as opposed to unclean (ἀκάθαρτα, 7.14). Moreover, there exists the possibility of 'saving' one's spouse (7.16).[44] Since Paul can describe this salvation as only a possibility, it is clear that he here denotes as holy someone who is not actually a community member. A comparison with 6.15-20 is significant: there sex with an outsider rendered the believer unholy (cf. 6.19) and compromised their union with Christ (just as in 5.1-13 the act of immorality, probably also with an outsider, revealed a so-called brother to be a πόρνος). Here in 7.14-16 sexual union with an outsider renders the outsider holy: rather than being polluted by intercourse with a non-believer and thus taken outside the circle of the holy, the believer brings their spouse and their children inside. The crucial difference is not hard to discern: in 6.15-20 the sexual encounter was an illicit one (as the very choice of the term πόρνη indicates) whereas in 7.14-16 the sexual relation is marriage and thus legitimate. What this indicates, though, is that while Paul uses arguments about holiness and bodily union with Christ to support and promote his sexual ethics, the substantive ethical convictions themselves are not actually derived from these arguments but are already assumed. *Why* does sex with a πόρνη threaten and destroy union with Christ while sex with one's unbelieving spouse does not? Simply because sex with a πόρνη is (deemed to be) illicit while sex with one's spouse is allowed. Paul does not demonstrate why one relation is bad and the other good; this distinction is the *presumption* from which his argument proceeds (see further §5.6).

The forceful imperative of 6.18, 'flee from sexual immorality' (φεύγετε τὴν πορνείαν), is closely parallel to a similarly forceful imperative in 10.14, 'flee from idolatry' (φεύγετε ἀπὸ τῆς εἰδωλολατρείας), an imperative located in the midst of a complex and important argument that we shall consider in depth in the following chapter.[45] Important here, however, are the parallels in the arguments Paul makes in both sections of the letter, dealing respectively with sexual immorality and idolatry. Bearing in mind what Paul has presented as the basis for avoiding sexual immorality, what does he present as the reasons for avoiding idolatry? Again the notion of union or participation is prominent: idolatry is fundamentally wrong because it

---

the case of someone whose partner has died (Paul clearly regards death as ending the marriage bond; see Rom. 7.2-4) Paul counsels against remarriage, though he does not forbid it (1 Cor. 7.39-40).

44. Again, *pace* Countryman (1988), purity notions influence Paul's ethics here. It is debated whether Paul is optimistic or not about this possibility of salvation (see, e.g., Kubo 1978).

45. On these parallels see Cheung 1999: 112–14.

involves κοινωνία with δαιμόνια (10.20),[46] a participation (μετέχειν) at their table (10.21), which is incompatible with belonging to the body of Christ. Participation in the Lord's supper is a κοινωνία in the blood and body of Christ, the bread in particular a demonstration of the identity of the Christian congregation as 'one body' (ἐν σῶμα, 10.17; see §4.1.2). Just as union with a πόρνη is incompatible with union with Christ, so is union with διαμόνια. The rites of Christian belonging, baptism and Lord's supper, provide no automatic protection against the dangers of participation in such competing unions (10.1-5); far from protecting the Corinthians against danger, they imply a requirement of loyalty, an avoidance of any competing or incompatible participation, with the threat of punishment arising from divine jealousy (10.1-13, 22).[47]

Recalling Barth, we may begin to consider what Paul regards as relevant in terms of marking group-identity, maintaining the boundary between insider and outsider. Here we return to 6.13-14, where Paul sets out an important distinction between food and sex, between the stomach and the body:[48]

> Foods for the stomach and the stomach for foods,
>   And God will destroy both these.
> But the body not for sexual immorality but for the Lord, and the Lord
> for the body;
>   And God raised the Lord and will also raise us up by his power.

As indicated elsewhere, and as we shall see in more detail in the following chapter, Paul considers food irrelevant morally, and as a marker of group-identity: 'food will not bring us close to God. We are no worse off if we do not eat, and no better off if we do' (1 Cor. 8.8, NRSV; cf. Rom. 14.6;[49] Rom. 14.14, 17, 20). Sex, or more specifically πορνεία, sexual immorality, is

---

46. Semi-divine beings, divinities, spirits, powers, etc. (BDAG, 210), not necessarily hostile or regarded negatively, though clearly so in this context, as in other Jewish and Christian writings; see further Newton 1998: 349–62; Lampe 2003.

47. Note also the striking references to Christ in 10.4 and 9, where Paul retells the story of Israel in the wilderness.

48. As in 1 Cor. 7.1 and 8.8 (on which see below), commentators have frequently suggested that parts of these verses contain quotations from the Corinthians (cf., e.g. Hurd 1965: 68; Newton 1998: 293; Thiselton 2000: 462, 647–48). Although, given the nature of 1 Corinthians as a response to Corinthian questions (see 7.1), it is likely that such phrases are incorporated into Paul's response, he nowhere refutes any such phrases with his characteristic rebuttal, μὴ γένοιτο (e.g., Rom. 3.4; 1 Cor. 6.15; Gal. 2.17, etc.), and a good case can be made for reading these verses as Paul's own coherent argument (see esp. May 2001 §6.4, etc.).

49. On the parallels between 1 Cor. 8.8 and Rom. 14.6, see Cheung 1999: 134–36. As Cheung notes, the formulation in 1 Corinthians reflects a context where Paul wishes to induce caution about the prospect of eating, compared with the more positive formulation in Romans, though that does not imply that 1 Cor. 8.8 is intended to imply a categorical 'do not eat', as Cheung suggests. See further ch. 6 below.

highly pertinent, however, since it concerns the body. The body's significance, 1 Cor. 6.14 implies, stems from the fact that it will be resurrected (cf. 1 Cor. 15.35-54).[50] As May puts it:

> Paul's point is that food is finally irrelevant but that πορνεία is not ... the issue here is the distinction between food and sex, and ... this governs all else. Food is trivial, a natural urge to be followed, lacking in any eternal consequences, irrelevant to the identity of the believer (8:8). Sex, however, goes to the root of who the believer is. His devotion to the Lord is incompatible with πορνεία. (May 2001 §6.4)[51]

It is, of course, easy to pick holes in Paul's logic here: the stomach is equally part of the body – whatever the meaning of σῶμα here, it must at least include the physical body, if Paul's conviction that sex makes two people one body, one flesh (6.16), is to carry any force – so one might well make the case that allowing unclean food to pollute the body, via the stomach, is also incompatible with the body's union with Christ. However, for whatever reasons, Paul does not regard the ingestion of food as something which affects the body's union with Christ; put differently, food per se is not of concern as an area of cultural practice in which the Christian groups are to indicate their distinctive identity.[52] Sexual activity and idolatry – union with human or 'divine' outsiders respectively – does, however, threaten to destroy the Christian's union with Christ and thus to undermine their identity and pollute the whole communal body.

---

50. Cf. Kirchhoff 1994: 127, who notes that the parallelism of vv. 13b and 14 indicates the different eschatological fates related to the two pairings compared here (stomach/food and body/Lord): 'Leib und Herr stehen seit der Taufe in Beziehung, und der Leib ist seitdem für die Auferweckung vorgesehen.' However, I think she goes on to press the parallelism in relationships between stomach/food and body/Lord too far.

51. Cf. also Newton 1998: 343, 375–76; otherwise Cheung 1999: 16, 133–35.

52. In this regard Paul does seem to have broken with Jewish tradition, in which food serves as a key marker of cultural distinctiveness. This is not, let it be stressed, to claim that Paul has somehow been 'liberated' from such cultural constraints, or has a more 'radical' view, or other such expressions of Christian superiority. Barth's work should suggest a less-loaded description: it is simply that there is some difference in the areas of cultural practice which are deemed to be relevant in terms of defining group identity. It is indicative, for example, that among Jewish writings from the period 200BCE–100CE even documents which take sharply different stances vis-à-vis Hellenistic culture and the Gentile world, such as *3* and *4 Maccabees* on the one hand and the *Letter of Aristeas* on the other, nonetheless agree on the importance of the literal observance of the food laws; allegorical explanations of the purpose of the food laws serve to strengthen not weaken their importance. Cf. *Ep. Arist.* 128-71; *3 Macc.* 3.3-7; *4 Macc.* 1.31-35; 5.1-29; Barclay 1996a: 138–50, 192–203, 369–80; Cheung 1999: 45–50. Some Jews did allegorize the Law so far as to give up its literal observance, according to Philo (*Migr. Abr.* 89-93), but Philo regards this as going beyond what is permissible within Jewish custom (cf. Segal 1990: 203). For further comments, and for qualifications of Cheung's arguments, see the brief excursus in Horrell forthcoming.

Thus, in terms of marking identity and boundaries, it is ideas and practices associated with the body and its union with Christ that seem to denote the key 'value orientations' which Paul deems crucial in establishing and maintaining the distinctiveness of the group. This union in one body is signalled positively in the rituals of baptism and Lord's supper (see §4.1) and is protected through the avoidance of what are deemed to be competing unions, destructive of bodily union with Christ – those defined as sexually immoral or idolatrous.

5.4 *Social Interaction with 'Outsiders'*

While the theme of ethics in relation to 'outsiders' will be our concern in a later chapter (ch. 8), it is pertinent here to consider briefly how the sense of distinctive group identity, expressed in the sharp rhetoric of difference, shapes and affects social practice. According to Barth, whose ideas were summarized in the previous section, we should not assume or expect the maintenance of distinct identity to imply a stance of social isolation in all aspects of social life but rather a structuring of interaction focused on those areas of values and practice taken to be salient for defining identity and maintaining a group boundary.

In investigating this subject it is instructive to return to some of the texts already considered in the previous section. In 1 Cor. 5.1-13, in the context of his instruction to the Corinthians concerning the offender in their midst, Paul has cause to clarify teaching given in his previous letter (5.9). This letter evidently warned the Corinthians not to 'mix' (συναναμίγνυσθαι) with the sexually immoral (πόρνοι) and other sinners. It seems, at least so far as we can tell from Paul's reporting, that the Corinthians, if they took any notice at all, might have taken this in terms of separation from immoral people in the world, from outsiders (5.10). Indeed, the kind of material found in 2 Cor. 6.14–7.1, with its stark warnings against being yoked (ἑτεροζυγοῦντες) with unbelievers (ἀπίστοις) and about the incompatibilities of light and darkness, could certainly be thought to imply just such a stance. This enigmatic text in 2 Corinthians could possibly be a fragment of this very 'previous letter' (cf. Hurd 1965: 235–37), though the process by which this fragment could have come to be incorporated into 2 Corinthians is not easy to envisage. In any case, whether the Corinthians misread Paul or whether Paul is now 'reinterpreting' his own prior communication, he now insists that he did not mean them to avoid mixing with such immoral people 'of this world', since this would require withdrawal from the world (1 Cor. 5.10). The contact that is to be shunned is contact with a 'so-called brother' (ἀδελφὸς ὀνομαζόμενος) who is actually a πόρνος, in other words, with someone who is dangerously dislocated in terms of their identity, a pollutant in the church, a πόρνος bearing the disguise of an ἀδελφός. And shunning contact includes the specific instruction not even to eat with such a person (5.11).

By implication, eating with outsiders who are known to be outsiders, and indeed enjoying social contacts with them, is not proscribed. Indeed, this is precisely what we find in 1 Cor. 10.25-28 (on which see ch. 6 below), where believers are given permission not only to eat everything sold in the market but also to accept invitations to meals with unbelievers and to eat whatever is set before them. To be sure, this latter permission is hedged with certain qualifications which we shall consider in the next chapter, but the permission is nonetheless significant and bears out the remarks above that food itself is not deemed by Paul a matter of ethical or identity-defining significance.

Even a marriage to an outsider should continue rather than be ended by divorce; here the dominical teaching against divorce forms a stronger ethical principle than any concern for distinction from outsiders (7.12-16). Clearly, the ideal for marriage is that it should be 'in the Lord' (ἐν κυρίῳ, 7.39), but where this is not the case the boundary of distinction and holiness is redrawn such that the outsider, and the children of the marriage, are inside the circle. Although sexual unions represent the kind of bodily union which is precisely the site where Paul draws the boundary lines around the Christian group, the 'theory' is adjusted, so to speak, to allow 'moral' sexual unions to continue. It is only unions labelled immoral which are presented as destroying the believer's bodily union with Christ (6.12-20).

This considerable degree of openness to continued interaction with 'outsiders' – even to the extent of expecting that they may be present during meetings of the congregation (1 Cor. 14.23) – presents the kind of picture Barth's work would lead us to expect. A strong sense of ideological distinction and group identity does not necessarily translate into isolationist or separatist social practice, and certainly not across all areas of social life. Rather, interaction is proscribed at precisely (and specifically) the places where it touches those forms of value and practice deemed essential for distinctive identity. The most important instances for Paul appear to be the two strongly associated in Jewish tradition with Gentile immorality: sexual immorality and idolatry. It is these which are depicted as constituting forms of union which are incompatible with the positive designator of Christian identity: bodily union with Christ.

5.5 *Ethical Norms: Distinctive or Shared?*

But this conclusion leaves us with another question: How distinctive are the ethical norms which would appear to underpin this basis for group distinctiveness? In other words, to what extent, if at all, does the call for distinction and the construction of a distinctive group-identity correlate with a distinctive set of ethical principles? To answer this question thoroughly would of course necessitate a whole series of studies of particular topics in which Paul's instructions were compared with the range of contemporary material in Jewish and Graeco-Roman sources. In the following short section, I shall draw on a number of specific and detailed studies, related to the topics explored in this chapter, which have attempted precisely this comparative task, in order to sketch what emerges as a plausible answer to this question. Indeed, despite plenty of debate over the detail, recent scholarship on the whole combines to form a reasonably clear and coherent picture.[53]

We have already seen how the language of turning from idolatry and avoiding sexual immorality stems primarily from Jewish tradition, in which it serves to distinguish 'the people' from 'the nations' (and, at the same time, to warn the former of the dire consequences of turning to such practices). The theme of avoiding idolatry in particular is clearly one which Paul owes to Judaism. The word $\epsilon \H{\iota}\delta\omega\lambda o\nu$ was used in non-Jewish Greek literature with a range of meanings, such as phantom, form, or image (LSJ, 483), generally 'in a positive, neutral, or merely factual manner ... [and] [o]nly very rarely to indicate a representation of the divine. It indicated something which was an image or representation of the real thing but not the real thing itself' (Newton 1998: 131; see pp. 128–34). In the Septuagint, however, $\epsilon \H{\iota}\delta\omega\lambda o\nu$ translates a range of Hebrew words used to designate images of gods, or the Gentiles' gods themselves.[54] The strongly negative stance towards such $\epsilon \H{\iota}\delta\omega\lambda\alpha$ derives both from the Torah's prohibitions against making images ($\epsilon \H{\iota}\delta\omega\lambda\alpha$)[55] and from the warnings against those among the people who turn from exclusive devotion to Yhwh to other gods ($\epsilon \H{\iota}\delta\omega\lambda\alpha$; e.g. Lev. 26.30; Deut. 32.19-21; 2 Kgs 17.9-12). Since the gods of the nations are, in a sense, only images, made by human hands, they can be ridiculed as nothing (e.g. Isa. 44.9-20; 46.1-13; Wis. 13.10-19), yet at the same time, because of Yhwh's jealousy, they constitute a dangerous temptation for the people of God (cf. Exodus 32; Num. 25.2-11; 1 Cor. 10.6-22).[56]

---

53. Notwithstanding the tendency to minimize or discount the significance of evidence on the 'other side' in some works dealing with either the Jewish or the Graeco-Roman materials; cf. §1.2-3 above.

54. Cf. F. Büchsel, *TWNT* 2: 374. See, e.g., the references to Laban's household gods, stolen by Rachel: התרפים; $\tau\grave{\alpha}\ \epsilon \H{\iota}\delta\omega\lambda\alpha$, Gen. 31.19, 34, 35; cf. θεούς in 31.30. Often אלהים is the Hebrew word translated: e.g., Num. 25.2; 1 Kgs 11.8.

55. Exod. 20.4; Lev. 19.4 (אליל); Deut. 5.8 (פסל).

56. Cf. Tomson 1990: 156–58 on two views Tomson discerns in Jewish tradition: the 'rational' view (idols are nothing) and the non-rational (idolatry involves contact with demons).

This polemic against idols and idolatry, serving both to distinguish the community from the nations and to warn insiders against apostasy, underpins Paul's understanding (cf. §5.1 above). Devotion to the one God, and the repudiation of the worship of other 'so-called' gods (cf. 1 Cor. 8.5-6), is a characteristic standpoint Paul shares with Jewish tradition. The differences are to be found in the fact that the line between insiders and outsiders is drawn by Paul around the (Jewish and Gentile) Christian community, rather than between Jews and Gentiles (cf. Barclay 1996a: 388), and in the ways Paul draws on ideas of union with Christ to develop arguments as to why idolatry is wrong; food itself does not seem to serve as a marker of group-distinctiveness (cf. §5.3 and n. 52).

When it comes to sexual morality, however, it becomes evident that Paul shares a good deal in common, not only with Jewish ethics but also with Graeco-Roman moral philosophy, though certain common emphases are notably missing.[57] A wide range of sources stress the importance of marriage as a duty, a stress absent from Paul's treatment, where the single state is preferable and marriage is a second-best option for those who cannot contain their desire. Nonetheless, Paul's view that marriage provides the appropriate context for sexual relations and thus serves as a means to avoid immorality is paralleled in both Judaism and certain Graeco-Roman moral philosophers (notably Musonius Rufus).[58] A view often found across these traditions, however, though notably absent in Paul's treatment, is that sex should be engaged in for the purpose of procreation only, and not to provide pleasure.[59] While sexual encounters outside the marital bond were apparently common in Graeco-Roman society, and were not by any means universally condemned, Yarbrough shows that the notions of chastity and faithfulness within marriage were certainly held as ethical ideals (1985: 57–60). These notions are strongly evident in Jewish texts, where the claim is made that Jews guard the purity of marriage more than do other nations (*Sib. Or.* 3.591-600) and where the

---

57. See esp. the important study of Yarbrough 1985; on the Jewish parallels, see Rosner 1994, and on the Stoic-Cynic parallels, Deming 1995.

58. See Yarbrough 1985: 7–29, 53–60; Musonius, *Disc.* 12: *On Sexual Indulgence* (text and translation in Lutz 1947); for Jewish examples note Prov. 5.15-20; Tob. 4.12; *T. Levi* 9.9-10 (cited also by Rosner 1994: 159).

59. See Yarbrough 1985: 11-12, 21-22, 48-49, 58; Ward 1990, who proposes that, unlike his contemporaries, 'Paul, in effect, redefined marriage as a context for the mutual satisfying of erotic desires' (pp. 286–87). Thiselton (2000: 494) calls this 'a startling assertion', but for an antidote to the rather wishful reading that sees Paul here providing a remarkably modern, positive view of sex as for mutual erotic enjoyment, see Martin 1997a, who stresses Paul's negative stance towards desire: marriage serves for Paul as a means to contain, even extinguish, passion. Pseudo-Aristotle (*Oeconomica* 1.3) also sees the union of man and woman as much more than a means of procreation: their relationship is also concerned with 'mutual help, goodwill, and co-operation'.

prohibition against adultery is prominent (Exod. 20.14; Lev. 2.10; Deut. 5.18, etc.; cf. Josephus, *Apion* 2.199-201). Abstaining from prostitutes is certainly claimed as a particular mark of Jewish distinctiveness in sexual morality (Yarbrough 1985: 13): Philo has Joseph remark that while the men of other nations are, from the age of fourteen, permitted to consort freely with prostitutes (πόρναις) and harlots (χαμαιτύπαις), the Hebrews do not tolerate such liaisons, putting women to death who ply such a trade, and coming pure to marriage, which is sought not for pleasure but for procreation (*Jos.* 42-43). Yet there are also examples of Graeco-Roman writers condemning all extramarital sexual encounters, whether with married women, other men, slaves, courtesans, or prostitutes, and appealing to what is generally accepted in doing so.[60] Paul's notion of what constitutes πορνεία thus presumes and repeats the Jewish moral tradition (Dautzenberg 1989: 284–96), but it is also paralleled elsewhere.

In his rigorous prohibition of divorce, Paul goes beyond the customary strictures of both Jewish and Graeco-Roman moral teaching, where divorce was presumed as a fact of everyday life.[61] Decisive here is the rigorous teaching of Jesus, which Paul refers to explicitly on this point, uniquely in his ethical instruction (1 Cor. 7.10-11). Nonetheless, we should also note the comparable evidence indicating a high regard for marriage in both Jewish and Graeco-Roman moral traditions. While the rabbis, for example, famously debated legitimate reasons for divorce, based on different interpretations of Deut. 24.1 (see *m. Git.* 9.10), it is also apparent that they regarded divorce as highly regrettable, a perspective which echoes earlier biblical texts (*b. Git.* 90b; Mal. 2.15-16).[62] Conversely, it should also be noted that, even in the same sentence with which he most clearly forbids

60. See esp. Musonius, *Disc.* 12 (in Lutz 1947); Dio Chrysostom, *Or.* 7.133–34. Musonius condemns all 'unlawful' sexual intercourse (p. 86, line 11), including relations which are evidently held by some as acceptable, like that of a man with his unmarried female slave (p. 86, line 29–p. 88 line 6); but the immorality of relations with slaves is something Musonius takes as 'well-known' (γνώριμος, p. 88, line 6). Dio refers to the business of keeping a brothel as one 'which all the world condemns as shameful'. Those who keep such places 'bring individuals together in union without love and intercourse without affection, and all for the sake of filthy lucre'. See Yarbrough 1985: 57–58, for further citations on this point, e.g., Pseudo-Aristotle, *Oeconomica* 3.2; see also Downing 1998: 101–10, on the ascetic strand in Cynicism which would teach against such liaisons (and also counsel against marriage); Kirchhoff 1994: 90–100.

61. Cf. Yarbrough 1985: 113: 'This absolute rejection of divorce is the one area in which Paul is clearly unlike all of his contemporaries. Both Jewish and Greco-Roman law provided for divorce with few restrictions.' The 'all' here is something of an overstatement, however; see below with n. 62.

62. See further Rosner 1994: 168, who also points to Deut. 22.19, 28, 29, which outlines situations where divorce is not permitted, and cites parallels from Qumran indicating opposition to divorce there. Thus, 'Paul was not alone among Jews in his day when he proscribed divorce.'

divorce, Paul has to make some concession to the reality that divorce occurs: 'do not separate ... but if you do ...' (1 Cor. 7.10-11). Other early Christian texts reflect the ongoing process of adapting rigour to reality, notably Mt. 5.32; 19.9, where the exception clause 'except for $\pi o \rho \nu \epsilon i \alpha$' is closely parallel to the Shammaite interpretation of legitimate reasons for divorce.

Perhaps the most precise parallels to Paul's teaching on marriage and sexual morality are found in the various discussions of the reasons for and against marriage, and of the situations in which it might be best not to marry. Despite the widespread view that marriage was a duty, the idea that there might indeed be cases where marriage should be avoided is not infrequently encountered, in Judaism and especially in the Stoic-Cynic discussions.[63] Yarbrough, for example, notes the rabbinic debate about whether or not one should study Torah and only then marry (1985: 22–23; e.g. *b. Qid.* 29b). Stephen Barton surveys a wide range of Jewish evidence roughly contemporary with Paul (Philo, Josephus and Qumran) and finds much material to support the view that family and household ties should be repudiated in certain circumstances, notably in service of a higher call or duty towards God (Barton 1994: 23–47). David Balch examines Philo's view of Moses' asceticism as a possible background to the discussion in 1 Corinthians 7 (Balch 1972: 358–61; Philo, *Vit. Mos.* 2.66-70). Brian Rosner also notes a range of Jewish material, concluding that 'ancient Judaism had considerable ascetic tendencies, countered by other elements in the Biblical tradition, but able to appeal to Biblical laws and examples' (Rosner 1994: 158; see pp. 153–58).

Rosner also notes that these 'ascetic elements were shared with the pagan world' (p. 158). Indeed, significant parallels to Paul's treatment of marriage have been identified in the Stoic-Cynic discussions of this topic.[64] For example, Balch, in another article, concludes that

---

63. May 2001 ch. 8 stresses the fact that marriage is regarded as a crucial means to support the social order, and thus sees Paul's opposition to marriage as a deeply anti-social stance which would have drawn sharp criticism. However, May somewhat marginalizes the parallel evidence concerning the avoidance of marriage in certain circumstances, which seems to indicate that such discussions (and resulting practices) were quite prominent in Paul's time. The Augustan legislation promoting marriage and the producing of children would hardly have been deemed necessary was there not a significant tendency to avoid (re)marriage, and not only at the margins of society. Indeed, commenting on this legislation, Tacitus comments that it 'failed, however, to make marriage and the family popular – childlessness remained the vogue' (*Ann.* 3.25). This may, of course, be a considerable exaggeration, but it cannot be entirely discounted. On the Augustan legislation, see Yarbrough 1985: 45–46 n. 78; Dio Cassius, *Rom. Hist.* 56.1-10.

64. Rosner's claim (1994: 150 n. 8), in the context of his argument for the primacy of the Jewish evidence, that 'the Yarborough [*sic*]/Balch case has been seriously undermined in a recent article by Roy Bowen Ward [Ward 1990] ... which takes them to task over their best

> in 1 Cor 7:32-35, Paul uses technical terms common in Stoic discussions concerning marriage. Antipater, Epictetus, Hierocles and Paul agree that 'distraction' from one's central duty or call is negative. The discussion is carried on to determine what is 'advantageous' or beneficial. One should deal with 'anxiety'. (Balch 1983: 439)

So, for example, while Epictetus considered that it was a civic duty to marry, he could imagine that present circumstances – 'like that of a battle field' (*Diss* 3.22.69) – might make it best for the Cynic philosopher not to marry (*Diss* 3.22.67-72).[65] Will Deming (1995) has explored the Stoic-Cynic debates about marriage in detail, arguing that they provide the closest context for understanding Paul's discussion in 1 Corinthians 7. While the Stoics generally held that marriage was a social duty for all, the Cynics stressed the value of self-sufficiency, of freedom from all such conventional responsibilities. The Cynic position was adopted by some Stoics, Deming argues, to the extent that they discussed certain 'adverse' circumstances in which it was best not to marry. Deming does not then propose the implausible thesis that Paul is entirely a Stoic-Cynic thinker on these matters, but rather that he joins these perspectives with his Judaeo-Christian convictions. So, for example, Paul parallels a Stoic-Cynic view in advising against marriage in the present adverse circumstances (1 Cor. 7.26), but Paul's perspective on these circumstances is shaped by the Judaeo-Christian apocalyptic theme of 'the hardships that were expected to beset the world in the period *before* the End' (Deming 1995: 182).

Evidence for shared or overlapping ethical norms, specifically in conjunction with a strong sense of distinction, may also be found in 1 Cor. 5.1-13. Commentators unanimously note that the sin which provokes Paul's strong reaction is regarded as a crime in both Jewish and Roman law (see §5.3 with n. 23). But the significance of this for our understanding of Paul's ethics is less frequently considered. Paul's point, of course, is not to show the Corinthians that his ethical judgments cohere with those of their wider society but rather to heighten the sense of outrage he feels and which they ought to feel (see §5.3). But at precisely this point – the only place in Paul's letters where an offender's sin is so grave as to require expulsion from the church[66] – Paul is making an ethical judgment which

---

piece of evidence, namely, Musonius', simply overlooks the range of evidence on which Yarbrough, Balch and others draw, and overstates the extent of Ward's critique. Even Rosner is forced to concede that, in terms of Paul's ethics being based on scripture, '1 Corinthians 7 turns out to be "the exception which proves the rule"' (p. 176).

65. See further Balch 1983: 430–31; Yarbrough 1985: 43 with n. 68. Barton also surveys a range of Graeco-Roman evidence which shows that the commitment to philosophy could be deemed to override the duty to marry (Barton 1994: 47–54).

66. The identification of the offender of 1 Corinthians 5 with the one referred to in 2 Cor. 2.5-11; 7.12, occasionally suggested (e.g. Lampe 1967: 353–54), is unlikely. But there is no

represents a point of moral agreement, shared 'common ground', between him and his contemporaries outside the church. Precisely here we see, ironically, the juxtaposition of a sense of distinct (and morally superior) identity and shared ethical norms.

This ironic juxtaposition can also be seen in the use Paul makes of so-called catalogues of vices and virtues.[67] It is widely agreed that in using this form Paul follows a form of expression already conventional in his day and found in a wide range of literature, both Graeco-Roman and Jewish. A variety of hypotheses has been proposed concerning the immediate influences on Paul in this regard, though none of the comparable catalogues provides an exact parallel to the content of any Pauline list *as a whole* (Zaas 1988).[68] In other words, Paul utilizes a traditional form but does not simply reproduce some supposedly standard content. Indeed, even the various lists in the New Testament utilize a wide range of diverse vocabulary (see Wibbing 1959: 87–88, 99–100). Paul's lists seem to show some degree of adaptation to their literary context – hence the prominence of πόρνοι in 1 Cor. 5.10, 11; and 6.9 – but are at the same time comprised, like their contemporary parallels, of various terms which stereotypically depict vice and virtue; they do not therefore reflect a series of particular problems or instances Paul seeks to correct.[69] As Conzelmann remarks, the lists serve as typical and exhortatory depictions (1975: 101). There are parallels, moreover, not only to the form of the list as such but also to specific terms Paul employs. As we have already seen, his emphasizing of πορνεία and εἰδωλολατρία (cf. Rom. 1.23-24; 1 Cor. 5.10-11; 6.9; Gal. 5.19-20) reflects a specifically Jewish ethical tradition, as does their connection with πλεονεξία (see Reinmuth 1985: 22–41); but other vices and virtues

indication that the offender in 2 Corinthians was expelled from the church, still less that Paul ordered his expulsion. More likely it was a case that the majority (in the end) sided with Paul and shunned this person who had insulted or opposed Paul, such that Paul now calls for the congregation to call off their hostility and accept the person once more (2 Cor. 2.5-8; further Horrell 1996: 299 with n. 22; 307–309). May (2001 §5.5) also makes the interesting observation that while the act committed by the offender of 1 Corinthians 5 is sufficient to redefine him as a πόρνος, and so to require his expulsion from the church, the act of taking fellow believers to court (1 Cor. 6.1-8) does not redefine a believer's identity as ἄδικος, or similar, but instead draws a *warning* from Paul.

67. See Rom. 1.29-31; 13.13; 1 Cor. 5.10-11; 6.9-10; 2 Cor. 6.6; 12.20-21; Gal. 5.19-23; Phil. 4.8, as listed, along with other NT instances, by Wibbing 1959: 78.

68. See, e.g., Vögtle 1936; Wibbing 1959, etc. For brief overviews, see Conzelmann 1975: 100–101; Zaas 1988: 623.

69. Zaas (1988) argues that the content of Paul's lists is not 'random', against the view expressed by Robin Scroggs: 'What is clear is that the users or creators of these lists do not carefully select the individual items to fit the context with which they are dealing. The lists were often, apparently, traditional ... Paul does not care about any specific item in the lists' (Scroggs 1983: 102, 104). This last phrase is an overstatement, but even Zaas concedes that 'Paul is not using these lists to argue against specific vices' (1988: 629).

indicate a more widely shared sense of what is good and bad. As Hans Dieter Betz puts it, referring to the extensive list of vices and virtues in Gal. 5.19-22: 'the individual concepts are not in any way specifically "Christian," but represent the conventional morality of the time' (1979: 282). In the Galatians list, for example, the 'vices' include hostility (ἔχθρα), strife (ἔρις), jealousy (ζῆλος), rage (θυμός), quarrelling (ἐριθεία), dissensions (διχοστασίαι), factions (αἱρέσεις), and envy (φθόνος), all of which are regarded and named as vices in Graeco-Roman literature.[70] And the corresponding list of virtues ends with what Betz refers to as 'three famous virtues from Hellenistic ethics': faithfulness (πίστις), gentleness (πραΰτης) and self-control (ἐγκράτεια) – this last, Betz notes, is 'especially important' (p. 288).[71] The most striking example of this shared vocabulary (and sense of moral values) is undoubtedly found in the list of praiseworthy things in Phil. 4.8 where, uniquely in his letters, Paul uses the language of virtue (ἀρετή), the central concept of Greek ethics (cf. Wibbing 1959: 119), in the context of a 'rhythmically arranged list of Hellenistic virtues'[72] which could almost all have 'been written as part of contemporary Stoic exhortation'

70. See, e.g., Diogenes Laertius, *Lives* 7.110-14 (cited in NW 2.1: 575–76) where ζῆλος, θυμός and φθόνος appear among the manifestations of the passions; Sophocles, *Oedipus at Colonus*, 1229-1238 (NW 2.1: 577) where the troubles of life include φθόνος, στάσεις, ἔρις, μάχαι (1232). Ἐριθεία, διχοστασία and αἵρεσις come from the arena of politics (on this language in Paul and in ancient politics, see Welborn 1987). Ἐριθεία is not a common word; according to BDAG, 392, it is found before the NT only in Aristotle, where it refers to 'a self-seeking pursuit of political office by unfair means'; see Aristotle, *Pol.* 5, 1302b, 4; 1303a, 15, etc. Διχοστασία (cf. στάσις, the more common term, though not used by Paul) refers to dissension or sedition (LSJ, 439, with examples). Αἵρεσις refers to political factions (BDAG, 27–28). For examples of vice lists, see also Epictetus, *Diss.* 2.16.45; 3.22.13; for Jewish examples, Wis. 14.25-26; Philo, *Sacr.* 32; 1QS 4.2-14; further Wibbing 1959.

71. Πίστις here conveys the sense 'faithfulness' or 'reliability' (BDAG, 818); cf. Aristotle, *Eud. Eth.* 7,2, 1237b, 12–13; Polybius, *Hist.* 7.12.7. Πραΰτης, 'gentleness, humility, courtesy, considerateness, meekness' (BDAG, 861) was a social and political virtue; cf. Plutarch, *Caesar* 57.3; *Pyrrhus* 23.3. 'Die sanftmütige Freundlichkeit [πραΰτης] steht als soziale Tugend im menschlichen Umgang bei den Griechen in hohem Rang' (F. Hauck and S. Schulz, *TWNT* 6: 646). L. Robert (1965: 223) notes: 'Elle [la douceur/πραΰτης] n'indique pas «l'idée de soumission et d'humilité», mais elle est surtout le fait du personnage puissant, qui veut être doux'. For ἐγκράτεια, see BDAG, 274; Aristotle, *Nic. Eth.* 7.1145a–1154b; Epictetus, *Diss.* 2.20.13; Philo, *Vit. Mos.* 1.154.

72. For examples comparable to this list, cf. Philo, *Vit. Mos.* 1.154; Seneca, *De Tranq. An.* 3,4; Cicero, *Tusc. Disp.* 5.23.67. An inscription from the first century BCE honouring the son of Herostratos Dorkalion also gives a clear indication of the regard for such virtues (cited by Deissmann 1923: 270 n. 2, who notes the close parallel in 2 Pet. 1.5-6): ἄνδρα ἀγαθὸν γενόμενον καὶ διενένκαντα πίστει καὶ ἀρετῇ καὶ δικαιοσύνῃ καὶ εὐσεβείᾳ καὶ ... τὴν πλείστην εἰσενεγμένον σπουδήν (who was a good man and who excelled in faithfulness and virtue and justice and piety and showed the greatest zeal; my trans.).

(Bockmuehl 1998a: 250).[73] Markus Bockmuehl rightly notes the 'profound' implications of this approach, its relevance for 'a Christian ethic that can at least in part be formulated in openly accessible terms': Paul here encourages his addressees 'to adopt and mature in all those qualities which are intrinsically good and benefit others' (p. 250).

The degree of similarity should not be over-pressed; as is often noted, Paul does not include in his lists the four cardinal virtues of Greek morality – φρόνησις (wisdom), ἀνδρεία (courage), σωφροσύνη (good sense) and δικαιοσύνη (justice) – and only partially reflects the corresponding set of four vices and the four passions.[74] And his lists of 'virtues and vices' are by no means simply repetitions of standard, conventional terms. Some words, as we have seen, reflect a specifically Jewish moral perspective. Moreover, the lists as a whole are cast into a Christian theological framework by Paul: the vices and virtues in Gal. 5.19-23 represent the works of the flesh and the fruit of the Spirit respectively; the vices in 1 Cor. 6.9-11 warrant exclusion from the kingdom of God; and the remarkably 'Hellenistic' list of virtues in Phil. 4.8 is framed by references to the God of peace, who will guard the Philippians' hearts and minds 'in Christ Jesus' (4.7, 9). Nonetheless, it is very widely recognized that in these lists of vices and virtues Paul utilizes a form common in exhortation of the time and shares to a considerable extent a common language used to define what was good and bad.[75]

Herein, of course, lies the irony, for Paul uses precisely this common form and common language to underpin a sense of distinction from the world, to contrast Christians' pre-conversion and post-conversion lives (1 Cor. 6.9-11; cf. Gal. 5.19-23), and to highlight the difference between the pure community and the wicked world (1 Cor. 5.10-11).[76] Yarbrough notes

---

73. Cf. also Fee 1995: 415: 'Take away the "finally, brothers and sisters," and this sentence would fit more readily into Epictetus's *Discourses* or Seneca's *Moral Essays* than it would into any of the Pauline letters – except this one. The six adjectives and two nouns that make up the sentence are as uncommon in Paul as most of them are common stock to the world of Greco-Roman moralism. However, they are also the language of Jewish wisdom.'

74. E.g. Fee 1995: 416 n. 15; Bockmuehl 1998a: 251. On the cardinal virtues, together with their corresponding vices (ἀφροσύνη, δειλία, ἀκολασία, ἀδικία), and the four passions (ἐπιθυμία, φόβος, λύπη, ἡδονή), see Wibbing 1959: 15–17; NW 2.1: 576 n. 1. These four virtues are taken over into Judaism in Wis. 8.7: 'if anyone loves righteousness (δικαιοσύνην), her labours are virtues (ἀρεταί), for she teaches self-control (σωφροσύνην) and prudence (φρόνησιν), justice (δικαιοσύνην) and courage (ἀνδρείαν); there is nothing more beneficial for human life than these things'. Some of these terms do appear in Paul, e.g., δικαιοσύνη (frequently, though with a particular, theologically orientated sense), ἀφροσύνη (2 Cor. 11.1, 17, 21), ἐπιθυμία (Rom. 1.24; 6.12; Gal. 5.16, 24, etc.), but nowhere with the sense that they comprise a stock list of virtues, vices, or passions.

75. Further areas of 'common ground' have been discerned in other aspects of Paul's instruction too; see §1.2-3.

76. A comparable dualism is evident in 1QS 4.2-14, leading Wibbing (1959: 108–14, etc.) to see the Qumran parallels as particularly significant.

a similar 'irony' in Paul's appeal to standards of sexual morality in 1 Thess. 4.3-8, 'for in spite of the similarity between Paul's treatment of marriage and that of the Hellenistic moralists, Paul claims that to follow the precepts he gives distinguishes believers from "the Gentiles who do not know God"' (Yarbrough 1985: 124). Since the moral values on which this distinction is based are, as we have seen, to a considable extent shared, the ironic tension can only be resolved if we perceive Paul's claim to be *not* so much that Christians live by *distinctive* ethical standards but rather that they live up to, and beyond, the ethical standards that others share but do not follow. Shared ethical standards are a prerequisite for any claim to moral superiority, one form in which a positive and *comparative* basis for group identity can be expressed. This is, however, always a risky claim, which threatens to be empirically falsified, as in 1 Cor. 5.1-13. That, perhaps, explains not only why Paul finds that case so deeply disturbing but also why he responds to it by redefining the identity of the offender – he is not really a Christian at all!

Studies of Pauline ethics have long recognized the considerable extent to which the substantive content of Paul's ethical instruction is shared with his contemporaries (cf. ch. 1 above). While there remains debate about the relative influence of Jewish and Graeco-Roman traditions, and about the extent of Paul's explicit knowledge of, say, Hellenistic moral philosophy, this basic conclusion is widely supported.[77] It is clear that Paul provides distinctive motivations and bases for ethics, grounding his sexual morality to a considerable degree in the notion of union with Christ and highlighting this notion of bodily union as a basis for the construction and maintenance of distinct Christian identity.[78] But the substance of what

77.   Thus Meeks, for example, claims that '[t]he moral admonitions that Paul teaches to his gentile converts could be heard in any synagogue (and, with few exceptions, from any moral philosopher of the Greek world ...' (1993: 20); Yarbrough considers that 'in practical terms, there was no real difference between the Pauline community and the Hellenistic moralists with regard to sexual morality' (1985: 84, cf. pp. 76–77). These claims are somewhat too sweeping, given Paul's distinctively Jewish emphasis on idolatry and its connection with sexual immorality and his unusually strong repudiation of divorce (as Yarbrough notes, p. 113), but their general point is correct.

78.   Cf. Moxnes 2003, who discusses how Paul could have used arguments from Jewish legal traditions or the common morality of everyday life to undergird his substantive instructions on sexual morality but does not: instead he depicts sexual activity in cosmic terms, as a form of union that competes with union with Christ, and thus as central to Christian identity. Cf. also Malherbe 2000: 238, who agrees to a considerable extent with Yarbrough, but stresses how Paul's discussion in 1 Thess. 4.3-8 'is shot through with religious and theological language that qualifies everything he says about his warrants for his instruction, and the motivation, manner and end of the behavior he inculcates'. Yarbrough, however, also notes that when Paul's instruction is compared with that of his contemporaries, 'the theological element in his treatment stands out sharply' (1985: 123).

Paul considers right and wrong, and the language in which he expresses what is vice and what is virtue, represent not a particular discourse which distinguishes his ethics from those of 'the world' but rather, to a considerable extent, a shared moral vocabulary. This rather well-supported historical conclusion has significant implications for the contemporary appropriation of Pauline ethics.

5.6 *Conclusion: Distinct Identity, Shared Ethics*

We have seen how prominent in Pauline discourse is a sense of distinction, the conviction that the Christian community forms a holy body in the midst of an immoral, unholy world. This sense of distinction serves specifically to undergird a strong sense of positive group identity, giving a sense of favourable comparison with outgroups. Furthermore, the sense of group identity and boundaries is specifically grounded in ideas and practices related to the body: the positive assertion of the union of believers with and in the body of Christ corresponds with negative censure of competing unions, whether of a sexually immoral or an idolatrous kind. However, we have also seen that social interaction remains in a number of respects open, being circumscribed specifically where it connects with the key ideas and practices taken as crucial for defining and maintaining group identity and boundaries. Moreover, precisely where we find Paul stressing the ethical distinctiveness of the Christian community we also find that ethical norms and instructions are to a considerable degree shared – thus providing the basis for a comparative sense of positive group identity.[79] 1 Corinthians 5 provides a fascinating and important example here, for while Paul's rhetoric and intentions are clearly focused on the purity of the community in distinction from the wicked world, at the same time he indicates explicitly that the ethical basis for his judgment is universally shared, in the wider world in which he operates. 1 Corinthians 6–7 reveal another important aspect of this collocation of distinct identity and shared ethics. Paul uses arguments about the believer's bodily union with Christ to underpin a sense of distinct Christian identity and to motivate and legitimate ethical norms and specific patterns of behaviour: no immoral liaisons and the containment of sex inside marriage. But the arguments he uses do not actually demonstrate why certain acts should be classed as ethical or unethical. Sex with a πόρνη destroys union with Christ while sex with an unbelieving spouse does not; on the contrary, the spouse is made holy through the connection with the believer. Paul's arguments here

---

79. Cf. Barclay 2001b: 158, who speaks of Paul's 'continual affirmation of distinctive Christian identity, a discourse of difference that can persist despite obvious similarities with outsiders in moral norms and social practices'.

simply presume that certain relations are wrong while others are legitimate; he assumes substantive ethical convictions about the legitimacy of sex within marriage, inherited from Judaism and also shared more widely, and gives them specifically Christian motivation and legitimation. In other words, Paul provides Christian bases for ethical judgments that are both taken to be self-evidently right and reflect common ground with those who do not share this Christian world-view. Put differently, we may say that insofar as Paul's treatment of sex expresses substantive ethical rules – do not visit prostitutes, do not divorce, etc. – it is rigorous, but hardly unique, in its socio-historical context. But insofar as it constructs Christian identity, through the overt signals and basic value orientations associated with bodily union with Christ, it constitutes a distinctive discourse (cf. also Moxnes 2003).

This juxtaposition of shared ethical norms and distinctive group identity provides a significant point at which to relate Pauline ethics to the contrasting contemporary approaches outlined in ch. 2. With its strong emphasis on the Christian community as distinctive, pure and holy in the midst of an immoral world, Paul's ethical discourse finds an echo in Hauerwas's shrill and polemical call for the church to be different, to be shaped by its own distinctive ethic, and to stand as 'a community of peace and truth in a world of mendacity and fear' (Hauerwas 1983: 100). Yet in both cases the rhetoric of distinction may be seen to obscure the extent to which ethical norms and values are shared in common with the broader society.[80] If we read Paul beneath the surface of this rhetoric, it emerges (and sometimes explicitly: 1 Cor. 5.1) that the ethical values and judgments upon which his call for distinctiveness is based are widely shared: the catalogues of vice and virtue, for example, indicate a common sense of what can be defined as good and bad. Given this realization, the liberal vision of a shared moral framework for society, what John Rawls calls an 'overlapping consensus' (Rawls 2001: 32–38), does not seem implausible or unrealistic, even though, as in Paul's case – and generally, as Habermas recognizes – norms are generated and motivated in various tradition-specific ways. Paul motivates certain patterns of conduct via his notion of union with Christ; but the specific, substantive ethical norms that are thus undergirded are to a significant degree more broadly accepted.

Indeed, some of these ethical convictions (such as the legitimacy of sex only in marriage) do not emerge from the theological tradition with which the ethics are motivated but are rather assumed as part of a taken-for-granted set of shared moral presumptions. This may, then, raise some questions about Hauerwas's depiction of authentically Christian ethics as

---

80. For a powerful critique of Hauerwas's tendency to sharpen the sense of opposition between Church and world, see Stout 2004: 147–61.

generated by the particular story which forms the community called Church. People can, as Rawls notes, have (or adduce) different, tradition-specific reasons to support a shared ethical value or common moral framework (cf. Rawls 2001: 32).

Our reading of Paul would suggest that it is in conjunction with the need to foster a sense of distinct *identity* that the language of distinction plays a particular role, while the underlying ethical values are less distinctive and more reflective of widely shared convictions. Indeed, the claim to a sense of distinct and positive identity – a comparative claim to superior group identity – is, at least in part, *dependent* on shared ethical values, since it essentially takes the form of the claim to moral superiority: 'we' are moral, 'they' are not – judged on the basis of shared norms, albeit 'ours' are more rigorous. But then, such claims in a sense reduce to an 'empirical' one – our tradition produces people of greater moral character than yours – which threatens to be falsified when someone like the Corinthian offender appears, just as it does in Hauerwas's case when he resorts to such a claim in defence of Christian truth: 'For those inclined to so dismiss my argument, I have no decisive response other than to ask if they represent practices that can produce a Dorothy Day' (2001: 231; see §2.4, p. 74 with n. 72 above).

In terms of our thinking about the issues raised by the communitarian-liberal debate, then, it would seem important to appreciate the ways in which a sense of distinct identity and a shared sense of what is good and bad can, and in Paul's case do, go together. The former is, of course, a key focus for communitarianism in general and Hauerwas in particular – identity and moral character formed in community by a particular tradition – while the latter is a key liberal and Habermasian concern – how to sustain a common, tradition-transcending moral framework within which distinct identities and traditions may coexist. To be sure, Paul (like Hauerwas) shows scant interest in the latter (though see further ch. 8), since his goal is, as we have already seen, to foster the solidarity and the positive sense of group identity of his small Christian congregations. Nonetheless, what we have seen of the ways in which he does this suggests that this 'communitarian' focus does not imply the impossibility of the liberal vision of a shared moral framework, but rather affirms its plausibility.

Chapter 6

SOLIDARITY, DIFFERENCE AND OTHER-REGARD: THE STRONG AND THE WEAK (1 CORINTHIANS 8–10; ROMANS 14–15)

Having considered various ways in which corporate solidarity is a fundamental theme in Pauline ethics and examined some of the ways in which this solidarity is presented in terms of identity-distinction from the world (albeit combined with a greater degree of shared ethical values than the rhetoric of distinction might imply), we turn in this chapter to questions concerned with difference and diversity within the Christian communities. In other words, given the stress on the solidarity and holiness of these congregations as one body in Christ, how does Paul treat issues and conflicts that arise because of differences in ethical conviction and practice? As we have already seen (§1.7) these questions have been forcefully brought to prominence in Boyarin's work, where Paul is seen as (laudably) fostering a universal human unity and solidarity but (regrettably) doing so in a way which effectively erases cultural difference. These questions are also relevant to our attempt to read Paul so as, in part, to think about the liberal-communitarian debate: the issue of how, and how far, ethical diversity and difference can be sustained – both in the passive sense of being tolerated and in the more active sense of being valued – is pertinent both to an assessment of Hauerwas's approach to ecclesial ethics and to the liberal project of creating a shared public framework within which different traditions and ways of life can coexist.

Two Pauline passages will occupy the bulk of our attention in this chapter: 1 Cor. 8.1–11.1; and Rom. 14.1–15.13.[1] These passages are of especial importance for any appraisal of Paul's ethics, though they are particularly relevant, as we shall see, to questions about difference and diversity. 1 Corinthians 8–10 constitutes the most extensive passage of moral argumentation in Paul's letters, focused on one specific issue (assuming that the chapters have a literary integrity; see below). Here, in contrast to a number of passages where Paul gives ethical exhortation in a concise, perhaps traditional, certainly unexplicated form (e.g. Rom. 12.9-21; 1 Thess. 4.1-12; 5.12-22), Paul develops an argument, in relation to a

---

1. In this chapter I draw on material in Horrell 1997b, 2002d, forthcoming.

question posed by the Corinthian Christians, for a particular kind of approach to Christian moral reasoning and practice. This focus and consistency of argument distinguishes this passage from 1 Corinthians 5–7, also a lengthy section with a topical coherence (issues concerning sexual morality), but where different arguments and concerns feature at different points (cf., e.g., 1 Cor. 5.13 with 6.2; 6.16 with 7.14). Romans 14.1–15.13 also represents a coherent and extended argument focused on a single basic issue and occurs in the most influential Pauline letter, a letter which, though certainly 'situational', forms 'the most sustained and reflective statement of Paul's own theology by Paul himself' (Dunn 1998a: 25), a carefully constructed and extended piece of argumentation. Again their character as focused and extended argument distinguishes 14.1–15.13 from the other main section of ethical instruction in Rom. 12.1–13.14: while this earlier section has a discernible structure, it treats a number of themes distinctly (e.g., 13.1-7).[2] Thus, in these two passages in 1 Corinthians and Romans, we see Paul as a moral philosopher, by which I intend to claim not that Paul is either like or unlike contemporary Graeco-Roman moral philosophers, but rather that here Paul engages in reflection and argument on issues of ethics and morality.[3]

These two passages are also closely related; it is widely recognized that in Romans 14–15 Paul draws on and reworks material from 1 Corinthians 8–10, using it to address a new and somewhat different situation.[4] Examples of the closest specific parallels are shown in Table 6.1.[5]

These and other parallels 'clearly indicate to what a great extent Rom. 14:1–15:13 repeats, rephrases, echoes the arguments of 1 Cor. 8; 9; 10:23–11:1' (Karris 1973: 75), even though it also contains a good deal that is distinctive.[6] It might be suggested, therefore, that by looking in some detail

---

2. See further Horrell 2003.

3. Contrast Meeks 1993: 3–5, who focuses on early Christian 'morality' rather than 'ethics', since he regards the latter as 'a reflective, second-order activity' (see §3.4 above); but precisely that kind of reflection is what we find here.

4. Cf., e.g., Conzelmann 1975: 137: 'This passage in Romans ... obviously represents a revision and further development of 1 Cor 8–10.' As Conzelmann notes, this is also an argument in favour of the unity of the 1 Corinthians passage (though not a decisive one, since some sections of 1 Cor. 8.1–11.1 are not paralleled in Romans 14–15). However, I do not share the view that in drawing on 1 Corinthians 8–10 in Romans 14–15 Paul is formulating general paraenesis, unrelated to any specific issues at Rome, as some have argued (see further §6.2 below).

5. For further parallels, see Karris 1973: 73–75.

6. It is notable that 1 Cor. 10.1-22 is not paralleled in Rom. 14.1–15.13. This may be partly explained by the different issues of concern – idolatry is an issue in 1 Corinthians 8–10 but not in Romans 14–15 – but it is also significant that the summarizing section of 1 Cor. 8.1–11.1 (10.23–11.1) does not reiterate points from this section of the argument (see further below).

Table 6.1 *Parallels between 1 Corinthians 8–10 and Romans 14–15*

1 Corinthians	Romans
'a stumbling block to the weak'	'a stumbing block or offence to [your] sibling'
πρόσκομμα ... τοῖς ἀσθενέσιν (8.9)	πρόσκομμα τῷ ἀδελφῷ ἢ σκάνδαλον (14.13)
'the weak one is destroyed ... a sibling* for whom Christ died'	'your sibling is grieved ... do not ... destroy that one for whom Christ died'
ἀπόλλυται ... ὁ ἀσθενῶν ... ὁ ἀδελφὸς δι' ὃν Χριστὸς ἀπέθανεν (8.11)	ὁ ἀδελφός σου λυπεῖται ... μὴ ... ἐκεῖνον ἀπόλλυε, ὑπὲρ οὖ Χριστὸς ἀπέθανεν (14.15)
'therefore if food causes my sibling to stumble, I will never eat meat again, lest I cause my sibling to stumble'	'it is good not to eat meat or drink wine or do anything by which your sibling is made to stumble'
διόπερ εἰ βρῶμα σκανδαλίζει τὸν ἀδελφόν μου, οὐ μὴ φάγω κρέα εἰς τὸν αἰῶνα, ἵνα μὴ τὸν ἀδελφόν μου σκανδαλίσω (8.13)	καλὸν τὸ μὴ φαγεῖν κρέα μηδὲ πιεῖν οἶνον μηδὲ ἐν ᾧ ὁ ἀδελφός σου προσκόπτει (14.21)
'let no one seek their own [good/benefit] but that of the other ... be imitators of me just as I am of Christ'	'let each of us please our neighbour for the good purpose of upbuilding; for Christ did not please himself ...'
μηδεὶς τὸ ἑαυτοῦ ζητείτω ἀλλὰ τὸ τοῦ ἑτέρου ... μιμηταί μου γίνεσθε, καθὼς κἀγὼ Χριστοῦ (10.24; 11.1)	ἕκαστος ἡμῶν τῷ πλησίον ἀρεσκέτω εἰς τὸ ἀγαθὸν πρὸς οἰκοδομήν· καὶ γὰρ ὁ Χριστὸς οὐχ ἑαυτῷ ἤρεσεν· (15.2-3)

*Another notable parallel between the two passages is the frequent use of ἀδελφός, four times in 1 Cor. 8.11-13, five times in Rom. 14.10-21; see further §4.2. I have adopted the inclusive rendering 'sibling' here, rather than 'brother', or the more clumsy 'brother or sister'.

at both of these passages I am giving undue weight to what is in fact one set of ideas and not two. I would turn that comment round, however: the fact that Paul adapted and re-presented in Romans a form of argument presented in 1 Corinthians shows the importance for Paul of this way of approaching certain kinds of ethical questions and disagreements. The moral norms and values evident in both these passages can and should be regarded as central to Pauline ethics.

It should also be noted, however, that these passages both deal with questions concerning food, which Paul treats differently from sexual morality. As we saw in the previous chapter, sexual immorality and idolatry are to be shunned, and are dealt with in terms related to the body and its participation in competing unions. Food per se does not have the same ethical significance and is thus the focus for the development of different forms of ethical argument (cf. §5.3).

6.1 *Idol-Food at Corinth: 1 Corinthians 8.1–11.1*

After turning explicitly at 1 Cor. 7.1 to the issues raised in the letter sent by the Corinthians to Paul ('Now concerning the matters about which you wrote'), at 8.1 Paul most likely deals with a further matter raised by the Corinthians, that of εἰδωλόθυτα, foods that have been offered to 'idols'.[7] Given the widespread practice of offering foods to various deities, eating meals in dining rooms or areas associated with various temple complexes, eating sacrificial food in private houses, selling such foods in the markets and so on, encountering such 'idol-food' was by no means uncommon, and it is understandable that it should arise as a topic in early Christian ethics.[8] What is less clear from the glimpses we have in the text is whether the Corinthian letter asked for Paul's advice on this issue, or asserted a particular stance which some of the Corinthians regarded as justified.

Paul's response to the Corinthians constitutes a long and complex passage which has generated much scholarly discussion.[9] It has proved notoriously difficult to determine what Paul's stance actually was regarding the eating of idol-food and participating in non-Christian meals and cultic acts in various settings. The diversity of scholarly views at least reveals for certain that Paul's instruction is less than crystal clear on these matters! There are also difficulties arising from the apparent contrasts between different sections of the passage: ch. 8 and the latter parts of ch. 10 (10.23-33) seem at least theoretically to accept a Christian's right to eat idol-food, even in an εἰδωλεῖον, while 10.1-22 is full of stern warnings against idolatry. And ch. 9 appears in some respects a digression from the main topic. These literary difficulties have led to various partition hypotheses, in which certain sections of the passage are assigned to different letters,[10] and to a range of studies which leave some parts of the

---

7. On the meaning of 'idols', see above §5.5. On the use of περὶ δέ to introduce topics from the Corinthians' letter, see Hurd 1965: 65–74, though note the caution of Mitchell 1989, who shows that the phrase as used in Greek letters does not necessarily indicate the beginning of a response to an issue raised in a letter but only the introduction of a new topic known to both reader and writer. But there are other reasons to regard 1 Cor. 8.1 as a likely reference to an issue raised by the Corinthians, not least the parallel in 7.1 combined with the serial use of περὶ δέ in 1 Corinthians (1 Cor. 7.1, 25; 8.1; 12.1; 16.1, 12; cf. also 1 Thess. 4.9; 5.1) and the indications that Paul cites Corinthian views in 1 Cor. 8.1, 4, etc.; see further Horrell 1996: 89–90.

8. Cf. Gooch 1993: 1–46; Newton 1998: 79–257; Fotopoulos 2003: 176–78 (for a brief summary of the contexts in which idol-food could have been encountered). Cf. Acts 15.20, 29; Rev. 2.14, 20; *Did.* 6.3. On attitudes to the issue in Judaism and early Christianity see Cheung 1999, though for qualifications of some of his arguments see Horrell forthcoming.

9. Recent monographs devoted to these chapters (not to mention articles) include Willis 1985a; Probst 1991; Gooch 1993; Gardner 1994; Yeo 1995; Newton 1998; Cheung 1999; Smit 2000; Fotopoulos 2003. Thus I think Derek Newton is simply inaccurate to say that '[j]udging by current output, 1 Corinthians 8–10 remains the least considered section of Paul's First Letter to the Corinthians' (1998: 26). Alex Cheung is more accurate when he reports that 'a plethora of studies on 1 Corinthians 8–10 has been produced in the past decade' (1999: 17).

10. E.g. Weiss 1910: xl–xliii, 210–13; Héring 1962: xiii–xiv, 75; Schmithals 1971: 90–96; Jewett 1978: 396–404; Sellin 1987: 2964–82.

passage out of consideration.[11] Most recent work, however, has affirmed the unity of the passage, and indeed of 1 Corinthians as a whole, a conclusion with which I fully concur. There are no compelling textual or literary grounds for the hypothesis of literary partition, and both the form of the argument – a broadly chiastic ABA' pattern with an apparent digression at its heart – and the tensions between its various parts are features encountered elsewhere in Paul, indeed in passages that seem to be classic examples of Pauline argumentation (e.g., 1 Corinthians 12–14; Rom. 1.18–3.20; 9–11).[12] Though complex, the passage is best understood as a coherent and integrated unit.

Questions have also been raised concerning whether the diversity Paul depicts among the Corinthians here, often referred to in terms of a conflict between the 'strong' and the 'weak',[13] is real or only a hypothetical construct of Paul's. John Hurd, for example, followed more recently by Peter Gooch, has argued that in fact the Corinthians were united on the issue of idol-food and that the 'weak' are a non-existent, hypothetical group created by Paul, who was trying to impose on the Corinthians a policy agreed at the apostolic council which contradicted his earlier practice and teaching at Corinth.[14] Of course Paul's own literary construction of the situation at Corinth is all that we have, and in a number of places in these chapters Paul does present situations as hypothetical, in the sense that they may or may not happen (e.g., 10.27–28). However, there are no compelling grounds to doubt that differences of opinion and practice existed at Corinth; indeed, much of Paul's exhortation would be rather pointless if it did not. If Paul's aim were, as Hurd suggests, to dissuade the Corinthians from eating idol-food, then to base the reasons for avoidance to a large extent on concern for a weaker sibling, when such 'weak' persons did not exist at Corinth, would leave the Corinthians rather free to disregard Paul's advice. Jerome Murphy O'Connor agrees: 'No evidence contradicts the traditional opinion that

11. E.g. Willis 1985a (but note 1985b); Murphy-O'Connor 1978b; Yeo 1995.

12. On the ABA' pattern cf. Fee 1987: 15–16 with n. 40. The extended arguments in Rom. 1.18–3.20 and 9.1–11.36 both contain passages which, when compared, stand in tension, even contradiction, with one another, but which can be seen to serve the overall direction and purpose of the argument, as they make a particular point at a particular stage (cf., e.g., Rom. 2.12-16 and 3.20, or 9.14-18 and 10.1-13). On the unity of this passage, see Hurd 1965: 131–42; Merklein 1984: 163–73; Schrage 1995: 212–15. Recent work on this passage by Gardner 1994, and on 1 Corinthians by Mitchell 1991, also affirms its unity.

13. E.g. Theissen 1982: 121–43. Only the term 'weak' ($\dot{\alpha}\sigma\theta\epsilon\nu\dot{\eta}\varsigma$) is actually used here (1 Cor. 8.11, cf. 8.7, 10), contrasted with those who have knowledge (8.1, 4, 11); the strong and the weak are explicitly contrasted in Rom. 15.1, though this is a strength or weakness in 'faith' (14.1).

14. Hurd 1965: 117–25; followed by Fee 1980: 175–76; Wright 1991: 133 n. 36; Gooch 1993: 61–72 (except on the issue of whether Paul himself ate idol-food at Corinth).

there were two groups within the Corinthian church. One group had no doubts about the legitimacy of eating idol-meat, the other had serious reservations' (1978b: 544).[15]

While scholars disagree as to the precise form and the number of places where Corinthian opinions are quoted by Paul, there is widespread agreement that in 8.1 and 8.4 at least Paul cites opinions which have been expressed by some – the so-called 'strong' – at Corinth:[16] 'we all have knowledge' (8.1b); 'there is no idol in the world[17] and there is no God but one' (8.4b).[18] However, disputes about the extent of Corinthian quotations here are perhaps less crucial for the interpretation of the passage than is sometimes assumed. For in 8.1, 4, 6 and 8 (where Corinthian quotations have been suggested) it does seem clear both that the opinions quoted are ones associated with the Corinthian 'strong' but also that they are opinions which Paul basically shares – even though he may qualify them and differ as to their implications for conduct. Here, as in 6.12, he does not counter a cited opinion with an emphatic μὴ γένοιτο (as, e.g., in Rom. 3.4, 6, 31; 6.2, 15; 7.7, 13; Gal. 2.17; 3.21) and he seems to include himself in the 'we' who have knowledge in 1 Cor. 8.1, 4 and 6 (just as he includes himself explicitly among the 'strong' in faith in Rom. 15.1).[19]

These statements – 'there is no idol in the world and there is no God but one' – represent the theological legitimation for the strong's assertion of their freedom to eat idol-food without restriction (cf. Brunt 1981: 22). And it is a theological legitimation which Paul essentially accepts and shares. He does not entirely affirm the declaration that there is no idol in the world – there are many so-called gods (1 Cor. 8.5; cf. 10.19-22)[20] – but certainly affirms the monotheistic confession of 8.6: 'but for us there is one God ...

---

15. Cf. also also Brunt 1981: 30 n. 18; Willis 1985a: 92–96.

16. See Hurd 1965: 68; Fee 1987: 365 with n. 30; Schrage 1995: 220–21. It is less likely that οἴδαμεν should be included within the quotation (see Fee 1987: 365 n. 31, against Willis 1985a: 67–70; see further Gardner 1994: 22–23, 34).

17. Probably in the sense 'has no real existence' rather than that 'an idol is a nothing'; see discussion in Murphy O'Connor 1978b: 546; Schrage 1995: 236.

18. The likelihood of Paul's quoting in 1 Cor. 8.4b is shown by the repetition of ὅτι ... καὶ ὅτι; see Giblin 1975: 530.

19. Héring 1962: 72 and Schrage 1995: 221 ('daß sich V 1b und V 7a formal widersprechen') are therefore not quite correct to suggest that there is a formal contradiction between 1 Cor. 8.1 and 8.7, thus establishing that the former *must* be a Corinthian quotation: the two statements may simply indicate that the 'we all' is a group which does not include everyone in the congregation.

20. On Paul's hedging around both sides of the question of idols' existence, cf. Schrage 1995: 226; also Wright 1991: 128: 'The pagan pantheon cannot simply be dismissed as metaphysically nonexistent and therefore morally irrelevant.'

and one Lord ...'.[21] That this theological knowledge underpins a specific stance towards idol-food – one which claims a freedom to eat – is confirmed by Paul's description of the contrary position: those who do not have this knowledge are unable to eat idol-food except as something belonging to an idol (τοῦ εἰδώλου) and thus in so acting they pollute or defile their weak consciousness (καὶ ἡ συνείδησις αὐτῶν ἀσθενὴς οὖσα μολύνεται, 8.7).[22]

Paul's response to the existence of these 'weaker' believers is not, however, to reiterate the importance of the credal knowledge which the strong already affirm, nor to argue for a particular stance towards idol-food itself on the basis of such theological knowledge.[23] Rather, it is to argue for a different kind of foundation and motivation for ethical decision-making, essentially a relational, other-regarding ethic with a specifically christological shape. However legitimate the theological grounding for the strong's freedom to eat, a higher priority in determining legitimate action is its impact on others, given that food in itself is ethically neutral: partaking or abstaining imply no particular benefit or deprivation per se (8.8).[24] What is crucial in this case is the effect one's conduct has on others, whose 'consciences' are weak. Βλέπετε, 'watch out' (8.9), is the first imperative Paul uses in this passage. The problem is that the strong's exercise of their authority, their ἐξουσία, may become a stumbling block to the weak; seeing the strong eating ἐν εἰδωλείῳ or elsewhere, they may be 'built up' – οἰκοδομηθήσεται, an ironizing of the term Paul uses so positively elsewhere – to eat idol-food even while conscious of its idolatrous connections. The conduct of the strong would therefore lead to the destruction of the weak. The negative force of having such an impact is strongly depicted in Paul's description of such a 'weak' one as 'a sibling

---

21. It has been suggested that this credal confession stems from the strong at Corinth (so, e.g. Willis 1985a: 84–86), but, even if they knew and affirmed it, it is more plausibly taken as an established formula with which Paul is in wholehearted agreement. Cf. Schrage 1995: 221: 'In V 6 greift Paulus wahrscheinlich nicht auf ein Argument der Korinther, sondern auf eine überkommene Formel zurück.' Murphy O'Connor, 1978a: 254–59, argues that the text is a pre-Pauline baptismal acclamation. His argument that it is 'soteriological' and not 'cosmological' is less convincing.

22. On the strong and cultic sense of pollution or defilement implied by the verb μολύνω, see Thiselton 2000: 640. On συνείδησις, see further §6.3.1 below.

23. Thus my interpretation runs counter to that of Wright 1991, who argues for the centrality of 1 Cor. 8.6 – a Christianized *Shema* – to Paul's argument here, as a 'reassertion of Jewish-style monotheism' (p. 125) and as the theological basis from which Paul addresses this situation (p. 121). As Schrage puts it: 'The question of whether it is right or wrong to eat flesh offered to idols is decided ultimately by reference to others, not to God' (1988: 196). See further Horrell 1997b.

24. Cf. Gardner 1994: 48–53; also Rom. 14.17; 1 Cor. 6.13; §5.3 above.

(ὁ ἀδελφός) for whom Christ died' (8.11),[25] and of such destructive action as constituting a 'sin against Christ'. This is, as Murphy-O'Connor (1978b: 563) notes, 'the only occasion on which Paul speaks of a "sin against Christ"', and it is significant to note that it is a *relational* concern – causing a fellow believer to stumble – that is described as a sin against Christ, rather than a particular act concerning idol-food itself. Thus, in a hyperbolic summary of his point, Paul declares that he himself would go to extreme lengths, giving up meat forever rather than be a cause of offence and stumbling to any of these sisters and brothers (8.13; cf. the extreme language of Rom. 9.3). Here the importance of costly regard for others depends implicitly on the foundational value of communal solidarity: the other is an ἀδελφός (cf. §4.2 above) and a part of the communal body which is Christ.[26] It is also significant to note that this 'stumbling', which is the weak sibling's destruction, consists not in their being 'offended' by the strong's actions but rather in their being encouraged to act in a similar way without a sufficiently robust consciousness. Whether an act is legitimate or not can depend, it seems, on the stance of the individual actor. This is a point to which we shall return (§6.3.1).

Thus, while Paul accepts as legitimate the theological principles cited by the strong as justifying their freedom to eat idol-food, and nowhere in this chapter questions their 'right' (ἐξουσία) so to do (1 Cor. 8.9), he insists that Christian ethics has a quite different basis. There are some who do not see the theological knowledge or its consequences in the same way as the strong, and, rather than seeking to educate or enlighten them so as to change their views and practice, Paul insists that a christologically based pattern of self-giving for one's siblings in Christ must be adopted. Even a practice for which one has an unquestionable 'right',[27] which has an unquestionable theological basis, must be set aside if it is a cause of

---

25. As well as the emphasis created through the repetition of the term ἀδελφός here (and in Rom. 14.10-21), note the personalizing force of using the singular form, as also in Rom. 14.10-21; 1 Cor. 6.5-6; 1 Thess. 4.6, and the further intensification of the ethical demand implied in this language through the use of personal pronouns: τὸν ἀδελφὸν μου (8.13, *bis*), τὸν ἀδελφὸν σου (Rom. 14.10 [*bis*], 15, 21). Cf. §4.2.

26. Cf. Murphy O'Connor 1978b: 563–65, who argues that it is the community as the body of Christ which is in view in Paul's reference to a 'sin against Christ'.

27. Following many commentators, and BDAG, 352, I have used the term 'right' to translate ἐξουσία in this passage, esp. in 1 Corinthians 9, where some such translation is required. Winter (1994: 166–77) also argues for the translation 'right', and suggests that Paul has a specific 'civic right' in view in 1 Cor. 8.9, 'a civic privilege which entitled Corinthian citizens to dine on "civic" occasions in a temple' (p. 166), connected probably with festivities during the Isthmian games. This seems to me possible, but hardly more than this; it is equally, and perhaps more, likely that the 'rights' in view are viewed as such on the basis of theological legitimation (8.4-6; 9.8-14). There is, of course, an important contemporary debate as to whether the notion of 'rights' has any legitimate part in Christian ethics.

stumbling. This approach to Christian ethics is in fact neatly summarized in the opening three verses of ch. 8, where Paul anticipates the longer argument to follow: right action is not a matter of knowledge but of love. In other words, the basis for discerning what is good and acceptable is not what one knows to be the case ('there is no idol in the world') and what is therefore justifiable – ethics based on theological knowledge – but rather a generous regard for the other, a self-giving love as embodied by Christ.

That this interpretation of ch. 8 is correct is also confirmed by what follows in ch. 9. This apparently digressive chapter plays a crucial part in the wider argument and is linked verbally and thematically to this wider literary context.[28] It is unfortunate, therefore, that a good many studies concentrate on chs 8 and 10 (or parts thereof) without giving attention to ch. 9 and its role here.[29] Paul's personal example is brought to bear on the discussion. After insisting firmly and somewhat defensively that he is a genuine apostle (9.1-3)[30] – an essential basis for the argument that follows – Paul proceeds to pile up reasons to justify the legitimacy of his right to material support from the church. Arguments from everyday life, from scripture, from temple and cult, and even – climactically – from a command of the Lord, all cumulatively combine to demonstrate that Paul has a right, an ἐξουσία, which is unquestionably legitimate (9.7-14). Yet Paul sets aside his right for the sake of the gospel, and particularly for the sake of the weak, enslaving himself to all, and hyperbolically asserts that he would rather die than be deprived of his boast in this regard (9.15-23).[31] This, then, is the imitation to which Paul calls the Corinthian strong at the end of the whole passage and which he sees as an imitation of Christ (11.1). They may have the 'right' to eat idol-food but must be prepared to set this

---

28. Verbal links include, e.g., ἐξουσία (1 Cor. 8.9; 9.4-6, 12, 18) and the various words related to the idea of 'offence': πρόσκομμα (8.9); ἐγκοπή (9.12); ἀπρόσκοπος (10.32); σκανδαλίζειν (8.13); also κερδαίνω (9.19-23). See further Willis 1985b: 39–40; Malherbe 1994; Schrage 1995: 213. Such links make the literary partition hypotheses seem less plausible (cf. n. 10 above). Cf. also the role of 1 Corinthians 13 within chs 12–14.

29. Cf. n. 11 above. The corresponding problem besets an examination of 1 Corinthians 9 which does not locate it explicitly within the wider argument in which it functions (e.g. Robbins 1996).

30. On the arguments concerning whether this chapter should be seen primarily as a defence or as an example, see Horrell 1996: 204–206. Schrage, 1995: 280–91, suggests that the 'defence' mentioned in 9.3 relates to vv. 1-3, whereas vv. 4-27 are primarily an *exemplum*. Many scholars recognize the implication here that there are some doubts about Paul's apostleship at Corinth; e.g. Barrett 1971: 200; Fee 1987: 392–401. He must insist on this fact if the following section (vv. 4-23) is to carry any force. Paul is also probably on the defensive concerning his refusal of material support at Corinth (see further Horrell 1996: 210–16). I cannot see any evidence for the view that Paul is defending himself against criticism that he ate idol-food in this chapter, as argued by Hurd 1965: 130–31; Fee 1987: 363, 393, 425, etc.; contrast Gooch 1993: 93–95.

31. On 1 Cor. 9.14-15 see further §7.2 below.

right aside out of concern for others, especially for their 'weaker' siblings in the church.

At 10.1 the focus and thrust of Paul's argument seem quite clearly to shift, in a way which has led some to propose that 10.1-22 belongs to a different letter altogether. However, this section is not entirely disjunctive; rather, it picks up the train of thought begun in 9.24-27, specifically the danger of being found in the end ἀδόκιμος, that is, excluded from the company of those who are saved. This is clearly the theme of 10.1-13, an argument against complacency drawn from the experiences of the Israelites in the wilderness. The language of 10.1-4 represents a careful and deliberate attempt to parallel the Israelites' experiences with the rituals of baptism and Lord's supper in which the Corinthians have shared. Just as all of the Corinthians have been baptized in the name of Jesus Christ (1 Cor. 1.13–14; 12.13), and all share in the Lord's supper (1 Cor. 10.16-17; 11.17-34), so *all* of the Israelites also shared in the rituals of membership and belonging. After the laboured repetition of 'all', πάντες, five times in vv. 1-4, the rhetorical impact of v. 5, beginning with the adversative ἀλλ' οὐκ, can hardly be missed. Despite the fact that all shared equally in these signs of belonging, 'God was not pleased with the majority of them, for their bodies were scattered in the desert'. And straightaway the explicit link is made: these things happened, Paul tells his readers, as examples for us, τύποι ἡμῶν, in order to warn us against the forms of behaviour, the 'evil desires' (v. 6), for which the Israelites were judged and condemned: idolatry, sexual immorality, putting *Christ* (τὸν Χριστόν)[32] to the test, and grumbling. The lesson is clearly drawn out: so then, ὥστε,[33] 'if you think you are standing, watch out that you do not fall' (v. 12, NRSV). The whole passage is a warning against complacency: the Israelites all partook in the rituals of community membership just as much as the Corinthians, yet this was no guarantee of salvation. Each person should be aware of the potential precariousness of their position within the community – just as Paul is too (μή πως ... ἀδόκιμος γένωμαι, 9.27).[34]

32. Verse 9; which some scribes found too odd and changed to κύριος. Cf. 8.12 and the warning against 'sinning against Christ'.
33. Cf. Gardner 1994: 152: 'The word Ὥστε shows the centrality of v 12 to Paul's argument.'
34. Martin's view that Paul regards 'gnosis' as a 'prophylactic talisman' (1995a: 179–89) – on which cf. also n. 76 below – thus needs some qualification, in view of the dangers here described. The activity for which the strong claim an ἐξουσία would indeed 'pollute' (μολύνεται) the weak (8.7-12; cf. Rom. 14.23). Yet part of the point of 1 Cor. 10.1-22, surely, is to warn the strong against complacency. Their gnosis is precisely *not* a 'prophylactic' protection, at least not in the situations in view in 10.1-22.

It is notable, however, that the explicit focus of this whole section is on idolatry rather than idol-food as such (cf. 10.7, 14).[35] While 8.1–13 focused on the issue of eating in various contexts, including ἐν εἰδωλείῳ, here Paul talks of those who participate in sacrifice (note θύω; 10.20) and share 'the table of δαιμονίων' (10.21); as Derek Newton observes, 'Paul's emphasis is thus very much on those involved in the actual act of making and eating sacrifices'.[36] This is the form of activity which Paul without exception prohibits (cf. Newton 1998: 198–99; further pp. 331–71). As we have already seen (§5.3) Paul depicts idolatry in terms of a form of participation which is incompatible with the believer's participation in Christ, initiated in baptism and affirmed in the Lord's supper (10.16-17).

In 10.23 Paul begins to recapitulate and summarize his argument.[37] He begins by twice citing the Corinthian slogan 'all things are permissible', πάντα ἔξεστιν, quoted already in 6.12. As with the opinions Paul cites in 8.1 and 8.4, he does not negate or oppose this slogan, but qualifies it by insisting that there are more important values, higher priorities, which must inform ethical practice. It is not a matter of whether one has the freedom, or the right, to do something (ἔξεστιν), whether it is justifiable, but of whether it is for the common good (συμφέρει; cf. 1 Cor. 12.7: πρὸς τὸ

---

35. *Pace* Bockmuehl (2000: 168 with n. 101), it is not enough to cite 1 Cor. 10.14 as an indication that 'idol food is certainly *not* a matter of indifference for Paul'. Due weight must be given to the fact that Paul focuses here on εἰδωλολατρία, and not εἰδωλόθυτα, in the midst of a discussion primarily concerned with the latter (8.1, 4).

36. Newton 1998: 338. Newton has clarified, through a thorough study of the socio-historical and archaeological evidence, how the situation in view here differs from that depicted in 1 Corinthians 8, 'reclining ἐν εἰδωλείῳ'. In this latter case Newton shows what a variety of settings could be included in such a designation, and how those partaking in meals in such contexts might or might not be eating food that had been directly taken from the sacrificial act (pp. 79–257, 298–305). In many cases, only a small group of worshippers or cultic officials took part in the sacrificial act and ate of the sacrificial offerings; others might eat other food, and might do so in adjacent rooms, or in the open air, or in other settings which evinced no close connection with the cultic act itself (pp. 198–99, 202, 230, 233–39, etc.). In 10.1-22, Newton argues, participation in cultic acts of sacrificing and eating are in view. Thus the difference between the two sections of the passage is that '1 Corinthians 8 dealt with the issue of temple *eating*, whereas 1 Cor. 10.1-22 tackled the problem of actual sacrificial acts accompanied by eating' (pp. 198–99; cf. also Lampe 2003: 597 [thesis 1.1]). Most interpreters, by contrast, have been unable to see how any distinction could be drawn between eating ἐν εἰδωλείῳ and participating in the table of demons (e.g., recently, Cheung 1999: 28–32, 36–38, 92–94, etc.).

37. Cf. Hurd 1965: 128: 'Closer comparison reveals that the whole of 1 Cor. 10.23–11.1 is a point by point restatement and summary of the argument of 1 Cor. 8 and 9.' See also Watson 1989: 312. Notable in this concluding section is the lack of any reference back to 10.1-22. All the reiterations and repetitions relate to chs 8 and 9 (cf. Hurd 1965: 128–31). Schrage suggests that after making clear the necessary limits, especially the rejection of participation in pagan cultic meals (in 10.1-22), Paul turns back in the conclusion to the more fundamental statements of ch. 8 and summarizes and clarifies these with concrete examples (1995: 461).

συμφέρον), whether it builds up the community (οἰκοδομεῖ). Thus 10.23 parallels and reiterates 8.1: the basis for ethics is not knowledge but love. These values are fundamental to Paul's understanding of Christian ethical practice, which is essentially a relational, communal matter and is not primarily about an individual's own rights or benefits.[38] Indeed, as the concise imperative of 10.24 declares, it is an ethic oriented fundamentally to 'the other', and to the benefit and support of the other rather than of the self. This ethic is grounded, for Paul, in Christology. Hays suggests that there are 'two fundamental norms to which he [sc. Paul] points repeatedly: the unity of the community and the imitation of Christ' (1997a: 41).[39] We might use the terms 'solidarity' and 'other-regard' respectively. These basic principles of Pauline ethics are thus summarized in vv. 23 and 24: the solidarity and well-being of the community (συμφέρει ... οἰκοδομεῖ) and the other-regard which is an imitation of Christ (μηδεὶς τὸ ἑαυτοῦ ζητείτω ἀλλὰ τὸ τοῦ ἑτέρου).[40]

In v. 25 Paul turns to more specific and practical conclusions, dealing first with the issue of meat purchased in the market and second with invitations to meals from unbelievers. In the first case the Christian is free to buy and consume anything sold in the market without feeling the need to raise questions about it or to consider the possible objections of others.[41] Paul justifies this advice with a quotation from scripture (Ps. 24.1). While this verse was used in rabbinic literature 'to justify the use of benedictions over food' (Barrett 1982: 52), Paul seems to use it here as a scriptural basis for declaring all foods sold in the market place 'clean' and acceptable for the Christian (cf. Mk 7.14-20; Acts 10.14-15; Rom. 14.14).[42] In the case of

---

38. Cf. the uses of οἰκοδομή and οἰκοδομέω elsewhere in 1 Corinthians: 3.9; 14.3-5, 12, 17, 26. Hays (1997a: 57 n. 27) points out that this language refers to 'the edification of the community as a whole'.

39. Wright 1991: 135, also points to the christological basis of the argument here: 'Underlying it all is the same principle which Paul articulated in Philippians 2.1–5, and for which he drew up the "lordly example" of Christ in Philippians 2.5-11: one must gladly give up one's rights for the sake of the unity of the body of Christ.' See further Hays 1994; §7.1 below.

40. Close parallels are found in Rom. 15.2 and Phil. 2.4, both passages where the paradigm of Christ's self-giving is expounded; see further ch. 7 below.

41. The instruction in 1 Cor. 10.28 to desist from eating if someone mentions the origins of the food seems most likely to be linked only with the immediately preceding scenario in v. 27, on which see below, and not with v. 25 also. Verses 27 and 28 describe a situation in hypothetical terms (though an entirely realistic and likely one) – εἴ τις καλεῖ ... ἐὰν δέ τις ὑμῖν εἴπῃ ... – while v. 25 gives a straightforward imperative.

42. See further Lohse 1956; Barrett 1982 (contrast Tomson 1990: 205–206). Bockmuehl (2000: 169) argues that 'the burden of proof' lies squarely on those who believe Paul could have countenanced Christians eating blood, or other foods prohibited in Jewish legal traditions that applied to Gentiles (Bockmuehl sees Paul's rule for Jewish Christians as obedience to the whole Torah; p. 171). Paul's own statements, however, seem clear enough to

invitations to meals hosted by unbelievers, Paul allows the freedom to go, 'if you wish' (καὶ θέλετε πορεύεσθαι), and to eat whatever is served (1 Cor. 10.27). Although 10.1-22 certainly makes clear that pagan cultic sacrificial gatherings are not included in this permission, it is not necessarily to be assumed that the only invitations Paul has in view here are those to a private home (as do many interpreters).[43] On the contrary, it is entirely possible that invitations to various kinds of social and celebratory occasions in a variety of settings are included.[44] It is not the venue that determines whether an invitation can be accepted or not (*pace* Witherington 1993, et al.) but rather the character of the meal – with participation in actual sacrifice prohibited.[45] In the case of these invitations which one may accept, the only reason given here for 'not eating' is if someone (τις)[46] points out that the food has been offered to an idol (ἱερόθυτον – a more positive term, denoting 'sacrificed to a divinity', than the implicitly negative εἰδωλόθυτον). Then one should abstain, for the sake of the other person's συνείδησις; that is, not because you yourself are in danger from such food, but out of concern for the other.

The rhetorical questions which follow in vv. 29b-30 have puzzled commentators for years.[47] Duane Watson's (1989) analysis of the use of such questions in ancient rhetoric has shown that the lack of direct answer to the questions need not be problematic. Watson suggests that here the questions 'allow Paul to progress in his argumentation from the specific

place the burden of proof on the opposite side, not only here, but also in Rom. 14.14, 20, where he declares all foods clean, at least to the 'strong in faith' among whom he counts himself. Tomson finds such 'radicalism ... very unlikely', and thus seeks an alternative interpretation of Romans 14 (1990: 247–48). But given the world-shattering reorientation – death, indeed! – Paul describes as taking place in his encounter with Christ (cf., e.g., Gal. 2.18-21; Phil. 3.7-11), and notwithstanding the fact that Paul's theology and ethics remain thoroughly rooted in biblical and Jewish tradition, it is unclear to me why such 'radical' change should be sociologically unlikely.

43. See Schrage 1995: 468 n. 523. Examples include Fee 1980; 1987: 359–63; Wright 1991: 134–35; Gardner 1994: 176, 183.

44. Cf. Newton 1998 (see n. 36 above); Borgen 1994, esp. pp. 55–56; Martin 1995a: 183; Schrage 1995: 468–69, 461. Schrage suggests: 'Zudem paßt dann auch die Zurückhaltung (εἰ θέλετε) besser, weil die Grenze des Erlaubten hier eher zu verschwimmen droht' (p. 469).

45. Cf. Newton 1998 (see n. 36 above); Fisk 1989 (p. 63, etc.).

46. There has been much discussion as to whether the 'someone' Paul has in mind here is a Christian or a non-Christian. I think the evidence just tips in favour of a Christian; see Horrell 1996: 147 with n. 109 (with references there); similarly Schrage 1995: 469–70. But a decision on this point is relatively unimportant: it is entirely possible that Paul includes *anyone*, Christian or not, in this hypothetical category.

47. Cf. Thiselton 2000: 788. Schrage describes 1 Cor. 10.29b as 'sehr schwierig', but insists that the difficulty of the questions does not justify the hypothesis that they are a secondary interpolation (1995: 471 with n. 537).

examples of 10:23-29a to the more general principles of 10:31–11:1'.[48] But the questions seem to interject a perspective like that of the strong, which Paul has already sharply qualified: one's 'freedom' to act should certainly be curtailed because of the consciousness of others (8.7-13), just as Paul, though free, has enslaved himself to all (9.19-23) and abandoned his legitimate rights (9.4-18). And the mere fact that one offers an appropriate thanks to God for what(ever) one eats does not justify one's actions in a way that makes the concerns and attitudes of others irrelevant. Paul's first general principle, in the conclusion to the passage as a whole (10.31–11.1), does, however, concede something of the importance and force of these questions. The Christian's calling, in whatever they do, is indeed to glorify God and not to please people (10.31). But this also implies, of course, that Christian living is not primarily about exercising one's legitimate freedom and enjoying one's rights, but about glorifying God. Next Paul reiterates his basic conviction, so central to this whole passage, that one should avoid causing offence or stumbling either to Jews, or to Greeks, or to the church of God (10.32).[49] Just as Paul believes that he does, so they too must seek to please others rather than seeking their own benefit, in order that others may be saved, a pattern of behaviour clearly stamped by the pattern of Christ's self-giving action (10.33; cf. Rom. 15.2-3). Thus the concluding sentence urges imitation of Paul, recalling his personal example as given in 1 Corinthians 9, and revealing explicitly that he regards his own practice as an imitation of Christ (11.1).[50]

There are a number of conclusions and themes important for our understanding of Pauline ethics to be drawn from this lengthy passage, some of which will be dealt with after the following study of Romans 14–15, since they also emerge in that latter text. First, we should note that Paul does present some 'absolutes' in terms of permissible and impermissible conduct regarding idol-food. The permissive absolute is the imperative to 'eat everything sold in the market place' ($\pi\tilde{\alpha}\nu$ $\tau\grave{o}$ $\grave{\epsilon}\nu$ $\mu\alpha\kappa\acute{\epsilon}\lambda\lambda\wp$ $\pi\omega\lambda o\acute{\upsilon}\mu\epsilon\nu o\nu$ $\grave{\epsilon}\sigma\theta\acute{\iota}\epsilon\tau\epsilon$ [1 Cor. 10.25] – note the emphatic $\pi\tilde{\alpha}\nu$ and the imperative $\grave{\epsilon}\sigma\theta\acute{\iota}\epsilon\tau\epsilon$). Here there is an absolute limit on the extent to which the concerns of

48. Watson 1989: 313; see further pp. 310–18, summarized on p. 318.
49. Note the parallel with the groups listed in 9.20-22; cf. Hurd 1965: 130; further in relation to the theme of outsiders, §8.3 below.
50. See further ch. 7 below. Brian Dodd (1998: 157–58) argues that 1 Cor. 11.1 does not appeal for an imitation of Christ but rather justifies the appeal to imitate Paul on the grounds that he is 'of Christ' (cf. 1 Cor. 1.12; 2.16; 3.23; 6.15; 7.22; 12.27; 15.23; 2 Cor. 10.1, 7). However, *pace* Dodd (p. 158), in only two of the above list of occurrences (given by Dodd) of Χριστοῦ in 1 and 2 Corinthians is there any sense of the phrase being a 'technical term', a 'cipher' (1 Cor. 15.23; 2 Cor. 10.7) and the parallelism conveyed by καθὼς κἀγώ in 11.1 (cf. 10.33) speaks more strongly for the usual interpretation, which takes imitation to be implied in the second clause as stated in the first. If Dodd's reading were correct, we would have expected ἐγὼ γάρ rather than καθὼς κἀγώ.

others, elsewhere in this passage so crucially determinative, can be allowed to control one's freedom (cf. 10.29b). The prohibitive absolute is to flee from idolatry (10.14), by which Paul appears to mean to avoid participation in cultic sacrificial acts (see above, with n. 36). In both of these cases, the permissive and the prohibitive, the imperative's validity remains, with or without any concerned others: even if a weaker sibling objects to one's freedom to purchase any food from the market, that freedom is unassailable; conversely, even if no 'weaker' siblings are caused to stumble by one's participation in a cultic sacrifice, it is prohibited nonetheless.

Inside the limits framed by these instructions are situations where it is the concerns of the other which are crucial: there is no absolute or intrinsic reason why certain actions are sinful in themselves, but they should be avoided if they are a cause of stumbling to others. The first of these relational instructions concerns the eating of εἰδωλόθυτα in settings that may include an εἰδωλεῖον (8.10: the verb κατακείμενον, reclining, implies the activity of dining/eating). Here, Paul essentially accepts as legitimate the theological principles by which the so-called 'strong' justify their freedom to eat idol-food and thus agrees that they have a legitimate ἐξουσία to act in this way. But the exercise of this ἐξουσία is very firmly limited by the stumbling it may cause for the weak. The second activity is attending dinners or banquets when invited by an unbeliever (10.27-29). Here too, as in the case already outlined by Paul in ch. 8, it is the consciousness of the other which is crucial for determining legitimate practice. If someone points out that the food is ἱερόθυτον then one should desist from eating, not for the sake of one's own consciousness, but that of the other. It is difficult to determine whether this hypothetical 'someone' is a Christian or a non-Christian – the former seems most likely to be primarily in mind (see n. 46 above) – but if the latter may at least be included among those in view then, unlike in ch. 8, here Paul's concerns are with the impact of Christians' actions *outside* as well as inside the church (see further ch. 8). These relational instructions, it is important to note, occupy the bulk of Paul's attention and argumentative energy in chs 8 and 9 and in the summarizing advice of 10.23–11.1.[51]

This focus on an 'other-regarding' morality helps to explain why commentators have found it so difficult to agree on what constitutes 'Paul's position regarding idol-food' (Cheung 1999: 171).[52] In attempting

---

51.   Cf. n. 37 above on the lack of reiteration of points from 10.1-22.

52.   For Cheung it is self-evident that the early Church needed 'a clear-cut answer to the rightness or wrongness of the act of consumption of idol food' (p. 168), just as contemporary Asian Christians need a clear-cut answer (viz. prohibition); he sees 'Western secular materialism' as the reason why commentators have underestimated 'the sinfulness of eating idol food' (p. 303). But it should be clear that the perceived 'need' for a clear-cut answer is

to elucidate this, scholars often fail to appreciate the extent to which Paul refuses to approach the issue in this way.[53] To be sure, there are some reasonably clear absolutes, which Paul legitimates and undergirds theologically (10.26) and christologically (10.16-17), but much of his argument is based on the presumption that 'right' practice can only be determined in relation to the context of human relationships in which one is enmeshed, the possible injury that one's actions may cause to others. Even if this communal context were to be such that eating idol-food would often need to be avoided, it is nonetheless extremely important to appreciate the basis on which Paul argues for its (conditional) avoidance and the relational concerns on which he focuses. Also worth noting is that while Paul's concerns are very much focused on the others within the church, they are not exclusively so: seeking the benefit of 'the many' outside the community is also imperative (10.32-33; cf. §8.3 below).

More specifically, it becomes clear in this passage how this 'other-regarding' morality has a fundamentally christological foundation. Just as the solidarity, unity and purity of the community are grounded in the notion of being one in Christ (chs 4–5 above) so the imperative to allow the consciousness of the 'other', the weaker sibling, to determine one's actions is christologically underpinned. Just as Christ gave himself even to death for such a person (8.11) so the Christian's responsibility is to look to the interests of the other, even when that means abandoning one's own legitimate rights and sacrificing one's legitimate freedom (9.15-23; 10.24; 10.33–11.1).[54] This is a central theme in Pauline ethics which we shall explore in more detail in the following chapter.

The community solidarity which Paul both presumes and fosters here (not least through the emphasis placed on the designation ἀδελφός) is not, then, to be sustained through bringing everyone into line with a certain

Cheung's and not Paul's. Other writers approaching the issue from non-Western contexts have stressed the ambiguities and complexities which make any 'clear-cut' position difficult to elucidate and justify (e.g., Newton 1998; Yeo 1994; 1995: 217–20).

53. Cf. further Meeks 1988. However, I am not convinced that Meeks's label 'polyphonic' for Paul's ethics in these chapters is entirely apposite. Meeks valuably draws attention to the diversity of moral viewpoints expressed and discussed in the passage, and suggests that one of Paul's aims is to create a moral community – a community 'strong' enough to conduct its own moral reflection – rather than to give the community a ruling. Yet, while Paul does indeed refuse, in one sense, to give a simple ruling about idol-food, he does not merely present various moral voices here. Rather, he provides a different kind of moral imperative: a christologically patterned imperative for other-regard which should (within limits) determine ethical practice. The imperative to 'look to the interests of the other' is not simply one option among a range of voices but an unquestionable and fundamental metamoral value. See further §9.1 below.

54. The christological basis of Paul's ethics here is also stressed by Söding 1994, though he focuses rather heavily on 8.11 (see e.g. p. 88).

level of moral awareness and its correlative practice; Paul does not seek to educate those with a 'weak' moral consciousness. It is not this ethical unanimity that Paul sees as required for the community's unity and consensus (cf. 1 Cor. 1.10; §4.3). Rather, solidarity is to be sustained through fostering the kind of other-regard which allows such differences of conviction and practice to remain, though this other-regard requires that the practice of the strong be compromised insofar as it endangers the weak.

6.2 *The Strong and the Weak in Rome: Romans 14.1–15.13*

It is widely recognized that Romans 12–15 forms the major section of ethical instruction in the letter to the Romans, founded on the theological exposition that has preceded (cf. 12.1: παρακαλῶ οὖν ...).[55] While the whole text from 12.1–15.13 is rightly seen as devoted to ethical matters, 14.1 begins a major new section focused on specific issues affecting the internal relations of the Roman churches (though doubtless also relevant to other churches Paul knew).[56] It is difficult to know whether to include 15.7-13 as part of this specific section, since it forms 'an effective conclusion to the body of the letter as a whole' (Dunn 1988: 706). Yet it also, more specifically, constitutes a fitting conclusion to the ethical argument of 14.1–15.6, which itself represents an ethical instantiation of the message of Romans as a whole (see below). Consequently 15.7-13 should be considered along with 14.1–15.6.

Some have argued that this section of Romans constitutes 'general paraenesis', a generalizing adaptation of the material from 1 Corinthians without any specific orientation to the context in Rome.[57] This seems less likely than that the instruction is shaped with regard to what Paul knew or perceived to be relevant issues at Rome: recent scholarship has inclined to see Romans as a whole as shaped by such contextual factors. Specifically, tensions between Jewish and Gentile Christians, which may have arisen

---

55. The pattern of theology followed by ethics, or indicative followed by imperative, is, however, rather less apparent in most of the Pauline letters (that is, aside from Romans and Galatians) than is sometimes suggested (e.g. Dunn 1988: 715: 'Paul has completed his theological exposition ... Those in the Roman congregation who already knew his style would expect him to turn to some practical counsel'). Even in Romans, ethics has already been a concern before 12.1, for example, in 6.1-14.

56. Ulrich Wilckens rightly sees 14.1 as the beginning of a new section, a piece of exhortation directed to specific issues at Rome, after the somewhat more general paraenesis of 12–13 (1982: 79).

57. E.g., Karris 1973; Meeks 1987: 291, 299 n. 3. Against this view see, e.g., Dunn 1988: 795. Wilckens (1982: 79) puts it well: 'Zweifellos visiert Paulus aktuelle Probleme in Rom an. Doch er sieht sie als denen gleichartig, mit denen er zuvor in Korinth so intensiv zu tun hatte (vgl. 1 Kor 8–10).'

when Jewish Christians expelled from Rome after Claudius' edict began to return to the city, and to what had in the meantime been a largely Gentile dominated church, provide a plausible reason for Paul's emphasis in Romans on God's impartial treatment of both Jew and Gentile (Rom. 2.9-11; 3.9, 29; 10.12), the need for Gentile converts not to become arrogant (11.13-32), and for the two groups to welcome and accept one another (14.1–15.13).[58] Moreover, while tensions between Jewish and Gentile Christians were hardly unique to Rome, it is difficult to explain why Paul reshapes the material from 1 Corinthians in the way he does, leaving out much and adding a good deal that is new, addressing the specific issues of food and days, unless he has some specific disputes in view.

The issue, then, in Rom. 14.1–15.13 concerns people who hold different convictions with regard to food and the observance of special days. The subject of food provides the link with 1 Corinthians 8–10, while the main difference is that here in Romans there is no explicit connection with idolatry, as there is in 1 Corinthians. Those Paul calls the 'weak'[59] abstain from certain foods (they 'eat only vegetables'; Rom. 14.2) and observe certain days as special (14.5) while the 'strong' (οἱ δυνατοί), among whom Paul counts himself (15.1), regard all foods as acceptable and all days as alike (14.2, 5). It seems clear from the passage, *pace* Mark Nanos (1996: 95–119) and Neil Elliott (1999) (who argue that the 'weak' are non-Christian Jews), that both groups are Christian believers: Paul gives exhortations to both groups (14.3, 10, etc.); describes both groups as practising their different customs 'for the Lord' (14.6; cf. 14.4), clearly Christ;[60] denotes both groups as ἀδελφοί (14.10, 13, 15, 21), a term which Paul characteristically reserves for members of the Christian congregations;[61] and grounds his exhortation in the example and attitude of Christ (15.1-7). What is less clear is the extent to which the two groups should be identified as Jewish and Gentile respectively. Against such a straightforward identification is the fact that Paul locates himself among the strong – those who eat anything and keep no special days. Mark Reasoner

---

58. See, e.g., Wiefel 1991; Wedderburn 1988: 44–65. Paul Minear (1971) valuably shows the importance of Romans 14–15 for illuminating the context to which Paul's whole letter is addressed. However, Minear's outline of five distinct groups, to whom different aspects of Paul's instruction were addressed, goes beyond what the text itself suggests and permits as a plausible reconstruction.

59. 'The weak in faith' in 14.1; 'the powerless' or 'incapable' (ἀδύνατοι) in 15.1.

60. Note the distinction between κύριος and θεός in 14.6 and the statement in 14.9: εἰς τοῦτο γὰρ Χριστὸς ἀπέθανεν καὶ ἔζησεν, ἵνα καὶ νεκρῶν καὶ ζώντων κυριεύσῃ.

61. Romans 9.3 is unique in Paul's letters in using ἀδελφοί to denote Jews, rather than Christians. However, it is here immediately clarified and qualified with the phrase τῶν συγγενῶν μου κατὰ σάρκα. It is therefore unconvincing to see this as a parallel supporting the idea that the ἀδελφοί in chs 14–15 may include non-Christian Jews (*pace* Nanos 1996 and Elliott 1999, cited above).

(1999) has recently explored the evidence concerning vegetarianism, asceticism, observance of special days and so on in first-century Rome, concluding that while the 'weak' doubtless included some Jewish Christians the group may well have also included non-Jews who had their own reasons for avoiding meat and observing special days. However, not only does Reasoner's own evidence point rather strongly to the centrality of Jewish concerns in Rom. 14.1–15.13,[62] but the text of Romans itself seems to confirm that issues relating to the relationship between Jews and Gentiles are central to Paul's purposes in writing the letter (see, e.g., Rom. 1.16; 2.9-10; 3.1, 9, 29; 9.24; 10.12; 15.7-13). While both 'strong' and 'weak' groups may certainly each have contained Jews and Gentiles, the issue at stake in Rom. 14.1–15.13 concerns 'the observance or non-observance of the Jewish law', as John Barclay, among others, has persuasively shown (Barclay 1996b: 289). Although the Jewish law does not, of course, prohibit the consumption of all meat (and wine – if this is also at issue in Rome: cf. 14.21) the practice of Jews restricting their diet to avoid all meat and wine when eating in Gentile contexts is well known from Daniel (1.8-16) and Esther (Esth. 4.17x LXX) as well as Josephus (*Life* 14).[63] The motivation for such practice was evidently to ensure that Jewish dietary laws were not violated and to avoid the idolatrous connections of Gentile meat and wine.

This conclusion is important insofar as it indicates that Paul's concern here cannot be regarded as addressing merely trivial ethical disagreements. It is not simply a matter of whether some prefer to eat this or that, or to mark certain days or not, but rather a question of difference among Christians who hold different convictions concerning obedience to the Jewish law, which clearly specifies obligations concerning food and sabbath (Lev. 11.1-47; 23.1-3; Deut. 5.12-15; 14.3-21; cf. *m. Hul. passim*, esp. 7–10), and which is of immense religious, cultural and social significance.[64] The two groups to which Paul refers in Romans 14–15 represent two ends of the spectrum of reactions: one abstains entirely from

62. Cf. Reasoner 1999: 128–38, 146–58. In addition, Reasoner's argument that the 'strong' and the 'weak' are sociological designations, with the weak lower on the social scale than the strong (see pp. 218–19), does not carry conviction, since Reasoner himself shows both that 'in first century Rome there were strong precedents for vegetarianism even in the upper classes' (p. 205) and that 'the Jewish sabbath was popular among some of the upper levels of Roman society' (p. 151).

63. Cf. also Hegesippus' testimony concerning James, brother of Jesus, who 'drank no wine or strong drink, nor did he eat flesh' (in Eusebius, *HE* 2.23.5) and *T. Isaac* 4.5, where Isaac is described as one 'who would not eat meat or drink wine all his life long'.

64. See further Barclay 1996b: 305–308. *Pace* Bockmuehl (2000) and Tomson (1990) it is difficult to see here support for the notion that Paul regards Jewish Christians as obliged to follow the whole Torah while Gentile Christians should follow only those commands deemed applicable to them: Paul, a Jew, includes himself among the strong who regard *all* foods as

meat and wine, in order to avoid breaking the law and contamination; the other regards all food and drink as clean and acceptable.

On the specific issues of food and days, Paul makes his own ethical convictions plain: 'I know and am persuaded in the Lord Jesus that nothing is unclean in itself' (14.14); 'all things are clean' ($\pi\acute{\alpha}\nu\tau\alpha$ $\mu\grave{\epsilon}\nu$ $\kappa\alpha\theta\alpha\rho\acute{\alpha}$: 14.20). And, of course, there is the judgment implicit in his choice of the labels 'strong' and 'weak' (in faith! 14.1; cf. 15.1: 'we the strong ...'). However, it is significant that he does not mount an argument in favour of this ethical conviction, just as in 1 Corinthians 8–10 he did not develop the strong's theologically based argument for freedom to eat idol-food. Here too Paul does not invest his argumentative energies into demonstrating that 'all foods are clean' and to arguing that all should therefore eat without observing Jewish customs and regulations. Instead his energies again go into mounting an argument for an other-regarding morality, with strong theological, specifically christological foundations, which seeks to enable ethical diversity to remain within a context of corporate solidarity. His concern does seem to be the properly *moral* question, as Habermas denotes it, of 'the legitimate ordering of coexisting forms of life'.[65]

As in 1 Cor. 8.1-3, here too Paul effectively summarizes the main points of his argument in the opening verses of the passage (Rom. 14.1-3). He opens with the call to welcome or accept ($\pi\rho\sigma\lambda\alpha\mu\beta\acute{\alpha}\nu\epsilon\sigma\theta\epsilon$) the weak in faith and not to argue over disagreements ($\delta\iota\alpha\lambda\sigma\gamma\iota\sigma\mu\sigma\acute{\iota}$) (14.1), then outlines the issue of contention at Rome, where some eat anything, others only vegetables (14.2). There then follows a more specific exhortation to each side of this disagreement: those who eat freely are not to despise ($\mu\grave{\eta}$ $\dot{\epsilon}\xi\sigma\upsilon\theta\epsilon\nu\epsilon\acute{\iota}\tau\omega$) those who do not eat; those who restrict their eating are not to judge ($\mu\grave{\eta}$ $\kappa\rho\iota\nu\acute{\epsilon}\tau\omega$) those who eat without restriction. And the basic theological foundation for this is that God has accepted or welcomed ($\pi\rho\sigma\epsilon\lambda\alpha\beta\acute{\epsilon}\tau\sigma$) each of these types of person, with their different practices (14.3). These basic terms and exhortations recur as the more detailed argumentation progresses (see 14.10, 13; 15.7).

Paul then proceeds to show why judgment of one another is inappropriate, one of the prominent themes of this passage.[66] All of his addressees are someone else's servants – they belong to the Lord – and the

---

clean (14.20), a view which does not appear to acknowledge the validity of even the 'minimal' requirements of the Noachide commandments or the Apostolic Decree (Acts 15.20, 29). Cf. n. 42 above; further §1.2.

65. Habermas 1993: 60. See further §6.4 below.

66. A theme explored especially by Meeks 1987. See Rom. 14.3-5, 10, 13, 22. A negative view of judging others has already been presented in 2.1-11. Paul's hearers were there led to a critical impression of the anonymous person who judges, and then later (in 14.1–15.7) find this critique of judgment turned on their own practices towards one another. I owe this observation to Robert Jewett.

right to judge them therefore belongs solely to their master; the κύριος alone decides whether they 'stand' or 'fall', and Paul is confident that they will all 'stand', since the Lord has the power to ensure this (14.4). In other words, not only is it inappropriate for believers to judge one another at all but their negative judgment is misplaced in any case. Each person, Paul insists, whichever way they act with regard to foods and special days, acts 'in honour of the Lord' (κυρίῳ – an associative dative, or dative of respect: the action is done to, for, or in relation to, the Lord; 14.6). Christian life is essentially life lived not for oneself, but for the Lord. It here becomes clear that the Lord to whom each person's actions are directed is Christ, who by his dying and rising has become Lord over both the living and the dead (ἵνα καὶ νεκρῶν καὶ ζώντων κυριεύσῃ, 14.9).[67]

While in other contexts Paul does call for judgment to be exercised over other Christians (most firmly and famously in 1 Cor. 5.11-13: see §5.3) here he seeks to legitimate different patterns of ethical conduct and to remove any basis for judgment or criticism. He does so by outlining a form of ethical relativism, which seems, interestingly, to acknowledge the constructed nature of ethical convictions regarding food, but at the same time to insist on their reality for those who hold them. Nothing is unclean δι' ἑαυτοῦ, 'in itself', Paul writes, expressing a conviction he holds 'in the Lord Jesus' (possibly echoing Mk 7.15; Paul certainly agrees with the Markan gloss in 7.19).[68] But it *is* unclean (κοινός) to the one who reckons it so (Rom. 14.14). This is a concise, but nonetheless powerful, expression of an approach to morality which seeks to legitimate a variety of ethical stances without denying their importance, their reality even, to those who hold them.[69] We might perhaps label it, albeit oxymoronically, a constructivist realism: things really are such, to the one who reckons them so.[70] This is why people should be fully convinced in their own minds about the stance they adopt (14.5); this is why it is so important for people to act in accordance with their convictions. Not to do so, not to act according to faith, is to *sin*, Paul insists: πᾶν δὲ ὃ οὐκ ἐκ πίστεως ἁμαρτία

---

67. Cf. too the distinction between κύριος and θεός in 14.6; and note also how Paul's composite citation in 14.11 expresses acclamation of both 'the Lord' and 'God'. Paul has achieved this by adding the common phrase ζῶ ἐγώ λέγει κύριος (see e.g. Num. 14.28; Isa. 49.18; Jer. 22.24; Ezek. 5.11; Zeph. 2.9) to Isa. 45.23 LXX (which adds the closing words τῷ θεῷ to the Hebrew text).

68. For a study of the echoes and allusions to Jesus' teaching in Romans 12–15 see Thompson 1991.

69. It is possible that Paul derived this idea from the wording of Lev. 11.4-8 etc. where the repeated conclusion in the list of unclean animals is not that they are 'unclean' as such, but 'unclean for you' (טמא הוא לכם; ἀκάθαρτον τοῦτο ὑμῖν).

70. Peter Tomson speaks of Paul's 'pluralist rationalism', seeing Paul's ingenious solution here as providing a '"neutral" rationale which allows both gentile and Jewish diets' (1990: 245, 250).

ἐστίν (14.23). While the word συνείδησις, used in 1 Cor. 8.7-10, does not reappear here, the idea is comparable: whether an act is legitimate or not depends on the stance of the actor (see further §6.3.1 below).

But Paul is not concerned solely to legitimate the concurrent practice of different ethical convictions. He is primarily concerned to secure and strengthen the unity and solidarity of the Christian community while at the same time sustaining this diversity of ethical practices. In other words, the unity of the community is not to be fostered through the adoption of a common stance on this issue of ethical dispute but fostered precisely in the face of this diversity. There are various bases on which Paul mounts his appeal for solidarity. All are servants of the same κύριος, and the welcome extended to all by God (in Rom. 14.3) or by Christ (in 15.7) is a paradigm for the practice of acceptance and welcome which Paul seeks to engender among the Roman Christians. All are ἀδελφοί – Paul's favourite designation for members of the Christian communities, which is here emphatically repeated, as in 1 Cor. 8.11-13 (see Rom. 14.10 *bis*, 13, 15, 21). It is the status of the other as an ἀδελφός – moreover, an ἀδελφός 'for whom Christ died' (Rom. 14.15; cf. 1 Cor. 8.11) – that indicates the shame of judging and despising them (cf. 1 Cor. 6.5-8). And while Paul does not argue for the adoption of a particular ethical stance regarding food, he does, as in 1 Corinthians 8–10, urge the practice of other moral values which he sees as imperative for the building up of the community. His main concern is that his addressees pursue the things of peace and the things for building one another up (Rom. 14.19; cf. 15.2; 1 Cor. 8.1; 10.23). A unity of mind and purpose is the goal to which Paul looks (Rom. 15.5-6; cf. 1 Cor. 1.10), but – unless the bulk of his argument here is to become simply redundant – this unity is clearly not to be a uniformity.

The moral value which Paul sees as fundamental to achieving this divinely willed and scripturally announced goal, this unified community that at the same time protects the diversity within it, is that of other-regarding love, a self-sacrificial looking to the interests and well-being of the other. This theme is prominent throughout Rom. 14.13–15.7, culminating in the explicitly christological appeal of 15.1-7. What his hearers should 'judge' (κρίνατε), Paul suggests, presenting a positive version of the activity previously censured, is not one another but rather the importance of not placing any stumbling block in the way of a sister or brother (14.13). Although one may be free 'in the Lord Jesus' to eat anything, if doing so causes grief to an ἀδελφός for whom Christ died then the action no longer expresses the practice of ἀγάπη (14.14-15 – οὐκέτι κατὰ ἀγάπην περιπατεῖς). Their practice with regard to matters like food should not destroy 'the work of God', which is, presumably, this οἰκοδομή, this building up of the community comprising all those whom God has welcomed in Christ. The similarities with 1 Corinthians (esp. 8.9-13) are readily apparent.

In Rom. 14.14 Paul expressed the idea that while nothing was unclean 'in itself' it was unclean to the one who reckoned it so. That idea is developed in the direction of an other-regarding, relational morality in 14.20. Here Paul reiterates the idea that in themselves all things are clean (πάντα καθαρά) but then adds that it is a bad thing (κακόν) if a person's eating becomes a cause of stumbling (πρόσκομμα). The criterion for action is not simply whether or not it is 'unclean' to the individual but rather, and more decisively, the impact it has on others. Hence the assertion, comparable to 1 Cor. 8.13, that it is a good thing (καλόν) not to eat meat or drink wine or do anything if it might cause an ἀδελφός to stumble (Rom. 14.21). In practice, then, the solution to the tensions among those who are more or less scrupulous regarding food is for the 'strong' to accommodate their actions to take account of the concerns of the 'weak' (at the Christian communal meals; cf. Barclay 1996b: 302–303), just as in 1 Corinthians 8–10 the strong are to give up their right to eat idol-meat if and when it causes a weaker sibling to stumble.

This other-regarding practice is grounded especially in the example of Christ, which Paul presents explicitly in the opening verses of Romans 15. His exhortation that 'we the strong ought to bear the weaknesses of the weak and not to please ourselves' (15.1) is reminiscent of 1 Cor. 10.33 and also Gal. 6.2, where bearing one another's burdens is stated as the way to fulfil the 'law of Christ' (see further §7.3). The following instruction here to each person not to please themselves but their neighbour, for the good purpose of building up the neighbour (Rom. 15.2), as well as echoing the commandment Paul sees as encapsulating the whole of the Law (Lev. 19.18; Rom. 13.8-10), is justified by an appeal to the practice of Christ, 'who did not please himself' (Rom. 15.3). Imitating this pattern of other-regarding conduct is the fundamental moral responsibility. In other words, the christological basis of Paul's moral argument here undergirds not so much an individual's stance on specific ethical matters but more a *pattern of relating, an 'other-regard', which is morally imperative*. As in 1 Corinthians 8–10 (though there framed by absolutes, permissive and prohibitive), here too the Christian's duty is not specified as some particular ethical stance in relation to the substantive issue (food) but rather as a duty concerning Christ-like other-regard.

The basis for ethical action is not one's own convictions and judgments in regard to a substantive issue but rather one's responsibilities towards others – not knowledge, but love, to reiterate the summary of this approach to ethics given in 1 Cor. 8.1-3. The Pauline Christian cannot do ethics monologically, reflecting in isolation on what is right and wrong, but can only make that discernment as a situated participant, in the context of human relationships: what is right or wrong in terms of one's conduct cannot be specified in the abstract, but only in terms of a particular community setting, in relation to the others with whom one is placed.

Overall, then, what Paul seeks to do in Rom. 14.1–15.13 is to foster the corporate solidarity of the Christian congregation in Rome while legitimating differences of ethical practice. He seeks to undercut the basis on which some judge or despise others, and urges the priority of mutual up-building and the pursuit of peace, in order that those with differences might nonetheless welcome and accept one another; this theme of welcoming acceptance both opens and closes the passage (14.4; 15.7). What Paul does present as morally imperative is the practice of other-regarding love, seen paradigmatically in the self-giving of Christ, a relational moral imperative which provides the basis for both the fostering of solidarity and the respect of difference. This vision of a united community in which people with different convictions mutually welcome and accept one another, and together offer praise and glory to God through Christ, finally culminates in a series of scriptural quotations which describe the Gentiles (τὰ ἔθνη) and God's people Israel (ὁ λαὸς αὐτοῦ) together praising God (15.9-12). The quotations are chosen so as to reinforce the message, central to Romans as a whole, that God's purpose was always to bring Jew and Gentile together in one worshipping community (cf. Rom. 1.16; 2.9-11; 3.9, 29-30; 9.22-25; 10.12; 11.25-32).[71]

6.3 *Significant Themes: Conscience, Freedom, Tolerance, Difference*

After seeking to appreciate, through exegetical engagement, the moral arguments Paul mounts in 1 Corinthians 8–10 and Romans 14–15, we may valuably turn to consider a number of themes that emerge in these texts and which are particularly relevant to a reading of Pauline ethics in the context of contemporary debate. The significance of these themes in this contemporary context will be assessed in the concluding section of this chapter.

6.3.1 *Conscience, faith and stumbling*

One of the fascinating characteristics of the argument in 1 Cor. 8.1–11.1 is Paul's repeated use of the word συνείδησις, generally translated 'conscience' (e.g. KJV, NAS, RSV, NRSV, etc.). Indeed, eight of the fourteen appearances of the word in the seven undisputed Pauline letters are found

---

71. The scriptural quotations here are connected by the keyword ἔθνη but also express the idea of the Gentiles joining with Israel (ὁ λαός αὐτοῦ) in praise and hope (see especially the second quotation, from Deut. 32.43 LXX), and so relate to Paul's aim here and throughout Romans, to unite Jews and Gentiles within the Christian congregation. Cf. Moo 1996: 878: Paul cites the OT 'to show that the inclusion of Gentiles with Jews in the praise of God has always been part of God's purposes'.

in this passage.[72] The fact that the word is not used in the parallel texts in Romans 14–15 suggests that Paul may well be picking up here a word used by the Corinthians.[73] There has been considerable discussion of exactly what the term συνείδησις means in Paul and in other ancient authors. It is clear from 1 Cor. 8.7-12 that it must have a sense for Paul somewhat different from that generally implied by the modern use of the word 'conscience': those with a 'weak' συνείδησις are not those with a slack or indisciplined approach to morality, or with a weak 'inner moral voice', but almost the opposite. Their weak συνείδησις means that they are acutely aware of the connections between idol-food and idols, and therefore cannot eat the former without defiling their συνείδησις. The best way to understand the word appears to be as 'self-awareness' or 'moral consciousness', linked with the idea of knowing – the root from which the word derives[74] – in the sense of what a person knows, or is aware of, in themselves.[75] Thus συνείδησις can refer, not entirely unlike the modern 'conscience', to a (moral) knowledge or awareness affirmed from within oneself – what one knows to be the case (e.g., Rom. 2.15; 9.1; 2 Cor. 1.12) – or to the 'awareness' people will acquire concerning the character and conduct of those they observe (2 Cor. 4.2; 5.11). In 1 Corinthians 8, then, συνείδησις must be understood in connection with the 'knowledge' (γνῶσις) which some have and others do not (8.1-7). Those who have a 'strong συνείδησις' – Paul does not use this phrase but it is the implied counterpart to the 'weak συνείδησις' (8.7, 10, 12) – have a robust awareness of the non-existence of idols and can thus eat idol-food without contaminating their συνείδησις. Those with a weak awareness, however, connect idol-food with idols (8.7) and are thus defiled if they eat.[76] In 10.25 and 27, then, Paul

---

72. The references are: Rom. 2.15; 9.1; 13.5; 1 Cor. 8.7, 10, 12; 10.25, 27, 28, 29 (*bis*); 2 Cor. 1.12; 4.2; 5.11.

73. So, e.g., Jewett 1971: 436–37; Eckstein 1983: 232; *pace* Lohse 1989: 207–208.

74. Schrage, for example, notes that σύνοιδα, in reflexive form, means 'sich bewußt sein', such that συνείδησις has 'die Grundbedeutung «Wissen um etwas», «Bewußtsein um etwas»' (1995: 257 with n. 269). Cf. also Maurer, *TWNT* 7: 898. One should beware, however, of using etymology as a guide to meaning.

75. Cf. BDAG, 967–68, and the discussions in, e.g., Maurer, *TWNT* 7: 897–918; Jewett 1971: 402–46; Horsley 1978; Eckstein 1983; Gooch 1987; Tomson 1990: 195–96; Gardner 1994: 42–48; Martin 1995a: 180–82; Thiselton 2000: 640–44. Thiselton (2000: 642–43) notes that modern research has pointed to the sense of consciousness or self-awareness as the most apposite renderings for συνείδησις. He suggests the term 'moral consciousness' for 1 Corinthians 8–10 (p. 785, etc.).

76. Thus Martin is right to suggest that the crucial factor distinguishing the strong's participation (which does not defile them) from that of the weak (which does defile) is knowledge ('gnosis'); moreover, '[t]he Strong cannot simply hand over their gnosis to the Weak, as if it could be taught; rather, in Paul's rhetoric, people either have it or do not have it' (1995a: 187). However, Martin's view of this gnosis as serving as a 'prophylactic talisman' (pp. 179–89) needs some qualification; see n. 34 above.

means that Christians are free to buy and eat whatever is sold and served without the need to inquire or ask so as to become aware of the origins of the food (μηδὲν ἀνακρίνοντες διὰ τὴν συνείδησιν).[77] In 10.28-29 Paul makes clear that in situations where the concerns of others require the Christian to abstain from eating, the reason to abstain lies not in the Christian's own awareness about the food but in that of the other.

What is particularly significant, as we have already noted, is that for Paul the differing kinds of 'awareness' possessed by different individual actors render an action acceptable or unacceptable, defiling or non-defiling, depending on the stance of the actor rather than on any objective rightness or wrongness inherent in the act itself (1 Cor. 8.7-12). A similar notion is expressed in Romans 14, though here the term used is not συνείδησις but πίστις, 'faith'. Some have the faith (πιστεύει) to eat everything, while the weak in faith eat only vegetables (14.1-2); some distinguish (κρίνει) special days; others judge (κρίνει) all days alike (14.5). Such stances cannot be objectively declared right or wrong – even though in Paul's view the 'objective' truth is that all foods are clean (14.14, 20) – since the acceptability of an act depends on the actor's own convictions, the standpoint they are convinced of in their own individual mind (ἐν τῷ ἰδίῳ νοΐ, 14.5). The one who acts contrary to their own convictions and faith does something condemnable (14.14, 22–23). Strong faith – the faith to eat everything – corresponds to a strong συνείδησις.

This is also the context in which to understand what Paul means by 'causing a sibling to stumble', another prominent theme of both passages. As we have already noted, it is clear that this is not meant in the sense of doing something which someone else finds objectionable or offensive. Causing one's sibling to stumble consists rather in leading them to do something for which their συνείδησις or their faith is not sufficiently strong. Thus, when the weak person does something which is for them contaminating, they face condemnation and destruction as a Christian sibling (1 Cor. 8.10-12; Rom. 14.13-15, 20-23).

6.3.2 *Freedom*

It is sometimes asserted that freedom is a key value in Paul's ethics, even, according to Allen Verhey, 'the most fundamental of the Christian values' for Paul, followed by 'the most important value', love (Verhey 1984: 107–108). In 1 Corinthians 8–10, indeed, though not in Romans 14–15, Paul refers to his 'freedom' (9.1, 19; 10.29). However, the extent to which freedom should be considered a significant or substantive value in Pauline

---

77. Thiselton (2000: 779) translates μηδὲν ἀνακρίνοντες, 'without asking about it to reach a judgment'; see his comments on p. 785.

ethics is limited. In the first place, some of the Pauline references to being set free depict not a freedom as such, but rather a change of ownership: believers are freed from slavery to sin, in order to become slaves to righteousness, slaves who belong to God (Rom. 6.18-22; cf. 1 Cor. 6.20; 7.23). Other references highlight the freedom from the Law which Paul claims for Christians, especially in the context of the argument of Galatians, where the attraction of Law-observance is depicted as a return to slavery (Gal. 2.4; 5.1; Rom. 7.3).[78] The 'freedom' Paul claims for himself in 1 Cor. 9.1 (οὐκ εἰμὶ ἐλεύθερος;) must be interpreted as in some sense parallel to the ἐξουσία which the Corinthian strong possess. Paul has a freedom to enjoy his apostolic rights (ἐξουσίαι, 9.4-6), and also a freedom 'in the Lord Jesus' to eat all foods (so Rom. 14.14),[79] just as the Corinthians have an ἐξουσία, a 'right' or 'freedom of choice', in relation to idol-food (1 Cor. 8.9; cf. 10.29).[80] There is, then, a sense in which Paul, and all Christians, have a 'freedom' which relates to their right to act, in ways which go beyond what the Law allows (cf. also Gal. 2.17-19) – it is notable that Paul does not negate the Corinthian 'slogan' πάντα ἔξεστιν ('everything is permitted'; 1 Cor. 6.12; 10.23); we might have expected a μὴ γένοιτο – but only in certain areas (cf. §5.3). However, the imperative of other-regard requires that even legitimate freedom be given up, to a considerable extent, though not entirely (the freedom to eat everything sold in the market seems to be unassailable; see above). Paul clearly does not regard his freedom as any kind of absolute value: like all Christians, he belongs to his master, God/Christ (Rom. 14.8; 1 Cor. 6.20; Phil. 3.8, etc.), and even his apostolic task is one over which he has no freedom, no choice (1 Cor. 9.16-17).[81] Moreover, he has enslaved himself to all, in order to seek their salvation,

78. In Gal. 4.21-31 Paul uses the story of Abraham's two sons, one from the slave woman and one from the free, as an allegory of the contrast between the 'slavery' of the Israelites, who have the present Jerusalem as their 'mother', and the 'freedom' of the Christians, whose mother is the Jerusalem above. But the contrast is not simply between slavery and freedom, but rather, as 4.1-7 makes clear, between being immature children, little different in status from slaves, and becoming sons, inheriting the awaited promise. The freedom in view in 2 Cor. 3.17 is most likely that which, in Paul's view, comes with the new dispensation in the Spirit, contrasted with the death which comes via the Mosaic 'letter'.

79. Whether this latter freedom is in view in 1 Cor. 9.1 is open to dispute; Schrage thinks it unlikely, suggesting that the freedom to *reject* his apostolic rights is what is in view here (1995: 287). But for the example to work, Paul's 'freedom' must represent something parallel to the Corinthians' ἐξουσία, the (positive) right or freedom to do something substantive.

80. Cf. Thiselton 2000: 650; BDAG, 352. Paul's freedom and the Corinthians' ἐξουσια come together in the 'freedom' mentioned in 1 Cor. 10.29.

81. An ἀνάγκη has been placed upon him, and he is worthy of no reward, since he acts ἄκων, 'under compulsion', rather than ἑκών, 'voluntarily'. As Käsemann memorably puts it: 'One can demand no reward from *ananke*, one can only bow to it or rebel against it' (1969: 231). For further discussion and references, including to those who argue that Paul means to portray himself as working ἑκών rather than ἄκων, see Horrell 1996: 207.

specifically by accommodating his conduct and compromising his freedom in different ways for the sake of various groups, especially the weak (9.19-23).[82] This is evidently the pattern of Christ-like conduct to which Paul calls the Corinthian strong, and which he similarly urges upon the Christians in Galatia: 'for you were called to freedom, brothers and sisters; only do not [use/regard] your freedom as an opportunity for the flesh, but through love be slaves to one another' (διὰ τῆς ἀγάπης δουλεύετε ἀλλήλοις, Gal. 5.13).

6.3.3 *Tolerance and intolerance*

Tolerance and intolerance, such important terms for contemporary liberal politics and morality, are not terms Paul actually uses, and it has been suggested that it is anachronistic to look for such values in Paul (Barton 1998). However, a number of Paul's arguments in the texts we have examined concern the value which we label tolerance:[83] first, that a range of ethical stances is acceptable (depending on the individual actor's own convictions); second, that people should not despise or condemn those whose stance is different from their own (Rom. 14.3); third, that regard for others is a key reason for altering one's own behaviour, even when that behaviour is in itself legitimate and justifiable.[84] There are, however, a number of questions and issues that arise when we explore this 'tolerance' further, questions fundamentally concerned with what we may call the limits of tolerance and intolerance.

First, there is a question about the extent to which regard for others should reshape one's own conduct. It is easy to imagine how the principle of not causing a brother or sister to stumble could be invoked in all sorts of situations to justify all sorts of restrictions. Romans 14–15 reflects some tension concerning the extent to which restriction should be practised: on the one hand, 'it is good not to eat meat or drink wine or do anything by which your sibling is caused to stumble' (Rom. 14.21); on the other hand, each person should be fully convinced in their own mind of the rightness of their actions, and none should judge or despise the other (14.3-5, 10). In 1 Corinthians 8–10 Paul does a little more to establish limits, both permissive and prohibitive, around the extent to which the concerns of others should

---

82. See further Martin 1990: 117–35; Horrell 1996: 207–209.

83. Cf. *OED*, 3330: tolerance is 'the disposition or ability to accept without protest or adopt a liberal attitude towards the opinions or acts of others'. A 'tolerant' person is one 'who tolerates opinions or practices different from his or her own'.

84. Barton (1998: 128) claims that '[i]ts christocentricity is what makes love and sacrifice *for the sake of the truth* the central imperatives of Pauline morality, rather than tolerance' (my emphasis). But at least in the two major passages on which we have focused in this chapter, it would be truer to Paul to use the phrase 'for the sake of the (weaker) sibling'.

determine one's conduct. Yet this remains a difficulty for a morality built so strongly around an imperative of other-regard.

Second, there is a question about the limits of Paul's 'tolerance'. It is clear that in the realm of sexual ethics, as we saw in the previous chapter, there is a good deal less room for a diversity of convictions. People may legitimately decide to marry or not to marry, but they may not insist on their right to liaisons with πόρναι, nor on their freedom to divorce. A similar absoluteness pertains in the case of idolatry. But the apparent tolerance of Romans 14–15 may also be contrasted with the vehement argument of Galatians, and specifically of Gal. 2.11-21, where food and meals are also an issue, just as Paul's declaration in 1 Cor. 10.33 that he tries to please everyone in everything contrasts sharply with his belligerent refusal to please people as expressed in Gal. 1.10.[85] These apparently contradictory positions, tolerance and intolerance, stem, however, from a common and coherent basis: that the ground for community solidarity is being in Christ and that food is a matter of ethical indifference (cf. §§4.3; 5.3). To take this last point first: despite his attempts to promote mutual acceptance and regard, there is a superiority concerning Paul's own ethical stance implicit in Romans in the terms 'strong' and 'weak'. Even if we render the term ἀσθενής as 'delicate', as Peter Tomson (1990: 193–98) suggests, and even if Mark Nanos is right to detect a critical edge in Paul's use of the word 'strong' – a critique of arrogance and presumption on the part of the Gentile Christians (cf. Rom. 11.20-25; 12.3; etc.; Nanos 1996: 98–101) – nonetheless along with the attempt to legitimate diversity comes an apparent conviction that Paul's stance represents a strength of *faith* that the weak's does not. And in 1 Corinthians, the strong's ἐξουσία is based on unquestionable theological convictions, just as are Paul's apostolic rights; they are abandoned only because of others' weakness. So Paul's 'tolerance' does not entirely avoid presenting his own ethical conviction as preferable, or at least as the position which demonstrates most consistently the consequences of faith in the Lord Jesus (Rom. 14.14) or belief in the one God and the one Lord (1 Cor. 8.6). More significantly still, his tolerance *depends* on this conviction: it is only from a perspective which regards food in some 'absolute' sense as morally indifferent that one can adopt the relativist and tolerant stance we find especially in Romans 14–15 (cf. Schrage 1988: 194; quoted below, n. 97). In the incident at Antioch, conversely, Paul's opponents do not accept that food is a matter of indifference, since a certain level of attention to these matters is necessary if Jewish and Gentile Christians are to share table fellowship (cf. §4.3 above with n. 69). Paul insists unbendingly that both Jew and Gentile

---

85. Cf. the consideration of Paul's apparent inconsistency, based on a comparison of 1 Cor. 9.19-23 and Gal. 2.11-14, in Richardson 1980.

attain their status as members of this community only on the basis of believing in Christ, and not on the basis of the Law (Gal. 2.16). Paul's conviction that the basis for solidarity and identity is Christ,[86] so firmly asserted in Galatians, provides the grounds for his 'tolerance' in Romans, where different customs with regard to food, no longer defining of identity and belonging, are in themselves indifferent and so can be treated with a Christ-like generosity. In other words, Paul's tolerance operates only within the framework of an intolerance that insists on Christ alone as the basis for community solidarity, a basis which also implies the proscription of actions deemed to threaten this union (cf. ch. 5 above).

6.3.4 *Identity and difference*

This leads us to further issues which relate to the nature of Paul's tolerance, issues raised by John Barclay and especially by Boyarin (see §1.7) concerning the implications of Paul's instruction in relation to identity and difference. Barclay, writing specifically on Romans 14–15, notes Paul's attempt to protect 'Law-observance and Jewish Christianity', but argues that in the end 'Paul effectively undermines the social and cultural integrity of the Law-observant Christians in Rome'. This is because Paul both requires of Jewish Christians the cultivation of 'a deep bond of unity with people fundamentally neglectful of the Law' and also 'relativizes' the Jewish cultural heritage, presenting it as 'merely one option, one preference among others'.[87] Boyarin develops this last issue more widely, arguing, as we have seen, that Paul's desire to unite diverse peoples as one in Christ implies the corollary that all other cultural specificities are to be eradicated, or at least emptied of their integrity:

> What will appear from the Christian perspective as tolerance, namely Paul's willingness – indeed insistence – that within the Christian community all cultural practice is equally to be tolerated, from the rabbinic Jewish perspective is simply an eradication of the entire value system which insists that our cultural practice is our task and calling in the world and must not be abandoned or reduced to a matter of taste. The call to human Oneness, at the same time that it is a stirring call to

86. To avoid an implicit Christian superiority, we should note that this is simply Paul's conviction. In other words, it would be entirely possible to base the solidarity of the community around, say, common, or at least compatible, obedience to Torah. Paul, for whatever reasons, rejects this possibility and insists that being in Christ is the only legitimate basis.

87. Barclay 1996b: 303–308. Cf. also Watson 1986: 94–98, who argues that the aim of Paul's instruction is to unite two divided congregations into one 'Paulinist' congregation, where the Pauline principle of freedom from the law is accepted.

equality, constitutes a threat as well to Jewish (or any other) difference. (Boyarin 1994: 32)

The suggestion, then, is that Paul's apparently tolerant framework, with its attempt to protect difference, in fact does so only by relativizing these differences of cultural tradition, identity and ethics, such that they become matters of indifference.

There are a number of points to make by way of response, but in the end the force of Barclay's and Boyarin's argument must be affirmed. This affirmation, though, also brings us to another important point of comparison between Paul and liberalism (see §6.4 below). First, one must question Boyarin's rather pointed phrase 'a matter of taste'. For in Rom. 14.1–15.13 Paul does *not* quite say that one's practice with regard to food is simply a matter of personal taste or preference. He not only states that things *are* unclean to the one who reckons them so, but also insists that people *must* act in accordance with their faith-convictions; not to do so is to sin (14.23). (Is this so very far from Boyarin's insistence that certain groups of people have a particular 'task and calling in the world'?) In 1 Corinthians, support is added to the notion that acting in a way which is not in accord with one's moral consciousness is a serious and dangerous matter (8.10-13). A second response is to note that it is the 'strong' upon whom Paul places most of the burden of changing practice, in acknowledgment of, and sensitivity to, the convictions of the 'weak'. In other words, the practices of the weak – the law-observant – are protected more thoroughly than the practices of the strong.

Furthermore, while Boyarin reads Paul as a cultural critic of Judaism, from within, it is not insignificant to note that Paul is writing to people who already share a commitment to Christ; in this sense at least he writes from a 'Christian' perspective.[88] Among *these* people, then, it is indeed true to say that their Jewish or Gentile identity is to a significant degree relativized (to use Barclay's term) because of their common commitment to

---

88. Cf. Boyarin 1994: 1–12, 262 n. 6. This is perhaps a rather significant point, since it determines the basic interpretative position from which Paul is viewed. Obviously there are great complexities involved in discerning the extent to which Paul's theology fits within, or breaks from, the Judaism(s) of his time, and much scholarly ink has been spilt on precisely this question. But insofar as Paul is founder and instructor of communities containing both Jews and Gentiles, who find their common identity and unity not in Jewish markers of belonging but in faith and baptism in Christ, then there is at least some kind of theological and sociological distinction between the groups Paul is addressing and the Judaism contemporary with them (cf. 1 Cor. 10.32). Paul's theology is, of course, a thoroughly Jewish theology, but one which is (to use Terence Donaldson's felicitous term) 'reconfigured' to centre on Christ (Donaldson 1997). Given these basic observations, Paul should perhaps be judged not so much as a cultural critic of Judaism as by the ways in which he addresses the issues of morality and difference within the communities to which he writes, those who share his 'Christian' commitment. Ironically, therefore, those who see Paul's argument in Romans 14–15 as

Christ, a commitment which takes primacy, at least in Paul's view, over all others (Rom. 1.6; 10.9-17; Phil. 3.7-4.1). Within these Christian communities, therefore, the foundation of solidarity, the basis for identity and belonging, is being 'in Christ' (hence the insistent argument of Gal. 2.11-21). This 'Christian' allegiance now forms the members' most fundamental and determinative identity-designation (cf. §5.3), even though their identity is described using essentially Jewish terms (cf. §4.2).[89] Given this basis for unity and community, it is significant that Paul tries to create the kind of moral space within which distinctive convictions and practices can coexist with mutual respect and love. Yet Barclay and Boyarin are essentially right to maintain that these distinctive cultural and ethical practices are relativized insofar as they take their place beneath the encompassing and non-negotiable umbrella of being in Christ, upon which community solidarity depends.

In both of the major passages we have examined in this chapter, Paul preserves the space for a certain kind of difference, not least in terms of ethical conviction. Legitimate action in regard to idol-food is determined, on an individual level, by the dictates of one's own moral consciousness: what is permissible to one person would destroy another, since it would entail their acting against their συνείδησις. The way to preserve the community's solidarity in this situation is, according to Paul, not to rule that one pattern of practice (and hence of conviction) regarding idol-food should be accepted, but rather to require an accommodation to the concerns of the weak on the part of the strong. Their differences remain – and the substantive convictions of the strong are, after all, more clearly 'correct', from Paul's point of view – although the extent to which convictions can be practised is situationally and relationally determined. Romans 14–15 makes it clear that such ethical differences can be reflective of cultural and identity-defining practices. Here Paul more clearly develops a form of ethical relativism within which differences of conviction can remain, again in the context of a communal solidarity sustained not via ethical unanimity but through the practice of other-regarding love.

In relation to the issues raised by Boyarin and by Castelli (1991), this suggests that Paul's discourse is in some senses one which allows, indeed

concerned with relations between Christians and (non-Christian) Jews (see n. 61 above) may make Paul *more* and not less problematic in terms of the implications of his thought for Jewish culture and identity.

89. Indeed, in exploring Paul's sense of identity, Dunn (1999) vindicates Boyarin's argument that Paul essentially spiritualizes the essence of Jewishness, such that its actual cultural embodiedness becomes a matter of indifference: Paul thought of himself as a Jew (only) 'if he could make clear that the trappings [*sic!*] of Jewish identity, most explicitly the practice of circumcision and food laws, could be equally taken on or put off without affecting the integrity of that Jewishness either way' (Dunn 1999: 192).

preserves, difference, but also in some sense requires 'sameness'. A sameness is required in terms of commitment to Christ, since this is, for Paul, the unassailable basis for identity, belonging and community solidarity. A sameness is also required in terms of conformity to the metanorm of 'other-regard': this moral norm is obligatory for all, but precisely *this* norm provides the moral framework within which differences reflecting the diverse stances of an individual's faith or moral conscious- ness can be preserved.[90] This, indeed, is the kind of conformity for which Paul looks in his appeals to imitation (see ch. 7 below). And what is noteworthy, moreover, is that this kind of 'sameness' – an obligatory moral framework which precisely provides the means to preserve difference – is not so different in character and structure from the kind of framework which liberal (and indeed 'postmodern') tolerance of difference presumes, as we shall see briefly below.

6.4 *Conclusion*

The corporate solidarity which we have already identified as a fundamental norm in Pauline ethics (ch. 4) is both presumed and reflected in the texts we have considered in this chapter. The believers' identity as ἀδελφοί, their shared membership of the community of those who have been welcomed and accepted by Christ, and so on, forms the essential basis upon which the space for diversity and difference is built. The differences in view stem primarily from each person's συνείδησις (1 Corinthians) or faith (Romans) which render certain actions acceptable or unacceptable for them. In both of these major passages Paul's argumentative energies are directed not towards a resolution of the differences through outlining a concrete instruction on the substantive issue at hand ('you should eat all kinds of food', 'you should not eat idol-food', or whatever). Rather Paul argues for a pattern of relating within which these differences of conviction can remain, even though the practices that reflect these convictions must often be restricted out of concern for others. Indeed, the primary moral imperative that emerges is for a costly other-regard which requires the restriction of one's own freedom out of concern for the injury that may be caused to others. Just as the value of corporate solidarity has a fundamentally christological basis, as we saw in ch. 4, so too does this other-regard, shaped and inspired as it is by the example of Christ (see further ch. 7 below). Corporate solidarity does not then imply uniformity

---

90. Thus it is not quite right to say that the way in which faith is to be instantiated in works is, for Paul, 'under-determined', with 'a built-in "uncertainty principle" that allows for different expressions of a common faith' (Barclay 2001b: 162). It is rather the obligatory metanorms that provide circumscribed room for difference.

(cf. also §4.4), not even in matters of ethical conviction, but implies precisely a community within which differences can remain, because of the generous other-regard which offers a welcome to the other (Rom. 14.3; 15.7) and which inspires the avoidance of even legitimate conduct rather than force the other to a conformity which will in their case mean destruction. But there are strict limits to the degree of tolerable diversity, which pertains only in regard to issues which Paul regards as in themselves matters of indifference.

If we now consider how Paul's moral arguments appear in the context of the liberal-communitarian debate, it is clear that they are not exactly 'like' either approach in the debate nor (to focus more specifically) like either Habermas's or Hauerwas's mode of doing ethics. Nonetheless, at a general level what Paul is doing in the passages we have studied in this chapter is clearly akin to a Hauerwasian approach to ethics: Paul's concern is with the community of the church, with the character of relationships among its members, and he grounds his ethical arguments on the particular myth or story from which this community derives its identity – God's welcoming act in Christ, Christ's death for others, Christ's position as the believer's κύριος and God's role as judge of all, and so on. This 'tradition' engenders certain virtues – most notably that of other-regard – which (are meant to) sustain a certain kind of community. Yet precisely because of this basic similarity it is significant to note the extent to which Paul does not invest his energies into arguing for a certain ethical stance on the part of all Christians; instead he focuses on the ways in which the values of solidarity and other-regard provide precisely a basis for sustaining within a united community diversity and difference, even in terms of ethical convictions; his argument, especially in Romans, even expounds a form of ethical relativism. This concern contrasts somewhat with what Linda Woodhead calls Hauerwas's 'homogenising discourse' about the Church, a discourse which insufficiently reflects or values the plurality within the Christian tradition and communities, and with the mode of communication – a kind of diatribal and deliberately shocking rhetoric – with which he challenges his readers.[91] While Paul, of course, can be blunt, assertive and threatening (e.g. 1 Cor. 4.21; 5.1-13; Gal. 3.1-5), in the two passages where he develops a moral argument at greatest length his overriding concern is to foster the kind of non-judgmentalism and generous other-regard which will precisely protect the diverse and different stances which individual believers take,

---

91. Woodhead 2000: 183; also Albrecht 1995, 1997; cf. further §2.4 above with n. 80. Jeffrey Stout refers to the 'rhetorical excess' which characterizes the work of Hauerwas, MacIntyre and Richard Rorty (2004: xi) and notes that 'Hauerwas likes to shock first and qualify later' (p. 149).

according to their varied moral consciousness (συνείδησις) or faith (πίστις). This is hardly an overriding concern in Hauerwas's work.[92]

Furthermore, there are clear parallels between the central concerns and values of liberalism and those which emerge in Paul's arguments in these texts. Liberalism places considerable emphasis on the individual's right to choose their own vision of the good life, though these various visions have to be pursued within the constraints of the values embodied in the public framework of justice, which is meant to ensure that one person's pursuit of their good does not unfairly impinge upon the freedom or rights of another. Somewhat differently, of course, though with a structural similarity, Paul attempts, especially in Romans 14–15, to protect the different ways of life which individuals and groups follow, as guided by their 'faith', or, as in 1 Corinthians, by their 'conscience' (συνείδησις). And he does this by insisting on an all-encompassing framework of obligatory moral norms – recognition of the common membership of all within the community (solidarity) and the practice of generous regard for the other. Notwithstanding the significant differences, Paul's understanding of conscience (συνείδησις) and of rights (ἐξουσίαι) and freedom bear comparison with their significance in liberalism: for Paul, the individual's convictions, or awareness, render certain acts right or wrong *for them*, and those whose moral consciousness allows it have the freedom or right to act in a certain way. Yet this freedom must be curtailed to the extent that its practice leads others to act against their consciousness. The (liberal) idea of freedom of conscience, that individuals can legitimately hold differing convictions, but are allowed to practise these convictions only insofar as they are judged not to impact illegitimately on others, is not dissimilar. To be sure, Paul calls for a very extensive restriction of one's legitimate freedom out of regard for others. It is not so much a case of ensuring equal rights (so Habermas)[93] but of the strong being prepared never to use their rights (1 Cor. 9.15), to enslave themselves to others (1 Cor. 9.19), in imitation of the example of Paul and of Christ (1 Cor. 11.1). Nonetheless, while this is certainly a point of contrast, liberalism too places definite and 'intolerant' limits on the practice of freedom (see further below).

In terms of specific comparison between Paul's ethics and Habermas's discourse ethics the differences are more apparent than any similarities.

92. Thus Stout (2004: 157) sharply criticizes Hauerwas for his frequent offences 'against the vocation of charitable interpretation' in dealing with writers, theologians and others, who take different perspectives, especially those which represent some form of political or theological liberalism.

93. For example, citing the instance of abortion as one where no agreement between conflicting views seems possible, Habermas states that what is required is a way to secure 'the integrity and the coexistence of ways of life and worldviews that generate different ethical conceptions ... under conditions of equal rights' (1993: 60).

Paul shows little sign of any interest in the rational testing of the different norms generated by different traditions through argumentative and participative discourse, with the aim of establishing a consensus, though he does at least hint at the congregation's role in testing (corporately) what he and others say (1 Cor. 10.15; cf. 14.29). Nonetheless, as we have seen previously, there are points at which comparison is more fruitful. Habermas's distinction between ethics and morality is, for example, illuminating to the extent that it highlights one specific similarity between what Paul is doing here and what Habermas attempts in his programme for discourse ethics. Habermas, we recall, distinguishes between questions of ethics – questions bound up with the individual's sense of the good and with their sense of identity – and questions of morality – questions about the regulation of conflicts arising when 'my actions affect the interests of others' (Habermas 1993: 5). Discourse ethics' concern with the latter means that it should rightly be seen as a 'discourse theory of morality' (Habermas 1993: vii).[94] Just as discourse ethics (*sic!*) is concerned with the moral question of 'the legitimate ordering of coexisting forms of life' (Habermas 1993: 60), so Paul's concern in both 1 Corinthians 8–10 and Romans 14–15 is not primarily to resolve or rule on the substantive and specific issues of ethics but rather to argue for the practice of the kind of *morality* which he sees as essential to the maintenance of community harmony given continuing differences. Other-regard is in this sense precisely a *moral* value (for comments on the differences and similarities between Paul and Habermas in regard to this value, see §7.5 below).

A further point of comparison concerns the limits of tolerance and the implications for different cultural traditions of what appears a framework for tolerance, an issue raised in connection with Paul especially by Boyarin. Benhabib is perhaps more candid than Habermas in stressing that the moral norms of discourse ethics, which are substantive and not merely procedural, place limits on the acceptable legitimacy of norms associated with particular 'ways of life'.[95] In a context of liberal democracy, as Benhabib illustrates, this would mean, for example, that an ethical practice that contradicted the principle of equal respect and equal rights would not be tolerated (1992: 38–46). Benhabib's formulation of the principle is as follows: 'where there is a clash between the metanorms of communicative ethics and the specific norms of a moral way of life, the latter must be subordinated to the former' (p. 45). Thus there are firm limits to the liberal 'tolerance' of plurality and difference. Although expressed (of course) in very different language, this principle can be seen to operate, *mutatis mutandis*, in Pauline morality. As long as the 'metanorms' of solidarity in

94. See Habermas 1993: 4–9; 1991: 103–109; §2.2 above.
95. See Benhabib 1992: 45; §2.2 above, pp. 61–62.

Christ and of Christ-like other-regard provide the overarching framework, the differing practices of Jewish and Gentile Christians can and should be sustained and protected (so Romans 14–15). But where the practices of one way of life are perceived to clash with these metanorms – as in the incident at Antioch (Gal. 2.11-14) – then the latter are determinative, and the culturally-specific norms must give way.[96] This is one sense in which Paul, not unlike liberalism, constructs a framework for a (circumscribed) tolerance, within which differences can be sustained, precisely by insisting ('intolerantly') on certain overarching moral values and commitments. Thus the modern (liberal) notion of tolerance is not as foreign to Paul's thought as Stephen Barton, for example, suggests.[97] (Even postmodernism, with its stress on the value of difference and its critique of coercion towards sameness [cf. Castelli 1991] 'presupposes', as Benhabib notes, 'a super-liberalism, more pluralistic, more tolerant, more open to the right of difference and otherness' but does so precisely by assuming the 'hyper-universalist and superliberal values of diversity, heterogeneity, eccentricity and otherness' [1992: 16].)

This connects with another question about the character of both Pauline and liberal tolerance, already raised by Boyarin, namely, whether the 'tolerant' framework in which different cultural traditions have to take their place actually empties those traditions, and their associated identities, of their integrity by making them merely a matter of taste or personal conviction, one acceptable option. We have already given a qualified affirmation to Boyarin's argument concerning Paul in this regard. What is significant here is to note how this argument is closely paralleled in

---

96. So, rightly, Holmberg 1998, who sees Paul's response to the Antioch incident as requiring that 'Jewish identity must cede to the common Christian identity' (p. 414). Cf. also Boyarin 1994: 112–14.

97. Barton 1998. Barton is right, of course, to stress that 'Paul's categories of thought are not those of modern liberal secular pluralism' and that we are 'at risk of subverting the subject of our study' if we assume the latter as our agenda (p. 123). However, if we make explicit our concern with both contexts of moral thought, notwithstanding the important differences between them, then Paul's approach to morality becomes more interestingly comparable with 'liberal' notions of tolerance than Barton allows. Barton also seems to miss Paul's stress on the need for conduct shaped by a regard for the other, etc., stressing instead a concern for the truth and 'to lay down rules' (cf. pp. 128, 130, etc., see also n. 84 above).

Schrage is also concerned not to read Paul anachronistically, when he states that 'there are some areas of life where a variety of practice is possible, but only – *as we must add if we are not to modernize Paul* – when fundamental ethical principles are not involved' (1988: 194, my emphasis). But this comment implies that a difference between Paul and moderns is that the latter allow a variety of practice with regard to 'fundamental ethical principles'. Yet, rather like Paul, in fact, it is, in modern liberalism too, only non-fundamental principles which are considered as legitimately subject to a variety of practice, as Benhabib's statements show. Practices which contradict the 'fundamental ethical principles' of liberalism are not tolerated. See further Mendus 1989, esp. pp. 102–109.

Hauerwas's critique of liberalism. For Hauerwas, liberalism's apparent tolerance and guaranteed 'freedom of religion' reduce Christianity to a matter of personal choice, and belief in God to something which fundamentally 'does not matter'.[98] Just as Boyarin argues that in Paul's thought religious and cultural differences are emptied of their integrity as they are brought under the encompassing unity constituted in Christ, so, according to Hauerwas, the same happens to Christian integrity within the encompassing framework of liberalism. Benhabib's comments (see above) essentially affirm what for Hauerwas is a critique: Christianity (and, of course, other religious traditions) can only constitute one legitimate option, a matter of personal conviction, while the values of liberalism itself are non-negotiable, trumping when necessary the values of the traditions encompassed under its umbrella of belonging. Thus, what Paul does to Judaism, liberalism does to Christianity.[99]

The closely parallel critiques – Boyarin's of Paul, Hauerwas's of liberalism – illustrate again the comparable structure of both Pauline and liberal morality. The reasons why this structural similarity exists may lie in the comparable social achievements that are sought in each case. Paul, like political liberalism, sought to unite diverse religious and social groups within a new form of human solidarity which at the same time transcended these differences. Consequently, if we share, with Boyarin, a sense of the importance of a 'deeply felt human solidarity', then, given the continuing fact of religious and cultural diversity, we may perhaps ask whether such a common, tradition-transcending solidarity is possible *without* some such relativization of the various traditions held together by a broader notion of belonging. Or conversely, if we repudiate liberalism's attempts in this regard, in defence of Christianity's integrity, should we not also reject Paul's comparable and earlier attempt, in defence of Judaism's integrity?

---

98. Hauerwas 2001: 231; 1999: 8, etc.; cf. §2.3 above, p. 63 with n. 46.

99. One may of course ask how valid the comparison is, given the extent to which Christianity shares key elements of Judaism's religious story while liberalism does not so relate to Christianity. The parallel is certainly less than exact, but there are nonetheless important similarities, especially in the ways in which each 'new' tradition (Christianity, then liberalism) is seen as bringing some form of eschatological fulfilment by universalizing the essential (moral) content of the 'older' tradition through transcending its specific cultural and religious forms. So Dunn, for example, sees Paul as 'bringing Israel's promised destiny to its eschatological completion' (1998c: 264), a task which involved rejecting the importance of the 'trappings of Jewish identity' – circumcision and food laws especially – in favour of an 'essence' of Jewishness 'determined from within' (Dunn 1999: 192; see more fully below, §9.3.3, n. 12). Habermas recognizes that the moral values of modern liberalism owe much to their Judaeo-Christian origins, but sees the task of philosophy as being to translate religious language into the language of public reason, such that these moral values can be justified not on the (now unconvincing) basis of a particular religious tradition but on the basis of rational and universalizable principles (see §2.2, pp. 62–63 above).

Chapter 7

OTHER-REGARD AND CHRIST AS MORAL PARADIGM

In both of the passages that occupied our attention in the previous chapter appeals were made to the example of Christ as a paradigm of other-regard. In Rom. 15.1-3 this appeal to Christ's example is explicit: all should seek to please their neighbour and not themselves, 'for Christ did not please himself' (v. 3). In 1 Cor. 8.1–11.1 the more direct example is that of Paul himself (9.1-23) and only in the final appeal to imitate Paul is it stated that his conduct is itself intended as a imitation of Christ (11.1).[1] The task of this chapter is to consider, through engagement with certain key passages, how, and how far, Paul grounds and motivates the value of other-regard by appealing to Christ as the paradigm for Christian attitude and action.[2] This 'other-regard', I argue, along with 'corporate solidarity' (see ch. 4), constitutes the second key metanorm of Pauline ethics.

An earlier phase of New Testament scholarship saw a notable tendency to deny the significance of *imitatio Christi* in Pauline thought and to reject the idea that Christ's self-giving, or the actions of the historical Jesus, serve for Paul as an ethical example.[3] As we shall see in more detail below, Phil. 2.5-11 is a particular *crux interpretum* in this latter regard. Recent studies, however, opposing this earlier tendency, have been much more inclined to affirm, in variously nuanced ways, the importance of the imitation of Christ in Pauline ethics, though this trend is by no means uncontested.[4]

---

1. See §6.1, n. 50 for arguments against the view that imitation of Christ is not in view here.

2. On the term 'other-regard' and its appropriateness, see §7.5 below. Hays (1989: 225 n. 36) describes the principle (which he sees as *imitatio Christi*) as 'renunciation of privilege for the sake of others'.

3. Especially influential in this regard are the article on μιμέομαι κτλ. by W. Michaelis, *TWNT* 4: 661–78/*TDNT* 4: 659–74, and Käsemann's critical analysis of Phil. 2.5-11 (Käsemann 1960: 51–95, on which see §7.1 below). For an overview of research on the theme of imitation of Christ ('Nachahmung Christi'), see Merk 1989: 173–93, who notes, *inter alia*, how debates on this question connect with debates about the Jesus–Paul relationship.

4. E.g. Hurtado 1984; Kurz 1985; Wolff 1989; Hooker 1990: 7, 47 n. 7, 90–93; Fowl 1990: 92–101; 1998; Matera 1996: 174–83; Hays 1997a: 28–31. For a contrasting perspective, see e.g. Martin 1997b: 287–92; Dodd 1998: 158 (quoted in the conclusions below, §7.5), both of whom follow a reading of Philippians 2 similar to that of Käsemann.

Direct appeals to imitation (using μιμέομαι, μιμητής, etc.) in Paul's letters are limited in number and focused mostly on Paul himself as the example to be followed.[5] In 1 Thessalonians, the language of imitation appears, though not as an appeal but rather within the lengthy opening thanksgiving, where Paul reports how the Thessalonians received the gospel (1.2–2.16). Their imitation consists in enduring suffering, while receiving the gospel with joy; in doing this they became imitators (μιμηταί) of Paul and his co-workers (1.6; cf. 1.1) and of the Lord (τοῦ κυρίου), and also of the churches in Judaea (2.14). Moreover, through their commendable practice they have in turn become an example (τύπος) to others (1.7).[6] Aside from 1 Cor. 11.1, 1 Thess. 1.6 is the only explicit mention of imitating Christ/the Lord in Paul. What is more common as an appeal is the call to imitate Paul (1 Cor. 4.16; 11.1; Phil. 3.17; 4.9; Gal. 4.12) and others who set a comparable example (Phil. 3.17). This means that any claim that the imitation of Christ is an important theme in Pauline ethics, or that the value of other-regard has a fundamentally christological foundation, will need to find a convincing basis in the texts beyond the limited number of explicit appeals to imitation of Christ. Such a claim will also need to consider what it is about Paul's own practice that he intends to present as a model for imitation, and whether and how this is in turn shaped by the paradigm of Christ.

We shall therefore examine a number of passages where the example of Christ's self-giving can be argued to play a significant role in Paul's moral exhortation, and consider how this christological paradigm informs Paul's ethics. We shall begin with Philippians 2, where there has been debate over whether or not the depiction of Christ serves an ethical purpose. Examinations of 1 Cor. 9.14-15 and of the law of Christ (Gal. 6.2; 1 Cor. 9.21) will then enable us to reflect on the significance of the paradigm of Christ's self-giving for others in relation to other possible sources for Paul's ethics: the words and teaching of Jesus and the Jewish law. Finally, a study of 2 Cor. 8.9 in the context of Paul's instructions regarding the collection will reveal important facets of what Paul sees as the goal of a Christ-like practice of other-regard, related specifically to the impulse towards equality (cf. ch. 4 above). These various exegetical studies together indicate how central the value of other-regard is to Pauline ethics, and also how this value is christologically undergirded. Finally, then, we will be in a position to reflect on the ways in which Christ functions as moral exemplar

---

5. For a treatment of the key texts, see Merk 1989: 193–203; Castelli 1991: 89–117; Brant 1993, etc.

6. Merk 1989: 193, rightly notes that 'μιμητής-Sein und τύπος-Sein' are here related, in that the imitator in turn becomes a τύπος to be imitated.

in Pauline ethics, and what the significance of this is when considered in the light of the contrasting approaches of liberals and communitarians.

7.1 *Philippians 2.5-11 and Christ as Exemplar*

It would be hard to overstate the importance and impact of Phil. 2.5-11: it is, in terms of its prominence in historical and theological discussions, among the most influential texts in the Pauline letters and a central witness to early Christology. It is also, as Markus Bockmuehl remarks, 'a passage which in the twentieth century has been the subject of an uncontainable deluge of scholarly debate, quite possibly more so than any other New Testament text' (1998a: 115).[7] Behind the mass of contemporary literature, there are, Ralph Martin (1998b: 1) notes, two early landmarks in critical discussion of this text: Ernst Lohmeyer's *Kyrios Jesus*, first published in 1928, and Ernst Käsemann's 'Kritische Analyse von Phil. 2, 5-11', which appeared in 1950.[8] The abiding influence of Lohmeyer's work stems largely from his original proposal, since very widely accepted, that the passage represents an early Christian hymn, a *carmen Christi*, 'a piece of early Christian psalmody (*urchristlicher Psalmdichtung*)' (Lohmeyer 1961: 7).[9] A central argument of Käsemann's essay concerns the ethical interpretation of this hymn, namely, the idea that Paul presents Christ here as an ethical example (*Vorbild*), an interpretation that Käsemann vigorously opposes.

To a large extent, discussions of the origin, form and structure of the text are irrelevant for our purposes here, as are the debates over the christological significance of words and phrases within it – what does it mean to say that Christ was 'in the form of God' ($\dot{\epsilon}\nu$ μορφῆ θεοῦ), that he did not consider it a ἁρπαγμός to be equal with God (2.6), that he emptied himself (2.7), that he is (now) the Lord to whom every knee shall bow (2.10–11) and so on? Despite disagreement over these (significant) details, and various scholarly proposals concerning the (original) poetic structure of the hymn, the general shape of the 'story' it tells is clear enough (see below). It is, nonetheless, important at least to clarify that the identification of the text as a *pre*-Pauline hymn – and even this is hardly secure – should not prevent our reading it as a part of Paul's letter and as having a function within the wider text in which it is located. While there

---

7. As well as in the commentaries, a good recent orientation to this discussion is provided by the essays in Martin and Dodd 1998, and by Martin 1997b.

8. See Lohmeyer 1961; Käsemann 1960. Brown 1998 and Morgan 1998, respectively, offer a critical discussion of these two works. Cf. also Hurtado 1984: 114–16.

9. Cf. the judgment of Hofius 1991: 1: 'Die erstmals von E. Lohmeyer vertretene These, daß Paulus in Phil 2,6-11 einem ihm bereits vorgegebenen urchristlichen Hymnus zitiert, hat in der Forschung fast allgemein Anerkennung gefunden.'

seem good grounds for regarding it as formulated prior to the writing of Philippians, whether by Paul or by unknown others,[10] recent scholarship has tended, rightly, to insist that it must be interpreted if not as the product of Paul's own authorship then at least as a text *affirmed* by Paul and made his own in the context of the letter.[11]

Käsemann's argument is more directly relevant, since it concerns whether and how Paul presents Christ here as an ethical example. It is one of Käsemann's primary aims to argue against what he calls the 'ethical idealism' (*ethischer Idealismus*) which characterizes most interpretations of the text (Käsemann 1960: 57), including that of Lohmeyer, whose work Käsemann regards as in many respects crucial and important.[12] While Käsemann has fundamentally theological reasons for opposing this interpretation, he brings exegetical arguments against it particularly on the basis of vv. 5 and 9-11. Verse 5 is elliptical, the second clause lacking a verb. Something must therefore be supplied to make sense of what Paul writes, and, while there have been a variety of proposals, the crucial question is whether Paul intends to convey a parallelism between the attitude the Philippians should have and that of Christ, as is required by the ethical reading (see further below). Käsemann argues, to the contrary, that 'in Christ Jesus' (ἐν Χριστῷ ᾽Ιησοῦ) here has the sense of a 'technical formula', as is common in Pauline usage, and thus denotes the sphere in which believers live; it has a soteriological character. The verb implied, then, is not 'was' (ἦν) – your attitude should be the same as *was* in Christ Jesus – or other possibilities yielding a similar meaning (e.g., ἐφρονήθη), but rather, Käsemann suggests, φρονεῖτε or φρονεῖν δεῖ, which would convey the sense that the mindset the Philippians should have is 'that which it is

10. The poetic structure of the text, though the extent of this structuring is debatable, points to a text shaped by repetition and use, perhaps in worship; and while the text clearly plays an important role within the paraenetic argument in which Paul sets it, it constitutes a self-contained passage which goes beyond what would seem required simply to support the point Paul is making (cf. e.g. Rom. 15.1-3; 2 Cor. 8.9, for much briefer references to the 'story' of Christ in support of moral exhortation).

11. So, e.g., Fee 1995: 193 n. 3: 'Since Paul dictated these words ... we may assume that he *chose* to use these very words, even if they had existed in prior form.' Similarly, and quoted by Fee here, Hooker 1978: 152. Cf. also Wright 1991: 97–98; Hurtado 1984: 119.

12. Käsemann (1960: 53) refers to Lohmeyer's work as a 'Wendepunkt' in the interpretation of this text. On Käsemann's analysis as a whole, and on the ethical idealism which he opposes, see esp. Morgan 1998; also Hurtado 1984: 114–16; Martin 1997b: 90–92; Fowl 1990: 79–85 and more briefly Fowl 1998: 140. Käsemann's view of the hymn's function as 'kerygmatic' rather than 'ethical' became the dominant position for a time, not least because of the affirmation of his view in Martin 1997b (1st edn, 1967): 289–92; cf., e.g., Losie 1978: 52–53.

necessary to have "in Christ Jesus"'.[13] The hymn which follows does not then present Christ as a moral example, but rather presents the mythical scheme of the salvation event; it is this which forms the basis for Paul's paraenesis, and not some depiction of Christ as ethical *Vorbild*. Verses 9-11 add weight to this thesis. They hardly fit with the ethical interpretation of the hymn, which must relegate them to the status of an excursus or appendix (cf. Käsemann 1960: 91–92). But in terms of a presentation of the mythical scheme in which Christ becomes incarnate, humbled to death on a cross, then exalted and enthroned as Lord of all, they are obviously as central and indispensable as the preceding section. Thus, according to Käsemann, 'it becomes clear that the hymn conveys eschatology and soteriology, not ethics' (p. 94). The basis for Paul's appeal to the Christians in Philippi to demonstrate an attitude of humility is not that Christ demonstrates a similar pattern and is worthy of imitation but rather that through God's saving action in Christ, of which they are here reminded, they have been brought from the old age into the new, rescued from the dominion of the powers and brought into the sphere of Christ's lordship, 'in Christ'.[14]

Before we dismiss Käsemann too swiftly – for indeed most recent work has reasserted the validity of an ethical reading of this text[15] – we should pause to appreciate the theological convictions which drive his reading and specifically his opposition to the ethical interpretation.[16] Like Karl Barth, Käsemann is deeply opposed to the kind of theological liberalism that reduces the gospel to an 'ethical idealism', and which inclines therefore to read a passage like Phil. 2.5–11 as conveying (merely) a moral message.[17]

---

13. See Käsemann 1960: 90–91, cf. p. 57, where he affirms Barth's reading on this point. Käsemann considers that this view 'hat sich heute durchgesetzt', contra Lohmeyer (p. 91). Cf. e.g. NEB: 'Let your bearing towards one another arise out of your life in Christ Jesus'; Beare 1959: 73: 'Let this be the disposition that governs in your common life, as is fitting in Christ Jesus'. For similar interpretations, see also Gnilka 1968: 108–10; Martin 1997b: 289–91, and more recently Dodd 1998: 160.

14. Cf. Käsemann 1960: 95: 'Hier wird nicht ein ethisches Vorbild aufgerichtet. Damit wäre der Raum der alten Welt noch nicht verlassen. Hier wird bezeugt, daß die Welt dem Gehorsamen gehört und er Herr ist, damit wir gehorsam würden. Gehorsam werden wir jedoch nicht durch ein Vorbild, sondern durch das Wort, das uns als ihm gehörig bezeugt.'

15. E.g. Hooker 1978; Hurtado 1984; Fowl 1990: 49–101; 1998; Meeks 1991; Fee 1995: 196, 200; Bockmuehl 1998a: 123, etc. In subsequent editions of Martin's 1967 monograph, in which Käsemann's rejection of the ethical reading was supported, Martin also moves towards an accommodation of the 'ethical', as well as the 'soteriological', interpretation (Martin 1997b: xii, xlix).

16. On this, see esp. Morgan 1998, though Morgan also considers that Käsemann's rejection of the ethical reading is in the end implausible. Cf. also Hurtado 1984: 114–16.

17. So Morgan 1998: 43: 'dialectical theology's repudiation of liberal Protestantism's ethical idealism stands as godfather to this interpretation [sc. Käsemann's rejection of the ethical reading of Philippians 2]'.

That, Käsemann insists, is not the Christian gospel, and sanitizes its radical, apocalyptic, world-shattering message: that liberation from enslavement to the powers of the old age comes about (only) through a change of lordship (*Herrschaftswechsel*), and that with this change of lordship comes the possibility of obedience.

Käsemann is surely right that this text cannot properly be *reduced* to the status of an ethical example. While an ethical interpretation of the Christ-hymn is, in the end, much more plausible than Käsemann's reading, Käsemann's arguments should stand against any such reductionism.[18] Käsemann is also right to insist that these verses present a myth. For Käsemann this is meant in the Bultmannian sense and is asserted in the context of heated debates over Bultmann's identification of myth in the New Testament and proposals for a demythologizing hermeneutic (see further Morgan 1998; Bultmann 1985: 1–43). Drawing on the rather different view presented by Wendy Doniger, we can nonetheless affirm that the text presents a myth – a story believed to be true, and which shapes the identity and conduct of the people who affirm it (see §3.1). Despite the intensive debate, the basic shape of this story is clear; as Stephen Fowl puts it, 'what we have here is a down/up pattern with the change in direction occurring in the transition between vv. 8 and 9' (Fowl 1998: 142; cf. also Meeks 1991: 329–30). The first half of the story concerns Christ's descent, his self-emptying, his taking the form of a slave and humbling himself to the point of his death ($\mu\acute{\epsilon}\chi\rho\iota\ \theta\alpha\nu\acute{\alpha}\tau\sigma\upsilon$). As Bockmuehl notes (1998a: 125–26), 'the pivot and turning point' in the text is found in the final line of v. 8, where the descent emphatically culminates in the repeated reference to Christ's death, specified as 'death on a cross' ($\theta\alpha\nu\acute{\alpha}\tau\sigma\upsilon\ \delta\grave{\epsilon}\ \sigma\tau\alpha\upsilon\rho\sigma\hat{\upsilon}$). The second half describes the consequent ascent and exaltation, the enthronement of Christ as universal Lord and his being given 'the name above all names'. This short text therefore presents in concise and poetic form the central Christian myth: Christ's becoming human and going to his death, his exaltation by God as Lord. Its form as poetry, or at least 'rhythmic prose' (Hooker 1978: 157), suggests some pre-history in which it took shape as a summary of this myth, and its (concise) content and focus explain why it is so rich in terms that – not least because of the tightly packed expression – generate intense theological debate.

This view of the text enables us to develop a richer sense of what it might mean to describe this text as ethical, compared with the 'mere example' interpretation that Käsemann rightly rejected. As a rich and compact expression of the Christian myth, shared and proclaimed, whether 'liturgically' or otherwise, in the context of Christian gatherings, this text

---

18. Cf. Meeks 1991: 331: 'he [sc. Käsemann] rightly insisted that Christ is not presented in the hymn as merely a moral *Vorbild*, the exemplar of a virtue or an attitude to be emulated.'

shapes the beliefs, identity and behaviour of those who affirm it; it has to do with both world-view and ethos, to echo Geertz's terms (see §3.3). In this sense, it is about soteriology, eschatology *and – pace* Käsemann – ethics. Verses 9-11 are not then problematic for an ethical interpretation along these lines, though they are for a 'mere example' ethic. They belong in the text since they depict a crucial part of the story, which cannot end simply with death on a cross. But more than this, while Christ's 'story' is in one sense unimitatable, the pattern of faithful endurance through suffering leading to resurrection glory is precisely one to which Paul points the Philippians and sees mirrored in his own, as well as Christ's, experience (Rom. 8.18-39; Phil. 3.10-11, 21, etc.).[19]

What kind of ethical interpretation does the text, and Philippians as a whole, then suggest? First we return to v. 5. Most recent commentators have not been persuaded by Käsemann's reading, but have insisted that the Greek more likely implies a form of ethical reading: that the pattern of thinking to which Paul calls the Philippians in vv. 1-4 ($\tauο\hat{υ}το$ in v. 5 points back, not forwards)[20] is that which was (or is)[21] also in Christ.[22] Looking back to vv. 3-4, then, it becomes clear that the specific pattern of moral conduct which Paul sees exemplified in Christ is one characterized by 'humility' ($\tauαπεινοφροσύνη$) – a self-lowering in which each person considers others before themselves and looks not to their own (things)[23] but to those of others. This self-lowering other-regard is paradigmatically demonstrated in the central story of the faith, in Christ Jesus himself, whose self-lowering takes the extreme form of a movement from the form of God (and equality with God) to the form of a slave, a person 'bereft of rights and social status' (Matera 1996: 179). This 'social humility', that is, the lowering of oneself before (and for the sake of) those who are socially equal or inferior is *not*, it is widely agreed, seen as positive or morally

---

19. This is perhaps also why Paul follows the hymn with an exhortation to the Philippians to 'work out your own salvation with fear and trembling' (2.12; cf. 3.12-16). On the relevance of 2.9-11 to an ethical reading of the passage, see also Hurtado 1984: 125.

20. So Hawthorne 1983: 80; Fee 1995: 201 n. 33; Bockmuehl 1998a: 122. Otherwise Losie 1978.

21. Bockmuehl (1998a: 123–24) argues for the present rather than imperfect tense to be supplied here.

22. Hawthorne, for example, against the interpretation of $\dot{ε}ν$ Χριστο$\hat{υ}$ Ἰησο$\hat{υ}$ pressed by Käsemann, insists that the 'grammatical parallelism' between $\dot{ε}ν$ $\dot{υ}μ\hat{ι}ν$ and $\dot{ε}ν$ Χριστο$\hat{υ}$ Ἰησο$\hat{υ}$ demands that the two phrases be treated alike and thus makes impossible the 'incorporation-in-Christ' reading (1983: 81). The καί (here meaning 'also') adds further weight to this interpretation, 'that the frame of mind set forth in vv. 3-4 is precisely that which one *also* has seen in Christ Jesus' (Fee 1995: 200).

23. As in 1 Cor. 10.24, a closely parallel phrase, Paul does not specify a noun here (interests, concerns, rights, etc.) but speaks simply of $\tau\grave{α}$ $\dot{ε}αυτ\hat{ω}ν/\tau\grave{α}$ $\dot{ε}τέρων$ (cf. 1 Cor. 10.24: $\tau\grave{ο}$ $\dot{ε}αυτο\hat{υ}/\tau\grave{ο}$ $\dot{ε}τέρου$).

commendable in Graeco-Roman ethics,[24] nor does it exist with any degree of prominence as a virtue in pre-Christian Jewish tradition – though it has clear precedents and precursors there.[25] Yet it comes to prominence as a central Christian virtue, not least in Paul, precisely because it is demonstrated paradigmatically in the story of Christ's self-giving for others – his shameful and ignominious death becoming in Christianity a positive model for imitation.[26]

Despite James Dunn's vigorous argument for a non-incarnationalist reading of Phil. 2.6-11,[27] and despite the difficulty in determing exactly what ἐν μορφῇ θεοῦ implies about Christ's status, most scholars accept that 2.6 describes Christ's pre-existence (or his 'pretemporal existence': so Martin 1998b: 3).[28] N.T. Wright's treatment of the crucial term ἁρπαγμός has also been influential in adding considerable weight to the view that Christ is depicted here as 'not taking advantage of' or exploiting his equality with God, rather than as grasping for something he did not possess, as in Dunn's Adamic reading (Wright 1986/1991: 56–98). One related question, then,

---

24. Cf., e.g., Schrage 1961: 204–205; Bockmuehl 2000: 138 n. 87; W. Grundmann, *TWNT* 8: 1–6; and esp. Ortwein 1999, for a major study of 'renunciation of status' (*Statusverzicht*) as a value in the NT and its environment (cf. Theissen 1999: 71–78, on this value as central to early Christian ethics). Ortwein comments: 'Demut wird in der paganen Antike nur sehr selten positiv bewertet.' The few positive references are to humility before the gods or under the law. 'Als Haltung vor den Menschen wird sie als Haltung der Unterlegenen den Überlegenen gegenüber gefordert, mit einer Ausnahme (Agesilaios) aber negativ bewertet. Als Haltung der Überlegenen gegenüber den Unterlegenen läßt sie sich m.W. nicht nachwiesen' (p. 87). For examples of ταπεινοφροσύνη used pejoratively, see Josephus, *War* 4.494; Epictetus, *Diss.* 3.24.56.

25. The extent to which the social virtue of humility is evident in pre-Christian Judaism is debated, with e.g. Wengst 1988 and Dawes 1991a, 1991b, arguing for its Hebrew Bible origins (though Dawes rejects Wengst's view that it originated in the solidarity of the oppressed poor = the humiliated). Dickson and Rosner (2003) have recently argued that, while some kinds of humility are certainly evident, humility as *social* humility – the lowering of oneself before a lesser or equal – appears positively only in Sir. 4.8. On the developments towards humility as a social virtue in Jewish tradition, Ortwein (1999) again offers a full survey (see the conclusions in this regard on pp. 156–58, 320–22).

26. For uses of the ταπειν- root in Paul, see Rom. 12.16; 2 Cor. 7.6; 10.1; 11.7; 12.21; Phil. 2.3, 8; 3.21; 4.12. In terms of presenting humility as a positive virtue, Rom. 12.16; 2 Cor. 11.7; and Phil. 2.3 are significant. Kurz (1985: 120) is simply inaccurate when he states that '[t]he ταπειν- root appears only in Philippians and mostly in chaps. 2–3'. The pattern of conduct which humility epitomizes is also much more widely presented as exemplary, through Paul's references to Christ's self-giving for others, and to his own social self-lowering, suffering, labour, etc. Cf. also Schürmann 1974: 294–300; Wolff 1989.

27. See Dunn 1980: 114–21; 1998a: 281–88; 1998b.

28. See, e.g., Casey 1991: 112–13; Fee 1995: 203 n. 41; Bockmuehl 1998a: 126: 'Among the majority of scholars there is still widespread agreement that we are dealing with Christ's state or condition in relation to God, *prior to* his state or condition as a servant'. For a critique of Dunn's view see Hurst 1998.

concerns whether it is the heavenly-then-incarnate Christ or the earthly, historical Jesus who forms the pattern for Christian imitation. Certainly here, as elsewhere, Paul does not point to any specific actions of the historical Jesus as examples to follow, only to his central act of self-giving, 'to death on a cross'.[29] But it makes little sense to try to distinguish heavenly Christ and earthly Jesus in this connection, despite the suggestions of interpreters to the contrary.[30] Rather, Paul regards the self-giving of Christ Jesus,[31] through incarnation to death on the cross, as one seamless act, a paradigmatic demonstration of self-giving for others (cf. 2 Cor. 8.9; Gal. 4.4-5; §7.4 below).

But this same pattern is also demonstrated by Paul himself, and by Timothy and Epaphroditus. Just as Paul's very identity is fundamentally rooted in Christ (Phil. 1.20-21; 3.7-9), so he too is 'conformed' to the pattern of Christ's death in hope of attaining the resurrection (3.10, 21); he chooses the less personally preferable path for the sake of the Philippians (1.24-25); he strains *upwards* ($\check{\alpha}\nu\omega$) towards the heavenly prize (3.14). Timothy is concerned for the Philippians' welfare, unlike 'those who seek their own interests ($\tau\grave{\alpha}$ $\dot{\epsilon}\alpha\upsilon\tau\hat{\omega}\nu$)' (2.19-21). Epaphroditus has served Paul's needs and ministered to him when the Philippians could not (2.25-30), specifically giving himself to the point of death ($\mu\dot{\epsilon}\chi\rho\iota$ $\theta\alpha\nu\acute{\alpha}\tau\omega$, 2.30; cf. 2.8) for the work of Christ. 'In sending these coworkers to Philippi', then, as Frank Matera notes, 'Paul provides the community with concrete examples of his moral exhortation' (1996: 181). The Philippians are called to follow these and similar examples, to become together imitators of Paul (3.17).[32] Hence the following 'inclusive description of Paul and the letter's recipients', in 3.20-21, 'echoes the hymn' of 2.6-11: as Christ was in the form of God, yet humbled himself to death and was subsequently exalted, so he will transform the body of those who have followed his pattern of self-lowering humility ($\tau\alpha\pi\epsilon\acute{\iota}\nu\omega\sigma\iota\varsigma$), conforming ($\sigma\acute{\upsilon}\mu\mu\rho\rho\phi\nu$) them to his glory (Meeks 1991: 333).[33]

---

29. Cf. Matera 1996: 179: 'For Paul, Christians are to imitate the self-emptying of Christ. To this extent, the Pauline notion of imitating Christ is rooted in Christ's redemptive act rather than in specific moral or ethical examples taken from Jesus' earthly life.'

30. Cf. Schrage 1961: 238–41. For an overview of discussion, see Merk 1989: 184–87. Kümmel (1965: 451) rightly comments, 'daß Paulus den irdischen Jesus und den erhöhten Herrn als Einheit sieht', against the view that only the pre-existent Christ serves as ethical *Vorbild* and that the concrete person of the historical Jesus is of no significance. Similarly, Schürmann 1974: 288.

31. Paul's inclusion of the name Jesus here may not be insignificant, serving to negate the drawing of any distinction between 'heavenly Christ' and 'earthly Jesus'; cf. Hooker 1978: 154; also 2 Cor. 8.9.

32. Note esp. the phrase $\check{\epsilon}\chi\epsilon\tau\epsilon$ $\tau\acute{\upsilon}\pi\omega\nu$ $\dot{\eta}\mu\hat{\alpha}\varsigma$, so the $\tau\acute{\upsilon}\pi\omega\varsigma$ is not only Paul himself. $\Sigma\upsilon\mu\mu\iota\mu\eta\tau\alpha\acute{\iota}$ could possibly imply 'become fellow-imitators with me, of Christ', though the adjoining $\mu\omega\upsilon$ makes this unlikely (see Hawthorne 1983: 160; Fee 1995: 364 n. 10).

33. Cf. further Kurz 1985; Hooker 1978: 155. For the meaning of $\tau\grave{\omega}$ $\sigma\hat{\omega}\mu\alpha$ $\tau\hat{\eta}\varsigma$ $\tau\alpha\pi\epsilon\iota\nu\acute{\omega}\sigma\epsilon\omega\varsigma$ $\dot{\eta}\mu\hat{\omega}\nu$ in this context, see Doble 2002.

The parallels between the depiction of Christ in 2.6-11 and Paul's self-description in 3.2-16 should not be overpressed.[34] There are clearly differences. But the point is not to claim 'that the two subjects have done the same thing or thought the same thoughts but that the dramatic structure of the two "plots" is analogous, though not the same' (Meeks 1991: 333). And the determinative 'plot' is the story of Christ, whose self-giving to death and subsequent vindication form the lens, the master-pattern, through which Paul makes sense of his own experiences and (re)tells the story of his own life, and which he in turn commends as the pattern for the Philippians to imitate.[35] We may perhaps best speak of a 'conformity' to Christ (so Hooker 1978: 155–57):[36] 'the story of Christ narrated in 2:6-11 functions as an exemplar, a concrete expression of a shared norm from which Paul and the Philippians can make analogical judgments about how they should live' (Fowl 1998: 145–46; cf. 1990: 92–101).[37]

Wayne Meeks has drawn attention to the frequent use of the verb $\phi\rho o\nu\epsilon\omega$ in Philippians, a frequency comparable only with the later chapters of Romans (Meeks 1991: 332).[38] In both letters, the verb concerns the kind of attitude, the sort of mindset which should shape conduct (Rom. 12.3, 16; 15.5; Phil. 2.2, 5; 3.15; etc.). This $\phi\rho o\nu\eta\sigma\iota\varsigma$, or 'practical wisdom' – Paul does not, however, use the noun – was, as Meeks notes, 'an important concept in Greco-Roman moral philosophy' (p. 333; see, e.g., Aristotle, *Nic. Eth.* 6.5.1 [1140a, 24]; 6.8.1 [1141b, 23]; LSJ, 1956). The frequent uses of the verb in Philippians, and the manner in which it is used, support Meeks's proposal, 'that this letter's most comprehensive purpose is the shaping of a Christian *phrōnesis* [*sic*], a practical moral reasoning that is

34. So Dodd 1998, in criticism, e.g., of Kurz 1985, who draws rather too close a parallel between Christ's giving up his equality with God and Paul's giving up his Jewish credentials (p. 115), though his general argument about the examples of Christ and Paul serving as the main bases for exhortation in Philippians, exemplars of a kenotic pattern of self-abasement leading to exaltation, seems to me convincing.

35. Cf. also Oakes 2001, who sees a 'threefold parallel between Christ, Paul and the Philippians' as the 'main thematic structure of the letter' (p. xiii; see pp. 103–28, 175–210). Further, in relation to Galatians and Romans, see Barclay 2002; Horrell 2002c. Though I disagree with Barclay on the extent to which there is a story which underpins Paul's theology, we agree that Paul's personal story is shaped and told as one 'moulded by the story of the crucified Christ' (Barclay 2002: 146; cf. 155–56; Horrell 2002c: 166). Thus it is the story of Christ, rather than the narrative of Paul's own life, on which Paul draws to interpret and describe his experience (*pace* Wright 1992: 404).

36. Cf. also Matera 1996: 174: 'because he has conformed himself to the pattern of Christ's death, Paul invites others to imitate him by conforming themselves to Christ'.

37. Cf. also Hawthorne 1983: 79: 'The hymn, therefore, presents Christ as the ultimate model for moral action.'

38. See Phil. 1.7; 2.2 (*bis*), 5; 3.15 (*bis*), 19; 4.2, 10 (*bis*); Rom. 8.5; 11.20; 12.3 (*bis*), 16 (*bis*); 14.6 (*bis*); 15.5.

"conformed to [Christ's] death" in hope of his resurrection' (p. 333; cf. Fowl 1998: 145–48). It is perhaps not surprising, then, that it is here in Philippians that Paul uniquely uses the language of virtue (ἀρετή, 4.8): as the Christians in Philippi affirm and celebrate the story of Christ's descent and ascent, humiliation and exaltation, so they are to conform their character and practice to the moral exemplar of Christ, and thus cultivate the virtues embodied in him – humility, other-regard, confidence and joy in suffering and so on. And the purpose of all this is to enable the community to live in unity and harmony, despite the pressures and threats from without and within (Phil. 1.27–2.4; 3.1–4.9, etc.; cf. Matera 1996: 177–78). The *carmen Christi* in 2.6-11 is, then, central to the letter as a whole, and specifically to the moral exhortation within it. In the story of Christ's self-lowering, self-giving, even to death, and his subsequent vindication, the Philippians are to see the determinative plot which shapes Paul's and their own moral reasoning.

7.2 *1 Corinthians 9.14-15 and Paul's Imitation of Christ*

We have already seen briefly how Paul's example, set out in 1 Corinthians 9, is used to present a pattern of conduct to which he calls the Corinthian strong: the setting aside of one's own rights out of concern for the other, specifically for one's (weaker) siblings (see §6.1). The example set out in chapter 9 is that which Paul appeals to the Corinthians to imitate, and which he regards as in turn an imitation of Christ (11.1). There are aspects of this text, however, which warrant more detailed examination. We shall focus initially and especially on 9.14-15.[39] This text is relevant, first, to a consideration of the way in which Paul regards the words or commands of Jesus and of the extent to which they shape his conduct. Second, as we read this text in its literary context, it enables us to say more about what Paul does consider as his imitation of Christ.

In 9.14 we reach the climax of the list of reasons Paul gives to justify his right to support from the communities which he visits. Wolfgang Schrage is correct to note that Paul evidently intends to build upwards, giving gradually more and more weighty justifications for his rights, in moving from reasons based in everyday life and common logic (9.7) to the Law of Moses (9.8-10) and finally to the command of the Lord (9.14).[40] The citation of the Lord's command, then, provides 'the decisive authority' (Schrage 1995: 308) which 'clinches the argument' (Fee 1987: 412): if ever

---

39. In this section I draw on material from Horrell 1997b.
40. Schrage 1995: 295: 'Vermutlich zielt Paulus doch eher auf eine beabsichtige Steigerung von Alltags- und Vernunftgründen über das Mosegesetz bis zum Herrenwort.' (Cf. also p. 308.)

there were a right, an $\dot{\epsilon}\xi o \upsilon \sigma \acute{\iota} \alpha$, that could be unquestionably legitimated, this is it.[41]

Given that Paul refers here to what the Lord commanded ($\dot{o}$ κύριος διέταξεν) the following verse creates a striking juxtaposition: 'but I have not used any of these [rights, or, reasons to justify a right to support] (ἐγὼ δὲ οὐ κέχρημαι οὐδενὶ τούτων)'.[42] Paul seems to regard an instruction of the Lord as a 'right' ($\dot{\epsilon}\xi o \upsilon \sigma \acute{\iota} \alpha$) which can be set aside (cf. Dungan 1971: 20–40; Theissen 1982: 43–44). Perhaps this is because, as some have suggested, he regards the command as addressed to the congregations, thus giving the Apostles a 'right' to material support. However, I shall argue below that this is an unlikely, and certainly an incomplete, explanation.

The basic reason for this surprising juxtaposition is connected with the exemplary purpose of this whole passage. As W.L. Willis puts it: 'Paul has established his rights so strongly so that *he can make something* of his renunciation of them' (1985b: 35). Just as the Corinthian strong's $\dot{\epsilon}\xi o \upsilon \sigma \acute{\iota} \alpha$ is grounded on fundamental and unquestionable theological principles (8.6) so is Paul's right ($\dot{\epsilon}\xi o \upsilon \sigma \acute{\iota} \alpha$) to support grounded on an equally unquestionable basis: the Lord's command. Consequently, Paul's appeal to them to set aside their justifiable rights is no more than he does himself.

But does this actually mean that in doing this Paul ignores, or even disobeys, a command of the Lord? These verses provide an interesting test case concerning not only the references to Jesus tradition in Paul's letters but also the kind of authority Paul attributes to these dominical commands. As in the other (few) comparable instances where Paul makes explicit reference to Jesus' teaching, aside from 1 Cor. 11.23-25, there is here no direct quotation of gospel tradition, only a summary of what the Lord's instruction was (cf. 1 Cor. 7.10-11; 1 Thess. 4.15-17; perhaps Rom. 14.14; §1.4 above). Despite this lack of material repetition, it is generally and most plausibly assumed that Paul is referring to Jesus tradition preserved in the synoptic gospels and not to an *agraphon* or unknown

---

41. 'V 14 nennt Paulus nun ... die entscheidende Instanz in seinem Beweisgang, nämlich ein Herrenwort' (Schrage 1995: 308). The use of διατάσσω, Schrage rightly argues, also shows that it is mistaken to regard this citation as just a further 'and by the way ... (beiläufig)' addition to the list (pp. 308–309).

42. The referent of τούτων is not explicitly stated and must therefore be inferred. The usual, and most convincing, interpretation is to take Paul as referring to 'rights', as is clearly the case in vv. 12 and 18; see Schrage 1995: 319–20. Alternatively τούτων might refer to the preceding list of grounds on which a right to support could be legitimated. On this reading, τούτων and ταῦτα (v. 15a and b) refer to the same thing, namely, the reasons Paul has given which would support a claim to material support. Dungan 1971: 21–22 n. 2 makes this argument, against which see Fee 1987: 416 n. 12. Dungan comments that: 'The translation, "I have not used any of these rights" ... is inaccurate if for no other reason because Paul is speaking of only one right anyway.' However, this assertion is easily countered: Paul mentions three 'rights' in 9.4–6.

saying. This tradition is found in the mission instructions given to the twelve in Mt. 10.1-15, Mk 6.7-11; and Lk. 9.1-5, or to the seventy in Lk. 10.1-12. It is often suggested that the 'proverb' attributed to Jesus in Lk. 10.7//Mt. 10.10 underlies Paul's allusion:[43] 'the worker is worthy of his wage/food' (ἄξιος γὰρ ὁ ἐργάτης τοῦ μισθοῦ αὐτοῦ [Luke]/τῆς τροφῆς αὐτοῦ [Matthew]).[44] Scholars have debated whether Matthew's or Luke's version of the saying is most likely reflected in Paul's text,[45] though the 'ambiguity of the evidence' perhaps confirms the fact that Paul cannot be said to depend entirely on one extant version of this discourse, but 'shows points of contact with more than one account'.[46]

If it were specifically this proverb to which Paul alludes here, as many suggest, then it could be argued that the force of Jesus' word is to stress the responsibility upon congregations to support their missionary leaders. Certainly the proverb appears in later literature as an isolated saying used to justify the material support of Christian leaders (1 Tim. 5.18; cf. *Did.* 13.1).[47] Against the idea, then, that Paul is himself disregarding a word of the Lord, Gordon Fee maintains that '[a]s "command" the word of Jesus referred to here does not have to do with *his* (Paul's) action but *theirs* ... the command is not given *to* the missionaries but *for* their benefit'.[48] F.F. Bruce similarly suggests that the 'command' was 'essentially intended as a permission from the outset' (1974: 73). So, according to Seyoon Kim, 'Paul's failure to avail himself of it is hardly a "disobedience" to it' (1993: 475).

There are, however, reasons why this interpretation is unsatisfactory. First, there is the grammar of Paul's own formulation in 1 Cor. 9.14 which

---

43. E.g. Resch 1904: 51; Dautzenberg 1969: 216; Harvey 1982: 211; Fee 1987: 413; Barrett 1971: 208. Otherwise Goulder 1974: 145.

44. A few texts bring Matthew into line with Luke.

45. Dungan concludes that 'Matthew's version of the saying "the workman is worthy of his food" is the saying Paul is presupposing in 1 Cor. 9.14' and suggests that Paul's argument in 1 Cor. 9.3-12 would have appeared as 'an artistic elaboration on the two aspects of this proverb: workman and food' (Dungan 1971: 79–80). He suggests, as with the Lord's teaching on divorce, that the Corinthians were already aware of this 'command' of Jesus (pp. 27–28, 147). B. Fjärstedt, however, has outlined in detail the parallels in vocabulary between Luke 10 and 1 Corinthians 9, and it may be suggested that the Lukan form is at least as likely to underlie Paul's thought here (see Allison 1982: 6–10). Paul's use of the word μισθός (1 Cor. 9.17-18) would seem to favour Luke over Matthew.

46. Allison 1982: 13, who explains this with reference to the fact that no one synoptic account is wholly more primitive than the others. 'Each version contains early and late elements.'

47. In neither place is the proverb explicitly attributed to Jesus. 1 Tim. 5.18 appears to quote it as scripture. See esp. Harvey 1982.

48. Fee 1987: 413 n. 96. He asserts that 'Jesus' word itself is not a "command" but a proverb' (p. 413).

suggests that it is the missionaries themselves who are the objects of the Lord's instruction (cf. Schrage 1995: 278, 310):

οὕτως καὶ ὁ κύριος διέταξεν τοῖς τὸ εὐαγγέλιον καταγγέλλουσιν ἐκ τοῦ εὐαγγελίου ζῆν.

This is often translated as if 'those who proclaim the gospel' were only the indirect addressees of the command: 'In the same way, the Lord commanded that those who proclaim the gospel should get their living by the gospel' (NRSV, identical in RSV).[49] However, since διατάσσω (to order, instruct, command, direct, etc.) normally uses the dative case for those addressed (cf. BDAG, 237), a translation which makes 'those who proclaim the gospel' the direct target of the Lord's command should be a natural choice, unless the context demands a different rendering. Clear examples of this usual usage are close at hand: 1 Cor. 16.1: ὥσπερ διέταξα ταῖς ἐκκλησίαις τῆς Γαλατίας ('as I instructed the churches of Galatia'); Tit. 1.5: ὡς ἐγώ σοι διεταξάμην ('as I directed you'; cf. also Mt. 11.1; Acts 7.44; 24.23).[50] In avoiding this rather natural translation here in 1 Cor. 9.14, some translations are also led to soften the sense of the latter part of the verse (so, e.g., NRSV: 'should get their living by the gospel'). The Greek would be much better rendered with the straightforward translation:

So also the Lord commanded those who proclaim the gospel to live from the gospel.[51]

This rendering is confirmed by the synoptic tradition to which Paul here alludes. Indeed, a second reason to doubt that the command refers only to a permission (indirectly) given to the missionaries, which primarily implies a direct responsibility incumbent upon the congregations, is that in the synoptic mission instructions the addressees are those who are sent out (the twelve, and the seventy). They are *commanded* (παραγγέλλω in Mk 6.8 and Mt. 10.5) not to take even the minimum of possessions, not even the staff, cloak and pouch characteristic of the Cynic preacher.[52] Given the concise summary of this instruction which Paul presents, and the lack of any specific citation of the 'worker is worthy' proverb in 1 Cor. 9.14, it is more likely that Paul is alluding to (some form of) this whole block of

---

49. Cf. also NIV, REB, Barrett 1971: 208.

50. There are also occasions, though far fewer, where an indirect object after διατάσσω occurs, naturally in the dative: e.g. Lk. 8.55: διέταξεν αὐτῇ δοθῆναι φαγεῖν, though here the aorist passive infinitive δοθῆναι makes the sense clear.

51. Is the more common translation actually influenced by the desire to avoid the implication that Paul is being disobedient to a command of the Lord?

52. See, e.g., Epictetus, *Diss.* 3.22.10. The synoptic accounts vary: Mk 6.8-9 allows a staff and sandals, forbidden in Mt. 10.10 and Lk. 9.3; 10.4. Cf. Harvey 1982: 218; Crossan 1993: 117–19.

instruction than that the proverb alone is in view.[53] The proverb, in its synoptic context, clearly *explains* to the disciples the reason why they can confidently obey this command: their work for the kingdom will earn their support, and they may, indeed *must*, by their charismatic property-less lifestyle demonstrate their trust in God, which is also trust in the generosity of sympathizers wherever they stay (as the mission instructions make clear; Mt. 10.11-13; Mk 6.10; Lk. 9.4; 10.5-8; cf. esp. Theissen 1982: 27–67). While obligations are thus indirectly placed upon the sympathizers of the Jesus movement who remain resident in the towns and villages, it cannot be claimed that the instruction is in any way directly addressed to them, though there are other passages 'which stress the reward which is gained by supplying the needs of his [sc. Jesus'] followers' (Harvey 1982: 219; see, e.g., Mt. 10.40-42; Mk 9.41).

A third reason for suggesting that the command of Jesus was regarded as addressed to the apostles (including Paul) is the Corinthians' subsequent anger against Paul, though it must be conceded that on this point the evidence is not conclusive. Their criticism of Paul over the issue of his self-support (which implies, of course, his refusal of their support) seems already to be emerging in 1 Corinthians 9 but it intensifies after the writing of 1 Corinthians and is a major issue on which Paul defends himself in the heated letter contained in 2 Corinthians 10–13 (see 11.7-12; 12.13-18). The Corinthians are apparently aware of other apostles who conform to the pattern of the Lord's instruction on this matter (1 Cor. 9.5, 12). Certainly there are a range of largely social reasons why some of the Corinthians are offended by Paul's rejection of their support: not only does Paul spurn the offer of patronage but he also insists on labouring at his trade, an activity which some of the Corinthians perhaps found rather demeaning for a true apostle (cf. Marshall 1987; Horrell 1996: 199–237). However, we might question David Dungan's assertion that 'nowhere in the context of the attack upon Paul, whether conducted by the angry Corinthians or by the Jerusalem opposition, is he charged with *disobeying the command of the Lord*' (1971: 39). On the contrary, there are aspects of his self-defence in

---

53. Indeed Dale Allison (1982: 12–13) argues that 'Paul knew some version of the missionary discourse' and that the parallels imply 'not only a use of Matt. 10.10 = Luke 10.7 by Paul but familiarity with its larger context'. Otherwise Tuckett 1984. Only on the grounds that the 'worker is worthy' proverb was regarded at this time as an isolated saying could one accept the comments of Haraguchi 1993: 183–84: 'Die paulinische Überlieferung betont die Norm oder Pflicht der Verkündiger (vgl. ὁ κύριος διέταξεν) auf Kosten der Gemeinde zu leben, während die synoptische Tradition das recht der Wanderprediger begründet, sich von der Gemeinde unterhalten zu lassen (vgl. ἄξιος γὰρ ὁ ἐργάτης).' It seems much more likely to me that Paul knows and agrees with the synoptic tradition which regards the instruction to live from the gospel as a command of Jesus addressed to the apostles. Paul, however, is prepared to set this command aside, treating it as a right which he chooses not to use.

2 Corinthians 10–13 that may at least hint at such accusations. Gerd Theissen has drawn attention to these hints: 'Whenever he [sc. Paul] speaks of the superlative apostles (2 Cor. 11.15; 12.11) he goes on to speak about his renunciation of his right to support, and does so in such a way as to defend himself against the charge of ἁμαρτία or ἀδικία' (Theissen 1982: 45): 'Did I commit a sin (ἢ ἁμαρτίαν ἐποίησα) by humbling myself so that you might be exalted, because I proclaimed God's good news to you free of charge (δωρεάν)?' (2 Cor. 11.7). 'The catchword ἁμαρτία may in this instance have come from the Corinthian community, since Paul usually uses it to refer to the comprehensive power of sin rather than a specific transgression' (Theissen 1982: 45–46).[54] Was Paul's rejection of the lifestyle for travelling missionaries commanded by Jesus regarded (understandably) as sinful?

It appears, then, that Paul does regard the word of Jesus as a command addressed to the apostles (a group in which he insists he is included: 9.1-3). He knows that the Lord instructed those who proclaim the gospel to 'live' from the gospel. He regards this command as the most impressive and decisive among a list of reasons to justify what he treats as a 'right' – something over which he has freedom to decide (others disagreed) – a right which he refuses to 'use' on account of a higher priority: proclaiming the gospel to all 'free of charge' (ἀδάπανον, 9.18). Even something which Jesus commanded may, for this reason, be set aside. Schrage, notably, agrees: 'one cannot get around the conclusion that an obligatory and not optional command of the Lord finds its own limits in the service of the proclamation of the gospel'.[55]

But then the crucial question is: What kind of understanding of the gospel is it that leads Paul to believe that his pattern of conduct, and specifically his setting aside the command of the Lord, is required? Paul's answer to this question begins to emerge in the following verses (esp. 9.19-23). Paul does not 'use' his ἐξουσία (9.18) nor exploit his freedom, but rather has enslaved himself to all (9.19). This self-lowering to the place of a

---

54. Thus Theissen suggests that 'Paul has been reproached not for renouncing a privilege but for an offence against the norms of the early Christian itinerant charismatic movement' (1982: 44).

55. Schrage 1995: 310: 'Man kommt nicht um die Erklärung herum, daß selbst ein verpflichtendes und nicht in die Beliebigkeit abzuschiedendes Gebot des Herrn seine Grenze am Dienst der Verkündigung des Evangeliums findet'. In response to the previously published version of my argument (Horrell 1997b), Thiselton (2000: 695 n. 173) suggests that the argument is problematic due to a failure to distinguish 'between mandatory and permissive injunctions'. However, such a (probably anachronistic) distinction is nowhere indicated in the texts: both Paul and the synoptic writers simply present this injunction as something Jesus commanded.

slave has the purpose of gaining as many as possible (9.19).[56] More specifically, Paul adapts his behaviour variously, according to the expectations of different groups, such that he may gain them all (9.20-22). In this list too there is a rhetorical climax in the final phrase 'to the weak I became weak', the only phrase in the series without the qualifying ὡς, and the one which most directly relates to the wider argument of 1 Corinthians 8–10.[57] What this weakness specifically implies may be further glimpsed in 1 Cor. 4.8-13, where Paul contrasts his own (and the apostles') experiences with those of the Corinthians, or at least, those among the Corinthians who are 'puffed up' (4.18-19, using φυσιόω [twice], as in 8.1).[58] Here, in a hardship or *peristasis* catalogue,[59] Paul speaks graphically of the weakness, deprivation and humiliation which are his apostolic lot (cf. also 2 Cor. 4.8-12; 6.4-10). The catalogue includes reference to his hard physical labour (cf. Ebner 1991: 69) – 'working with our own hands' (1 Cor. 4.12) – and to his responding to slander and persecution with blessing and endurance (4.12-13), and culminates in the description of the apostles as 'the scum of the earth' (4.13). This social humiliation is not merely what happens to be Paul's experience but represents a deliberate 'self-lowering',[60] as the reference to his manual labour makes clear. This is a chosen policy which, as 2 Cor. 11.7 explicitly indicates, Paul regards as a form of self-humbling (ἐμαυτὸν ταπεινῶν). The self-lowering of which manual labour is a part is, then, for Paul an essential part of his proclamation (or better, embodiment) of the gospel, a deliberate 'becoming weak to the weak', important enough to be insisted upon even when it is the cause of offence to some of the Corinthians[61] and even if it requires one to go against the instruction of Jesus.

---

56. It is debated whether κερδαίνω (used repeatedly through vv. 19-22) has essentially an evangelistic reference (so Black 1983; 1984: 118–19) or a broader reference both to evangelism/conversion and to restoring right community relationships (cf. Gardner 1994: 99; Mt. 18.15). In view of the wider context of the discussion in 1 Corinthians 8–10 the latter seems to me preferable, since Paul is not concerned only to illustrate his missionary technique but also to show how his continuing practice represents an example of self-sacrificial regard for others, specifically for the weak – precisely the conduct to which he calls the Corinthian strong.

57. As noted, e.g., by Fee 1987: 422 n. 5; Conzelmann 1975: 161 n. 28; Gardner 1994: 103. It is surprising that Thiselton (2000) fails to notice this point. See further Horrell 1996: 208–209.

58. On this passage see further Horrell 1996: 200–204.

59. On these catalogues in Paul and other ancient literature, see esp. Hodgson 1983; Fitzgerald 1988; Ebner 1991. Hodgson (1983: 63) lists Pauline examples as: Rom. 8.35; 1 Cor. 4.10-13; 2 Cor. 4.8-9; 6.4-5, 8-10; 11.23-29; 12.10; and Phil. 4.12.

60. On this, see Martin 1990: 122–23; Judge 1984: 14.

61. Cf. further Martin 1990: 118–24; Horrell 1996: 210–16.

And why is this pattern of conduct so central to Paul's apostolic self-understanding and presentation of the gospel? Because it represents precisely a conformity to the pattern of Christ's self-giving for others, his self-lowering and humiliation unto death. In other catalogues, most clearly in 2 Cor. 4.8-10, Paul explicitly talks of his hardships and sufferings as an indication that he manifests the dying (νέκρωσις) of Jesus in his own body (cf. also 2 Cor. 6.9). The parallels between Paul's self-description and Phil. 2.7-8 are especially notable: like Christ, Paul has taken the form and position of a slave (πᾶσιν ἐμαυτὸν ἐδούλωσα, 1 Cor. 9.19) and followed the pattern of self-humbling for the sake of others (2 Cor. 11.7; cf. Dautzenberg 1969: 222, 225). The calls for imitation of Paul found in 1 Cor. 4.16 and Phil. 3.17 are calls for the imitation of this pattern of self-humbling, self-giving practice, seen supremely in Christ but also exemplified in the conduct of Paul and his co-workers.[62] Thus Paul can call for imitation of him as he in turn imitates Christ (1 Cor. 11.1). In the context of 1 Cor. 8.1–11.1, specifically of chapter 9, Paul indicates that the ethical imperative of Christ-like other-regard has priority over the theological or scriptural justifications which might otherwise legitimate a particular practice (cf. §6.1). In 1 Cor. 9.9, as Hays correctly observes, Paul cites scripture but then 'follows a course opposed to what the text – on his own reading – requires' (Hays 1989: 166). Hays continues: 'What this extraordinary fact demonstrates is that Paul allows the *imitatio Christi* paradigm (renunciation of privilege for the sake of others) to override all particular ethical rules and prescriptions, even when the rule is a direct command of scripture' (p. 225 n. 36). Hays's perceptive comment should nonetheless be both qualified and expanded. The scripture Paul cites in 1 Cor. 9.9 does not give a *direct* command concerning the duty of missionaries or leaders to rely on the community for support, nor about the duty of the community to provide that support. Despite Paul's comment ('God isn't concerned about oxen, is he?'), the text in Deut. 25.4 *is* (at least at the explicit level) about the treatment of labouring animals; Paul applies it to an analogous human situation, only to reject the pattern of conduct the principle requires.[63] Hays's comment applies more forcefully, in fact, to the command of Jesus, which *is* directly concerned with the conduct of travelling missionaries: Paul allows the *imitatio Christi* paradigm to override all particular ethical rules and prescriptions, even when the rule is a direct command of the Lord Jesus. This forceful claim may, however, also be misleading if it is taken to imply that 'all particular ethical rules and prescriptions' can be abandoned and replaced simply with

---

62. On the parallel examples of Paul and Christ in Philippians, see esp. Kurz 1985, and §7.1.

63. On the parallels with rabbinic exegesis, see Instone Brewer 1992.

the imperative to imitate Christ. As Schrage (1961) argued in relation to the claim of Bultmann and others that Pauline ethics could be reduced to the love command (see §1.1 above), this emptying of concrete content does not do justice to the material. More plausible is to view this moral demand as something akin to what Benhabib calls a 'metanorm' – a fundamental principle which sets the framework within which human relationships and specific ethical rules must function. And when, as Paul clearly perceived in this case, there is a clash between a metanorm and a specific ethical rule, 'the latter must be subordinated to the former' (Benhabib 1992: 45; cf. §2.2 above).

7.3 *The Law of Christ (Galatians 6.2; 1 Corinthians 9.21)*

Paul refers only twice to 'the law of Christ': once, directly, in Gal. 6.2 (ὁ νόμος τοῦ Χριστοῦ) and once in the somewhat more opaque expression ἔννομος Χριστοῦ (1 Cor. 9.21) – 'subject to the law of Christ', or perhaps 'inside Christ's law' (or 'jurisdiction').[64] There is therefore only a slender textual basis on which to build a view of what Paul meant to convey by this phrase – a fact that should induce caution in any attempt to do this – but considering its possible meanings provides a valuable probe into significant questions concerning Pauline ethics (cf. Stanton 2001). The various interpretations of the phrase may be grouped into four main proposals,[65] leaving aside certain suggestions with little substance or relevance, such as the idea that the phrase in Gal. 6.2 originates with Paul's opponents (so, e.g., Betz 1979: 300–301). Quite apart from the lack of evidence to substantiate this latter idea, a similar methodological point applies as in the case of Phil. 2.6-11 (and not least in view of Paul's use of a similar phrase in 1 Cor. 9.21): whatever its origins, Paul makes this phrase his own and uses it in a positive way.[66]

First is the view, espoused, as we have already seen, by W.D. Davies and C.H. Dodd, that the law of Christ refers to the teachings of Jesus, which

---

64. Cf. BDAG, 337–38. E.P. Sanders describes the phrase ἔννομος Χριστοῦ as 'virtually untranslatable' (1983: 100). Richard Longenecker (1984: 13) suggests the literal rendering 'in-lawed to Christ', though this would be a better translation of the less likely reading Χριστῷ (D², Ψ, Majority Text, Syriac Peshitta [see NA²⁷]).

65. For other, somewhat different, summaries of the various proposals, see Barclay 1988: 127–31; Martyn 1997a: 548.

66. Cf. Hays 1987: 274: 'even if the phrase *does* come from the opponents, Paul uses it in a thoroughly positive and nonpolemical way'. Whether the use is 'nonpolemical' is questionable, however, since Paul's argument is directed throughout against those tempted to place themselves 'under law' (Gal. 4.21); even Hays describes 'the law of Christ' as 'an ironic rhetorical formulation' (p. 275).

constitute for Paul a new Torah (see §1.4).[67] The problems with this view are, however, decisive: not only is there little evidence to support Davies's suggestion of the Jewish expectation of a messianic Torah, but also Paul makes very few *explicit* references to Jesus' teaching (see §1.4), and, as we have just seen, shows himself prepared to reinterpret and even reject that teaching.

A second influential interpretation is that the law of Christ refers to the love-command as taught and exemplified by Christ. Martin Luther, for example, in his 1535 commentary on Galatians, declared that '[t]he law of Christ is the law of love', pointing to the command given by Jesus in John 13.34-35 (see Luther 1953: 539). More recently, Schrage comments that '[t]he law of Christ is the love-command', but adds that this must be more precisely defined in the sense of 'conformity to Christ' (*Christus-konformität*), since for Paul Christ's act defines what love is (Schrage 1995: 345).[68]

The third view, which in varied forms comes closest to commanding widespread current assent, is that the law here refers to the Jewish/Mosaic law, and that 'when Paul talks of "fulfilling the law of Christ" he means "fulfilling the law in the way exemplified (and taught?) by Christ", i.e. fulfilling it through love' (Barclay 1988: 133–34).[69]

A fourth view, argued most fully by Richard Hays (1987), is that the 'law' of Christ in Gal. 6.2 refers 'not [to] the torah of Moses, not [to] a body of rules, but [to] a regulative principle or structure of existence, in this case the structure of existence embodied paradigmatically in Jesus Christ' (p. 276); the phrase is thus 'a formulation coined (or employed) by Paul to refer to this paradigmatic self-giving of Jesus Christ' (p. 275).[70]

---

67. As Stanton (2001: 49) notes, this view is found already in Justin Martyr, who refers to Christ as 'the new lawgiver' (ὁ καινὸς νομοθέτης, *Dial.* 14.3, cf. 12.2), though he also refers to Christ as himself 'the new law' (ὁ καινὸς νόμος, *Dial.* 11.4; Stanton 2001: 52).

68. Cf. also Furnish 1968: 64; Mußner 1988: 399: 'Das „Gesetz Christi" ist das Gesetz der gegenseitigen Liebe'.

69. Cf., similarly, Stanton 1996: 116; 2001: 57; Dunn 1993: 323; Lohse 1996: 386–89; Sanders 1983: 97–98; Martyn 1997a: 549: 'in Gal 6:2 Paul refers to the Law as it has been taken in hand by Christ himself' (cf. pp. 554–58).

70. Cf. also Schürmann 1974, who argues that it is the (inextricably connected) conduct and word of Jesus, specifically his exemplary conduct ('exemplarisches Verhalten', p. 283), that serve 'als Vorbild und Maßstab sittlichen Verhaltens' (p. 286) and to which Paul refers in the phrase 'the law of Christ'. 'Die Liebe der Selbstaufgabe und Selbsterniedrigung Christi ist nach Paulus letzte Norm und Kraftquelle sittlichen Verhaltens' (p. 294). Richard Longenecker (1990: 275–76) argues that the law of Christ here stands for those 'prescriptive principles stemming from the heart of the gospel (usually embodied in the example and teachings of Jesus) ... ', quoting in this connection what he elsewhere defines as 'New Testament ethics' itself (1984: 15). Winger (2000) argues that Paul uses 'the law of Christ' as 'a way of referring to the practice which Paul believes should govern the community of believers ... In short, this is a name for living by the Spirit' (p. 538), not a law that could be summarized in any kind of

It should already be evident that the different proposals are not entirely separable: elements of them all can be (and are) combined, as in the quotation from Barclay above. Similarly, James Dunn comments on Gal. 6.2:

> Paul refers in this shorthand way to the Jesus-tradition as indicating how Jesus interpreted the law in his teaching and actions ... this does not mean a law other than the Torah, the (Jewish) law. It means that law as interpreted by the love command in the light of the Jesus-tradition and the Christ-event. (Dunn 1993: 322–23)

It may, then, be a question of trying to determine where Paul's focus lies, rather than deciding on one interpretation to the complete exclusion of the others.

We may best begin with the reference in Galatians, where Paul gives more direct indication as to the substance of the law of Christ than he does in 1 Cor. 9.21 (to which we shall, however, return). The imperative addressed to the Galatians, in the section of the letter devoted to ethical exhortation (Gal. 5.13–6.10), is to 'bear one another's burdens (ἀλλήλων τὰ βάρη βαστάζετε)'. This is the conduct which will fulfil (ἀναπληρώσετε) the law of Christ (6.2). Some commentators (e.g. Mußner 1988: 398–99) argue for a close connection with the previous verse, which deals with 'restoring' a person who is caught in 'transgression' (παράπτωμα): the burdens to be shared are thus specifically those of others' sins and moral failures. But in view of the fact that the section from 6.1-10 consists of a series of brief and rather loosely connected injunctions, and also of the parallels in Rom. 15.1 and 1 Cor. 12.26 (cf. Barclay 1988: 132 n. 82), it is probably more convincing to take the burden-bearing to have a rather broader reference.[71] The pattern of conduct is urged as a mutual or reciprocal (*wechselseitig*) activity, as Mußner (1988: 399) rightly notes; ἀλλήλων ('one another's') stands emphatically at the beginning of the sentence.

But does this likely imply an echo of Jesus' *teaching*? There are, of course, passages in the gospels where Jesus describes his mission as one of service and self-giving for others, and calls his disciples to a similar pattern of self-lowering (Mk 10.42-45). But the lack of precise verbal parallels and of any indication that Paul knows of a Jesus-saying on the theme of bearing others' burdens make a conscious echo unlikely.

An echo of Jesus' teaching might be discerned in Paul's earlier reference to the command to love the neighbour as the fulfilment of the law (Gal.

---

rule or norm. But this becomes too loose and general an interpretation, and one through which Winger cannot find any coherent connection with the comparable phrase in 1 Cor. 9.21 (pp. 545–46) – on which see below.

71. Both Burton (1921: 329) and Longenecker (1990: 274–75), for example, see the 'burdens' as related specifically to the topic of v. 1 but also as having a broader reference.

5.14; cf. Rom. 13.8-10, both citing Lev. 19.18): many scholars point to Jesus' declaration that love of God and love of neighbour are the most important commandments (Mt. 22.36-40; Mk 12.28-31; cf. Lk. 10.26-28) as a likely source for Paul's similar conviction about love of neighbour as the heart of the law (e.g., Dunn 1988: 779; 1993: 291). Thus Paul's call for love (Gal. 5.14) and specifically for bearing one another's burdens (Gal. 6.2) might be seen as 'indicating how Jesus interpreted the law in his teaching and actions' (Dunn 1993: 322). There is, however, even in connection with the references to love of neighbour, no clear indication that Paul's exhortations are directly dependent on Jesus' teaching: neither in Gal. 5.14 nor in Rom. 13.8-10 does Paul give any hint of an awareness that his summary of the heart of the law echoes a similar declaration by Jesus.[72] Nor does Paul anywhere link loving God and loving the neighbour. And, in any case, given the Jewish parallels linking and highlighting love of God and of neighbour (e.g. *T. Iss.* 5.2; *T. Dan* 5.3), or emphasizing the command to love the neighbour as a central principle in the law (*Jub.* 7.20; 20.2; *Gen. Rab.* 24.7), or for discerning the heart of the law in the Golden Rule (*b. Shab.* 31a), it is by no means necessary to assume that Paul's principle derives directly or indirectly from Jesus, though this remains a possibility.[73]

A further question is whether Paul intends a reference to the Jewish law in Gal. 6.2. Undoubtedly Paul speaks of the Jewish law, the Torah, in Gal. 5.14, when he cites Lev. 19.18 as a 'sentence' (λόγος) in which the law has been brought to fulfilment (cf. Rom. 13.10):[74] this λόγος now stands as the

---

72. Such an indication might have been given through the use of phrases such as ἐν κυρίῳ Ἰησοῦ (Rom. 14.14), ὁ κύριος διέταξεν (1 Cor. 9.14), ἐν λόγῳ κυρίου (1 Thess. 4.15); cf. also 1 Cor. 7.10. Furnish (1973: 97), commenting on Gal. 5.14, notes: 'It is surprising that Paul here makes no reference to Jesus' teaching and makes no use of the Great Commandment as such. The commandment to "love God" (Deut. 6:5) is not cited here or anywhere else in the Pauline letters.'

73. See further Barclay 1988: 135–36; Martyn 1997a: 515–18; and specifically on the golden rule, Dihle 1962. Dunn (1988: 779; 1993: 291–92), however, comments on the lack of prominence given to Lev. 19.18 in Jewish literature prior to the time of Paul, compared with its prominence in the NT, suggesting the influence of Jesus' teaching on this prominence. On the significance of the command to love the neighbour in Jewish texts, despite the limited number of explicit citations of Lev. 19.18, see esp. Söding 1995: 56–66, who argues that, especially in the *Testaments of the Twelve Patriarchs*, the impression emerges that love of neighbour is the most important thing that Torah demands, though Söding also notes that nowhere is it suggested that love of neighbour could serve to encapsulate all moral instruction (p. 66). Theissen (2003b) argues that Jesus' emphasis on the double command to love God and the neighbour reflects (Palestinian) Jewish tradition, though Jesus presents it in a distinctive way. Theissen argues for the authenticity of the 'Doppelgebot' and tentatively suggests its specific origins in the teaching of John the Baptist.

74. *Pace* Hübner 1984: 36–41, who argues that ὁ πᾶς νόμος in Gal. 5.14 is not the Mosaic law, in contrast to the νόμος of Gal. 5.3. For criticisms, see Barclay 1988: 136–37.

fundamental moral imperative. But is it this same law which is referred to in Gal. 6.2, now, in some sense seen from a new perspective, as belonging to, or being (re)interpreted by, Christ? As we have seen, most recent scholars have given an affirmative answer to this question, partly on the basis of the close parallel with Gal. 5.14,[75] and partly in view of the fact that (virtually) all of the thirty preceding uses of the word νόμος in Galatians have referred to the (Jewish) law.[76]

These are considerable reasons in favour of this view. Nevertheless, there are also reasons to doubt it. Much depends, of course, on the weight given to the phrase τοῦ Χριστοῦ. How much does this designation determine how the verse is to be read, in comparison with other references to νόμος? It is important to note that Paul nowhere (this verse aside) unambiguously connects the name of Christ positively with the Jewish law: it is the law of God (Rom. 7.22, 25),[77] the law of Moses (1 Cor. 9.9). But Christ is the τέλος νόμου (the end or goal of the law, Rom. 10.4), the one who redeems from the curse of the law (Gal. 3.13) and the one in whom Paul has died to the law (Gal. 2.19-20). The significance of the parallels between Gal. 5.14 and 6.2 can also be variously assessed. It is clear that in 5.14 Paul speaks of the Jewish law, claiming that it 'stands fulfilled' (πεπλήρωται) in the one sentence 'love your neighbour as yourself' (Lev. 19.18). It is possible, as J.L. Martyn has argued, that the perfect tense here intends a reference to Christ's act of self-giving love, in which he '*has brought the law to completion*', such that 'love has *taken the place of the commandments*' (Martyn 1997a: 489, 522; 1997b: 235–49).[78] But even if the referent here is Christ's act rather than any on the part of the Galatians, the parallel in Rom. 13.8-10 makes clear that Paul sees this sentence as epitomizing the Christian's obligation. Yet here again the perfect tense of πληρόω is used:

---

75.   See, e.g., Barclay 1988: 131–42 (esp. 134 n. 89); Stanton 1996: 116: 'Since "fulfilling the law" in 5:14 refers to the law of Moses, the use of the similar verb in 6:2 strongly suggests that "law" here also refers to the law of Moses'.

76.   See esp. Martyn 1997a: 555: 'Gal 6:2 is the thirty-first of Paul's references in Galatians to *nomos*, and in all of the other significant instances the reference is to *the* law.' The references are: Gal. 2.16 (3 times), 19 (twice), 21; 3.2, 5, 10 (twice), 11, 12, 13, 17, 18, 19, 21 (3 times), 23, 24; 4.4, 5, 21 (twice); 5.3, 4, 14, 18, 23. After 6.2 the only further use of νόμος is in 6.13. The second use of νόμος in Gal. 3.21 is a more general reference, though in a discussion where the law is clearly the subject. One might debate whether 5.18 and 23 are possibly more general references too, but it is indisputable that the consistent referent of νόμος throughout Galatians is the Torah.

77.   In Galatians Paul is reluctant to say even this much, stating that the law 'was ordained by angels, through the hand of a mediator. And a mediator implies more than one party; but God is one' (3.19-20).

78.   'In general', Martyn notes, arguing for the force of the perfect to be taken seriously, 'commentators adopt the domesticated reading represented in the texts in which the verb has been changed into the present tense (DFG et al.)' (1997a: 489 n. 58).

the one who loves the neighbour *has fulfilled* the law (νόμον πεπλήρωκεν, 13.8). As Stephen Westerholm has pointed out, Paul does not give the imperative to 'fulfill the law' but rather states that 'when one loves one's neighbor, the whole law is fully satisfied in the process' (1987: 235).[79] This is evidently a fulfilment which does not imply an obligation to obey all of the law, as the rejection of circumcision, food laws and sabbath observance reveals.[80] As Westerholm (1987) shows, Paul can thus speak of a fulfilment of the law on the part of Christians, a fulfilment which is a *result* of their conduct (Rom. 8.4; 13.8, 10; Gal. 5.14), but never refers to their obligation to 'do' the law (cf. Rom. 10.5; Gal. 3.10, 12; 5.3), nor to their being 'under' it (Rom. 6.14-15; 1 Cor. 9.20; Gal. 5.18) (Westerholm 1987).[81]

If Gal. 6.2 were also taken to refer to the Jewish law, then questions arise, first, as to why Paul (on this view) essentially repeats the sentiment of 5.14 again[82] and, second, why there are significant differences between the two verses. Galatians 5.14 refers to the whole (Jewish) law, to its standing fulfilled (πεπλήρωται: perfect) and to love of neighbour; 6.2 refers to the law *of Christ*, to bearing one another's burdens and to this practice as one which *will* fulfil (ἀναπληρώσετε: future) this law – the tense of the verb marks a significant contrast with Gal. 5.14 and Rom. 13.8 (cf. above). The need to explain these differences and the inadequacy of reading Gal. 6.2 as little more than a repetition of 5.14 suggest that something more distinctive may be in view in the reference to the law of Christ.

For the law of Christ to mean something other than the Jewish law, it must at least be plausible to take Paul as using νόμος to refer to something other than Torah here. As Martyn has stressed, the fact that the previous references in Galatians virtually all use νόμος to mean *the* law is a strong point against this idea. Alternatively, however, the unique addition of the crucial phrase τοῦ Χριστοῦ here means that this verse may well be seen as stating something distinctive. It is a question of the relative weight assigned to these two contrasting considerations. As is often noted, one has to go to Romans to find clear instances where Paul uses νόμος with a number of

---

79. Thus Westerholm's argument challenges Sanders's claim that Paul's response to questions about behaviour is essentially 'fulfill the law!' (Sanders 1983: 84; Westerholm 1987: 235).

80. So, e.g., Westerholm 1984: 242–44; 1987: 233. While there are important Jewish parallels to the identification of a great command as the heart of the law (see above), the differences are equally important. As Barclay notes, 'the rabbis ... never intended their summarizing statements to mean that other parts of the law should be wilfully ignored' (1988: 136). Similarly, and forcefully, Martyn 1997a: 515–18.

81. Cf. further §1.2 above, with comments on Gal. 5.3 and 1 Cor. 7.19.

82. Note once again Barclay's suggestion that fulfilling the law of Christ 'means "fulfilling the law in the way exemplified (and taught?) by Christ", i.e., fulfilling it through love' (1988: 133–34) – which, if correct, means that 6.2 adds nothing substantial not already said in 5.14, except to connect the name of Christ explicitly with this teaching.

different referents: Rom. 3.27 posits a distinction between the law of works and the law of faith; Rom. 7.22-25 presents a variety of νόμοι (the law of God, the law of sin, the law in my members, and the law of my mind); and Rom. 8.2 contrasts the law of the spirit of life with the law of sin and death. It is widely agreed that νόμος here refers not to the Jewish law but means something like 'principle' or 'norm' – a 'law' that structures and determines one's existence and practice in different spheres, not unlike the 'law of gravity' (cf., e.g., Sanders 1983: 15 n. 26; Fitzmyer 1993: 482–83). Granted this, as Hays remarks, 'it becomes entirely reasonable to read *nomos tou Christou* analogously' (1987: 275 n. 25).

Martyn has, however, argued against this reading of νόμος in Romans, in support of the view that sees a reference to the Jewish law in Gal. 6.2, insisting that all these uses of νόμος in Romans also refer to *the* law (1997a: 548–49, 554–58). According to Martyn, references to 'the law of ...' in Rom. 3.27; 7.23, 25; and 8.2 all mean 'the law in the possession of', 'as it has been taken in hand by', or 'determined by' (pp. 556–57). So the law of sin and death refers to the (Jewish) law as taken in hand by the corrupting power of sin; and likewise the law of Christ refers to the law 'as it has been taken in hand by Christ himself' (p. 549). While this can work with some of the references in Romans, it can hardly do justice to Paul's talk of 'another law' (ἕτερον νόμον, 7.23), nor to his question about 'what kind of law' (ποῖος νόμος, 3.27). Moreover, Martyn's logic slides from observations about the use of the genitive to refer to the law's origin or source,[83] via his argument that the sense of the genitive 'shades over into the sense of determination', to his suggestion that the genitive conveys the sense 'in the possession of' (pp. 556–57). The former sense works well, say, for 1 Cor. 9.9: 'the law of Moses' is the law whose origin or source, humanly speaking, was Moses, while to speak of the law in the hands or the possession of Moses is highly strained.

There are, then, good reasons to think that the phrase 'the law of Christ' may be employed by Paul to refer to something distinctive, to a principle or law grounded or originating in Christ. The differences between Gal. 5.14 and 6.2 – not least the striking designation of the law of 6.2 as 'of Christ' – strongly suggest that 6.2 does more than reiterate the content of 5.14. Hays suggests that 'the law of Christ' 'functions as an ironic rhetorical formulation addressed to "those who want to be under law" (4:21)' (1987: 275). We may perhaps doubt whether it is intended to be ironic, but the idea that the law of Christ stands in antithesis to the law to

---

83. Cf. Josephus, *Ant.* 11.121 (τῶν Μωυσέος νόμων), 124 (τῷ νόμῳ τοῦ θεοῦ), 130 (τὸν τοῦ θεοῦ νόμον), examples to which Martyn appeals. See further Winger 1992: 43–44, 159–96, who distinguishes between the 'genitive of source' and the genitive used 'to specify the realm in which the νόμος referred to operates' (p. 44). Winger illustrates the various ways in which νόμος is used and its various referents in Paul.

which the Galatians are (strangely, in Paul's view) tempted to enslave themselves (5.1-6) resonates with the similar juxtapositions Paul constructs in Rom. 3.27; 7.25; and 8.2. This is *not*, of course, an antithesis in the sense that what the law of Christ requires is opposed to what the Jewish law teaches (cf. Gal. 3.21): as 5.14 makes clear, Torah finds its fulfilment in the command to love of neighbour, which is precisely the pattern of conduct Christians see epitomized in Christ's self-giving and are exhorted to emulate. But it is an antithesis in a similar way to that formulated in 1 Cor. 9.21, which, I shall claim, adds support to this reading: the contrast is between being obligated to, or 'under' *the* law, and living in obligation to Christ's law.

Hays shows convincingly that Galatians as a whole supports the idea that what Paul has in view in 6.2 is 'Christ's example of burden-bearing'. This example 'establishes a normative pattern (*nomos*) which all who are in Christ are called to "fulfill" in their relationships with others' (p. 287). The theme of Christ's redemptive self-giving appears, as Hays notes, at the opening of the letter (1.3-4), and again in 2.20; 3.13-14; and 4.4-5 (p. 277). 'The pattern of Christ's action is a pattern of submission to God and of accepting suffering for the sake of others' (p. 278). As in Phil. 2.6-11, the focus here is 'on the decisive significance of Christ's incarnation and death'; 'nothing is said about any *teachings* of Jesus on humility and servanthood, nor is there any reference to historical incidents in Jesus' ministry' (p. 278). Equally important are the indications that Paul understands his own life and experience in terms of 'a conformity to the normative pattern of Christ's obedient self-sacrifice' (p. 281): he has been crucified with Christ and the life he now lives is Christ's life in him (2.19-20). Indeed, the basis for Paul's missionary activity is God's decision to reveal his Son *in* (and through) Paul – this is probably the best way to make sense of the ἐν ἐμοί in 1.16, rather than with the common rendering 'to me' (e.g., RSV/NRSV).[84] Paul's appeal to the Galatians to 'become as I am' just as he has become as they are (4.12) may also be interpreted as a further exemplification of the christological pattern: Christ became what we are in order that we may become what he is.[85] Paul has become like them in becoming 'as one without the law', that is, a Gentile (1 Cor. 9.21; cf. Gal. 2.14-19) – Hays points to Phil. 3.7-8 as evidence that Paul regards such a step as one of self-sacrifice

---

84. Cf. Hays 1987: 281, who comments that 'the *en* is surely instrumental'; Barclay 2002: 141 notes that 'in me' is probably the best rendering 'from the hindsight of 2:20 and 4:19'. Cf. also 2 Cor. 13.3. In favour of 'to me', see Martyn 1997a: 158. De Boer (2002: 31) argues that ἐν ἐμοί 'means "in my former way of life"', that is, 'that God invaded my life as a zealous Pharisee and persecutor of the church with the Son of God'. The ἐν ἐμοί in 2.20 then means that Christ now lives 'in the activity of Paul the apostle' (p. 32).

85. Cf. Gal. 4.4-6; Hays 1987: 281. On this pattern of 'interchange' in Paul, see esp. Hooker 1990: 1–69.

(p. 281) – and can now appeal to them to become like him, to follow his own exemplification of this pattern of Christian existence (cf. 5.13). Hays also notes the close parallel between Gal. 6.14 ('the world is crucified to me and I to the world') and 5.24 ('those who belong to Christ have crucified the flesh') as a further example of the way in which 'Paul treats his own experience as paradigmatic for Christian experience in general' (p. 282). Thus, just as Paul's experience is of being conformed to the pattern of Christ's self-giving death (1.16; 2.19-20), so his hope for the Galatian community is that 'Christ be formed among you (ἐν ὑμῖν)' (4.19). Thus their pattern of conduct will be one of being slaves to one another in love (5.13), bearing one another's burdens in conformity to the basic principle or 'normative pattern' (νόμος) seen in Christ (cf. pp. 283, 286–87).

Although I find these arguments persuasive, given the nature of the case and the lack of definitive evidence, the possibility that the Jewish law is in view in Gal. 6.2 cannot be excluded; to claim otherwise would be disingenuous. It is worth pointing out, therefore, that, even if this majority view is correct, it would still be entirely plausible to read Gal. 6.2 as indicating the centrality of Christ's self-giving for others as a model for Christian practice. Whether this is seen as the basic principle (νόμος) to which Paul points, or as the heart of the Jewish law (νόμος) as expressed in the love-command and exemplified (and taught?) by Christ, the central point stands in either case: the pattern of conduct to which Paul summons the Galatians is that seen in Christ.

Hays's interpretation of Gal. 6.2 can, however, be further supported when we consider the other occurrence of a comparable phrase in 1 Cor. 9.21. As Hays suggests is the case in Gal. 6.2, here too it is clear that the formulation ἔννομος Χριστοῦ is coined in antithesis to other designations. The most immediate is Paul's declaration that he became ὡς ἄνομος ('like one without the law'). To counter any impression that he is thereby 'lawless' (ἄνομος) or free from moral obligation he insists that he is not ἄνομος θεοῦ but ἔννομος Χριστοῦ. (In view of the arguments above about the referent of νόμος in Gal. 6.2 it is notable here that Paul does not say ἔννομος θεοῦ, which would more clearly suggest the Torah [cf. Rom. 7.22, 25]; once again the phrasing suggests that something distinctive is in mind when Paul speaks of *Christ's* νόμος.) This whole phrase (1 Cor. 9.21) stands in contrast to 9.20, where Paul states that he became ὡς Ἰουδαῖος and ὡς ὑπὸ νόμον ('like a Jew ... like one under the law') but immediately counters the impression that he is actually obligated to the Jewish law by insisting that he is not himself under the law (μὴ ὢν αὐτὸς ὑπὸ νόμον).[86] So while Paul can become

---

86.   Tomson (1990: 274–79) argues that the ὡς in v. 20a, and the phrase μὴ ὢν αὐτὸς ὑπὸ νόμον (v. 20), are later insertions, but the textual evidence to support this is weak and Tomson's view seems unduly influenced by his desire to portray Paul as a Torah-observant Jew.

like someone under the law he is not himself under the law, and while he can become like someone without the law, he is not himself lawless but 'in the law of Christ'. Being ἔννομος Χριστοῦ denotes the form of Paul's moral obligation, and stands in distinction to being under *the* law.

Paul does not give any specific indication here as to what it means for him to be ἔννομος Χριστοῦ. But our study of the larger passage in which the phrase is set will already have suggested a plausible answer (see §6.1; §7.2): Paul's fundamental obligation, summarized in 10.33, is to set aside his own rights and interests in seeking the benefit of others. This is precisely the conduct which Paul has described in 9.1-19 and which he calls the Corinthian 'strong' to follow (8.7-13; 10.23-24); this is the principle that guides his attempts to please everyone in everything and which generates his missionary adaptability (9.19-23; 10.33). And the shape of this obligation is given by the pattern of Christ's self-giving for others.[87] Thus this pattern of practice is, for Paul, an imitation of Christ, and, as such, a pattern which the Corinthians too should imitate (11.1). The wider context of 1 Cor. 9.21 thus adds further plausibility to the idea that the νόμος of Christ to which Paul conforms is exactly what Hays has seen as the law of Christ in Gal. 6.2: a normative pattern determined by 'the paradigmatic self-giving of Jesus Christ' (Hays 1987: 275).

7.4 *The Collection (2 Corinthians 8.9-15): Self-Giving and Equality*

It is clear that Paul invested a significant amount of time and energy in organizing a collection for 'the poor among the saints' in Jerusalem (Rom. 15.26).[88] As such, and as a practical activity concerned with the redistribution of money between Christian communities, its importance for a study of Paul's ethics should be obvious.[89] The details and history of this collection project are hard to reconstruct, and utilizing the evidence of Acts alongside that of the epistles raises particular difficulties. For example, Acts 11.27-30 refers to relief sent from Antioch to Jerusalem during a time of famine, delivered by Barnabas and Saul. Is this, as John Knox argued, a chronologically misplaced reference to the delivery of the

---

87. Cf. Hays's comment on 1 Cor. 9.21: 'By using the expression "under Christ's law" … Paul … is asserting that the pattern of Christ's self-sacrificial death on the cross has now become the normative pattern for his own existence' (1997b: 154).

88. In this section, I draw on material from Horrell 1995b. Major works on the collection are Georgi 1992; Nickle 1966; Beckheuer 1997; Joubert 2000.

89. It is surprising that Matera (1996) pays no significant attention to 2 Corinthians 8–9, Paul's most significant discussion of the collection, especially given Matera's emphasis on the importance of imitating Christ in Paul's ethics (cf. 2 Cor. 8.9 and further below).

collection itself, the correct occasion for which was the visit of Paul to Jerusalem reported in Acts 21.15 (Knox 1989: 49–52)?[90] Alternatively, Dieter Georgi argues that Acts 11.27-30 refers to an Antiochene collection (not, he maintains, delivered by Barnabas and Saul); an 'effort undertaken in Antioch after and in accordance with the Jerusalem agreement' recorded in Gal. 2.1-10 (Georgi 1992: 44; see pp. 43–48). Keith Nickle also takes Acts 11.27-30 to refer to an earlier Antiochene collection, but suggests that this Antioch famine relief was sent prior to Paul's agreement in Jerusalem to commence his larger collection project (Nickle 1966: 23–32, 59–60).

The origins of Paul's collection efforts are usually placed in the so-called 'apostolic council', the meeting held in Jerusalem and reported in Gal. 2.1-10, probably the same meeting recounted in Acts 15.1-29, though portrayed somewhat differently there and without mention of any collection (see Knox 1989: 47–49; Lüdemann 1989: 171–72). After his initial concern that he might have been found to have been 'running in vain' (Gal. 2.2), Paul was relieved to find his role as apostle to the Gentiles accepted and affirmed, without any additions or subtractions being made to his gospel (Gal. 2.6-9). The only thing urged upon him by the so-called 'pillars' of the Jerusalem church, Peter, James and John, was that he should 'remember the poor', something which, Paul tells us, he was in any case eager to do (Gal. 2.10). This agreement is generally seen as marking the beginning of the collection project.[91] However, since there is no explicit reference to *the* collection here, and the verb μνημονεύωμεν is in the present tense (implying 'we should continue to remember'),[92] it may well be, as Fern Clarke has suggested (2000: 188–93; 2001), that the phrase should be taken in a more general sense to refer to the agreed missionary priority of concern for the poor, a concern Paul insists he already shares and is more

---

90. There is much to be said for Knox's solution to the problem of reconciling the evidence of Acts with that of the epistles, reducing the five visits to Jerusalem recorded in Acts (9.26-30; 11.29-30; 15.1-29; 18.22; 21.15–23.31) to three, corresponding with the three reported in the epistles (Rom. 15.25-28; Gal. 1.18; 2.1-10). Knox suggested that the collection delivery reported in Acts 11 belonged chronologically with the visit mentioned in Acts 21, and that the conference reported in Acts 15 should be placed chronologically at the time of the visit mentioned in Acts 18. Further support to this three-visit framework is given by Jewett 1979; Lüdemann 1984, despite the significant differences in their respective chronologies (cf. also Jewett 1986: 53–59). For a brief summary, see Horrell 2000a: 30–32.

91. Cf., e.g., Betz 1979: 101; Beckheuer 1997: 57, 270. Joubert (2000: 17) writes as if Paul explicitly states this to be the case: 'μόνον τῶν πτωχῶν ἵνα μνημονεύωμεν. According to Paul, this requirement/command of Peter (Gal 2,10) led to the commencement of his collection for Jerusalem' (see further pp. 73–115, esp. p. 88). And this is rather crucial for Joubert's view of the collection as an act whereby Paul seeks 'to repay his "debt of gratitude" towards Jerusalem' (p. 204), thus enabling him and his churches to become benefactors in response to Jerusalem's benefaction.

92. Cf. Burton 1921: 99; Nickle 1966: 59 n. 55.

than willing to continue. The collection project itself would then be the most visible and significant instance (as far as our records allow us to conclude) of Paul's commitment to enact this concern.

Involvement in the collection spread at least to the churches of Galatia, Achaia and Macedonia. Paul's instructions to the Corinthians, he tells us, are a repeat of those he has already given to the churches of Galatia (1 Cor. 16.1-4). The same passage also suggests that the Corinthians have already heard of the collection project and have perhaps sought further information from Paul in the letter they wrote to him.[93] The collection may have broken down in Galatia, perhaps because of the conflicts in which Paul's letter to the Galatians is embroiled. It certainly broke down for a time in Corinth. The cause there too was almost certainly conflict with Paul and disaffection with him in the congregation, in particular the painful visit which caused Paul such grief, and led to his withdrawal from Corinth (2 Cor. 2.1-11). In 2 Corinthians 8–9, however, we witness the rekindling of the collection project, and Paul's attempt to ensure that the collection is ready when he arrives from Macedonia (2 Cor. 9.2-5). From Rom. 15.25-26 we learn that both Macedonia and Achaia (the province in which Corinth was situated) did indeed make their contributions to the collection, and that as Paul wrote Romans he was preparing to travel to Jerusalem to deliver the gifts. The sum involved is hard to judge, as is the reception Paul, his travelling companions and the money received when they arrived in Jerusalem. The silence of Acts on the collection (see only Acts 24.17) has led some to suspect that it was not well received, and that Paul's hopes were disappointed (cf. Rom. 15.30-32).[94]

The various references Paul makes to the collection indicate its importance to him, and also provide key evidence for any reconstruction of the relative chronology of Paul's letters.[95] But most relevant here are questions concerning the reasons why Paul regarded the collection as important, what he saw as its aims, and how he motivated members of the churches to contribute. In terms of Paul's own vision of the collection's

---

93. On the introductory formula περὶ δέ (1 Cor. 7.1; 16.1, etc.), see Hurd 1965: 65–74; §6.1 n. 7 above. Even if Mitchell (1989) is right to question Hurd's argument that the phrase marks topics raised in the Corinthians' letter, it remains the case that the phrase signals that the topic is already familiar to author and reader.

94. Georgi argues that 'the total sum gathered for the collection must have been considerable' (1992: 123; on the reception the collection may have received, see pp. 122–27). Nickle, however, believes that 'the amount given was not great' (1966: 129; and on the partial success of the collection, see pp. 155–56). Joubert (2000: 204–15) suggests that a compromise solution was reached, with Paul 'paying for the Nazirite vows of four Torah-observant members of the Jerusalem community (Acts 21,23-24)' (p. 214).

95. See Lüdemann 1984, esp. pp. 77–100. On the collection's importance to a more general chronology of Paul's life, see also Buck 1950; Hyldahl 1986: 112–27.

purpose, three main reasons have been suggested (cf. further Nickle 1966: 100–43).

One reason suggested for the collection is primarily eschatological and rooted in a particular view of salvation history. The collection may be linked with the themes expressed in Romans 9–11. From Paul's perspective, the mission to the Jews had not been a success; on the whole they had rejected the gospel. The Gentiles, in contrast, had received and accepted the good news. The collection, accompanied by representatives from the Gentile churches, would fulfil the prophets' vision of the nations going up to Jerusalem 'in the last days' (Isa. 2.2-4; Mic. 4.1-3) (cf. Munck 1959: 301–308; Bruce 1968: 23–25).[96] It would provoke the Jews to jealousy (Rom. 10.19; 11.11-16) and thus lead to their salvation. The delivery of the collection, as a symbolic representation of the pilgrimage of the redeemed Gentiles to Zion, would play an instrumental role in God's plan of salvation, and in hastening the consummation of the End. Whether this was central to Paul's own understanding of the collection may be doubted, however, not least because he planned, once the collection had been delivered, to visit the Roman church on his way to begin a mission in Spain (Rom. 15.24, 28) – so the collection is hardly seen by Paul as a final eschatological pilgrimage. Indeed, this reasoning does not emerge explicitly in Paul's own discussions of the collection.

A second reason has to do with the unity of the Church. It is clear that there were tensions between Paul and the Jerusalem church leaders, tensions which arose not least because of their different understandings of the basis on which the Gentiles could be full members of this new community in Christ (see Gal. 2.1-21, etc.). The collection, then, may be seen as Paul's attempt to demonstrate 'the solidarity of all believers in the one Body of Christ' (Nickle 1966: 154; cf. Berger 1977: 199; Gnilka 1996; et al.), to show to the Jerusalem church the fruit the gospel has borne among the Gentiles, and to encourage the Jerusalem church to recognize the Pauline churches as part of the whole Church of Christ. One may see the collection as a deliberately 'political', even provocative, act whereby Paul sought to convince 'the Jerusalem church of the legitimacy of the law-free congregations he had founded, so that they would stop trying to undermine them' (Watson 1986: 175). Hence Paul's fears that the collection will not be accepted by those in Jerusalem (Rom. 15.30-31): to accept the collection (perhaps under pressure of dire need) would be to accept the validity of the Pauline congregations, to reject it would be to refuse to recognize them.

---

96. Cf. also Beckheuer (1997), who argues that the book of Isaiah has especially shaped Paul's theology of the collection (e.g. p. 273).

Certainly the collection both presumes and aims to reinforce the 'international' solidarity of Christians, a solidarity which is explicitly forged between Jewish and Gentile believers, between churches in Jerusalem and elsewhere. In Romans 15, Paul explains that the Gentiles are indebted to those in Jerusalem for their spiritual things ($\pi\nu\epsilon\upsilon\mu\alpha\tau\iota\kappa\acute{\alpha}$; 15.27); the collection is an attempt by the Gentiles to share their material things ($\sigma\alpha\rho\kappa\iota\kappa\acute{\alpha}$) with those to whom they are already spiritually indebted (cf. also 2 Cor. 8.14, on which see below). In the very concrete business of sharing money and material goods, then, Paul urged his congregations to express their unity and solidarity not only within the churches (cf. Gal. 6.6) but also across the miles. Thus the collection reinforces on an inter-community level the theme of solidarity, which we have already argued to have a central place in Pauline ethics (ch. 4 above).

Nonetheless, the reason which emerges most explicitly as Paul's fundamental motivation for the collection is the desire to relieve the poverty of the poor among the saints in Jerusalem: the aim of the collection is simply to give material assistance to those who are in need.[97] Its closest Jewish parallel may have been the practice of almsgiving, as Klaus Berger argues.[98] Such a focus on relief of extreme material poverty as the major reason for the collection is challenged by the possibility that the term 'the poor' (οἱ πτωχοί; cf. Heb. אביונים) was a self-designation of the Jerusalem Christians, virtually synonymous with other pious epithets such as οἱ ἅγιοι, and not a socio-economic description (cf. Gal. 2.10).[99] However, Leander Keck (1965, 1966) has shown this to be extremely unlikely, and, in any case, Paul specifically states that the collection is for 'the poor among the saints in Jerusalem' (Rom. 15.26; cf. also Lüdemann 1984: 78–79; Joubert 2000: 89–90). Analyses of the economic situation of the inhabitants of Judaea and specifically Jerusalem, and evidence concerning periodic famines, notably in the late 40s CE, confirm that life-threatening poverty very likely affected many of the lower classes in Jerusalem as well as elsewhere.[100] Assuming Luke is right to report that the Jerusalem church took responsibility for its own needy members (Acts

97. Joubert (2000: 1–16) offers a critique of most perspectives on the collection, which have emphasized its theological significance and motivations over against its material and social dimensions; he mentions my earlier article (Horrell 1995b) as 'a ray of hope' in this respect (p. 4 n. 15).

98. Berger 1977; cf. Hyldahl 1986: 124–25. Contrast Nickle 1966: 74–99, who argues that the Temple tax is the closest analogy to Paul's collection in the Judaism of his time.

99. This view was classically argued by Holl 1928: 58–60, who proposed that οἱ ἅγιοι and οἱ πτωχοί were equivalent and specific designations of the Jerusalem Urgemeinde, the latter adopted from the Jewish view of the אביונים. Cf. also Betz 1979: 101–102.

100. See Jeremias 1969: 111–12; Murphy-O'Connor 1991: 75–76; Joubert 2000: 107–13. More generally, and in relation to the Pauline churches in the context of the Roman empire, see Meggitt 1998; Friesen 2004.

4.34-35; 6.1) – such charitable practice among Christians is more widely evidenced, of course – it is not surprising that it came to need urgent assistance from elsewhere.[101] Nevertheless, while the relief of material poverty thus emerges as the major focus of the collection, it is likely that Paul also saw special significance in rendering aid to Jerusalem. Famines were, after all, common elsewhere too, but we have no indication that Paul organized any other such collections; indeed, he accepts the Macedonians' contribution to the collection for Jerusalem, despite their own 'deep poverty' (2 Cor. 8.2). In this latter regard, however, we should also note that Paul stresses heavily that the Macedonians 'begged' to be allowed to take part (αὐθαίρετοι μετὰ πολλῆς παρακλήσεως δεόμενοι ἡμῶν ..., 8.3-4), suggesting – notwithstanding the rhetorical purpose of this emphasis – some reluctance on Paul's part to allow those already so poor to contribute (so Nickle 1966: 62). This would seem to confirm a basic intention to redistribute in such a way as to relieve a particularly pressing case of poverty.

Given this primary focus on the relief of material poverty, what grounds does Paul present to legitimate the collection project, and to motivate participation in it? And how does he depict its goals? The crucial text here is 2 Corinthians 8–9 (especially 8.9-15), Paul's most extended discussion of the collection.[102] Throughout this discussion, and especially in conclusion, Paul portrays the collection in richly theological terms:[103] it is the harvest of righteousness (9.10), causing an abundance of thanksgiving to God (9.11, 12) and bringing glory to God (9.13). Participation in the collection is described as 'the obedience of your confession of the gospel of Christ' (9.13). Above all, it is no less than 'the grace of God' (8.1; cf. 8.4, 6, 7, 19; 9.14),[104] χάρις being repeatedly used to describe the collection as an act of generosity in response to, and dependent upon, God's 'inexpressible gift' (9.15). As Ivor Jones notes, 'both chapters show Paul's deep concern that the Collection for the Saints should not only be an act of charity but an act overflowing in praise to God' (Jones 1973: 43). The intrinsically and unavoidably material act of giving money is thus depicted as no merely

---

101. Luke's portrayals of the community of goods in the earliest church in Jerusalem (Acts 2.44-45; 4.32) are often seen as idealized. This may well be so, but the practice of mutual sharing, hospitality, etc., as well as more radical forms of self-giving for other believers (*1 Clem.* 55.2), are evidenced, as well as criticized, in our sources (Rom. 12.13; Gal. 6.6; *Did.* 11.4-6; 12.1-5; 13.1-2; for criticism see, e.g., Lucian, *Peregrinus*, 13, 16)

102. Our primary focus here will be on the ways in which Paul depicts and motivates the collection, leaving largely to one side other questions, such as the practical arrangements for making the collection, the sending of Titus and two ἀδελφοί and the implications of this for the literary integrity and chronological ordering of 2 Corinthians (on which see Horrell 1996: 296–312).

103. See the list of terms Paul uses to describe the collection in Dahl 1977: 37–38.

104. On the centrality of χάρις in these chapters, see Rhyne 1987: 409.

practical undertaking but one which is expressive of the most fundamental theological themes of the gospel.

Paul's first way of inspiring the Corinthians to give is to tell them of the grace of God at work among the Macedonians (8.1-5). The Macedonians begged Paul to permit them to share in the grace and fellowship of serving the saints through the collection (8.4), and it is their enthusiasm that has led to Titus being urged to return to Corinth to complete the task of organizing the collection which he previously began there (8.6). While the description of the Macedonians' 'deep poverty' (8.2) no doubt serves a rhetorical point here, heightening the motivating comparison – if such poor people have insisted on contributing, then surely you Corinthians should do so (cf. 8.14; 9.1-5) – but there is no reason to doubt that it also reflects economic reality (see further Meggitt 1998; Friesen 2004). A further motivation for the Corinthians to give takes the form of flattery: since they already abound in everything ('in faith and word and knowledge' etc.), so they should also abound in this 'grace' which is the collection (8.7). Their giving should not arise in response to a command on Paul's part, but should rather emanate from their own eagerness and love (8.8; cf. Phlm. 8-9).

A key motivational statement follows in 2 Cor. 8.9, where Paul presents the example of Christ as a model for generous giving to the collection: 'for you know the grace ($\chi \acute{\alpha} \rho \iota \varsigma$) of our Lord Jesus Christ who, being rich ($\pi \lambda o \acute{u} \sigma \iota o \varsigma$), for your sakes became poor ($\dot{\epsilon} \pi \tau \acute{\omega} \chi \epsilon \upsilon \sigma \epsilon \nu$), so that you through his poverty ($\pi \tau \omega \chi \epsilon \acute{\iota} \alpha$) might become rich ($\pi \lambda o \upsilon \tau \acute{\eta} \sigma \eta \tau \epsilon$)'. Scholars have debated whether Paul here refers to the incarnation,[105] or to the form of death which Christ accepted.[106] As is the case in the comparable passage in Phil. 2.6-8, the idea of the pre-existent Christ becoming human seems most likely to be in view here, though, again as in Philippians 2, the self-lowering of Christ encompasses incarnation *and* death, the whole life of Jesus, in one seamless act (cf. Gal. 4.4-5). This christological pattern may aptly be described as one of 'interchange': 'Christ became what we are, in order that, in him, we might become what he is' (see Hooker 1990: 1–69). The basic similarity between 2 Cor. 8.9 and Phil. 2.6-8 is clear – the depiction of Jesus Christ's self-lowering – but in each case Paul depicts this act in terms which reflect the behaviour he wishes to inculcate in his readers (cf. §7.1 above). In Philippians, appealing for humility ($\tau \alpha \pi \epsilon \iota \nu o \phi \rho o \sigma \acute{u} \nu \eta$, 2.3), Christ's exemplary act is described as one of self-humbling ($\dot{\epsilon} \tau \alpha \pi \epsilon \acute{\iota} \nu \omega \sigma \epsilon \nu$ $\dot{\epsilon} \alpha \upsilon \tau \acute{o} \nu$, 2.8). Here in 2 Corinthians 8, where Paul is talking about the collection as an instantiation of grace ($\chi \acute{\alpha} \rho \iota \varsigma$) intended to help those who are poor ($\pi \tau \omega \chi \acute{o} \varsigma$) Paul describes Christ's act in precisely these terms. We

---

105. So, e.g., Craddock 1968: 165; Furnish 1984: 417; Martin 1986: 263.
106. So Dunn 1980: 121–23; Murphy-O'Connor 1991: 83.

should also note that close-by in the same letter[107] Paul also describes his own apostolic experience in exactly the same language (ὡς πτωχοὶ πολλοὺς δὲ πλουτίζοντες, 2 Cor. 6.10). Once again, then, as in Philippians, Paul dares to depict the character and effects of his own (and his co-workers') activity in the same terms as Christ's.

But what does Paul mean here by 'rich' and 'poor'? It is certainly hard to interpret the verse as implying that Christ gave up material wealth, and still more unsatisfactory to suggest that the purpose of his becoming poor was to make Christians economically rich (cf. Craddock 1968: 164). Alternatively, we should be wary of over-spiritualizing the verse and losing the connection with the material realities without which it has no force as a motivation for action in regard to the collection. For one thing is certain: Paul considers that this christological statement is *relevant* as a motivation for the giving of money – that could hardly be more material. As C.T. Rhyne puts it: 'Paul dares to suggest a vital connection between the Christ event and his overdue collection. Material and spiritual are unapologetically lumped together' (Rhyne 1987: 409). The self-lowering of Christ from his incarnation to the point of his humiliating death, a self-emptying which can be described as a form of impoverishment – social and material, as well as spiritual – brings a form of spiritual enrichment, and can serve as a model for the self-giving of Christians in material matters (Rom. 15.27).

However, the christological pattern so presented in this context implies an appeal much more encompassing and demanding than a request for almsgiving, for the giving of what one can spare. It is a demand for the giving of oneself, a self-emptying like the *kenosis* of Christ (Phil. 2.7), a giving in which one actually becomes poor (cf. Hooker 1990: 47, 69). Again we should note how this pattern of (social) self-lowering is one which Paul believes himself to have followed, not only in his (involuntary) sufferings but also in his deliberate practice of manual labour, in becoming weak to gain the weak (see §7.2 above). Thus Paul's appeal to Christ's example here would seem to imply that the Corinthians too may actually experience a material change in their position as a result of their Christ-like, costly self-giving. They may find themselves, at least to some extent and in some ways, impoverished.

---

107. The literary composition of 2 Corinthians has been much discussed, and a number of different partition theories compete for acceptance. I find a basic partition of the letter into two (chs 1–9 and 10–13) most plausible, though the enigmatic 6.14–7.1 may also be a fragment of a different letter again. I have also previously argued for the view that chs 10–13 should be placed prior to chs 1–9 and regarded as the painful letter to which Paul refers in 2 Cor. 2.4, 9; 7.8, 12 (Horrell 1996: 296–312; also esp. Watson 1984).

That this is indeed an implication Paul recognizes in his statement of the christological *exemplum* is made clear by the way the text proceeds.[108] After urging the Corinthians to complete the task they began 'last year' (8.10-12) – when Titus initiated the collection project among them (8.6), prior to the breakdown of relations with Paul (see Horrell 1996: 304–307) – Paul proceeds immediately to clarify his request in relation to the self-impoverishment the christological paradigm may seem to require. He is not, he insists, asking the Corinthians to bring affliction ($\theta\lambda\hat{\iota}\psi\iota\varsigma$) upon themselves, in order to bring others relief ($\check{\alpha}\nu\epsilon\sigma\iota\varsigma$); his desire is that there should be 'equality' ($\iota\sigma\acute{o}\tau\eta\varsigma$, 8.13-15). These three verses give an important indication as to what Paul sees as the intended result of the collection and more generally as the aim of Christ-like self-giving.

The concept of equality/fairness ($\iota\sigma\acute{o}\tau\eta\varsigma$) was strongly developed in Greek thought, especially in the legal context.[109] It did not necessarily mean something equivalent to the modern notion of equality, however, but conveyed the sense of 'proper balance' or 'fairness', as in the reference in Col. 4.1 to masters treating their slaves 'justly and fairly' (NRSV, $\tau\grave{o}$ $\delta\acute{\iota}\kappa\alpha\iota o\nu$ $\kappa\alpha\grave{\iota}$ $\tau\grave{\eta}\nu$ $\iota\sigma\acute{o}\tau\eta\tau\alpha$).[110] Similarly, 'equality' is linked with 'justice/ righteousness' ($\delta\iota\kappa\alpha\iota o\sigma\acute{\upsilon}\nu\eta$) by Philo, for whom 'the mother of justice is equality' ($\iota\sigma\acute{o}\tau\eta\varsigma$ ... $\mu\acute{\eta}\tau\eta\rho$ $\delta\iota\kappa\alpha\iota o\sigma\acute{\upsilon}\nu\eta\varsigma$, *Spec. Leg.* 4.231; cf. *Rer. Div. Her.* 161, 163). For Philo, however, 'equality' is essentially to be seen as the ordering work of God the Creator (*Spec. Leg.* 231-237; *Rer. Div. Her.* 141-206; Georgi 1992: 138–40). Such a view of 'equality' can easily become deterministic, affirming the order of the world as it is, rather than challenging it: God apportions to each their lot, and the right 'balance' consists in treatment according to one's rightful position (cf. Jones 1973: 43). Paul, however, does not present such a view, even though he sees 'equality' as the motivating source of the collection project (2 Cor. 8.13: $\grave{\epsilon}\xi$ $\iota\sigma\acute{o}\tau\eta\tau o\varsigma$).[111] He talks of an equality which arises from the redistribution of surplus: those who have a surplus ($\pi\epsilon\rho\acute{\iota}\sigma\sigma\epsilon\upsilon\mu\alpha$) in the present should supply the lack of others ($\dot{\upsilon}\sigma\tau\acute{\epsilon}\rho\eta\mu\alpha$), aware that at some point, or in some different way, the reverse may occur (8.14; cf. Rom. 15.27). Thus Paul seems to envisage a kind of 'mutualism' in which reciprocal giving may periodically continue, according to need and circumstance (cf. Meggitt 1998: 155–78).[112]

---

108. On this model as an *exemplum* here, cf. Betz 1985: 61.

109. See G. Stählin, *TDNT* 3: 346; Georgi 1992: 85.

110. Cf. BDAG, 481; Ps-Phocylides 137; more generally, Aristotle, *Pol.* 1.1260b, 3-7; Seneca, *Ep.* 47.1.

111. Georgi (1992: 88–89) argues that $\grave{\epsilon}\xi$ $\iota\sigma\acute{o}\tau\eta\tau o\varsigma$ in 2 Cor. 8.13 is virtually equivalent to $\grave{\epsilon}\kappa$ $\theta\epsilon o\hat{\upsilon}$.

112. Cf. also 2 Cor. 9.13, which suggests that the collection is but one instance of a sharing with all ($\epsilon\grave{\iota}\varsigma$ $\alpha\grave{\upsilon}\tau o\grave{\upsilon}\varsigma$ $\kappa\alpha\grave{\iota}$ $\epsilon\grave{\iota}\varsigma$ $\pi\acute{\alpha}\nu\tau\alpha\varsigma$). There is, however, only limited evidence concerning the broader practice of this economic mutualism in the Pauline communities, and Meggitt is hard

The aim, for Paul, of economic redistribution is not that Christians with something to give might impoverish themselves, but that a state of equality might be attained. The self-lowering of the relatively wealthy is a means of achieving this equality, which is rooted in the will of God, but is to be realized through responsible human action. It is this, rather than some eschatological pilgrimage of Gentiles to Zion, that Paul depicts as the goal of the collection.

Like Philo, Paul quotes Exod. 16.18 as a scriptural illustration of the equitable distribution which is the divine will: 'the one who had much did not have too much, and the one who had little did not have too little' (2 Cor. 8.15; cf. Philo, *Rer. Div. Her.* 191). Philo sees this Exodus passage as an example of the perfect distribution accomplished by the divine *logos*. In this, despite introducing his *logos*-theology, he is perhaps closer to the meaning of the original than Paul: in Exodus 16 it is a divinely wrought providential miracle which ensures that 'each had collected as much as they needed to eat'. Paul quotes the verse, however, as a vision of what human action, in the form of the collection, should achieve: the divine objective of equality is to be realized through generous acts of redistribution, acts of grace inspired by the grace of God.

After outlining to the Corinthians the practical arrangements regarding those whom he is sending to organize the final preparation of the collection at Corinth (2 Cor. 8.16–9.5), Paul gives the Corinthians one more reason for generosity: 'the one who sows sparingly will also reap sparingly, and the one who sows bountifully will also reap bountifully' (9.6). But their giving must be freely and lovingly undertaken, as was Christ's giving of himself (Gal. 1.4; 2.20; cf. Mk 10.45; 1 Tim. 2.6; etc.), for 'God loves a cheerful giver' (2 Cor. 9.7, an approximate citation of Prov. 22.8a [LXX], a Greek addition to the Hebrew text). This is not intended as an excuse for restricted giving, as if God would prefer those who can only happily give a little to give only a little. Paul puts things rather differently: where the grace of God abounds, there people of their own free-will will abound in good deeds (2 Cor. 9.8), like the righteous one whom scripture describes as scattering gifts freely to the poor (9.9).[113]

---

pressed to find further support for his claim that it constitutes a prominent form of economic relationship among the Pauline communities. Nonetheless, there is certainly evidence for material sharing both within communities and with Paul (Gal. 6.6; Phil. 2.25; 4.15-18; cf. above n. 101), and also for the expectation that moral responsibilities are to be practised reciprocally (Rom. 12.10, 16; 13.8; 15.2, 7; 1 Cor. 12.25; Gal. 5.13; 6.2; Phil. 2.3; 1 Thess. 3.12; 4.9, etc.).

113. A quotation of Ps. 112.9 (111.9 LXX), where the righteous person is the subject. 2 Corinthians 9.10 may suggest that it is God's righteousness which is referred to in v. 9; see discussion in Furnish 1984: 448–49.

The paradigm of Christ's self-giving thus plays a central role in Paul's appeal to the Corinthians to give generously to the collection. Once again this exemplar serves to define the shape of moral obligation and to undergird the practice of other-regard. Also important here, however, is Paul's clarification of the goal of this self-giving on the part of the Corinthians: its intended outcome is not their own abasement but rather a form of equality. The significance of this, along with other points that have emerged in this chapter, will be explored briefly below.

7.5 *Conclusion*

These various examples have hopefully substantiated the claim that 'other-regard' constitutes a key moral norm in Pauline ethics. Like the corporate solidarity explored in ch. 4, this other-regard, depicted specifically in terms of self-lowering and reversal of positions, also conveys a certain impulse towards the goal of equality (see further below). Other-regard is not, however, promoted as an abstract or rational moral principle (as, say, in the Golden Rule) but rather as a pattern of behaviour which constitutes a conformity to the pattern of Christ's self-giving. Indeed, the various examples surveyed have illustrated how centrally Christ functions as an ethical exemplar in Paul's letters, specifically as a paradigm of self-giving for others. The explicit calls to imitation of Christ, few as they are, are only the tip of a much larger iceberg. Indeed, the appeal to conform to the pattern of Christ's story of humiliation for the sake of others through to vindication is often conveyed indirectly, through the example of Paul, who considers his own life and practice to mirror this christological paradigm. In Philippians, the story of Christ in 2.6-11 serves as the fundamental basis for moral exhortation, supported by the examples of Paul and his co-workers; in Galatians, and elsewhere, Paul presents himself as conformed to the pattern of Christ, having been crucified with him, and longs for the same formation of Christ among the Galatians. Christ's self-giving defines the specific shape of their moral obligation. Similarly in 1 Corinthians 8–10 and 2 Corinthians 8–9, and elsewhere too (not least Romans 14–15), the christologically shaped pattern of regard for others defines and motivates moral action.

Brian Dodd's rejection of the importance of this theme, in the context of an argument for a Käsemannian interpretation of Philippians 2, is therefore unconvincing on a number of levels. Dodd does not wish to deny that 'Christ's example' is 'used in ethical admonition by Paul', but claims that it appears 'sparingly and briefly in just a few places (Rom. 15:1-3; 2 Cor. 8:9; cf. Eph. 4:32–5:1). If we add to these Phil. 2:5-8, all use Christ's example *in a very limited way* to extol the virtue of his self-abasement out of regard for benefiting others' (Dodd 1998: 158, my emphasis). Not only does Dodd fail to perceive the extent to which the normative pattern of Christ's self-giving is woven into the fabric of Pauline ethics but he also restricts the significance of this pattern. Self-giving out of regard for others is no minor virtue in Paul's ethics but rather a metanorm, a key moral value which fundamentally determines the shape of Christian relating.

We may, nonetheless, debate the best terminology to describe this christologically-shaped morality. 'Imitation of Christ' or 'Christ as example' are both open to criticism, not least because they imply that what is in view is (merely) an act of copying or following, which hardly does full justice to the theme as Paul presents it (here Käsemann's critique of the 'ethical example' reading remains pertinent). Perhaps most adequate is to speak of 'conformity' to the normative pattern of Christ's self-giving for others, for this at least gives some sense of the way Paul envisages the 'story' of Christ as that which fundamentally (re)shapes his and all Christians' identity and practice.[114] Christ is a moral paradigm in the sense that the pattern of his own obedient existence, from self-lowering through death to vindication, provides the determinative shape which all Christian lives should follow, in that they are lives lived 'in Christ' (cf. Phil. 3.9-11). There are clearly also a variety of ways in which one might choose to denote the value I have labelled other-regard, the most obvious of which is love. As we have seen, Paul describes Christ's (and his own) act(s) of self-lowering in various ways, according to the context in which he places the description. And he does, of course, frequently appeal for the virtue of love to be practised within the Christian assemblies (e.g., Rom. 12.9-10; 1 Cor. 13.1–14.1; 16.14; Gal. 5.6, 13; 1 Thess. 4.9-10). But there are two reasons for choosing 'other-regard' as the descriptor. One is that it forms a concise expression very close to the virtually untranslatable ones Paul himself uses in some of the key appeals we have examined (1 Cor. 10.24; Phil. 2.4; cf. p. 210 with n. 23 above). The second is that, as Hays points out, love is a vague and overused term, which requires definition and substance to be made meaningful (Hays 1997a: 202; see §1.6 above): 'other-regard' is a concise way of defining what love implies, according to Paul (cf. 1 Cor. 13.5: οὐ ζητεῖ τὰ ἐαυτῆς). To take but one example, Paul's declaration of Christ's love for him is given substance by specifying that Christ 'gave himself for me' (Gal. 2.20).

The label other-regard also hints at a response to Elizabeth Castelli's critique of Paul's calls for imitation as a coercive discourse of power which implies a drive to erase difference and construct sameness (Castelli 1991). The crucial questions concern what kind of imitation is called for and what kind of sameness is in view. There is indeed, as we have already seen in the

---

114. Cf. Hays 1987: 281; Barclay 2002. See also, e.g., Hooker 1990: 92; Hurtado 1984: 125–26, for arguments in favour of 'conformity' rather than 'imitation'.

preceding chapter, a 'sameness' in the sense that certain moral values are presented as obligatory for all within the community, a demand we have paralleled with the liberal insistence on the universal acceptance of certain metamoral values. To put it differently, there is an insistence on a certain basis for solidarity, within which a tolerance of difference operates (see §6.4 above). But the imitation in view concerns an imitation of self-giving and self-lowering *for the sake of the other*, which is a practice which precisely creates the room for difference to be sustained within a context of communal solidarity. Moreover, imitating the practice of self-giving for others demands what Stephen Fowl (echoing John Milbank) calls 'non-identical repetition' (Fowl 1998: 148): the basic shape of the moral exemplar is given, but what conformity to this paradigm will require can only be determined in the context of particular situations and relationships. This is well illustrated in 1 Corinthians 9, where it becomes clear that such imitation may even – according to Paul – require a conscious rejection of specific ethical instructions given in the tradition (§7.2 above).

There are nonetheless dangers in calls for the imitation of Christ's self-giving. There is the danger, as Nietzsche supposed, and criticized, that Christian morality can thus be seen as centrally concerned with self-abasement and weak humility. This is especially pernicious when obedience to the pattern of Christ's self-giving and acceptance of suffering is urged (by the powerful) upon the socially weak, thus legitimating and sustaining oppression and abuse (cf. 1 Pet. 2.18-23).[115] These dangers need to be fully and carefully considered,[116] though Paul's particular presentation of the christological paradigm – whatever its subsequent developments – largely avoids them: first, self-lowering is a pattern of behaviour Paul urges particularly on those who are socially or economically 'higher', and one which he seeks to follow himself (cf. also ch. 6 above) – and the weakness in view is not that of passivity but that of 'lowly' social practice (in Paul's case, manual labour); secondly, as 2 Cor. 8.9-13 makes clear, the aim of this lowering is not abasement per se, but redistribution with a view to the establishment of equality.

When we reflect on the findings of this chapter in the light of the liberal-communitarian debate, and specifically the contrasting approaches of Habermas and Hauerwas, it should be clear that the material surveyed above illustrates especially clearly the closeness of Paul's approach to ethics to that of Hauerwas. Philippians 2 provides perhaps the most obvious example. Here the Christian myth, the story of the descending and

---

115. For a penetrating critique of 1 Peter in this respect, see Corley 1995. Cf. also Martin's (1998a) critique of Hays (1997a), discussed above in §1.6.

116. They are somewhat ignored in Philippa Carter's otherwise valuable book on the 'servant-ethic' in the NT (Carter 1997).

ascending Christ, told and retold in the context of Christian worship and communal practice, inculcates the practice of certain kinds of moral virtues (humility, serving others, etc.) through nurturing a particular kind of character, a character which is conformed to that of the moral exemplar, Christ. Given this close similarity, two further reflections are significant. One is that it is interesting to observe how in this most 'Hauerwasian' mode – the shaping of moral character through participating in a story – Paul's ethics finds its most distinctive virtues, when compared with his non-Christian contemporaries, namely, the coming to prominence of (social) humility (see p. 211 above, with nn. 24–26).

Secondly, however, it is notable how this most distinctively Christian morality in Paul has at least the potential to legitimate and sustain patterns of suffering and oppression through an appeal to imitate Christ's self-giving through suffering. In this connection it is relevant to recall the feminist criticism of Hauerwas, that his tradition-focused ethics – not least through its deliberate eschewal of appeals to 'liberal' values: equality, freedom and justice – fails sufficiently to acknowledge and challenge the forms of domination and violent oppression that that tradition sustains (see Albrecht 1995; 1997; §2.4, pp. 76–79 above). Is it the case that where ethics is at its most 'ecclesial', least open to being challenged and recast in the light of broader ethical discussion, the potential to sustain or legitimate oppression is also most apparent? (Cf. esp. p. 77 above.)

When it comes to Habermas, the contrasts with Paul's christomorphic ethics are initially most striking. Habermas's 'rational morality' (*Vernunftmoral*) stipulates that valid moral norms are 'in the common interest and – precisely because they are equally good for all – do not impose supererogatory demands' (Habermas 1993: 34; 1991: 136). As such, Habermas insists, such a morality brings to an end the morality of sacrifice ('Insofern besiegelt die Vernunftmoral die Abschaffung des Opfers' [1991: 136]). Paul, as we have seen, sees precisely such self-sacrifice as the Christian's obligation, following the example of Christ. Nonetheless, points of contact may also be discerned. First, Habermas himself describes as morally admirable the actions of someone who, in situations of 'unjust suffering' or 'barbarous living conditions', goes beyond what 'rational morality' would require and makes sacrifices in the interests of his neighbour (1993: 34–35; 1991: 137; cf. 2002: 164–65). Second, Paul, as we have seen, regards self-giving not as a means to bring tribulation upon oneself, as if such suffering were per se morally commendable, but rather as a means to give to others in the interests of their benefit and in order to achieve equality. Just as is soteriologically the case with Christ's self-giving – 'he became what we are, in order that we might become what he is' – the point of self-lowering, socially and economically, is to bring benefit to others, such that a (new) form of human solidarity may be constructed (cf. §4.3; §7.4 above). Thus, Habermas and Paul agree – though they (of course) express this thought very differently – that self-sacrifice is commendable *in situations where human relations are distorted*, and that the aim of such action is to restore or create a form of equitable solidarity within which such self-sacrifice will no longer be required.

That brings us to one final concluding question: Given the prominence of a christologically undergirded other-regard in Paul's ethics, can we still sustain the claim that solidarity is the first and most fundamental value (so ch. 4 above)? The answer is yes, because the appeal for other-regard presumes the existence and value of communal solidarity. Other-regard is primarily a community-focused virtue, practised in relation to 'one another', that is, towards one's (weaker) siblings, other members of the Christian movement; it is a means by which unity and equality can be created and sustained within the community. That in turn raises the question of how Paul perceives the Christian's responsibility towards outsiders, and whether (more broadly) he has anything to say about universal ethical responsibilities. These are issues to which we turn in the following chapter.

Chapter 8

ETHICS AND OUTSIDERS

The ecclesial focus of Paul's ethics can hardly be missed. Throughout our consideration of key themes and values from solidarity through to other-regard the subject of Paul's concern has evidently been the formation, relationships and behavioural norms of the assemblies of Christians. Even when he deals with topics that we might describe as 'individual' ethics, say in the realm of sexual morality, it is clear that Paul's preoccupation is as much with the purity of the corporate ecclesial body as with that of the individual (see ch. 5 above).[1] For this reason it is understandable that studies of Pauline ethics, and of Paul generally, have largely neglected the theme of views of 'outsiders' (that is, the non-Christian 'general public').[2] Most studies of Pauline or New Testament ethics include a consideration of the Christians' 'political responsibilities' – for which Rom. 13.1-7 provides the key text – but other facets of this theme are seldom considered.[3] This is, however, an unfortunate neglect, as I shall hope to show in this chapter. Certain aspects of the topic of views of outsiders have already been dealt with in ch. 5, specifically the pejorative designations which form part of what I called the rhetoric of distinction and, in contrast, the permission or encouragement for Christians to continue

---

1. Hahn (2002: 697–729) organizes his treatment of NT ethics into three main sections, dealing in turn with the life of the individual Christian, life in the community (*Gemeinschaft*), and life in the orders of the world. Surveying Paul's 'concrete ethics', Schrage (1988: 217–39) considers issues of 'individual ethics'; sexual ethics (marriage, divorce, etc.); work, property and slavery; and political ethics (cf. below); comparable topics are dealt with by Hahn in terms of 'life in the orders of the world'. Such treatments tend to obscure the extent to which, even in such areas of practical instruction, Paul's focus is ecclesial-communal, a *Gemeindeethik*.

2. Cf. Furnish 2002b: 106: 'No extensive, comprehensive study has been undertaken of how Paul regarded those who belonged in what I have proposed as the fourth category [of possible types of "outsiders"], namely, the general "public"'. Furnish then examines relevant material in 1 Thessalonians and 1 Corinthians. There have, however, as Furnish notes, been a number of studies of the social interaction between Christians and outsiders, and of the differing kinds of depictions of the world evident in different Pauline churches (e.g. Still 1999; Vos 1999; Adams 2000). An important stimulus to these investigations was the study of Barclay 1992 (cf. also Barclay 1993b).

3. See, e.g., Verhey 1984: 120–21; Lohse 1991: 131–38; Schrage 1988: 235–39.

relatively open social interaction with outsiders and the evidence to show that to a considerable degree ethical norms were shared in common. The task of this chapter is to explore some further aspects of this theme, beginning with that of 'universal ethics'. By this, I mean ethics deemed (by Paul) to be applicable to all people. In other words, our question will be: Do we find in Paul any sense that all people can, should, or do have the scope to recognize common, universal ethical norms? This is not, as we shall see, best conceived in terms of appeals to 'natural law', though there is some overlap with that subject; nor am I here concerned with Paul's appeal to nature as one argument to convince recalcitrant Christians (1 Cor. 11.14).[4] The crucial texts for our purposes come from Romans. The distinction from the exploration of common ethical norms in ch. 5 is that there we were largely concerned with shared norms that *we* can discern, often against the flow of Paul's rhetoric. Here we are concerned to see whether Paul himself appeals to 'universal' standards. The second aspect to be explored is the (again explicit) exhortations concerning Christians' relations with outsiders. In this case there are a number of short but pertinent texts to be considered throughout the Pauline letters.

This topic has obvious relevance to our attempt to read Paul's ethics in the context of the liberal-communitarian debate and specifically the contrasting approaches of Habermas and Hauerwas, since the debate fundamentally concerns what kind of public discourse about ethics is possible and desirable. It relates directly, for example, to questions about whether Paul's ethics are distinctive, deriving from the specific narrative tradition embodied in the ecclesial community, or whether they share and presume common ethical standards and can have (or claim) a more general appeal. It also impinges upon any consideration of the nature of Christians' involvement in, and responsibility towards, their wider societies. Finally, it is important when we come to consider, as we shall in our final chapter, what the different possible models might be for appropriating Pauline ethics in our contemporary societies.

8.1 *Universal Knowledge: Romans 1–2*

The first text to which we turn is Romans 1–2, within which 1.19-21 and 2.14-15 are of especial interest. The main body of the letter to the Romans opens at 1.18, following the announcement of the main theme of the letter in 1.16-17 (cf. e.g. Fitzmyer 1993: 253, 269). The subject of this substantial opening section is announced in the 'programmatic proposition' of 1.18

---

4. On the subject of natural law in the NT and second-Temple Judaism, see esp. Bockmuehl 2000: 87–143, with treatment of Paul on pp. 127–40.

(Michel 1978: 96): the wrath of God, which is being revealed against all human wickedness and suppression of the truth. This declaration is justified in the following verses, which explain why this wrath can legitimately be directed towards humankind. What can be known about God, God's 'knowability' (τὸ γνωστόν; cf. BDAG, 204) is evident (φανερόν) to, in, or among them (ἐν αὐτοῖς, v. 19). This knowledge, then, is knowledge of God, and is attained through the things God has made (τοῖς ποιήμασιν, v. 20). Invisible qualities, God's eternal power and divinity, 'are perceived with the eye of reason' (BDAG, 493, νοούμενα καθορᾶται) or, in Fitzmyer's deliberately literal rendering, 'being intellectually apprehended are perceived' (1993: 280). This indicates well the essential sense here: though invisible (ἀόρατα) these divine qualities are perceived (καθορᾶται)[5] through a process of rational reflection (νοούμενα).[6] Dunn insists that Paul must have intended his readers 'to think in terms of some kind of rational perception of the fuller reality in and behind the created cosmos', thus echoing Stoic convictions also evident in Hellenistic Judaism (1988: 58).[7] Since this perception of God's invisible nature comes through the creation and is thereby accessible to people, it is rightly labelled 'some sort of natural theology' (Dunn 1988: 56). It comes, however, only because God has made it evident, that is, perceptible (ἐφανέρωσεν, v. 19), which is somewhat different – according to Paul's usage – from saying that God has 'revealed' it, for which ἀποκαλύπτω would be the expected word (cf. Rom 1.17-18; Bockmuehl 1988).[8] The crucial point for Paul to demonstrate is that people are therefore 'without excuse' (ἀναπολόγητος, v. 20; cf. Rom. 2.1). Humanity's knowledge of God must be presumed in order for Paul then to assert that, given this, people neither glorified nor gave thanks to God, such that their insight was obscured (1.21).[9] This led to God's 'handing them over' to reap the consequences of their refusal to offer the worship to which their knowledge should have led them (1.24, 26, 28). Here, following a pattern well established in Jewish tradition (cf. §5.1 above), refusal to

5. Fitzmyer (1993: 280) notes the oxymoronic play on two words from the root ὁράω here, against Käsemann 1974: 37.

6. See further BDAG, 493, and esp. the parallel in Ps-Aristotle, *De Mundo* 399a.30–399b.24 (quoted in NW 2.1: 18–19 and also, less extensively, by Käsemann 1974: 35).

7. Cf. also Fitzmyer 1993: 280; Wis. 13.5; Philo, *Leg. All.* 3.32 (§§97-99); *Praem. Poen.* 7 (§§41-46); *Op. Mund.* 12-13 (§§67-71); Plutarch, *Numa* 8.7-8; Cicero, *Tusc. Disp.* 1.27.66-67; 1.28.70; Plotinus 3.2.1; 3.2.3. For these and further parallels, see NW 2.1: 11–22.

8. Bockmuehl (1988: 99) rejects the common view that φανερόω and ἀποκαλύπτω are synonymous in Paul, suggesting that the former has the sense of 'making perceptible' (*Wahrnehmbarmachung*), though he later refers to Rom. 1.19 as a case of 'divine revelation' (2000: 130).

9. Cf. Wilckens 1978: 106: 'Sie [die Menschen] *kennen* Gott, aber sie widersprechen in ihrem Verhalten dieser Kenntnis, indem sie Gott nicht "als Gott" verherrlichen und ihm danken'.

acknowledge the one true God results in idolatry (1.22-23) which in turn leads to sexual immorality (1.24-28) and all kinds of wickedness (1.29-31). The appeal to 'nature' (φύσις), here (1.26), is, as Bockmuehl notes, an appeal to the 'created order' (2000: 130).[10] The key point Paul needs to prove is again explicit in the 'concluding sentence' of v. 32 (Michel 1978: 96): people can be judged guilty *precisely and only* because they *knew* God's just decree (τὸ δικαίωμα τοῦ θεοῦ ἐπιγνόντες). This decree is specifically 'that those who do such things deserve to die', but this itself presumes an awareness of what God deems to be immoral conduct (cf. Schrage 1961: 193).

A second sub-section of this introductory argument commences at 2.1, where Paul turns to 'an imaginary listener or interlocutor, who loudly applauds his description of the pagan's moral failure' (Fitzmyer 1993: 296). Having drawn on stock Jewish denunciation of Gentile idolatry and immorality (cf. esp. Wis. 13–15), Paul now begins to develop the argument that this applies equally to those who know and possess the law, since God's judgment is impartial and is based on what a person has or has not done.[11] 'Having' (cf. 2.14) or even 'hearing' the law (2.13) brings Jews no privileged standing (2.6-13; cf. 2.25-29). This assertion is supported in 2.14-15, where Paul strikingly claims that even those (Gentiles) who do not have the law can know and obey its standards (cf. *4 Ezra* 3.36).[12] Although they do not 'have' the law they may 'do by nature the things of the law' z(φύσει τὰ τοῦ νόμου ποιῶσιν, 2.14).[13] 'By nature' (φύσει) here means, in

10. Sexual relations between men and between women are thus seen as going against this natural order, in a way comparable with other Jewish texts, which link sexual immorality more generally with idolatry, and often make reference to the sins of Sodom (Gen. 19.1-9), or to the Watchers (Gen. 6.1-5); in both these cases, however, the sin in view is not necessarily that of homosexual acts, but of transgressing rules of hospitality or social justice (in the case of Sodom, cf. Ezek. 16.49-50) or the boundary between human and non-human (in the case of the Watchers). Cf., e.g., Wis. 14.12-27; *T. Reub.* 5.1-6; *T. Naph.* 3.2-5; Philo, *Abr.* 26 (§§133-36); Josephus, *Apion* 2.24; Jude 6-7; Bockmuehl 2000: 130 with nn. 59–60. On 'order' in creation, see also Philo, *Op. Mund.* 12 (§§67-68). These 'perversions' may be paradigmatic, in a way that adultery, say, is not, since they are deemed to represent precisely a transgression of the created order. But whether this perspective is relevant or convincing in terms of the contemporary discussion of homosexuality is a moot point (cf. e.g. the contrasting arguments of Hays 1997a: 379–406 and Martin 1995b).

11. Whether Paul's imaginary interlocutor is a Jew (from 2.1 onwards) is disputed, though this target becomes explicit at 2.17. It seems to me most plausible to take vv. 1-16 as an 'implicit indictment of Jews, which becomes overt in v. 17' (Fitzmyer 1993: 297; cf. Dunn 1988: 90–91), despite the arguments of Stowers (1994: 100–107, 127–28) to the contrary (for a wider critique of Stowers's reading of Romans, see Hays 1996).

12. As Dunn (1988: 105) notes, these verses allude again to the same kind of 'broader religiosity already evoked in 1:19-20, 28 and 2:7, 10'.

13. φύσει is best taken with the words that follow it, rather than those that precede (rightly, Wilckens 1978: 133 with n. 309; Dunn 1988: 98; Fitzmyer 1993: 310, against Cranfield 1975: 156–57, et al.).

effect, 'naturally' (Bockmuehl 2000: 131). This is because 'they are the law for themselves' (Dunn 1988: 99; ἐαυτοῖς εἰσιν νόμος), by which Paul means that through and in their own selves they come to knowledge of *the* law, the Jewish Torah. As Schrage puts it, this 'is not the norm and demand of some natural law or even an autonomous ethic, but the divine law' (1961: 193). Bockmuehl makes a similar point: 'Paul's concern ... is not some sort of separate "natural law", but rather a "natural" or common-sense *knowledge* of the one Law of God' (2000: 131). There are indeed three ways in which they know this Torah-defined good and evil, even without the law's explicit guidance: they know it because the law[14] is 'written in their hearts', because of the confirming testimony of their moral consciousness (συνείδησις; cf. §6.3.1), and because of the way their thoughts (λογισμοί) operate both to accuse or to defend (v. 15).[15] This 'self-criticism' anticipates the last judgment (cf. Käsemann 1974: 61; Wis. 1.5-10), to which Paul now refers in v. 16: the day when all people, their hidden secrets laid bare, will face judgment according to what they have done (cf. vv. 12-13).

It is, of course, clear that Paul presents these arguments in order to establish an essentially negative conclusion: that all people, Jew and Gentile alike, stand liable to God's judgment (Rom. 3.19; cf. 11.32). This is the necessary starting point for a presentation of the 'good news' (τὸ εὐαγγέλιον) as God's answer to this dire situation (Rom. 1.16-17; 3.21-26). Paul is not concerned to establish a positive case for universal ethics. Nor is his argument for universal failure necessarily convincing. The possibility of 'righteous' Gentiles, 'who do naturally what the law requires', is, even Paul implies, 'not only a theoretical and hypothetical one, but one which is actually grasped and realised in practice' (Schrage 1961: 192; cf. also Dunn 1988: 99). Nor would Jewish readers likely be convinced that they all stood condemned, despite Paul's string of scriptural citations (3.10-18), since most would hardly steal, commit adultery, or desecrate temples (2.21-22), and those who broke the law (cf. 2.27) knew well that the law had its own

---

14. That is, τὸ ἔργον τοῦ νόμου, the deed, practice or content of the law (cf. BDAG, 390–91; Wilckens 1978: 134 n. 315: 'der Inhalt der Tora'). The singular of ἔργον here (with positive nuance) contrasts with Paul's use of the plural ἔργα νόμου elsewhere, always with negative force, as Dunn rightly notes (1988: 100; see, e.g., Rom. 3.20, 28; Gal. 2.16; 3.2, 5, 10).

15. Commentators disagree as to whether this latter phrase should be regarded as describing 'the role of the conscience in greater detail' (Fitzmyer 1993: 311) or as a further 'way of speaking about the moral consciousness evident among those outside the law' (Dunn 1988: 102; cf. Wilckens 1978: 136: 'Beide haben Zeugenfunktion, das Gewissen zusammen mit den Gedanken'). It seems most plausible to take the verse as indicating three distinct, though related, ways in which the Gentiles have the moral knowledge the law provides, as even Fitzmyer suggests (1993: 311).

means to atone for transgression.[16] Nonetheless, the significance of this passage for Pauline ethics should not be denied. Whether Paul is right or wrong to depict all people as failing to live up to moral standards, the crucial point is that he argues – and *has* to argue – for a universal sense of what is right and wrong, and a universal knowledge of God. Were this knowledge not accessible to all, then all could not justifiably be judged. The knowledge of God is through a form of natural theology, since it comes via reflection on the visible things of creation, though only by God's decision to make it evident therein. The knowledge of right and wrong is knowledge not of a natural law as such, but of the Jewish law. The content of this law is conveyed by God to those who do not 'have' the law itself – God is surely the implied agent who 'writes' it on people's hearts (cf. Jer. 31.33) – and it is affirmed by the conscience and the thoughts found in human beings themselves. The specific ethical standards Paul might have in mind are not made explicit, though we can make some reasonable deductions as to what they might, at least in essence, be.[17] The starting point for human wickedness is the refusal to recognize and worship God, so the first commandment (Exod. 20.3-6; Deut. 5.7-10) would seem to be implicit as a standard here. The mention of stealing and committing adultery in 2.21-22, and again in 13.9 (there together with murder and coveting), also point to the Decalogue (Exod. 20.14-15; Deut. 5.18-19),[18] which, Paul later declares, is epitomized in the command to love the neighbour (Lev. 19.18; Rom. 13.8-10; cf. Gal. 5.14; §7.3 above). So the injunctions to love or fear God and to love one's neighbour, prominent in the *Testaments of the Twelve Patriarchs*[19] as well as in Jesus' summary of the law (Mk 12.29-31), would seem to offer comparable epitomes of the moral imperatives Paul considers to be universally knowable, with the Decalogue's specified sins against the neighbour (stealing, coveting, etc.) being encapsulated in the love-command (Lev. 19.18), or in some form of the Golden Rule (cf. Tob. 4.15; Sir. 31.15; Mt. 7.12; Lk. 6.31; Rom. 13.10;

---

16.   Cf. further Sanders 1977: 442–47, 474–511; 1983: 123–32, 149–54. There is a good deal to be said for Sanders's argument that Paul is reasoning (to at least a significant degree) 'from solution to plight': convinced that God has acted in Christ to save all people, Paul must now demonstrate that all people needed saving, the logical starting point for his argument. Otherwise, as Paul recognizes, the implication is that Christ died for nothing (Gal. 2.21).

17.   Thus, at least by looking to the wider context in Romans, I think we can go somewhat further than Bockmuehl suggests when he comments on Rom. 2.14-15: 'With respect to the positive *substance* of Pauline ethics, however, there is not in fact a great deal to learn here' (2000: 131).

18.   Cf. Dunn 1988: 114, though the third link Dunn notes to the Decalogue, 'committing sacrilege' (ἱεροσυλεῖς), is less directly paralleled in the prohibitions against idolatry.

19.   *T. Rub.* 6.9; *T. Iss.* 5.2; 7.6; *T. Dan* 5.3; *T. Benj.* 3.3-5; cf. also *T. Sim.* 4.4, 7; *T. Zeb.* 8.5; *T. Gad* 4.1-7; 6.1-7; 7.1-7; *T. Jos.* 17.2-3; *T. Benj.* 8.1. Note also *Jub.* 7.20; 20.2. See further Söding 1995: 56–66, esp. 58 with n. 70.

Dihle 1962). Paul, however, as we have already had cause to note (§7.3, p. 225 with n. 72), does not speak of the command to 'love God' (Deut. 6.5) nor link love for God and for neighbour: a Pauline summary of these universal moral imperatives would therefore be to worship God (cf. Rom. 1.21, 25) and to love one's neighbour.

8.2 *Universal Obligations: Romans 13.1-7*

Among the notorious texts penned (or rather, dictated [Rom. 16.22]) by Paul, Rom. 13.1-7 has a certain prominence, not least because of this text's dubious impact on the Church's relations with oppressive and iniquitous regimes.[20] The moral problem is most sharply expressed by John O'Neill: 'These seven verses have caused more unhappiness and misery in the Christian East and West than any other seven verses in the New Testament by the licence they have given to tyrants, and the support for tyrants the Church has felt called on to offer as a result of the presence of Romans 13 in the canon' (O'Neill 1975: 209). O'Neill's answer is to remove the verses from the letter, along with many other sections of Paul's Roman epistle; others too have reckoned this section an interpolation, or at least an 'alien body', an odd intrusion, in Paul's text.[21] However, the linguistic connections with their context and the lack of textual evidence for their omission render unlikely the view that these verses are an interpolation.[22] Even Käsemann's view of the section as a self-contained block (1974: 340) is unconvincing in the light both of the connections between this passage and its literary context and of its congruence with Pauline teaching elsewhere (see §8.3-4 below).

One common interpretative strategy, adopted not least because of the *Wirkungsgeschichte* O'Neill rightly deplores, is to insist that Romans 13 does not offer a theology of political power or of the state, but is essentially a contextual response to specific pressures in Rome in the late 50s CE and an attempt to protect Christians (and perhaps Jews too) in the city from

---

20. E.g., in apartheid South Africa, on which see Botha 1994, who presents various approaches to Romans 13 as a necessary prequisite for an ethical reading of the text. In this section I draw on some of the material in Horrell 2003.

21. E.g. Kallas 1965. Käsemann (1974: 340) describes Rom. 13.1-7 as 'ein selbständiger Block ... ein Fremdkörper in der paulinischen Paränese', though not as an interpolation.

22. So, rightly, e.g., Dunn 1988: 758–59. Romans 12.9-21 begins and ends with references to Christians doing what is good (τὸ ἀγαθόν), a clear link to 13.1-7, where the authorities are not a cause of fear to those who do good (τὸ ἀγαθὸν ἔργον, 13.3; cf. 13.4). Similarly, 13.7 is linked to the following section via the references to what one owes (τὰς ὀφειλάς, v. 7; ὀφείλετε, v. 8).

unnecessary persecution.[23] This response, which takes many forms, is an understandable attempt at 'damage limitation', an effort to restrict any broader theology of the state being drawn from this passage. Nonetheless, there are difficulties with such a move, over and above the general point that all of Paul's writing is similarly contextual – including the principles we may find more conducive (e.g. Gal. 3.28). As we shall see in more detail, Paul speaks here in strikingly generalized terms, thus making this text unusually amenable to claims of universal applicability.[24]

Chapters 12–13 of Romans seem to have a roughly chiastic structure (ABCB′A′), opening and closing with the theme of transformation (12.1-2; 13.13-14), inside which is the theme of love, first along with a series of practical admonitions that embody it (12.9-21), and second as the commandment that summarizes the whole law (13.8-10). If these approximately balancing sections form the AB/B′A′, then the section in the middle is evidently 13.1-7, linked by key words to both what precedes and what follows it.[25] Moreover, on each side of 13.1-7 is found material concerning the relations of Christians to outsiders, specifically in 12.14-21 (on which see §8.4 below) and more generally in 13.8-10 with its reference to love for the neighbour.[26]

It is nonetheless difficult to see 13.1–7 as constituting a central and decisive, even if apparently digressive, contribution to the argument of these two chapters, as is the case in other Pauline ABA′ constructions (1 Cor. 8–10 [ch. 9]; 1 Cor. 12–14 [ch. 13]), unless the exhortation to be subject to the state is a central concern for Paul in this wider section of instruction.[27] Even then, the passage hardly illuminates the surrounding contexts in the way that 1 Corinthians 9 and 13 do theirs (cf. §6.1 above). It is, however, possible to see Rom. 13.1-7 as dealing with a crucial test case of the Christians' external relations, and thus as providing a key exemplar of the instructions surrounding it. The call to be a community which clings

---

23. Examples, though with important differences among them, include Elliott 1997 (cf. further 1994); Friedrich, Pöhlmann and Stuhlmacher 1976.

24. Cf. Schrage 1988: 235: 'one cannot evade the problem by assuming that Romans 13 responds to special dangers arising within the Christian community at Rome'.

25. See further Horrell 2003: 83–87. Gerd Theissen presented a similar analysis of the 'Ringkomposition' of 12.1–13.14 in his (unpublished) lectures on 'Ethik des Neuen Testaments' (University of Heidelberg, 2003).

26. Romans 13.8-10 is not, of course, concerned only, or even primarily, with relations with outsiders, but the use of the term 'neighbour' (vv. 9-10), taken from Lev. 19.18, cited in v. 9, suggests that Paul's concerns are wider than those solely relating to Christians' dealings with 'one another'.

27. This might be the case if Paul is concerned in Romans to counteract rumours that he is a lawless person who promotes evil (cf. Rom. 3.8; Wengst 1987: 82; Brown and Meier 1983: 105–27) or if disturbances over the payment of taxes were a central concern of Paul's paraenesis here (cf. n. 39 below).

to what is good and maintains the practice of peaceable non-retaliation (12.14-21; see below) means that the Roman Christians can and should submit to the authorities whose God-given responsibility is to reward the good and punish evil;[28] and their call to be people whose only outstanding debt is the constant obligation to give themselves to the other in love (13.8-10) means that they should honour their debts to the state.

The section opens, however, with an emphatically *universal* address: 'let *every person* (πᾶσα ψυχή) be subject to the governing authorities' (v. 1a).[29] Although Paul is obviously writing specifically to the Christians in Rome, and can have no expectation of giving instruction to the 'general public' (cf. 12.1, 3, etc.), formulating the exhortation in this general way is nonetheless notable, and unusual.[30] In a similar vein, the following point about the status of such authorities is also made in general, universally applicable terms – 'there is no authority except from God' – though the next phrase should probably be interpreted as deliberately including the current Roman regime under this description (cf. Cranfield 1979: 663): 'those that exist', that is, the currently existing authorities, 'have been arranged (τεταγμέναι) by God' (v. 1b). As Bockmuehl notes, 'Paul grounds his instructions in what he clearly regards as a universal creational given: political authority is the exclusive gift and prerogative of God' (2000: 136). And the absence of any 'christological reasoning' in this whole passage further suggests an intentionally universal argument (cf. Bockmuehl 2000: 136) – Paul seems capable of so adjusting his mode of argument, as is often noted with respect to Rom. 10.17–11.36 (Stendahl 1976: 4).

Furthermore, Paul expresses in surprisingly unqualified terms the authorities' role in praising good conduct and punishing bad (13.3-4). Given that Paul had already suffered imprisonment and beatings at the

28.   Cf. Wengst 1987: 81: 'relations with people outside the community ... are not to be different from those within the community, despite the aggression with which they meet [*sic*]. As a particular case of behaviour towards such people generally, Paul considers attitudes to those holding power in the state'.

29.   Πᾶσα ψυχή stands emphatically at the opening of the sentence. It is now widely agreed that earthly, political authorities are in view in these verses, rather than angelic or spiritual powers (Dunn 1988: 760; cf. also Cranfield 1979: 656–59).

30.   Cf. the frequent use of ἀδελφοί, etc. (see §4.2 above), and the contrast between the third-person format used in Rom. 13.1-5 and the second-person forms that characterize what precedes and follows it. The universality of Paul's address here is noted by G. Delling, *TWNT* 8: 45: submission is commanded 'nicht speziell den Christen, sondern jedermann' (cf. also Wilckens 1982: 32). Cranfield (1979: 656) disagrees, insisting that 'in the context of Romans, "every Christian (in Rome)"' is intended. He agrees, however, that '[t]he phrase is emphatic'. Dunn's comment sagely encompasses both perspectives: 'The counsel is all-embracive [*sic*], though here naturally the Christian audience is primarily in view' (1988: 760). Gerd Theissen also stresses the significance of the presentation of this teaching as universally applicable (lectures on 'Ethik des Neuen Testaments', University of Heidelberg, 2003).

hands of Roman 'justice' (2 Cor. 6.5; 11.23, 25),[31] it is striking that he can speak here without any hint of reserve or irony of the state as God's servant in rewarding good and punishing evil.[32] Nor does Paul explicitly limit the extent of submission to the governing authority,[33] although the early Christians soon glossed this text with the 'Petrine clause' of Acts 5.29 to formulate the view that obedience is owed only insofar as the authorities do not command or require anything that goes against the will of God.[34] The theological basis Paul gives is simply 'that there is no such actual power without God, that those in authority are virtually appointed by God to their function' (Wengst 1987: 83). As Klaus Wengst rightly goes on to comment (and despite exegetical efforts to relieve Paul of this dubious achievement):[35] 'by doing that without caveat, qualification and dialectic, he [Paul] at least exposes himself to the danger of providing theological legitimation for *de facto* power no matter how it may have come into being and how it may be used' (1987: 83–84). Nonetheless, it should be appreciated that the (Jewish) perspective Paul presents here *both* legitimates *and* limits the rulers' authority at one and the same time. Insofar as Paul – along with many other Jewish writers[36] – regards rulers as there because God has given them their position, he does add a certain

31. Further evidence of Paul's imprisonments is of course found in Philippians, Philemon and Acts: the crucial point about 2 Corinthians is that it is undoubtedly written prior to Romans and by Paul himself. Those who comment, as many do, that this text was written before Nero's persecution ignore this rather obvious fact: Paul had already experienced the governing authorities' enactment of 'justice' and might well have questioned the presumption that it rewards good and punishes evil.

32. Cf. further Wengst 1987: 72–89. Elliott speaks of Paul's 'absurdly positive comments' (1997: 196). As Cranfield notes, 'Paul seems to take no account of the possibility of the government's being unjust and punishing the good work and praising the evil' (1979: 664).

33. It should, however, be noted that Paul calls for submission (using ὑποτάσσω) rather than obedience (using ὑπακούω); note the distinction in the deutero-Pauline household codes, where wives are called to submit (Eph. 5.24; Col. 3.18), but children and slaves to obey (Eph. 6.1, 5; Col. 3.20, 22). While an unqualified call for submission hardly encourages a stance of critique or disobedience, it does at least indicate that Paul's concern is more with accepting one's place within a given 'order' (τάγμα) than with a blanket call for obedience per se (cf. also Rom. 13.1-2: ὑπὸ θεοῦ τεταγμέναι εἰσίν ... τῇ τοῦ θεοῦ διαταγῇ). Cf. Käsemann 1974: 339.

34. Cf. Wilckens 1982: 45 with n. 190, who cites Hippolytus, Origen, et al. Much later, the Geneva Bible of 1560, for example, added the marginal comment to Rom. 13.5: 'so farre as lawfully wee may: for if unlawful things be commanded us, we must answere as Peter teacheth us, It is better to obey God than men'. The politics of translation become clear in this connection: one of the motivations for the KJV was to counter such 'seditious' interpretations. See Wink 1992: 114 with n. 38, from where the Geneva Bible quotation is taken.

35. E.g., Elliott 1994: 226: 'Only the arrogant presumptions of our own privilege have allowed us to hear these verses as a sacred legitimation of power.'

36. See, e.g., Prov. 8.15-16; Isa. 45.1; Dan. 2.21; 4.17, 25, 32; Wis. 6.3; Josephus, *War* 2.140; 5.367; further Dunn 1988: 761.

divine legitimation to Roman imperial domination. But, equally, by insisting that it is God who has granted the rulers their role, Paul, again along with the same Jewish writers (see e.g. Dan. 4.1-37; Wis. 6.1-6; etc.), relativizes their position: it is theirs not on the grounds of their own might or (pseudo-divine) status – as Roman imperial ideology claims – but only because God has chosen to allow it to be so; and what God has granted God can equally take away – and may well do so soon (cf. Rom. 13.11-14; 1 Cor. 2.6; 15.24; 1 Thess. 5.2-3).

Yet more significant for our purposes here is Paul's presumption that non-Christian governing authorities recognize correctly what is good and what is evil. What Paul (strikingly) presents as a simple fact he must at least see as a real possibility, even if he might acknowledge that the authorities do not always live up to this depiction of their role (herein, of course, lies one area for criticism of ruling powers, at least implicitly sanctioned in this text). As in Rom. 2.14-15, then, we have further evidence that Paul regards the recognition and practice of good and evil as evident among non-Christian Gentiles. Even more clearly than in 2.14–15, where the idea is formulated in the context of a negative argument for universal sinfulness, here the assumption is a positive one: that the governing authority *does* act on the basis of its correct recognition of good and evil. As it does this, it acts as 'God's servant' to avenge God's wrath (ἔκδικος εἰς ὀργήν) upon those who do evil (13.4). The obvious parallels of language between 12.19 and 13.4 indicate, as F.F. Bruce concisely comments, that '[t]he state thus is charged with a function which has been explicitly forbidden to the Christian'.[37] But in so acting as God's representative, the ruling power is presumed to share God's sense of good and evil.

Both the fear of suffering wrath and one's own moral consciousness, then, are reasons to submit to the authorities (13.5). And the authorities' role as God's 'officials' (λειτουργοί)[38] means that taxes should be paid. Many have seen here the real point of Paul's instruction,[39] but this seems a reductionistic reading, not least since this arises only as a supporting

---

37.   Bruce 1963: 238. Bruce explicitly makes the point that Paul gives no direct indication as to how a Christian ruler might reconcile the instructions of chs 12 and 13. Cf. also Yoder 1972: 199: 'It is inconceivable that these two verses [12.19 and 13.4], using such similar language, should be meant to be read independently of one another.' For Yoder this 'makes it clear that the function exercised by government is not the function to be exercised by Christians ... the text cannot mean that Christians are called to do military or police service' (p. 205). Cf. also Hays 1997a: 317–46, esp. 342–43 and further n. 77 below.

38.   Paul uses both singular and plural forms in these verses to describe the authorities/ authority (ἐξουσίαι/ἐξουσία, ἄρχοντες, διάκονος, λειτουργοί), without any apparent distinction in mind.

39.   E.g., Furnish 1979: 126, 131–35; cf. also Friedrich, Pöhlmann and Stuhlmacher 1976. Reports of disturbances over the payment of taxes in Rome in the late 50s CE may certainly make this point especially pertinent (Tacitus, *Ann.* 13.50-51).

reason (εἰς τοῦτο γάρ) to indicate why subordination to the authority, as God's servant, is the appropriate course of action.[40] The final exhortation, indeed, is cast once again in very general terms (v. 7).

The text represents a 'universal ethics', then, in at least two senses. First, in the sense that all political authority is seen as ordered by God and as able, at least potentially, to enact God's justice and to recognize correctly what is good and what is evil. A common sense of good and evil, knowable by non-Christian and Christian alike, is therefore presumed here. Secondly, in the sense that, given this universal declaration about political authority, the duty to submit to such authority is a universal human obligation. The fact that Paul addressed this instruction specifically to the Roman Christians does not negate this observation about the formulation of his text: the Christians at Rome are urged to do what Paul presents as a duty for all people.

8.3 *Concern for the Reaction of Outsiders*

In terms of demonstrating an explicit concern about the reaction of outsiders to Christians' conduct,[41] there are three Pauline texts which are particularly pertinent: 1 Thess. 4.11-12; 1 Cor. 10.32; and 1 Cor. 14.22-25. Although the concern (variously) expressed in these texts is distinctive in its focus on the reaction of outsiders, it should not be seen as an isolated or uncharacteristic theme in Paul's writing. Rather, as will become clear, it coheres with other aspects of the topic of ethics and outsiders.

It is widely agreed that 1 Thessalonians is Paul's earliest letter and that it reflects an imminent eschatological expectation and an apocalyptic fervour on the part of the Thessalonians, a world-view conveyed in Paul's missionary preaching. The Thessalonian Christians have, since their conversion, experienced hostility and conflict in their relations with their non-Christian neighbours, a social experience rendered comprehensible, and even in part created, by their apocalyptic and dualistic world-view (see Jewett 1986; Barclay 1992, 1993b; Still 1999).[42] The letter is characterized

---

40. As Dunn notes (1988: 766), the γάρ indicates that the verb τελεῖτε must be taken as indicative, not imperative; similarly, Fitzmyer 1993: 669, who comments: 'Paul takes it for granted that the Christians of Romans have been paying taxes'; cf. also Schrage 1988: 235. Friedrich, Pöhlmann and Stuhlmacher, however, translate v. 6: 'Deshalb müßt ihr auch Steuern bezahlen' (1976: 160).

41. On this general theme and its appearance in early Christian texts, see van Unnik 1980.

42. Jewett interprets the Thessalonian church's experience in the light of the model of millenarian movements, with an apocalyptic outlook leading to a radical rejection of the current world order. However, he rejects the common view that the Thessalonians held an imminent eschatology and suggests instead that at least some in the church propounded a realized eschatology (1986: 97, 176–77).

by contrasting depictions of insiders – the ἀδελφοί who will escape the wrath to come – and outsiders – 'the rest' (οἱ λοιποί) who have no hope and face wrathful destruction (cf. 1 Thess. 1.9-10; 4.5, 12-13; 5.2-10; Barclay 1993b: 517). Thus the rhetoric of distinction is strongly evident here (cf. ch. 5 above).

It is therefore significant to find a concern for outsiders also expressed in various ways in this letter (see further §8.4 below). At the close of the key section of ethical instruction (4.1-12), Paul urges the Thessalonians, apparently repeating previous instruction, to aim 'to live quietly, to busy yourselves with your own affairs (πράσσειν τὰ ἴδια), and to work with your own hands' (4.11). The purpose of this conduct is that they should meet their own needs and conduct themselves (περιπατῆτε) 'properly' or 'decently towards those outside'[43] (εὐσχημόνως πρὸς τοὺς ἔξω, 4.12; cf. Rom. 13.13;[44] Col. 4.5). There may be various reasons why Paul gave this instruction, various aspects of the Thessalonians' conduct he wishes to confront: some of the Thessalonians may have abandoned work in view of the imminent expectation (cf. 1 Thess. 5.14; 2 Thess. 3.6-12);[45] their world-view may have inclined them not only to a passive understanding of their 'social alienation' but also to an aggressive and 'provocative evangelism' (so Barclay 1993b: 520–25) – at the very least they may have been inclined 'to respond to the non-Christian criticism to which they were subject' (Still 1999: 214). These latter possibilities would explain why Paul urges them to 'mind their own business'. A positive 'missionary' motivation for this instruction is certainly not explicit in the text;[46] indeed, if Barclay is right, then Paul's concern is almost the opposite – to stop the Thessalonians being such zealous and aggressive missionaries! Yet it would seem reasonable, not least given the evangelistic motivation evident in other

---

43. As Malherbe (2000: 251) notes, a distinction between 'with a view to the outsiders' and 'in the view of the outsiders' is not clear here. What Paul seeks to prevent, Malherbe rightly notes, is criticism of the Thessalonians' behaviour.

44. The similarity between 1 Thess. 4.12 and Rom. 13.13 (εὐσχημόνως περιπατήσωμεν), along with the focus on loving the neighbour in Rom. 13.8-10, suggests that a similar concern for outsiders' view of Christians' behaviour is implied in Romans, as well as 1 Thessalonians.

45. Cf., e.g., Best 1972: 175–77; Jewett 1986: 172–76, though Jewett sees the 'cessation of economic activity' (p. 174) as a sign of 'millenarian radicalism' (p. 176) and as reflecting a realized rather than futurist eschatology (see n. 42 above). The pertinence of this issue to 1 Thessalonians depends in part on the (disputed) authenticity of 2 Thessalonians and in part on whether ἄτακτος in 1 Thess. 5.14 (cf. 2 Thess. 3.6, 11) refers specifically to the abandonment of work (so, e.g., Bruce 1982: 122–23); it may be translated 'idle' or more generally 'disorderly, unruly', see BDAG, 148. Jewett (1986: 104–105) argues for the meaning 'rebellious' or 'insubordinate', but agrees that ceasing work was one manifestation of their world-view (see above).

46. Cf. Furnish 2002b: 113: 'nor is there any hint [in 1 Thess. 4.9-12] that the Apostle wants his converts to be models of good behavior in order to attract outsiders to the gospel'.

texts concerned with outsiders' reactions (see below),[47] to see at least a 'passive' missionary motivation here: by living quietly, supporting themselves and keeping out of other people's noses, the Thessalonian Christians will avoid causing offence, as far as possible, and thus remove a hindrance to others' acceptance of the gospel (cf. Holtz 1986: 180–81; Best 1972: 177). A further observation is also pertinent: in his conviction that following his instructions will engender 'appropriate' conduct towards outsiders, Paul 'is presupposing a certain congruence between the norms that prevail in society at large and the ethos that distinguishes the believing community' (Furnish 2002b: 112).[48] Although the content of shared norms is here only minimally evident – essentially it is a matter of keeping inoffensively quiet – the assumption of a commonly shared sense of what is good is one which we have already seen in Romans 2 and 13 and which will also be seen to underpin the notion of doing good to all (see §8.4).

The idea of avoiding offence or causing hindrance is a more explicit concern in 1 Cor. 10.32. Here, in concluding his treatment of an issue which has primarily concerned relationships among Christians (cf. 1 Cor. 8.11-13; §6.1 above), Paul urges the Corinthians to act in such a way that they give no offence to Jews or to Greeks or to the assembly of God (ἀπρόσκοποι καὶ Ἰουδαίοις γίνεσθε καὶ Ἕλλησιν καὶ τῇ ἐκκλησίᾳ τοῦ θεοῦ, 1 Cor. 10.32). It is often noted that this formulation already expresses embryonically the notion that would later develop into the explicit description of Christians as a third race, sociologically distinct from both Jews and Greeks.[49] But the expressed desire for peaceful coexistence with outsiders is less frequently discussed. Yet given the somewhat different characteristics, so far as we can discern them, of the Christian groups at Thessalonica and at Corinth (see esp. Barclay 1992), the occurrence of similar instruction in both letters is significant. The brief instruction in 1 Cor. 10.32 clearly echoes Paul's earlier and more famous description of his accommodatory missionary stance, becoming all things to all people (9.19-22), and is explicitly part of the imitation to which he calls the Corinthians (10.32–11.1). The same three groups are broadly in view in both passages

---

47. See also van Unnik 1980.

48. Cf. Malherbe 2000: 251: 'Paul ... inculcates behavior that would be acceptable to social norms'; Schnelle 1990: 298: in grounding his instruction with a consideration (*Rücksichtnahme*) for the judgment of non-Christian Gentiles 'geht Paulus offensichtlich von einer Gemeinsamkeit ethischer Normen bei Heiden und Christen aus'. A similar point is made by Schulz 1987: 303, though he sees this as a reflection of Paul's presupposition that 'das ungeschriebene Sittengesetz der Heiden' is the same (*gleich*) 'mit dem geschriebenen Moralgesetz von Sinai'. In view of Schulz's concern to distinguish an early phase of Pauline ethics (evident in 1 Thessalonians) from the later phase (evident in the other genuine letters), this is an ironic conflation of Romans with 1 Thessalonians.

49. Sanders 1983: 171–79; Horrell 2000b: 341; see, e.g., Aristides, *Apol.* 2; Tertullian, *Ad Nat.* 8; *Scorp.* 10.

(cf. Hurd 1965: 130): Jews (9.20), Greeks ('those outside the law', 9.21) and the assembly of God ('the weak', 9.22; cf. 8.9). The 'weak', of course, are only a part of the congregation, but they constitute the focus of concern for Paul, in his attempt to convince the strong to follow his own pattern of adaptability for the sake of others. The weak (in 9.22) may also include outsiders, since Paul's own pattern of accommodation, outlined in 9.19-23 and summarized in 10.32-33, has both a missionary and community-building purpose (see §7.2 above, n. 56). Imitating Paul in seeking to 'please everyone in everything' (10.33) is a pattern of conduct intended to further these purposes.[50]

A second instance of concern for the reaction of outsiders in 1 Corinthians comes in the midst of the discussion about prophecy and tongues and their uses in the congregational meetings (1 Cor. 12.1–14.40, esp. 14.1-40). The first reference to an outsider's presence in the assembly might appear to come in 14.16, where Paul questions the value of a thanksgiving uttered 'in the spirit' ($\dot{\epsilon}\nu$ $\pi\nu\epsilon\dot{\nu}\mu\alpha\tau\iota$) since 'the one who occupies the place of the $\dot{\iota}\delta\iota\dot{\omega}\tau\eta\varsigma$', lacking understanding of what is said, cannot then add an Amen. The $\dot{\iota}\delta\iota\dot{\omega}\tau\eta\varsigma$ is an 'outsider' (e.g. NRSV) in the sense that they are excluded from sharing the meaning of the prayer; they are not 'in the know' (cf. BDAG, 468). But the focus here on upbuilding ($\dot{o}\iota\kappa\delta\delta\omega\mu\dot{\epsilon}\omega$, v. 17) suggests that the person is a member of the congregation (cf. Furnish 2002b: 121). The distinction between $\dot{\iota}\delta\iota\dot{\omega}\tau\alpha\iota$ ('outsiders') and $\ddot{\alpha}\pi\iota\sigma\tau\iota$ ('unbelievers') drawn in vv. 23-24 also speaks against interpreting $\dot{\iota}\delta\iota\dot{\omega}\tau\alpha\iota$ to mean outsiders in the sense of 'unbelieving non-members'. In the latter verses, at least, it seems that the two categories correspond to the uninitiated ($\dot{\iota}\delta\iota\dot{\omega}\tau\alpha\iota$) – perhaps those 'on the margins of the community' (Furnish 2002b: 122; cf. BDAG, 468)[51] – and unbelieving outsiders ($\ddot{\alpha}\pi\iota\sigma\tau\iota$).[52] A number of points of interest emerge in this generally

---

50. Trying to please Jews and Greeks on the issue of idol-food is perhaps an impossible goal, though Paul's solution of eating whatever is served at meals, *unless* anyone points out that it is sacrificial food, might indicate an attempt to do that (within the absolutes he sets down; see §6.1). The concern for outsiders might partly explain, along with the (predominant) concern for relations inside the community, why Paul's instruction on the substantive issue is less than forthright. Clearly, Paul's policy of adaptability, as set out in 1 Cor. 9.20-22, would be regarded (by some) as offensively vacillating: how can one be (only) 'on occasion' $\dot{\omega}\varsigma$ Ἰουδαῖος and at other times $\dot{\omega}\varsigma$ ἄνομος? This chameleon-like flexibility indicates that Paul's identity and practice are no longer defined by these categories, but rather by a 'being in Christ' which Paul understands to demand precisely this adaptability. See further Horrell forthcoming.

51. One need not anachronistically assume an order of catechumenates, or anything so formally constituted. Thiselton (2000: 1114–15, 1127) suggests the meaning 'uninitiated'.

52. *Pace* Conzelmann (1975: 243), who comments that '[n]o difference of meaning is perceptible between ἰδιώτης, "layman", and ἄπιστος, "unbeliever"'. Cf. also Barrett (1971: 324), who translates the two nouns together as 'unbelieving outsiders'. Nor is it necessary

confusing passage (vv. 20-25).[53] One is Paul's presumption that unbelieving outsiders may well be present during the worship meetings of the congregation, including (most probably) the Lord's supper celebration.[54] Nor should this be surprising, once we have shed some modern assumptions about the privacy of domestic space (see Osiek and Balch 1997: 24–35, 193–204), though it does make clear that these assemblies were not, in Paul's view at least, secretive cult-groups from whose meetings outsiders must be firmly excluded. A second point of interest is Paul's concern about the impact of Christians' behaviour upon such outsiders as may be present. One reason to prophesy rather than use tongues, aside from the fact that the latter excludes those not 'in the know' (vv. 16-17), is that an outsider hearing tongues is liable to conclude that the group is 'mad' (μαίνεσθε). This probably implies not madness as such, but rather that members of the group are ecstatic and possessed, acting like worshippers in a Dionysiac cult.[55] Comprehensible prophecy, in contrast, may lead to the outsider's conversion (vv. 24–25). Once again, then, the purpose of acting with a view to the reaction of outsiders is twofold: to prevent undue criticism of the Christian community and to win outsiders for the faith.

8.4 *Doing Good to All*

The previous examples of instruction to consider the impact of one's actions upon outsiders express a concern about others in primarily negative terms: the avoidance of unnecessary criticism. (A somewhat more

---

(*pace* Barrett 1971: 324) to take Paul as using the word differently in v. 16 and in vv. 23-24: in both places it could refer to those on the fringes of the community (cf. Klauck 1984: 101; Thiselton 2000: 1114–15, 1127). While the contextually required referent in v. 16 is simply the one excluded from understanding the prayer, it seems more likely that the word is used consistently across these nine verses than that two different meanings come into play.

53. Paul's logic here is certainly obscure, if not altogether confused, cf. Thiselton 2000: 1122. Barrett (1971: 322–27) finds a coherent reading.

54. Cf. Furnish 2002b: 122; Schrage 1999: 411; Lindemann 2000: 309; Barrett 1971: 325–26; contra Allo 1956: 386, who maintains that unbelievers 'n'étaient pas admis à l'acte solennel du «repas du Seigneur». Rather, after the first part of the gathering – the proper meal, after which, according to Allo, came the eucharist – 'ceux qui n'étaient pas membres de l'église ou chrétiens venus d'une autre église (et peut-être ἰδιῶται à Corinthe) aient été congédiés, puis les portes fermées'. That the meal of 11.17-34 would include, or be followed by, the worship described in 14.1-40 is most likely (cf. Lampe 1991b), and there are simply no grounds in the text for taking Allo's view about the exclusion of outsiders from the eucharistic gathering (whether, and to what extent, they participated is another question, to which Paul's text gives no answers).

55. So, e.g., Barrett 1971: 326; Klauck 1984: 102; Witherington 1995: 284; see further Kroeger and Kroeger 1978; Fiorenza 1983: 227–30.

positive concern to influence conversion is apparent, however, in 1 Cor. 14.24-25.) Although a missionary motivation seems to be evident, at least in the (again essentially negative) sense of minimizing any hinderance to their acceptance of the gospel, this 'concern for outsiders' conveys no positive exhortation to ethical action for their good. But this more positive theme, which coheres with, but also goes beyond, the theme of concern for the reaction of outsiders, is indeed woven throughout the Pauline letters.

We might well note, first, how the appeals for a generous, Christ-like 'other-regard' in some cases at least allow the implication that this 'other-regard' pertains to those outside as well as inside the Christian community, even though, as we have already seen (chs 6–7 above), its primary focus is on regard for Christian brothers and sisters.[56] Much more explicit expressions of ethical responsibility towards outsiders, however, are found in the various appeals to show love, or do good, to all people.

Beginning again with Paul's earliest letter, 1 Thessalonians, we find the Thessalonians urged to 'abound in love ($\tau\hat{\eta}$ $\dot{\alpha}\gamma\dot{\alpha}\pi\eta$) for one another and for all ($\epsilon\dot{\iota}\varsigma$ $\dot{\alpha}\lambda\lambda\dot{\eta}\lambdaους$ $\kappa\alpha\dot{\iota}$ $\epsilon\dot{\iota}\varsigma$ $\pi\dot{\alpha}\nu\tau\alpha\varsigma$)' (3.12); later, in the concluding list of summary exhortations, they are told to 'repay no one evil for evil, but always strive to do good ($\tau\dot{o}$ $\dot{\alpha}\gamma\alpha\theta\dot{o}\nu$) to one another and to all ($\epsilon\dot{\iota}\varsigma$ $\dot{\alpha}\lambda\lambda\dot{\eta}\lambdaους$ $\kappa\alpha\dot{\iota}$ $\epsilon\dot{\iota}\varsigma$ $\pi\dot{\alpha}\nu\tau\alpha\varsigma$)' (5.15).[57] This latter verse presents an ethical exhortation to non-retaliation that clearly became an established and traditional element in early Christian paraenesis, as we will see in more detail in connection with Rom. 12.17 (below). It may be, as Furnish suggests (2002b: 110–11; cf. Holtz 1986: 256), that the parallels between these verses imply that 'the good' ($\tau\dot{o}$ $\dot{\alpha}\gamma\alpha\theta\dot{o}\nu$) is more or less equivalent to love ($\dot{\alpha}\gamma\dot{\alpha}\pi\eta$) – certainly this seems more likely than that 'the good' (at least here) refers specifically to civic benefactions on the part of the wealthy.[58] Thomas Söding also argues

---

56. E.g., in Phil. 2.3-4 the focus is on relations with 'one another' ($\dot{\alpha}\lambda\lambda\dot{\eta}\lambdaους$, v. 3), but the norm of looking 'not to your own [interests; cf. p. 210 n. 23 above] but to those of others' is stated in unspecific terms, as in 1 Cor. 10.24, where the connection with 10.32-33 suggests a wider circle of concern than solely the Christian $\dot{\alpha}\delta\epsilon\lambda\phioί$. In Rom. 15.1-2 the topic is relations among Christians, described as 'strong' and 'weak' (see §6.2 above), but the appeal for other-regard uses the term $\pi\lambda\eta\sigmaίον$ (neighbour) rather than $\dot{\alpha}\delta\epsilon\lambda\phiός$, or similar, echoing the earlier appeal for love of neighbour in 13.8-10 (cf. §8.2 n. 26 above). There too the focus is on the duty to love 'one another' ($\dot{\alpha}\lambda\lambda\dot{\eta}\lambdaους$, 13.8), but the statement that 'love does no wrong to the neighbour' (13.10), which picks up the word $\pi\lambda\eta\sigmaίον$ from Lev. 19.18, cited in the previous verse, again suggests, or at least allows, a wider sphere of applicability.

57. As well as the commentaries, see the recent discussion of these texts in Söding 1995: 67–100; Furnish 2002b: 109–11.

58. As argued by Winter (1994: 25–40) in relation to Rom. 13.3-4; and 1 Pet. 2.14-15, and also to 2 Thess. 3.13 (pp. 57–59). Cf. also Clarke 1993: 159–69, on Rom. 5.7. Neither Winter nor Clarke, it should be noted, makes this claim in relation to 1 Thess. 5.15 (this text is not in fact mentioned, though Clarke cites Gal. 6.10 as a further 'possible parallel' for the use of benefaction terminology; p. 168).

that what Paul has in mind in urging the Thessalonians to act 'properly (εὐσχημόνως) towards those outside' (4.12) is, in view of the content of 4.9-12 and 3.11-13, undoubtedly ἀγάπη (Söding 1995: 87). Whether or not Söding is right to argue that Paul envisages in 4.9–12 an 'overflowing' of love from within and among the community to those outside (1995: 84–90), he is certainly correct to conclude, in the light of 3.11–13, that the Thessalonian Christians' 'conduct in relation to non-Christians is to be defined by agape, even and precisely when they are slandered, despised, and discriminated against by them' (p. 90).[59] Questioning the universality of Paul's injunction, Furnish claims that 'there is nothing in the context [of 1 Thess. 3.12] to support the view, expressed by many commentators, that "all" refers to the whole of humankind'. Rather, he insists, 'the sense is more likely local than universal, namely "all" of those non-Christians with whom the Thessalonians are in daily and continuing contact' (2002b: 109). But this is an unnecessary and vacuous distinction. Quite obviously, the 'all' whom this instruction specifically has in view are those with whom the Thessalonians have contact – they are unlikely to have a chance to show love towards non-Christians in Alexandria, Rome or wherever! But the fact that a universally applicable ethical imperative is (necessarily) enacted in a local context, with its own specific pressures, does not negate its formulation and validity as a principle relevant to Christian interaction with 'all' humankind. Wherever any of the Thessalonians happened to be, or to travel, the same obligation would apply, in regard to whomever they met. Indeed, the similar formulations in other Pauline letters indicate that this is no 'local' injunction, appropriate only in view of the particular situation the Thessalonians face, but one which is to characterize Christian conduct everywhere and in relations with all people.

The fact that an injunction to do good to all people is necessarily enacted as opportunity arises, that is, in local contexts, is indeed acknowledged in the form of the exhortation in Gal. 6.10, where it forms the concluding exhortation in the final block of instructions (6.1-10) before the close of the letter (6.11-18). 'As we have time (καιρόν)', that is, 'opportunity',[60] Paul writes, 'let us do good (τὸ ἀγαθόν) to all (πρὸς πάντας), especially to those of the household of faith (πρὸς τοὺς οἰκείους τῆς πίστεως)'. Coming '[a]s the conclusion to the parenetical section', Betz

---

59. Cf. also Holtz 1986: 144. There seems little ground in the text for restricting the focus of 'all' to 'pagans who were present in the Christian assemblies' (so Malherbe 2000: 213; cf. pp. 312, 322). The 'all' (πάντας) in v. 14 may well refer to the three groups of Christians listed there, who need patient admonition from their fellow believers (cf. Furnish 2002b: 110 with n. 9). But the focus is clearly wider in v. 15, given the traditional paraenesis about non-retaliation, as well as the contrast repeated elsewhere between ἀλλήλους and πάντας.

60. For this meaning of ὡς καιρὸν ἔχομεν, see Betz 1979: 310 with n. 186; BDAG, 497 (1b), with references there.

notes, 'the statement sums up in a general way, and in the form of a final appeal, what the Apostle regards as the ethical task of the Christian community' (1979: 310). The instruction is similar in content to those found in 1 Thess. 3.12 and 5.15: the appeal to do good (or to love) applies especially to interaction within the Christian movement but also to relations with all people (cf. Mußner 1988: 407). The phrase 'to one another and to all' (1 Thess. 3.12; 5.15) is reversed and differently expressed in Gal. 6.10, in essence, 'to all and especially to one another'. The phrase 'those of the household of faith', however, as a general designation of Christians, perhaps implies a less locally focused perspective, compared with 'one another'. But the general obligation towards all people is the same. Betz stresses 'the universality of its application: the Christian is expected to do good to all mankind'. Or, as Mußner puts it, echoing Gal. 5.14, the neighbours, to whom the command for love of neighbour applies, are all people (*alle Menschen*) (1988: 407). Interestingly, Betz suggests a theological underpinning for this conviction: 'The universal character of God's redemption corresponds to the universality of Christian ethical and social responsibility' (1979: 311).[61]

Less closely parallel, but still comparable, is the injunction in the closing exhortations in Philippians, the letter in which Paul most closely echoes the language of Greek ethics (Phil. 4.8; see §5.5 above): 'let your gentleness be known by all people ($\pi\hat{\alpha}\sigma\iota\nu$ $\dot{\alpha}\nu\theta\rho\dot{\omega}\pi\sigma\iota\varsigma$)' (4.5). The quality of $\dot{\epsilon}\pi\iota\epsilon\iota\kappa\acute{\epsilon}\varsigma$[62] – gentleness, courtesy, forbearance, etc. (BDAG, 371) – is positively used in Jewish and Christian literature, describing the character of God (Ps. 85.5 [LXX]; Wis. 12.18; 2 Macc. 2.22; 10.4; *Odes* 7.42), Christ (2 Cor. 10.1), rulers (*3 Macc.* 3.15; 7.6), or righteous people (Wis. 2.19), and also in other Greek and Roman texts, where it can have the sense of 'fairness' (Thucydides 5.86).[63] Plutarch refers to a temple of Clemency ($\tau\grave{o}$ $\tau\hat{\eta}\varsigma$ $\dot{\epsilon}\pi\iota\epsilon\iota\kappa\epsilon\acute{\iota}\alpha\varsigma$ $\dot{\iota}\epsilon\rho\acute{o}\nu$) decreed as a thank-offering for (Julius) Caesar's gentleness ($\pi\rho\alpha\acute{o}\tau\eta\varsigma$, *Caesar* 57). This same 'gentle forbearance' (Fee 1995: 406) – 'making allowances despite facts that might suggest reason for a different reaction' (BDAG, 371); 'the opposite of an insistence on strict justice' (Bockmuehl 1998a: 245, citing Aristotle, *Nic. Eth.* 5.10 [see 1137a, 32–1138a, 3]) – is to characterize Christians' conduct. Paul means not merely, or even primarily, that outsiders should be able to *see* the 'gentleness' with which Christians treat one another, but rather that Christians should demonstrate this quality *towards all people*, that is, towards outsiders, even when others' treatment of them is not so

---

61. Betz's comments are echoed by Longenecker 1990: 283.

62. The neuter substantive $\tau\grave{o}$ $\dot{\epsilon}\pi\iota\epsilon\iota\kappa\acute{\epsilon}\varsigma$, used here, is equivalent to the noun $\dot{\eta}$ $\dot{\epsilon}\pi\iota\epsilon\acute{\iota}\kappa\epsilon\iota\alpha$.

63. For the sense 'clemency', see, e.g., Thucydides 3.40; 3.48, where the danger of being unduly swayed by such a consideration is highlighted.

courteous.[64] This 'making allowances', acting graciously and courteously, thus expresses in different terms the notion that Christians are to avoid retaliation and show love to all whom they encounter.

These themes are spelt out most fully in Rom. 12.14-21. A series of concise and loosely structured aphorisms begins in v. 9 with a focus on the need for love ($\dot{\alpha}\gamma\dot{\alpha}\pi\eta$), specifically the sibling-love ($\phi\iota\lambda\alpha\delta\epsilon\lambda\phi\dot{\iota}\alpha$) shown towards 'one another' ($\epsilon\dot{\iota}\varsigma\ \dot{\alpha}\lambda\lambda\dot{\eta}\lambda\text{ov}\varsigma$, v. 10), and continues with exhortations to cultivate the kinds of virtues necessary to sustain the solidarity, hope and spiritual vitality of the congregation (vv. 9-13). While the focus is thus initially on the character and qualities of relationships among 'insiders', it switches through vv. 14-17 to focus on relations with 'outsiders' (cf. Wilckens 1982: 22–23; Zerbe 1992: 186).[65] The theme which connects all the admonitions concerning relations with non-Christians is that of 'responding with positive good to all hostile acts', a theme 'repeated with variations no less than four times (vv 14, 17, 19, 21)' (Dunn 1988: 755). Verses 14 and 17 echo the teaching in the Sermon on the Mount/Plain concerning love of enemies, non-retaliation and responding to abuse with blessing: v. 14 exhibits notable parallels with Mt. 5.44 and Lk. 6.27-28, while v. 17 repeats the theme of non-retaliation, detailed in Mt. 5.38-48 and Lk. 6.27-36.[66] It is debated whether Paul here exhibits a *direct* dependence on Jesus' teaching[67] but it is certain that the specific instruction 'not to repay evil with evil' quickly became an established element in early Christian teaching: the tradition is reproduced, in similar form, in Rom. 12.17, 1 Thess. 5.15 and 1 Pet. 3.9 (see further Piper 1979: 4–18; 1980: 218–

---

64. The need for forbearance in the Christians' relations with one another may also be in view, given the internal disagreements Paul addresses in 4.2-3, but $\pi\tilde{\alpha}\sigma\iota\nu$ $\dot{\alpha}\nu\theta\rho\dot{\omega}\pi\sigma\iota\varsigma$ indicates a focus outwards, towards all people (cf. Bockmuehl 1998a: 244; Fee 1995: 406 with n. 27). On the theme of suffering in Philippians, and the evidence to suggest that the Philippian Christians were suffering because of their treatment by outsiders, see Oakes 2001: 77–102.

65. The first clear reference to relations with outsiders is in v. 14; the call to show hospitality (v. 13b) could conceivably extend beyond the Christian network, though its primary focus is probably on receiving travelling Christians (cf. Mt. 25.35; Mk 6.10-11; 9.41; Rom. 16.23; 1 Tim. 3.2; 5.10; Tit. 1.8; Heb. 13.2; 1 Pet. 4.9). The focus returns to relations among insiders ($\epsilon\dot{\iota}\varsigma\ \dot{\alpha}\lambda\lambda\dot{\eta}\lambda\text{ov}\varsigma$) in Rom. 12.16 (and probably also in v. 15), then shifts back to outsiders in vv. 17-21. Thus the transition from the topic of insider-relations to that of outsider-relations is effected through a 'chain-link' construction, on which see Longenecker forthcoming.

66. On Paul's 'ethic of non-retaliation and peace' in Rom. 12.14-21, see Zerbe 1992.

67. In favour of this conclusion, see, e.g., Dunn 1988: 745. For more cautious views, see, e.g., Söding 1995: 247; Walter 1989: 56; Wenham 1995: 250–52; Wilckens 1982: 22–23. Wilckens, for example, maintains that behind v. 14 'steht deutlich ein Jesuswort' which quickly found its way into the general exhortations of Christian paraenesis. 'Darum ist keineswegs sicher, ob sich Paulus hier bewußt war, ein *Herrenwort* zu zitieren.' Wenham suggests that Rom. 12.17 constitutes a probable echo of the Jesus-tradition.

23). In both 1 Thessalonians and Romans it is immediately linked with an exhortation to do good (τὸ ἀγαθόν/τὸ καλόν)[68] to all people. The formulation in Romans is especially significant, since it enables us to determine whether Paul means that Christians are to do what is 'good' – as defined in distinctively Christian terms – towards all; or whether he means that they should do (towards all) what is commonly recognized as 'good'. Clearly, each of these alternatives would imply a rather different assessment of the significance of the injunctions in relation to the liberal-communitarian debate (see §8.5 below). The injunctions to do good to all in 1 Thessalonians and Galatians, moreover, allow either possibility. But in Romans Paul specifies that his addressees are to 'take into consideration (προνοούμενοι) what is good ἐνώπιον πάντων ἀνθρώπων'. It has been argued that this should be understood to mean 'do what the gospel defines as good in front of all people' (cf. Cranfield 1979: 645–46),[69] or as if the genitive plural were here equivalent to the dative (Michel 1978: 390; Wilckens 1982: 24), thus implying 'do good to all people' (ihnen gegenüber, im Verhältnis zu ihnen).[70] But these suggestions are forced and unconvincing, especially in the light of parallel uses in Pauline and other biblical texts (see esp. Dunn 1988: 748). Proverbs 3.4, echoed here and in 2 Cor. 8.21, provides clear support for what Dunn rightly calls 'the most natural sense' in Rom. 12.17 – 'in the sight or opinion of all':

καὶ προνοοῦ καλὰ ἐνώπιον κυρίου καὶ ἀνθρώπων
and take thought for what is good in the Lord's sight and in the sight of people (Prov. 3.4, LXX)

προνοοῦμεν γὰρ καλὰ οὐ μόνον ἐνώπιον κυρίου ἀλλὰ καὶ ἐνώπιον ἀνθρώπων
for we take thought for what is good not only in the Lord's sight but also in the sight of people (2 Cor. 8.21; cf. also Polycarp, *Phil.* 6.1)

As Dunn notes, '[s]ince ἐνώπιον κυρίου clearly means "what God regards as noble," ἐνώπιον ἀνθρώπων can hardly be taken in a different sense'

---

68. τὸ καλόν (used in Rom. 12.17; also in 1 Thess. 5.21) is equivalent to τὸ ἀγαθόν (used in 1 Thess. 5.15; also in Rom. 12.9, 21), as is the case in Rom. 7.14-21, where both words are used with similar meaning (cf. Dunn 1988: 748). Cf. also Gal. 6.9 and 10; Mußner 1988: 406–407: 'τὸ ἀγαθόν = τὸ καλόν ... τὸ καλόν ist alles Gute im ethischen Sinn'.

69. Cranfield accepts that ἐνώπιον must mean 'in the sight of', but considers that Paul can 'hardly' mean 'that Christians are to take thought for those things which are agreed by all men to be good ... for Paul was well aware of the darkening of men's minds (cf. 1.21) and the need for the human mind to be renewed, if it is to recognize and approve the will of God (cf. 12.2)' (pp. 645–46). But this common sense of what is good seems precisely what Paul means; nor is this as unexpected as Cranfield implies, in view of other passages in Romans and elsewhere.

70. Wilckens 1982: 24. Wilckens concedes, however: 'Doch ist eine solche Bedeutung von ἐνώπιον sonst nicht bezeugt.'

(p. 748).[71] 2 Corinthians 4.2 also adds support to the conviction that what Paul has in mind in Rom. 12.17 is the view of the good which outsiders themselves hold, since there the purpose of truthful openness is to commend oneself not only to God but also to the awareness or (moral) consciousness of all people (πρὸς πᾶσαν συνείδησιν ἀνθρώπων).[72] Dunn thus rightly concludes that in Rom. 12.17, as elsewhere in Romans (see §8.1-2 above), 'Paul shows himself ready to appeal to a widespread sense of what is morally right and fitting' (p. 748).

The focus on relations with 'all people' is further emphasized in v. 18, where the same words (πάντων ἀνθρώπων) appear once more. The Christians in Rome are urged to live peaceably with all people, insofar as determining that is within their power. This requires the renunciation of vengeance, which should be left instead to God (12.19) or to the governing powers, acting on God's behalf (13.4).[73] Instead, an enemy's aggression is to be met with generosity and kindness – with deeds of love (*Liebeswerke*; Wilckens 1982: 26). The closing exhortation well summarizes the recurrent theme and moral imperative: not to be overcome by evil (τὸ κακόν), but to overcome evil with good (τὸ ἀγαθόν, v. 21). Given this theme, the most likely interpretation of the enigmatic statement that in giving one's enemy food and drink one will 'heap burning coals on their head' (v. 20; Prov. 25.21-22) is not that one will intensify their guilt and eventual punishment but rather that one's act may lead to their repentance and reconciliation (cf. 1 Pet. 2.12; 3.13-17).[74]

---

71. Cf. Fitzmyer 1993: 656–57; also Thrall 2000: 552, who sees 2 Cor. 8.21 as emphasizing 'the need for conduct to be seen as honourable by one's fellow men and women as well as by the Lord'. Furnish (1984: 424) notes that the emphasis lies on the second phrase in Paul's Greek – ἀλλὰ καὶ ἐνώπιον ἀνθρώπων.

72. See further Thrall 1994: 301–302, who gives good reasons why this phrase should not be read as a reference to 'the Christian consciences of the Corinthians' but rather 'to the consciences of people in general'. Paul therefore reflects the assumption 'that there is some general human capacity for recognising the gospel as the truth'.

73. On the parallels between these two verses, see §8.2 above and also n. 77 below.

74. For arguments in favour of this interpretation, see, e.g., Cranfield 1979: 648–50; Wilckens 1982: 26; Dunn 1988: 750–51; Furnish 1973: 107–108; and esp. Klassen 1963. Klassen draws on evidence concerning an Egyptian repentance ritual to illuminate the background to Prov. 25.21-22, and concludes: 'The coals of fire were evidence in the original ritual that repentance had taken place and for Paul they probably signified that the enemy had been made into a friend' (p. 349). According to Str-B (3: 302) the Targum of Prov. 25.21-22 ends 'und Gott wird ihn dir übergeben oder: wird ihn dir zum Freunde machen', adding support to the interpretation that sees the aim as reconciliation rather than revenge. It is also notable that Paul omits the final phrase of Prov. 25.22 ('and the Lord will reward you'), again suggesting that he is thinking not in terms of gaining (revenge? justice?) for oneself but of doing good for the sake of the other. For the interpretation in terms of eschatological judgment, see Piper 1979: 115–19.

8.5 *Conclusion*

A number of conclusions emerge from the material surveyed in this chapter: I present them here in a logical order, rather than in the order of the preceding sections from which they derive. First, we have seen the prominence of the theme, variously expressed, of acting with consideration for the reaction of outsiders, or (more positively) of seeking to do good to all people. Concern about the reaction of outsiders is important in order to avoid criticism of the Church and to win outsiders for the faith, or at least not to hinder their acceptance of it. The instruction to do good to all, however, is not presented with such apologetic or missionary motives, but rather as a positive Christian obligation. In this case, the way in which Christians are to act towards outsiders is an extension of the way they are to treat one another: with love, goodness and forbearance. Even when they suffer abuse from outsiders, they are to avoid retaliation. The sphere of moral responsibility is concisely conveyed in the almost formulaic phrase 'to one another and to all' (εἰς ἀλλήλους καὶ εἰς πάντας; see §8.4 above): the primary focus is on relations within the community, but it extends beyond, without limits. The occurrence of comparable injunctions to act with consideration towards 'all people' throughout Paul's letters – 1 Thessalonians (3.12; 5.15), Galatians (6.10), 1 Corinthians (10.32 [cf. 1.22]), Romans (12.17-18) and Philippians (4.5) – indicates that this moral responsibility is, in Paul's view, incumbent on all Christians, whatever their specific situation and whether or not they appear to be suffering from the abuse of outsiders.[75] Sensitivity to the contextual shaping and distinctive characteristics of each of Paul's letters should not lead us to ignore such pervasive convictions.

Secondly, it is apparent that the appeal to do good to all means specifically acting in a way which all will acknowledge and recognize as good. In other words, implicit – especially in 1 Thess. 4.12, Phil. 4.5 and (most clearly) Rom. 12.17 – is a conviction that there is common ground, *Gemeinsamkeit*, in the ethical values held by Christians and by all people, a shared sense of what is good and evil. This conviction as to a commonly shared and universally accessible sense of right and wrong also comes to expression in Romans 1–2. Knowledge of God (1.19-21) and of God's decree (1.32) is accessible to all, indeed, attained by all, since only then is their judgment legitimate. Gentiles as well as Jews have access to the discernment of good and evil conveyed in God's law (2.14-15). 'Worship God and love your neighbour' seems the best concise summary of the moral knowledge Paul presumes as universally shared.

75.　This would seem to be the case, e.g., for the Thessalonians and Philippians, but not for the Corinthians (see further Barclay 1992; Vos 1999).

Thirdly, beyond the sense that the knowledge of right and wrong is shared in common, Paul also indicates that non-Christians can and do act in accordance with these insights. Their knowledge is not merely a basis for their condemnation. The possibility of right action in accordance with God's standards of good and evil, even among Gentiles, is implied in Rom. 2.14-15 and is (strikingly) presumed in Rom. 13.1-4. There Paul depicts as a matter of fact that ruling authorities share God's perception of what is good and what is evil, and can therefore praise the former and punish the latter, acting thereby as God's agents. The corollary of this is that the duty to be subject to such authorities is presented as a universal human obligation.

Notable by its absence is explicit christological motivation for these responsibilities towards outsiders and ruling authorities. The injunctions to take care about outsiders' reactions, and to do them good, are generally conveyed concisely without explicit justification and motivation, though christological and theological motivations could readily be adduced: Christ's refusal to return violence with violence (cf. 1 Pet. 2.19-24), his self-giving for the sake of others (cf. chs 6–7 above), his universal lordship (Rom. 10.12; Phil. 2.10-11), etc. In the case of Rom. 13.1-7, however, the lack of explicitly christological reasoning may well reflect Paul's sensitivity to the fact that he is constructing an argument with universal validity.

In terms of the significance of these conclusions when we read Paul's ethics in the context of the liberal-communitarian debate, a number of points may be made. First, Paul's presentation of the Christian's duty to do good to all, to act peaceably even when faced with violence and abuse, is clearly congruent with a Hauerwasian perspective: Christians are called to be the Church, which means to be a peaceable, non-violent people in the midst of a world of violence (see §2.3 above). Nonetheless, the ecclesial focus which dominates Hauerwas's ethics may be suspected of turning attention away from the expressions of concern for all people which we have seen to pervade Paul's letters (if, admittedly, in concise form). As we have already seen (§2.4), the focus on the Church as a 'political alternative', 'an alternative politics' (Hauerwas 1999: 35, 6) means that attention is not directed towards the possibilities for discerning shared values and common moral ground in the public political sphere; it is 'theological politics', not 'political theology' (cf. §2.3 above, p. 68).[76] Hays's study (1997a), for example, in many ways congruent with and influenced by a Hauerwasian

---

76. For example, Hauerwas's comment that 'a worldwide network of local churches … is the vision of peace … it would be unthinkable for people in such a network to kill one another for any loyalties that are not determined by the network itself' (Hauerwas 2000: 332), while it hopefully conceives of the Christian church as a bulwark against war between nation-states, leaves unmentioned the issues concerning the tensions between those who are and are not a part of this Christian network.

approach to ethics (cf. §1.6; §2.3 above), interprets Paul's ethics (and the ethics of the New Testament generally) as focused more or less entirely on the community of faith – though we should reiterate that this neglect of the theme of 'ethics and outsiders' characterizes many studies of Pauline ethics (cf. p. 246 n. 2 above). The focal images of community, cross and new creation consolidate this ecclesial-community focus, leaving little room for creation and world as positive spheres of influence and concern in Pauline ethics (cf. Gundry-Volf 1999; Cranfield 1998; further below).

Hauerwas's ecclesial ethics shares with communitarianism generally the conviction that moral values are generated by specific traditions and embodied in particular communities, and thus highlights the distinctiveness of Christian ethics. This correlates with a sharp distinction between Church and world; the former is (or should be) a community formed by the practices engendered by its own narrative and displaying a character which sets it starkly apart from the world. Similarly, for Hays, the Church is fundamentally 'a counter-cultural community of discipleship' (1997a: 196). Criticism of an apparent 'sectarianism' here may or may not be entirely on target (see §2.4 above). But what seems clear is that what Fergusson refers to as Hauerwas's 'over-concentration on the distinctiveness of the church' (Fergusson 1997b: 244; cf. 1998: 67) leads to a focus on how Christians are to live *as Church* and a neglect of the ways in which they are to live as citizens of their societies, specifically as members who share moral 'common ground' with others in their society.

Indicative of this problem is the absence, noted by Charles Cranfield, from Hays's (lengthy) treatment of New Testament ethics of any 'serious exegesis of those New Testament passages which seem to indicate that the Christian has an obligation to the civil authority' – most notably Rom. 13.1-7 (Cranfield 1998: 169).[77] More broadly, in Hays's appropriation of New Testament ethics, the Christian is conceived as having responsibilities as a member of the (counter-cultural) ecclesial community and not as a member of a broader society, in which they might participate precisely as citizens who share with others a sense of the good and certain social obligations.

Indeed, more significant in terms of raising questions about the ecclesial ethics of Hauerwas (and Hays) are the indications that Paul not only urges Christians to do good to all people but also considers that a sense of what

77. In mounting an argument for Christian pacifism, for example, Hays (1997a: 317–46) highlights Rom. 12.14-21, but passes swiftly over Rom. 13.4, noting only that while 'the governing authority bears the sword to execute God's wrath (13:4) that is not the role of believers' (p. 331). In this, like other prominent proponents of Christian pacifism, Yoder and Hauerwas, Hays presumes that Christians act as members of the Church but cannot legitimately act as members or representatives of governments or states. Cf. Yoder 1972: 205, cited above, n. 37. On this subject, see further Horrell 2003.

is good and evil constitutes 'common ground' shared by all people. It is not merely that Christians are called to do good towards all people – this much can certainly be affirmed from a Hauerwasian perspective – but rather that what Christians should do is, to a considerable degree, recognized as good by all people (Rom. 12.17). The evidence surveyed in this chapter suggests that the existence of common ground in ethics is not merely something that historical criticism can unearth, working against the flow of Paul's rhetoric (cf. §5.5-5.6 above), but something Paul explicitly acknowledges and uses as an essential starting point for an argument about the validity of the gospel (Rom. 2.13-16). This would seem to suggest that the liberal goal of achieving at least an 'overlapping consensus' (Rawls 2001: 32–38) on ethical norms is not to be dismissed as merely a post-Enlightenment illusion.

In terms of a specific comparison between Paul and Habermas, there are – of course – profound differences, but also notable points of convergence. Habermas proposes a procedural ethic as a means to test, through rational discourse and argumentation, the general validity of ethical norms, themselves deriving from various traditions and ways of life. It is a posttraditional, postmetaphysical, rational morality (*Vernunftmoral*), based on the univeral presuppositions of human communication, that has the potential to sustain a moral consensus (see §2.2 above). For Paul, the knowledge and acknowledgment of God is the foundational point for human morality; and the universally accessible recognition of good and evil, defined and measured by God's law, is given by God. Yet the knowledge of God's law is confirmed and affirmed by the moral consciousness (συνείδησις) and rational reflections (λογισμοί) of human beings (Rom. 2.15; cf. 1.20); thus Paul reflects the conviction that human consciousness and rationality are sufficiently universal and competent to affirm universal moral standards. Furthermore, he urges his Christian addressees to 'test' or 'prove' what is good and what corresponds to the will of God (Rom. 12.2; Gal. 6.4; Phil. 1.10; 1 Thess. 5.21).[78] This they can do because their minds are renewed and enlivened by the Spirit, but this does not equate with a corresponding assumption on Paul's part that non-Christians are entirely unable to discern the good (Rom. 2.15, 18; 12.17, etc.).[79]

Once again, while seeing how Pauline ethics coheres in key respects with an ecclesial-communitarian approach, we can also discern important ways in which there are resonances with liberal concerns and convictions.

---

78. These references to testing what is good form important evidence for Theissen's proposal that Paul's ethics represent a synthesis of a biblical 'Gebotsethik' and a Greek 'Einsichtsethik'; see Theissen 2003c.

79. *Pace* Cranfield 1979: 645–46 (quoted in n. 69 above), who allows this assumption to determine his reading of Rom. 12.17.

Moreover, it seems, reading Paul from an ecclesial perspective, as in Hays's important treatment, tends to engender a neglect of two themes on which we have focused in this chapter: first, the widespread injunctions to do good *to* all people; second, the acknowledgment that a sense of what *is* good is shared in common.

Chapter 9

SOLIDARITY AND DIFFERENCE: PAUL AMONG LIBERALS AND COMMUNITARIANS

It remains to draw together the conclusions of this study, as they relate to its key aims: to investigate (exegetically) the shape and content of Paul's ethics; to undertake this exegetical inquiry in the light of contemporary approaches to (political) ethics, particularly as represented in the liberal-communitarian debate; and (thus) to consider how a contemporary appropriation of Pauline ethics might proceed. Without pretending that these aims are, or even could be, distinctly separated,[1] I shall present conclusions relating to each of the three aspects in turn. These summary conclusions cannot, of course, repeat the more substantial reflections which appear before, especially in the concluding section of each chapter; nor do they follow the plan of the book by way of resumé. Instead, they present a series of theses, conclusions and proposals which follow from the preceding discussions.

9.1 *The Shape of Pauline Ethics: Seven Theses*

First, I offer some conclusions about the shape of Pauline ethics, as these follow from the exegetical studies undertaken, of course, in the light of the particular questions and agenda to which this study is directed. I present these not as a summary of the sequence of the preceding exegetical chapters but in the form of seven theses, each of which is briefly explained and justified.

---

1. Hence the exegetical studies in chs 4–8 were *preceded* by chs 1–3, such that the exegesis is seen to be shaped by the questions arising from the perspective chosen and the context of contemporary debate. This avoids giving the impression, as, e.g., in Hays 1997a, that the first task is to 'listen' to the text(s) and (only) then to outline an approach to interpretation (cf. the critical comments of Martin 1998a; §1.6 above).

9.1.1 *The 'metanorms' of Paul's ethics are most concisely described as the imperatives of corporate solidarity and other-regard.*

These two imperatives emerge as the fundamental and obligatory norms of Pauline ethics. 'Corporate solidarity', with impulses towards egalitarianism (see ch. 4; §7.4), and set in the context of a sense of distinction between community and world (see ch. 5), has been too much overlooked as a basic foundation for Paul's ethics; even studies which stress their communal focus have seldom given due attention to the ways in which Paul attempts to foster and restore this solidarity. 'Other-regard' holds together a number of values often recognized as key in Pauline ethics, namely, love, love of neighbour, social humility, renunciation of status, etc. and provides a general label which encapsulates what Paul denotes as the essential content of this imperative (see §7.5). In both cases, these moral imperatives are grounded in Paul's theology, and especially his Christology (see below). Solidarity and other-regard are metanorms (cf. Benhabib 1992: 45) in the sense that they determine the moral framework for the community, setting the parameters within which other ethical convictions can be articulated and practised (see below). In view of the aim to bring Pauline ethics into conversation with other (contemporary) approaches to ethics, and the questions and issues raised by Boyarin's study (see §1.7), these metanorms are denoted here (and throughout this study) in terms which reflect their moral content rather than the specific language of Paul's mythic discourse;[2] thus they are made more widely meaningful and comparable.

9.1.2 *Corporate solidarity does not imply the erasure of difference: Paul is concerned to sustain diversity within the ecclesial community, including differences of ethical convictions and cultural practices, though only insofar as these fall within the limits of tolerable diversity determined in part by the obligatory metanorms.*

The imperative of solidarity does not equate with sameness, nor imply the erasure of difference; corporate solidarity is explicitly the solidarity of a diversely membered body (§4.4). Indeed, Paul invests significant argumentative energy, in his most lengthy ethical discourses, in attempts not to

---

2. This contrasts, e.g., with two of Hays's focal images, 'cross' and 'new creation', which reflect the specific content of Pauline theology (see Hays 1997a; §1.6 above). Cf. also §1.1, p. 15 with n. 26.

rule on the substantive issue of dispute but to articulate a moral framework which allows differences of ethical conviction and practice to remain, within certain limits. Within these limits, it is the moral consciousness (1 Corinthians) or faith (Romans) of the believer that determines whether an act is legitimate for them (cf. §6.3.1). The basic imperatives of solidarity and other-regard in part determine whether and when such diversity is allowed: different convictions regarding food are acceptable (Rom. 14.1–15.13) unless their practice destroys the solidarity of the community in Christ (Galatians 2); regard for the other (and the potential damage to their moral consciousness) can require the restriction of one's own freedom to act, no matter how legitimate that action might otherwise be (1 Cor. 8.1–11.1). In these cases, notably regarding food, Paul presses for conformity not to specific rules of ethical practice (eating, not eating, etc.) but to the metanorm of other-regard. This can be seen as a form of 'sameness' – not unlike the 'sameness' required by liberalism – only in the sense that conformity to this norm is required to sustain a 'tolerance' towards the difference of the other (see §6.3.4-6.4). The limits of tolerable diversity are also shaped by Paul's conviction that union with Christ (the basis for solidarity) is the crucial basis for distinguishing Christian identity (see ch. 5). Thus, actions which are deemed to threaten or destroy this union, notably in the realm of idolatry or sexual immorality, are proscribed. In these cases, however, the substantive ethical convictions themselves are not derived from the Christian myth itself, but rather from Judaism and other contemporary moral traditions (see §5.5, further §9.1.7).

9.1.3 *Within the context of corporate solidarity, other-regard is the moral imperative that enables the other to remain different, even in relation to ethical convictions. Yet this also implies the relativization of these different identities and ethical stances, insofar as they are regarded as different possibilities encompassed within a wider basis for solidarity and identity, where certain moral obligations are incumbent upon all.*

Solidarity is sustained not through a drive towards sameness and erasure of difference, but through the practice of a generous other-regard: it is this Paul presents as morally imperative – a certain kind of 'conformity' (cf. above) – rather than that Christians adopt the same stance towards all ethical issues. It is indeed this other-regard which requires that believers cease to judge or condemn the other, for holding an ethical stance they regard as inadequate or sinful, and instead adopt a stance of tolerance and acceptance (see §6.3.3-6.3.4). Paul's appeals for imitation are appeals for an imitation precisely of the self-lowering other-regard which sustains rather than erases this diversity (§7.5). To this extent, diversity and difference are sustained and protected. Moreover, Paul does not – *pace* Boyarin – reduce these ethical and cultural differences to mere 'matters of taste' (cf. §1.7; §6.3.4); they cannot be simply adopted or dropped at will, but are obligatory, or potentially sinful, depending on the stance determined by one's moral consciousness or faith. Nonetheless, Boyarin and Barclay are right to insist that Paul relativizes these different stances by presenting them as equally valid possibilities (for the one whose faith or conscience allows) for members of a community whose identity and moral obligations are determined by a common basis for communal solidarity and belonging: being in Christ (see §6.3.3-6.3.4). Following Jewish food laws becomes a matter which some do and some do not, thus requiring the practice of tolerance; while demonstrating solidarity in Christ – not least through sharing the Christian meal! – and a Christ-like other-regard are nonnegotiable obligations. It is the convictions and associated practices expressive of union with Christ that are determinative in terms of group identity and community-boundaries, such that other cultural/ethical practices no longer have this identity-defining significance (see §5.3).

9.1.4 *The solidarity of the Christian community is depicted as that of a pure and holy community, standing in sharp distinction from the world. Yet the rhetoric of distinction is counterbalanced by the indications that ethical values are to a considerable extent shared in common and that social interaction remains in various respects open.*

A frequent theme in Paul's letters, and specifically in his ethics, is that of the distinction between the holy community and the wicked world (see ch. 5). The positive designations of the community acquire their profile by contrast with the negative designations applied to outsiders, thus illustrating Henri Tajfel's argument that positive group identity is always constructed through *comparison* (see §5.2). While this might seem to imply that the Christian community has a distinctive ethic, its own set of norms and values, this is not entirely the case (cf. §5.5; ch. 8). Rather, the rhetoric of distinction often presumes a shared set of ethical values and builds a sense of positive group identity on the notion that 'we' live up to the (most rigorous) ethical standards, while 'they' fail to do so. This precariously empirical claim – we are more moral than they are – threatens to be falsified by the brute facts of reality, as in 1 Corinthians 5, though Paul seeks to redeem it by redefining the sinner as an outsider and not a Christian (§5.3).

The strong sense of distinction from the world does not, however, correlate with a stance of social isolation. Rather, as Frederik Barth's work suggests, group boundaries and distinct identity are maintained through specific and salient areas of cultural/ethical practice. In Paul's case, these have to do with expressions of union with Christ, with correlative proscriptions against what are deemed to represent competing unions. In other respects, open social interaction is allowed and encouraged (§5.4).

9.1.5 *Although Paul's ethics are focused on the ecclesial community, there are explicit indications that he sees a common knowledge of good and evil as accessible to, and attained by, humanity in general. He also exhorts Christians to do 'good' to all, by which he means that which all will recognize and affirm as good.*

While historical criticism can help to uncover the extent to which ethical values are shared, beneath the rhetoric of distinction Paul uses – as, for example, in the catalogues of vice and virtue (§5.5) – there are also places where Paul himself makes explicit appeal to common standards of good and evil. The conviction that standards of good and evil are universally known is a crucial basis for Paul's negative indictment of all humankind in Romans 1–3 (§8.1). Even if Paul's purpose is to show that none has lived up to these standards, the fact that they are depicted as commonly agreed is of significance in questioning the notion that Paul conceives of 'Christian' ethics as having a distinct content, incommensurable with other systems and standards. Indeed, in Romans 13 (§8.2) he strikingly presumes that the (non-Christian!) ruling authorities recognize good and evil and react accordingly, indicating again a sense of coherence between Christian and wider societal ethical standards. Moreover, in exhorting Christians to do good to all – a recurrent theme in his letters too seldom discussed in studies of Paul's ethics – Paul not only appeals for a practice of peaceable, nonretaliatory gentleness, even in response to hostility and aggression, but also indicates once again that what Christians do as 'good' will be recognized as such by all people, which is to say that some 'moral consensus' concerning the good is presumed to exist (§8.4).

9.1.6 *Paul's ethics are thoroughly grounded in the myth which constitutes Paul's 'theology', the story which establishes the world-view and the ethos he promotes. His reflective moral arguments also depend upon this theology for their content and motivations. Christology is especially important in giving shape and substance to Paul's ethics.*

The indications that Paul presumes a commonly shared sense of good and evil do not, however, undermine the thesis, long recognized in New Testament studies, that Paul's ethical exhortation is thoroughly grounded in his theology (cf. §1.1). Indeed, Paul's arguments for universal knowledge of ethical standards are derived from the myth which conveys the story of God's dealings with humankind: knowing God but refusing to acknowledge and worship God represents the origin of human sin (Rom. 1.18-32); the knowledge of good and evil is written in human hearts by God's agency (Rom. 2.15), and so on. More fundamentally still, while his convictions as to the substantive content of the good may be considerably shared with his contemporaries, Paul's exhortations, arguments and appeals are all formulated on the basis of the story which constitutes his theology. It is God's saving action in Christ, and the participation of believers in those events, that gives content and shape to ethical appeals, which are, in effect, appeals to act in ways congruent with this myth – imitating Christ's self-giving and God's gracious welcome, dying to sin and living anew in the Spirit, and so on.

I have not, however, unlike many studies of Pauline ethics, given space to outlining specifically how eschatology, the Spirit, and so on, function as motivating bases for ethical exhortation. This is in part because these represent aspects of the mythology rather than the ethics themselves; thus they convey motivations for acting ethically rather than indications as to what *constitutes* ethical action. In other words, to stress (with Paul) that ethical living is enabled by the Spirit's power and motivated by the coming End conveys nothing about the kind of conduct that ought actually to result but only indicates that one ought (and ought to be able) to conduct oneself in a correct manner, whatever that may be.[3] It is also in part

3. Barclay (2001b: 155), for example, writes that 'Paul's strategy of moral formation depends greatly on the work of the Spirit, whose effect is not only to inspire and energize but also to bring about a "transformation" of the believer (2 Cor 3:18) ... Paul's prime educational aid is the guidance and instruction of the Spirit'. This may well be how Paul sees it, with his world-view formed by his particular mythological convictions. But to study Paul's *ethics* requires a study of the substantive ways in which human conduct is shaped and directed, and in this regard it is not clear that 'the Spirit' implies any specific pattern of action, or determines in what 'transformation' shall consist.

because in attempting to engage Pauline ethics in a conversation with other approaches to ethics I have sought to express the exhortations of these ethics in terms that are meaningful outside the bounds of theological discourse.

In this respect, however, Paul's Christology stands out, since it does contribute not only to the motivational structure of Pauline ethics but also to their substantive shape.[4] Paul draws on the whole range of ideas in his mythological story in order to argue and exhort, but Christology is especially prominent, not least in terms of determining the metanorms of Pauline ethics. The notion of incorporation into Christ, specifically into his 'body', provides the basis for a conception of solidarity in which diverse groups are united as one (§4.1). And being 'one in Christ' provides a key reason why this solidarity must be sustained in the face of division and discord (§4.3). In the self-giving death of Christ Paul finds the determinative paradigm of other-regard; conformity to this paradigm, which is conformity to Christ, is fundamental to Christian identity and practice (see esp. ch. 7). Thus the two metanorms of solidarity and other-regard derive substantially from Paul's Christology.

9.1.7 *While Paul's theology and especially Christology shape the substance of his ethics at the level of metanorms, provide the basis for moral argument and motivation, and determine the ways in which distinctive identity is conceived and practised, they cannot explain why Paul holds certain specific ethical convictions, for example, concerning what constitutes sexual immorality. These reflect substantive convictions shared with, and derived from, his contemporary world, especially Judaism.*

The metanorms, and the exhortative and motivational shape, of Pauline ethics are thus determined by Paul's theology and especially his Christology. Union with Christ, for example, provides the ideological basis for distinctive identity and group-definition, and provides a reason why, for example, union with a πόρνη, or with δαιμόνια, is to be shunned (cf. §5.3; §9.1.4). But these christological convictions cannot actually explain *why* Paul regards union with a πόρνη as destructive of union with Christ, while union with a marital partner (even an unbelieving one) is not. This distinction can only reflect a *presumption* on Paul's part that a marital union is ethically acceptable while union with a πόρνη is not. This

---

4. The centrality of Christology to Pauline ethics is noted, e.g., by Schrage 1988: 181 ('christology is for Paul the fundamental ethical principle') and by Hays 1997a: 46 ('the fundamental norm of Pauline ethics is the christomorphic life').

presumption, along with others evident in Paul's ethics, derives especially from Paul's Judaism, where the strictures against idolatry and sexual immorality are prominent, though it also exhibits points of similarity with ethical convictions expressed by Graeco-Roman moral philosophers (see §5.5). Exploring the extent of these parallels has not been an aim of this study, and this final thesis is therefore especially dependent on the work of others. Nonetheless, despite the diverse viewpoints in scholarship on the subject (see §1.2-3) and disagreements as to the extent of distinctiveness in Pauline ethics, it can be stated in a form which would command very wide assent: while the motivational stucture of Paul's ethics draws on distinctively Christian convictions, their substantive content overlaps considerably with other contemporary traditions. This conclusion, combined with others already stated, is significant when it comes to considering how Paul's ethics might enable us to think about the liberal-commuitarian debate and how they might be appropriated today.

9.2 *Paul among Liberals and Communitarians*

The next task, then, is to set our study of Pauline ethics explicitly alongside the liberal-communitarian debate and specifically the contrasting approaches of Habermas and Hauerwas, as outlined in ch. 2 above. Again, I present a number of concise conclusions, each of which is then briefly discussed.

9.2.1 *Paul's ethics exhibit a fundamental congruence with Hauerwas's ecclesial ethics and (thus) share basic characteristics of the communitarian approach.*

Paul's ethics, not least in relation to their most basic goals of building ecclesial solidarity and fostering other-regard, are founded upon the story of God's saving deeds in Christ, especially Christ's self-giving death. The ethos of the community is shaped, for example, through the participation of its members in rituals which embody the central Christian myth or story (§4.1), and the value of other-regard is inculcated through appeal to the example of Christ (ch. 7). Christian character and virtue are developed through a process of conformity to Christ, whose paradigmatic self-giving for others is commemorated in worship and ritual, and through imitation of Paul and his co-workers, in whom the christomorphic pattern can also be seen. Just as Hauerwas's ecclesial ethics is narrative dependent, and focused on the formation of the character of the Church, so too is Paul's. Thus Paul, like Hauerwas, exemplifies a communitarian-type ethic, in which moral identity is formed within a tradition-constituted community, and through its character-forming practices.

This conclusion, however, though it needs to be stated as a fundamental outcome of the comparison, is unsurprising and (therefore) relatively unilluminating. More significant, given this congruence, are the following additional conclusions, in which this congruence is qualified and problematized in various ways.

9.2.2 Notwithstanding the basic similarity of approach, there are various respects in which Paul's way of doing ethics raises critical questions about the convictions and priorities of Hauerwas's ecclesial ethics, not least concerning its polemic against liberalism.

In the passages where Paul most fully constructs a moral argument, 1 Corinthians 8–10 and Romans 14–15 (ch. 6 above), it is notable that his concern is not to resolve the substantive ethical issue under dispute, but rather, through inculcating a stance of other-regard in a context of communal solidarity, to construct a moral framework within which a degree of diversity and difference can remain. This includes, as is especially clear in Romans 14–15, differences of ethical conviction and cultural practice, which are rendered valid (and, indeed, obligatory) for an individual depending on their particular stance of 'faith' (Romans) or 'conscience' (1 Corinthians). Thus Paul's argumentative energies in the sphere of ethics are to a considerable extent directed precisely towards sustaining a diversity of conviction and practice within the Church, which contrasts somewhat with the substantive priorities of Hauerwas's ethics, as feminist critics of Hauerwas have pointed out (cf. §2.4, pp. 77–79).

Paul's 'rhetoric of distinction' (see ch. 5 above), with its depiction of the Church as a pure and holy community in the midst of a wicked world, exhibits clear resonances with Hauerwas's tendency to draw stark distinctions between Church and world, to polarize Christian and 'secular' arguments, thus strengthening a sense of incommensurability between the two realms of discourse and specifically between Christianity and modern liberalism. Yet we have also seen in Paul tendencies which run counter to this rhetoric of distinction. Not only is it clear that, frequently, beneath the appeals for distinctiveness lie shared ethical convictions which, in themselves, are not specifically tradition or narrative dependent (see, e.g., 1 Cor. 5.1; §5.5) but Paul himself explicitly argues on the basis of a universal sense of right and wrong, accessible to all humankind (§8.1-2). Moreover, in urging Christians to do good to all people, Paul also makes clear that Christians share with others convictions as to what constitutes 'goodness' (Rom. 12.17; §8.4). Thus, notwithstanding their ecclesial focus, there is also a good deal in Pauline ethics which points towards the possibility, and the desirability, of finding 'common cause' with outsiders and discerning shared areas of 'moral consensus' (Fergusson 1998: 73, 75; §2.4, p. 76). And, of course, this goal – the establishing of moral consensus among groups and individuals who nonetheless retain their own tradition-specific identities, views of the good and so on – is a key concern for liberalism in general and Habermas in particular.

9.2.3 *There are clear and basic differences between Paul's ethics and the liberal approach represented by Habermas's discourse ethics, but there are also notable and significant structural and substantive similarities.*

Just as there is an obvious and unsurprising congruence between Paul's and Hauerwas's approach to ethics, so too at one level the differences between Pauline ethics and discourse ethics are clear and fundamental. Paul's ethics find their rationale, their motivation, and at least some of their substance, in the specific 'metaphysical' myth of God's saving act in Christ, while Habermas's discourse ethics is based on what are argued to be the universal pragmatic presuppositions of human communication and as such is argued to provide a rational procedure for testing the validity of ethical norms in a society where traditional and metaphysical justifications no longer carry authority (see §2.2). Despite Paul's occasional references to 'testing' God's will and his indications that human rationality is able to discern the good that God's law conveys, the extent of any overlap in terms of a *Vernunftmoral* (rational morality) is strictly limited (cf. §8.5).

Nonetheless, there are areas of similarity to be considered. One such area concerns the focus on 'consensus' which is, for Habermas, the goal of rational discourse concerning ethical norms and is also evident in Paul's repeated appeals for unity and harmony, for the kind of communal unity in which all will 'think the same' (see §4.3). Just as for Habermas (and Benhabib and others) this consensus does not imply sameness, so too for Paul 'thinking the same' does not imply the erasure of difference, but rather, as in liberalism, the kind of consensus within which ('tolerable') differences can be valued and sustained. More specifically, the 'moral intuitions' that discourse ethics sees as implied in the pragmatic presuppositions of communicative action, and around which, according to Habermas, every morality revolves, are closely paralleled in Paul's basic concern to foster solidarity and other-regard (cf. §2.2, pp. 60–61). Habermas expresses these values as 'equality of respect, solidarity, and the common good' (Habermas 1990: 201). Benhabib's 'universal moral respect' and 'egalitarian reciprocity' are comparable (1992: 29). So too are the Pauline principles of solidarity and other-regard, though these are focused within the ecclesial community rather than in society as a whole. A more Pauline description of these basic moral values might be: a sense of corporate belonging where each person has equal regard and respect, and where there is a constant and generous regard for the other (cf. chs 4, 7).

Also comparable is the concern to sustain diversity and difference within certain absolute limits, or, to put it somewhat pithily, tolerance within a framework of intolerance (see ch. 6). While Paul is perhaps too well known for his absolute limits and negative prohibitions, it is less often made explicit that political liberalism, for all its emphasis on plurality, tolerance and diversity, also depends on the acceptance of certain metamoral values as fundamental and absolute. Paul's moral argument in Romans 14–15 in particular exhibits a structural similarity with liberal morality. In Paul's case, the 'tolerant' stance with regard to food depends on a non-negotiable demand for a solidarity and other-regard rooted in Christ, and on accepting that divergent cultural practices are relativized insofar as they become different possibilities beneath a wider canopy of identity and belonging (cf. §6.3; §9.1.3). Habermas's conviction that valid norms are only such if they result from the uncoerced and equal participation of all may or may not reflect presuppositions inherent in the nature of human communication, but what is clear, as Benhabib has candidly shown, is that these (moral) principles override those of specific ways of life, when and if there is a clash between the two (see §2.2, pp. 61–62). In other words, they provide the 'intolerant' or inflexible framework within which diverse ethical convictions can be practised and held.

That there are these structural and substantive similarities between Pauline and liberal moralities is not entirely surprising. Both Hauerwas and Habermas, among many others, acknowledge that the moral values of modern liberalism are, to at least some extent, products of the Judaeo-Christian tradition. Tracing the *Wirkungsgeschichte* of specifically Pauline ideas in this regard would require another kind of study; here the important point is to note that Hauerwas's ecclesial ethics, with its strident polemic against liberalism, fails to do justice to these similarities (as too does Harink 2003; cf. pp. ix–x above). This is not, let me hasten to stress, to claim that political liberalism somehow represents a particularly 'Christian' form of social organization, such that the Church's political duty might be regarded as supporting that system and its (forceful) promulgation around the world, a claim that Hauerwas, among others, has powerfully criticized. Indeed, as we have seen (§6.4), another area of structural similarity would seem to be that liberalism relativizes the status of Christianity just as Paul relativized the status of Judaism for Jewish Christians: both forms of ethics are thus, for different groups of people, problematic (cf. §9.3.3 below). The point here is simply to insist that the distinction between the values and practices of Christianity (as seen in

Paul) and liberalism cannot be drawn as sharply as some forms of ecclesial ethics imply.[5]

9.2.4 *Notwithstanding the similarities between Pauline and liberal ethics, Paul's approach to ethics supports certain criticisms of the liberal project emanating from the communitarian perspective.*

Insofar as Paul's ethics exemplify a communitarian-type ethic, they support certain communitarian, and specifically Hauerwasian, convictions and thus reinforce certain questions raised about the liberal project and specifically about Habermas's hopeful vision of the way in which reasoned argument can lead to moral consensus. Positively, Paul's ethics exemplify the notion that moral virtue is formed and motivated through participation in a story-formed community: through their ritual appropriation of the Christian myth, members of the Christian assemblies forge a corporate identity 'in Christ', where, for example, Christ's humility and self-giving become a paradigm to which they are to conform (e.g. Phil. 2.4-11). This is much more than a (mere) ethical example which they are urged to follow; rather it expresses the story which determines their identity and character and thus shapes their moral priorities (cf. §7.1). Negatively, Paul's ethics thus reinforces the questions about liberalism's ability to foster moral character (cf. §2.4, pp. 72–73 above). How does liberalism inspire people to

---

5.   In his discussion of abortion, for example, Hays (1997a) suggests that the Church might form a 'countercommunity of *witness* ... through its active assumption of responsibility for the needy and its willingness to receive women and children who otherwise would become the victims of the regnant cultural systems' (pp. 458–59). Cf. Hauerwas 1981: 208–209, further 196–229, whom Hays cites in his treatment of this topic. For Hauerwas, the Christian community recognizes a 'duty ... to accept and welcome a child into the world ... as a gift' (p. 227), whereas '[f]rom the world's perspective the birth of a child represents but another drain on our material and psychological resources'. I do not wish to deny the 'political' importance of the Christian story in forming and training people who sense a positive and communal obligation to welcome children with joy – as Hauerwas shows, this is a more fundamental Christian contribution to the debate than endlessly arguing about when 'life' begins – especially in view of the consumerist-individualist ideology which tends to inculcate the view that having children is a matter of an individual's choice to acquire, or not. But what Hays's appeal ignores is the extent to which the welfare support systems of many 'liberal' states – and I speak primarily from knowledge of the UK context – already embody and practise, often in partnership with Church-based and other charitable organizations, precisely that for which he calls as a countercultural act: the willingness to undertake responsibility for the care of children, either through supporting them in living with their (often vulnerable) parent(s), or in providing alternative care. Naturally one can criticize the ways in which these support systems operate in practice, but to deny that they (and those who work in them) represent an attempt to do what Hays commends is an instance where – to echo my own analysis of Paul – the rhetoric of distinction obscures shared values and commitments.

demonstrate other-regard? Does liberalism depend on the various traditions encompassed within its sphere of belonging to generate substantive ethical convictions and, indeed, to foster people of moral character? If so, and in the light of the parallel moves Paul seems to make (notably in Romans 14–15), we may perhaps affirm Hauerwas's argument that it effectively undermines these traditions by relativizing them as simply various acceptable options (cf. §6.4). Alternatively it may be suggested that despite the apparent aim to provide (merely) a just public framework within which different 'ways of life' may be sustained, liberalism allows – or promotes? – the values of global capitalism to form most decisively the character and interaction of its citizens. The question posed by both the communitarian critique and by Pauline ethics is, then: How are the (liberal) values of plurality, tolerance and difference, and the social solidarity which they presume, to be fostered, motivated and exemplified, if not through some kind of traditioned story, embodied in rituals and communally shared?[6]

9.3 *Models for the Appropriation of Pauline Ethics*

In the light of the preceding sections, I want to conclude by suggesting three possible models for the appropriation of Pauline ethics. Each of these models, like this study as a whole, finds its basis in an engagement with Paul's texts, but also represents an attempt to show how the tradition of Paul's thought might be developed in such a way as to respond to contemporary situations and dilemmas.[7] More specifically, however, while retaining throughout a rootedness in the tradition of Pauline thought, the models represent, respectively, approaches which in key respects think 'with', 'beyond' and then 'against' Paul. It will be evident that the model which most closely resembles thinking 'with' Paul is the most congruent with Hauerwas's ecclesial ethics, though it also

6. One anecdotal example, hence relegated to a footnote: I recall watching the Millennium celebrations, televised from around the world. Many celebrations included traditional forms of music and dance, expressions of diverse cultures. England's showpiece was a wall-of-fire and firework display on the Thames. Quite apart from the technical failures that diminished the impressiveness of the show, what struck me was how empty this was in terms of its reflection of tradition, identity and culture, let alone the moral values that such tradition might convey. The question is, of course, more easily posed than answered: What could have been done that might have reflected (and fostered) something of a sense of shared identity and 'local' solidarity? What community- and identity-forming 'stories' might people living in England have recalled and celebrated together, and with people throughout the world, without implying or reviving racist notions of religious or cultural imperialism?

7. Here I echo Jean Porter's description of what Alasdair MacIntyre is doing in his reading of Aquinas (Porter 1993: 525; cf. p. 4 above).

raises certain critical questions for that tradition. The second model, which thinks 'beyond' Paul, offers a mediating position between communitarian and liberal concerns, not unlike David Fergusson's (1998) contribution to that contemporary debate. The third model is in some ways opposite to the first, and clearly goes not only beyond but also 'against' Paul's own perspectives. In considering how Paul's ethics might inform an ethic for a contemporary, plural society it connects with key liberal aims, while also raising questions pertinent to the realization of those aims, not least since it also implies clearly communitarian convictions (cf. §9.2.4).

9.3.1 *Paul's ethics for the 'politics called church'*

Just as the approach that underpins Paul's ethics coheres at a basic level with Hauerwas's ecclesial ethics (see §9.2.1 above) so the mode of contemporary appropriation that remains closest to the original intentions and character of Pauline ethics is that which reads them as a form of ecclesial ethics. By this I mean, of course, an ethics concerned primarily with the formation and development of the ecclesial community, and with individual Christians insofar as they are members of this 'body'. Paul wrote to communities of Christians and, despite an occasional reference to what seem to be universal ethical obligations (Rom. 13.1; §8.2), it is these specific communities whose practice he expects and intends to influence. It is the solidarity of the ecclesia that Paul seeks to promote, differences among the members of the ecclesia that he intends to sustain, and other-regard between weaker and stronger siblings that he aims to foster. And Paul frequently depicts the Christian community as a community of light, of the pure and holy, of the saved, in the midst of a world of wickedness and darkness, whose ignorant inhabitants are heading for destruction (see ch. 5 above). Paul is equally clear, however, that the Christian's obligation is to do good and act peaceably towards all. To this extent, like Hauerwas, he is not concerned with withdrawal from the world but with the obligation to be the Church in the world.

Even when we read 'with' Paul and thus affirm an ecclesially-focused ethics, however, there are ways in which our study of Pauline ethics raises some suggestive considerations and issues. First, the focus on the metamoral values of solidarity and other-regard coheres with Hauerwas's desire to move away from a focus on 'moral quandaries' (1983: 4) and, furthermore, implies that the fundamental moral challenge is to foster forms of communal solidarity within which legitimate differences can be valued and sustained. This is the kind of political ethics which constructs the 'politics called church';[8] these are the moral foundations upon which specific ethical issues can be debated. Indeed, the extent to which Paul invests his argumentative energies into constructing a framework for the toleration of diversity within the context of communal solidarity might raise important questions about the *priorities* for an ecclesial ethics of a Pauline kind. Second, while Paul sees certain forms of practice as key for sustaining distinct Christian identity – primarily the avoidance of idolatrous or sexually immoral unions deemed incompatible with union with Christ – his sense of what is ethical and unethical, say in the realm of sexual morality, derives to a considerable extent not from the Christian story as such but rather from his contemporary world (cf. §9.1.7 above). Indeed, Paul explicitly indicates that perceptions of what is good and evil are shared in common by all, Christian and non-Christian alike (ch. 8). Thus, while an ecclesial ethics may be similarly concerned to foster a sense of distinct Christian identity, and, following Paul, may draw on the myth of union with Christ to do so, it need not necessarily reproduce the specific ethical conventions Paul presumes, since these have no specifically Christian character but are in many cases part of the overlapping moral consensus of Paul's time. Indeed, to do so may lead to anachronistic attempts to reproduce ancient morality rather than a specifically Christian one.[9] Similarly, an ecclesial ethics may need to acknowledge the extent to which contemporary Christian convictions about what is good are shared with, and informed by, widely shared moral norms. This begins to point in the direction of setting Paul's presumptions against Paul's rhetoric, in the sense that Paul's rhetoric of distinction is counterbalanced by his own indications that standards of good and evil are, in fact, widely shared among his contemporaries.

8.   For this phrase see Hauerwas 2001: 17; further §2.3, pp. 68–69 above.

9.   For a comparable point in the context of a different argument, see Bultmann's reasons why the mythology presumed by the NT writers should not and cannot be appropriated by modern Christians: 'there is nothing specifically Christian about the mythical world picture, which is simply the world picture of a time now past that was not yet formed by scientific thinking' (Bultmann 1985: 3). The same applies to ethical assumptions shared by NT and other ancient writers. Such anachronism is often discussed in the context of the homosexuality debate, in considering whether what Paul and other biblical writers had in view was anything like modern homosexuality. But it is less often noted that this chronological and cultural divide equally affects subjects like marriage and divorce, where it is too easily presumed that Paul is addressing the same 'ethical issue' as we do. Not only are the cultural presumptions vastly different (cf. e.g. Countryman 1988; Martin 1997a), but differences in the legal minimum age of marriage, etc., make straightforward comparison invalid. Roman law allowed marriage for girls/women at twelve, for boys/men at fourteen, although the *average* age at which first marriages occurred was likely to have been somewhat higher than these minima (see Saller 1994: 26–41). For similar cautions about attempts to reproduce early Christian ethics, see Meeks 1993: 215–18.

9.3.2 *Paul's ethics for the church and the world*

A second model for the appropriation of Pauline ethics, one concerned not only with ecclesially-focused ethics but with the possible contribution of these ethics to the formation of the kind of 'moral consensus which alone can sustain a pluralist culture' (Fergusson 1998: 75), might indeed build on the indications Paul gives that his substantive ethical convictions are widely shared, and that what is good and evil can be universally recognized and agreed. As we have seen (ch. 8), Paul explicitly argues for universally accessible and recognizable ethical standards, and in appealing to Christians to do good to all reveals the conviction that what constitutes 'good' is subject to at least a degree of consensus. To build on these ideas in developing a view of potential moral consensus involves going beyond Paul, however, since his own explicit focus is so often on the distinctiveness of the ecclesial community (as also in Hauerwas's work); the notion of shared ethical convictions is mostly overshadowed (though not altogether obscured) by this predominant perspective. Nonetheless, even where Paul most strongly appeals for the purity of the ecclesial community, his appeal also intimates that the ethical norm is shared by all (1 Cor. 5.1-13): in effect, his appeal is for the members of the Christian community to do better than their contemporaries at meeting common ethical standards (see further §5.3). Perhaps most significantly, what this reveals is the extent to which Pauline ethics constructs a distinct sense of in-group identity while at the same time sharing (and presuming) widely held ethical values (see further ch. 5). And this would suggest that a key liberal goal is not unachievable, despite that fact that Paul's (and Hauerwas's) rhetoric often implies the opposite: to sustain a variety of diverse traditions and identities within the framework of an 'overlapping consensus' on ethical values and norms. In Paul's case we can see that ethical practices are motivated in tradition-specific ways – through the notion of union with Christ, and so on – while the substance itself is, to at least a considerable extent (cf. §9.1.4-7), widely accepted. On this model, the challenge to Christian ethics would be to go beyond Paul (and beyond Hauerwas?) in not only strengthening a sense of distinct identity and motivating ethics in specifically 'Christian' ways but also agreeing to seek out and make explicit the extent to which the substance of ethical conviction forms (or could form) part of a broader moral consensus. (One possible way forward here, which would not involve ceding the priority of the Christian story to the broader story of liberalism and thus allowing the latter to relativize the truth of the former, would be to focus on how the

Christian story itself can narrate, affirm and learn from the good that is found *extra muros ecclesiae*.)[10]

9.3.3 *Paul's ethics for a plural society*

But if the communitarian critique of liberalism is in some essential respects correct – and we have at least seen reason to affirm it from a Pauline point of view (§9.2.4) – then the question remains how the (liberal?) social framework that constitutes and preserves this moral consensus is itself to be fostered and sustained. The previous model would imply that each person, or group, will have their own tradition-specific reasons for sharing an ethic that (at least in part) represents what is good for all: it represents an ecclesial ethic which can also make a contribution to the formulation of a shared ethic for society as a whole. Another possibility is to consider how Paul's ethics might serve as a model for such a social ethic itself. Ogletree, as we have already seen (§1.6, pp. 33–34), makes suggestions along these lines, arguing that Paul's treatment of 'cultural pluralism' offers potential for 'the imaginative development of social thought' in modern societies faced with similar issues of community and pluralism (1983: 158), though it is clear that he is talking about a specifically *Christian* project. A 'Christian social ethic' may be developed by drawing on 'developments within the early Christian communities themselves' as analogies (p. 192). In other words, what Ogletree suggests is that the most fruitful approach for developing a Christian social ethic may not be the one implied in the previous two sections – taking the hints about shared ethics, attitudes to outsiders, rulers, etc., from Paul and developing them further in a new context – but rather one in which the early Christian communities themselves are treated as analogous to modern societies. On this model, the ways in which Paul deals with diversity in the assemblies might be suggestive for ways of dealing with diversity in contemporary societies, and so on. Paul's attempts to articulate an ethic in which diverse ways of life, dictated by a person's 'faith', or 'conscience', are respected within a framework of communal solidarity could provide generative material for our continuing reflections on similar challenges. We might therefore take from our reading of Paul's ethics the idea that human solidarity requires some shared myth, embodied in rituals, that narrates and forms that solidarity, and which may at the same time provide strong grounds for the

---

10. One example of such potential within Christian theology is explored by Geoff Thompson, in his (1995) study of Karl Barth's secular parables of the kingdom (cf. also Thompson 2000, on engaging the world with Justin Martyr, George Lindbeck and Hans Frei). Fergusson (1998: 22–33, 166–67) also makes positive mention of Barth's ideas in this connection.

treasuring of difference, within limits, whether through the notion of differences of faith, conscience, or whatever. We might then conclude that to generate an ethic appropriate to our plural, indeed global, society, we need to articulate new stories, new myths, about human solidarity and difference which avoid the notion that only Christ can provide their basis, and in so doing go not only beyond but also against Paul.[11] This would imply a more radical, innovative approach, constructing a new shared story with the resources and traditions at hand, and recognizing that any new basis for human solidarity does indeed relativize any other religious, cultural and ethical convictions – just as proved to be the case with the new story with which Paul strove to unite Jews and Gentiles in one communal body. This would be one form the 'communitarianization of liberalism' (cf. Bell 1993: 8) might take, a form compatible with what Nigel Biggar describes as 'the project of recovering liberalism's lost theological horizon and rescuing it in non-secularist form' (2000: 160), though Biggar's comment presumes a religious, and, one suspects, Christian, form of rescue package. This may sound an entirely wishful, if not objectionable, possibility. Certainly it carries its dangers, as do all attempts at myth-making – but then, old myths as well as new ones have been used to support appalling atrocities, and perhaps myths and rituals constructed to foster forms of human solidarity and instil the value of regard for the Other would be better than the myths that currently capture our imagination: the myth of the American superhero (see Lawrence and Jewett 2002), the myths of consumerism and so on. In such a project, the Pauline tradition, for all its inadequacies and problems, could, I hope to have shown, have a good deal to offer. Christians may find objectionable, of course, the notion that the resources of their tradition, along with others, might be used to formulate a new story, one which encompassed, and at the same time relativized, their identity within a wider circle of human belonging. But then they should be reminded that this is no less than Paul envisioned for Judaism, for all his attempts to 'protect' the practice of Jewish Christians. If they can celebrate this social achievement, the formation of new communities in which Jews and Greeks were united by a new solidarity in Christ – a 'fulfilment' of Judaism's heritage in transcending its ethnic and national boundaries[12] – then a further form of

---

11. To return to Boyarin (1994; see §1.7), this makes some attempt to reflect on how the 'human solidarity' Boyarin treasures might be sustained and nurtured. Boyarin criticizes Paul's notion of universal incorporation into Christ as a basis for solidarity but has little to say on alternative ways in which solidarity might specifically be fostered.

12. Cf. the comments of Dunn 1998c: 'Paul saw his own apostolic work not as a disowning of his heritage, but precisely as its fulfillment' (p. 258); 'Paul's criticism of Judaism was ... a criticism of the xenophobic strand of Judaism, to which Paul himself had previously belonged ... Paul was in effect converting from a closed Judaism to an open Judaism'

social achievement, in which Christians too take their place among those whose differences remain, but who are now united under a new basis for human solidarity, might equally be a cause for celebration.

(p. 261); 'his was the privilege of bringing Israel's promised destiny to its eschatological completion' (p. 264). And this involved rejecting the importance of the 'trappings of Jewish identity' – circumcision and food laws especially – in favour of an 'essence' of Jewishness 'determined from within' (Dunn 1999: 192). These positive comments confirm exactly the achievement which is for Boyarin a focus for criticism.

BIBLIOGRAPHY

Aasgaard, R. 1997 'Brotherhood in Plutarch and Paul: Its Role and Character', in Moxnes 1997: 166–82.
— 'My Beloved Brothers and Sisters! A Study of the Meaning and Function of Christian Siblingship in Paul, in its Greco-Roman and Jewish Context', University of Oslo: PhD dissertation (now JSNTSup 265; London: T. & T. Clark International, 2004).
— 2002 '"Role Ethics" in Paul: The Significance of the Sibling Role for Paul's Ethical Thinking', *NTS* 48: 513–30.
Adams, E. 2000 *Constructing the World: A Study in Paul's Cosmological Language*, SNTW, Edinburgh: T. & T. Clark.
— and D.G. Horrell, eds 2004 *Christianity at Corinth: The Quest for the Pauline Church*, Louisville, KY: Westminster John Knox.
Adams, N. 1996 'Eschatology and Habermas' Ideal Speech Situation', *Modern Believing* 37: 3–10.
— 2003 'Recent Books in English by Jürgen Habermas', *SCE* 16.1: 72–79.
Adorno, T.W. 1980 *Minima Moralia*, Gesammelte Schriften 4; Frankfurt: Suhrkamp.
Albrecht, G.H. 1995 *The Character of Our Communities: Toward an Ethic of Liberation for the Church*, Nashville: Abingdon.
— 1997 'Article Review, *In Good Company: The Church as Polis*', *SJT* 50: 219–27.
Allison, D.C. 1982 'The Pauline Epistles and the Synoptic Gospels: The Pattern of the Parallels', *NTS* 28: 1–32.
Allmen, D. von 1981 *La Famille de Dieu: La Symbolique familiale dans le Paulinisme*, OBO 41; Göttingen: Vandenhoeck & Ruprecht.
Allo, E.B. 1956 *Saint Paul: Première Épître aux Corinthiens*, Paris: Gabalda.
Amadon, J., and R. Eklund 2001 'Annotated Bibliography on Biblical Ethics', *Ex Auditu* 17: 163–74.
Apel, K.-O. 1990 'Is the Ethics of the Ideal Communication Community a Utopia? On the Relationship between Ethics, Utopia, and the Critique of Utopia', in Benhabib and Dallmayr 1990: 23–59.
— 1992 'Die Diskursethik vor Herausforderung der "Philosophie der Befreiung". Versuch einer Antwort an Enrique Dussel', in Fornet-Betancourt 1992: 16–54.
— and M. Kettner, eds 1992 *Zur Anwendung der Diskursethik in Politik, Recht und Wissenschaft*, Frankfurt: Suhrkamp.
Arens, E., ed. 1989a *Habermas und die Theologie: Beiträge zur theologischen Rezeption, Diskussion und Kritik der Theorie kommunikativen Handelns*, Düsseldorf: Patmos.

— 1989b 'Theologie nach Habermas. Eine Einführung', in Arens 1989a: 9–38.

— 1991 *Erinnerung, Befreiung, Solidarität: Benjamin, Marcuse, Habermas und die politische Theologie*, Düsseldorf: Patmos.

— 1997 'Critical Theory and Political Theology between Modernity and Postmodernity', in Batstone and Mendieta 1997: 222–42.

Atkins, R.A. 1991 *Egalitarian Community: Ethnography and Exegesis*, Tuscaloosa and London: University of Alabama Press.

Attridge, H.W. 2002 'Review of Troels Engberg-Pedersen, *Paul and the Stoics*', *RBL* 9: at http://www.bookreviews.org.

Avis, P. 1999 *God and the Creative Imagination: Metaphor, Symbol and Myth in Religion and Theology*, London and New York: Routledge.

Balch, D.L. 1972 'Backgrounds of I Cor. VII: Sayings of the Lord in Q; Moses as an Ascetic ΘΕΙΟΣ ΑΝΗΠ in II Cor. III', *NTS* 18: 351–64.

— 1983 '1 Cor 7:32-35 and Stoic Debates about Marriage, Anxiety, and Distraction', *JBL* 102: 429–39.

Banks, R. 1994 *Paul's Idea of Community*, revised edn; Peabody, MA: Hendrickson.

Barclay, J.M.G. 1988 *Obeying the Truth: A Study of Paul's Ethics in Galatians*, SNTW; Edinburgh: T. & T. Clark.

— 1991 'Paul, Philemon, and the Dilemma of Christian Slave Ownership', *NTS* 37: 161–86.

— 1992 'Thessalonica and Corinth: Social Contrasts in Pauline Christianity', *JSNT* 47: 49–74.

— 1993a 'Jesus and Paul', in *DPL*: 492–503.

— 1993b 'Conflict in Thessalonica', *CBQ* 55: 512–30.

— 1995 'Paul among Diaspora Jews: Anomaly or Apostate?', *JSNT* 60: 89–120.

— 1996a *Jews in the Mediterranean Diaspora: From Alexander to Trajan (323 BCE to 117 CE)*, Edinburgh: T. & T. Clark.

— 1996b '"Do We Undermine the Law?" A Study of Romans 14.1–15.6', in Dunn 1996: 287–308.

— 2001a 'Review of T. Engberg-Pedersen, *Paul and the Stoics*', *BibInt* 9: 233–36.

— 2001b 'Matching Theory and Practice: Josephus's Constitutional Ideal and Paul's Strategy in Corinth', in Engberg-Pedersen 2001: 139–63.

— 2002 'Paul's Story: Theology as Testimony', in Longenecker 2002: 133–56.

Barcley, W.B. 1999 *'Christ in You': A Study in Paul's Theology and Ethics*, Lanham, New York, Oxford: University Press of America.

Barrett, C.K. 1971 *The First Epistle to the Corinthians*, BNTC; London: A. & C. Black.

— 1982 *Essays on Paul*, London: SPCK.

Bartchy, S.S. 1973 *ΜΑΛΛΟΝ ΧΡΗΣΑΙ: First-Century Slavery and the Interpretation of 1. Cor. 7.21*, SBLDS 11; Missoula, MT: University of Montana.

— 1999 'Undermining Ancient Patriarchy: The Apostle Paul's Vision of a Society of Siblings', *BTB* 29: 68–78.

Barth, F. 1969 *Ethnic Groups and Boundaries*, London: Allen & Unwin.

Barton, S.C. 1992 'The Communal Dimension of Earliest Christianity: A Critical Survey of the Field', *JTS* 43: 399–427.

— 1994 *Discipleship and Family Ties in Mark and Matthew*, SNTSMS 80; Cambridge: CUP.

— 1995 'Historical Criticism and Social-Scientific Perspectives in New Testament Study', in J.B. Green, ed., *Hearing the New Testament: Strategies for Interpretation*, Grand Rapids, MI: Eerdmans: 61–89.

— 1997 'Social-Scientific Criticism', in S.E. Porter, ed., *Handbook to Exegesis of the New Testament*, Leiden: Brill: 277–89.

— 1998 'Paul and the Limits of Tolerance', in G.N. Stanton and G.G. Stroumsa, eds, *Tolerance and Intolerance in Early Judaism and Christianity*, Cambridge: CUP: 121–34.

Bassler, J.M. ed. 1991 *Pauline Theology, Vol. 1: Thessalonians, Philippians, Galatians, Philemon*, Minneapolis: Fortress.

Batstone, D., and E. Mendieta, eds 1997 *Liberation Theologies, Postmodernity and the Americas*, London and New York: Routledge.

Bauckham, R.J. 1999 *James*, London and New York: Routledge.

Baur, F.C. 1831 'Die Christuspartei in der korinthische Gemeinde, der Gegensatz des petrinischen und paulinischen Christentums in der ältesten Kirche, der Apostel Petrus in Rom', *Tübinger Zeitschrift* 4: 61–206 (repr. in F.C. Baur, *Historischkritische Untersuchungen zum Neuen Testament* [Ausgewählte Werke, vol. 1; Stuttgart-Bad Cannstatt: Friedrich Frommann Verlag, 1963]: 1–146).

Beare, F.W. 1959 *A Commentary on the Epistle to the Philippians*, BNTC; London: A. & C. Black.

Becker, J. 1989 *Paul Apostle to the Gentiles*, Louisville, KY: Westminster/ John Knox.

Beckheuer, B. 1997 *Paulus und Jerusalem: Kollekte und Mission im theologischen Denken des Heidenapostels*, Frankfurt: Lang.

Beker, J.C. 1980 *Paul the Apostle: The Triumph of God in Life and Thought*, Edinburgh: T. & T. Clark.

Bell, D. 1993. *Communitarianism and Its Critics*, Oxford: Clarendon.

Benhabib, S. 1986 *Critique, Norm, and Utopia: A Study of the Foundations of Critical Theory*, New York: Columbia University Press.

— 1992 *Situating the Self: Gender, Community and Postmodernism in Contemporary Ethics*, Cambridge: Polity.

— and F. Dallmayr, eds 1990 *The Communicative Ethics Controversy*, Cambridge, MA: MIT Press.

Berger, K. 1977 'Almosen für Israel: Zum historischen Kontext der paulinischen Kollekte', *NTS* 23: 180–204.

Berger, P.L. 1967 *The Sacred Canopy: Elements of a Sociological Theory of Religion*, New York and London: Doubleday.

— 1969 *A Rumour of Angels: Modern Society and the Rediscovery of the Supernatural*, Harmondsworth: Penguin.

— 1974 *Pyramids of Sacrifice: Political Ethics and Social Change*, Harmondsworth: Penguin.

— and T. Luckmann 1966 *The Social Construction of Reality: A Treatise in the Sociology of Knowledge*, New York: Doubleday/Harmondsworth: Penguin.

Berkman, J. 2001 'An Introduction to *The Hauerwas Reader*', in Berkman and Cartwright 2001: 3–16.

— and M. Cartwright, eds 2001 *The Hauerwas Reader: Stanley Hauerwas*, Durham, NC, and London: Duke University Press.

Best, E. 1972 *The First and Second Epistles to the Thessalonians*, BNTC; London: A. & C. Black.

Betz, H.D. 1975 'The Literary Composition and Function of Paul's Letter to the Galatians', *NTS* 21: 353–79.

— 1979 *Galatians*, Hermeneia; Minneapolis: Fortress.

— 1985 *2 Corinthians 8 and 9*, Hermeneia; Minneapolis: Fortress.

— 1988 'Das Problem der Grundlagen der paulinischen Ethik (Röm 12,1-2)', *ZTK* 85: 199–218.

— 1989 'The Foundations of Christian Ethics according to Romans 12:1-2', in P.E. Devenish and G.L. Goodwin, eds, *Witness and Existence: Essays in Honour of Schubert M. Ogden*, Chicago and London: University of Chicago Press: 55–72.

Biggar, N. 2000 'Is Stanley Hauerwas Sectarian?', in Nation and Wells 2000: 141–60.

Black, D.A. 1983 'A Note on "the Weak" in 1 Corinthians 9,22', *Bib* 64: 240–42.

— 1984 *Paul, Apostle of Weakness: Astheneia and Its Cognates in the Pauline Literature*, New York, Frankfurt, etc.: Lang.

Blasi, A., J. Duhaime and P.-A. Turcotte, eds 2002 *Handbook of Early Christianity: Social Science Approaches*, Walnut Creek, CA: Alta Mira.

Blount, B.K. 2001 *Then the Whisper Put on Flesh: New Testament Ethics in an African American Context*, Nashville: Abingdon.

Bockmuehl, M.N.A. 1988 'Das Verb φανερόω im Neuen Testament: Versuch einer Neuauswertung', *BZ* 32: 87–99.

— 1995 'The Noachide Commandments and New Testament Ethics: With Special Reference to Acts 15 and Pauline Halakah', *RB* 102: 72–101 (Repr. in Bockmuehl 2000: 145–73.)

— 1997 'New Testament Ethics. Review Article on *The Moral Vision of the New Testament* by R. Hays', *ExpTim* 109: 86.

— 1998a *The Epistle to the Philippians*, BNTC; London: A. & C. Black.

— 1998b 'Review of K. Finsterbusch, *Die Thora als Lebensweisung*', *JTS* 49: 784–87.

— 2000 *Jewish Law in Gentile Churches*, Edinburgh: T. & T. Clark.

Boer, M.C. de 2002 'Paul, Theologian of God's Apocalypse', *Int* 56: 21–33.

Borgen, P. 1994 '"Yes," "No," "How Far?"': The Participation of Jews and Christians in Pagan Cults', in Engberg-Pedersen 1994: 30–59.

Bornkamm, G. 1969 *Early Christian Experience*, London: SCM.

— 1991 'The Letter to the Romans as Paul's Last Will and Testament', in Donfried 1991: 16–28.

Botha, J. 1994 *Subject to Whose Authority? Multiple Readings of Romans 13*, Atlanta, GA: Scholars.

Boyarin, D. 1994 *A Radical Jew: Paul and the Politics of Identity*, Berkeley, CA: University of California Press.

Brant, J.A. 1993 'The Place of *Mimêsis* in Paul's Thought', *SR* 22: 285–300.

Braxton, B.R. 2000 *The Tyranny of Resolution: 1 Corinthians 7:17-24*, SBLDS 181; Atlanta, GA: SBL.

Bronner, S.E. 1994 *Of Critical Theory and Its Theorists*, Oxford and Cambridge, MA: Blackwell.

Brown, C. 1998 'Ernst Lohmeyer's *Kyrios Jesus*', in Martin and Dodd 1998: 6–42.

Brown, R. 1996 'Tajfel's Contribution to the Reduction of Intergroup Conflict', in Robinson 1996: 169–89.

Brown, R.E., and J.P. Meier 1983 *Antioch and Rome*, London: Chapman.

Browning, D., and F.S. Fiorenza, eds 1992 *Habermas, Modernity, and Public Theology*, New York: Crossroad.

Bruce, F.F. 1963 *The Epistle of Paul to the Romans*, London: Tyndale.

— 1968 'Paul and Jerusalem', *TynBul* 19: 3–25.

— 1974 *Paul and Jesus*, Grand Rapids, MI: Baker.

— 1982 *1 & 2 Thessalonians*, WBC 45; Waco, TX: Word.

Brunt, J.C. 1981 'Love, Freedom, and Moral Responsibility: The Contribution of 1 Cor. 8–10 to an Understanding of Paul's Ethical Thinking', SBLSP 20: 19–33.

Buck, C.H. 1950 'The Collection for the Saints', *HTR* 43: 1–29.

Bultmann, R. 1924 'Das Problem der Ethik bei Paulus', *ZNW* 23: 123–40.

— 1952 *Theology of the New Testament*, Vol. 1; London: SCM.

— 1960 *Jesus Christ and Mythology*, London: SCM.

— 1966 'Das christliche Gebot der Nächstenliebe' (first published 1930), in Bultmann, *Glauben und Verstehen*, Vol. 1; Tübingen: Mohr Siebeck: 229–44.

— 1985 *New Testament and Mythology and Other Basic Writings*, ed. and tr. S.M. Ogden, London: SCM.

— 1995 'The Problem of Ethics in Paul', in Rosner 1995: 195–216.

Burridge, R.A. 1998 'Review of *The Moral Vision of the New Testament*, by R.B. Hays', *Journal of Theology for Southern Africa* 102: 71–73.

— forthcoming *The Imitation of Jesus: An Inclusive Approach to New Testament Ethics*, Grand Rapids, MI: Eerdmans/London: T. & T. Clark.

Burton, E. 1921 *A Critical and Exegetical Commentary on the Epistle to the Galatians*, ICC; Edinburgh: T. & T. Clark.

Cairns, D. 1974 'The Thought of Peter Berger', *SJT* 27: 181–97.

Callaghan, A.D. 1997 *Embassy of Onesimos: The Letter of Paul to Philemon*, Valley Forge, PA: TPI.

— 2000 'Paul, *Ekklēsia*, and Emancipation in Corinth', in Horsley 2000: 216–23.

Campbell, D.A. 2002 'The Story of Jesus in Romans and Galatians', in Longenecker 2002: 97–124.

Campbell, W.S. 1991 *Paul's Gospel in an Intercultural Context*, Frankfurt: Lang.

Carrington, P. 1940 *The Primitive Christian Catechism*, Cambridge: CUP.

Carter, C.A. 2001 *The Politics of the Cross: The Theology and Social Ethics of John Howard Yoder*, Grand Rapids, MI: Brazos.

Carter, P. 1997 *The Servant-Ethic in the New Testament*, New York: Lang.

Casey, P.M. 1991 *From Jewish Prophet to Gentile God*, Cambridge: Clarke.

Castelli, E.A. 1991 *Imitating Paul: A Discourse of Power*, Louisville, KY: Westminster/John Knox Press.

Catchpole, D.R. 1975 'The Synoptic Divorce Material as a Traditio-Historical Problem', *BJRL* 57: 92–127.

— 2004 'Who and Where Is the "Wretched Man" of Romans 7, and Why Is "She" Wretched?', in G.N. Stanton, B.W. Longenecker and S.C. Barton, eds, *The Holy Spirit and Christian Origins: FS James D.G. Dunn*, Grand Rapids, MI: Eerdmans, 168–80.

Cavanaugh, W. 2001 'Stan the Man: A Thoroughly Biased Account of a Completely Unobjective Person', in Berkman and Cartwright 2001: 17–32.

Chang, H.-K. 1995 'Neuere Entwürfe zur Ethik des Neuen Testaments im deutschsprachigen Raum. Ihre Sichtung und kritische Würdigung', University of Erlangen: dissertation.

Cheung, A.T. 1999 *Idol Food in Corinth: Jewish Background and Pauline Legacy*, JSNTSup 176; Sheffield: SAP.

Clarke, A.D. 1993 *Secular and Christian Leadership in Corinth: A Socio-Historical and Exegetical Study of 1 Corinthians 1–6*, AGAJU 18; Leiden: Brill.

— 2004 'Equality or Mutuality: Paul's Use of "Brother" Language', in P.J. Williams, A.D. Clarke, P.M. Head, D. Instone-Brewer, eds, *The New Testament in Its First Century Setting: Essays on Context and Background in Honour of B.W. Winter on His 65th Birthday*, Grand Rapids, MI: Eerdmans, 151–64.

Clarke, F.K.T. 2000 'God's Concern for the Poor in the New Testament: A Discussion of the Role of the Poor in the Foundation of Christian Belief (Early to Mid-First Century CE)', University of Exeter: PhD dissertation.

— 2001 '"Remembering the Poor". Does Galatians 2.10a allude to the Collection?', *Scripture Bulletin* 31.1: 20–28.

Collier, G.D. 1994 '"That We Might Not Crave Evil." The Structure and Argument of 1 Corinthians 10.1–13', *JSNT* 55: 55–75.

Conzelmann, H. 1975 *A Commentary on the First Epistle to the Corinthians*, Hermeneia; Philadelphia: Fortress.

Corley, K. 1995 '1 Peter', in E.S. Fiorenza, ed., *Searching the Scriptures, Vol. 2: A Feminist Commentory*, London: SCM: 349–60.

Countryman, L.W. 1988 *Dirt, Greed and Sex: Sexual Ethics in the New Testament and Their Implications for Today*, Philadelphia: Fortress.

Craddock, F.B. 1968 'The Poverty of Christ: An Investigation of II Corinthians 8:9', *Int* 22: 158–70.

Cranfield, C.E.B. 1975 *A Critical and Exegetical Commentary on the Epistle to the Romans*, Vol. 1, ICC; Edinburgh: T. & T. Clark.

— 1979 *A Critical and Exegetical Commentary on the Epistle to the Romans*, Vol. 2, ICC; Edinburgh: T. & T. Clark.

— 1998 'A Response to Professor Richard B. Hays' *The Moral Vision of the New Testament*', in Cranfield, *On Romans: And Other New Testament Essays*, Edinburgh: T. & T. Clark: 167–75.

Cronin, C. 1993 'Translator's Introduction', in Habermas 1993: xi–xxxi.

Crossan, J.D. 1993 *Jesus: A Revolutionary Biography*, San Francisco: Harper.

Cruz, H. 1990 *Christological Motives and Motivated Actions in Pauline Paraenesis*, Frankfurt: Lang.

Dahl, N.A. 1950 'Der Name Israel: Zur Auslegung von Gal 6,16', *Judaica* 6: 161–70.

— 1977 *Studies in Paul*, Augsburg: Fortress.

Dallmayr, F. 1990 'Introduction', in Benhabib and Dallmayr 1990: 1–20.

Dautzenberg, G. 1969 'Der Verzicht auf das apostolische Unterhaltsrecht. Eine exegetische Untersuchung zu 1 Kor 9', *Bib* 50: 212–32.

— 1989 'Φεύγετε τὴν πορνείαν (1 Kor 6, 18). Eine Fallstudie zur paulinischen Sexualethik in ihrem Verhältnis zur Sexualethik des Frühjudentums', in Merklein 1989: 271–98.

Davies, W.D. 1955 *Paul and Rabbinic Judaism*, 2nd edn; London: SPCK.

Davis, N. 1991 'Contemporary Deontology', in Singer 1991: 205–18.

Dawes, S.B. 1991a ''ĂNĀWĀ in Translation and Tradition', *VT* 41: 38–48.

— 1991b 'Humility: Whence This Strange Notion?', *ExpTim* 103: 72–75.

De Angelis, G. 1999 'Die Vernunft der Kommunikation und das Problem einer diskursiven Ethik', University of Heidelberg: dissertation.

Deidun, T.J. 1981 *New Covenant Morality in Paul*, Rome: Biblical Institute Press.

Deissmann, G.A. 1923 *Licht vom Osten*, 4th edn; Tübingen: Mohr.

Deming, W. 1995 *Paul on Marriage and Celibacy: The Hellenistic Background of 1 Corinthians 7*, SNTSMS 83; Cambridge: CUP.

Dibelius, M. 1928 *Urchristentum und Kultur*, Heidelberg: Carl Winters.

Dickson, J.P., and B.S. Rosner 2003 'Did Humility Exist before the New Testament? Stephen B. Dawes Revisited', paper presented to SNTS conference, Bonn 2003. Part forthcoming as 'Humility as a Social Virtue in the Hebrew Bible', *VT*.

Dihle, A. 1962 *Die goldene Regel. Eine Einführung in die Geschichte der antiken und frühchristlichen Vulgarethik*, Göttingen: Vandenhoeck & Ruprecht.

Doble, P. 2002 '"Vile Bodies" or Transformed Persons? Philippians 3.12 in Context', *JSNT* 86: 3–27.

Dodd, B.J. 1998 'The Story of Christ and the Imitation of Paul in Philippians 2–3', in Martin and Dodd 1998: 154–61.

Dodd, C.H. 1936 *The Apostolic Preaching and Its Developments*, London: Hodder & Stoughton.

— 1950 *Gospel and Law*, Cambridge: CUP.

— 1968 *More New Testament Studies*, Manchester: Manchester University Press.

Donaldson, T.L. 1997 *Paul and the Gentiles: Remapping the Apostle's Convictional World*, Minneapolis: Fortress.

Donfried, K.P. ed. 1991 *The Romans Debate: Revised and Expanded Edition*, Edinburgh: T. & T. Clark.

Doniger, W. 1998 *The Implied Spider: Politics and Theology in Myth*, New York: Columbia University Press.

Doohan, H. 1989 *Paul's Vision of Church*, GNS 32; Wilmington, DE: Michael Glazier.

Douglas, M. 1966 *Purity and Danger*, London: Routledge and Kegan Paul.

Downing, F.G. 1998 *Cynics, Paul and the Pauline Churches*, London and New York: Routledge.

— 2001 'Review of T. Engberg-Pedersen, *Paul and the Stoics*', *JTS* 52: 278–80.

Dungan, D.L. 1971 *The Sayings of Jesus in the Churches of Paul: The Use of the Synoptic Tradition in the Regulation of Early Church Life*, Oxford: Blackwell.

Dunn, J.D.G. 1970 *Baptism in the Holy Spirit*, London: SCM.

— 1980 *Christology in the Making*, London: SCM.

— 1988 *Romans*, 2 vols; WBC 38A and 38B; Dallas, TX: Word.

— 1990 *Jesus, Paul and the Law*, London: SPCK.

— 1993 *The Epistle to the Galatians*, BNTC; London: A. & C. Black.

— 1994 'Jesus Tradition in Paul', in B. Chilton and C.A. Evans, eds, *Studying the Historical Jesus: Evaluations of the State of Current Research*, Leiden: Brill: 155–78.

— ed. 1996 *Paul and the Mosaic Law*, WUNT 89; Tübingen: Mohr.

— 1998a *The Theology of Paul the Apostle*, Edinburgh: T. & T. Clark.

— 1998b 'Christ, Adam, and Preexistence', in Martin and Dodd 1998: 74–83.

— 1998c 'Paul: Apostate or Apostle of Israel?', *ZNW* 89: 256–71.

— 1999 'Who Did Paul Think He Was? A Study of Jewish-Christian Identity', *NTS* 45: 174–93.

Ebner, M. 1991 *Leidenslisten und Apostelbrief. Untersuchungen zu Form, Motivik und Funktion der Peristasenkataloge bei Paulus*, Würzburg: Echter.

Eckstein, H.-J. 1983 *Der Begriff Syneidesis bei Paulus*, WUNT 2.10; Tübingen: Mohr.

Elgvin, T. 1997 '"To Master His Own Vessel". I Thess 4.4 in Light of New Qumran Evidence', *NTS* 43: 604–19.

Elliott, J.H. 2003 'The Jesus Movement Was Not Egalitarian but Family Oriented', *BibInt* 11: 173–210.

Elliott, N. 1994 *Liberating Paul: The Justice of God and the Politics of the Apostle*, New York: Orbis/Sheffield: SAP.

— 1997 'Romans 13:1-7 in the Context of Imperial Propaganda', in Horsley 1997a: 184–204.

— 1999 'Asceticism among the "Weak" and the "Strong" in Romans 14–15', in L.E. Vaage and V.L. Wimbush, eds, *Asceticism and the New Testament*, London and New York: Routledge: 231–51.

Ellis, E.E. 1986 'Traditions in 1 Corinthians', *NTS* 32: 481–502.

Elster, J. 1986 *Karl Marx: A Reader*, Cambridge: CUP.

Engberg-Pedersen, T. 1993 'Proclaiming the Lord's Death: 1 Corinthians and the Forms of Paul's Theological Argument', in Hay 1993: 103–32.

— ed. 1994 *Paul in His Hellenistic Context*, SNTW; Edinburgh: T. & T. Clark.

— 2000 *Paul and the Stoics*, Edinburgh: T. & T. Clark.

— ed. 2001 *Paul beyond the Judaism/Hellenism Divide*, Louisville, KY: Westminster John Knox.

— 2002a 'Response to Reviews of Troels Engberg-Pedersen, *Paul and the Stoics*', *RBL* 9: at http://www.book.reviews.org.

— 2002b 'Response to Martyn', *JSNT* 86: 103–14.

Esler, P.F. 1994 *The First Christians in Their Social Worlds*, London and New York: Routledge.

— 1996 'Group Boundaries and Intergroup Conflict in Galatians: A New Reading of Galatians 5:13–6:10', in M.G. Brett, ed., *Ethnicity and the Bible*, Leiden: Brill: 215–40.

— 1998 *Galatians*, London and New York: Routledge.

— 2003a 'Social Identity, the Virtues, and the Good Life: A New Approach to Romans 12:1–15:13', *BTB* 33: 51–63.

— 2003b *Conflict and Identity in Romans*, Minneapolis, MN: Fortress.

— 2004 'Paul and Stoicism: Romans 12 as a Test Case', *NTS* 50: 106–24.

Fape, M.O. 1999 *Paul's Concept of Baptism and Its Present Implications for Believers*, Lewiston/Queenston/Lampeter: Mellen.

Fatum, L. 1997 'Brotherhood in Christ: A Gender Hermeneutical Reading of 1 Thessalonians', in Moxnes 1997: 183–97.

Fee, G.D. 1980 'Εἰδωλόθυτα Once Again: An Interpretation of 1 Corinthians 8–10', *Bib* 61: 172–97.

— 1987 *The First Epistle to the Corinthians*, NICNT; Grand Rapids, MI: Eerdmans.

— 1995 *Paul's Letter to the Philippians*, NICNT; Grand Rapids, MI: Eerdmans.

Fergusson, D.A.S. 1997a 'Communitarianism and Liberalism: Towards a Convergence?', *SCE* 10.1: 32–48.

— 1997b 'Another Way of Reading Stanley Hauerwas?', *SJT* 50: 242–49.

— 1998 *Community, Liberalism and Christian Ethics*, Cambridge: CUP.

Ferrera, A. 1985 'A Critique of Habermas' Diskursethik', *Telos* 64: 45–74.

Finsterbusch, K. 1996 *Die Thora als Lebensweisung für Heidenchristen*, SUNT 20; Göttingen: Vandenhoeck & Ruprecht.

Fiorenza, E.S. 1983 *In Memory of Her: A Feminist Theological Reconstruction of Christian Origins*, London: SCM (2nd edn 1995).

— 1990 'Missionaries, Apostles, Co-Workers: Romans 16 and the Reconstruction of Women's Early Christian History', in A. Loades, ed., *Feminist Theology: A Reader*, London: SPCK: 57–71.

Fiorenza, F.S. 1992a 'Introduction: A Critical Reception for a Practical Public Theology', in Browning and Fiorenza 1992: 1–18.

— 1992b 'The Church as a Community of Interpretation: Political Theology between Discourse Ethics and Hermeneutical Reconstruction', in Browning and Fiorenza 1992: 66–91.

Fisk, B. 1989 'Eating Meat Offered to Idols: Corinthian Behaviour and Pauline Response in 1 Corinthians 8–10 (A Response to Gordon Fee)', *Trinity Journal* 10: 49–70.

Fitzgerald, J.T. 1988 *Cracks in an Earthen Vessel: An Examination of the Catalogues of Hardships in the Corinthian Correspondence*, SBLDS 99; Atlanta, GA: Scholars.

Fitzmyer, J.A. 1993 *Romans*, AB 33; New York: Doubleday.

Fornet-Betancourt, R., ed. 1992 *Diskursethik oder Befreiungsethik?*, Aachen: Augustinus Buchhandlung.

Forrester, D.B. 2000 'The Church and the Concentration Camp: Some Reflections on Moral Community', in Nation and Wells 2000: 189–207.

Fotopoulos, J. 2003 *Food Offered to Idols in Roman Corinth*, WUNT 2.151; Tübingen: Mohr.

Fowl, S.E. 1990 *The Story of Christ in the Ethics of Paul: An Analysis of the Function of the Hymnic Material in the Pauline Corpus*, JSNTSup 36; Sheffield: SAP.

— 1998 'Christology and Ethics in Philippians 2: 5-11', in Martin and Dodd 1998: 140–53.

Frankemölle, H. 1970 *Das Taufverständnis des Paulus. Taufe, Tod und Auferstehung nach Röm 6*, SBS 47; Stuttgart: Katholisches Bibelwerk.

Frazer, E., and N. Lacey 1993 *The Politics of Community: A Feminist Critique of the Liberal-Communitarian Debate*, New York, London, etc.: Harvester Wheatsheaf.

Friedrich, J., W. Pöhlmann and P. Stuhlmacher 1976 'Zur historischen Situation und Intention von Röm 13,1-7', *ZTK* 73: 131–66.

Friesen, S. 2004 'Poverty in Pauline Studies: Beyond the So-Called New Consensus', *JSNT* 26: 323–61.

Furnish, V.P. 1968 *Theology and Ethics in Paul*, Nashville: Abingdon.

— 1973 *The Love Command in the New Testament*, London: SCM.

— 1979 *The Moral Teaching of Paul*, Nashville, TN: Abingdon.

— 1984 *II Corinthians*, AB 32A; New York: Doubleday.

— 1989 'The Jesus–Paul Debate: From Baur to Bultmann', in Wedderburn 1989a: 17–50.

— 1990 'Belonging to Christ: A Paradigm for Ethics in First Corinthians', *Int* 44: 145–57.

— 1993 *Jesus according to Paul*, Cambridge: CUP.

— 2002a 'Review of Troels Engberg-Pedersen, *Paul and the Stoics*', *RBL* 9: at http://www.bookreviews.org.

— 2002b 'Inside Looking Out: Some Pauline Views of the Unbelieving Public', in J.C. Anderson, P. Sellew and C. Setzer, eds, *Pauline Conversations in Context: Essays in Honor of Calvin J. Roetzel*, JSNTSup 221; London: SAP: 104–24.

Gaca, K.L. 2002 'Review of Troels Engberg-Pedersen, *Paul and the Stoics*', *RBL* 9: at http://www.bookreviews.org.

Gardner, P.D. 1994 *The Gifts of God and the Authentication of a Christian: An Exegetical Study of 1 Corinthians 8–11.1*, Lanham, New York, London: University Press of America.

Gayer, R. 1976 *Die Stellung des Sklaven in den paulinischen Gemeinden und bei Paulus*, Frankfurt: Lang.

Gebauer, R. 1993 *Letzte Begründung. Eine Kritik der Diskursethik von Jürgen Habermas*, München: Wilhelm Fink.

Geertz, C. 1973 *The Interpretation of Cultures*, New York: Basic Books.

Georgi, D. 1992 *Remembering the Poor: The History of Paul's Collection for Jerusalem*, Nashville, TN: Abingdon.

Giblin, C.H. 1975 'Three Monotheistic Texts in Paul', *CBQ* 37: 527–47.

Giddens, A. 1987 *Social Theory and Modern Sociology*, Cambridge: Polity.

Gill, R. 1974 'Berger's Plausibility Structures: A Response to Professor Cairns', *SJT* 27: 198–207.

— 1975 *The Social Context of Theology*, London: Mowbrays.

— 1977 *Theology and Social Structure*, London: Mowbrays.

Glad, C. 1995 *Paul and Philodemus: Adaptability in Epicurean and Early Christian Psychagogy*, NovTSup 81; Leiden: Brill.

Glancy, J.A. 1998 'Obstacles to Slaves' Participation in the Corinthian Church', *JBL* 117: 481–501.

Gnilka, J. 1968 *Der Philipperbrief*, HTKNT 10/3; Freiburg/Basel/Wien: Herder.

— 1996 'Die Kollekte der paulinischen Gemeinden für Jerusalem als Ausdruck ekklesialer Gemeinschaft', in Kampling and Söding 1996: 301–15.

Gooch, P.D. 1993 *Dangerous Food: 1 Corinthians 8–10 in Its Context*, SCJ 5; Waterloo, Ontario: Wilfrid Laurier University Press.

Gooch, P.W. 1987 '"Conscience" in 1 Corinthians 8 and 10', *NTS* 33: 244–54.

Goulder, M.D. 1974 *Midrash and Lection in Matthew*, London: SPCK.

Gundry-Volf, J. 1999 'Putting the *Moral Vision of the New Testament* into Focus: A Review', *BBR* 9: 277–87.

Habermas, J. 1981 *Theorie des kommunikativen Handelns*, 2 vols, Frankfurt: Suhrkamp.

— 1983 *Moralbewußtsein und kommunikatives Handeln*, Frankfurt: Suhrkamp.

— 1984 *The Theory of Communicative Action, Vol. 1: Reason and the Rationalization of Society*, London: Heinemann.

— 1987 *The Theory of Communicative Action, Vol. 2: Lifeworld and System: A Critique of Functionalist Reason*, Cambridge: Polity.

— 1990 *Moral Consciousness and Communicative Action*, Cambridge: Polity.

— 1991 *Erläuterungen zur Diskursethik*, Frankfurt: Suhrkamp.

— 1992 'Transcendance from Within, Transcendance in This World', in Browning and Fiorenza 1992: 226–50.

— 1993 *Justification and Application: Remarks on Discourse Ethics*, Cambridge: Polity.

— 1995 'Reconciliation through the Public Use of Reason: Remarks on John Rawls's *Political Liberalism*', *Journal of Philosophy* 92: 109–31.

— 1997 'Israel and Athens, or to Whom Does Anamnestic Reason Belong? On Unity in Multicultural Diversity', in Batstone and Mendieta 1997: 243–52.

— 2002 *Religion and Rationality: Essays on Reason, God, and Modernity*, Cambridge: Polity.

Hahn, F. 1996 'Die Einheit der Kirche nach dem Zeugnis des Apostels Paulus', in Kampling and Söding 1996: 288–300.

— 2002 *Theologie des Neuen Testaments. Band II: Die Einheit des Neuen Testaments*, Tübingen: Mohr.

Halter, H. 1977 *Taufe und Ethos: Paulinische Kriterien für das Proprium christlicher Moral*, Freiburg: Herder.

Haraguchi, T. 1993 'Das Unterhaltsrecht des frühchristlichen Verkündigers. Eine Untersuchung zur Bezeichnung ἐργάτης im Neuen Testament', *ZNW* 84: 178–95.

Harink, D. 2003 *Paul among the Postliberals*, Grand Rapids, MI: Brazos.

Harris, G. 1991 'The Beginnings of Church Discipline: 1 Corinthians 5', *NTS* 37: 1–21.

Hartman, L. 1992 *'Auf den Namen des Herrn Jesus'. Die Taufe in den neutestamentlichen Schriften*, SBS 148; Stuttgart: Katholisches Bibelwerk.

Harvey, A.E. 1982 '"The Workman Is Worthy of His Hire": Fortunes of a Proverb in the Early Church', *NovT* 24: 209–21.

Hasenstab, R. 1977 *Modelle paulinischer Ethik: Beiträge zu einem Autonomie-Modell aus paulinischem Geist*, Mainz: Matthias-Grünewald.

Hauerwas, S. 1975 *Character and the Christian Life*, third reprinting with a new Introduction, Notre Dame, IN: University of Notre Dame Press, 1994.

— 1981 *A Community of Character: Toward a Constructive Christian Social Ethic*, Notre Dame, IN: University of Notre Dame Press.

— 1983 *The Peaceable Kingdom: A Primer in Christian Ethics*, Notre Dame, IN: University of Notre Dame Press.

— 1987 'Will the Real Sectarian Stand Up?', *TToday* 44: 87–94.

— 1990 'The Testament of Friends', *Christian Century* 107: 212–16.

— 1993 *Unleashing the Scripture: Freeing the Bible from Captivity to America*, Nashville, TN: Abingdon.

— 1994 *Dispatches from the Front: Theological Engagements with the Secular*, Durham, NC, and London: Duke University Press.

— 1997 'Failure of Communication or a Case of Uncomprehending Feminism?', *SJT* 50: 228–39.

— 1998a *Sanctify Them in the Truth: Holiness Exemplified*, Edinburgh: T. & T. Clark.

— 1998b 'Christian Ethics in America (and the JRE): A Report on a Book I Will Not Write', *JRE* 25.3: 57–76.

— 1999 *After Christendom? How the Church Is to Behave If Freedom, Justice, and a Christian Nation Are Bad Ideas*, reissued with a new preface 1999; Nashville, TN: Abingdon.

— 2000 'Where Would I Be without Friends?', in Nation and Wells 2000: 313–32.

— 2001 *With the Grain of the Universe: The Church's Witness and Natural Theology*, Grand Rapids, MI: Brazos.

— and C. Pinches 1997 *Christians among the Virtues: Theological Conversations with Ancient and Modern Ethics*, Notre Dame, IN: University of Notre Dame Press.

Hawthorne, G.F. 1983 *Philippians*, WBC 43; Waco, TX: Word.

Hay, D.M. ed. 1993 *Pauline Theology, Vol. 2: 1 and 2 Corinthians*, Minneapolis: Fortress.

— and E.E. Johnson, eds 1995 *Pauline Theology, Vol. 3: Romans*, Minneapolis: Fortress.

Hays, R.B. 1983 *The Faith of Jesus Christ: An Investigation of the Narrative Substructure of Galatians 3:1–4:11*, SBLDS 56; Chico; CA: Scholars (2nd edn; Grand Rapids, MI: Eerdmans, 2001).

— 1987 'Christology and Ethics in Galatians: The Law of Christ', *CBQ* 49: 268–90.

— 1989 *Echoes of Scripture in the Letters of Paul*, New Haven and London: Yale University Press.

— 1994 'Ecclesiology and Ethics in 1 Corinthians', *Ex Auditu* 10: 31–43.

— 1996 '"The Gospel Is the Power of God for Salvation to Gentiles Only?" A Critique of Stanley Stowers' *A Rereading of Romans*', *CR* 9: 27–44.

— 1997a *The Moral Vision of the New Testament: A Contemporary Introduction to New Testament Ethics*, Edinburgh: T. & T. Clark.

— 1997b *First Corinthians*, Interpretation; Louisville, KY: John Knox.

— 2004 'Is Paul's Gospel Narratable?', *JSNT* 27: 217–39.

Héring, J. 1962 *The First Epistle of Saint Paul to the Corinthians*, London: Epworth.

Hjort, B.G. 2000 *The Irreversible Sequence. Paul's Ethics: Their Foundation and Present Relevance*, Frankfurt: Lang.

Hochschild, R. 1999 *Sozialgeschichtliche Exegese: Entwicklung, Geschichte und Methodik einer neutestamentlichen Forschungsrichtung*, Göttingen: Vandenhoeck & Ruprecht.

Hodgson, R. 1983 'Paul the Apostle and First Century Tribulation Lists', *ZNW* 74: 59–80.

Hofius, O. 1991 *Der Christushymnus Philipper 2,6-11*, 2nd edn; Tübingen: Mohr.

Hogg, M.A., and D. Abrams 1988 *Social Identifications: A Social Psychology of Intergroup Relations and Group Processes*, London and New York: Routledge.

Höhn, H.-J. 1985 *Kirche und kommunikatives Handeln: Studien zur Theologie und Praxis der Kirche in der Auseinandersetzung mit den Sozialtheorien Niklas Luhmanns und Jürgen Habermas*, Frankfurt: Knecht.

Holl, K. 1928 *Gesammelte Aufsätze zur Kirchengeschichte, Vol. 2: Der Osten*, Tübingen: Mohr.

Holmberg, B. 1978 *Paul and Power: The Structure of Authority in the Primitive Church as Reflected in the Pauline Epistles*, Lund: CWK Gleerup.

— 1998 'Jewish *Versus* Christian Identity in the Early Church?', *RB* 105: 397–425.

— 2004 'The Methods of Historical Reconstruction in the Scholarly "Recovery" of Corinthian Christianity', in Adams and Horrell 2004: 255–71.

Holtz, T. 1986 *Der erste Brief an die Thessalonicher*, EKKNT 13; Zürich/ Neukirchen-Vluyn: Benziger/Neukirchener.

Honneth, A. 1995 'The Other of Justice: Habermas and the Ethical Challenge of Postmodernism', in White 1995a: 289–323.

Hooker, M.D. 1978 'Philippians 2:6-11', in E.E. Ellis and E. Gräßer, eds, *Jesus und Paulus. FS W. G. Kümmel*, Göttingen: Vandenhoeck & Ruprecht: 151–64.

— 1990 *From Adam to Christ: Essays on Paul*, Cambridge: CUP.

— 1991 *The Gospel according to St Mark*, BNTC; London: A. & C. Black.

Horrell, D.G. 1993 'Converging Ideologies: Berger and Luckmann and the Pastoral Epistles', *JSNT* 50: 85–103 (repr. in S.E. Porter and C.A. Evans, eds, *New Testament Interpretation and Methods*, Sheffield: SAP, 1997: 102–20).

— 1995a 'The Lord's Supper at Corinth and in the Church Today', *Theology* 98: 196–202.

— 1995b 'Paul's Collection: Resources for a Materialist Theology', *EpRev* 22.2: 74– 83.

— 1996 *The Social Ethos of the Corinthian Correspondence: Interests and Ideology from 1 Corinthians to 1 Clement*, SNTW; Edinburgh: T. & T. Clark.

— 1997a '"The Lord Commanded … But I have not Used … " Exegetical and Hermeneutical Reflections on 1 Cor 9.14-15', *NTS* 43: 587–603.

— 1997b 'Theological Principle or Christological Praxis? Pauline Ethics in 1 Cor 8.1–11.1', *JSNT* 67: 83–114.

— ed. 1999 *Social-Scientific Approaches to New Testament Interpretation*, Edinburgh: T. & T. Clark.

— 2000a *An Introduction to the Study of Paul*, London: Continuum.

— 2000b '"No Longer Jew or Greek": Paul's Corporate Christology and the Construction of Christian Community', in D.G. Horrell and C.M. Tuckett, eds, *Christology, Controversy and Community: New Testament Essays in Honour of David R. Catchpole*, NovTSup 99; Leiden: Brill: 321–44.

— 2001a 'Berger and New Testament Studies', in Woodhead, Heelas and Martin 2001: 142–53.

— 2001b 'From ἀδελφοί to οἶκος θεοῦ: Social Transformation in Pauline Christianity', *JBL* 120: 293–311.

— 2002a 'Social Sciences Studying Formative Christian Phenomena: A Creative Movement', in Blasi, Duhaime and Turcotte 2002: 3–28.

— 2002b '"Becoming Christian": Solidifying Christian Identity and Content', in Blasi, Duhaime and Turcotte 2002: 309–35.

— 2002c 'Paul's Narratives or Narrative Substructure? The Significance of "Paul's Story"', in Longenecker 2002: 157–71.

— 2002d 'Solidarity and Difference: Pauline Morality in Romans 14–15', *SCE* 15.2: 60–78.

— 2003 'The Peaceable, Tolerant Community and the Legitimate Role of the State: Ethics and Ethical Dilemmas in Romans 12.1–15.13', *RevExp* 100.1: 81–99.

— 2004 'Review of D. Harink, *Paul among the Postliberals*', *JTS* 55: 663–8.

— forthcoming 'Idol-Food, Idolatry and Ethics in Paul', in S.C. Barton, ed., *Idolatry in the Bible, Early Judaism and Christianity*, London: T. & T. Clark.

Horsley, R.A. 1978 'Consciousness and Freedom among the Corinthians: 1 Corinthians 8–10', *CBQ* 40: 574–89.

— ed. 1997a *Paul and Empire: Religion and Power in Roman Imperial Society*, Harrisburg, PA: TPI.

— 1997b '1 Corinthians: A Case Study of Paul's Assembly as an Alternative Society', in Horsley 1997a: 242–52.

— 1998 'Paul and Slavery: A Critical Alternative to Recent Readings', *Semeia* 83/84: 153–200.

— ed. 2000 *Paul and Politics: Ekklesia, Israel, Imperium, Interpretation*, Harrisburg, PA: TPI.

Horster, D. 1984 *Habermas zur Einführung*, 3rd edn; Hannover: SOAK.

— 1990 *Habermas zur Einführung*, Hamburg: Junius.

Horton, J., and S. Mendus, eds 1994a *After MacIntyre: Critical Perspectives on the Work of Alasdair MacIntyre*, Cambridge: Polity.

— 1994b 'Alasdair MacIntyre: *After Virtue* and After', in Horton and Mendus 1994a: 1–15.

Houlden, J.L. 1975 *Ethics and the New Testament*, Oxford: Mowbrays (reissued 1992: Edinburgh: T. & T. Clark).

Hübner, H. 1984 *Law in Paul's Thought*, SNTW; Edinburgh: T. & T. Clark.

— 1987 'Paulusforschung seit 1945. Ein kritischer Literaturbericht', *ANRW* II.25.4: 2649–840.

Hunter, A.M. 1961 *Paul and His Predecessors*, London: SCM.

Hurd, J.C. 1965 *The Origin of 1 Corinthians*, London: SPCK.

— and P. Richardson, eds 1984 *From Jesus to Paul: Studies in Honour of Francis Wright Beare*, Ontario: Wilfrid Laurier University Press.

Hurst, L.D. 1998 'Christ, Adam, and Preexistence Revisited', in Martin and Dodd 1998: 84–95.

Hurtado, L. 1984 'Jesus as Lordly Example in Philippians 2:5-11', in Hurd and Richardson 1984: 113–26.

Hyldahl, N. 1986 *Die paulinische Chronologie*, Leiden: Brill.

Instone Brewer, D. 1992 '1 Corinthians 9.9-11: A Literal Interpretation of "Do Not Muzzle the Ox"', *NTS* 38: 554–65.

Jacoby, H. 1899 *Neutestamentliche Ethik*, Königsberg: Thomas & Oppermann.

Jeremias, J. 1960 *Die Abendmahlsworte Jesu*, 3rd edn; Göttingen: Vandenhoeck & Ruprecht.

— 1969 *Jerusalem in the Time of Jesus*, London: SCM.

Jervis, L.A. 1993 "'But I Want You to Know ...'": Paul's Midrashic Intertextual Response to the Corinthian Worshipers (1 Cor 11:2-16)', *JBL* 112: 231–46.

Jewett, R. 1971 *Paul's Anthropological Terms*, AGAJU 10; Leiden: Brill.

— 1978 'The Redaction of 1 Corinthians and the Trajectory of the Pauline School', *JAAR* 44.4 Supplement B.

— 1979 *Dating Paul's Life*, London: SCM.

— 1986 *The Thessalonian Correspondence: Pauline Rhetoric and Millenarian Piety*, Philadelphia: Fortress.

Johnson, E.E., and D.M. Hay, eds 1997 *Pauline Theology Vol. 4: Looking Back, Pressing On*, Atlanta, GA: Scholars.

Jones, I.H. 1973 *The Contemporary Cross*, London: Epworth.

Joubert, S. 2000 *Paul as Benefactor: Reciprocity, Strategy and Theological Reflection in Paul's Collection*, WUNT 2.124; Tübingen: Mohr.

Judge, E.A. 1984 'Cultural Conformity and Innovation in Paul: Some Clues from Contemporary Documents', *TynBul* 35: 3–24.

Juncker, A. 1904/1919 *Die Ethik des Apostels Paulus*, 2 vols; Halle: Max Niemeyer.

Kallas, J. 1965 'Romans XIII.1-7: An Interpolation', *NTS* 11: 365–74.

Kampling, R., and T. Söding, eds 1996 *Ekklesiologie des Neuen Testaments. FS Karl Kertelge*, Freiburg, Basel, Wien: Herder.

Kant, I. 1911 *Grundlegung der Metaphysik der Sitten*, in *Kant's Gesammelte Schriften: Werke Band 4*, Berlin: Georg Reimer.

Karris, R.J. 1973 'Romans 14:1–15:13 and the Occasion of Romans', *CBQ* 25: 155–78; cited from the reprint in Donfried 1991: 65–84.

Käsemann, E. 1960 'Kritische Analyse von Phil. 2,5-11', in *Exegetische Versuche und Besinnungen*, Vol. 1; Göttingen: Vandenhoeck & Ruprecht: 51–95.

— 1969 *New Testament Questions of Today*, London: SCM.

— 1974 *An die Römer*, 3rd edn, HNT 8a; Tübingen: Mohr.

Keck, L.E. 1965 'The Poor among the Saints in the New Testament', *ZNW* 56: 100–29.

— 1966 'The Poor among the Saints in Jewish Christianity and Qumran', *ZNW* 57: 54–78.

— 1974 'On the Ethos of Early Christians', *JAAR* 42: 435–52.

— 1996 'Rethinking "New Testament Ethics"', *JBL* 115: 3–16.

Kettner, M. 1992 'Einführung', in Apel and Kettner 1992: 9–28.

Kim, S. 1993 'Jesus, Sayings of', *DPL*: 475–80.

Kirchhoff, R. 1994 *Die Sünde gegen den eigenen Leib. Studien zu* πόρνη *und* πορνεία *in 1 Kor 6,12-20 und den sozio-kulturellen Kontext der paulinischen Adressaten*, SUNT 18; Göttingen: Vandenhoeck & Ruprecht.

Kittredge, C.B. 2000 'Corinthian Women Prophets and Paul's Argumentation in 1 Corinthians', in Horsley 2000: 103–109.

Klassen, W. 1963 'Coals of Fire: Sign of Repentance or Revenge?', *NTS* 9: 337–50.

Klauck, H.-J. 1982 *Herrenmahl und hellenisticher Kult: Eine religionsgeschichtliche Untersuchung zum ersten Korintherbrief*, NTAbh 15; Münster: Aschendorff.

— 1984 *1. Korintherbrief*, NEchtB 7; Würzburg: Echter.

Knapp, M. 1993 *Gottes Herrschaft als Zukunft der Welt. Biblische, theologiegeschichtliche und systematische Studien zur Grundlegung einer Reich-Gottes-*

Theologie in Auseinandersetzung mit Jürgen Habermas' Theorie des kommuni-kativen Handelns, Würzburg: Echter.

Knox, J. 1989 *Chapters in a Life of Paul*, revised edn; London: SCM.

Kopalski, V. 2001 *What Are They Saying about Paul and the Law?*, New York/ Mahwah, NJ: Paulist.

Kroeger, R., and C. Kroeger 1978 'An Inquiry into Evidence of Maenadism in the Corinthian Congregation', SBLSP 14 (vol. 2): 331–38.

Kubo, S. 1978 'I Corinthians vii: 16: Optimistic or Pessimistic?', *NTS* 24: 539–44.

Kümmel, W.G. 1965 'Jesus und Paulus', *NTS* 10: 163–81. Cited from repr. in Kümmel, *Heilsgeschehen und Geschichte: Gesammelte Aufsätze 1933–1964*, Marburg: Elwert: 439–56.

Kurz, W.S. 1985 'Kenotic Imitation of Paul and of Christ in Philippians 2 and 3', in F.F. Segovia, ed., *Discipleship in the New Testament*, Philadelphia: Fortress: 103–26.

Lampe, G.W.H. 1967 'Church Discipline and the Interpretation of the Epistles to the Corinthians', in W.R. Farmer, C.F.D. Moule and R.R. Niebuhr, eds, *Christian History and Interpretation: Studies Presented to John Knox*, Cambridge: CUP: 337–61.

Lampe, P. 1987 *Die stadtrömischen Christen in den ersten beiden Jahrhunderten*, WUNT 2.18; Tübingen: Mohr.

— 1991a 'The Roman Christians of Romans 16', in Donfried 1991: 216–30.

— 1991b 'Das korinthische Herrenmahl im Schnittpunkt hellenistisch-römischer Mahlpraxis und paulinischer Theologia Crucis', *ZNW* 82: 183–213.

— 2003 'Die dämonologischen Implikationen von I Korinther 8 und 10 vor dem Hintergrund paganer Zeugnisse', in A. Lange, H. Lichtenberger and K.F.D. Römheld, eds, *Die Dämonen: Die Dämonologie der israelitisch-jüdischen und frühchristlichen Literatur im Kontext ihrer Umwelt*, Tübingen: Mohr: 584–99.

Lanci, J.R. 1997 *A New Temple for Corinth: Rhetorical and Archaeological Approaches to Pauline Imagery*, New York: Lang.

Lassen, E.M. 1991 'The Use of the Father Image in Imperial Propaganda and in 1 Corinthians 4:14-21', *TynBul* 42: 127–36.

Lategan, B.C. 1990 'Is Paul Developing a Specifically Christian Ethic in Galatians?', in D.L. Balch, E. Fergusson and W.A. Meeks, eds, *Greeks, Romans, and Christians: Essays in Honor of Abraham J. Malherbe*, Minneapolis: Fortress: 318–28.

Lawrence, J.S., and R. Jewett 2002 *The Myth of the American Superhero*, Grand Rapids, MI: Eerdmans.

Lindemann, A. 1986 'Die biblische Toragebote und die paulinische Ethik', in W. Schrage, ed., *Studien zum Text und zur Ethik des Neuen Testament. FS Heinrich Greeven*, Berlin, New York: De Gruyter: 242–65 (repr. in Lindemann 1999: 91–114).

— 1995 'Die Kirche als Leib. Beobachtungen zur "demokratischen" Ekklesiologie bei Paulus', *ZTK* 92: 140–65 (repr. in Lindemann 1999: 132–57).

— 1999 *Paulus, Apostel und Lehrer der Kirche*, Tübingen: Mohr.

— 2000 *Der erste Korintherbrief*, HNT 9/1; Tübingen: Mohr.

Llewelyn, S.R. 2001 'The Use of Sunday for Meetings of Believers in the New Testament', *NovT* 43: 205–23.

Lohmeyer, E. 1961 *Kyrios Jesus. Eine Untersuchung zu Phil. 2,5-11*, Darmstadt: Wissenschaftliche Buchgesellschaft.
Lohse, E. 1956 'Zu 1 Cor 10 26.31', *ZNW* 47: 277–80.
— 1989 'Die Berufung auf das Gewissen in der paulinischen Ethik', in Merklein 1989: 207–19.
— 1991 *Theological Ethics of the New Testament*, Minneapolis: Fortress.
— 1996 'Das Gesetz Christi. Zur theologischen begründung christlicher Ethik im Galaterbrief', in Kampling and Söding 1996: 378–89.
Longenecker, B.W. 1996 'Defining the Faithful Character of the Covenant Community: Galatians 2.15-21 and Beyond', in Dunn 1996: 75–97.
— ed. 2002 *Narrative Dynamics in Paul: A Critical Assessment*, Louisville, KY: Westminster John Knox.
— forthcoming *Chains That Bind: Chain-Link Construction in New Testament Texts*, Waco, TX: Baylor University Press.
Longenecker, R.N. 1984 *New Testament Social Ethics for Today*, Grand Rapids, MI: Eerdmans.
— 1990 *Galatians*, WBC 41; Dallas, TX: Word.
Losie, L.A. 1978 'A Note on the Interpretation of Phil 2.5', *ExpTim* 90: 52–54.
Lovering, E.H., and J.L. Sumney, eds 1996 *Theology and Ethics in Paul and His Interpreters: Essays in Honor of Victor Paul Furnish*, Nashville, TN: Abingdon.
Lüdemann, G. 1984 *Paul, Apostle to the Gentiles: Studies in Chronology*, London: SCM.
— 1989 *Early Christianity according to the Traditions in Acts: A Commentary*, London: SCM.
Luther, M. 1953 *A Commentary on St. Paul's Epistle to the Galatians*, 1535 edn; London: Clarke.
Lutz, C.E. 1947 *Musonius Rufus, the Roman Socrates*, Yale Classical Studies 10; New Haven: Yale University Press.
MacDonald, D.R. 1987 *There Is No Male and Female: The Fate of a Dominical Saying in Paul and Gnosticism*, HDR 20; Philadelphia: Fortress.
MacDonald, M.Y. 1988 *The Pauline Churches: A Socio-historical Study of Institutionalisation in the Pauline and Deutero-Pauline Writings*, SNTSMS 60; Cambridge: CUP.
MacIntyre, A. 1985 [1981] *After Virtue: A Study in Moral Theory*, 2nd edn; London: Duckworth.
— 1988 *Whose Justice? Which Rationality?*, London: Duckworth.
— 1990 *Three Rival Versions of Moral Enquiry*, London: Duckworth.
— 1994 'A Partial Response to My Critics', in Horton and Mendus 1994a: 283–304.
Malherbe, A.J. 1986 *Moral Exhortation: A Greco-Roman Sourcebook*, Philadelphia: Westminster.
— 1987 *Paul and the Thessalonians: The Philosophic Tradition of Pastoral Care*, Philadelphia: Fortress.
— 1989 *Paul and the Popular Philosophers*, Minneapolis: Fortress.
— 1992 'Hellenistic Moralists and the New Testament', *ANRW* II.26.1: 267–333.
— 1994 'Determinism and Free Will in Paul: The Argument of 1 Corinthians 8 and 9', in Engberg-Pedersen 1994: 231–55.

— 2000 *The Letters to the Thessalonians*, AB 32B; New York: Doubleday.

Malina, B.J. 1981 *The New Testament World: Insights from Cultural Anthropology*, London: SCM (2nd, revised edn, Louisville, KY: Westminster John Knox, 1993).

— 1986 *Christian Origins and Cultural Anthropology: Practical Models for Interpretation*, Atlanta, GA: John Knox.

Malina, B.J. and J.H. Neyrey 1988 *Calling Jesus Names: The Social Value of Labels in Matthew*, Sonoma, CA: Polebridge.

— 1996 *Portraits of Paul: An Archaeology of Ancient Personality*, Louisville, KY: Westminster John Knox.

Marshall, I.H. 1980 *Last Supper and Lord's Supper*, Exeter: Paternoster.

Marshall, P. 1987 *Enmity in Corinth: Social Conventions in Paul's Relations with the Corinthians*, WUNT 2.23; Tübingen: Mohr.

Martin, D.B. 1990 *Slavery as Salvation: The Metaphor of Slavery in Pauline Christianity*, New Haven and London: Yale University Press.

— 1991 'Tongues of Angels and Other Status Indicators', *JAAR* 59: 547–89.

— 1995a *The Corinthian Body*, New Haven and London: Yale University Press.

— 1995b 'Heterosexism and the Interpretation of Romans 1: 18-32', *BibInt* 3: 332–55.

— 1997a 'Paul without Passion: On Paul's Rejection of Desire in Sex and Marriage', in Moxnes 1997: 201–15.

— 1998a 'Review of Richard B. Hays, *The Moral Vision of the New Testament*', *JBL* 117: 358–60.

— 2001a 'Review Essay: Justin J. Meggitt, *Paul, Poverty and Survival*', *JSNT* 84: 51–64.

— 2001b 'Paul and the Judaism/Hellenism Dichotomy: Toward a Social History of the Question', in Engberg-Pedersen 2001: 29–61.

Martin, R.P. 1986 *2 Corinthians*, WBC 40; Waco, TX: Word.

— 1997b *A Hymn of Christ: Philippians 2:5-11 in Recent Interpretation and in the Setting of Early Christian Worship*, 1st edn (as *Carmen Christi*), SNTSMS 4; Cambridge: CUP, 1967; 2nd edn, Grand Rapids, MI: Eerdmans, 1983; 3rd edn, Downers Grove, IL: IVP.

— 1998b '*Carmen Christi* Revisited', in Martin and Dodd 1998: 1–5.

— and B.J. Dodd, eds 1998 *Where Christology Began: Essays on Philippians 2*, Louisville, KY: Westminster John Knox.

Martyn, J.L. 1997a *Galatians*, AB 33A; New York: Doubleday.

— 1997b *Theological Issues in the Letters of Paul*, Edinburgh: T. & T. Clark.

— 2002 'De-apocalypticizing Paul: An Essay Focused on *Paul and the Stoics* by Troels Engberg-Pedersen', *JSNT* 86: 61–102.

Marx, K. 1969 'Thesen über Feuerbach', in K. Marx and F. Engels, *Werke*, Vol. 3; Berlin: Dietz: 5–7.

Marxsen, W. 1989 *'Christliche' und christliche Ethik im Neuen Testament*, Gütersloh: Gerd Mohn.

— 1993 *New Testament Foundations for Christian Ethics*, Edinburgh: T. & T. Clark.

Matera, F.J. 1996 *New Testament Ethics: The Legacies of Jesus and Paul*, Louisville, KY: Westminster John Knox.

May, A.S. 2001 'The Body for the Lord: Sex and Identity in 1 Corinthians 5–7', University of Glasgow: PhD dissertation (now JSNTSup 278; London: T. & T. Clark International 2004).

McCarthy, T. 1990 'Introduction', in Habermas 1990: vii–xiii.

McDonald, J.I.H. 1998 *The Crucible of Christian Morality*, London and New York: Routledge.

Meeks, W.A. 1974 'The Image of the Androgyne: Some Uses of a Symbol in Earliest Christianity', *History of Religions* 13: 165–208.

— 1982 '"And Rose up to Play": Midrash and Paraenesis in 1 Corinthians 10: 1-22', *JSNT* 16: 64–78.

— 1983 *The First Urban Christians*, New Haven and London: Yale University Press.

— 1986 *The Moral World of the First Christians*, Philadelphia: Westminster.

— 1987 'Judgement and the Brother: Romans 14:1–15:13', in G.F. Hawthorne and O. Betz, eds, *Tradition and Interpretation in the New Testament*, Grand Rapids, MI: Eerdmans/Tübingen: Mohr: 290–300.

— 1988 'The Polyphonic Ethics of the Apostle Paul', *The Annual of the Society of Christian Ethics*: 17–29.

— 1991 'The Man from Heaven in Paul's Letter to the Philippians', in B.A. Pearson, ed., *The Future of Early Christianity: Essays in Honor of Helmut Koester*, Minneapolis, MN: Fortress: 329–36.

— 1993 *The Origins of Christian Morality: The First Two Centuries*, London and New Haven: Yale University Press.

— 1996a 'The Ethics of the Fourth Evangelist', in R.A. Culpepper and C.C. Black, eds, *Exploring the Gospel of John: Essays in Honor of D. Moody Smith*, Louisville, KY: Westminster John Knox: 317–26.

— 1996b 'The "Haustafeln" and American Slavery: A Hermeneutical Challenge', in Lovering and Sumney 1996: 232–53.

— 2001 'Corinthian Christians as Artificial Aliens', in Engberg-Pedersen 2001: 129–38.

Meggitt, J.J. 1998 *Paul, Poverty and Survival*, SNTW; Edinburgh: T. & T. Clark.

— 2001 'Response to Martin and Theissen', *JSNT* 84: 85–94.

Mendus, S. 1989 *Toleration and the Limits of Liberalism*, Atlantic Highlands, NJ: Humanities Press International.

Merk, O. 1968 *Handeln aus Glauben. Die Motiveriungen der paulinischen Ethik*, Marburg: Elwert.

— 1989 'Nachahmung Christi. Zu ethischen Perspektiven in der paulinischen Theologie', in Merklein 1989: 172–206.

Merklein, H. 1984 'Die Einheitlichkeit des ersten Korintherbriefes', *ZNW* 75: 153–83.

— ed. 1989 *Neues Testament und Ethik. FS Rudolf Schnackenburg*, Freiburg, Basel, Wien: Herder.

Metzger, B.M. 1994 *A Textual Commentary on the Greek New Testament*, 2nd edn; Stuttgart: Deutsche Bibelgesellschaft.

Michel, O. 1978 *Der Brief an die Römer*, 14th edn, 5th revision, KEK 4; Göttingen: Vandenhoeck & Ruprecht.

Milbank, J. 1990 *Theology and Social Theory: Beyond Secular Reason*, Oxford: Blackwell.

Minear, P.S. 1971 *The Obedience of Faith: The Purposes of Paul in the Epistle to the Romans*, London: SCM.

Miscamble, W.D. 1987 'Sectarian Passivism?', *TToday* 44: 69–77.

Mitchell, M.M. 1989 'Concerning περὶ δέ in 1 Corinthians', *NovT* 31: 229–56.

— 1991 *Paul and the Rhetoric of Reconciliation: An Exegetical Investigation of the Language and Composition of 1 Corinthians*, HUT 28; Tübingen: Mohr.

— 1996 'Review of Neil Elliott, *Liberating Paul*', *CBQ* 58: 546–47.

Mitton, C.L. 1973 'New Wine in Old Wineskins: IV. Leaven', *ExpTim* 84: 339–43.

Moiser, J. 1983 'A Reassessment of Paul's View of Marriage with Reference to 1 Cor. 7', *JSNT* 18: 103–22.

Moo, D.J. 1996 *The Epistle to the Romans*, Grand Rapids, MI: Eerdmans.

Moon, J.D. 1995 'Practical Discourse and Communicative Ethics', in White 1995a: 143–64.

Morgan, R. 1998 'Incarnation, Myth, and Theology: Ernst Käsemann's Interpretation of Philippians 2:5-11', in Martin and Dodd 1998: 43–73.

Moxnes, H. ed. 1997 *Constructing Early Christian Families*, London and New York: Routledge.

— 2003 'Asceticism and Christian Identity in Antiquity: A Dialogue with Foucault and Paul', *JSNT* 26: 3–29.

Mulhall, S., and A. Swift 1996 *Liberals and Communitarians*, 2nd edn; Oxford: Blackwell.

Müller, J.-W. 2001 'Jürgen Habermas', *Prospect* (March 2001): 44–48.

Munck, J. 1959 *Paul and the Salvation of Mankind*, London: SCM.

Murphy-O'Connor, J. 1978a 'I Cor.,VIII,6: Cosmology or Soteriology?', *RB* 85: 253–67.

— 1978b 'Freedom or the Ghetto (1 Cor.,VIII,1-13; X,23–XI,1.)', *RB* 85: 543–74.

— 1980 'Sex and Logic in 1 Corinthians 11:2-16', *CBQ* 42: 482–500.

— 1991 *The Theology of the Second Letter to the Corinthians*, Cambridge: CUP.

Mußner, F. 1988 *Der Galaterbrief*, 5th edn, HTKNT 9; Freiburg, Basel, Wien: Herder.

Nanos, M.D. 1996 *The Mystery of Romans: The Jewish Context of Paul's Letter*, Minneapolis: Fortress.

Nation, M.T. 2000 'Stanley Hauerwas: Where Would We Be without Him?', in Nation and Wells 2000: 19–36.

Nation, M.T., and S. Wells, eds 2000 *Faithfulness and Fortitude: In Conversation with the Theological Ethics of Stanley Hauerwas*, Edinburgh: T. & T. Clark.

Neirynck, F. 1986 'Paul and the Sayings of Jesus', in A. Vanhoye, ed., *L'Apôtre Paul: Personnalité, style et conception du ministère*, Leuven: Leuven University Press: 306–20.

Newton, D. 1998 *Deity and Diet: The Dilemma of Sacrificial Food in Corinth*, JSNTSup 169; Sheffield: SAP.

Neyrey, J.H. 1990 *Paul in Other Words: A Cultural Reading of His Letters*, Louisville, KY: Westminster/John Knox.

Nickle, K. 1966 *The Collection: A Study in Paul's Strategy*, London: SCM.

Nolland, J. 1995 'The Gospel Prohibition of Divorce: Tradition History and Meaning', *JSNT* 58: 19–35.

Oakes, P. 2001 *Philippians: From People to Letter*, SNTSMS 110; Cambridge: CUP.

Ogletree, T.W. 1983 *The Use of the Bible in Christian Ethics*, Minneapolis: Fortress/ Oxford: Blackwell.

O'Neill, J.C. 1975 *Paul's Letter to the Romans*, Harmondsworth: Penguin.

O'Neill, O. 1991 'Kantian Ethics', in Singer 1991: 175–85.

Ortwein, G.G. 1999 *Status und Statusverzicht im Neuen Testament und seiner Umwelt*, NTOA 39; Göttingen: Vandenhoeck & Ruprecht.

Osiek, C., and D.L. Balch 1997 *Families in the New Testament World: Households and House Churches*, Louisville, KY: Westminster John Knox.

Pagels, E.H. 1974 'Paul and Women: A Response to Recent Discussion', *JAAR* 42: 538–49.

Parsons, M. 1995 'Being Precedes Act: Indicative and Imperative in Paul's Writing', in Rosner 1995: 217–47.

Paulsen, H. 1980 'Einheit und Freiheit der Söhne Gottes – Gal 3.26-29', *ZNW* 71: 74–95.

Petersen, N. 1985 *Rediscovering Paul: Philemon and the Sociology of Paul's Narrative World*, Philadelphia: Fortress.

Phipps, W.E. 1982 'Is Paul's Attitude toward Sexual Relations Contained in 1 Cor 7.1?', *NTS* 28: 125–31.

Pickett, R. 1997 *The Cross in Corinth: The Social Significance of the Death of Jesus*, JSNTSup 143; Sheffield: SAP.

Piper, J. 1979 *'Love Your Enemies': Jesus' Love Command in the Synoptic Gospels and in the Early Christian Paraenesis*, SNTSMS 38; Cambridge: CUP.

— 1980 'Hope as the Motivation of Love: 1 Peter 3:9-12', *NTS* 26: 212–31.

Plant, R. 2001 *Politics, Theology and History*, Cambridge: CUP.

Pleasants, N. 1998 'From Critical Theory to Habermas's Critical Social Theory: A Change of Paradigm', *Imprints* 3: 49–78.

Polaski, S.H. 1999 *Paul and the Discourse of Power*, Sheffield: SAP.

Porter, J. 1993 'Openness and Constraint: Moral Reflection as Tradition-Guided Inquiry in Alasdair MacIntyre's Recent Works', *JR* 73: 514–36.

Probst, H. 1991 *Paulus und der Brief: Die Rhetorik des antiken Briefes als Form der paulinischen Korintherkorrespondenz (1 Kor 8–10)*, WUNT 2.45; Tübingen: Mohr.

Quirk, M.J. 1987 'Beyond Sectarianism?', *TToday* 44: 78–86.

Räisänen, H. 1992 *Jesus, Paul and Torah: Collected Essays*, JSNTSup 43; Sheffield: JSOT.

Rasmusson, A. 1994 *The Church as Polis: From Political Theology to Theological Politics as Exemplified by Jürgen Moltmann and Stanley Hauerwas*, Lund: Lund University Press.

Rawls, J. 1993 *Political Liberalism*, NewYork: Columbia University Press.

— 1995 'Reply to Habermas', *Journal of Philosophy* 92: 132–80.

— 2001 *Justice as Fairness: A Restatement*, ed. E. Kelly, Cambridge, MA: Harvard University Press.

Reasoner, M. 1999 *The Strong and the Weak: Romans 14.1–15.13 in Context*, SNTSMS 103; Cambridge: CUP.

Reese-Schäfer, W. 1991 *Jürgen Habermas*, Frankfurt: Campus.

— 2001 'Kommunitarismus: I. Philosophisch, II. Ethisch', RGG^4 4: cols 1530–32.

Rehg, W. 1994 *Insight and Solidarity: A Study in the Discourse Ethics of Jürgen Habermas*, Berkeley, Los Angeles, London: University of California Press.

Reinmuth, E. 1985 *Geist und Gesetz. Studien zu Voraussetzungen und Inhalt der paulinischen Paraenese*, Berlin: Evangelische Verlagsanstalt.

Resch, A. 1904 *Der Paulinismus und die Logia Jesu in ihrem gegenseitigen Verhältnis*, TU 12; Leipzig: Hinrichs.

Rhyne, C.T. 1987 'II Corinthians 8:8-15', *Int* 41: 408–13.

Richardson, P. 1980 'Pauline Inconsistency: 1 Corinthians 9:19-23 and Galatians 2:11-14', *NTS* 26: 347–62.

— 1983 'Judgment in Sexual Matters in 1 Corinthians 6:1-11', *NovT* 25: 37–58.

— 1986 'On the Absence of "Anti-Judaism" in 1 Corinthians', in P. Richardson with D. Granskou, eds, *Anti-Judaism in Early Christianity. Vol. 1: Paul and the Gospels*, SCJ 2; Ontario: Wilfrid Laurier University Press: 59–74.

Riches, J.K. 2003 'Asceticism and Christian Identity in Antiquity: A Response', *JSNT* 26: 35–38.

Robbins, V.K. 1996 *The Tapestry of Early Christian Discourse*, London and New York: Routledge.

Robert, L. 1965 'D'Aphrodisias à la Lycaonie', *Hellenica* 13.

Robinson, W.P. ed. 1996 *Social Groups and Identities: Developing the Legacy of Henri Tajfel*, Oxford: Butterworth Heinemann.

Roetzel, C.J. 1995 'Paul and the Law: Whence and Whither?', *Currents in Research: Biblical Studies* 3: 249–75.

— 1998 *Paul: The Man and the Myth*, Columbia: University of South Carolina Press.

Rogerson, J.W. 1995 'Discourse Ethics and Biblical Ethics', in J.W. Rogerson, M. Davies and M. Daniel Carroll R., eds, *The Bible in Ethics*, Sheffield: SAP: 17–26.

Rohrbaugh, R.L. ed. 1996 *The Social Sciences and New Testament Interpretation*, Peabody: Hendrickson.

Rosner, B.S. 1994 *Paul, Scripture and Ethics: A Study of 1 Corinthians 5–7*, AGAJU 22; Leiden: Brill.

— ed. 1995 *Understanding Paul's Ethics: Twentieth-Century Approaches*, Grand Rapids, MI: Eerdmans/Carlisle: Paternoster.

Ross, D. 1949 *Aristotle*, 5th edn; London: Methuen.

Saller, R.P. 1994 *Patriarchy, Property and Death in the Roman Family*, Cambridge: CUP.

Sampley, J.P. 1991 *Walking between the Times: Paul's Moral Reasoning*, Minneapolis: Fortress.

Sanders, E.P. 1977 *Paul and Palestinian Judaism*, London: SCM.

— 1983 *Paul, the Law and the Jewish People*, London: SCM.

— 1990 'Jewish Association with Gentiles and Galatians 2:11-14', in R.T. Fortna and B.R. Gaventa, eds, *The Conversation Continues: Studies in Paul and John in Honor of J. Louis Martyn*, Nashville, TN: Abingdon: 170–88.

— 1991 *Paul*, Oxford: OUP.

— and M. Davies 1989 *Studying the Synoptic Gospels*, London: SCM.

Sanders, J.T. 1975 *Ethics in the New Testament*, London: SCM (reissued with a new preface 1986).

Sandnes, K.O. 1997 'Equality within Patriarchal Structures: Some New Testament Perspectives on the Christian Fellowship as a Brother- or Sisterhood and a Family', in Moxnes 1997: 150–65.

Schäfer, K. 1989 *Gemeinde als »Bruderschaft«. Ein Beitrag zum Kirchenverständnis des Paulus*, Frankfurt: Lang.

Schäfer, P. 1974 'Die Torah der messianischen Zeit', *ZNW* 65: 27–42.

Schelke, K.H. 1954 'Bruder', *RAC* 2: 631–40.

— 1970 *Theologie des Neuen Testaments. Vol. 3: Ethos*, Düsseldorf: Patmos.

Schmeller, T. 1995 *Hierarchie und Egalität. Eine sozialgeschichtliche Untersuchung paulinischer Gemeinden und grieschisch-römischer Vereine*, SBS 162; Stuttgart: Katholisches Bibelwerk.

Schmithals, W. 1971 *Gnosticism in Corinth*, Nashville, TN: Abingdon.

Schnackenburg, R. 1962 *Die sittliche Botschaft des Neuen Testaments*, 2nd edn (1st edn 1954), München: Max Hüber.

— 1965 *The Moral Teaching of the New Testament*, New York: Herder and Herder.

— 1986/1988 *Die sittliche Botschaft des Neuen Testaments*, revised edn, 2 vols; Freiburg: Herder.

Schnelle, U. 1990 'Die Ethik des 1. Thessalonicherbriefes', in R.F. Collins, ed., *The Thessalonian Correspondence*, BETL 87; Leuven: Leuven University Press: 295–305.

Schoberth, W. 2001 'Kommunitarismus: III. Religionsphilosophisch, fundamental-theologisch, praktisch-theologisch', RGG^4 4: cols 1532–33.

Schrage, W. 1961 *Die konkreten Einzelgebote in der paulinischen Paränese*, Gütersloh: Gerd Mohn.

— 1988 *The Ethics of the New Testament*, Edinburgh: T. & T. Clark.

— 1991 *Der erste Brief an die Korinther (1 Kor 1,1–6,11)*, EKKNT 7.1; Zürich and Neukirchen-Vluyn: Benziger/Neukirchener.

— 1995 *Der erste Brief an die Korinther (1 Kor 6,12–11,16)*, EKKNT 7.2; Zürich and Neukirchen-Vluyn: Benziger/Neukirchener.

— 1999 *Der erste Brief an die Korinther (1 Cor 11.17–14.40)*, EKKNT 7.3; Zürich and Neukirchen-Vluyn: Benziger/Neukirchener.

Schulz, S. 1987 *Neutestamentliche Ethik*, Zürich: Theologischer Verlag.

Schürmann, H. 1974 '"Das Gesetz des Christus" (Gal 6,2). Jesu Verhalten und Wort als letztgültige sittliche Norm nach Paulus', in J. Gnilka, ed., *Neues Testament and Kirche. FS Rudolf Schnackenburg*, Freiburg, Basel, Wien: Herder: 282–300.

Scroggs, R. 1972 'Paul and the Eschatological Woman', *JAAR* 40: 283–303.

— 1975 'The Earliest Christian Communities as Sectarian Movement', in J. Neusner (ed.), *Christianity, Judaism and Other Greco-Roman Cults: Studies for Morton Smith at Sixty*, Leiden: Brill: 1–23 (repr. in Horrell 1999: 69–91).

— 1983 *The New Testament and Homosexuality*, Philadelphia: Fortress.

Segal, A.F. 1990 *Paul the Convert: The Apostolate and Apostasy of Saul the Pharisee*, New Haven and London: Yale University Press.

Sellin, G. 1987 'Hauptprobleme des Ersten Korintherbriefes', *ANRW* II.25.4: 2940–3044.

Sherif, M. 1956 *Experiments in Group Conflict*, San Francisco: Freeman.

Singer, P. ed. 1991 *A Companion to Ethics*, Oxford: Blackwell.

Smit, J.F.M. 2000 *'About the Idol Offerings': Rhetoric, Social Context and Theology of Paul's Discourse in First Corinthians 8:1–11:1*, Leuven: Peeters.

Söding, T. 1994 'Starke und Schwache. Der Götzenopferstreit in 1 Kor 8–10 als Paradigma paulinischer Ethik', *ZNW* 85: 69–92 (repr. in Söding, *Das Wort vom Kreuz. Studien zur paulinischen Theologie*, WUNT 93; Tübingen: Mohr, 1997: 346–69).

— 1995 *Das Liebesgebot bei Paulus. Die Mahnung zur Agape im Rahmen der paulinischen Ethik*, NTAbh 26; Münster: Aschendorff.

South, J.T. 1992 *Disciplinary Practices in Pauline Texts*, Lewiston, NY: Mellen.

— 1993 'A Critique of the "Curse/Death" Interpretation of 1 Corinthians 5.1-8', *NTS* 39: 539–61.

Spicq, C. 1958–59 *Agape dans le Nouveau Testament*, 3 vols; Paris: Gabalda.

— 1970 *Theologie Morale du Nouveau Testament*, 4th edn, 2 vols; Paris: Gabalda.

Stanton, G.N. 1996 'The Law of Moses and the Law of Christ – Galatians 3.1–6.2', in Dunn 1996: 99–116.

— 2001 'What Is the Law of Christ?', *Ex Auditu* 17: 47–59.

Stendahl, K. 1976 *Paul among Jews and Gentiles*, Philadelphia: Fortress.

Still, T.D. 1999 *Conflict at Thessalonica: A Pauline Church and Its Neighbours*, JSNTSup 183; Sheffield: SAP.

Stout, J. 2004 *Democracy and Tradition*, New Forum Books; Princeton and Oxford: Princeton University Press.

Stowers, S.K. 1994 *A Rereading of Romans*, New Haven and London: Yale University Press.

— 1998 'Paul and Slavery: A Response', *Semeia* 83/84: 295–311.

— 2002 'Review of Troels Engberg-Pedersen, *Paul and the Stoics*', *RBL* 9: at http://www.bookreviews.org.

Strecker, C. 1999 *Die liminale Theologie des Paulus. Zugänge zur paulinischen Theologie aus kulturanthropologischer Perspektive*, FRLANT 185; Göttingen: Vandenhoeck & Ruprecht.

Strecker, G. 1972 *Handlungsorientierter Glaube. Vorstudien zu einer Ethik des Neuen Testaments*, Berlin: Kreuz Verlag Stuttgart.

Swartley, W.M. ed. 1992 *The Love of Enemy and Nonretaliation in the New Testament*, Louisville, KY: Westminster John Knox.

Taatz, I. 1991 *Frühjudische Briefe. Die paulinischen Briefe im Rahmen der offiziellen religiösen Briefe des Frühjudentums*, NTOA 16; Göttingen: Vandenhoeck & Ruprecht.

Tajfel, H. 1981 *Human Groups and Social Categories*. Cambridge: CUP.

Tannehill, R.C. 1967 *Dying and Rising with Christ: A Study in Pauline Theology*, BZNW 32; Berlin: Töpelmann.

Taylor, C. 1989 *Sources of the Self*, Cambridge: CUP.

Theissen, G. 1979 *Studien zur Soziologie des Urchristentums*, WUNT 19; Tübingen: Mohr.

— 1982 *The Social Setting of Pauline Christianity*, Edinburgh: T. & T. Clark.

— 1993 *Social Reality and the Early Christians*, Edinburgh: T. & T. Clark.

— 1999 *A Theory of Primitive Christian Religion*, London: SCM.

— 2001 'The Social Structure of Pauline Communities: Some Critical Remarks on J.J. Meggitt, *Paul, Poverty and Survival*', *JSNT* 84: 65–84.

— 2003a 'Social Conflicts in the Corinthian Community: Further Remarks on J.J. Meggitt, *Paul, Poverty and Survival*', *JSNT* 25: 371–91.

— 2003b 'Das Doppelgebot der Liebe. Jüdische Ethik bei Jesus', in Theissen, *Jesus als historische Gestalt. Beiträge zur Jesusforschung*, FRLANT 202; Göttingen: Vandenhoeck & Ruprecht: 57–72.

— 2003c 'Early Christian Ethos: A Synthesis of Biblical and Greek Morality?', unpublished paper.

Thiselton, A.C. 2000 *The First Epistle to the Corinthians*, NIGTC; Grand Rapids, MI: Eerdmans.

Thompson, G. 1995 '"... as open to the world as any theologian could be"? Karl Barth's Account of Extra-Ecclesial Truth and Its Value to Christianity's Encounter with Other Religious Traditions', PhD thesis, University of Cambridge.

— 2000 'A Question of Posture: Engaging the World with Justin Martyr, George Lindbeck and Hans Frei', *Pacifica* 13: 267–87.

Thompson, M.B. 1991 *Clothed with Christ: The Example and Teaching of Jesus in Rom 12.1–15.13*, JSNTSup 59; Sheffield: JSOT.

Thrall, M.E. 1994 *A Critical and Exegetical Commentary on the Second Epistle to the Corinthians*, Vol. 1, ICC; Edinburgh: T. & T. Clark.

— 2000 *A Critical and Exegetical Commentary on the Second Epistle to the Corinthians*, Vol. 2, ICC; Edinburgh: T. & T. Clark.

Thurston, B. 1998 *Women in the New Testament*, New York: Crossroad.

Tomson, P.J. 1990 *Paul and the Jewish Law: Halakha in the Letters of the Apostle to the Gentiles*, Assen/Maastricht: Van Gorcum/Minneapolis: Fortress.

— 1996 'Paul's Jewish Background in View of His Law Teaching in 1 Corinthians 7', in Dunn 1996: 251–70.

Troeltsch, E. 1931 *The Social Teaching of the Christian Churches*, Vol. 1, London: Allen & Unwin/New York: Macmillan.

Tuckett, C.M. 1984 'Paul and the Synoptic Mission Discourse?', *ETL* 60: 374–81.

Turner, J.C. 1996 'Henri Tajfel: An Introduction', in Robinson 1996: 1–23.

Turner, J.C. and R.Y. Bourhis 1996 'Social Identity, Interdependence and the Social Group: A Reply to Rabbie et al.', in Robinson 1996: 25–63.

Unnik, W.C. van 1980 'Die Rücksicht auf die Reaktion der Nicht-Christen als Motiv in der altchristlichen Paraenese', in Unnik, *Sparsa Collecta: The Collected Essays of W.C. van Unnik*, Vol. 2, NovTSup 30; Leiden: Brill: 307–22.

Verhey, A. 1984 *The Great Reversal: Ethics and the New Testament*, Grand Rapids, MI: Eerdmans.

Vielhauer, P. 1940 *Oikodome. Das Bild vom Bau in der christlichen Literatur vom Neuen Testament bis Clemens Alexandrinus*, Karlsruhe-Durlach: Tron (repr. in Vielhauer, *Oikodome. Aufsätze zum Neuen Testament*, ed. G. Klein; München: Kaiser, 1979: 1–168).

Vögtle, A. 1936 *Die Tugend- und Lasterkataloge im Neuen Testament*, NTAbh 16.4-5; Münster: Aschendorff.

Vos, C.S. de 1999 *Church and Community Conflicts: The Relationships of the Thessalonian, Corinthian, and Philippian Churches with Their Wider Civic Communities*, SBLDS 168; Atlanta, GA: Scholars.

— 2001 'Once a Slave, Always a Slave? Slavery, Manumission and Relational Patterns in Paul's Letter to Philemon', *JSNT* 82: 89–105.

Walter, N. 1989 'Paul and the Early Christian Jesus-Tradition', in Wedderburn 1989a: 51–80.

Ward, R.B. 1990 'Musonius and Paul on Marriage', *NTS* 36: 281–89.

Watson, D.F. 1989 '1 Corinthians 10:23–11:1 in the Light of Greco-Roman Rhetoric: The Role of Rhetorical Questions', *JBL* 108: 301–18.

Watson, F.B. 1984 '2 Cor x–xiii and Paul's Painful Letter to the Corinthians', *JTS* 35: 324–46.

— 1986 *Paul, Judaism and the Gentiles: A Sociological Approach*, SNTSMS 56; Cambridge: CUP.

— 1994 *Text, Church and World: Biblical Interpretation in Theological Perspective*, Edinburgh: T. & T. Clark.

— 1997 'Review of *The Moral Vision of the New Testament: A Contemporary Introduction to New Testament Ethics*, by Richard B. Hays', *SCE* 10: 94–99.

— 2000a *Agape, Eros, Gender: Towards a Pauline Sexual Ethic*, Cambridge: CUP.

— 2000b 'The Authority of the Voice: A Theological Reading of 1 Cor 11.2-16', *NTS* 46: 520–36.

— 2002 'Is There a Story in These Texts?', in Longenecker 2002: 231–39.

Wedderburn, A.J.M. 1987 *Baptism and Resurrection: Studies in Pauline Theology against Its Greco-Roman Background*, WUNT 44; Tübingen: Mohr.

— 1988 *The Reasons for Romans*, Edinburgh: T. & T. Clark.

— ed. 1989a *Paul and Jesus: Collected Essays*, JSNTSup 37; Sheffield: JSOT.

— 1989b 'Introduction', in Wedderburn 1989a: 11–15.

— 1989c 'Paul and Jesus: The Problem of Continuity', in Wedderburn 1989a: 99–115.

— 1989d 'Paul and Jesus: Similarity and Continuity', in Wedderburn 1989a: 117–43.

Weiss, J. 1910 *Der erste Korintherbrief*, KEK 5; Göttingen: Vandenhoeck & Ruprecht.

Welborn, L.L. 1987 'On the Discord in Corinth: 1 Corinthians 1–4 and Ancient Politics', *JBL* 106: 85–111 (repr. in Welborn, *Politics and Rhetoric in the Corinthian Epistles*, Macon, GA: Mercer University Press, 1997).

Wells, S. 1998 *Transforming Fate into Destiny: The Theological Ethics of Stanley Hauerwas*, Carlisle: Paternoster.

— 2002 'Review of S. Hauerwas, *With the Grain of the Universe*', *SCE* 15.2: 79–81.

Wendland, H.-D. 1970 *Ethik des Neuen Testaments*, Göttingen: Vandenhoeck & Ruprecht.

Wengst, K. 1987 *Pax Romana and the Peace of Jesus Christ*, London: SCM.

— 1988 *Humility: Solidarity of the Humiliated*, London: SCM.

Wenham, D. 1995 *Paul: Follower of Jesus or Founder of Christianity?*, Grand Rapids, MI: Eerdmans.

Wernle, P. 1897 *Der Christ und die Sünde bei Paulus*, Freiburg/Leipzig: Mohr Siebeck.

Westerholm, S. 1984 'Letter and Spirit: The Foundation of Pauline Ethics', *NTS* 30: 229–48.

— 1987 'On Fulfilling the Whole Law', *SEÅ* 51–52: 229–37.

White, S.K. 1988 *The Recent Work of Jürgen Habermas*, Cambridge: CUP.

— ed. 1995a *The Cambridge Companion to Habermas*, Cambridge: CUP.

— 1995b 'Reason, Modernity, and Democracy', in White 1995a: 3–16.

Wibbing, S. 1959 *Die Tugend- und Lasterkataloge im Neuen Testament*, BZNW 25; Berlin: Töpelmann.

Wiefel, W. 1991 'The Jewish Community in Ancient Rome and the Origins of Roman Christianity', in Donfried 1991: 85–101.

Wilckens, U. 1978 *Der Brief an die Römer (Röm 1–5)*, EKKNT 6.1; Zürich/ Neukirchen-Vluyn: Benziger/Neukirchener.

— 1982 *Der Brief an die Römer (Röm 12–16)*, EKKNT 6.3; Zürich/Neukirchen- Vluyn: Benziger/Neukirchener.

Willis, W.L. 1985a *Idol Meat in Corinth: The Pauline Argument in 1 Corinthians 8 and 10*, SBLDS 68; Chico, CA: Scholars.

— 1985b 'An Apostolic Apologia? The Form and Function of 1 Corinthians 9', *JSNT* 24: 33–48.

— 1996 'Bibliography: Pauline Ethics 1964–1994', in Lovering and Sumney 1996: 306–19.

Winger, M. 1992 *By What Law? The Meaning of Nomos in the Letters of Paul*, SBLDS 128; Atlanta, GA: Scholars.

— 2000 'The Law of Christ', *NTS* 46: 537–46.

Wink, W. 1992 'Neither Passivity nor Violence: Jesus' Third Way (Matt. 5:38-42 par.)', in Swartley 1992: 102–25.

Winter, B.W. 1994 *Seek the Welfare of the City: Christians as Benefactors and Citizens*, Grand Rapids, MI: Eerdmans.

— 2001 *After Paul Left Corinth: The Influence of Secular Ethics and Social Change*, Grand Rapids, MI: Eerdmans.

Winter, S.C. 1987 'Paul's Letter to Philemon', *NTS* 33: 1–15.

Wire, A.C. 1990 *The Corinthian Women Prophets: A Reconstruction through Paul's Rhetoric*, Minneapolis: Fortress.

Witherington, B. 1981 'Rite and Rights for Women – Galatians 3.28', *NTS* 27: 593–604.

— 1988 *Women in the Earliest Churches*, SNTSMS 59; Cambridge: CUP.

— 1993 'Not So Idle Thoughts about *EIDOLOTHUTON*', *TynBul* 44: 237–54.

— 1995 *Conflict and Community in Corinth: A Socio-Rhetorical Commentary on 1 and 2 Corinthians*, Grand Rapids, MI: Eerdmans.

— 1998 *Grace in Galatia: A Commentary on Paul's Letter to the Galatians*, Edinburgh: T. & T. Clark.

Wolff, C. 1989 'Humility and Self-Denial in Jesus' Life and Message and in the Apostolic Existence of Paul', in Wedderburn 1989a: 145–60.

— 2000 *Der erste Brief des Paulus an die Korinther*, 2nd edn, THKNT; Leipzig: Evangelische Verlagsanstalt.

Wolter, M. 1997 'Ethos und Identität in paulinischen Gemeinden', *NTS* 43: 430– 44.

Woodhead, L. 2000 'Can Women Love Stanley Hauerwas? Pursuing an Embodied Theology', in Nation and Wells 2000: 161–88.
— P. Heelas and D. Martin, eds 2001 *Peter Berger and the Study of Religion*, London and New York: Routledge.
Wright, N.T. 1986 'ἁρπαγμός and the Meaning of Philippians 2:5-11', *JTS* 37: 321–52.
— 1991 *The Climax of the Covenant: Christ and the Law in Pauline Theology*, Edinburgh: T. & T. Clark.
— 1992 *The New Testament and the People of God*, London: SPCK.
— 1995 'Review of *A Radical Jew: Paul and the Politics of Identity*, Daniel Boyarin', *RRT* 2.3: 15–23.
Wuthnow, R. 1986 'Religion as Sacred Canopy', in J.D. Hunter and S.C. Ainlay, eds, *Making Sense of Modern Times: Peter L. Berger and the Vision of Interpretive Sociology*, London and New York: Routledge and Kegan Paul: 121–42.
Yarbrough, O.L. 1985 *Not like the Gentiles: Marriage Rules in the Letters of Paul*, SBLDS 80; Atlanta, GA: Scholars.
Yeo, K.-K. 1994 'The Rhetorical Hermeneutic of 1 Corinthians 8 and Chinese Ancestor Worship', *BibInt* 2: 294–311.
— 1995 *Rhetorical Interaction in 1 Corinthians 8 and 10: A Formal Analysis with Preliminary Suggestions for a Chinese, Cross-Cultural Hermeneutic*, Leiden: Brill.
Yoder, J.H. 1972 *The Politics of Jesus*, Grand Rapids, MI: Eerdmans.
Young, N.H. 2003 '"The Use of Sunday for Meetings of Believers in the New Testament": A Response', *NovT* 65: 111–22.
Zaas, P.S. 1984 '"Cast Out the Evil Man from Your Midst" (1 Cor 5.13b)', *JBL* 103: 259–61.
— 1988 'Catalogues and Context: 1 Corinthians 5 and 6', *NTS* 34: 622–29.
Zerbe, G. 1992 'Paul's Ethic of Nonretaliation and Peace', in Swartley 1992: 177–222.

Indexes

INDEX OF MODERN AUTHORS

Aasgaard, R. 111–14
Abrams, D. 138
Adams, E. 28, 89, 116, 246
Adams, N. 57, 60, 62
Adorno, T.W. 4
Albrecht, G.H. 66, 70, 73, 77, 78, 199, 244
Allison, D.C. 26, 148, 216, 218
Allmen, D. von 111, 112
Allo, E.B. 261
Amadon, J. 8
Apel, K.-O. 49, 56, 57, 59, 60
Arens, E. 4, 53, 62, 63
Atkins, R.A. 99
Attridge, H.W. 21
Avis, P. 85

Balch, D.L. 157, 158, 261
Banks, R. 111
Barclay, J.M.G. 19, 21, 23, 25, 85, 87, 89, 120, 125, 127, 137, 139, 151, 155, 163, 184, 188, 195–98, 213, 222, 224–27, 229, 242, 246, 257–59, 268, 276, 278
Barcley, W.B. 9
Barrett, C.K. 109, 114, 174, 177, 216, 217, 260, 261
Bartchy, S.S. 99, 105, 111, 115, 125–27
Barth, F. 140, 141, 150, 151, 153, 277
Barton, S.C. 28, 157, 158, 193, 202
Bassler, J.M. 89
Bauckham, R.J. 23
Baur, F.C. 116
Beare, F.W. 208
Becker, J. 89
Beckheuer, B. 231, 232, 234
Beker, J.C. 87, 88

Bell, D. 47–52, 54, 78, 79, 290
Benhabib, S. 48, 50, 51, 53, 54, 59–62, 70, 72, 99, 118, 124, 201–203, 222, 274, 282, 283
Berger, K. 234, 235
Berger, P.L. 83–85
Berkman, J. 64
Best, E. 258, 259
Betz, H.D. 20, 21, 24, 104, 105, 120, 160, 222, 232, 235, 239, 263, 264
Biggar, N. 75, 77, 290
Black, D.A. 220
Blount, B.K. 9, 37, 125, 130
Bockmuehl, M.N.A. 2, 9, 16–18, 27, 35, 36, 119, 120, 160, 161, 176, 177, 184, 206, 208–11, 247–51, 254, 264, 265
Boer, M.C de 229
Bornkamm, G. 88, 107
Botha, J. 252
Bourhis, R.Y. 92
Boyarin, D. 1, 5, 41–44, 46, 54, 99, 121, 125, 126, 166, 195–97, 201–203, 274, 276, 290, 291
Brant, J.A. 205
Braxton, B.R. 125
Bronner, S.E. 53, 54
Brown, C. 206
Brown, R. 138
Brown, R.E. 253
Browning, D. 63
Bruce, F.F. 216, 234, 256, 258
Brunt, J.C. 171
Büchsel, F. 154
Buck, C.H. 233
Bultmann, R. 3, 7, 10–14, 25, 46, 85, 87, 94, 209, 222, 287
Burridge, R.A. 32, 36
Burton, E. 124, 125, 224, 232

INDEX OF ANCIENT REFERENCES